Century 21™ *plus*

Computer Applications with Document Formatting

JACK P. HOGGATT, ED.D.

Professor of Business Communication
University of Wisconsin
Eau Claire, Wisconsin

•

JON A. SHANK, ED.D.

Professor of Education
Robert Morris University
Moon Township, Pennsylvania

•

KARL BARKSDALE

Technology Consultant
Springville, Utah

THOMSON
─────★─────™
SOUTH-WESTERN

Australia · Brazil · Canada · Mexico · Singapore · Spain · United Kingdom · United States

THOMSON

SOUTH-WESTERN

Century 21™ Plus: Computer Applications with Document Formatting

Jack Hoggatt, Jon Shank, Karl Barksdale

VP/Editorial Director:
Jack W. Calhoun

VP/Editor-in-Chief:
Karen Schmohe

Acquisitions Editor:
Jane Congdon

Project Manager:
Dave Lafferty

Consulting Editor:
Jean Findley,
Custom Editorial Productions, Inc.

Marketing Manager:
Michael Cloran

Marketing Coordinator:
Linda Kuper

Marketing Communications Manager:
Elizabeth A. Shipp

Senior Production Editor:
Martha Conway

Production Manager:
Tricia Boies

Senior Manufacturing Coordinator:
Charlene Taylor

Manager of Technology, Editorial:
Liz Prigge

Technology Project Editor:
Scott Hamilton

Web Coordinator:
Ed Stubenrauch

Art Director:
Stacy Jenkins Shirley

Photography Manager:
Deanna Ettinger

Permissions Editor:
Linda Ellis

Copyeditor:
Gary Morris

Production House:
GGS Book Services

Cover Designer:
Grannan Graphic Design, Ltd.

Cover Images:
© Getty Images, Inc.

Internal Designer:
Grannan Graphic Design, Ltd.

Photo Researcher:
Terri Miller

Printer:
Quebecor World, Versailles
Versailles, KY

For more information about our
products, contact us at:

Thomson Higher Education
5191 Natorp Boulevard
Mason, Ohio 45040
USA

Microsoft is a registered trademark of Microsoft Corporation in the U.S. and/or other countries.

The names of all products mentioned herein are used for identification purposes only and may be trademarks or
registered trademarks of their respective owners. Thomson South-Western disclaims any affiliation, association,
connection with, sponsorship, or endorsement by such owners.

A Century of Innovation

Century 21™ Computer Applications, 8E Hoggatt and Shank

Century 21

From turn-of-the-century progress to a new millennium of computer success, *Century 21* delivers a proven brand of tradition and innovation that has helped more than 85 million people.

For decades *Century 21* educational tools have been breaking new ground with innovative materials. *Century 21* continues an unmatched tradition of excellence, driven by a responsiveness to teaching needs.

Built on more than 100 years of teaching experience and backed by a leader in business education publishing, *Century 21* delivers the latest content using proven presentation methods and the technology tools of tomorrow.

Now the latest edition of this market leader promises more. Hallmark strengths—such as *Century 21's* unique cycle approach to learning and cross-curricular themes—combine with more computer applications, a fresh emphasis on emerging technologies, and enhanced communication skills.

Experience the power that a century of innovation can bring to your course with *Century 21 Computer Applications*.

Your Choice of Solutions and Support

One Trusted Name. Everything You Need.

Here are a few of the innovative choices available from *Century 21's* complete line of learning resources, simulations, technology, and teaching support:

Century 21 Computer Applications and Keyboarding, Comprehensive, Lessons 1-150, 3 semester text (ISBN 0-538-43946-7)

Century 21 Keyboarding and Word Processing, Essentials, Lessons 1-75, 1 semester text (ISBN 0-538-43959-9)

Century 21 Plus, Computer Applications (ISBN 0-538-43960-2)

Wraparound Instructor's Edition, Century 21 Computer Applications and Keyboarding for:
   Comprehensive Text, Lessons 1-150 (ISBN 0-538-44029-5)
   Essentials Text, Lessons 1-75 (ISBN 0-538-44030-9)
   C21 Plus (ISBN 0-538-44031-7)

Instructor's Manual and Solutions Key (ISBN 0-538-44032-5); C21 Plus (ISBN 0-538-44374-4)

CheckPro™ document-checking software (Windows site license) (ISBN 0-538-44039-2); C21 Plus (ISBN 0-538-44373-1)

Instructor's Resource CD-ROM (ISBN 0-538-44038-4); C21 Plus (ISBN 0-538-44243-3)

ExamView Electronic Testing Software (ISBN 0-538-44244-1); C21 Plus (ISBN 0-538-44245-X)

Complete Instructor's Resource Kit (includes *Spanish Language Supplement, E-Terms Dictionary, Exploring Cultural Diversity, Placement/Performance Tests, Roll of Honor, Mouse Pad, Instructor's Manual and Solutions Key,* and *Instructor's Resource CD-ROM*) (ISBN 0-538-44042-2) (Lessons 1-150 only)

Innovation That Stands Alone

Proven Cycle Approach —
Stronger Instruction at Every Turn

Learn. Improve. Enhance. Build.

No one does a better job of ensuring that your students understand and effectively use what they've learned. *Century 21's* unique **cycle approach** reflects a strength in instructional design based on decades of learning success.

Students begin with a foundation in the **basics**, then revisit content to **improve** skills. Students return to content again to **enhance** abilities, and finally learn to **build** upon the knowledge already developed.

Cross-Curricular Connection

Part One focuses on specific cross-curricular topics to strengthen students' skills while applying their abilities in other disciplines. These include:

Social Studies

Science and Math

Environment and Health

Century 21

Strengths That Set Century 21 Apart and Your Students Ahead

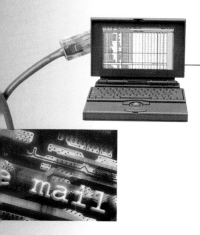

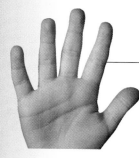

Interactive Innovation — with Integrated Computer
Applications

- **Expanded coverage of computer applications is integrated throughout the text.** Students effectively prepare for the business world with computer applications integrated into each instructional unit.
- **Non-software-specific approach** provides ultimate flexibility in the classroom and later in the workplace, as students focus on mastering the techniques rather than learning a specific software program.
- **Emerging technologies** including speech recognition, Internet, e-mail, database, electronic presentations, spreadsheets, and advanced word processing are addressed to prepare students for tomorrow's business environment.
- **Coverage of input technologies** equips students to integrate the power of PCs and PDAs.

Skill-Building — Including Balanced-Hand
and Other Specialized Focus Exercises

Skill-building builds speed and accuracy. Balanced-hand skills ensure equal use of right and left hands for maximum proficiency

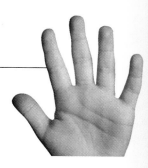

Walk Through a Century of Innovation
for a Lifetime of Learning

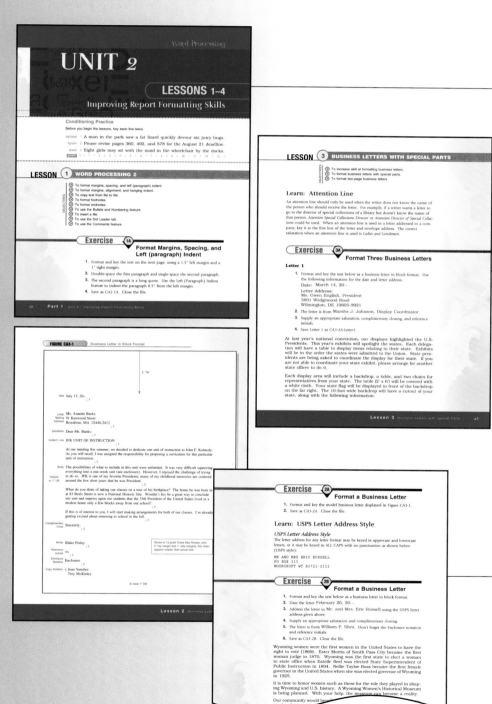

Unit Opener

- **Conditioning practice** reinforce keyboarding skills.
- **Lessons** follow within a unit.
- **Scales** identify gross words a minute (gwam) to measure keying productivity.

Lesson Opener

- **Lesson Objectives** identify key areas of learning throughout.
- **Learn** introduces a new topic.
- **Exercises** are within lessons.

Exercises

- **Model documents** give overviews of document formats.
- **Step by step instructions** tell how to complete an exercise.
- Documents illustrate **cross-curricular themes**.

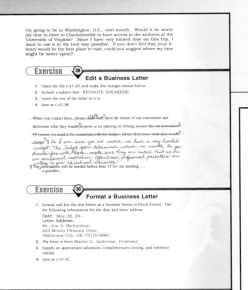

Script and Rough Draft

- **Script and rough-draft copy** provide real-world keying experience.

Internet Features

- **Internet Activities** enhance lessons and follow cross-curricular themes.
- **Icons** identify data files.

Assessment

- Lessons for assessments **integrate software applications**.

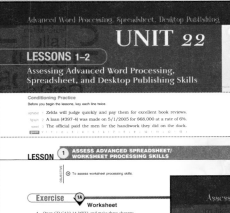

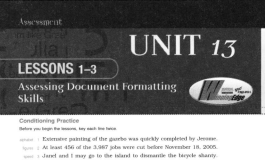

- **Winning Edge Activities** and performance indicators throughout the text prepare students for competitive BPA and FBLA events.

A Century of Advantages *Applied*

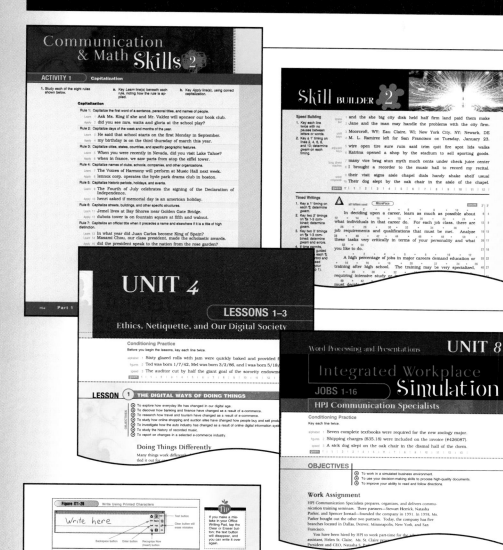

- **Communication and math skills** are incorporated into lessons.

- **Skill Builders** help students improve keying technique and speed.

- **Computer concepts, history, and ethics** are covered.

- **Networking and web design** are also covered.

- **Workplace Simulations** reflect current technology and actual job situations.

- **Handwriting and speech recognition** are covered.

- **Scanning, photos, and digital imaging** are also covered.

- **Microsoft OneNote** introduces electronic notetaking software.

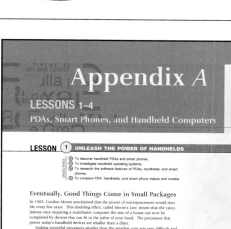

- **Leadership, careers and employability, keyboarding skill building,** and the use of **PDA's** are presented.

A Century of Innovation with the Technology to *Take You Further*

A Century of Strong Support

Prepare your students for a lifetime of computer success with innovative, key technology solutions that reflect the business needs of a new decade.

Century 21 Computer Applications, 8E

NEW *MicroType 4™*

New, updated software now gives instructors the option to view student reports online with a new Web reporting function. Lessons cover alphabetic, numeric, skillbuilding, and keypad instruction using graphics, games, audio, video, and a word processor with timer. Available for Windows.

Century 21, 8E Web Site

www.c21key.swlearning.com

Updated, this dynamic site provides instructors and students with even more online opportunities for interaction, instruction, and the latest teaching tools. Placement and Performance Tests, solutions, PowerPoint presentation slides, *Exploring Cultural Diversity*, certificates, *MicroPace 2.0* timed-writing templates, lesson plans, and more are available.

NEW *CheckPro™ for 8E*

New software allows instructors to save time by instantly checking documents keyed from the text. Revised software for use with the eighth edition checks most Word documents for accuracy, and now checks other documents with additional features. Available for Windows.

NEW Technology bundle – *Check-Pro with MicroType 4*

The best of both software programs in one package.

NEW *ExamView* Electronic Testing Software

This latest test-creation and online testing software allows instructors to produce reliable, balanced tests quickly and reduce grading time.

Instructor's Resource CD

This resource provides access to all key instructor support and teaching tools from one easy location! On the CD, you'll find *Exploring Cultural Diversity*, *Instructor's Manual and Solutions Key*, certificates, *Workplace Enrichment*, correlations and data files, formatting templates, *MicroPace-Pro 2.0* timed-writing templates, lesson plans, and PowerPoint presentations.

Adobe® eBooks for *Century 21, 8E*

Instructors can enrich the traditional course with digital material that offers the same rich photos, graphics, and easy-to-read fonts as the printed text! Students view **eBooks** on their computers using the free Adobe Acrobat Book Reader.

MicroPace Pro 2.0™

This dynamic diagnostic and skill-building software helps students improve accuracy and speed as it identifies errors and guides students to specific areas that need improvement. Paced and timed writings, drills, and practices are included. For Windows or Macintosh.

KeyChamp 2.0™

Students improve their speed as the software analyzes two-stroke key combinations (digraphs) and recommends speed-building drills. Available for Windows or Macintosh.

Everything You and Your Students Need for *Keyboarding Success*

The Century 21 Family

Century 21 Computer Applications 8E

Century 21 Computer Applications and Keyboarding Comprehensive, *Lessons 1-150*	0-538-43946-7
Century 21 Computer Keyboarding Essentials, *Lessons 1-75*	0-538-43959-9
Century 21 Plus Computer Applications	0-538-43960-2
Adobe eBook, *Lessons 1-150*	0-538-44189-5
Adobe eBook, *Lessons 1-75*	0-538-44190-9
Workplace Enrichment Activities	0-538-44023-6
Spanish Language Supplement*	0-538-44024-4
E-Terms Booklet* (softcover, 1-color, 64 pages)	0-538-44025-2
Exploring Cultural Diversity* (softcover, 1-color, 32 pages)	0-538-44026-0
Style Manual (softcover, 1-color, 32 pages)	0-538-44027-9
Placement/Performance Tests*, *Lessons 1-150*, (32 pages)	0-538-44028-7
Placement Tests, Century 21 Plus (16 pages)	0-538-44375-8
Wraparound Instructor's Edition, *Lessons 1-150*, (hard top-spiral bound cover, 4-color, 640 pages)	0-538-44029-5
Wraparound Instructor's Edition, *Lessons 1-75*, (hard top-spiral bound cover, 4-color, 324 pages)	0-538-44030-9
Wraparound Instructor's Edition, Century 21 Plus, (hard side spiral bound cover, 4-color, 768 pages)	0-538-44031-7
Instructor's Manual and Solutions Key*, *Lessons 1-150* (softcover, 1-color, 448 pages)	0-538-44032-5
Instructor's Manual and Solutions Key, C21 Plus (softcover, 1-color, 256 pages)	0-538-44374-4
Roll of Honor*	0-538-44033-3
PC Keyboard Wall Poster	0-538-44035-X
Model Document Posters	0-538-69926-4
Mouse Pad*	0-538-44037-6
CheckPro Site License, Windows, *Lessons 1-150*	0-538-44039-2
CheckPro Site License, Windows, Century 21 Plus	0-538-44373-1
MicroType 4 Site License, Windows	0-538-44050-3
Instructor's Resource CD* (includes Data and Solutions Files, Lesson Plans, and PowerPoint), *Lessons 1-150*	0-538-44038-4
Instructor's Resource CD, Century 21 Plus	0-538-44243-3
ExamView, *Lessons 1-150*	0-538-44244-1
ExamView, Century 21 Plus	0-538-44245-X
Instructor's Resource Kit (box), *Lessons 1-150*	0-538-44042-2

Technology Bundle

CheckPro Site License/MicroType 4 Site License, Windows, *Lessons 1-150*	0-538-44195-X
CheckPro Site License/MicroType 4 Site License, Windows, Century 21 Plus	0-538-44447-9

*Included in Instructor's Resource Kit (Lessons 1-150)

Preface

Century 21 Plus Computer Applications with Document Formatting represents **a new way of beginning** a course on computer applications from the authors of the long established and highly successful *Century 21 Computer Applications and Keyboarding* series. The emphasis is on new technologies, offering minimal keyboarding reinforcement for those students who need to learn advanced computer applications. This new text is targeted to students who have had keyboarding and some basic computer applications instruction in another course.

Lessons focus on computer concepts and applications with the reinforcement and instructional design that are well known with the *Century 21* family. Each lesson is consistently structured with objectives and a series of hands-on exercises. Interesting new topics include computer concepts, ethics, speech and handwriting input technologies, and PDAs. Available on the website are additional activities and topics for discussion.

The topics exceed the South-Western scope and sequence standards for computer literacy, which correspond to the National Educational Technology Standards (NETS) for computer education. Many Microsoft Office Specialist topics are also supported.

For this new edition, some familiar instructional elements include Skill Builders, Communication and Math Skills exercises, and Internet Activities. Model documents illustrate correct formatting.

Note that this text is "generic" for Microsoft® Office—meaning that it is based on Microsoft Office 2003 for Windows, but can also be used with XP. All figures are from Microsoft Office 2003 for Windows.

The *Century 21* family includes a full range of high-quality supplementary items to enhance your courses, including a website at www.c21key.swlearning.com. Thank you for choosing *Century 21*. We know that you will find this text an exciting addition to your classes.

ABOUT THE AUTHORS

Dr. Jon A. Shank is a Professor of Education at Robert Morris University in Moon Township, Pennsylvania. For more than 20 years, he served as Dean of the School of Applied Sciences and Education at Robert Morris. Dr. Shank retired as Dean in 1998 to return to full-time teaching. He currently teaches methods courses to students who are studying to become business education teachers. Dr. Shank holds memberships in regional, state, and national business education organizations. He has received many honors during his career, including Outstanding Post-Secondary Business Educator in Pennsylvania.

Dr. Jack P. Hoggatt is Department Chair for the Department of Business Communications and Assistant Dean at the University of Wisconsin-Eau Claire. He has taught courses in Business Writing, Advanced Business Communications, and the communication component of the university's Masters in Business Administration (MBA) program. Dr. Hoggatt has held offices in several professional organizations, including the Wisconsin Business Education Association.

Dr. Jon Shank (left), Karl Barksdale (standing) and Dr. Jack Hoggatt

He has served as an advisor to local and state student business organizations. Dr. Hoggatt is involved with his community and the school activities of his children.

Karl Barksdale was a former Development Manager for the Training and Certification team at WordPerfect Corporation and a Marketing Manager in the Consumer Products division. Prior to his stint at WordPerfect, he obtained a master's degree in curriculum from the University of Utah and applied his degree as the Secondary Curriculum Coordinator for Provo School District. After his association with WordPerfect, Karl returned to education as a Business Education instructor. Since that time he has authored over 50 business and computer education textbooks for South-Western Educational Publishing, Course Technology, Speaking Solutions, and a variety of other publishers.

REVIEWERS

Jeff Aronsky
La Mesa Junior High School
Santa Clarita, CA

Brenda Bertine
Crystal River High School
Crystal River, FL

Bladen Crockett
NC Department of Public
   Instruction
Raleigh, NC

Chris Ericson
Centennial Public School
Utica, NE

Sandy Hull
Grant Community High
   School
Fox Lake, IL

Christi Larson
Waterloo East High School
Waterloo, IA

Dr. James R. Smith
Orange County District
Hillsborough, NC

Ana Solomon
Neighborhood Centers
   Adult School
Oakland, CA

Mary Wincapaw
Juneau Business High
   School
Milwaukee, WI

Contents

Word Processing, Presentations, and Spreadsheets

Documents You Need to Know

The document types indicated on the left can be found in the sections and pages noted on the right.

UNIT 1

LESSONS 1–3

Computer Basics: Prerequisites to Success

Conditioning Practice

Before you begin the lessons, key each line twice.

alphabet	1	Jacques paid a very sizeable sum for the meetings next week.
fig/sym	2	The desk (#539A28) and chair (#61B34) usually sell for $700.
speed	3	Pamela did the work for us, but the neighbor may pay for it.

gwam 1' | 1 | 2 | 3 | 4 | 5 | 6 | 7 | 8 | 9 | 10 | 11 | 12 |

LESSON 1 DIGITOOLS AND OPERATING SYSTEMS

OBJECTIVES

- ⊙ To learn critical computer terms and vocabulary.
- ⊙ To examine why computers are important in our society and our daily lives.
- ⊙ To review the five things computers do.
- ⊙ To learn the basic functions of an operating system.
- ⊙ To change default settings for passwords, audio devices, and appearance.

Computers in Our Lives

A state-of-the-art computerized fire alert system was installed in a recently remodeled apartment complex. The system monitors hundreds of sensors tirelessly, day and night without fatigue.

A smoldering electrical fire starts as the residents sleep late into the night. A whiff of smoke glides past one of the sensors. At this mere hint of a serious problem, the computers simultaneously alert fire officials, sound the evacuation alarm for the sleepy residents, and strategically set off sprinklers near the source of the blaze.

In a nearby fire station, a computerized GPS system with a mapping database provides the firefighters with the best possible route to the smoldering danger, saving time and lives and reducing property damage.

After the blaze, the Fire Chief pops opens a battlefield-ready tablet PC—a ruggedly engineered computer that can be dropped from the top of a fire truck without sustaining damage. The Chief activates a speech program and voice-types an electronic report that can be shared with insurance companies, law enforcement, apartment

© PHOTODISC GREEN /GETTY IMAGES BUSINESS & OCCUPATIONS 2 V43

owners, building inspectors, and electrical engineers so each can learn exactly what happened and can work to prevent such fires in the future.

This single example demonstrates just how dependent we are on computers. We depend on them for our safety, our work, our education, and our interaction with each other. To compete in the world of the future, you need to understand what computers do, how they work, and how you can get the most out of the technologies of the 21st Century.

Learn: What Computers Actually Do

In a way, **computers** are simple devices. *They are just machines that follow a set of instructions.* They can't think for themselves. They compute in **binary** language, which means they use the digits 0 and 1 to accomplish everything they do. (We will talk more about that curiosity in Part 2.) For the present, it's enough to know that computers generally do five things:

- receive **input**
- **process** inputs
- produce an **output**
- **store** information
- **distribute** outputs

computers

binary

What makes today's computers so special is that they do these five things extremely well; in many ways, better and faster than human beings. As a result, we have come to depend on them for critical aspects of our lives.

© PRNEWSFOTO/MICROSOFT CORP.

Old Hardware Versus New-Style DigiTools

Before they can work, computers need three elements:

- Hardware
- Operating systems
- Applications

peripherals

Personal Computer or **PC**

CPU (Central Processing Unit)

All the material parts of a computer and its **peripherals** (like a scanner or printer) are hardware devices. If you can physically touch it, it's hardware. In the early 1980s, when the **Personal Computer** or **PC** first came to prominence, PC hardware consisted of a **CPU (Central Processing Unit)** resting on a board with supporting memory and other communications components, like video and sound cards. Computers were clunky and awkward looking.

All of these components were placed inside a big box. In those days, it took a big box to fit the bulky components inside. A monochrome (one-color) monitor was added as an output display device, and a keyboard was needed for input. A decade later, the mouse was added as another input device.

Consider how much PCs have changed. Over time, computers became faster and smaller. Powerful computers can now fit in the palm of your hand, like a PDA or smart phone. They can be mobile, like an ultralight laptop or a tough tablet PC—such as the one used by the fire chief in the introduction. Some models can now substitute speech recognition and digital pen technologies for keyboards and

the mouse as input devices. Even smaller devices, such as wristwatches, can also be computer enhanced. (View a few samples in Figure PR1-1.)

There is simply no one thing that can be called a computer anymore. Today, computers are found in many forms and styles. Like different tools in a carpenter's toolbox, each fits a different need. We call all of these new computerized tools **Digital Communications Tools** or **DigiTools** for short. And you need to become proficient with these new tools.

Digital Communications Tools or **DigiTools**

Take Control with Your OS

All computerized DigiTools have one thing in common: an **Operating System** or **OS**. An OS provides the essential link between you and your hardware. The OS gives you a starting point, a way to communicate with your digital devices. Without an operating system, nothing happens.

Operating System or **OS**

An OS is a piece of software that communicates what you want your DigiTools to do. When you start a typical PC, the first thing you'll probably notice is a login and password routine. (See Figure PR1-2.) Operating systems provide this security so unauthorized users are kept out of your system.

After the OS registers your login name and password, it lets you into your own personal **desktop** or welcome screen. The Desktop is created by the OS. A desktop allows you to navigate your PC, tablet PC, or other DigiTool with ease. You can see a typical *Windows* desktop from a tablet PC in Figure PR1-3 on the next page.

desktop

Desktop and welcome screens introduce you to your computer's **interface**. An interface provides the way in which you and your computer communicate with each other. For example, the *Windows* interface uses **icons** or pictures to communicate commands to the user. These icons take the form of buttons, a taskbar, various toolbars, and other visual devices that make using a computer as intuitive as possible. Review the names of the icons shown in Figure PR1-3.

interface

icons

Desktop icons can start key applications

Start button

Input panel icon (tablet PC users only)

Taskbar application icons

Date and quick start icons

Is It Acceptable or Not?

acceptable use policy or **AUP**

network

Internet

An **acceptable use policy** or **AUP** is a document listing the rules or terms of use that must be followed to use a **network** or the **Internet**.

A network is a collection of computers connected together. The Internet is a worldwide system that connects networks together for information-sharing purposes.

Most networks and Internet connections are controlled by public or private organizations that establish rules for their use. Many people are surprised to learn that there are many things they can't do over the Internet from work, school, or library. The rules can be a bit confusing, so AUPs are provided to clarify the terms of use. Most acceptable use policies share some common goals:

- Guard your password carefully.

- Do not let others use your computer account without permission from a supervisor.

- Never use your computer to lie, distort, or offend others.

- Use your computer for official business only. Personal business is limited or not allowed.

- Do not forward suspicious-looking messages or e-mail.

- Do not steal information from the computer files of others.

- Do not download graphics, music, videos, software, or other copyrighted information from the Internet without written permission.

- Always log out of your computer at the end of each session.

Because each business and organization has slightly different rules, obtain a copy of the official AUP from your network administrator or Internet service provider and review its terms of use so you'll be clear on what is and is not acceptable.

Exercise 1A

Start Up and Shut Down

1. Review any terms of use or acceptable use policy required to use your computer network or Internet connection.

2. Start your computer and log into your user account. (Learn the login and password procedure for your computer from your network administrator or instructor.)

3. Review and memorize the parts of your computer's desktop. Compare your desktop with Figure PR1-3.

4. Notice the little arrow on your screen? This is called a **mouse pointer** on traditional PCs and a **pen pointer** on a tablet PC. Practice moving the mouse or digital pen pointer.

   • Mouse users: Move the mouse pointer to each corner of the screen. When you run out of room on your mouse pad, lift your mouse, move it back a few inches, place it back on the mouse pad, and slide the mouse pointer further toward the corner.

   • Digital pen users: Hover your digital pen approximately 1/2" above the surface of the screen, and move the pen pointer to each corner of the screen without touching the screen's surface.

5. Shut down the computer by choosing **Start**, **Turn Off Computer** and **Turn Off**.

It's Your Default

Operating systems provide a variety of settings, options, or ways to get things done. To help beginners, an OS provides **default** interface settings. Default settings are picked by the software engineers who design the OS. These settings are their best guesses as to what you will want these settings to be under ordinary circumstances.

However, you're not ordinary at all! It's your default; you can change these settings if you like. For example, one of the primary purposes of an OS is to talk to the hardware connected to your computer, such as your printer. If there are multiple printers on your network, one will be selected as your default printer. But what if you want to print on a color printer down the hallway from your office? By changing the default printer setting, you can use the printer that best fits your needs.

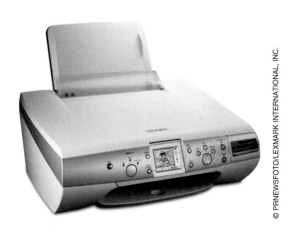

© PRNEWSFOTO/LEXMARK INTERNATIONAL, INC.

The **Control Panel** can help you make changes in your printer settings as well as make other important changes to your PC's interface. To open the Control Panel, log into your Windows computer and choose Start, Control Panel. When the Control Panel window opens, you will see a series of powerful utilities, explained in Figure PR1-4 on p. 6.

After the Control Panel window opens, you can choose from a variety of options explained in Figure PR1-4.

mouse pointer

pen pointer

If you are a new digital pen user, remember that a *tap* is like a mouse click, a *double tap* is like a double mouse click, and a click and drag motion requires a *touch and drag* with a digital pen. To perform the equivalent of a mouse right click on a tablet PC, touch the digital pen on the surface of the screen and wait for a circle of dots to appear. Then lift the pen to reveal pop-up menus.

default

Control Panel

The Control Panels can be viewed in either **Classic** or **Categories** views by selecting this option in the top, left-hand corner of the open Control Panel window. The examples in this prerequisites unit are shown in Categories view as seen in Figure PR1-4. Leave your Control Panel in Categories view for the exercises that follow.

Choose Categories view

Changes the look of your interface

Connects to shared computers and the Internet

Allows the installation of new software

Allows the configuration of multimedia devices

Helps maintain and repair the system

Manages PC security settings

Adapts the PC for handicapped individuals

Allows the setup of printers and other hardware peripheral devices

Allows multiple, secure, individual user accounts

Manipulates the date, time, and time zone settings

> **Tip**
>
> What if you change a default setting and realize later that it was a mistake? In every OS there are buttons that allow you to return to the original default settings.

For example, if you choose Printers and Other Hardware, followed by View Installed Printers and Faxes, you'll be taken to a screen that will allow you to choose between various printers. You can make one of these printers your default by choosing your desired printer's icon and selecting Set as Default from the File menu. (See Figure PR1-5.)

You will need proper access rights or security clearance to change a few of your OS default settings. If you're working on a school or business network, you may not be able to change some of these OS settings. System administrators often lock these utilities because they are powerful tools that can completely change the operation of a computer. (See Figure PR1-6.)

Figure PR1-5   Use Your OS Interface to Change Your Printer Settings

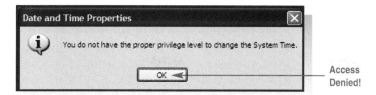

Access Denied!

Appearance and Themes: Cosmetic Surgery for Your PC

In the next exercise, you will change a few settings using your Control Panel options. For instance, by opening the Appearance and Themes control panel, you can change the resolution of your screen, change the desktop's background, and even add your own graphics! It's fun and makes your working environment more interesting. It's like giving your PC a facelift! (See Figure PR1-7.)

Exercise 1B

Using Control Panel

1. Turn on your computer and log into your system once again. After your PC starts up, choose **Start**, **Control Panel** and then **Appearance and Themes**.

2. Choose **Change the Desktop Background**. The Display Properties dialog box will then appear.

3. Choose **Red moon desert** or some other background from the Background images list. Then choose **Apply** followed by **OK** to transfer that image to your desktop.

4. Return to your desktop by closing the Display Properties and the Control Panel windows by clicking their **Close** boxes, as marked in Figure PR1-7.

Figure PR1-7   Change the Appearance of Your PC's Desktop

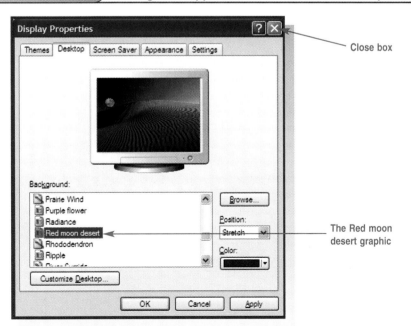

Close box

The Red moon desert graphic

When you open a Control Panel utility, you will view a **dialog** box, such as the one seen in Figure PR1-7. A dialog box presents options that you can choose from; however, nothing changes without input from you. And if you decide you don't want to make any changes, choose Cancel to close the dialog box without jeopardizing your current settings.

Sound Check

The Control Panel allows you to manage the hardware connected to your computer. For example, if your speaker volume is too high or too low, the first place to go is to the Control Panel for Sounds and Audio Devices.

Exercise 1C

Sounds and Audio

1. Choose **Start**, **Control Panel** and then **Sounds**, **Speech**, **and Audio Devices**. The Sounds and Audio Devices Properties dialog box will appear.

2. Choose **Adjust the System Volume** and then the **Volume** tab, as seen in Figure PR1-8.

3. In the Device Volume section, move the slider to an appropriate volume. (*Note:* If you have speakers, you can choose the **Speaker Volume** button and adjust the individual speaker volume settings for your speakers.)

4. Return to your desktop by closing the Sounds and Audio Devices Properties dialog box and the Control Panel window by clicking their **Close** boxes marked in Figure PR1-8.

Figure PR1-8   The Sounds and Audio Devices Dialog Box

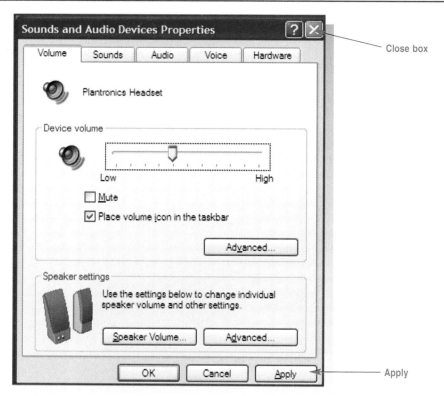

Learn: Change Your Password

A password is a series of letters and/or numbers you can use to protect your files. Your password is your first line of defense on any computer. If you have access rights, you can change your password if you feel that your security has been compromised. Remember these password tips before you continue with the next exercise:

- Don't share your password with anyone.
- Don't write your password down and leave it in an obvious place.
- Don't create an obvious password that someone may guess easily.
- Don't create an unnecessarily long password that will be difficult to key.

Note: The instructions in Exercise 1D treat the Windows User Account dialog box. However, you may have an entirely different security system established by your system administrator. Your instructions may vary.

Exercise 1D

Passwords

1. Choose **Start**, **Control Panel** and then **User Accounts**.

2. Choose **Create a Password** or **Change Password**. The Create a Password for Your Account dialog box will then appear. (See Figure PR1-9.)

3. Key your password twice to make sure you enter it correctly, as instructed in the dialog box. (*Note:* Tap the TAB key to move from entry box to entry box. You can also click or tap in any dialog entry box to activate it.)

4. Key a word or phrase in the "hint" entry box that can help remind you of your password should you ever forget it.

5. Choose **Create Password** and then close any open dialog boxes.

6. Restart your computer. Restarting a computer is slightly different than shutting down. Choose **Start**, **Turn off Computer**, **Restart**. After the computer restarts or **reboots**, try your new password and see if it works as intended.

Figure PR1-9 — Create or Change Your Password

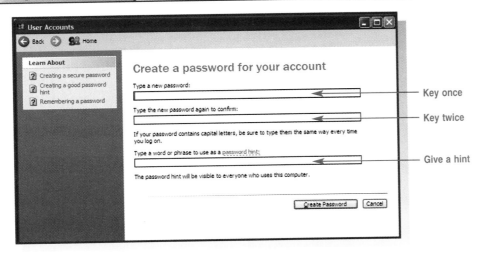

OBJECTIVE

⊘ To discover what applications do and how to open, minimize, maximize, and restore them.

applications

Apply Yourself

An operating system has another important function. The OS makes it possible to access or manage **applications**. Applications are specialized software programs, each with a specific purpose. (Read the *Critical Applications* table below.) In *Microsoft Windows*, view the available applications on your PC by selecting Start, All Programs, as seen in Figure PR1-10.

Application software includes all of the rich tools that people want to use on a PC. They are called alternatively **software** or **programs**. Some of the most essential applications that you will master in this text are previewed in the table below.

CRITICAL APPLICATIONS		
Application Name	**What It Does**	**How to Open It**
Microsoft Office **Word**	Word processing and document formatting	Start, All Programs, Microsoft Office, Microsoft Office Word
Microsoft Office **OneNote**	Notetaking and research	Start, All Programs, Microsoft Office, Microsoft Office OneNote
Internet Explorer	Web browsing	Start, Internet
Microsoft Office **Outlook**	Personal information management and e-mail	Start, All Programs, Microsoft Office, Microsoft Office Outlook
Microsoft Office **PowerPoint**	Multimedia presentations	Start, All Programs, Microsoft Office, Microsoft Office PowerPoint
Microsoft Office **Access**	Databases	Start, All Programs, Microsoft Office, Microsoft Office Access
Microsoft Office **Excel**	Spreadsheets	Start, All Programs, Microsoft Office, Start, Microsoft Office Excel
Dragon **NaturallySpeaking**	Speech recognition	Start, All Programs, Dragon NaturallySpeaking, Dragon NaturallySpeaking

Choose a folder
to reveal more
applications

Learn: Manipulating Applications

Applications open in *Windows* on the desktop; for example, both *Microsoft OneNote*
and *Microsoft Word* have been opened in Figure PR1-11. All open applications have
a **title bar** where information about the application is displayed. An application can
be moved from one part of the screen to another by clicking with a mouse (or
touching with a pen) and dragging an open application into position by its title bar.

    The OS also allows you to control the size of open application windows using the
Minimize, **Maximize**, and **Restore** options. There is also a **Close** button, which
makes it a snap to exit an application. Since the OS creates these controls, they look
similar from application to application. (See Figure PR1-11.) Here's how they work:

title bar

Close

Figure PR1-11   Operating System Controls on Open Applications

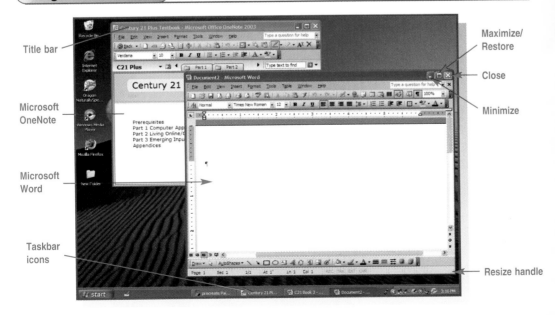

Title bar

Microsoft
OneNote

Microsoft
Word

Taskbar
icons

Maximize/
Restore

Close

Minimize

Resize handle

Maximize

Restore

resize handle

Minimize

- The **Maximize** button will expand the window to fill the entire screen. The button then becomes the **Restore** button.

- Choosing **Restore** will return the window to its previous size.

- Restored windows can be made almost any size by dragging the corner of an open application window by its **resize handle**.

- The **Minimize** button will make an application disappear! Actually, it just sends the application to the taskbar. One click (with a mouse) or one tap (with a digital pen) on the application's taskbar icon will restore it to its original window.

Exercise 2A

Opening an Application

1. Select **Start, All Programs, Microsoft Office, Microsoft Office Word**. (See Figure PR1-10.)

2. Choose the **Minimize** button to send *Microsoft Word* to the taskbar.

3. Click or tap the **Microsoft Word** icon from the taskbar to restore *Word*.

4. Choose the **Maximize/Restore** button twice and observe the difference in the action of these two options.

5. With *Microsoft Word* in the Restore mode, drag the corner **resize handle** in and out several inches and resize *Microsoft Word* to the approximate size seen in Figure PR1-11.

6. Click or tap the **title** bar and drag the restored and resized window to various parts of the screen. Move it left, right, up, and then down around the desktop.

7. Repeat steps 1–6 with each of the applications listed in the *Critical Applications* table on page 10. In the third column, the **path**—or the steps you need to follow to open the application—has been listed. If your computer system doesn't have one of these applications, skip that application. Close each application after you open it.

Learn: About Storage Media

Your computer's OS also communicates with the various storage devices on a computer. (See Figure PR1-12.) Storage devices are essential for preserving everything you've written, taken a picture of, or created using your favorite applications. Storage devices, also called **storage media**, include:

storage media

hard drives

compact discs or **CD-RW**

USB flash

- **hard drives** (often called the **local disk c:**)

- **compact discs** or **CD-RW** drives (the **RW** stands for **read/writable**)

- **USB flash** or thumb drives

- floppy disks (seldom used today)

- storage tapes (still used somewhat to store large amounts of data)

Exercise 2B

Storage Devices

1. To view the storage devices available to you, choose **Start**, **My Computer**. When the My Computer window appears, the storage devices available to you will be displayed. (See Figure PR1-12.) (*Note:* Other peripheral devices such as a PDA mobile device or a scanner will also be displayed on the screen.)

2. Close your My Computer window by selecting its **Close** box.

Figure PR1-12 View Your Storage Devices

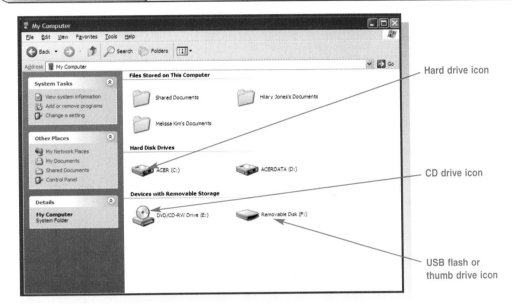

LESSON 3 FILE MANAGEMENT

OBJECTIVES

⊙ To create, rename, and delete folders.
⊙ To open, save, rename, copy, and delete a data file.
⊙ To go online to learn more about computers and how they work.

Learn: About Files and Folders

Information is stored on storage devices in the form of **files**. Applications can create new files. A file can include anything you have created, such as a report in *Word*, an *Excel* spreadsheet, a *PowerPoint* show, a photograph, a Web page, or a music file. When you save using an application, you are creating a file containing the information you want to preserve.

Folders are used to organize files. Properly named folders can make it easier for you to find your saved files. A folder is an imaginary place where files are stored.

By default, *Windows* users will save their files in the **My Documents** folder. The My Documents folder is the center of your file-saving activities. This is your home base, where you will save valuable files for later use.

Folders

My Documents

You can save many different types of files in your My Documents folder, as seen in Figure PR1-13. Notice that each different file type has a different style of icon. *Microsoft Word* documents have a little blue *W* attached to them. *Excel* documents have a green X. Another file type called PDF (Portable Document Format) is red and has a small PDF sign attached. Notice that the folder icons are generally yellow, and look like small file folders.

Note: Your system administrator may have assigned you a different folder in which to save your work. They will need to show you the exact location of this folder. The location you are shown will be your starting point, your equivalent of a My Documents folder.

Figure PR1-13 — My Documents Displays Your Available Files and Folders

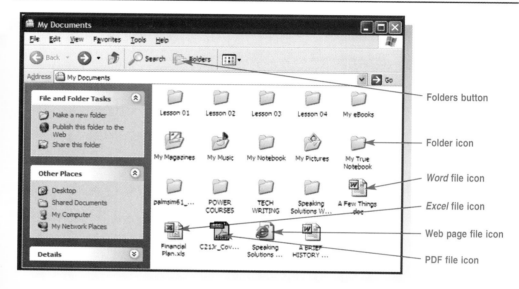

Exercise 3A
My Documents Folder

1. To view your My Documents folder, choose **Start**, **My Documents**. When the My Documents window appears, you will see a few default folders, and perhaps even a file or two, as seen in Figure PR1-13. Some of the default folders may include My Music, My Notebook, My Pictures, and perhaps My Library.

2. Close the My Documents folder using the **Close** button or by choosing **File**, **Exit**.

Learn: Manage, Copy, Move, and Delete Folders

You can use your My Documents window to view, manage, copy, move, and delete folders and subfolders. There are two types of folders: folders and subfolders. Any folder inside another folder can be called a subfolder of the folder in which it resides. Any folders inside the My Documents folder are subfolders of My Documents.

Folders and Subfolders

1. Choose **Start**, **My Documents**, and then click or tap the **Folders** button on the Standard buttons toolbar. This will reveal a list of folders and resources in the left pane as shown in Figure PR1-14.

2. Click or tap the plus sign (+) beside the My Documents folder and you'll view any folders or files inside the My Documents folder as a list in the left pane. When this happens, the + is changed to a –. (See Figure PR1-14.)

3. Choose the (–) beside the My Documents folder, and all the folders inside and their files in the left pane will be hidden.

4. Click or tap the **Desktop** icon in the left pane. All the resources available on your desktop will then be visible in the right pane.

5. Click or tap the **My Computer** icon in the left pane. All the storage media available to you will be visible in the right pane. (Review Exercise 2B.)

6. Choose **My Documents** again to return to your home base.

7. To display the folders and files in the right pane differently, click or tap the **Views** button on the Standard toolbar and choose **Details** as seen in Figure PR1-15 on the following page. (*Note:* The Details view provides the most information about each resource in your My Documents folder, including the file size, the file type, and the date it was created.)

8. Click or tap the **Views** button again. This time choose **Thumbnails**. This is a great way to preview graphics or picture images. (*Note:* For an example, open the **My Pictures** subfolder if you have one. Choose the **Thumbnails** view and see what happens.)

9. Click or tap the **Views** button and try all of the different viewing options. (See Figure PR1-15.) After seeing each, choose the view you like best.

INTERNET  **ACTIVITY**

Learn more about how computers work online by visiting http://www.c21key. swlearning.com. Click or tap on the icon for your textbook and choose the link that will take you to the *Online Technology Essays.*

Figure PR1-14 — View Your Computer's Resources in Different Ways

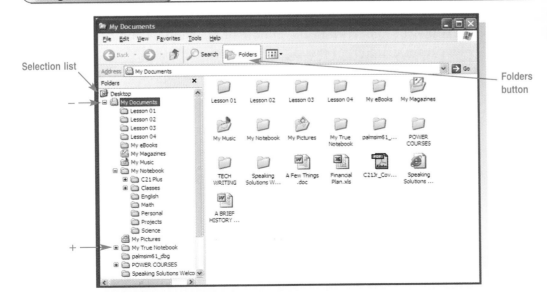

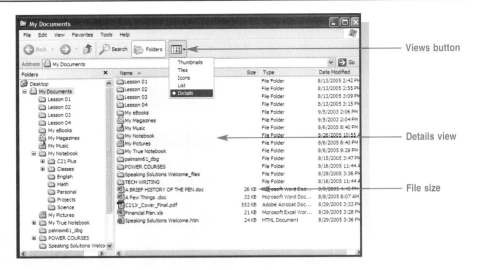

Learn: Create Folders and Subfolders

In the exercise that follows, you will get a chance to make new folders and organize them in a way that will help you in your studies. You will use your My Documents folder to create and organize folders and subfolders, delete unwanted folders, and rename a folder that may have been misnamed.

Exercise 3C

Create Folders and Subfolders

1. Choose **Start**, **My Documents** and then click or tap the **Folders** button on the Standard buttons toolbar so the File and Folder Tasks pane appears in the left side of the window, as seen in Figure PR1-16.

2. Click or tap the **Make a new folder** command marked in Figure PR1-16. (*Note:* You may also choose **File** from the menu bar followed by **New** and **Folder** or right-click in the middle of the window and choose **New**, **Folder** from the pop-up menu.)

3. Name the new folder **Century 21**. Then click or tap outside the folder to have the name accepted. (*Note:* You may also tap ENTER to have the name accepted.)

4. Choose the **Make a new folder** command again, but this time create a new folder called **Goodbye**. Click or tap outside the folder to have the name accepted.

5. Click or tap the **Goodbye** folder. Notice that a little red X appears in the Files and Folder Tasks pane. (See Figure PR 1-17.) This is the Delete button. Click or tap the **Delete** button. You'll then be asked if you really want to delete this folder. Choose **Yes**.

6. Open your new **Century 21** folder. Create four subfolders inside. Name them **Unit 1**, **Unit 2**, **Unit 3**, and **Unit 4**, as seen in Figure PR1-17.

TIP

Your OS will put deleted folders and files into the **Recycle Bin** for temporary storage. Your file or folder will not be permanently deleted until you open the Recycle Bin and choose **Empty Recycle Bin**.

Figure PR1-16   Create Folders and Subfolders

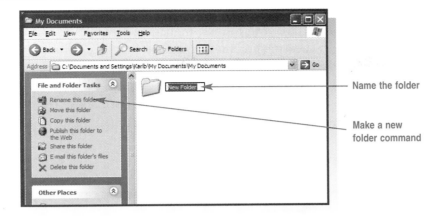

Name the folder

Make a new
folder command

Figure PR1-17   Create Subfolders

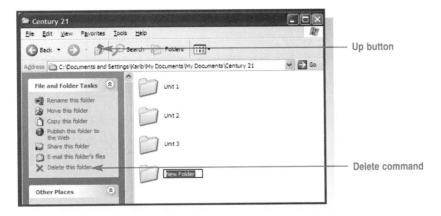

Up button

Delete command

7. To rename a folder, use the **Up** button (marked in Figure PR1-17) to move up one level so that you can now see your Century 21 folder as seen in Figure PR1-18.

8. Click or tap the **Century 21** folder and then select **Rename the folder** from the File and Folder Tasks pane. Rename the folder as **My Century 21 Folder**.

You can also choose Rename from the File menu or right-click any folder or filename to bring up a pop-up menu that will also give you access to the rename, delete, copy, and move options.

Figure PR1-18   Rename a Folder

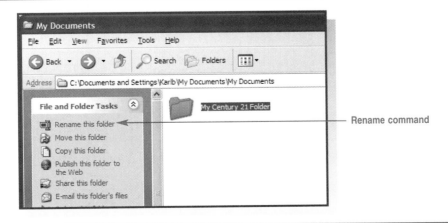

Rename command

Learn: Opening and Saving Data Files

Windows OS uses very similar commands for managing both files and folders. Because you know how to manage your folders, managing files will be a snap. However, before you can practice managing files, you must first save a file into one of your My Documents subfolders.

For this exercise you'll use *Microsoft Word* to open and save a data file into your Unit 1 subfolder. Data files have been included in many of the exercises throughout this text, so you need to know exactly where to find them.

Exercise 3D

Open and Save Data Files

1. Open the *Microsoft Word* application. (See Exercise 2A.)
2. Choose **File**, **Open** from the application's menu bar.
3. With the help of an instructor or system administrator, locate the Century 21 Data Files folder for this book.
4. Choose and open a file called **Computers**.
5. After the file opens, resave the file by choosing **File**, **Save As** from the menu bar.
6. In the Save As dialog box, choose **My Documents** from the left pane; then open your **My Century 21 Folder**, open your **Unit 1** folder, and select the **Save** button. (Review Figure PR1-19.)
7. Close *Microsoft Word*.

Figure PR1-19   Locate Your Subfolder in the Save As Dialog Box

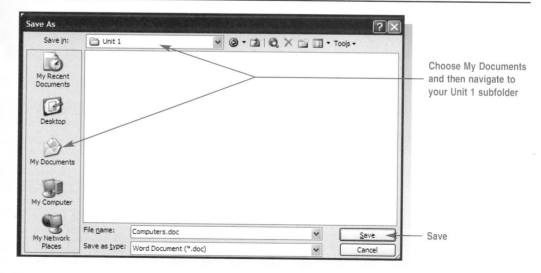

Rename, Copy, and Delete Files

1. Choose **Start**, **My Documents**, and then click or tap the **Folders** button on the Standard toolbar to display the File and Folder Tasks pane at the left side of the open window, as seen in Figure PR1-20. (Review Exercise 3B.)

2. Navigate the following path to your *Computers* file: Choose **Start**, **My Documents**, open your **My Century 21 Folder**, and then open the **Unit 1** subfolder. You should see your *Computers* file inside this folder as seen in Figure PR1-20.

3. Click or tap the **Folders** button again on the Standard toolbar to display the File and Folder Tasks pane as seen in Figure PR1-20. (Review Exercise 3C.)

4. Click or tap the **Computers** file. Then select **Rename the file** from the File and Folder Tasks pane. Rename the file as **What Computers Do**. Click or tap outside the filename box to have the name accepted.

5. Click or tap the **What Computers Do** file. Then click or tap the **Copy this file** command marked in Figure PR1-20. A series of dialog boxes will appear. Follow the instructions and save a copy of this file into your Unit 2 folder.

6. Return to your Unit 1 folder. Click or tap the **What Computers Do** file. Notice that a little red X appears in the Files and Folder Tasks pane. (See Figure PR 1-20.) This is the Delete button. Click or tap the **Delete** button. You'll be asked if you really want to delete this file. Choose **Yes**.

Tip

If you accidentally put a file in the wrong place, you can use the **Move this file** command to change its location in your file and folder structure. (The same option works with folders.) You can also drag and drop files into folders.

Congratulations! You have finished the prerequisites required to continue with this course of study.

Now that you are expert in creating and manipulating files and folders, organize your My Documents folder in preparation for this course.

1. Open your **My Documents** folder (or the folder where you will be saving your data).

2. Delete the four unit folders and the file you created in this Prerequisites section.

3. Create new folders and subfolders to correspond to the units in this book.

Figure PR1-20 Rename, Copy, and Delete a File

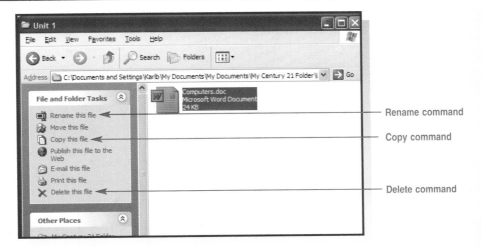

Tablet PC users, proceed to the handwriting recognition unit (Part 3 Unit 1). There you will hone your digital pen skills before continuing.

A Note About Microsoft OneNote

Microsoft OneNote is a new electronic notetaking application that can help you in our study of the units in this textbook. If you have *Microsoft OneNote* loaded onto your computer, you may wish to complete *Part 3, Unit 4: OneNote* before continuing to Part 1. *OneNote* is a study aid that can help you get the most out of this course or any class you may take in the future.

Part 1

Word Processing

UNIT 1

LESSONS 1-3

Improving E-Mail and Memo Formatting Skills

Conditioning Practice

Before you begin the lessons, key each line twice.

alphabet 1 Tom saw Jo leave quickly for her job after my dog won six prizes.

fig/sym 2 Check No. 203 ($1,486.17) and Check No. 219 ($57.98) are missing.

speed 3 Did their auditor sign the key element of the forms for the firm?

gwam 1' | 1 | 2 | 3 | 4 | 5 | 6 | 7 | 8 | 9 | 10 | 11 | 12 | 13 |

LESSON 1 WORD PROCESSING 1

OBJECTIVES
- To review underline, *italicize*, and **bold** features.
- To learn to copy text to another file.
- To learn Send to and Attachment features.

Exercise 1A

Underline, *Italicize*, and **Bold**

1. Key sentences 1–5 below; underline, *italicize*, and **bold** text as you key.

2. Save as *CA1-1A*. Close the file.

1. **Benjamin Britten's** *Four Sea Interludes* include *Dawn, Sunday Morning, Moonlight,* and *Storm.*
2. Chris O'Donnell, Renee Zellweger, Brooke Shields, and Mariah Carey star in *The Bachelor.*
3. The titles of **books** and **movies** should be underlined or *italicized.*
4. Any Given Sunday is a **drama**; Magnolia is a **comedy**; and Supernova is a **sci-fi.**
5. *Success* was written by Henry Wadsworth **Longfellow**; Samuel **Longfellow** wrote *Go Forth to Life.*

Learn: Copy and Paste, Cut and Paste

Use the **Copy** and **Paste** features to copy text from one file to another. Use the **Cut** and **Paste** features to move text from one file to another.

Steps to Copy, Cut, and Paste:

1. Select the text.
2. Copy or cut the selected text.
3. Open the document in which you want to place the copied (or cut) text.
4. Place the insertion point where you want to place the text.
5. Paste the text at the insertion point.

Exercise 1B
Copy Text to Another File

1. Open *CD-CA1-1*; copy sentences 6–10.
2. Open *CA1-1A*; place the copied text a double space below sentence 5.
3. Save as *CA1-1B*. Close the file.

Exercise 1C
Reinforce Copying Files

The initial words of each of the three paragraphs of the Gettysburg Address are shown below. The names of the files where these paragraphs can be found are shown in parentheses.

1. Open the files: *CD-CA1-1C-1*, *CD-CA1-1C-2*, and *CD-CA1-1C-3*.
2. Create a copy of the Gettysburg Address:
   a. Copy the paragraphs from *CD-CA1-1C-2* and *CD-CA1-1C-3*.
   b. Place them in the correct order in *CD-CA1-1C-1*. Leave a double space between paragraphs.
3. Save as *CA1-1C-4*. Close the file.

Paragraph 1: Four score and seven years ago, our fathers brought . . .
(*CD-CA1-1C-1*)
Paragraph 2: Now we are engaged in a great civil war, testing . . .
(*CD-CA1-1C-2*)
Paragraph 3: But in a large sense we cannot dedicate, we cannot . . .
(*CD-CA1-1C-3*)

Learn: Send To and Attachment Features

There are two methods for sending a file electronically to another person. A file created in your WP (word processing) software can be sent directly from that program using the Send To method. From the File menu, select Send To and then Mail Recipient. See Figures CA1-1a and CA1-1b below.

A file that has been created and saved can also be sent electronically using your e-mail software. After creating and addressing a new e-mail message, click the Attachment button and browse to find the WP file you wish to send. See Figure CA1-2. The recipient will be able to open the file in the WP program once the e-mail is received.

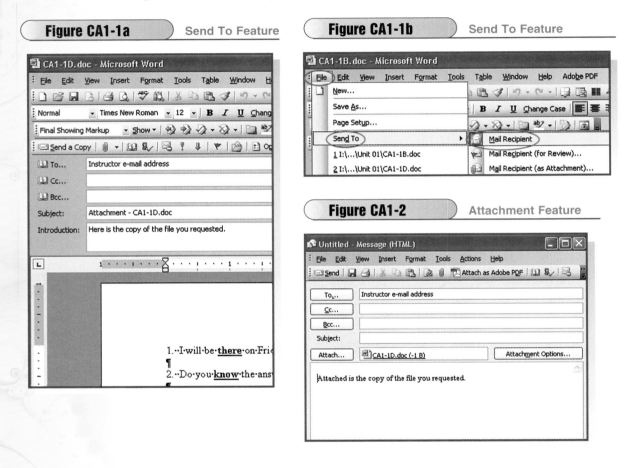

Figure CA1-1a — Send To Feature

Figure CA1-1b — Send To Feature

Figure CA1-2 — Attachment Feature

Exercise 1D

Send to and Attachment

1. Open the file *CD-CA1-1D*.

2. Delete the incorrect word choice and parentheses from each sentence; bold and underline the correct word choice.

3. Send the document containing *CD-CA1-1D* from your WP software to your instructor with this introduction: Here is the copy of the file you requested.

4. Save the document as *CA1-1D* and close it. Send an e-mail to your instructor with the message: Attached is the copy of the file you requested. *Attach CA1-1D*.

⊙ To process e-mail messages with attachments.

Learn: E-mail

E-mail (electronic mail) is used in most business organizations. Because of the ease of creating and the speed of sending, e-mail messages have partially replaced the memo and the letter. Generally, delivery of an e-mail message takes place within minutes, whether the receiver is in the same building or in another location anywhere in the world. An e-mail message is illustrated in Figure CA1-3.

Figure CA1-3   E-Mail

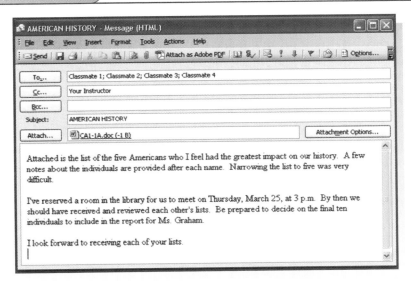

E-mail heading. The format used for the e-mail heading may vary slightly, depending on the program used for creating e-mail. The heading generally includes who the e-mail is being sent to (To:), what the e-mail is about (Subject:), and who copies of the e-mail are being sent to (Cc:). The name of the person sending the e-mail and the date the e-mail is sent are automatically included by the software. If you don't want the person receiving the e-mail to know that you are sending a copy of the e-mail to another person, the Bcc: feature can be used.

E-mail body. The paragraphs of an e-mail message all begin at the left margin and are single spaced with a double space between paragraphs.

Special E-mail Features

Several software features make communicating through e-mail fast and efficient.

E-mail address list. Names and e-mail addresses of persons you frequently correspond with may be kept in an address list or address book. An address can be keyed on the To: line by selecting it from the list.

E-mail copies. Copies of e-mail can be sent to additional addresses at the same time you send the original message. The Cc: (courtesy copy) and Bcc: (blind courtesy copy) features of e-mail software are used to send copies.

> **Cc:** If you want the recipient to know that you have sent the message to others, key the e-mail address of the other individuals on the Cc: line in the e-mail heading.

> **Bcc:** If you do *not* want the recipient to know that you have sent the message to others, key their e-mail addresses on the Bcc: line in the e-mail heading.

Attachments. Documents, such as reports, tables, spreadsheets, and databases, may be attached electronically to e-mail. Common names of this software feature are Attachments, Attached, and Attach file.

Forward. The Forward feature allows you to forward a copy of an e-mail message you received to other individuals.

Reply. The Reply feature is used to respond quickly to incoming e-mail. The incoming message (unless deleted) and your reply are sent to the sender of the original message. The originator's address does not have to be keyed. The original message quickly reminds the originator what the reply is about, so a brief reply is sufficient.

E-mail distribution list. When e-mail is sent to several addresses at once, list each address on the To: line, separated by semicolon.

> **To:** burrouta@uswest.net; dunwoocj@dellnet.com; williaak@earthlink.net; garciarf@aol.com

For sending e-mail often to the same group of people, the Recipient List feature (available on most e-mail software) saves time. All addresses in a group can be keyed on the To: line at once when the name of the recipient list is selected.

Exercise 2A

Create Attachment

1. In your word processing program, format and key the following text, using a 2" top margin and single spacing.
2. Double-space the heading.
3. Bold all names.

AMERICAN HISTORY
Your Name
March 18, 20--

Albert Einstein: American physicist whose theory of relativity led to the harnessing of nuclear energy.

Benjamin Franklin: A leading American statesman, inventor, philanthropist, publisher, author, revolutionary, and thinker.

Abraham Lincoln: The sixteenth President of the United States; helped keep the Union together during the Civil War, which led to the abolishment of slavery; recognized for his honesty and compassion.

Franklin Roosevelt: Thirty-second President of the United States; led the country during two critical periods in United States history (the Great Depression and World War II).

George Washington: Commander in Chief of the Continental Army during the American Revolution; first President of the United States.

4. Correct all spelling, keying, and formatting errors.
5. Save as *CA1-2A*. Close the file.

Exercise 2B

Send/Receive E-Mail with Attachment

1. Open your e-mail program.
2. Key the text below as an e-mail to four classmates; send a copy to your instructor.

Online Resources

See Bonus Exercises 2C-2D on E-Mail Attachments at www.c21key.bonus-exercises. swlearning.com.

Attached is the list of the five Americans who I feel had the greatest impact on our history. A few notes about the individuals are provided after each name. Narrowing the list to five was very difficult. ¶ I've reserved a room in the library for us to meet on Thursday, March 25, at 3 p.m. By then we should have received and reviewed each other's lists. Be prepared to decide on the final ten individuals to include in the report for Ms. Graham. ¶ I look forward to receiving each of your lists.

3. Include an appropriate subject line and attach *CA1-2A*.
4. Reply to all e-mail messages you receive.
5. Save as *CA1-2B* and close.

Note: If e-mail is not available, create a memo to four of your classmates.

LESSON 3 IMPROVE MEMO FORMATTING SKILLS

OBJECTIVES

- To increase proficiency at formatting memos.
- To format memo distribution lists.

Learn: Interoffice Memo

Memos (interoffice memorandums) are written messages used by employees within an organization to communicate with one another. A standard format (arrangement) for memos is presented below and illustrated in Figure CA1-4.

Memo Margins

Top margin (TM): 2"
Side margins (SM): default or 1"
Bottom margin (BM): about 1"

Memo Heading. The memo heading includes who the memo is being sent to **(TO:)**, who the memo is from **(FROM:)**, the date the memo is being sent **(DATE:)**, and what the memo is about **(SUBJECT:)**. Use ALL CAPS for all lines of the heading beginning at the left margin, and space as shown below.

TO:	Tab twice to key name.
	DS
FROM:	Tab once to key name.
	DS
DATE:	Tab once to key date.
	DS
SUBJECT:	Tab once to key subject in ALL CAPS.
	DS

Memo body. The paragraphs of the memo all begin at the left margin and are single spaced with a double space between paragraphs.

Reference initials. If someone other than the originator of the memo keys it, his/her initials are keyed in lowercase letters at the left margin, a double space below the body.

Special Memo Parts

In addition to the standard memo parts, several other parts enhance communicating with memos.

Attachment/enclosure notations. If another document is attached to a memo, the word *Attachment* is keyed at the left margin a double space below the reference initials (or below the last line of the body if reference initials are not used). If a document accompanies the memo but is not attached to it, key the word *Enclosure*.

2"

TO: Andrew Nelson, Manager
                  Amy McDonald, Assistant Manager
                  Judith Smythe, Assistant Manager

FROM :   Malcolm McKinley, Travel Agent

DATE: May 3, 20--

SUBJECT: CIVIL WAR BUS TOUR

Yes, I think there would be an interest in a bus tour of some of the battle campaigns of the Civil War. My recommendation would be to start with a six-day tour that includes some of the most famous battlefields.

Of course, the one that comes to mind right away is Gettysburg, where over 158,000 Union (George G. Meade) and Confederate (Robert E. Lee) soldiers fought courageously for their causes. This battle (July 1–3, 1863) resulted in an estimated 51,000 lives being lost. Being able to visit the place where President Lincoln delivered the Gettysburg Address would also be of real interest to those considering the trip. I've looked at several websites, and evidently something of interest is always going on in or near Gettysburg.

The other battlefields that I recommend including on the tour are Manassas (Virginia) and Antietam (Maryland). Both of these battlefields were key encounters of the Civil War.

Within the next week, I will provide you with more details on a tour such as the one I've briefly presented.

xx

c Timothy Gerrard
  Maria Valdez

Default or 1" LM

Default or 1" RM

At least 1" BM

Copy notation. A copy notation indicates that a copy of a memo is being sent to someone other than the addressee. Use c followed by the name(s) of the person(s) to receive a copy. Place a copy notation a double space below the last line of the enclosure notation or the reference initials if there is no enclosure. If there is more than one name, list names vertically. If you do not want the person to know you are sending it to others, use the bc (blind copy) notation on the copy only.

Memo distribution list. When a memo is sent to several individuals, a distribution list is used. Format the memo distribution list as shown below:

TO: Tim Burroughs
     Charla Dunwoody
     Alexandra Williams
     Ramon Garcia

Exercise 3A

Memos

1. Format and key the text below as an interoffice memo.
2. For the list, set tabs at 0.5" and 0.75".
3. Tab, key an asterisk, and then tab again before keying the name of each act.
4. Save as *CA1-3A*. Close the file.

TO: American History Students | FROM: Professor Perry | DATE: January 20, 20-- | SUBJECT: NEXT EXAM

Here is the information about next week's exam. The exam will cover Chapter 22, pages 702–727, and Chapter 23, pages 740–769.

The main emphasis of Chapter 22 is the New Deal. You will be expected to explain what the New Deal was, why some people criticized it while others praised it, and the impact of the New Deal on the U.S. economy.

Between 1933 and 1937, many pieces of legislation associated with the New Deal were passed. Make sure you know the purpose of each of the following acts.

    * Emergency Banking Act
    * Agricultural Adjustment Act
    * Federal Emergency Relief Act
    * Home Owners Refinancing Act
    * National Industrial Recovery Act
    * Emergency Relief Appropriation Act
    * National Labor Relations Act
    * Social Security Act

Chapter 23 covers World War II. We thoroughly discussed this chapter in class. Make sure you review your notes carefully.

If you are knowledgeable about these topics, you should do well on the exam. | xx

Exercise 3B

Memos

1. Format and key the text below as a memo to **Marsha Hanson, Director**. The memo is from **Jack Vermillion**.
2. Use the current date and a subject line of ANTHONY AND STANTON DISCUSSION.
3. Include a blind copy notation to **Kevin Hefner**.
4. Save as *CA1-3B*. Close the file.

Even though the Virginia Women's Museum is primarily for recognizing those women who contributed greatly to Virginia's history, I think it appropriate to recognize some early leaders of the women's movement on a national level.

Susan B. Anthony and Elizabeth Cady Stanton are two women who led the struggle for women's suffrage at the national level. They organized the National Woman Suffrage Association. Shouldn't they be recognized for their gallant efforts in our museum as well?

Please include a discussion of this issue on the next agenda. | xx

Exercise 3C

Memos

1. Format and key the text below as a memorandum.

Online Resources

See Bonus Exercises 4A-4C on E-Mail and Memos at www.c21key.bonus-exercises. swlearning.com.

TO: Andrew Nelson, Manager; Amy McDonald, Assistant Manager; Judith Smythe, Assistant Manager | FROM: Malcolm McKinley, Travel Agent | DATE: May 3, 20-- | SUBJECT: CIVIL WAR BUS TOUR

Yes, I think there would be an interest in a bus tour of some of the battle campaigns of the Civil War. My recommendation would be to start with a six-day tour that includes some of the most famous battlefields.

Of course, the one that comes to mind right away is Gettysburg, where over 158,000 Union (George G. Meade) and Confederate (Robert E. Lee) soldiers fought courageously for their causes. This battle (July 1–3, 1863) resulted in an estimated 51,000 lives being lost. Being able to visit the place where President Lincoln delivered the Gettysburg Address would also be of real interest to those considering the trip. I've looked at several websites, and evidently something of interest is always going on in or near Gettysburg.

The other battlefields that I recommend including on the tour are Manassas (Virginia) and Antietam (Maryland). Both of these battlefields were key encounters of the Civil War.

Within the next week, I will provide you with more details on a tour such as the one I've briefly presented. | xx

2. Send copies of the memo to **Timothy Gerrard** and **Maria Valdez**.
3. Save as *CA1-3C* and close.

UNIT 2

LESSONS 1–4

Improving Report Formatting Skills

Conditioning Practice

Before you begin the lessons, key each line twice.

alphabet	1	A man in the park saw a fat lizard quickly devour six juicy bugs.
fig/sym	2	Please revise pages 360, 492, and 578 for the August 21 deadline.
speed	3	Eight girls may sit with the maid in the wheelchair by the docks.

gwam 1' | 1 | 2 | 3 | 4 | 5 | 6 | 7 | 8 | 9 | 10 | 11 | 12 | 13 |

LESSON 1 WORD PROCESSING 2

OBJECTIVES

- To format margins, spacing, and left (paragraph) indent.
- To format margins, alignment, and hanging indent.
- To copy text from file to file.
- To format footnotes.
- To format endnotes.
- To use the Bullets and Numbering feature.
- To insert a file.
- To use the Dot Leader tab.
- To use the Comments feature.

Exercise 1A

Format Margins, Spacing, and Left (paragraph) Indent

1. Format and key the text on the next page, using a 1.5" left margin and a 1" right margin.

2. Double-space the first paragraph and single-space the second paragraph.

3. The second paragraph is a long quote. Use the Left (Paragraph) Indent feature to indent the paragraph 0.5" from the left margin.

4. Save as *CA2-1A*. Close the file.

Another speech of significant magnitude was delivered by Winston Churchill (1940, 572). His words not only lifted the spirits of the British but also were motivational to those committed to the Allied cause.

> We shall go on to the end, we shall fight in France, we shall fight on the seas and oceans, we shall fight with growing confidence and growing strength in the air, we shall defend our island, whatever the cost may be, we shall fight on the beaches, we shall fight on the landing grounds, we. . . .

Exercise 1B

Format Margins, Alignment, and Hanging Indent

1. Start a new word processing document. Set a 1.5" left margin and a 1" right margin.

2. Use the Align Right feature to place the page number (6) 1" from the top of the page at the right margin.

3. Center and key the title **REFERENCES** 2" from the top of the paper, and insert a double space after the title.

4. Use the Hanging Indent feature to format and key the text below.

5. Single-space each reference; double-space between each reference.

6. Save as *CA2-1B*. Close the file.

6

REFERENCES

Churchill, Winston. "We Shall Fight in the Fields and in the Streets." London, June 4, 1940. Quoted by William J. Bennett, *The Book of Virtues*. New York: Simon & Schuster, 1993.

Henry, Patrick. "Liberty or Death." Richmond, VA, March 23, 1775. Quoted in *North American Biographies*, Vol. 6. Danbury, CT: Grolier Education Corporation, 1994.

Lincoln, Abraham. "The Gettysburg Address." Gettysburg, PA, November 19, 1863. Quoted by Joseph Nathan Kane, *Facts About the President*, 7th ed. New York: The H. W. Wilson Company, 2001.

Copy Text from File to File

1. The text shown below completes the quote by Winston Churchill used in Exercise 1A. Open the file *CD-CA2-1C* and copy the text.
2. Open *CA2-1A* (the file created in Exercise 1A).
3. Paste the copied text at the ellipsis; then delete the ellipsis.
4. Save as *CA2-1C*. Close the file.

> shall fight in the fields and in the streets, we shall fight in the hills; we shall never surrender, and even if, which I do not for a moment believe, this island or a large part of it were subjugated and starving, then our Empire beyond the seas, armed and guarded by the British fleet, would carry on the struggle, until in God's good time, the New World, with all its power and might, steps forth to the rescue and the liberation of the old.

Learn: Footnote and Endnote Format

Use the Footnote and Endnote features to identify sources quoted in your text. WP (word processing) software automatically positions and prints each footnote at the bottom of the same page as the reference to it.

The software automatically prints endnotes on a separate page at the end of the report. WP software lets you edit, add, or delete footnotes and endnotes and automatically makes the changes in numbering and formatting.

Format Footnotes

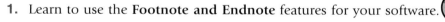

1. Learn to use the **Footnote and Endnote** features for your software.
2. Open the file *CD-CA2-1D*.
3. Insert the two footnotes shown below where indicated in the file.
4. Delete (*Insert footnote No. x*) from the copy.
5. Save as *CA2-1D*. Close the file.

[1]David J. Rachman and Michael H. Mescon, *Business Today* (New York: Random House, 1987), p. 529.

[2]Greg Anrig, Jr., "Making the Most of 1988's Low Tax Rate," *Money*, February 1988, pp. 56–57.

Learn: Superscript

Text may be placed slightly higher than other text on a line by using the Superscript feature. The superscript is commonly used for footnotes and endnotes not inserted with the Footnote and Endnote feature, and for mathematical formulas and equations.

Exercise 1E

Superscript and Endnotes

1. Learn to use the **Superscript** feature for your software.
2. Open the file *CD-CA2-1E*.
3. In your word processing program, change the three endnote numbers to superscripts.
4. Delete (**Apply superscript. . .**) from the copy.
5. Format endnotes 2 and 3 (below) on p. 2 of the file, below endnote 1.
6. Save as *CA2-1E*. Close the file.

ENDNOTES

[1]John Grove, "New Media for Your Messages," *The Secretary*, March 1993, p. 6.

[2]Grove, p. 7.

[3]Amy Gage, "Voice Mail Technology Can Be a Source of Frustration, Irritation," *St. Paul Pioneer Press*, August 3, 1994, p. 1C.

Learn: Bullets and Numbering

Bullets (special characters) are used to enhance the appearance of text. Bullets are often used to add visual interest or emphasis. Examples of bullets: ❖ ➤ ✓ •

Numbering is used to show the proper order of a series of steps. Use numbers instead of bullets whenever the order of items is important.

bullets

numbering

Exercise 1F

Use the Bullets and Numbering Feature

1. Format and key the text below using the **Bullets and Numbering** feature.
2. Double-space before and after each bulleted or numbered list.
3. Save as *CA2-1F*. Close the file.

Please contact the following freshmen to determine if they would like to try out for the play next week: *(insert bulleted list)* Anita Rawlins, Roberto Jimanez, Ho Chi

Then do the following:

1. Check files for names of freshmen in last year's play.

2. Contact them to see if they will participate this year.

3. Contact these sophomores to see if they are still interested: *(insert bulleted list)* Ted Roberts, Marsha Mallory, Clint Hernandez.

Learn: Insert a File

To insert an existing file into a file that you are currently working on, use the Insert File feature.

Exercise 1G

Insert a File

1. Key the text below (except the words printed in red).
2. Leave a 2" top margin.
3. Insert the *CD-CA2-1G-EXAM1* and *CD-CA2-1G-EXAM2* files where indicated in red.
4. Save as *CA2-1G* and close.

TABLE EXAMS

Here is a list of the software features you will need to know for the first exam on tables.

Insert **CD-CA2-1G-EXAM1** file.

For the second exam on tables, you will need to know the following table formatting software features.

Insert **CD-CA2-1G-EXAM2** file.

Learn: Dot Leader Tab

dot leader tab

The **dot leader tab** feature automatically places dot leaders (. . . .) between columns of designated text. The leaders lead the eyes from the text in the first column to the text in the second column. A *right* dot leader tab inserts the text to the left of the tab setting; a left dot leader tab inserts the text to the right of the tab setting.

Exercise 1H

Use the Dot Leader Tab

1. Format and key the text below.
2. Leave a 2" top margin and set a right dot leader tab at the right margin.
3. Leave a space before and after inserting the dot leader tab to enhance the appearance of the text.
4. Save as *CA2-1H*. Close the file.

TELEPHONE EXTENSIONS

Javier Pizzaro 9458
Mark Cortez 6351
Helen Etheridge 4187
Rachel LaBonte 3067

Learn: Comment Feature

Comments or annotations by the originator or a reviewer of a document can be included on a document with the **Insert Comment** feature. See Figure CA2-1.

Insert Comment

Exercise 1I

Use the Comment Feature

1. Open *CD-CA2-1I*.
2. Insert the comments shown below.
3. Save as *CA2-1I*. Close the file.

FIGURE CA2-1   Comment Feature

PLAINS INDIANS

Comment: The heading should be bolded and keyed in 14 point.

Comment: Leave a DS here rather than a QS.

The American Plains Indians are among the best known of all Indians. These Indians played a significant role in shaping the history of the West. Some of the more noteworthy Plains Indians were Big Foot, Black Kettle, Crazy Horse, Red Cloud, Sitting Bull, and Spotted Tail.

Comment: Consider changing Indians to Native Americans.

Big Foot

Comment: Bold the heading rather than underline.

Big Foot (?1825-1890) was also known as Spotted Elk.

LESSON 2 BOUND REPORT WITH TEXTUAL CITATIONS

OBJECTIVE

 To format a bound report with textual citations and references.

Learn: Format a Bound Report

Reports can either be bound or unbound. An **unbound report** is a short report of only a few pages, prepared without a cover or binding. A **bound report** is longer and the pages are fastened together at the left margin. In this lesson, you will learn to format bound reports and use features such as endnotes, footnotes, bullets, and comments.

unbound report
bound report

Bound Reports

Longer reports are generally bound at the left margin. The binding takes about one-half inch (0.5") of space. To accommodate the binding, the left margin is increased to 1.5" on all pages.

Standard Margins

Except for the left margin (default or 1" for unbound and 1.5" for bound), all margin settings are the same for unbound and bound reports. The right margin is default or 1". A top margin of 2" and a bottom margin of about 1" are customarily used on the first page of reports. All remaining pages are keyed with a 1" top and bottom margin. Because an exact 1" bottom margin is not always possible, the bottom margin may be adjusted to prevent a side heading or first line of a paragraph from printing as the last line on a page (**orphan**); or to prevent the last line of a paragraph from occurring at the top of a new page (**widow**). The Widow/Orphan software feature also may be used to prevent these problems.

orphan
widow

Page Numbering

The first page of a report is usually not numbered. However, if a page number is used on the first page, position it at the bottom of the page using center alignment. On the second and subsequent pages, position the page number at the top of the page using right alignment.

Internal Spacing

A double space is left between the report title and the first line of the body. Multiple-line titles are double spaced.

A double space is left above and below side headings and between paragraphs. The reports you key in this unit will have double-spaced paragraphs. However, paragraphs may be single space or double space. The paragraphs are indented 0.5".

Long quotes. Quoted material of four or more lines should be single spaced and indented 0.5" from the left margin. Double-space above and below the quoted material. The first line is indented an additional 0.5" if the quotation starts at the beginning of a paragraph.

Enumerated items. Indent enumerated items 0.5" from the left margin; block the lines at that point. Single-space individual items; double-space between items. Double-space above and below a series of items.

Headings and Subheadings

Main heading. Center the main heading in ALL CAPS. Bold the main heading and use 14 point.

Side headings. Begin side headings at the left margin. Capitalize the first letter of the first word and all other main words in each heading. Bold side headings.

Paragraph headings. Indent paragraph headings 0.5" from the left margin. Capitalize only the first letter of the first word and any proper nouns; bold the heading; and follow the heading with a bold period.

Learn: Documentation

Documentation is used to give credit for published material (electronic as well as printed) that is quoted or closely paraphrased (slightly changed). Three types of documentation will be used in this unit: textual citation, endnotes, and footnotes.

Textual citation. Reports can be written with textual citations included at the end of a paragraph. The textual citation method includes the name(s) of the author(s), the date of the referenced publication, and the page number(s) of the material cited as part of the actual text:

(Johnson, 2005, 165).

When the author's name is used in the text introducing the quotation, only the year of publication and the page number(s) appear in parentheses:

Johnson (2005, 165) said that . . .

For electronic references, include the author's name and the year.

Exercise 2A

Bound Report 1

1. Format the text below and on the next page as a bound report with textual citations.
2. Proofread your copy and correct any errors.
3. Save as *CA2-2A*.

PLAINS INDIANS

The American Plains Indians are among the best known of all Native Americans. These Indians played a significant role in shaping the history of the West. Some of the more noteworthy Plains Indians were big Foot, Black Kettle, Crazy Horse, Red Cloud, Sitting Bull, and Spotted Tail.

Big Foot

Big Foot (?1825–1890) was also known as Spotted Elk. Born in the northern Great Plains, he eventually became a Minneconjou Teton Sioux chief. He was part of a tribal delegation that traveled to Washington, D.C., and worked to establish schools throughout the Sioux territory. He was one of those massacred at Wounded Knee in December 1890 (Bowman, 1995, 63).

Black Kettle

Black Kettle (?1803–1868) was born near the Black Hills in present-day South Dakota. He was recognized as a Southern Cheyenne peace chief for his efforts to bring peace to the region. However, his

(continued on next page)

attempts at accommodation ~~failed~~ *were not successful* and his band was massacred at sand creek in 1864. Even though he continued to seek peace, he was killed with the remainder of his tribe in *the Washita Valley of* Oklahoma in 1868 (Bowman, 1995, 67).

Crazy Horse

Crazy Horse *(?1842–1877)* was also born near the Black Hills. His father was a medicine man; his mother was the sister of Spotted Tail. He was recognized as a skilled hunter and fighter. Crazy Horse believed he was im*m*une from battle injury and took part in all the major Sioux battles to protect the Black Hills *against white intrusion*. He was named ~~war~~ ~~supreme~~ *war* chief of the Oglalas in 1876 and led the Sioux and Cheyenne to victory at the battle of Rosebud in January that year. Perhaps he is ~~remembered most~~ *most remembered* for leading the Sioux and Cheyenne in the battle of the *Little* Bighorn where his warriors defeated Custer's forces. Crazy Horse is regarded a*s* the greatest leader of the Sioux and a symbol of the*ir* heroic resistance *(Bowman, 1995, 160–161).*

Sitting Bull Sitting Bull (?1831–1890) a leader of the Sioux, was born in the region of the Grand River in South Dakota (Encarta, 2004). He was *k*nown among the Sioux as a war*r*ior even during his youth. He was bitterly opposed to white encroachment but made peace in 1868 when the U.S. government *guaranteed* ~~gave~~ him a large reservation free of white settlers. When gold was discovered *in the Black Hills*, he joined the Arapaho *and Cheyenne* to fight the invaders (Bowman, 1995, 673). According to fellow tribesmen, the name Sitting Bull suggested an animal possessed of great endurance that planted immovably on its haunches to fight on to the death (Utley, 1993, 15).

Exercise 2B

Bound Report 1 (continued)

1. Open the file *CD-CA2-2B* and make the corrections on the next page.
2. Open the PLAINS INDIANS report *(CA2-2A)*, and copy and paste the Red Cloud text before the paragraph on Sitting Bull.
3. Proofread your copy and correct any errors.
4. Save as *CA2-2B*.

Red Cloud

Red Cloud (1822–1909) was born near the Platte River in present-day Nebraska. Because of his intelligence, strength, and bravery, he became the ~~the~~ chief of the Oglala Sioux. "Red Cloud's War" took place between 1865 and 1868. These battles forced the closing of the Bozeman trail and the signing of the Fort Laramie Treaty in 1868. In exchange for peace, the U.S. government accepted the territorial claims of the sioux (Bowman, 1995, 601).

Exercise 2C

Bound Report 1 (continued)

1. Open the file *CD-CA2-2C* and make the corrections shown below.
2. Copy and paste the text to the end of the "Plains Indians" report.
3. Proofread your copy and correct any errors.
4. Save as *CA2-2C*.

INTERNET **ACTIVITY**

Use the Internet to learn more about a person named in the "Plains Indians" report. Compose a paragraph or two about the individual.

Spotted Tail

Spotted Tail (?1833–1881) was born along the White River *either* in present-day South Dakota or near present-day Laramie, Wyoming. He became the leader of the Brulé Sioux and was one of the signers of the Fort Laramie Treaty of 1868. Eventually, he became the government-appointed chief of the agency Sioux and made frequent trips to Washington, D.C. in that capacity (Bowman, 1995, 688). Starting in 1870 spotted Tail became the statesman that made him the greatest chief the Brulés ever knew (Fielder, 1975, p. 29).

Learn: References Page Format

Each type of documentation (textual citation, endnotes, and footnotes) requires a references page. All references cited in the report are listed alphabetically by author surnames at the end of a report under the heading REFERENCES (centered, bold, 14 point). The REFERENCES page can also be called WORKS CITED or BIBLIOGRAPHY. Double-space between the heading and the first reference.

Use the same margins as for the first page of the report, and include a page number. Single-space each reference; double-space between references. Begin the first line of each reference at the left margin; indent other lines 0.5" (hanging indent).

1. Prepare a separate references page for your report from the information shown below.

2. Proofread the document and correct any errors.

3. Save as *CA2-2D*.

> Bowman, John S. (ed). *The Cambridge Dictionary of American Biography.* Cambridge: Cambridge University Press, 1995.
>
> Encarta, http://encarta.msn.com/encyclopedia_761578750/sittingbull.html (5 February 2004).
>
> Fielder, Mildred. *Sioux Indian Leaders.* Seattle: Superior Publishing Company, 1975.
>
> Utley, Robert M. *The Lance and the Shield: The Life and Times of Sitting Bull.* New York: Henry Holt and Company, 1993.

LESSON 3 — REPORT WITH FOOTNOTES

OBJECTIVES

⊙ To format a bound report with footnotes.
⊙ To format a references page.

Learn: Footnote Format

Footnotes are another type of documentation that can be used to identify sources quoted in your document. Your word processing software will automatically position and print each footnote at the bottom of the same page as its reference. Footnotes are identified by a superscript number, are single spaced, indented 0.5" from the margin, and include a double space between footnotes.

Figure CA2-2 shows a bound report with footnotes. Use this as a guide when you complete the next exercise.

2" TM

Main Heading

GLOBALIZATION
↓ 2

We live in a time of worldwide change. What happens in one part of the world

impacts people on the other side of the world. People around the world are influenced

Footnote
superscript

by common developments.[1]

The term "globalization" is used to describe this phenomenon. According to

Harris, the term is being used in a variety of contexts.[2] However, most often the term

is used to describe the growing integration of economies and societies around the

world.[3]

The business world uses this term in a narrower context to refer to the produc-

tion, distribution, and marketing of goods and services at an international level. Every-

1.5" LM

one is impacted by the continued increase of globalization in a variety of ways. The

Default
or
1" RM

types of food we eat, the kinds of clothes we wear, the variety of technologies that

we utilize, the modes of transportation that are available to us, and the types of jobs we

pursue are directly linked to "globalization." Globalization is changing the world we

live in.

Side Heading **Causes of Globalization**

Harris indicates that there are three mainf actors contributing to globalization.

These factors include:

Footnotes

[1]Robert K. Schaeffer, *Understanding Globalization* (Lanham, MD: Rowman & Littlefield Publishers, Inc., 1997), p. 1.

[2]Richard G. Harris, "Globalization, Trade, and Income," *Canadian Journal of Economics*, November 1993, p. 755.

[3]The World Bank Group, "Globalization," http://www.worldbank.org/ economicpolicy/globalization/ (February 5, 2004).

At least 1" BM

Format a Bound Report with Footnotes

1. Format and key the first page of the Globalization report shown in Figure CA2-2.

2. Use a 2" top margin, a 1.5" left margin, and a 1" right margin.

3. Continue keying the report using the rough draft copy below and on the next page.

- The reduction in trade and investment barriers in the post-world war II period.

- The rapid growth and increase in the size of developing countries' economies.

- Changes in technologies.[4]

Trade Agreements

Unfair Originally, each nation established its own rules governing foreign trade. Regulations and tariffs were often the out come, leading to the tariff wars of the 1930s. However,

During the 1950's a concerted effort was made to reduce these artificial barriers to trade, and as a result the quotas and other controls limiting foreign trade were gradually dismantled.[5]

Many trade agreements exist in the world today. There of those agrement (General Agreement on Tariffs and Trade [GATT], the European Community, and the North American Free Trade Agreement [NAFTA]) have had or will have a significant impact on the United States.

GATT. The first trade agreement of major significance was the General Agreement on Tariffs and Trade. The purpose of GATT was aimed at to lowering tariff barriers among its members. The success of the organization is evidenced by its membership. Originally signed by 23 countries in 1947, the number of participating countries continues to grow.

The Uruguay Round of GATT is the most ambitious trade agreement ever attempted. Some 108 nations would lower tariff and other barriers on textiles and agriculture goods; protect one another's intellectual property; and open their borders to banks, insurance companies, and purveyors of other services.[6]

(continued on next page)

The European Community. The European Community is another example of how trade agreements impact the production, distribution, and marketing of goods and services. The 12 member nations of the European Community have dismantled the internal borders of its members to enhance trade relations.

Dismantling the borders was only the first step toward an even greater purpose--the peaceful union of European countries.

4. Use this information for the footnotes:

Footnotes

[4]Harris, p. 763.

[5]*Encyclopedia Americana*, Vol. 26, "Trade Policy," (Danbury, CT: Grolier Incorporated, 2001), p. 915.

[6]Louis S. Richman, "Dangerous Times for Trade Treaties," *Fortune*, September 20, 1993, p. 14.

---

5. Proofread your document and correct any errors.
6. Save as *CA2-3A*. (*Note:* You will finish the report in Exercises 3B–3C.)

Exercise 3B

Format a Bound Report with Footnotes (continued)

1. Insert the file *CD-CA2-3B* after the last sentence of the "Globalization" document created in Exercise 3A (*CA2-3A*).
2. Make the changes shown on the next page.
3. Use the following information for footnotes 7–9:

---

[7]"Fact Sheet: European Community," Vol. 4, No. 7, Washington, D.C.: *U.S. Department of State Dispatch*, February 15, 1994, p. 89.

[8]Mario Bognanno and Kathryn J. Ready, eds., *North American Free Trade Agreement*, (Westport, CT: Quorum Books, 1993), p. xiii.

[9]Rahul Jacob, "The Big Rise," *Fortune*, May 30, 1994, pp. 74–75.

---

4. Save as *CA2-3B*.

The first step was accomplished by the Paris and Rome treaties, which established the European community and consequently removed the economic barriers. The treaties called for members to establish a common market; a common customs tariff; and common economic, agricultural, transport, and nuclear policies.[7]

NAFTA. A trade agreement that will have a significant impact on the way business is conducted in the United States is the North American Free Trade Agreement. This trade agreement involves Canada, the United States, and Mexico. Proponents of NAFTA claim that the accord will not only increase trade throughout the Americas, but it will also moderate product prices and create jobs in all three of the countries.[8]

Over the years a number of trade agreements have been enacted that promote trade. The result of these agreements has been an enhanced quality of life because of the increased access to goods and services produced in other countries.

Growth in Developing Countries' Economies

The growth in developing countries' economies is another major reason for globalization. According to Jacob, the surge means more consumers who need goods and services.[9] These needs appear because of the increase in per capita incomes of the developing countries.

Exercise 3C

Format a Bound Report with Footnotes (continued)

1. Format and key the text below and on the next page at the end of the "Globalization" report *(CA2-3B)*.

2. Use the following information for footnotes 10–11:

---

[10]"**India's Income Per Capita Way Behind China,**" http://in.news.yahoo.com/021204/43/1ysk5.html **(February 9, 2004).**

[11]**Pete Engardio, "Third World Leapfrog,"** *Business Week*, **May 18, 1994, p. 47.**

---

3. Proofread your report and correct any errors.

4. Save as *CA2-3C*.

According to the U.S. Department of Commerce, the world's ten biggest emerging markets include:

- Argentina
- Brazil
- China
- India
- Indonesia
- Mexico
- Poland
- South Africa
- South Korea
- Turkey

Of these emerging markets, the most dramatic increase is in the East Asian countries. India, for example, has been able to achieve higher growth in incomes, longer life expectancy, and better schooling through increased integration into the world economy.[10]

Recent technological developments have also contributed to globalization. Because of these developments, the world is a smaller place; communication is almost instant to many parts of the world. The extent of the technological developments can be sensed in Engardio's comments:[11]

> Places that until recently were incommunicado are rapidly acquiring state-of-the-art telecommunications that will let them foster both internal and foreign investment. It may take a decade for many countries in Asia, Latin America, and Eastern Europe to unclog bottlenecks in transportation and power supplies. But by installing optical fiber, digital switches, and the latest wireless transmission systems, urban centers and industrial zones from Beijing to Budapest are stepping into the Information Age. Videoconferencing, electronic data interchange, and digital mobile-phone services already are reaching most of Asia and parts of Eastern Europe.
>
> All of these developing regions see advanced communications as a way to leapfrog stages of economic development.

Summary

The world continues to become more globalized. The trend will continue because of three main factors: new and improved trade agreements, rapid growth rates of developing countries' economies, and technological advances. All of these factors foster globalization.

Format a References Page

1. Create a references page for the "Globalization" report. If necessary, review the information on page 21 for formatting references.

2. Using the information from the footnotes and the additional information presented below, prepare a References page for the report.

Engardio article **pp. 47–49**
"Fact Sheet" article **pp. 87–93**
Harris article **pp. 755–776**
Jacob article **pp. 74–90**
Richman article **p. 14**

3. Save as *CA2-3D*.

LESSON   **4** REPORT WITH ENDNOTES, TITLE PAGE, AND TABLE OF CONTENTS

OBJECTIVES

- ⊙ To format a bound report.
- ⊙ To format an endnotes page.
- ⊙ To format a references page.
- ⊙ To format a report summary.
- ⊙ To format a title page.
- ⊙ To format a table of contents.

Learn: Endnote Format

Endnotes are another way to identify sources quoted in your document. Your word processing software will automatically position and print endnotes on a separate page at the end of the report. Endnotes are identified by a superscript number.

The complete documentation for the reference is placed at the end of the report in a section labeled ENDNOTES. The references listed in the endnotes section are placed in the same order they appear in the report. A corresponding superscript number identifies the reference in the text.

The endnotes page has the same top and side margins as the first page of the report, except that it has a page number 1" from the top at the right margin. Each endnote is single spaced with a double space between endnotes. The first line of each endnote is indented 0.5" from the left margin (keyed to a superscript endnote number); all other lines begin at the left margin. Figure CA2-3 shows how endnotes are formatted. Use the figure as a guide when you complete the next exercise.

3

2" TM

ENDNOTES

1.5" LM

[1]Robert J. Samuelson, "Lost on the Information Highway," *Newsweek*, December 20, 1993, p. 111.

Default
or
1" RM

[2]Laurence A. Canter and Martha S. Siegel, *How to Make a FORTUNE on the Information Superhighway* (New York: Harper-Collins Publishers, Inc., 1994), p. 1.

[3]"Number of Internet Users Doubling Every 11 Months," http://www.glocalvantage.com/NumberofInternetUsersDoublingEvery11Months/ (February 6, 2004).

Exercise   4A

Format a Bound Report with Endnotes

1. Format the copy on the following pages as a bound report with endnotes. The first page of the report is shown formatted; you will need to format the second page of the report.

2. When you finish, use the Speller feature on your word processing program and proofread your document.

3. Save as *CA2-4A*.

INFORMATION SUPERHIGHWAY

Technology has a significant impact on our lives and will have an even greater impact in the future. During the early 1990s, the term "Information Highway" was first used to describe the next wave of technological advancements. As always there were those who were skeptical about what impact, if any, the Information Highway (also called the "Information Superhighway") would have on our lives.

One writer, as late as December 1993, indicated that he was not holding his breath. He doubted if the Information Superhighway would become a truly transforming technology; and if so, he felt, it may take decades. This writer went on to compare acceptance of the Information Superhighway to acceptance of the car.

> It takes time for breakthrough technologies to make their mark. Consider the car. In 1908 Henry Ford began selling the Model T. One early effort of low-cost cars was to rid cities of horses. A picture of a New York street in 1900 shows 36 horse carriages and 1 car; a picture of the same street in 1924 shows 40 cars and 1 carriage. This was a big deal. In 1900, horses dumped 2.5 million pounds of manure onto New York streets every day. Still, the car culture's triumph was slow.[1]

Other writers during the early 1990s were much more optimistic about the value of this superhighway, and began predicting what it would mean to all of us in the near future.

> The Information Superhighway is going to affect your life, whether you want it to or not. In the very near future you will talk to your friends and family, send letters, go shopping, get news, find answers to your questions . . . .[2]

Bound Report with Long Quotations, Endnotes

What is the Information Superhighway?

The Information Superhighway, more commonly called the **Internet**, is a large computer network made up of many smaller networks. By connecting to the Internet, an individual can access and exchange information with anyone else who is connected to the Internet. Currently, millions of individuals are connected; the number increases daily. In fact, the number of Internet users worldwide is said to be doubling every 11 months. In 1983, there were about 2,000 users; by 2000, estimates ranged from 200 million to 375 million.[3]

What has been the impact of the Superhighway?

The development of the Information Superhighway since 1993 has been much faster than many expected and has even exceeded the visions of those who were predicting its widespread use.

Many individuals use the Information Superhighway daily to send **e-mail** messages and attachments; to participate in **chat groups**; to shop; and to get the latest news, weather, and sports. Taking the Internet away from them would impact them almost as much as taking away the telephone, television, and mail delivery service. The Information Superhighway has been constructed, and "road improvements" will make it even better in the future.

Exercise 4B

Format an Endnotes Page

1. If necessary, review Figure CA2-3 on page 29 to see how to format endnotes.

2. Use the endnotes information below to prepare an endnotes page to go with your report.

> [1]Robert J. Samuelson, "Lost on the Information Highway," *Newsweek*, December 20, 1993, p. 111.
>
> [2]Laurence A. Canter and Martha S. Siegel, *How to Make a FORTUNE on the Information Superhighway* (New York: Harper-Collins Publishers, Inc., 1994), p. 1.
>
> [3]"Number of Internet Users Doubling Every 11 Months," http://www.glocalvantage.com/NumberofInternetUsersDoublingEvery11Months/ (February 6, 2004).

3. Save as *CA2-4B*.

Exercise 4C

Format a References Page (optional)

1. Use the endnotes information above to prepare a references page to go with your report.

2. Save as *CA2-4C*.

Format a Bound Report with Endnotes

1. Format the copy below and on the next page as a bound report with end-notes.
2. When you finish, use the Speller feature on your word processing program and proofread your document.
3. Save as *CA2-4D*.

DELIVERING THE MAIL

For years, people have used written communication as one of their primary means of exchanging information. Those using this form of communicating have depended on the U.S. mail to transport their messages from one place to another.

For much of American history, the mail was our main form of organized communication. Americans wanting to know the state of the world, the health of a friend, or the fate of their business anxiously awaited the mail. To advise a distant relative, to order goods, to pay a bill, to express views to their congressman or love to their fiancée, they used the mail. No American institution has been more intimately involved in daily hopes and fears.[1]

The history of the U.S. mail is not only interesting but also reflective of the changes in American society, specifically transportation. A variety of modes of transporting mail have been used over the years. Speed, of course, was the driving force behind most of the changes.

Steamboats

Congress used inventions to move the mail from place to place. In 1813, five years after Robert Fulton's first experiments on the Hudson River, Congress authorized the Post Office to transport mail by steamboat.[2] Transporting mail to river cities worked very well. However, the efficiency of using steamboats to transport mail between New York and San Francisco was questionable. "The distance was 19,000 miles and the trip could take as long as six to seven months."[3]

Railroads

Although mail was carried by railroads as early as 1834, it was not until 1838 that Congress declared railroads to be post roads.[4] Trains eventually revolutionized mail delivery. The cost of sending a letter decreased substantially, making it more affordable to the public.

No aspect of American life was untouched by the revolution that the trains brought in bringing mail service almost to the level of a free good. (For many years--ironically enough, until the Depression called for an increase in the cost of a first-class letter to three cents--an ordinary first-class letter went for two cents.)[5]

(continued on next page)

Pony Express

The Pony Express was one of the most colorful means of transporting mail. This method of delivery was used to take mail from St. Joseph, Missouri, westward.

April 3, 1860, remains a memorable day in the history of the frontier, for that was the day on which the Pony Express began its operations--westward from St. Joseph and eastward from San Francisco. Even in those days San Francisco had already become the most important city in California.[6]

With the East Coast being connected to the West Coast by railroad in 1869, the Pony Express had a relatively short life span.

Automobiles

The invention of the automobile in the late 1800s brought a new means of delivering mail in the United States.

An automobile was used experimentally for rural delivery as early as 1902 at Adrian, Michigan, and in 1906 the Department gave permission for rural carriers to use their automobiles. The change from horse and wagon to the motor car paralleled improvements in highways and the development of more reliable automotive equipment . . . .[7]

Airplanes

The next major mode of transporting used by the Postal Service was airplanes. Speed was the driving force behind using airplanes. ". . . so closely has speed been associated with the mails that much of the world's postal history can be written around the attempts to send mail faster each day than it went the day before."[8]

Electronic Mail

"People have always wanted to correspond with each other in the fastest way possible . . ."[9] A new way of communicating via the written word became available with the creation of the Internet. The creation of the Internet provides a way of transporting the written word almost instantaneously. Electronic Mail (e-mail) messages generally arrive at their destination within seconds of when they were sent. More and more written messages are being delivered via e-mail.

Exercise 4E

Format an Endnotes Page

1. If necessary, review Figure CA2-3 on pages 28–29 to see how to format endnotes.

2. Use the following information to prepare an endnotes page for your report.

[1]Wayne E. Fuller, *The American Mail* (Chicago: University of Chicago Press, 1972), p. ix.

[2]William M. Leary, *Aerial Pioneers* (Washington, D.C.: Smithsonian Institution Press, 1985), p. 238.

[3]Richard Wormser, *The Iron Horse: How Railroads Changed America* (New York: Walker Publishing Company, Inc., 1993), p. 26.

[4]Leary, p. 238.

[5]Albro Martin, *Railroads Triumphant* (New York: Oxford University Press, 1992), p. 94.

[6]Fred Reinfeld, *Pony Express* (Lincoln: University of Nebraska Press, 1973), p. 55.

[7]Carl H. Scheele, *A Short History of the Mail Service* (Washington, D.C.: Smithsonian Institution Press, 1970), p. 117.

[8]Fuller, p. 9.

[9]"Zen and the Art of the Internet," http://www.cs.indiana.edu/docproject/zen/zen-1.0_4.html (February 8, 2004).

3. Save as *CA2-4E*.

Exercise 4F

Format a Report Summary

1. Complete the report "Delivering the Mail" that you began in Exercise 4D. Open the *CD-CA2-4F* file and make the corrections to the text as shown below.

2. Copy the corrected text and paste it at the end of the "Delivering the Mail" report *(CA2-4D)*.

3. Save as *CA2-4F*.

Summary

(now the U.S. Postal Service)

The Post Office has been the primary means for transporting written messages for many years. As the information age continues to emerge technologies will play a significant roll in getting written messages from the sender to the reciever. Again this change is directly attributable to speed. Instead of talking in terms of months required for delivering a message from the east coast to the west coast, *we now talk in terms of* it now takes seconds. Today, e-mail and faxes as are just as important to a successful business operation as the Post Office.

Learn: Title Page Format

A cover or title page is prepared for most bound reports. To format a title page, center and bold the title (14 point) in ALL CAPS 2" from the top. Center the writer's name in capital and lowercase letters 5" from the top. The school name is centered a double space below the writer's name. The date should be centered 9" from the top. Margin settings are the same as the report body. (See Figure CA2-4.)

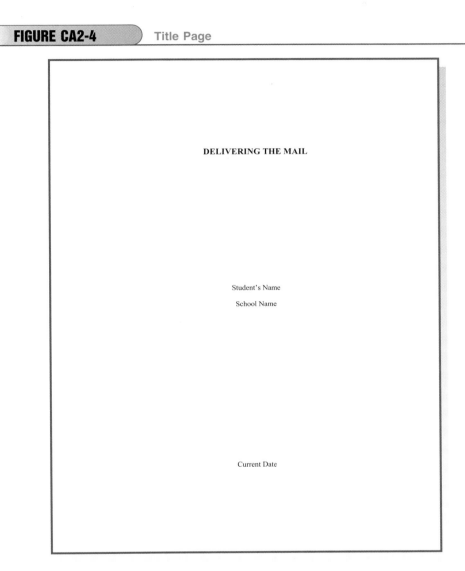

Exercise   4G

Format a Title Page

1. Use the guidelines above and as shown in Figure CA2-4 for formatting a title page.
2. Format and key a title page for "Delivering the Mail."
3. Save as *CA2-4G*.

Learn: Table of Contents Format

A table of contents lists the headings of a report and the page numbers where those headings can be found in the report. The side and top margins for the table of contents are the same as those used for the first page of the report.

Include TABLE OF CONTENTS (centered, bold, 14 point, 2" from top) as a heading. Then double-space before listing side and paragraph headings (if included). Side headings are double spaced beginning at left margin; paragraph headings are indented and single spaced with a double space above and below them. Page numbers for each entry are keyed at the right margin. Use a right dot leader tab to insert page numbers. (See Figure CA2-5.)

FIGURE CA2-5 Table of Contents

TABLE OF CONTENTS

Exercise 4H

Format a Table of Contents

1. Use the guidelines above and in Figure CA2-5 for formatting a table of contents.

2. Format and key the information in Figure CA2-5 as the table of contents for "Delivering the Mail." Verify the page numbers with your report page numbers.

3. Save as *CA2-4H*.

Online Resources

See Bonus Exercise 4I on Formatting a Table of Contents at www.c21key.bonus-exercises. swlearning.com.

Word Processing

UNIT 3

LESSONS 1–4

Improving Letter Formatting Skills

Conditioning Practice

Before you begin the lessons, key each line twice.

alphabet	1	Jack Fitzgerald always competed in the six big equestrian events.
fig/sym	2	Only 6,398 of the 14,652 men scored above 70 percent on the test.
speed	3	Dick is to make a turn to the right at the big sign for downtown.

gwam 1' | 1 | 2 | 3 | 4 | 5 | 6 | 7 | 8 | 9 | 10 | 11 | 12 | 13 |

LESSON ① WORD PROCESSING 3

OBJECTIVES
- ⊙ To use the Insert Date feature.
- ⊙ To learn to navigate in a document.
- ⊙ To use a macro.

Learn: Insert Date Feature

Use the **Insert Date** feature to enter the date into a document automatically. Some software has an Update Automatically option in addition to Insert Date. When the update option is used, the date is inserted as a date *field*. Each time the document is opened or printed, the current date replaces the previous date. The date on your computer must be current to insert the correct date in a document.

Some software provides an **Automatic Completion (AutoComplete)** feature, which also inserts the date automatically. When you start keying the month, Auto-Complete recognizes the word and shows it in a tip box above the insertion point. By tapping the Enter key, you enter the remainder of the month automatically, without keying it. When you tap the Space Bar, the tip box shows the complete date. Tapping the Enter key enters the complete date.

Insert Date

Automatic Completion (AutoComplete)

Exercise 1A

Insert Date

1. Key the text below using the Insert Date and AutoComplete features in your word processor. If AutoComplete is not available with your software, use the Insert Date feature.

2. Save as *CA3-1A*.

Part I
<Insert Date>

Mr. Sean McCarthy
633 Country Club Drive
Largo, FL 34641-5639

<Insert hard page break>

Part II
<Insert Date Field, Update Automatically>

Ms. Brittany Garcia
2130 Mt. Pleasant Drive
Bridgeport, CT 06611-2301

<Insert hard page break>

Part III
1. Today is <AutoComplete>.
2. Your balance as of <Insert Date Field, Update Automatically> is $42.83.
3. I received your check today, <Insert Date>.
4. You will need to make sure that today's date, <Insert Date Field, Update Automatically>, is included on the form.

Learn: Navigate a Document

The **Home**, **End**, **PageUp**, and **PageDown** keys can be used to *navigate* (move the insertion point quickly from one location to another) in a document.

The **CTRL** key in combination with the arrow keys can be used to move the insertion point to various locations.

Home
End
PageUp
PageDown
CTRL

Exercise 1B

Navigate a Document

1. Key sentence 1 on the following page and edit as instructed in sentences 2, 3, and 4. Use only the insertion point to navigate.

2. Save as *CA3-1B*. Close the file.

1. Key the following sentence.

   The basketball game is on Friday.

2. Make the following changes, using the insertion point move keys.

   The ^next^ basketball game is on Friday, February 20.

3. Make these additional changes, using the insertion point move keys.

   The next ^varsity^ basketball game is on Friday, February 20, at 7 p.m.

4. Make these changes.

   The next varsity basketball game is on ~~Friday~~, Saturday, February 20, at 7 p.m. against Sundance.

Learn: Use a Macro

The **Macro** feature of a software package allows the operator to save (record) keystrokes and/or commands and instructions for retrieval (playback) later. A macro can be as simple as a few words, such as a company name, or as complex as the commands to create a table that will be used over and over. By eliminating repetitive keying and formatting, a macro saves time.

Macro

Exercise 1C

Use a Macro

1. Define a macro for *The state capital of.*

2. Key each sentence below, inserting the macro for the repeated text.

3. Save as *CA3-1C.* Close the file.

---

1. **The state capital of** Alaska is Juneau.
2. **The state capital of** Arizona is Phoenix.
3. **The state capital of** Colorado is Denver.
4. **The state capital of** Delaware is Dover.
5. **The state capital of** Florida is Tallahassee.
6. **The state capital of** Hawaii is Honolulu.

Online Resources
See Bonus Exercise 1D on
Using a Macro at
www.c21key.bonus-exercises.
swlearning.com.

OBJECTIVE

⊙ To learn to format business letters.

Learn: Format a Business Letter

There are two types of letters: business letters and personal-business letters. The only difference between the two is that a business letter is printed on letterhead that includes the return address. Therefore, the return address does not need to be keyed. A model business letter is shown in Figure CA3-1.

Special Parts of Business Letters

In addition to the basic letter parts, business letters may include the special letter parts described below.

Subject line. The subject line specifies the topic discussed in the letter. Key the subject line in ALL CAPS, a double space below the salutation.

Reference initials. If the letter is keyed by someone other than its originator, their initials (keyboard operator's) should be placed in lowercase letters at the left margin a double space below the originator's name, title, or department.

Attachment/Enclosure notation. If another document is attached to a letter, the word *Attachment* is keyed at the left margin, a double space below the reference initials. If the document is not attached, the word *Enclosure* is used. If reference initials are not used, *Attachment* or *Enclosure* is keyed a double space below the writer's name.

Copy notation. A copy notation indicates that a copy of a letter is being sent to someone other than the addressee. Use *c* followed by the name of the person(s) to receive a copy. Place a copy notation a double space below the enclosure notation or the reference line if there is no enclosure:

```
c Hector Ramirez
  Ursula O'Donohue
```

2" TM

Date   July 15, 20--
    ↓ 4

Letter
Mailing   Ms. Annette Banks
Address   91 Kenwood Street
     Brookline, MA 02446-2412
      ↓ 2

Salutation   Dear Ms. Banks:
    ↓ 2

Subject Line   JFK UNIT OF INSTRUCTION
      ↓ 2

At our meeting this summer, we decided to dedicate one unit of instruction to John F. Kennedy. As you will recall, I was assigned the responsibility for proposing a curriculum for this particular unit of instruction.
    ↓ 2

Body   The possibilities of what to include in this unit were unlimited. It was very difficult squeezing everything into a one-week unit (see enclosure). However, I enjoyed the challenge of trying to do so. JFK is one of my favorite Presidents; many of my childhood memories are centered
Default
or 1" LM   around the few short years that he was President.
    ↓ 2

What do you think of taking our classes on a tour of his birthplace? The home he was born in at 83 Beals Street is now a National Historic Site. Wouldn't this be a great way to conclude our unit and impress upon our students that the 35th President of the United States lived in a modest home only a few blocks away from our school?
    ↓ 2

If this is of interest to you, I will start making arrangements for both of our classes. I'm already getting excited about returning to school in the fall.
    ↓ 2

Complimentary
Close   Sincerely,
    ↓ 4

Default
or 1" RM

Writer   Blake Finley
    ↓ 2

Reference
Initials   xx
    ↓ 2

Enclosure
Notation   Enclosure
    ↓ 2

Copy Notation   c Juan Sanchez
     Trey McKinley

> Shown in 12-point Times New Roman, with 2" top margin and 1" side margins, this letter appears smaller than actual size.

At least 1" BM

Exercise 2A
Format a Business Letter

1. Format and key the model business letter displayed in Figure CA3-1.

2. Save as *CA3-2A*. Close the file.

Learn: USPS Letter Address Style

USPS Letter Address Style

The letter address for any letter format may be keyed in uppercase and lowercase letters, or it may be keyed in ALL CAPS with no punctuation as shown below (USPS style):

```
MR AND MRS ERIC RUSSELL
PO BOX 215
MOORCROFT WY 82721-2152
```

Exercise 2B
Format a Business Letter

1. Format and key the text below as a business letter in block format.

2. Date the letter February 20, 20--.

3. Address the letter to Mr. and Mrs. Eric Russell using the USPS letter address given above.

4. Supply an appropriate salutation and complimentary closing.

5. The letter is from William P. Shea. Don't forget the Enclosure notation and reference initials.

6. Save as *CA3-2B*. Close the file.

Wyoming women were the first women in the United States to have the right to vote (1869). Ester Morris of South Pass City became the first woman judge in 1870. Wyoming was the first state to elect a woman to state office when Estelle Reel was elected State Superintendent of Public Instruction in 1894. Nellie Tayloe Ross became the first female governor in the United States when she was elected governor of Wyoming in 1925.

It is time to honor women such as these for the role they played in shaping Wyoming and U.S. history. A Wyoming Women's Historical Museum is being planned. With your help, the museum can become a reality.

Our community would benefit from the increased tourist activity. Thousands of tourists visit the nation's first national monument, Devil's Tower, each year. Since Moorcroft is only 30 miles from Devil's Tower, a museum would draw many of them to our city as they travel to and from the Tower.

National and state funds for the project are being solicited; however, additional funding from the private sector will be required. Please look over the enclosed brochure and join the Wyoming Women's Historical Museum Foundation by making a contribution.

Online Resources

See Bonus Exercises 2C, 2D, and 2E on Formatting Business Letters at www.c21key.bonus-exercises.swlearning.com.

LESSON ③ BUSINESS LETTERS WITH SPECIAL PARTS

- ⊙ To increase skill at formatting business letters.
- ⊙ To format business letters with special parts.
- ⊙ To format two-page business letters.

Learn: Attention Line

An attention line should only be used when the writer does not know the name of the person who should receive the letter. For example, if a writer wants a letter to go to the director of special collections of a library but doesn't know the name of that person, *Attention Special Collections Director* or *Attention Director of Special Collections* could be used. When an attention line is used in a letter addressed to a company, key it as the first line of the letter and envelope address. The correct salutation when an attention line is used is *Ladies and Gentlemen*.

Exercise 3A

Format Three Business Letters

Letter 1

1. Format and key the text below as a business letter in block format. Use the following information for the date and letter address.

   Date: March 14, 20--

   Letter Address:
   Ms. Gwen English, President
   3801 Wedgewood Road
   Wilmington, DE 19805-9921

2. The letter is from Marsha J. Johnson, Display Coordinator.

3. Supply an appropriate salutation, complimentary closing, and reference initials.

4. Save Letter 1 as *CA3-3A-Letter1*.

At last year's national convention, our displays highlighted the U.S. Presidents. This year's exhibits will spotlight the states. Each delegation will have a table to display items relating to their state. Exhibits will be in the order the states were admitted to the Union. State presidents are being asked to coordinate the display for their state. If you are not able to coordinate your state exhibit, please arrange for another state officer to do it.

Each display area will include a backdrop, a table, and two chairs for representatives from your state. The table (2' x 6') will be covered with a white cloth. Your state flag will be displayed in front of the backdrop on the far right. The 10-foot-wide backdrop will have a cutout of your state, along with the following information.

Delaware
Capital: Dover
State Nickname: The Diamond State
Admitted to the Union: No. 1 on December 7, 1787

Each delegation can decide what they want to exhibit on the table. We hope that you will include something to give to the people attending the convention. You know how attendees like freebies. We anticipate about eight hundred people at the convention.

We are excited about the state exhibits and hope that you and your officers will make **Delaware's** display the best one at the convention.

Letter 2

1. Revise Letter 1 by addressing it to the Pennsylvania State President:

    Mr. Todd Woodward, President
    810 Lexington Circle
    State College, PA 16801-3452

2. The letter should be changed to reflect the **Pennsylvania** information given below.

    Capital: Harrisburg
    State Nickname: The Keystone State
    Admitted to the Union: No. 2 on December 12, 1787

3. Save Letter 2 as *CA3-3A-Letter2*.

Letter 3

1. Format and key the text below as a business letter in block format. Use the Insert Date feature to insert the current date.

2. Use the following information for the letter address.

    Attention Special Collections Director
    University of Virginia Library
    Alderman, 2 East
    Charlottesville, VA 22903-0011

3. Supply a salutation, complimentary closing, and reference initials.

4. This letter is from Gregg G. Elway, Doctoral Candidate.

5. Save Letter 3 as *CA3-3A-Letter3*.

I'm doing my dissertation on the Civil War generals and their families. Of course, it is easy to gather the needed information on U. S. Grant and Robert E. Lee. So much has been written about these icons of the Civil War that the problem is deciding what to include.

However, I'm not having as much luck with some of the other generals. I'm particularly interested in Galusha Pennypacker, who was claimed to be the youngest general of the Civil War, and in John E. Wool, who was claimed to be the oldest Civil War general. I believe Pennypacker was from Pennsylvania and Wool from New York. From the little I've been able to gather, I believe Pennypacker didn't reach voting age until after the war and Wool was on active duty at the age of 77 when the war began.

I'm going to be in Washington, D.C., next month. Would it be worth my time to drive to Charlottesville to have access to the archives at the University of Virginia? Since I have very limited time on this trip, I want to use it in the best way possible. If you don't feel that your library would be the best place to visit, could you suggest where my time might be better spent?

Exercise 3B

Edit a Business Letter

1. Open the file *CA3-2D* and make the changes shown below.
2. Include a subject line: KEYNOTE SPEAKERS.
3. Leave the rest of the letter as it is.
4. Save as *CA3-3B*.

...When you contact them, please ~~share with~~ <ins>tell</ins> them the theme of our convention and determine what they ~~would~~ propose as an opening or closing session ~~for our convention.~~ ~~Of course, we need to be concerned with the budget; please determine what they would charge.~~ ¶ As I am sure you are aware, we have a very limited budget. The budget often determines whom we invite. As you discuss fees with them, make sure they are aware that we are an educational institution. Oftentimes, professional presenters are willing to give "educational discounts." ¶ The information will be needed before June 15 for our <ins>speaker</ins> meeting. ...

Exercise 3C

Format a Business Letter

1. Format and key the text below as a business letters in block format. Use the following information for the date and letter address.
   Date: May 28, 20--
   Letter Address:
   Mr. Jon A. Richardson
   283 Mount Pleasant Drive
   Oklahoma City, OK 73110-6661
2. The letter is from Martin G. Anderson, Professor.
3. Supply an appropriate salutation, complimentary closing, and reference initials.
4. Save as *CA3-3C*.

Thank you for your kind letter. I'm glad you enjoyed my presentation at last week's convention. It is always nice to receive positive feedback from colleagues.

As I mentioned in my presentation, integrating the Internet into my class has made learning history more interesting for students. Having students just read about history from a textbook wasn't getting the results I wanted. Students were bored, and quite frankly so was I. Now, after students read the chapters, I integrate Internet activities with my lectures. I further enliven my class with electronic presentations, newspapers, speakers, and field trips. This combination brings to life for the students the events and individuals that have shaped our history. As a result, student motivation has increased and so has mine.

One of the Internet addresses that you will find particularly beneficial is PBS's "The American Experience" (http://www.pbs.org/wgbh/amex/whoweare.html). It has been active since November 1995 and has received excellent reviews. The 35 feature sites contain stories of people and events that shaped our country. These sites definitely help bring to life some of the incredible men and women who made this country what it is today.

Check the site out and let me know what you think. I'll look forward to seeing you again at next year's convention.

Learn: Second-Page Headings

Occasionally, a letter (or memo) will be longer than one page. Only page 1 is keyed on letterhead; all additional pages should be keyed on plain paper with a second-page heading. Key the heading 1" from the top of the page single spaced in block format at the left margin. Include the name of the addressee, the page number, and the date. Double space below the date before continuing the letter:

Ms. Lindsay Grimaldi
Page 2
June 28, 20--

Exercise 3D

Format a Two-Page Business Letter

1. Format and key the text below as a business letter in block format. Remember to include a heading on the second page.

2. Use the following information for the date and letter address.
   Date: June 28, 20--
   Letter Address:
   Ms. Lindsay Grimaldi
   3647 Greenpoint Avenue
   Long Island City, NY 11101-4534

3. The letter is from Jon A. Richardson, Instructor.

4. Where noted, include the following list single-spaced:
   - The Film & More
   - Special Features
   - Timelines
   - Maps
   - People & Events
   - Instructor's Guide

5. Supply an appropriate salutation, complimentary closing, and reference initials.

6. Save as *CA3-3D*.

Last month while attending the history convention in Los Angeles, I went to a session titled "How to Bring History to Life." I thoroughly enjoyed the session and have since corresponded with the speaker, Mr. Martin Anderson. He led me to PBS's website titled "The American Experience." ¶ Three of the feature sites would integrate nicely into what we have planned for the last nine weeks of the school year. Each site includes:

Insert list here.

I've listed the sites below along with the description provided by PBS. Hopefully, you have access to the Internet at your summer home and will be able to take a quick look at the sites.

Lindbergh (http://www.pbs.org/wgbh/amex/lindbergh/filmmore/index.html) *At 25, Charles A. Lindbergh—handsome, talented, and brave—arrived in Paris, the first man to fly across the Atlantic. But the struggle to wear the mantle of legend would be a consuming one. Crowds pursued him; reporters invaded his private life. His marriage, travels with his wife, and the kidnapping and murder of their first child were all fodder for the front page.*

Eleanor Roosevelt (http://www.pbs.org/wgbh/amex/eleanor/filmmore/index.html) *Eleanor Roosevelt struggled to overcome an unhappy childhood, betrayal in her marriage, a controlling mother-in-law, and gripping depressions—all the while staying true to her passion for social justice. This biography includes rare home movies, contemporary footage, and . . . brings to vibrant life one of the century's most influential women.*

MacArthur (http://www.pbs.org/wgbh/amex/macarthur/filmmore/index.html) *No soldier in modern history has been more admired—or more reviled. Douglas MacArthur, liberator of the Philippines, shogun of occupied Japan, mastermind of the Inchon invasion, was an admired national hero when he was suddenly relieved of his command. A portrait of a complex, imposing, and fascinating American general.*

After reviewing the sites, let me know if you are interested in including them in your American History sections. I will arrange with the media center to have an Internet connection and large monitor available for all our sections on Friday of Weeks 5, 7, and 9. ¶ I enjoyed spending two months back on Utah State's campus. I decided to pursue my master's degree. After summer school, I took a quick trip to the Grand Canyon and Zion National Park. What beautiful country! ¶ I hope you are enjoying the final days of your summer vacation on Long Island.

INTERNET ACTIVITY

Search the Web to learn more about Lindbergh, Roosevelt, or MacArthur. Key a couple of paragraphs about the individual, including what you learned from the Web search.

Online Resources

See Bonus Exercise 3E on Editing Business Letters at www.c21key.bonus-exercises.swlearning.com.

OBJECTIVES
- ⟩ To learn personal-business letter formatting.
- ⟩ To increase proficiency in keying opening and closing lines of letters.

Learn: Format a Personal-Business Letter in Block Style

A letter written by an individual to deal with business of a personal nature is called a personal-business letter. Unlike a business letter, a personal-business letter is not keyed on business letterhead. Therefore, a return address must be included at the top of the letter. A model business letter is shown in Figure CA3-2 on page 50.

Block format is commonly used for formatting personal-business letters. Letters arranged in block format have all parts of the letter beginning at the left margin. The paragraphs are not indented.

Letter Margins

Side margin (SM): default or 1"
Top margin (TM): 2"
Bottom margin (BM): at least 1"

Rather than a top margin of 2", letters may be centered vertically using the Center Page feature. Inserting two hard returns below the last line of the letter places the letter in reading position.

Basic Parts of Personal-Business Letters

The basic parts of the personal-business letter are described below in order of placement.

Return address. The return address consists of a line for the street address and one for the city, state, and ZIP Code.

Date. Key the month, day, and year on the line below the city, state, and ZIP Code.

Letter mailing address. Key the first line of the letter mailing (delivery) address a quadruple space below the date. A personal title (Miss, Mr., Mrs., Ms.) or a professional title (Dr., Lt., Senator) is keyed before the receiver's name.

Salutation. Key the salutation (greeting) a double space below the letter mailing address.

Body. Begin the letter body (message) a double space below the salutation. Single space and block the paragraphs with a double space between them.

Complimentary close. Key the complimentary close a double space below the last line of the body.

Name of the writer. Key the name of the writer (originator of the message) a quadruple space below the complimentary close. The name may be preceded by a personal title (Miss, Mrs., Ms.) to indicate how a female prefers to be addressed in a response. If a male has a name that does not clearly indicate his gender (Kim, Leslie, Pat, for example), the title Mr. may precede his name.

Special Parts of Letters

In addition to the basic letter parts, letters may include the special letter parts described below.

Reference initials. If the letter is keyed by someone other than the person who wrote it, their initials (keyboard operator's) should be placed in lowercase letters at the left margin a double space below the originator's name. It is also correct to have the originator's initials in CAPS followed by the keyboard operator's initials in lowercase (JPH/jaz).

Attachment/Enclosure notation. If another document is attached to a letter, the word *Attachment* is keyed at the left margin, a double space below the reference initials. If the additional document is not attached, the word *Enclosure* is used. If reference initials are not used, *Attachment* or *Enclosure* is keyed a double space below the writer's name.

Exercise 4A

Format a Personal-Business Letter

1. Format and key the model business letter displayed in Figure CA3-2 on p. 50.
2. Save as *CA3-4A*.

Learn: Blind Copy Notation

When a copy of a letter is to be sent to someone without disclosing to the addressee of the letter, a **blind copy (bc) notation** is used. When used, *bc* and the name of the person receiving the blind copy are keyed at the left margin a double space below the last letter part on all copies of the letter *except* the original.

bc Arlyn Hunter
   Miguel Rodriguez

**blind copy (bc)
notation**

Exercise 4B

Format a Personal-Business Letter

1. Key in block format the letter shown on page 51. Use the following return address, date, and letter address.

Return address and date:
1116 Tiffany Street
Bronx, NY 10459-2276
May 3, 20--

Letter address:
Mr. Mitchell R. Clevenger
325 Manhattan Avenue
New York, NY 10025-3827

(continued on page 51)

2" TM

Return address   230 Glendale Court
Brooklyn, NY 11234-3721
February 15, 20--
↓ 4

Letter mailing address   Ms. Julie Hutchinson
1825 Melbourne Avenue
Flushing, NY 11367-2351
↓ 2

Salutation   Dear Julie
↓ 2

Body   It seems like years since we were in Ms. Gerhig's keyboarding class. Now I wish I had paid more attention. As I indicated on the phone, I am applying for a position as box office coordinator for one of the theatres on Broadway. Of course, I know the importance of having my letter of application and resume formatted correctly, but I'm not sure that I remember how to do it.
↓ 2

Default or 1" LM   Since you just completed your business education degree, I knew where to get the help I needed. Thanks for agreeing to look over my application documents; they are enclosed. Also, if you have any suggestions for changes to the content, please share those with me too. This job is so important to me; it's the one I really want.   Default or 1" RM
↓ 2

Thanks again for agreeing to help. If I get the job, I'll take you out to one of New York's finest restaurants.
↓ 2

Complimentary close   Sincerely
↓ 4

Writer   Rebecca Dunworthy
↓ 2

Enclosure notation   Enclosures

> Shown in 12-point Times New Roman, with 2" top margin and 1" side margins, this letter appears smaller than actual size.

At least 1" BM

2. Supply an appropriate salutation and complimentary closing. The letter is from Suzanne E. Salmon, History Student.

3. Include a blind copy notation to your instructor.

4. Save as *CA3-4B*.

For one of the assignments in my U.S. History class, I have to interview a person who is knowledgeable about an event included in our history book. It didn't take long for me to decide whom I was going to contact.

Who better to talk about *Operation Desert Storm* than a newsperson assigned to the region to cover the news during this period? Would you be willing to meet with me for about an hour to discuss the Persian Gulf War? I would like to learn more about the following topics:

• The events that led up to the confrontation

• The confrontation

• The impact on the people of Iraq

• The impact on the environment in the region

• The role of General Colin Powell, Chairman of the Joint Chiefs of Staff

• The role of General Norman Schwarzkopf, U.S. Field Commander

Of course, if there are other things that you would like to discuss to help me describe this event to the class, I would appreciate your sharing those topics with me also. I will call you next week to see if you will be available to meet with me.

Online Resources

See Bonus Exercise 4C on Formatting a Personal-Business Letter at www.c21key. bonus-exercises.swlearning.com.

UNIT 4

Improving Table Formatting Skills

Conditioning Practice

Before you begin the lessons, key each line twice.

alphabet	1	Zachary enjoyed picking six bouquets of vivid flowers at my home.
figures	2	I bought my first cards on July 25, 1980; I now have 3,467 cards.
speed	3	Dixie owns the six foals and the cow in the neighbor's hay field.

gwam 1' | 1 | 2 | 3 | 4 | 5 | 6 | 7 | 8 | 9 | 10 | 11 | 12 | 13 |

LESSON ① WORD PROCESSING 4

OBJECTIVES

- ⊙ To practice using table formatting features.
- ⊙ To use the Split and Join Cells features.
- ⊙ To use the Shading feature.
- ⊙ To use the Borders feature.
- ⊙ To use the Gridlines feature.

Learn/Review: Table Format Features

**Vertical alignment
Center Page**

Vertical placement. Use the **Vertical alignment** or **Center Page** feature to center a table vertically on the page. This will make the top and bottom margins equal.

Horizontal placement. Center the tables horizontally. The left and right margins will be equal.

Table

Column width and row height. Use the **Table** feature to change the height of the rows in a table. The height of all the rows of the table can be changed to the same height, or each row can be a different height. Adjust column width and row height to put more white space around data in the rows and columns. Additional white space makes data easier to read.

Vertical alignment. Within rows, data may be aligned at the top, center, or bottom. Title rows most often use center alignment. Data rows usually are either center- or bottom-aligned. Use the Table feature to change the vertical alignment of the text in cells. The text within a cell can be top-aligned, center-aligned, or bottom-aligned.

Horizontal alignment. Within columns, words may be left-aligned or center-aligned. Whole numbers are right-aligned if a column total is shown; decimal numbers are decimal-aligned. Other figures may be center-aligned. Use the **Center alignment** Table feature to center a table horizontally on the page. This will make the right and left margins equal.

Center alignment

Delete/Insert rows and/or columns. The table feature can be used to insert or delete rows and columns in a table. A row(s) can be inserted above or below an existing row. A column(s) can be inserted to the left or right of an existing column as needed. Delete empty rows or columns wherever they occur in a table.

Join cells. Use the Table feature to **join** cells (merge two or more cells into one cell). This feature is useful when information in the table spans more than one column or row. The main title, for example, spans all columns.

join

Adjust column widths. In a newly created table, all columns are the same width. You can change the width of one or more columns to accommodate entries of unequal widths.

Exercise 1A

Practice Table Formatting

1. Open the file *CD-CA4-1A* and make the following changes to the table to make it look like the table on the following page:
   a. Insert a new column to the right of the first column.
   b. Use **Department** for the column heading.
   c. Move the department names from column A to column B.
   d. Merge the cells of the first row (main title).
   e. Adjust column widths so the entire ZIP Code fits on one line with the city and state and all column headings fit on one line.
   f. Delete the blank row.
   g. Change the row height for all rows to 0.5".
   h. Change the vertical alignment to *center* for the column heading row and *bottom* for all entry rows.
   i. Center the table horizontally and vertically.
2. Save as *CA4-1A*. Close the file.

<table>
<tr><td colspan="4" align="center">DIRECTORY
OF
DEPARTMENT MANAGERS</td></tr>
<tr><td>Manager</td><td>Department</td><td>Address</td><td>Home Phone</td></tr>
<tr><td>Michael Ross</td><td>Accounting</td><td>310 Flagstaff Avenue
Saint Paul, MN 55124-3811</td><td>555-0102</td></tr>
<tr><td>Tanisha Santana</td><td>Finance</td><td>4123 Lakeview Road
Minneapolis, MN 55438-3317</td><td>555-0189</td></tr>
<tr><td>Preston Foster</td><td>Marketing</td><td>376 Norwood Avenue
Anoka, MN 55303-7742</td><td>555-0156</td></tr>
<tr><td>Natasha Ashford</td><td>Personnel</td><td>812 Dartmouth Drive
Hopkins, MN 55345-5622</td><td>555-0137</td></tr>
<tr><td>Jamal Richards</td><td>Purchasing</td><td>55 Wyndham Bay
Saint Paul, MN 55125-0052</td><td>555-0176</td></tr>
<tr><td>Brianne Bostwick</td><td>Publications</td><td>927 Prestwick Terrace
Minneapolis, MN 55443-4747</td><td>555-0123</td></tr>
</table>

Exercise 1B

Practice Table Formatting

1. Open the file *CD-CA4-1B* and change the table format to make it appear as shown below.

2. Center the table horizontally and vertically on the page.

3. Save as *CA4-1B*. Close the file.

<table>
<tr><td colspan="6" align="center">MAJOR LEAGUE BASEBALL</td></tr>
<tr><td colspan="3" align="center">National League</td><td colspan="3" align="center">American League</td></tr>
<tr><td>East</td><td>West</td><td>Central</td><td>East</td><td>West</td><td>Central</td></tr>
<tr>
<td>Atlanta
Florida
Montreal
New York
Philadelphia</td>
<td>Arizona
Colorado
Los Angeles
San Diego
San Francisco</td>
<td>Chicago
Cincinnati
Houston
Milwaukee
Pittsburgh
St. Louis</td>
<td>Baltimore
Boston
New York
Tampa Bay
Toronto</td>
<td>Anaheim
Oakland
Seattle
Texas</td>
<td>Chicago
Cleveland
Detroit
Kansas City
Minnesota</td>
</tr>
</table>

Learn/Review: Split Cells Feature

Use the Table feature to **split** cells. This feature is useful when information in the table is easier to read when placed in more than one cell. Any existing cell can be split (divided) into two or more smaller cells if necessary. The cell can be split horizontally (rows) or vertically (columns).

split

Exercise 1C

Use the Split and Join Cells Features

1. Open the *CD-CA4-1C* file.
2. Finish keying any columns that are incomplete using the information shown in the table below.
3. Use the Split Cells and Join Cells features of your software to complete the formatting. (You will shade the table as part of Exercise 1D.)
4. Center the table vertically and horizontally.
5. Save as *CA4-1C*. Close the file.

ACCOUNTING MAJOR					
General Electives (40 credits)				Business Core (32 credits)	Accounting Requirements (28 credits)
Category I (9 Credits)	**Category II** (9 Credits)	**Category III** (11 Credits)	**Category IV** (11 Credits)	Acct 201 Acct 202 Bcom 206	Acct 301 Acct 302 Acct 314
CJ 202 Math 111 Math 245	Biol 102 Chem 101 Geog 104	Econ 103 Econ 104 Psyc 100 Soc 101	No specific courses required.	Bcom 207 MIS 240 Bsad 300 Bsad 305	Acct 315 Acct 317 Acct 321 Acct 450
Category I – Communications and Analytical Skills Category II – Natural Sciences Category III – Social Sciences Category IV – Humanities				Fin 320 Mktg 330 Mgmt 340 Mgmt 341 Mgmt 449	Acct 460 Fin 326 Fin 327

Learn: Shading Feature

Use the **Shading** feature to enhance the appearance and to highlight selected columns, rows, or individual cells of tables to make them easier to read and to emphasize cell content. The Shading feature allows you to fill in areas of the table with varying shades of gray or with color. Shading covers the selected area. It may be the entire table or a single cell, column, or row within a table.

Shading

Exercise 1D

Use the Shading Feature

1. Open the data file *CD-CA4-1D*.

2. Shade alternate lines of the table as shown. Use 10% shading.

3. Save as *CA4-1D-Table1*.

4. Open your data file *CA4-1B* (from Exercise 1B).

5. Shade *National League* red and shade *American League* blue.

6. For both the National and American Leagues, shade *East* yellow, *West* green, and *Central* purple.

7. Save as *CA4-1D-Table2*.

8. Open your data file *CA4-1C* (from Exercise 1C). Apply shading as shown in the table displayed in 1C.

9. Save as *CA4-1D-Table3*.

TOP 10		
ALL TIME FILMS		
Movie	Year of Release	Lifetime Gross
Titanic	1997	$600,788,000
Star Wars: Episode IV–A New Hope	1977	$460,998,000
E.T., the Extra-Terrestrial	1982	$434,974,000
Star Wars: Episode I–The Phantom Menace	1999	$431,088,000
Spider-Man	2002	$407,681,000
The Lord of the Rings: The Return of the King	2003	$376,059,000
The Passion of the Christ	2004	$364,642,000
Jurassic Park	1993	$357,068,000
The Lord of the Rings: The Two Towers	2002	$340,655,000
Finding Nemo	2003	$339,714,000

Source: http://movieweb.com/movies/box_office/alltime.php, April 27, 2004.

Learn: Borders Feature

Borders may be applied around an entire table or around cells, rows, or columns within a table. Borders improve appearance as well as highlight the data within the borders.

Exercise 1E

Use the Borders Feature

1. Open file *CD-CA4-1E* from the data CD.
2. Complete the table so that it appears as shown below.
3. Save as *CA4-1E*.

FIFTH & SIXTH GRADE TOURNAMENT SCHEDULE **Altoona** February 26					
Middle School Gym **5th Grade**		**Time**	**High School Gym** **6th Grade**		
Score	**Teams**		**Teams**	**Score**	
	Bruce Somerset	**9:00**	Bruce Somerset		
	St. Croix Central St. Croix Falls		St. Croix Central St. Croix Falls		
	Menomonie Rice Lake	**10:10**	Menomonie Rice Lake		
	Altoona Eau Claire		Altoona Eau Claire		
	St. Croix Falls Bruce	**11:20**	St. Croix Falls Bruce		
	St. Croix Central Somerset		St. Croix Central Somerset		
	Rice Lake Eau Claire	**12:30**	Rice Lake Eau Claire		
	Menomonie Altoona		Menomonie Altoona		
	St. Croix Falls Somerset	**1:40**	St. Croix Falls Somerset		
	St. Croix Central Bruce		St. Croix Central Bruce		
	Rice Lake Altoona	**2:50**	Rice Lake Altoona		
	Menomonie Eau Claire		Menomonie Eau Claire		

Exercise 1F

Optional Activity 1

1. Open the file from Exercise 1E (*CA4-1E*).
2. Apply a different style border with a Box setting.
3. Save as *CA4-1F*.

Exercise 1G

Optional Activity 2

1. Open the file from Exercise 1F (*CA4-1F*).
2. Apply a border around the cells of the three games Altoona's sixth-grade team plays. Also apply a border around the times they play the games.
3. Save as *CA4-1G*.

Learn: Gridlines Feature

gridlines

Hide Gridlines

When you remove table borders (No Border or None), light gray lines, called **gridlines**, replace the borders. These gridlines give you a visual guide as you work with the table; they do not print. The gray gridlines can be turned off by activating the **Hide Gridlines** option. This allows you to see what the table will look like when it is printed.

Exercise 1H

Use the Gridlines Feature

1. Open the file from Exercise 1E (*CA4-1E*).
2. Apply the **None** border setting; then hide the gridlines.
3. Save as *CA4-1H*.

LESSON 2 — REVIEW TABLE FORMATTING FEATURES

OBJECTIVE

⊙ To improve table formatting skills.

Learn/Review: Table Formatting

Table
columns
rows
cells

Tables are used to organize and present information in a concise, logical way to make it easy for the reader to understand and analyze it. The table format can make information easier or more difficult to understand.

Use the **Table** feature to create a grid for arranging information in rows and columns. Tables consist of vertical columns and horizontal rows. **Columns** are labeled alphabetically from left to right; **rows** are labeled numerically from top to bottom. The intersection of columns and rows makes **cells**.

When text is keyed in a cell, it wraps around in that cell—instead of wrapping around to the next row. A line space is added to the cell each time the text wraps around.

To fill in cells, use the Tab key or right arrow key to move from cell to cell in a row and from row to row. (Tapping Enter will simply insert a blank line space in the cell.) To move around in a filled-in table, use the arrow keys, Tab, or the mouse (click the desired cell).

The Table feature can be used to edit or modify existing tables. Common modifications include the addition and deletion of rows and columns.

The formatting changes (bold, italicize, alignment, etc.) that you have learned to make to text can also be made to the text within a table. You can do this prior to keying the text into the table, or it can be done after the text has been keyed. After the table is complete, make changes by selecting the cell (or row or column) to be changed and then giving the software command to make the change.

Most of the tables in the following exercises are already organized; you simply need to create them to look like the examples in the text. However, some of the tables will require you to use your decision-making skills to organize the information before formatting and keying the tables. To complete this unit, you will need to understand the format features shown in the table in Figure CA4-1.

Exercise 2A

Review Table Formatting

1. Study the table format guides on pages 52–53 and the model table in Figure CA4-1. Note the parts of the table and how the table is centered horizontally and vertically on the page.

2. Key the table shown below.

   a. Determine the number of rows and columns needed.

   b. Create a table and fill in the information. Adjust column widths as needed.

   c. Center and bold the main title and column hearings.

   d. Change the row height to 0.3" for all rows.

   e. Change vertical alignment to *center* for the column headings and *bottom* for all other rows.

   f. Center the table horizontally and vertically.

3. Save as *CA4-2A*.

Note: When you complete a table in this unit, check your work. Correct all spelling, keying, and formatting errors before closing or printing the file.

CIVIL WAR PERSONALITIES

Name	Position
Davis, Jefferson	Confederate Commander in Chief
Grant, Ulysses S.	Union Army Commanding General
Jackson, Stonewall	Confederate Army General
Johnston, Joseph E.	Confederate Army General
Lee, Robert E.	Confederate Army Commanding General
Lincoln, Abraham	Union Commander in Chief
Longstreet, James	Confederate Army General
Mead, George	Union Army General
Sheridan, Philip H.	Union Army General
Sherman, William T.	Union Army General
Stuart, J. E. B. (Jeb)	Confederate Army General
Thomas, George H.	Union Army General

Source: *Encyclopedia Americana*, 1998.

Figure CA4-1 Three-Column Table Centered Horizontally and Vertically

Vertical Centering (equal top and bottom margins)

Main title / Secondary title / Column headings / Body

BROADWAY GROSSES		
July 14–20, 2003		
Production	***Gross This Week***	***Gross Last Week***
The Lion King	$1,121,811	$1,121,839
Mamma Mia!	1,035,381	1,026,647
Hairspray	997,902	1,004,684
The Producers	983,442	919,713
Gypsy	854,020	826,381
Nine	772,375	771,355
Movin' Out	767,794	737,234
42nd Street	758,580	694,469
Thoroughly Modern Millie	724,055	596,945
Aida	701,370	631,348
Totals	$8,716,730	$8,330,615

Horizontal Centering (equal side margins)

Source

Source: http://www.playbill.com/features/article/80911.html (29 July 2003).

Review Table Formatting

1. Create the table shown below using the following information:

   a. **Main title**: row height 0.9"; center vertical alignment; bold text.

   b. **Column headings**: row height 0.4"; center vertical alignment; bold text.

   c. **Data rows**: row height 0.3"; bottom vertical alignment; column B center horizontal alignment.

   d. **Table placement**: center the table horizontally and vertically.

2. Save as *CA4-2B*.

MAJOR LAND BATTLES of the CIVIL WAR	
Battle	**Dates**
Fort Sumter	*April 12–14, 1861*
First Bull Run (Manassas)	*July 21, 1861*
Harpers Ferry	*September 12–15, 1862*
Second Bull Run (Manassas)	*August 28–30, 1862*
Antietam	*September 17, 1862*
Fredericksburg	*December 11–15, 1862*
Chancellorsville	*April 30–May 6, 1863*
Gettysburg	*July 1–3, 1863*
Wilderness	*May 5–7, 1864*
Spotsylvania	*May 8–21, 1864*
Siege & Battles around Petersburg	*June 8, 1864–April 2, 1865*
Appomattox	*April 2–9, 1865*
Battles for Atlanta	*July 20–September 1, 1864*

Source: *Civil War Desk Reference*, 2002, p. 241.

Online Resources

See Bonus Exercise 2C on Table Formatting at www.c21key.bonus-exercises.swlearning.com.

LESSON ③ SORT TABLES AND APPLY SHADING

OBJECTIVES
- ⊙ To improve table formatting skills.
- ⊙ To sort information in a table.
- ⊙ To enhance tables with shading.

Learn: Sort Feature

The **Sort** feature arranges text in a table in a specific order. In a table column, text can be sorted alphabetically in ascending (A to Z) or descending (Z to A) order. Also, numbers and dates can be sorted numerically (chronologically), in either ascending or descending order.

Sort

Practice Table Editing

1. Open the file from Exercise 2A (*CA4-2A*).
2. Include the information shown below at the end of the table.
3. Sort the table to arrange the new entries alphabetically with the rest of the entries.
4. Save as *CA4-3A*.

McClellan, George B.	Union Army General
Forrest, Nathan Bedford	Confederate Army General
Johnston, Albert Sidney	Confederate Army General
McDowell, Irvin	Union Army General

Practice Table Formatting

1. Format and key the table shown below attractively on the page.
2. Adjust row height, column width, alignment, placement, etc.
3. Shade the column headings as shown.
4. Use a 12-point font for the headings and a 10-point font for the body and source note of the table.
5. Save as *CA4-3B*.

FAMOUS AMERICANS					
Thinkers and Innovators		**Politics**		**Arts and Entertainment**	
Name	**Life**	**Name**	**Life**	**Name**	**Life**
George W. Carver	1864–1943	Frederick Douglass	1817–1895	Louis Armstrong	1901–197
W. E. B. DuBois	1868–1963	Rosa Parks	1913–	Billie Holiday	1915–195
Madam C. J. Walker	1867–1919	Harriet Tubman	1823–1913	Duke Ellington	1899–197
Booker T. Washington	1856–1915	Thurgood Marshall	1908–1993	Ella Fitzgerald	1917–199(
Benjamin Banneker	1731–1806	Colin Powell	1937–	Bill Cosby	1937–
Mary McLeod Bethune	1875–1955	Shirley Chisholm	1924–	Alex Haley	1921–199:
Charles Drew	1904–1950	Martin Luther King, Jr.	1929–1968	Oprah Winfrey	1954–

Source: "Black History Innovators." *USA Today.* February 15, 2000. http://www.usatoday.com

Practice Table Formatting

1. Open the file from Exercise 3B (*CA4-3B*).
2. Alphabetize columns 1, 3, and 5 of the table by last name.
3. Save as *CA4-3C*.

Practice Table Formatting

 INTERNET ACTIVITY

1. Key the table below and insert the following three names besides the individual's accomplishments:
   - Albert Einstein
   - Thomas Alva Edison
   - Andrew Carnegie

2. Use the table format features that you have learned to arrange the information attractively on the page.

3. Save as *CA4-3D*.

Select one of the names listed in the table. Use the Internet to learn more about the individual you select. Compose a paragraph or two telling about his or her contribution to American history.

KEY PEOPLE IN
AMERICAN HISTORY

Name	Accomplishment	Life
Alexander Grayam Bell	Invented the telephone in 1977.	1847–1922
John Wilkes Boothe	Actor; Assassin of President Lincoln, April 14, 1865	1838–1865
	Scotish immigrant who built a fortune by building steel mills.	1835–1919
Crazy Horse	Sioux Indian chief who resisted government demands for his tribe to leave the Black Hills.	1842 1877
Jefferson David	President of the confederate States of America.	1808–1889
	American physicist; Theory of Relativity led to harnessing nuclear energy.	1879–1955
Thomas Jefferson	Third president of the United States; author of the Declaration of Independence.	1743–1826
Martin Luther King	Civil rights leader; belief in nonviolence was patterned after Mohandas Gandi.	1929–1968
Eleanor Roosevelt	Franklin D. Roosevelt's wife and a major champoin for civil rights and humanitarian issues.	1884–1962
Elizabeth stanton	American social reformer; led the struggle for women's sufferage with Susan B. Anthony.	1815–1902
	American inventor of the incandescent light bulb and the phonograph.	*1847–1931*

Source: Giese, James R., et al. *The American Century*, New York: West Educational Publishing, 1999, pp. 929–935.

Online Resources

See Bonus Exercise 3E on Table Formatting at www.c21key.bonus-exercises.swlearning.com.

LESSON 4 PRESENT INFORMATION IN TABLES

OBJECTIVES
- To improve table formatting skills.
- To use decision-making skills to organize information in a table.

Improve Table Editing Skills

1. Open the file from Exercise 3D (*CA4-3D*) and make the following changes.
   a. Delete *John Wilkes Booth* and *Thomas Jefferson* from the table.
   b. Add the three names shown below (alphabetical order).
   c. Make any adjustments necessary to make the table fit on one page.
2. Save as *CA4-4A*.

Tisquantum	*Taught the Pilgrims farming techniques; helped them establish treaties with native tribes.*	*1580–1622 (approx.)*
Sir Walter Raleigh	*English adventurer who settled the region from South Carolina north to present-day New York City under a charter from Queen Elizabeth I of England.*	*1554–1618*
John D. Rockefeller	*Oil magnate and philanthropist; founded Standard Oil Company in 1870.*	*1839–1937*

Improve Table Formatting Skills

1. Key the table below using the following information:
   a. **Column headings**: row height 0.4"; center vertical alignment; bold text.
   b. **Data rows**: row height 0.4"; bottom vertical alignment.
   c. **Table placement**: center table horizontally and vertically.
2. Save as *CA4-4B*.

WHAT AMERICANS REMEMBER

Top Five Events

Rank	Age Group			
	18-35	35-54	55-64	65 and Over
1	Oklahoma City Bombing	Oklahoma City Bombing	JFK Death	JFK Death
2	Challenger	JFK Death	Moon Walk	Pearl Harbor
3	Gulf War Begins	Challenger	Oklahoma City Bombing	WWII Ends
4	Reagan Shot	Moon Walk	Challenger	Moon Walk
5	Berlin Wall Falls	Gulf War Begins	MLK Death	FDR Death

Source: The Pew Research Center, "Public Perspectives on the American Century." August 20, 1999. http://www.people-press.org/mill1sec4.htm.

OBJECTIVES

⊘ To improve table formatting skills.

⊘ To format tables with borders and shading.

Exercise 5A

Improve Table Formatting Skills

1. Key the table shown below. Use the table format features that you have learned to arrange the information attractively on the page.

   a. Use a table border and shading similar to the illustration.

   b. Adjust column width so that each data entry fits on a single line.

   c. Save as *CA4-5A*.

PRESIDENTS 1953 - 2004				
President	**Dates in Office**	**Age at Inauguration**	**State of Birth**	**Vice President**
Dwight D. Eisenhower	1953–1961	62	Texas	Richard M. Nixon
John F. Kennedy	1961–1963	43	Massachusetts	Lyndon B. Johnson
Lyndon B. Johnson	1963–1969	55	Texas	Hubert H. Humphrey
Richard M. Nixon	1969–1974	56	California	Spiro T. Agnew
				Gerald R. Ford
Gerald R. Ford	1974–1977	61	Nebraska	Nelson A. Rockefeller
James E. Carter, Jr.	1977–1981	52	Georgia	Walter F. Mondale
Ronald W. Reagan	1981–1989	69	Illinois	George H. W. Bush
George H. W. Bush	1989–1993	64	Massachusetts	J. Danforth Quayle
William J. Clinton	1993–2001	46	Arkansas	Albert Gore, Jr.
G. W. Bush	2001–	54	Connecticut	Richard B. Cheney
Blue = Republican Party Affiliation		Red = Democratic Party Affiliation		

Source: *Time Almanac 2004*. New York: Time Inc., 2003, p. 112.

Improve Table Formatting Skills

1. Key the table shown below. Use the table format features that you have learned to arrange the information attractively on the page.

   a. Use a table border and shading similar to the illustration.

   b. Bold all text.

   c. Double-space between each data entry.

   d. Include the following source note outside the table:

   Source: Matthew T. Downey, et al. *United States History*, Minneapolis: West Publishing Company, 1997, p. 158.

2. Save as *CA4-5B*.

Online Resources

See Bonus Exercise 5C on Table Formatting and Bonus Exercises 6A, 6B and 6C on Enhanced Table Formatting at www.c21key. bonus-exercises.swlearning.com.

THE CONSTITUTION		
The Executive Branch	**The Legislative Branch**	**The Judicial Branch**
• President administers and enforces federal laws • President chosen by electors who have been chosen by the states	• A bicameral or two-house legislature • Each state has equal number of representatives in the Senate • Representation in the House determined by state population • Simple majority required to enact legislation	• National court system directed by the Supreme Court • Courts to hear cases related to national laws, treaties, the Constitution; cases between states, between citizens of different states, or between a state and citizens of another state

Communication & Math Skills 1

ACTIVITY 1 Simple Sentences

1. Study each of the guides for simple sentences shown below.
2. Key the *Learn* sentences, noting the subjects and predicates.

3. For *Apply* lines 9 through 11, combine the two sentences into one simple sentence with two nouns as the subject and one verb as the predicate.

4. Revise Sentence 12 by combining the two sentences into one simple sentence with two nouns as the subject and two verbs as the predicate.
5. Save as *CS1-ACT1*.

Simple Sentences

A simple sentence consists of one independent clause that contains a subject (noun or pronoun) and a predicate (verb).

Learn 1 Pam is president of her class.
Learn 2 Kevin walks to and from school.
Learn 3 Reading mystery novels is my favorite pastime.
Learn 4 The captain of the team is out with a badly sprained ankle.

A simple sentence may have as its subject more than one noun or pronoun (compound subject) and as its predicate more than one verb (compound predicate).

Learn 5 She bought a new easel. (single subject/single predicate)
Learn 6 Marv and I received two pictures. (compound subject/single predicate)
Learn 7 Ali cleaned and polished his trumpet. (single subject/compound predicate)
Learn 8 He and I cleaned and cooked the fish. (compound subject and predicate)

Apply 9 Jorge read AURA by Fuentes. Rosa read it, also.
Apply 10 Hamad writes his own poems. So does Janelle.
Apply 11 Sara talked with Mona at the concert. Lee talked with her, also.
Apply 12 Mel chooses and buys his own art supplies. Suzy also chooses and buys hers.

ACTIVITY 2 Compound Sentences

1. Study each of the guides for compound sentences shown below.
2. Key *Learn* lines 13–20, noting the words that make up the subjects and predicates of each sentence.

3. For *Apply* lines 21–24, combine the two sentences into a compound sentence. Choose carefully from the coordinating conjunctions and, but, for, or, nor, yet, and so.

4. Save as *CS1-ACT2*.

Compound Sentences

A compound sentence contains two or more independent clauses connected by a coordinating conjunction (and, but, for, or, nor, yet, so).

Learn 13 Jay Sparks likes to hike, and Roy Tubbs likes to swim.
Learn 14 The computer is operative, but the printer does not work.
Learn 15 You may read a book, or you may choose to paint.
Learn 16 The sky is clear, the moon is out, and the sea is very calm.

Each clause of a compound sentence may have as its subject more than one noun/pronoun and as its predicate more than one verb.

Learn 17 Ben and I saw the play, and Bob and Maria went to a movie.
Learn 18 Nick sang and danced, but the others played in the band.

Learn 19 You may play solitaire, or you and Joe may play checkers.
Learn 20 Bobby huffed and puffed, but Erin scampered up the hill.

Apply 21 Karen listened to Ravel's BOLERO. Matt read FORREST GUMP.
Apply 22 You may watch STAR TREK. You and Edie may play dominoes.
Apply 23 Ken may play football or basketball. He may not play both.
Apply 24 Melanie skated to CABARET music. Jon chose WEST SIDE STORY.

ACTIVITY 3   Complex Sentences

1. Study the guides for complex sentences shown below.

2. Key *Learn* lines 25–32, noting the subject and predicate of the independent clause and of the dependent clause for each sentence.

3. For *Apply* lines 33–36, combine the two sentences into a complex sentence.

4. Save as *CS1-ACT3*.

Complex Sentences

A complex sentence contains only one independent clause but one or more dependent clauses.

Learn 25 The book that you gave Juan for his birthday is lost.
Learn 26 If I were you, I would speak to Paula before the dance.
Learn 27 Miss Gomez, who chairs the art department, is currently on leave.
Learn 28 Students who use their time wisely usually succeed.

The subject of a complex sentence may consist of more than one noun or pronoun; the predicate may consist of more than one verb.

Learn 29 All who attended the party arrived on time and left after dessert.
Learn 30 If you are to join, you should sign up and pay your dues.
Learn 31 After she and I left, Cliff and Pam sang and danced.
Learn 32 Although they don't know it yet, Fran and Brett were elected.

Apply 33 My PSAT and SAT scores are high. I may not get into Yale.
Apply 34 They attended the symphony. They then had a light supper.
Apply 35 Mindy is to audition for the part. She should apply now.
Apply 36 You are buying a computer. You should also get software.

ACTIVITY 4   Composing

1. Key each line once (do not key the figure). In place of the blank line, key the word(s) that correctly complete(s) the sentence.

2. Save as *CS1-ACT4*.

1. A small mass of land surrounded by water is a/an _____.
2. A large mass of land surrounded by water is a/an _____.
3. The earth rotates on what is called its _____.
4. When the sun comes up over the horizon, we say it _____.
5. When the sun goes down over the horizon, we say it _____.
6. A device used to display temperature is a/an _____.
7. A device used to display atmospheric pressure is a/an _____.

ACTIVITY 5   Math: Adding and Subtracting Numbers

1. Open *CD-CS1-ACT5* and print the file

2. Solve the problems as directed in the file.

3. Submit your answers.

Skill BUILDER 1

Keyboard Review

Key each line twice.

A/Z	1	Zack had a pizza at the plaza by the zoo on a hazy day.
B/Y	2	Bobby may be too busy to buy me a bag for my boat trip.
C/X	3	Ricky caught six cod to fix for the six excited scouts.
D/W	4	Wilda would like to own the doe she found in the woods.
E/V	5	Evan will give us the van to move the five heavy boxes.
F/U	6	All four of us bought coats with fur collars and cuffs.
G/T	7	Eight men tugged the boat into deep water to get going.
H/S	8	Marsha wishes to show how to make charts on a computer.
I/R	9	Ira can rise above his ire to rid the firm of a crisis.
J/Q	10	Josh quietly quit the squad after a major joint injury.
K/P	11	Kip packed a backpack and put it on a box on the porch.
L/O	12	Lola is to wear the royal blue skirt and a gold blouse.
M/N	13	Many of the men met in the hall to see the new manager.
figures	14	I worked 8:30 to 5 at 1964 Lake Blvd. from May 7 to 26.
fig/sym	15	I said, "ISBN #0-651-24879-3 was not assigned to them."

Timed Writings

1. Key two 1' timings on each ¶; determine *gwam*.
2. Key two 2' timings on ¶s 1–2 combined; determine *gwam*.
3. Key two 3' timings on ¶s 1–2 combined; determine *gwam* and errors.
4. If time permits, key 1' guided timings on each ¶. To set a goal, add 2 to the *gwam* achieved in step 1.

A all letters used   MicroPace   gwam   2' | 3'

As you work for higher skill, remember that how well you   6 | 4
key fast is just as important as how fast you key. How well   12 | 8
you key at any speed depends in major ways upon the technique 18 | 12
or form you use. Bouncing hands and flying fingers lower the   24 | 16
speed, while quiet hands and low finger reaches increase speed. 31 | 20

Few of us ever reach what the experts believe is perfect   36 | 24
technique, but all of us should try to approach it. We must   42 | 28
realize that good form is the secret to higher speed with   48 | 32
fewer errors. We can then focus our practice on the improve- 54 | 36
ment of the features of good form that will bring success.   60 | 40

UNIT 5

LESSONS 1–4

Creating Electronic Presentations

Conditioning Practice

Before you begin the lessons, key each line twice.

alphabet	1	Rebecca enjoyed explaining her vast knowledge of the zoo marquee.
figures	2	Flight 784 is scheduled to leave at 10:35 from Gate 96, on May 2.
speed	3	The maid may make the usual visit to the dock to work on the map.

gwam 1' | 1 | 2 | 3 | 4 | 5 | 6 | 7 | 8 | 9 | 10 | 11 | 12 | 13 |

LESSON ① CREATE TEXT SLIDES

OBJECTIVES
- ⊙ To learn about electronic presentations.
- ⊙ To navigate through an existing electronic presentation.
- ⊙ To create a title slide.
- ⊙ To create a bulleted list slide.

Learn: Electronic Presentations

electronic presentations

Electronic presentations are computer-generated visual aids (usually slide shows) that can be used to help communicate information. Electronic presentations can combine text, graphics, audio, video, and animation to deliver and support key points. With the powerful features of presentation software such as *Microsoft Power-Point*, attractive and engaging presentations can be created with ease.

Presentations are an important part of communication in business. Presentations are given to inform, to persuade, and/or to entertain. Visual aids generally make a speaker more effective in delivering his/her message. That is because the speaker is using two senses (hearing and sight) rather than just one. The probability of a person understanding and retaining something seen as well as heard is much greater than if it is just heard. For example, if you had never heard of a giraffe before, you would have a better idea of what a giraffe was if the speaker talked about a giraffe and showed pictures of one than if the speaker only talked about what a giraffe was.

With presentation software, you can create visuals (slides) that can be projected on a large screen for a larger audience to view or shown directly on a computer monitor for a smaller audience. Web pages, color or black-and-white overheads, audience handouts, and speaker notes can be created using electronic presentation software.

Learn: Key Features of Electronic Presentation Software

Presentation software has many of the same features as word processing programs. Learning how to use presentation software is quite easy for individuals who have had experience with word processing software. Presentation software is set up in much the same way as word processing software, with similar menus, commands, toolbars, and Help features. Notice the similarities in Figure CA5-1 shown below.

Each labeled part of the *PowerPoint* window has a specific function. Refer to the labeled part in the figure as you read about the parts of the *PowerPoint* window.

- The **title bar** displays the program and filename.
- The **menu bar** displays menus that contain program commands.
- The Standard and Formatting **toolbars** provide quick access to commands.
- The **Outline tab** displays the number of each slide and the text that is included on each slide.
- The **Slides tab** displays small images of the slides that have been created.
- The **Slide pane** displays the current slide or the slide that you click in the Slides tab.
- **Placeholders** are boxes with dotted borders that are part of most slide layouts. These boxes hold title and body text or objects such as charts, tables, and pictures.

presentation
software

title bar
menu bar
toolbars
Outline tab

Slides tab
Slide pane

placeholders

Figure CA5-1   *PowerPoint* Window

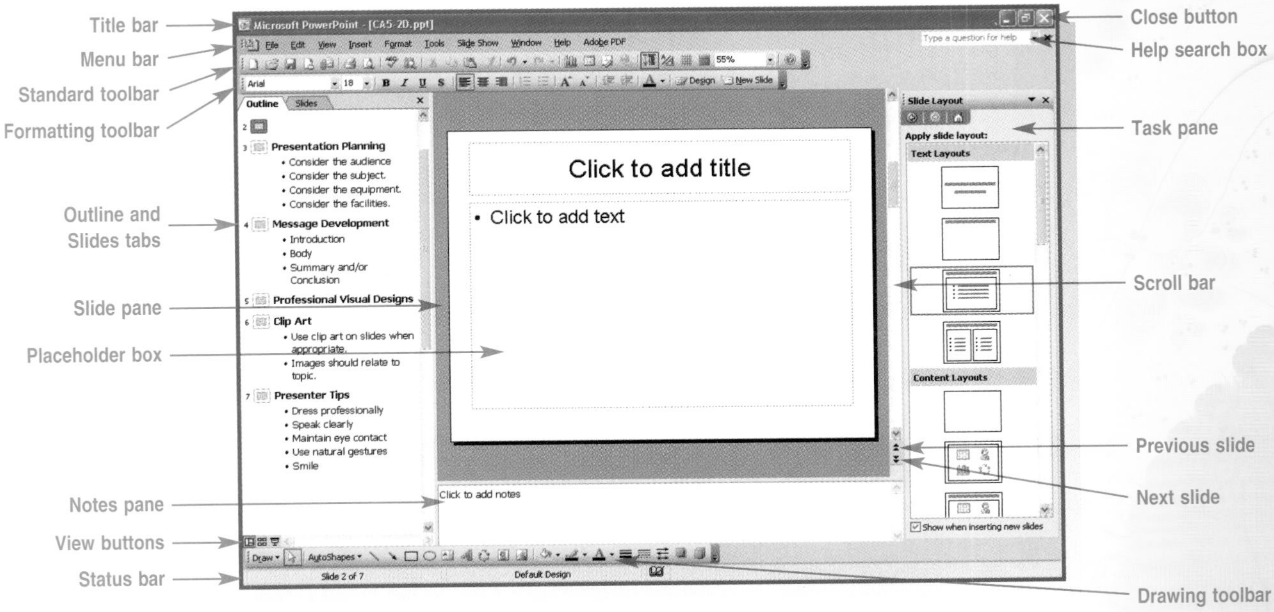

| Notes pane | • | The **Notes pane** allows you to key notes about the slide. |

Notes pane
- The **Notes pane** allows you to key notes about the slide.

View buttons
- The **View buttons** allow you to view the slides in several different ways, depending on what you are doing.

Drawing toolbar
- The **Drawing toolbar** contains buttons for commands that allow you to create and format drawing objects such as shapes, text boxes, and WordArt.

status bar
- The **status bar** displays helpful information such as the slide number and the design template name.

Close button
- The **Close button** closes the *PowerPoint* program.

Help search box
- The **Help search box** provides quick access to program Help.

task pane
- The **task pane** displays commonly used commands for *PowerPoint*. This pane will display such things as slide layouts, slide designs, and clip art.

scroll bar
- The **scroll bar** allows you to move the slides by clicking and dragging the bar or clicking the arrow buttons.

Previous Slide button
Next Slide button
- The **Previous Slide** and **Next Slide buttons** display the previous or next slide in the Slide pane.

Learn: View Options

There are different ways to view a presentation using the options on the View menu (as shown in Figure CA5-2) or the view buttons located in the lower left of the screen (as shown in Figure CA5-3). The different view options are useful for creating, editing, and viewing slides. The view options include:
- Normal View
- Slide Sorter View
- Slide Show View
- Notes Page View

Figure CA5-2 View Menu

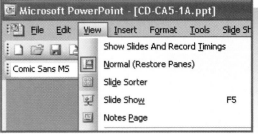

Figure CA5-3 View Buttons

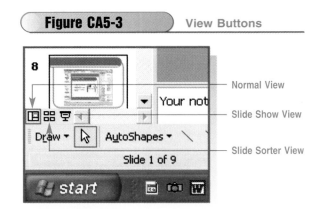

Normal View. The Normal View is used for creating and editing individual slides. See Figure CA5-4.

Slide Sorter View. The Slide Sorter View displays thumbnails of the slides that have been created. This view is used to view several slides at a time and is used for rearranging slides. It can also be used to apply features to several slides at a time. See Figure CA5-5.

Slide Show View. The Slide Show View is used to see how the slides will look on the full screen. The view can also be used to view and hear the effects of features and sounds applied to slides as the slide show is developed. This view is helpful for rehearsing and presenting your slide show. See Figure CA5-6.

Notes Page View. The Notes Page View displays one slide at a time with the accompanying notes displayed beneath the slide. You can print these pages and refer to the notes as the presentation is delivered. See Figure CA5-7.

 Figure CA5-4   Normal View

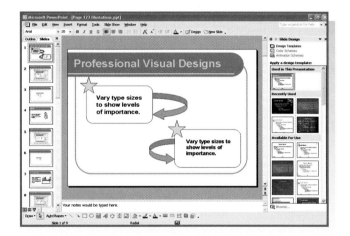

 **Figure CA5-5**   Slide Sorter View

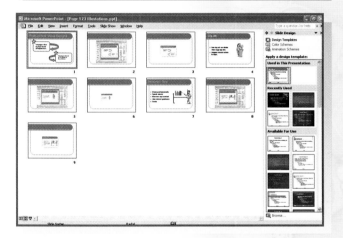

Figure CA5-6   Slide Show View

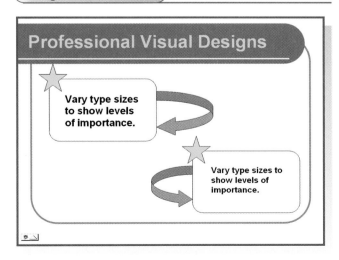

Figure CA5-7   Notes Page View

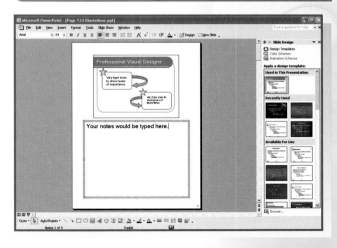

View Presentation

1. Read the information on viewing a presentation. Open *CD-CA5-1A* in your presentation software program. The file will open in Normal View. (Figure CA5-3 shows the View Buttons.)

2. Click **Slide Show View** and view the slide show. Left-click the mouse or tap the ENTER key to advance to the next slide.

3. Click **Slide Sorter View**. Use the scroll bar, if necessary, to see the last few slides.

4. Click **Normal View**; notice the notes beneath each slide. Read each note and then click the down arrow on the scroll bar to go to the next slide.

5. Close the file. Do not save.

Learn: Design Templates

design templates

Electronic presentation software comes with files containing **design templates** (see examples below). A design template is a set of design elements that can be applied to slides. A design template includes such things as a background design, font, font size, and color scheme. The design element also includes placeholder boxes for keying information and inserting graphics. Even though the design templates are preset, they can be changed or modified to better fit the needs of the user.

Learn: Slide Layout

layout

Layout refers to the way text and graphics are arranged on the slide. Presentation software allows the user to select a slide layout for each slide that is created. Some of the more common layouts (see examples below) include:

- Title slides
- Bulleted list slides
- Slides with clip art
- Slides for tables
- Slides for charts

Illustrations of Design Templates with Common Slide Layouts

The following illustrations display different design templates with some of the more common slide layouts. Review the figures and note the differences.

Learn: Title Slides

A title slide is to an electronic presentation as a title page is to a report. The title slide is placed at the beginning of slides and informs the audience. Generally, the title slide includes the presentation title and presenter name. Other information can be included if needed. Titles should be keyed in 40–48 point; subtitles, 25–34 point.

Design Template 1
(Title Slide Layout)

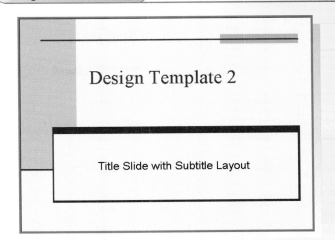

Design Template 2

Title Slide with Subtitle Layout

Design Template 3

- Bulleted List Slide Layout
- Bulleted List Slide Layout
- Bulleted List Slide Layout

Design Template 4
(Table Layout)

Salesperson	March Sales	April Sales
Van Noy	$135,385	$140,000
Eckersley	$118,375	$156,381

Exercise 1B

Create a Title Slide

1. Read the information above on slide layouts. Start a new presentation.
2. Select a professional-looking slide design template from those available in your software.
3. Select the title slide layout.
4. Create the title slide shown in Figure CA5-12.
5. Leave the file open to use in the next activity.

Professional Electronic
Presentations

Denise Strait
Multimedia Design Services

Learn: Bulleted Lists

Bulleted lists

Bulleted lists are lists of information that have a bullet (character -- • , ▶, ■, □) placed before them. Bulleted lists are used to guide discussion and to help the audience follow the speaker's ideas. If too much information is placed on a single slide, the text becomes difficult to read. Keep the information on the slide brief—do not write complete sentences. Be concise.

When creating lists, be sure to:

* Focus on one main idea.

* Add several supporting items.

* Limit the number of lines on one slide to six.

* Limit long wraparound lines of text.

* Set first-level topics in 30–34 point.

* Set second-level topics in 24–28 point.

Exercise   1C

Create Bulleted List Slides

1. Insert two slides with the bulleted list layout after the title slide you created in Exercise 1B.

2. Create the slides as shown in Figures CA5-13 and CA5-14. Reduce the font size if necessary to fit.

3. Save as *CA5-1C*. Keep the file open for the next exercise.

Figure CA5-13   Bulleted List 1

Presentation Planning

* Consider the audience.
* Consider the subject.
* Consider the equipment.
* Consider the facilities.

Figure CA5-14   Bulleted List 2

Message Development

* Introduction
* Body
* Summary and/or Conclusion

Exercise 1D

Change Template Design

1. Open *CA5-1C* from Exercise 1C, if it is not already open.

2. Change the template design to two other designs and see how the appearance changes with each template. (See Figures CA5-15 and CA5-16 for template design examples.)

3. Close the file without saving.

Figure CA5-15 Example 1

Message Development

- Introduction
- Body
- Summary and/or Conclusion

Figure CA5-16 Example 2

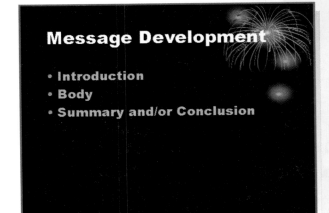

Learn: Design Templates on Microsoft Office Online

When an appropriate design template is not available on your computer, you can find other design templates on a Web site provided by Microsoft. To access these designs in *PowerPoint*, display the Slide Designs in the task pane. Scroll to the bottom of the design templates and click the Design Templates on *Microsoft Office Online* template design. This will take you to the *Microsoft PowerPoint Designs* page. Click the type of background you are looking for to view the various designs. Click the design template you want to use, and then click the Download Now button.

Exercise 1E

Change Template Design

1. Open *CA5-1C* from Exercise 1C.

2. Change the template design to one of the *Microsoft Office* design templates available online.

3. Save the file as *CA5-1E*. Close the file.

LESSON 2 — INSERT ART AND DRAWING OBJECTS

OBJECTIVES
- To understand how to use appropriate graphic images, lines, and boxes.
- To insert, position, and size graphic images, lines, and boxes.
- To create slides with graphic enhancements.

Learn: Graphics

Art, or graphics, can enhance a message and help convey ideas. Graphic images include clip art from your software collection (or other sources such as the Internet) as well as objects drawn using the Drawing toolbar. Photo images or even original artwork scanned and converted to a digitized image are other types of graphics that can be used in electronic presentations.

Use graphics only when they are relevant to your topic and contribute to your presentation. Choose graphics that will not distract the audience. Clip art can often be used to add humor. Be creative, but use images in good taste. An image isn't necessary on every slide in a presentation.

Exercise 2A

Insert Clip Art

1. Read the information above about clip art. Open *CA5-1C* from Exercise 1C.

2. Insert an appropriate piece of clip art from your software collection in each of the slides you created in Exercise 1C. Size and position the clip art attractively. (See the examples shown in Figure CA5-17.)

3. Save as *CA5-2A*.

Figure CA5-17   Clip Art Examples

Learn: Clip Art on Office Online

When appropriate clip art is not available on your computer, you can find clip art on a website provided by Microsoft. To access these images, in *PowerPoint*, click the Insert Clip Art button on the Drawing toolbar. Click the Clip art on Office Online link at the bottom of the Clip Art task pane. This link will take you to the Microsoft Clip Art and Media page. Search for clip art using an appropriate term. For example, to find images about giving a presentation, use the term *presentation*.

Exercise 2B

Insert Online Clip Art

1. Read the information above about clip art from *Office Online*. Open *CA5-2A* from Exercise 2A.

2. Delete the clip art you inserted for Exercise 2A.

3. Use the Clip Art on Office Online feature to find clip art to replace the images you deleted.

4. Save as *CA5-2B*. Close the file.

Learn: Drawing Tools and AutoShapes

Electronic presentation software has drawing tools and AutoShapes that can be used to create lines, arrows, boxes, borders, and other simple shapes, as shown in Figure CA5-18. Text boxes, color, patterns, and clip art can be added to many of these objects. These features are used to help communicate your ideas.

- **Shapes** like arrows can focus an audience's attention on important points.

- **Lines** can be used to separate sections of a visual, to emphasize key words or to connect elements.

- **Boxes**, too, can separate elements and provide a distinctive background for text.

- **Decorative borders** can call attention to the contents of a box.

shapes

lines

boxes

decorative borders

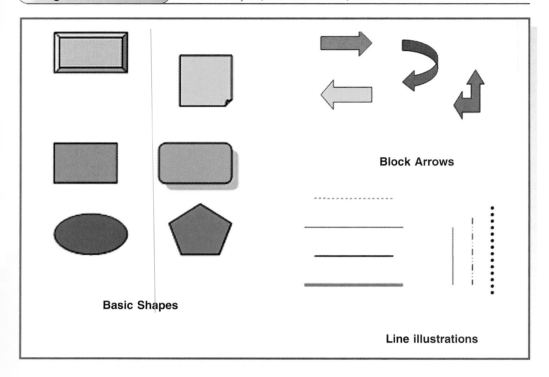

The Drawing toolbar is generally located at the bottom of the screen and has the features shown in Figure CA5-19 below.

Figure CA5-19   Drawing Toolbar in Powerpoint

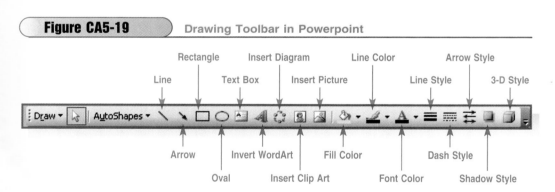

Exercise 2C

Use Drawing Tools and AutoShapes

1. Read the information above about drawing tools and AutoShapes. Open *CA5-2A* from Exercise 2A.

2. Create a simple logo for Multimedia Design Services. Use a circle, box, or other shape and add a fill to it. Put clip art or text on or around the shape. Place your logo attractively on the title slide.

3. Save as *CA5-2C*.

Create Text Boxes

1. Open *CA5-2C* from the last exercise.
2. Insert a slide with a title only layout (not a title slide) as the fourth slide.
3. Use the draw and/or AutoShapes features to create the slide shown in Figure CA5-20. Use the Arial font (24-point bold and 20-point bold) for the text boxes. Make the stars yellow. Use a color of your choice for the arrows.
4. Save as *CA5-2D*; keep the file open for the next activity.

Exercise 2E

Create Slides with Clip Art

1. Insert two slides with a text and clip art layout at the end of the presentation (CA5-2D).
2. Create the slides as shown in Figures CA5-21 and CA5-22. Insert an appropriate piece of clip art from your software collection or from Clip Art Office Online in each slide. Size the images as needed and position them properly.
3. Save as *CA5-2E*. Close the file.

Figure CA5-20	Text Boxes and Autoshapes

Professional Visual Designs

Vary type sizes to show levels of importance.

Vary type sizes to show levels of importance.

Figure CA5-21	Clip Art Example 1

Clip Art

- Use clip art on slides when appropriate.
- Images should relate to topic.

Figure CA5-22	Clip Art Example 2

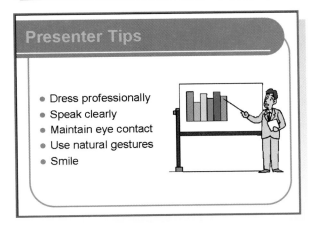

Presenter Tips

- Dress professionally
- Speak clearly
- Maintain eye contact
- Use natural gestures
- Smile

⊙ To learn how to change slide backgrounds.
⊙ To learn how diagrams and tables can portray processes and ideas.
⊙ To create diagrams using the choice, stair steps, cluster, and flowchart designs.
⊙ To create tables to enhance a presentation.

Learn: Slide Backgrounds

Presentation software allows you to use different backgrounds for your slides. The background feature is one of the options found under Format in the menu bar. (See Figures CA5-23, CA5-24, and CA5-25). This feature can be used to change the color of the background or to select one of the Fill Effects for the background. Once selected, the color or the fill can be applied to only one of the slides or to all the slides in the presentation. The fill effects include:

- Gradient
- Texture
- Pattern
- Picture

Figure CA5-23   Format Menu

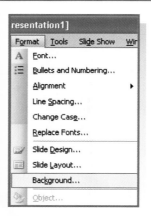

Figure CA5-25   Fill Effects Menu

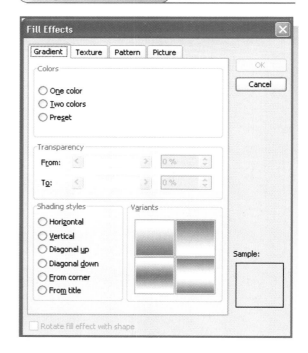

Figure CA5-24   Background Menu

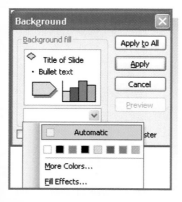

Exercise 3A

Change Slide Backgrounds

1. Read the information above about changing slide backgrounds. Start a new presentation. Select the design template shown below in Figure CA5-26 or a similar one.

2. Select the bulleted list layout (text and title).

3. Key the slide shown in Figure CA5-26.

4. Change the background color of the slide following the steps outlined on slide 1.

5. Insert a new slide.

6. Select the bulleted list layout.

7. Key the slide shown in Figure CA5-27.

8. Change the background texture of the slide following the steps outlined on slide 2.

9. Save as *CA5-3A*. Close the file.

 Figure CA5-26   Slide Background Color

> ## To Change Slide Background Color
> - Click Format on menu bar
> - Click Background
> - Click the ▼
> - Click More Colors
> - Click the desired color and click OK
> - Click Apply

 Figure CA5-27   Slide Background Texture

> ## To Change Slide Background Texture
> - Click Format on menu bar
> - Click Background
> - Click the ▼
> - Click Fill Effects
> - Click Texture
> - Click the desired texture and click OK
> - Click Apply

Learn: Diagrams

A **diagram** is a drawing that explains a process or idea. Diagrams can help an audience understand relationships or a sequence of events. Text can be arranged in boxes that are connected with lines or arrows to help the audience visualize the individual steps in a process or the parts of an idea.

diagram

While diagrams can become very complex, the best ones are quite simple. When creating diagrams, be sure to:

- Arrange text in boxes or other appropriate shapes.
- Show connections with lines and directional arrows.
- Use fonts and colors that work well with the rest of the presentation.

Learn: Choice Diagram

The diagram shown in Figure CA5-28 is a choice diagram. In this type of diagram, a choice must be made between two options. The arrows pointing in opposite directions indicate an either/or situation. This same technique can be used to represent conflict.

Exercise 3B

Create a Choice Diagram

1. Read the information above on creating a choice diagram. Start a new presentation. Select a design template suitable for creating slide 1 as shown above in Figure CA5-28.
2. Change the background texture of the slide to one of your choice.
3. Choose the bulleted list layout.
4. Move the box in which you will key the bulleted text to the bottom of the slide.
5. Use the Drawing or AutoShapes tools to create the choice diagram in the space above the bulleted list.
6. Key the bulleted list.
7. Save as *CA5-3B*. Close the file.

Learn: Stair Steps Diagram

The diagram shown in Figure CA5-29 shows a series of ideas. The stair steps diagram begins with a box at the bottom containing the text for the first idea being explained. Additional boxes with text are positioned to look like stairs going up. For a slide show, you could prepare four separate slides so that the stair steps appear one at a time as the discussion progresses. After completing the first slide, copy and paste it. Make the changes for the second slide; then copy and paste it to make the third slide, etc.

Figure CA5-28   Choice Diagram (Slide 1)

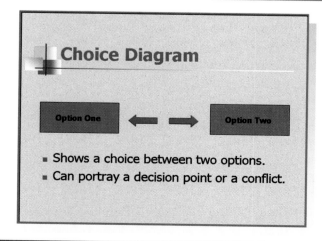

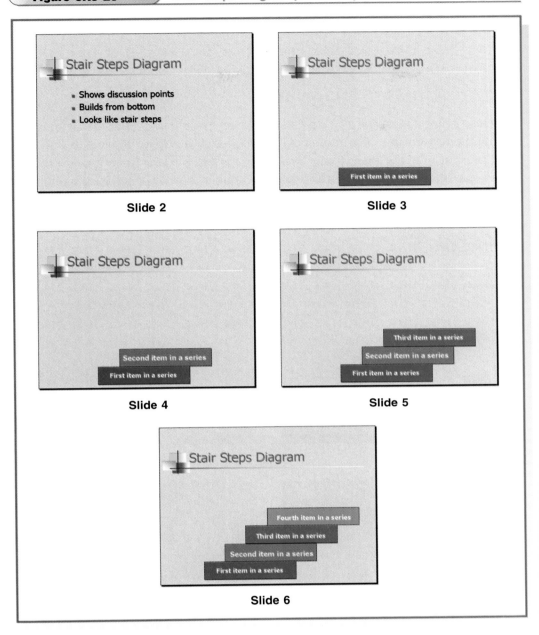

Slide 2

Slide 3

Slide 4

Slide 5

Slide 6

Exercise   3C

Create a Stair Steps Diagram

1. Study the information above on creating a stair steps diagram. Open *CA5-3B* from Exercise 3B and insert a slide for slide 2. Create slide 2 as shown in Figure CA5-29, using the bulleted list layout.

2. Use the Drawing or AutoShapes tools to create the stair steps diagram for slides 3–6. *Hint:* Use the following steps to create the boxes:

    a. Create the bottom box.

    b. After creating the first box, copy and paste it to make the remaining boxes (steps).

    c. Edit the text and color of the pasted boxes.

3. Save as *CA5-3C*. Close the file.

Learn: Cluster Diagram

The cluster diagram shown in Figure CA5-30 begins with an oval at the center containing the text for the main topic being explained. Additional ovals with text are positioned around the main topic. By creating a separate slide each time an item is added, each item can appear as it is discussed rather than having all items appear at once.

Figure CA5-30   Cluster Diagram (Slides 1–6)

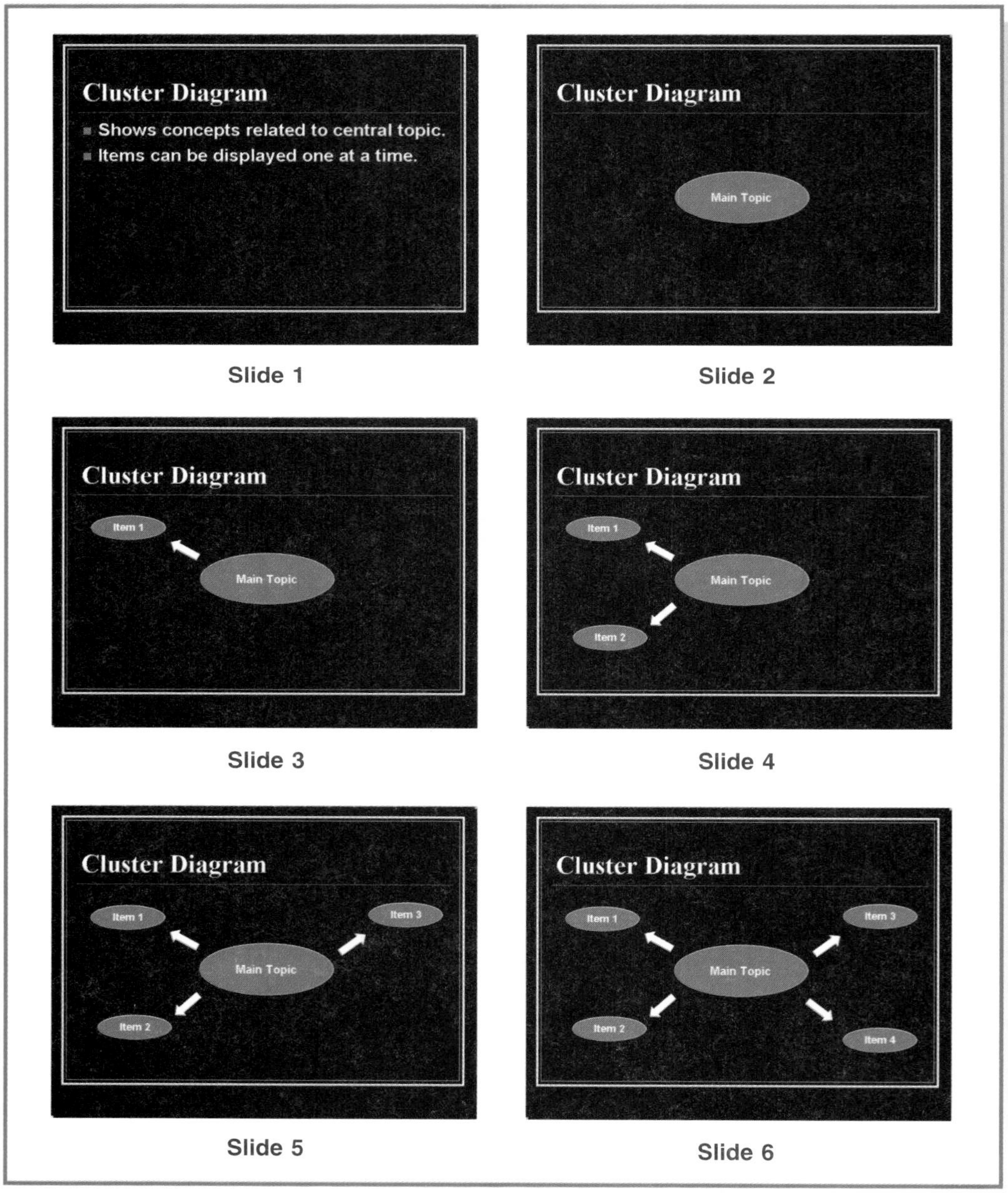

Exercise 3D

Create a Cluster Diagram

1. Read the information above about creating a cluster diagram. Start a new presentation.

2. Select a design template.

3. Choose an appropriate slide layout and create slide 1, as shown in Figure CA5-30.

4. Choose an appropriate slide layout and create slides 2–6.

5. Save as *CA5-3D*. Close the file.

Learn: Flowchart

The flowchart in Figure CA5-31 shows steps in a process, connected by arrows. Flowcharts can use pictures or shapes. In a flowchart with shapes, each shape has a certain meaning. An oval shows the beginning or end of a process. A parallelogram shows input or output. A diamond shows a decision to be made, worded as a question. Two arrows, one marked *Yes* and one marked *No*, extend from the diamond to the flowchart step that results from the decision. A rectangle shows a step that does not require a decision.

Exercise 3E

Create a Flowchart

1. Read the information above on creating a flowchart. Start a new presentation.

2. Select a design template.

3. Create a title slide using FLOWCHARTS for the title. Use your name and date for the subtitle.

4. Select an appropriate slide layout and create four additional slides using the drawing tools and AutoShapes features. The fourth slide should look like Figure CA5-31. Slide 1 would only include *Start*. Slide 2 would include *Start* and *Step*. Slide 3 would include *Start*, *Step*, and *Input*. (*Formatting Note:* This is a horizontal flowchart. A flowchart may also be shown vertically.)

5. Save as *CA5-3E*. Close the file.

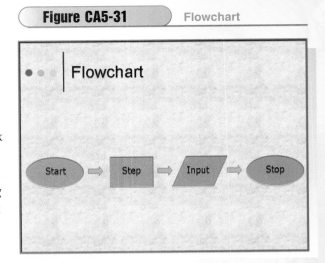

Figure CA5-31 Flowchart

Learn: Tables

Tables can be used in presentations to compare and contrast facts or figures and to list data (see Figure CA5-32). Some presentation software includes a table layout slide. In other software, you must create the table in a word processing or spreadsheet program and import it into your presentation.

Exercise 3F

Create a Table

1. Read the information above about creating a table. Start a new presentation.
2. Select a design template.
3. Insert a table layout slide.
4. Create the slide shown in Figure CA5-32.
5. Save as *CA5-3F*. Close the file.

Figure CA5-32   Table

Sales Report

Month	Jacket Sales	Vest Sales
November	375,000	325,000
December	425,000	372,000
January	400,000	275,000
February	275,000	125,000
March	100,000	75,000

LESSON 4 CREATE CHARTS AND GRAPHS

OBJECTIVES

- To learn which graph or chart to use for particular situations.
- To learn to create graphs.
- To learn various graph elements.

Learn: Charts and Graphs

Numeric information can be easier to understand when shown as a **graph** or **chart** rather than in text or a table. The relationship between data sets or trends can be compared with *bar*, *line*, or *area graph*s or *pie charts*. Each type of graph or chart is best suited for a particular situation.

bar graph

line and area graphs

pie chart

- **Bar graph**—comparison of item quantities
- **Line and area graphs**—quantity changes over time or distance
- **Pie chart**—parts of a whole

Common Graph Elements. Elements common to most graphs are identified on the bar graph shown below. They include:

- **X-axis**—the horizontal axis; usually for categories
- **Y-axis**—the vertical axis; usually for values
- **Scale**—numbers on the Y- or X-axis representing quantities
- **Tick marks**—coordinate marks on the graph to help guide the reader
- **Grids**—lines that extend from tick marks to make it easier to see data values
- **Labels**—names used to identity parts of the graph
- **Legend**—the key that identifies the shading, coloring, or patterns used for the information shown in the graph

X-axis
Y-axis
scale
tick marks
grids
labels
legend

Examine Figure CA5-33; then see if you can locate the various graph elements in the software you are using.

Figure CA5-33   Graph Elements

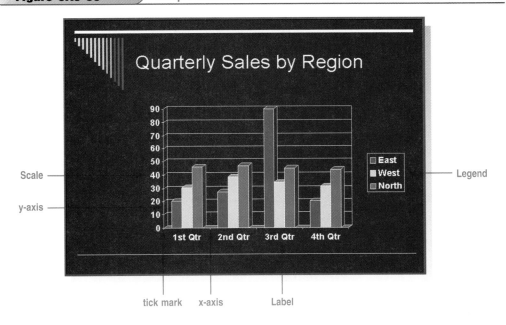

Learn: Bar Graphs

bar charts

Bar graphs (also called **bar charts**) compare one or more sets of data that are plotted on the horizontal X-axis and the vertical Y-axis. The X-axis usually contains category information (such as years or months); the Y-axis usually contains measured quantity values (numbers).

Vertical bars (columns) are easy to interpret; the baseline on the Y-axis should begin at zero for consistent comparisons when several graphs are used. Special effects can be added, but a simple graph is effective for showing relationships.

A cluster of bars on each point on the X-axis can show multiple data sets. When multiple data sets are used, the colors must provide an adequate contrast to be viewed from a distance, and yet blend with the other colors used in the presentation.

Presentation software offers three-dimensional (3D) versions of bar, line, and area graphs, and pie charts. A 3D graph or chart (as shown in Figure CA5-34) often has a more contemporary look than a two-dimensional version (as shown in Figure CA5-35).

Exercise 4A

Create a Bar Graph

1. Read the information above about creating a bar graph. Start a new presentation.
2. Using the information displayed in Figure CA5-35, create the 3D bar graph shown in Figure CA5-34 below.
3. Change the chart type to a 2D bar graph.
4. Change the bar colors to colors of your choice.
5. Display data values above the bars.
6. Save as *CA5-4A*. Close the file.

Figure CA5-34 3D Bar Graph

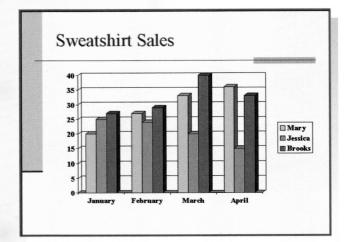

Figure CA5-35 2D Bar Graph

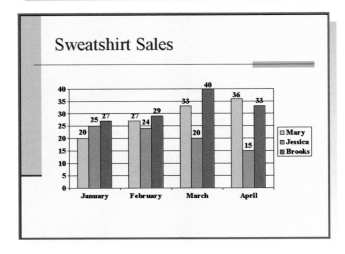

Learn: Line Graphs

Line graphs display changes in quantities over time or distance. Usually the X-axis shows a particular period of time or distance. The Y-axis shows measurements of quantity at different times or distances. See Figure CA5-36 for an example. The baseline of the Y-axis should be zero to provide a consistent reference point when several graphs are used in a presentation.

When the numbers for the X-axis are entered, lines appear connecting the values on the graph to reflect the changes in amounts. A grid with vertical lines helps the viewer interpret quantities.

Several sets of data can be displayed by using lines in different colors.

Exercise 4B

Create a Line Graph

1. Read the information above about creating a line graph. Start a new presentation.

2. Create a line graph showing the number of employees using the following data:

- 1980   30
- 1985   38
- 1990   45
- 1995   42
- 2000   40
- 2005   47

3. Include vertical lines and vertical drop lines in the graph.

4. Save as *CA5-4B*. Close the file.

Figure CA5-36 Line Graph

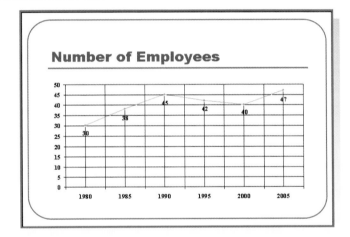

Exercise 4C

Create an Area Graph

1. An area graph is a variation of the line graph. The area beneath the lines is colored in. Change the line graph you created in Exercise 4B (*CA5-4B*) to an area graph (see example in Figure CA5-37).

2. Do not display the data values.

3. Save as *CA5-4C*. Close the file.

Learn: Pie Charts

Pie charts are best used to display parts of a whole. They show clearly the proportional relationship of only one set of values. Without any numbers displayed, the chart shows only general relationships. In the example shown in Figure CA5-38 below, the different colors used for the pie slices are identified in a legend. Colors used on the pie should provide adequate contrast between the slices. Consider also the color scheme of your entire presentation so that the pie chart will coordinate with other visuals.

Create a Pie Chart

1. Read the information above about creating a pie chart. Start a new presentation.

2. Create the pie chart as shown in Figure CA5-38.

    Chart data:
    Freshman   25
    Sophomore   40
    Junior   35
    Senior   50

3. Save as *CA5-4D*.

Figure CA5-37   Area Graph

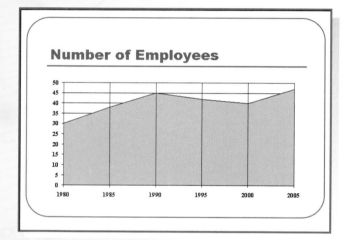

Figure CA5- 38   Pie Chart

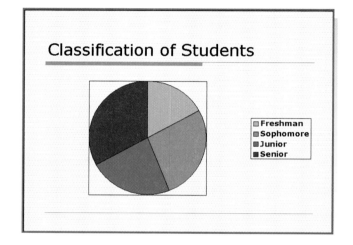

Exercise 4E

Create a Pie Chart

Figure CA5-39   3D Exploding Pie Chart

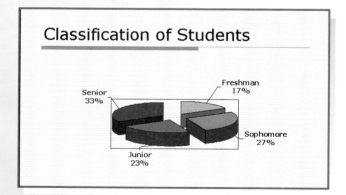

1. Change the pie chart you created in Exercise 4D (*CA5-4D*) to give it a 3D appearance and to emphasize the pie slices by exploding them. See the example of an exploding pie chart in Figure CA5-39.

2. Remove the legend.

3. Display labels and percentages with each slice.

4. Save as *CA5-4E*. Close the file.

Online Resources

See Bonus Exercise 5A on Creating an Electronic Presentation at www.c21key. bonus-exercises.swlearning.com.

Presentations

UNIT 6

LESSONS 1–4
Presentations/Multimedia

Conditioning Practice

Before you begin the lessons, key each line twice.

alphabet 1 Gavin Zahn will buy the exquisite green jacket from the old shop.

figures 2 Check No. 183 was used to pay Invoices 397 and 406 on October 25.

speed 3 Glen may pay the haughty neighbor if the turn signals work right.

gwam 1' | 1 | 2 | 3 | 4 | 5 | 6 | 7 | 8 | 9 | 10 | 11 | 12 | 13 |

LESSON 1 CREATE ELECTRONIC PRESENTATION

OBJECTIVES

 To create an electronic presentation.

 To add slides to an existing electronic presentation.

Exercise 1A

Create a Presentation

1. Using your electronic presentation software, create Slides 1–12 shown in Figure CA6-1. The slides will be used again in Lessons 2–4.

2. Save as *CA6-1A*.

Source for Slide 3:
http://www.whitehouse.
gov/government/exec.
html

Source for Slide 8:
http://www.whitehouse.
gov/government/judg.
html

(continued on next page)

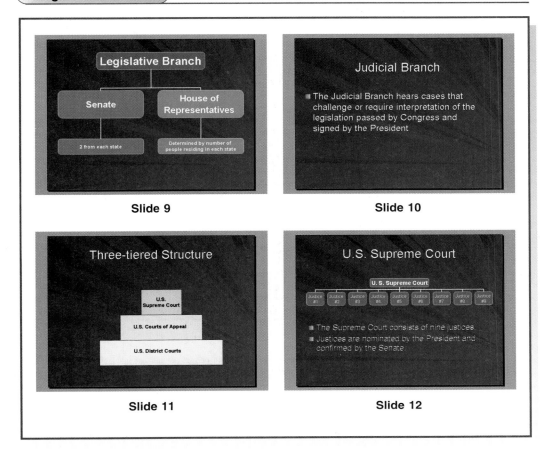

Slide 9

Slide 10

Slide 11

Slide 12

Source for Slide 10:
http://www.whitehouse.
gov/government/legi.
html

Learn: Insert Slides

Additional slides may be inserted in a presentation when the slide show is being created or anytime after the slide show has been created. To insert a slide, click on the **Slides Tab** in the Outline and Slides Pane. Then move the pointer to the place where the new slide is to be inserted and click the mouse. Then click on the New Slide icon. Each time you click on the New Slide icon, a new slide will appear.

Exercise 1B

Insert Slides

1. Open *CA6-1A* if it is not already open and insert a new slide between Slides 2 and 3. Create the Executive Branch title slide shown on the next page in Figure CA6-2.

2. Insert a new slide between slides 7 and 8 and create the Legislative Branch slide shown on the next page in Figure CA6-2.

3. Create a similar slide for the Judicial Branch and insert it between Slides 9 and 10.

4. Save as *CA6-1B*.

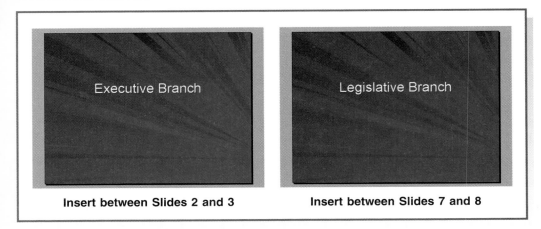

Insert between Slides 2 and 3   Insert between Slides 7 and 8

LESSON ENHANCING PRESENTATIONS WITH PICTURES AND ANIMATION/TRANSITIONS

OBJECTIVES

⊘ To copy and paste pictures from the Internet.

⊘ To learn how to use the transition and animation features to enhance a slide show.

⊘ To learn how to print slide show notes.

Learn: Electronic Presentation Enhancements

Electronic presentations can be enhanced by using the capabilities of the presentation software. Enhancements, however, should not be overdone. To enhance a presentation, consider adding:

- Slide animations
- Slide transitions
- Hyperlinks
- Pictures
- Sound
- Timing

Learn: Add Pictures

Pictures. In addition to clip art, pictures can be inserted in an electronic presentation using scanners, cameras, files, and the Internet. Movies can also be inserted into a presentation. Care must be taken not to violate copyright laws.

To copy a picture to place on a slide:

1. Right-click on the picture.

2. Click **Copy**.

3. Go to the slide where you want to place the picture.

4. Right-click.

5. Click **Paste**.

6. Click on the picture and drag to the desired location .

Learn: Slide Animations and Transitions

Slide animations. Rather than have a slide appear all at once in its entirety, animations can be used to make text, graphics, and other objects appear one at a time. This allows the presenter to control how the information is presented as well as add interest to the presentation.

A variety of animations are available to choose from. For example, the text and objects can be animated to fade in, spin, float, ascend, descend, or do a variety of other animations. **Animation schemes** are schemes that are preset. They range from very subtle to very glitzy. The scheme chosen should add interest without taking away from the message of the presenter. **Custom animation** allows for several different animations to be included on each slide.

Slide transitions. Slide transition is the term used to describe how the display changes from one slide to the next slide. When no transition is applied, slides go from one directly to the next. Transition effects make it appear as though the next slide dissolves in or appears through a circle, for example. There are numerous transitions to choose from.

Learn: Insert Hyperlink

Hyperlinks. A hyperlink is colored, underlined text that you click on to take you from the current location in the electronic file to another location. This means that a presenter can create hyperlinks to take the presentation from the current slide to an Internet site that relates to what he/she is talking about. A hyperlink can also take you to another place within the presentation.

Exercise

Show Slide Enhancement

1. Open the *CA6-1B* file from the last exercise.
2. Read above about how to add transitions and animations to your slide show.
3. Make the changes outlined at the right of the slides shown below in Figure CA6-3 and insert pictures as illustrated.
4. In Slide Sorter view, add a transition to all slides except the first. Include at least three types of transitions.
5. Animate the bulleted items so they appear one at a time for Slides 2, 7, and 8.
6. Have the three boxes of the three-tiered structure appear one at a time.
7. Read above about inserting a hyperlink.
8. Insert a slide (title and text layout) following Slide 7 (2nd Executive Agencies slide). Use **President's Cabinet** for the main heading. For the first bulleted item, insert a hyperlink to http://www.whitehouse.gov/government/cabinet_html
9. Save as *CA6-2A*.

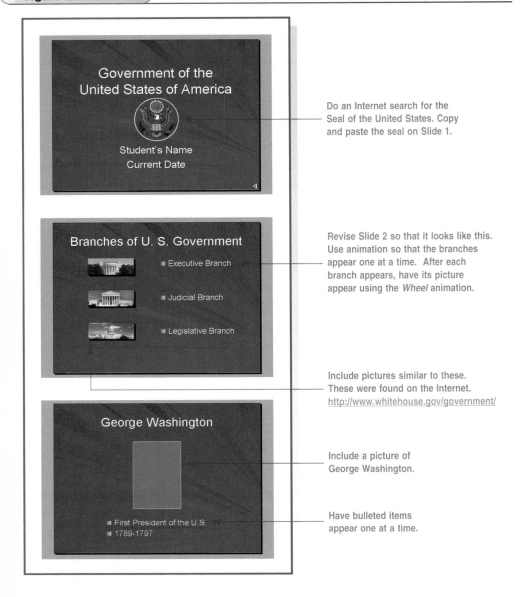

Do an Internet search for the Seal of the United States. Copy and paste the seal on Slide 1.

Revise Slide 2 so that it looks like this. Use animation so that the branches appear one at a time. After each branch appears, have its picture appear using the *Wheel* animation.

Include pictures similar to these. These were found on the Internet. http://www.whitehouse.gov/government/

Include a picture of George Washington.

Have bulleted items appear one at a time.

Learn: Add Notes

Notes for the presenter can be added to the slides of the electronic presentation file. This can be done in one of two ways. The first way is to simply click beneath the slide where it says *Click to add notes* and add the notes that you want included. You can also add notes by clicking Notes Page on the View menu and then clicking in the placeholder where it says *Click to add notes*. If the notes are too small to read as you key, increase the size by using the Zoom feature.

Add Notes

1. You will be giving a presentation to foreign exchange students at your school using the slide show you just created (*CA6-2A*). Read on the previous page about adding notes. Create "Notes Pages" using the notes shown below for each slide.

2. Copy the first slide and insert it at the end of your presentation as Slide 17.

3. Print copies of your notes pages to have available for Lesson 4.

4. Save as *CA6-2B*.

Notes Pages

1. The government of the United States as we know it today has evolved over time. Its beginnings date back prior to the U.S. gaining its independence from England.

2. Today we have three branches of government. They include:

   • the Executive Branch

   • the Legislative Branch, and

   • the Judicial Branch.

3. Let's start by talking about the Executive Branch.

4. As you can see, the President of the United States is in charge of the Executive Branch. He serves as Commander in Chief of the Armed Forces, appoints cabinet members, and oversees various executive (government) agencies that we will be discussing later on in the presentation.

5. The first Commander in Chief of the Armed Forces was our first President, George Washington. Interestingly enough, he was named the army's Commander in Chief by the Second Continental Congress before he was elected president.

6. This slide shows a diagram of the 14 Executive Agencies.

7. The Executive Agencies include:

   (The first seven Executive Agencies will fly in one at a time.

   Look at the screen and say each agency as it appears on the screen.)

8. **(The last seven agencies will fly in one at a time on Slide 8.**

   Continue to read them one at a time as they appear.)

9. Let's take a look at the President's Cabinet.

10. Now that we know a little about the Executive Branch, let's talk briefly about the Legislative Branch of government.

(continued on next page)

---

11. The Legislative Branch consists of Congress. Congress has two parts—the Senate and the House of Representatives.

12. As shown on this slide, there are two senators elected from each state. They are elected for a term of six years. The terms of the senators are staggered so that one-third of the Senate seats are up for election every two years. With each state having two senators, each state is given equal representation regardless of size or population.

   The House of Representatives on the other hand is based on the population of each state. As the population changes within states, the number of representatives allocated to that state may also change.

13. The third branch of our government is called the Judicial Branch.

14. The Judicial Branch hears cases that challenge or require interpretation of the laws passed by Congress. The Judicial Branch has the responsibility of protecting the rights of all Americans that were granted by the Constitution.

15. The judicial system is three-tiered; the first tier is the U.S. District Courts. Trials take place in these courts. If a person loses in a district court, he/she can usually appeal the decision. These appeals are heard in U.S. Courts of Appeal. Finally, there is the U.S. Supreme Court.

16. The Supreme Court consists of nine justices who have been nominated by the President and confirmed by the Senate. Even though there are many cases submitted to the Supreme Court, very few cases are ever acted upon by this court.

17. This is a very brief overview of our government. You will learn much more about it during the time you spend here. And we hope to learn about your country as well. Welcome to the United States.

LESSON ③ ENHANCING PRESENTATIONS WITH SOUND

OBJECTIVES

⊙ To insert sound from the clip organizer.
⊙ To record sound.
⊙ To play a CD audio track during parts of the slide show.

Learn: Add Sound to a Presentation

Sound. Another way to enhance a presentation is through the use of sound. When people hear something as well as see it, they are much more likely to retain it.

Also, the sound capability allows a presenter to bring variety and credibility to his or her presentation. Hearing John F. Kennedy say "Ask not what your country can do for you, ask what you can do for your country" has a much greater impact than if you or I say it. Having background music play as you show pictures has more of an impact than just showing the pictures.

There are several different types of sounds that can be included with your presentation. These include:

- Sound from the *clip organizer*
- Sound from a *file*
- Sound from a *CD Audio Track*
- Sound that you record—*Recorded Sound*

Sounds from clip organizer—prerecorded sounds available with the software.

Sounds from a file—sounds that you have recorded and saved as a file that can be linked to the presentation.

Sounds from a CD audio track—music that is played directly from a CD. Specific parts of the CD can be specified for playing.

Recorded sounds—With recording capability, words (using your voice or the voice of someone else), sounds, or music can be recorded to specific slides.

As with graphics and movies, care must be taken not to violate copyright laws when using sounds you do not record yourself.

Learn: Timing Feature

Timing. The timing feature controls the speed with which slides replace other slides. Setting times tells the software how long each slide will remain on the screen.

Exercise 3A

Insert Sound

1. Insert "America the Beautiful" from the sound clip organizer on the first and last slide of the presentation created for Lessons 1 and 2 (*CA6-2B*). Have the sound start automatically for Slide 1 and manually for Slide 16.

2. Save as *CA6-3A*.

Online Resources

See Bonus Exercise 3B on Recording Sound at www. c21key.bonus-exercises. swlearning.com.

LESSON 4   DELIVERING A PRESENTATION

OBJECTIVE ⊙ To give a presentation using electronic slides.

Learn: Preparing for a Presentation

Speaker notes. The notes that you created for the "Government of the United States of America" presentation should only be used as an aid when you are practicing your presentation. They should remind you of what you want to say during your practice sessions.

You will know when you have practiced the presentation enough, because you will be able to give the presentation by simply looking at the slides as they appear on the screen. The words on the slides will act as an outline and remind you of the key points you want to make.

Don't be concerned about giving the presentation word for word as it appears in the notes. If you do, it comes off as being memorized. Memorized speeches sound unnatural; the speaker is not able to develop a rapport with the audience. Experts generally advise speakers to have the opening memorized.

This allows the speaker to have a strong opening and appear knowledgeable and confident. If the speaker does memorize the opening, he/she should practice it so that it seems natural. This can be done by pausing in appropriate places and using vocal variety—speed, volume.

Definitely don't make the mistake that is often made by beginning presenters. They often bring the speaker notes to the podium with them and then find it much more comfortable to read to, rather than present to, the audience. Speakers who read to their audience are unable to maintain eye contact with the audience and so lose their credibility (believability).

By being well prepared and only glancing at the screen as the next slide comes up, the speaker seems natural. This also allows the speaker to focus on the audience rather than on what he/she is going to say.

Exercise 4A
Practice Presenting

1. Review the information above about practicing a presentation.
2. Practice giving the "Government of the United States of America" presentation that you created in Lessons 1 and 2.

Exercise 4B
Give a Presentation

1. Review the evaluation sheet displayed below.
2. Break up into groups of three. Each student in your group will give the presentation that was developed in Lessons 1–2. While one student is giving the presentation, the other two will evaluate it using the form shown below.
3. The evaluation form is available as the data file *CD-CA6-4B*.

Presentation Evaluation Form

	Excellent	Good	Average	Below Average	Poor
The beginning of the speech is					
The visual aids are					
The speaker's enthusiasm is					
The speaker's eye contact is					
The speaker's gestures are					
The speaker's confidence is					
The conclusion of the speech is					
The speaker's vocal variation is					

Additional Comments:

Online Resources

See Bonus Exercises 5A, 5B, and 5C on Planning, Creating, and Delivering a Presentation at www.c21key.bonus-exercises. swlearning.com.

Communication & Math Skills 2

1. Study each of the eight rules shown below.

a. Key *Learn* line(s) beneath each rule, noting how the rule is applied.

b. Key *Apply* line(s), using correct capitalization.

Capitalization

Rule 1: Capitalize the first word of a sentence, personal titles, and names of people.

Learn 1 Ask Ms. King if she and Mr. Valdez will sponsor our book club.

Apply 2 did you see mrs. watts and gloria at the school play?

Rule 2: Capitalize days of the week and months of the year.

Learn 3 He said that school starts on the first Monday in September.

Apply 4 my birthday is on the third thursday of march this year.

Rule 3: Capitalize cities, states, countries, and specific geographic features.

Learn 5 When you were recently in Nevada, did you visit Lake Tahoe?

Apply 6 when in france, we saw paris from atop the eiffel tower.

Rule 4: Capitalize names of clubs, schools, companies, and other organizations.

Learn 7 The Voices of Harmony will perform at Music Hall next week.

Apply 8 lennox corp. operates the hyde park drama club in boston.

Rule 5: Capitalize historic periods, holidays, and events.

Learn 9 The Fourth of July celebrates the signing of the Declaration of Independence.

Apply 10 henri asked if memorial day is an american holiday.

Rule 6: Capitalize streets, buildings, and other specific structures.

Learn 11 Jemel lives at Bay Shores near Golden Gate Bridge.

Apply 12 dubois tower is on fountain square at fifth and walnut.

Rule 7: Capitalize an official title when it precedes a name and elsewhere if it is a title of high distinction.

Learn 13 In what year did Juan Carlos become King of Spain?
Learn 14 Masami Chou, our class president, made the scholastic awards.

Apply 15 did the president speak to the nation from the rose garden?
Apply 16 mr. chavez, our company president, wrote two novels.

Rule 8: Capitalize initials; also, letters in abbreviations if the letters would be capitalized when the words are spelled out.

Learn 17 Does Dr. R. J. Anderson have an Ed.D. or a Ph.D.?
Learn 18 She said that UPS stands for United Parcel Service.

Apply 19 we have a letter from ms. anna m. bucks of washington, d.c.
Apply 20 m.d. means Doctor of Medicine, not medical doctor.

2. Key Proofread & Correct, using correct capitalization.
  a. Check answers.

b. Using the rule number(s) at the left of each line, study the rule relating to each error.

c. Rekey each incorrect line, using correct capitalization.

Proofread & Correct

Rules

1,6	1	has dr. holt visited his studio at the hopewell arts center?
1,3,5	2	pam has made plans to spend thanksgiving day in fort wayne.
1,2,8	3	j. c. hauck will receive a b.a. degree from usc in june.
1,4,6	4	is tech services, inc. located at fifth street and elm?
1,2,7	5	i heard senator dole make his acceptance speech on thursday.
1,3,6	6	did mrs. alma s. banks apply for a job with butler county?
1,3	7	she knew that albany, not new york city, is the capital.
1,3	8	eldon and cindy marks now live in santa fe, new mexico.
1,6	9	are you going to the marx theater in mount adams tonight?
1,2,6	10	on friday, the first of july, we will move to Keystone Plaza.

3. Save as *CS2-ACT1.*

ACTIVITY 2   Listening

1. Listen carefully to the sounds around you for 3 minutes.

2. As you listen, key a numbered list of every different sound you hear.

3. Identify with asterisks the three loudest sounds you heard.
4. Save as *CS2-ACT2.*

ACTIVITY 3   Composing

1. Key items 1 and 2 as paragraph 1 of a short composition, supplying the information needed to complete each sentence.

2. Key item 3 as paragraph 2, supplying the information needed.
3. Key item 4 as paragraph 3, supplying the information needed.

4. Proofread, revise, and correct.
5. Save as *CS2-ACT3.*

1 My name, (first/last), is (African/Asian/European/Hispanic, etc.) in origin.

2 My mother's ancestors originated in (name of country); my father's ancestors originated in (name of country).

3 I know the following facts about the country of my (mother's/father's) ancestors:
  1. (enter first fact here)
  2. (enter second fact here)
  3. (enter third fact here)

4 If I could visit a country of my choice, I would visit (name of country) because (give two or three reasons).

ACTIVITY 4   Math: Multiplying and Dividing Numbers

1. Open *CD-CS2-ACT4* and print the file.

2. Solve the problems as directed in the file.

3. Submit your answers.

Skill BUILDER 2

Speed Building

1. Key each line twice with no pauses between letters or words.
2. Key a 1' timing on lines 2, 4, 6, 8, and 10; determine *gwam* on each timing.

space bar
1 and the she big city disk held half firm land paid them make
2 Jane and the man may handle the problems with the city firm.

shift keys
3 Moorcroft, WY; Eau Claire, WI; New York City, NY; Newark, DE
4 M. L. Ramirez left for San Francisco on Tuesday, January 23.

adjacent keys
5 wire open tire sure ruin said trim quit fire spot lids walks
6 Katrina opened a shop by the stadium to sell sporting goods.

long direct reaches
7 many vice brag stun myth much cents under check juice center
8 I brought a recorder to the music hall to record my recital.

word response
9 their visit signs aisle chapel dials handy shake shelf usual
10 Their dog slept by the oak chair in the aisle of the chapel.

gwam 1' | 1 | 2 | 3 | 4 | 5 | 6 | 7 | 8 | 9 | 10 | 11 | 12 |

Timed Writings

1. Key a 1' timing on each ¶; determine *gwam*.
2. Key two 2' timings on ¶s 1-3 combined; determine *gwam*.
3. Key two 3' timings on ¶s 1-3 combined; determine *gwam* and errors.
4. If time permits, key two 1' guided timings on each ¶; one for control and one for speed (add 4 to your rate in step 1).

A all letters used (MicroPace)   gwam 2' | 3'

In deciding upon a career, learn as much as possible about	6 | 4
what individuals in that career do. For each job class, there are	12 | 8
job requirements and qualifications that must be met. Analyze	19 | 13
these tasks very critically in terms of your personality and what	26 | 17
you like to do.	27 | 18
A high percentage of jobs in major careers demand education or	33 | 22
training after high school. The training may be very specialized,	40 | 27
requiring intensive study or interning for two or more years. You	47 | 31
must decide if you are willing to expend so much time and effort.	53 | 35
After you have decided upon a career to pursue, discuss the	59 | 39
choice with parents, teachers, and others. Such people can help	66 | 44
you design a plan to guide you along the series of steps required	72 | 48
in pursuing your goal. Keep the plan flexible and change it when-	79 | 53
ever necessary.	80 | 54

gwam 2' | 1 | 2 | 3 | 4 | 5 | 6 |
3' | 1 | 2 | 3 | 4 |

UNIT 7

LESSONS 1–4

Assessing Document Formatting and Electronic Presentation Skills

Conditioning Practice

Before you begin the lessons, key each line twice.

alphabet 1 Bugs quickly explained why five of the zoo projects cost so much.

figures 2 Jo's office phone number is 632-0781; her home phone is 832-4859.

speed 3 Pamela may go with us to the city to do the work for the auditor.

gwam 1' | 1 | 2 | 3 | 4 | 5 | 6 | 7 | 8 | 9 | 10 | 11 | 12 | 13 |

LESSON 1 ASSESSMENT: E-MAILS, MEMOS, LETTERS

OBJECTIVE

 To assess e-mail, memo, and letter formatting skills.

Exercise 1A

Assess Memo Formatting Skills

1. Format the text below as a memo to Kathleen Maloney from Miguel Gonzalez.

2. Date the memo May 5, 20--; use BUDGET REQUEST for the subject line.

3. Save as *CA7-1A*.

As I searched the Internet for teaching resources, I came across some audiocassettes that would be an excellent addition to my World History course. The audiocassette collection, *The World's 100 Greatest People*, currently sells for $295, plus sales tax and shipping and handling charges of $9.95.

(continued on next page)

According to the advertisement (http://www.4iq.com/iquest16.html), "The 50 tapes included in this collection represent an audio treasury of 100 biographies detailing the life, time, achievement, and impact of some of history's greatest personalities, including philosophers, explorers, inventors, scientists, writers, artists, composers, and religious, political, and military leaders." These tapes could be used in many classes outside the Social Studies Department. Perhaps some of the other departments would be willing to share the cost of the tapes.

When you have a few minutes, I would like to discuss how we should proceed to get these tapes in time for next year.

Exercise 1B

Assess Letter Formatting Skills

1. Format the text below as a two-page letter to:

   Mr. Michael Kent, President
   Quote of the Month Club
   97 Liberty Square
   Boston, MA 02109-3625

   a. Use March 3, 20-- for the date.

   b. The letter is from Patricia Fermanich, who is the Program Chair. Use Dear Michael for the salutation and Sincerely for the complimentary closing.

2. Save as *CA7-1B*.

Arrangements for our April **Quote of the Month Club** meeting are progressing nicely. The meeting will be held at the Pilgrims' Inn in Plymouth on Saturday, the 15th. The Inn offers excellent accommodations and food. I worked out special pricing with the manager. The cost will be $199.50 per member. This includes a single room, lunch and dinner on Saturday, and a continental breakfast on Sunday. I've asked the Inn to reserve 25 rooms for our members and guests. They will hold them until April 10. I've enclosed the Inn's brochure and list of food options. We can discuss them at the officers' meeting in Boston next week.

Members didn't like the format of our last meeting, so I'm proposing this plan: Each person attending will be assigned to a team, and each team will be given four quotes. The team will select one quote and prepare a five-minute presentation explaining the meaning of the quote (their opinion). Each team will select a member to present to the entire group. Teams will evaluate each presenter in writing, rather than with oral comments. Some presenters at the last meeting felt uncomfortable being critiqued in front of the entire group.

(continued on next page)

I selected these four quotations:

- **Walter Elias Disney**--"Our greatest natural resource is the mind of our children."

- **Ayn Rand**--"Throughout the centuries there were men who took first steps down new roads armed with nothing but their own vision."

Insert the two bulleted quotations shown below.

These topics should provide for excellent discussions leading up to the presentations. When you send the meeting notice, please send the quotes so the members will have time to think about them prior to the meeting.

I'm looking forward to our officers' meeting next week. I may be a few minutes late since I have a 4 p.m. meeting that I must attend.

- *Wendell Lewis Willkie—"Our way of living together in America is a strong but delicate fabric. It is made up of many threads. It has been woven over many centuries by the patience and sacrifice of countless liberty-loving men and women."*

- *Althea Gibson—"No matter what accomplishments you make, somebody helps you."*

Exercise 1C

Assess E-Mail Formatting Skills

1. Send the text displayed below as an e-mail to your instructor. If you do not have e-mail software, prepare the text as a memo to Sachiko Yang.

2. Use April 24, 20-- for the date and RESPONSE TO YOUR QUESTION for the subject.

3. Save as CA7-1C.

Your question is a good one. Yes, Nellie Tayloe Ross of Wyoming and Miriam (Ma) Ferguson of Texas were elected on the same day, November 4, 1924. However, Ms. Ross took office 16 days before Ms. Ferguson; therefore, Ms. Ross is considered the first woman governor in the United States, and Ms. Ferguson is considered the second. It should also be noted that Ms. Ross completed her husband's term as governor of Wyoming prior to being elected in 1924.

If you have other questions before the exam on Friday, please let me know. I hope you do well on it.

LESSON 2 ASSESSMENT: REPORTS

OBJECTIVE

 To assess report formatting skills.

Assess Report Formatting Skills

1. Format the text below as a bound report with footnotes.

   a. Use FOUR OUTSTANDING AMERICANS for the title.

   b. Include the following footnotes where appropriate:

[1]Susan Clinton, *The Story of Susan B. Anthony* (Chicago: Children's Press, 1986), p. 5.

[2]Jim Powell, "The Education of Thomas Edison," April 25, 2000.

[3]"An Overview of Abraham Lincoln's Life," June 2, 2005.

2. Save as *CA7-2A*.

Many outstanding Americans have influenced the past, and many more will impact the future. Choosing the "Four Greatest Americans" does injustice to the hundreds of others who left their mark on our country and diminishes their contributions. This report simply recognizes four great Americans who ~~made~~ helped make America what it is today.

Without these four individuals, America perhaps would be quite different ~~than what it is today.~~ from the country we know. The four individuals included in this report are: Susan B. Anthony, Thomas A. Edison, Benjamin Franklin, and Abraham Lincoln.

Susan B. Anthony

Susan B. Anthony is noted for her advancement of women's rights. She and Elizabeth Cady Stanton organized the national woman suffrage association. The following quotation shows her commitment to the cause.

   At 7 a.m. on November 5, 1872, Susan B. Anthony broke the law
   by doing something she had never done before. After twenty
   years of working to win the vote for women, she marched to the
   polls in Rochester, New York, and voted. Her vote—for Ulysses
   S. Grant for president—was illegal. In New York state, only
   men were allowed to vote.[1]

Anthony continued to fight for women's rights, however, for the next 33 years of her life. Even though she died in 1906 and the amendment granting women the right to vote (nineteenth amendment) was not passed until 1920, that amendment is often called the Susan B. Anthony Amendment in honor of Anthony's efforts to advance women's rights.

Thomas Alva Edison

Imagine life without the incandescent light bulb, phonograph, kinetoscope (a small box for viewing moving films), or any of the other 1,090 inventions patented by Edison. Life certainly would be

(continued on next page)

different without these inventions or later inventions that came as a result of ~~his~~ _Edison's_ work.

Interestingly enough, most of Edison's learning _took_ place at home under the guidance of his mother. "Nancy Edison's secret: she was more dedicated than any teacher was likely to be, and she had the flexibility to experiment with various ways of nurturing her son's l~~i~~ve for learning."[2]

Benjamin Franklin

Benjamin Franklin was a man of many talents. He was an inventor, printer, diplomat, philosopher, author, postmaster, and leader. A few of his more noteworthy accomplishments included serving on the committee that created the Declaration of Independence; _publishing_ Poor Richard's Almanac; and _inventing_ the lightning rod, ~~the~~ Franklin stove, ~~the~~ odometer, and bifocal glasses.

Abraham Lincoln

For many Americans the impact of Abraham Lincoln is as great today as it was during his life time.

Abraham Lincoln is remembered for his vital role as the leader in preserving the Union and beginning the process that led to the end of slavery in the United States. He is also remembered for his character, his speeches and letters, and as a man of humble origins whose determination and perseverance led him to the nation's highest office.[3]

DS Lincoln is a great example of one who dealt positively with adversity in his personal and professional life. His contributions towards the shaping of America will be long remembered.

Exercise 2B

Format a References Page

1. Format a references page from the information below.

Clinton, Susan. *The Story of Susan B. Anthony.* Chicago: Children's Press, 1986.

"An Overview of Abraham Lincoln's Life." June 2, 2005. http://home.att.net/~rjnorton/Lincoln77.html.

Powell, Jim. "The Education of Thomas Edison." April 25, 2000. http://www.self-gov.org/freeman/9502powe.htm.

2. Save as *CA7-2B*.

Exercise 2C

Format a Title Page

1. Format a title page for the report.

2. Save as *CA7-2C*.

OBJECTIVE

⊘ To assess table formatting skills.

Exercise 3A

Assess Table Formatting Skills

1. Format the table shown below.
    a. Adjust column widths: columns A and B, 2"; column C, 1.75".
    b. Adjust row height: 0.3" (all rows).
    c. Use the horizontal and vertical alignment in cells as shown.
    d. Apply bold and shading (gray—5%) and a double-line border around every cell (as shown).
    e. Center the table horizontally and vertically.
2. Save as *CA7-3A*.

Fan Balloting

MAJOR LEAGUE ALL-CENTURY TEAM

Position	Player	No. of Votes
Catcher	Johnny Bench	1,010,403
	Yogi Berra	704,208
Pitcher	Nolan Ryan	992,040
	Sandy Koufax	970,434
First Baseman	Lou Gehrig	1,207,992
	Mark McGwire	517,181
Second Baseman	Jackie Robinson	788,116
	Rogers Hornsby	630,761
Shortstop	Cal Ripken Jr.	669,033
	Ernie Banks	598,168
Third Baseman	Mike Schmidt	855,654
	Brooks Robinson	761,700
Outfield	Babe Ruth	1,158,044
	Hank Aaron	1,156,782
	Ted Williams	1,125,583
	Willie Mays	1,115,896
	Joe DiMaggio	1,054,423
	Mickey Mantle	988,168

Source: *USA Today.* 25 October 1999. http://www.usatoday.com/sports/baseballmlbfs28.htm.

Assess Table Formatting Skills

1. Format the table shown below.

   a. Adjust column widths: column A and B, 1"; columns C and D, 0.75"; columns E and F, 1.25".

   b. Adjust row height: 0.25" (all rows).

   c. In cells, use bottom vertical alignment and the horizontal alignment shown.

   d. Apply bold and shading (gray—5%, gray—10%, red, and light blue) and a border around every cell (as shown).

   e. Center the table horizontally and vertically.

2. Save as CA7-3B.

UNITED STATES FEMALE GOVERNORS
1925–2000

Name		Party Affiliation		State	Years Served
Last	First	Dem.	Rep.		
Collins	Martha	X		Kentucky	1984–1987
Ferguson	Miriam	X		Texas	1925–1927 1933–1935
Finney	Joan	X		Kansas	1991–1995
Grasso	Ella	X		Connecticut	1975–1980
Hollister	Nancy		X	Ohio	1998–1999
Hull	Jane		X	Arizona	1997–present
Kunin	Madeleine	X		Vermont	1985–1991
Mofford	Rose	X		Arizona	1988–1991
Orr	Kay		X	Nebraska	1987–1991
Ray	Dixy	X		Washington	1977–1981
Richards	Ann	X		Texas	1991–1995
Roberts	Barbara	X		Oregon	1991–1995
Ross	Nellie	X		Wyoming	1925–1927
Shaheen	Jeanne	X		New Hampshire	1997–present
Wallace	Lurleen	X		Alabama	1967–1968
Whitman	Christine		X	New Jersey	1994–present

Source: "GenderGap in Government." March 31, 2004. http://www.gendergap.com/government/governor.htm.

Assess Table Formatting Skills

1. Format the table shown below using the table format features that you have learned to arrange the information attractively on the page.
2. Save as *CA7-3C*.

SALARY COMPARISON

Employee	Proposed Salary		Current Salary	
	Salary	Rank	Salary	Rank
Douglas, Jason	$39,790	8	$39,000	7
Hazelkorn, Rebecca	41,230	7	38,500	8
Jackson, Charla	37,952	9	37,000	9
Loomis, Scott	25,796	10	23,000	10
Market, Michael	47,682	5	45,500	4
Nelson, Tim	62,265	1	59,725	1
Reed, Maja	52,980	3	51,900	2
Sutherland, Tara	54,769	2	51,695	3
Tekulve, Jaycee	49,780	4	44,500	6
Welsch, Gary	47,290	6	45,000	5

LESSON 4 ASSESSMENT: ELECTRONIC PRESENTATIONS

OBJECTIVE

 To assess electronic presentation creation skills.

Assess Electronic Presentation Creation Skills

1. Create the ten slides shown below. The design template was downloaded from Microsoft Office Online Education templates.

   a. If the design template is not available to you, select an appropriate one from those that are available.

   b. The music, "America the Beautiful," for Slides 1 and 10 was downloaded from Microsoft Office Online. If not available, use other appropriate background music.

c. Use appropriate graphics to replace any of the ones shown below that are not available.

d. Instructions for each slide are given beneath the slide.

2. Save as *CA7-4A*.

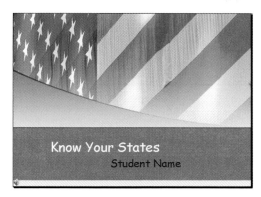

Slide 1

Slide Design: U.S. Flag - Microsoft Office Online.

Music: "America the Beautiful," start playing automatically

Transition: Shape Diamond

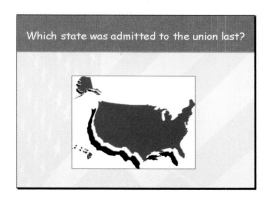

Slide 2

Transition: Comb Horizontally

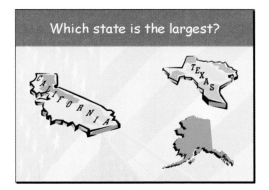

Slide 3

Transition: Cover Left-Down

Custom Animation: Have each state appear one at a time using the *Wheel* entrance effect.

Slide 4

Transition: Wedge

Three Largest States	
State	Approximate Area in Square Miles
Alaska	656,400
Texas	268,600
California	163,700

Slide 5

Transition: Newsflash, medium speed

Custom Animation: Have each state appear one at a time using the *Magnify* entrance effect.

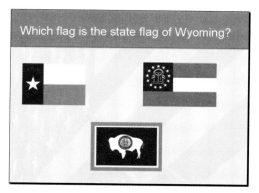

Slide 6

Transition: Wheel Clockwise, 8 spokes

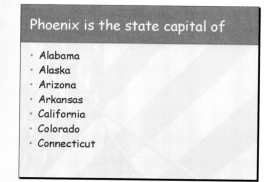

Slide 7

Transition: Box Out

Custom Animation: Have each state name appear one at a time using *Zoom* effect.

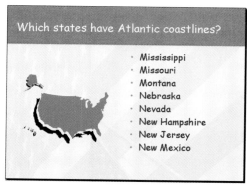

Slide 8

Transition: Blinds Horizontal

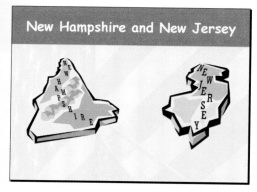

Slide 9

Transition: Push Down

Custom Animation: Have each state name appear one at a time using *Split* effect.

Slide 10

Transition: Strips Right-Down

Music: "America the Beautiful," start playing automatically

UNIT 8

Integrated Workplace Simulation

HPJ Communication Specialists

Conditioning Practice

Key each line twice.

alphabet	1	Seven complete textbooks were required for the new zoology major.
figures	2	Shipping charges ($35.18) were included on the invoice (#426087).
speed	3	A sick dog slept on the oak chair in the dismal hall of the dorm.

gwam 1' | 1 | 2 | 3 | 4 | 5 | 6 | 7 | 8 | 9 | 10 | 11 | 12 | 13 |

OBJECTIVES

⊙ To work in a simulated business environment.
⊙ To use your decision-making skills to process high-quality documents.
⊙ To improve your ability to read and follow directions.

Work Assignment

HPJ Communication Specialists prepares, organizes, and delivers communication training seminars. Three partners—Stewart Herrick, Natasha Parker, and Spencer Jorstad—founded the company in 1991. In 1998, Ms. Parker bought out the other two partners. Today, the company has five branches located in Dallas, Denver, Minneapolis, New York, and San Francisco.

You have been hired by HPJ to work part-time for the administrative assistant, Helen St. Claire. Ms. St. Claire processes documents for the President and CEO, Natasha S. Parker, as well as for Erika Thomas, the Minneapolis branch manager.

During your training program, you were instructed to use the unbound format for reports and block format for all company letters. Ms. Parker likes all her letters closed as follows:

```
Sincerely


Natasha S. Parker
President & CEO
```

When a document has more than one enclosure, format the enclosure notation as follows:

```
Enclosures: Agenda
            Hotel Confirmation
```

General processing instructions will be attached to each document you are given to process. Use the date included on the instructions for all documents requiring a date.

Use your decision-making skills to format documents attractively whenever specific instructions are not provided. Since HPJ has based its word processing manual on the Century 21 textbook, you can also refer to this text in making formatting decisions. You are expected to produce error-free documents. Even though you have a spell checker, you should proofread all documents carefully. HPJ has gone to great lengths to create the company image. The documents you create are part of that image. Errors are not accepted.

Use the Help features in your software to review a feature that you have forgotten or to learn new features you may need. Refer to Electronic Presentations as needed to create the electronic presentation.

HPJ Files and Website

Some jobs will require you to use documents stored in HPJ's company files. Some documents will require you to gather information from the company's Web site at http://www.hpj.swep.com. Name all the files you create with HPJ-, followed by the job number (*HPJ-JOB1, HPJ-JOB2*, etc.).

Getting Started

Create macros for closing lines and other text (HPJ Communication Specialists) that you will use often.

Job 1

HPJ   From the desk of
Helen St. Claire

Prepare an updated name and address list of the CEO and branch managers. Please get this information from the website and create a table similar to the one attached. Addresses are shown at the top of each Web page. Keep a copy of the list for your reference.

Suggestion: Create a macro for each branch manger's address to use for later jobs.

June 5   *HSC*

HPJ COMMUNICATION SPECIALISTS
CEO and Branch Manager Address List
June 5, 20--

Ms. Natasha S. Parker, President & CEO HPJ Communication Specialists Address City, State ZIP	Name of Branch Manager, Branch Manager HPJ Communication Specialists Address City, State ZIP
Name of Branch Manager, Branch Manager HPJ Communication Specialists Address City, State ZIP	Name of Branch Manager, Branch Manager HPJ Communication Specialists Address City, State ZIP
Name of Branch Manager, Branch Manager HPJ Communication Specialists Address City, State ZIP	Name of Branch Manager, Branch Manager HPJ Communication Specialists Address City, State ZIP

Job 2

Dear

Each of you has indicated a need for additional personnel. I've heard your requests. With this quarter's increase in seminar revenues, I am now in a position to respond to them. Five new communication specialist positions, one for each branch, have been added.

Since training for the positions takes place here at the home office, it is more cost-effective to hire communication specialists from this area. I will take care of recruitment and preliminary screening. However, since each of you will work closely with the individual hired, I think you should make the final selection.

When you are here for the annual meeting, I'll schedule time for you to interview eight individuals. If you are not satisfied with any of the eight, we will arrange additional interviews. I should have a job description created within the next week. When it is completed, I'll send it to you for your review.

Job 3

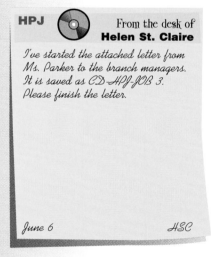
Technology. The changed marketplace is demanding that we explore new ways of delivering our seminars. How can we better use technology to deliver our product? This may include putting selected seminars online, inter- and intra-company communication, etc.

Company growth. What steps can we take to increase company growth? Last year revenues grew by 15 percent; our expenses grew by 8 percent.

Employee incentives. Last year we implemented a branch manager profit-sharing plan. Some of you have indicated that we need to expand this profit-sharing plan to include our communication specialists.

Regional expansion. Some of the regions have been very successful. How do we capitalize on that success? Is it time to divide the successful regions?

International expansion. HPJ has put on several seminars overseas--at a very high cost. Is it time to start thinking about creating a branch of **HPJ** at a strategic overseas location?

I am proud of what we have been able to accomplish this year. The foundation is in place, and we are ready to grow. Each of you plays a critical role in the success of **HPJ**. Thank you for your dedication and commitment to making our company the "leader in providing corporate and individual communication training." Best wishes for continued success. I'm looking forward to discussing **HPJ**'s future at this year's annual meeting. If you have additional items that you would like included on the agenda, please get them to me before June 15.

Job 4

HPJ COMMUNICATION SPECIALIST bf

bf   (DS) Job Description (DS)

HPJ Communication Specialists work cooperatively with other branch members
to develop and deliver communication seminars throughout the United States.

A. II. Duties and Responsibilities
   a. Research seminar topics
   b. Develop seminars
   c. Prepare electronic presentations for seminars
   d. Prepare seminar manual
   e. Present seminars

H. I. Position Requirements
   a. College degree
   b. Excellent oral and written communication skills
   c. Excellent interpersonal skills
   d. Technology skills
   e. Knowledge of business concepts

Job 5 & 6

SUBJECT: JOB DESCRIPTION FOR COMMUNICATION SPECIALISTS

I've attached a draft of the job description for the communication
specialists that we will be hiring for each branch. I wanted to give each
of you an opportunity to review it before we advertise for the positions in
the newspaper.

If there are additional responsibilities that you would like to see included
with the job description before we post it, please let me know by Friday.
The advertisement will run in the <u>Star</u> on Sunday and appear on its Job
Board website next week. I'm confident that we will have an even
greater interest in the positions than we had when we hired a couple of
communication specialists last January.

Job 7

HPJ

From the desk of
Helen St. Claire

Create the attached New Seminar Description table. You will need to copy seminar descriptions from our website. Add color and other enhancements. Your document may be posted on the Web page if NSP approves.

June 7   *HSC*

NEW SEMINAR DESCRIPTIONS

Seminar Title	Seminar Description	Cost per Person
Business Etiquette: You Cannot Not Communicate!		$99
Gender Communication: "He Says, She Says"		$75
International Communication		$75
Listen Up!		$99
Technology in the Workplace		$125

Job 8

HPJ

From the desk of
Helen St. Claire

Format the attached agenda for the annual meeting in outline format.

June 8   *HSC*

AGENDA

I. Greetings
II. Overview of past year
III. Seminars
    a. Enhancement
    b. Expansion
    c. Client base
IV. Leadership
V. Company growth
    a. Regional expansion
    b. International expansion
VI. Employee incentives
    a. Branch managers
    b. Communication specialists
VII. Technology
VIII. Miscellaneous
IX. Adjournment

Job 9

Attached is the agenda for the annual meeting. I didn't hear from any of you about additions to the agenda; so if you have items to discuss, we can include them under Miscellaneous.

Your accommodations have been made for the McIntyre Inn. Your confirmation is enclosed. A limousine will pick you up at the Inn at 8:30 a.m. on Monday. Activities have been planned for Monday and Wednesday evenings. Tuesday and Thursday mornings have been left open. You can arrange something on your own, or we can make group arrangements. We'll decide on Monday before adjourning for the day.

I'm looking forward to seeing you on the 26th.

Job 10

HPJ Communication Specialists
Interview Schedule for **Jamal Carter**
June 29, 20--, Room 101

Time	Name of Interviewee
1:00–1:15	Joan Langston
1:20–1:35	Tim Wohlers
1:40–1:55	Mark Enqvist
2:00–2:15	Stewart Peters
2:20–2:35	Felipe Valdez
2:40–2:55	Katarina Dent
3:00–3:15	Jennifer Kent
3:20–3:35	Sandra Baylor

Job 11

Seminar Objectives for:
TECHNOLOGY IN THE WORKPLACE
Minneapolis Branch

1. Discuss the role of communication technology in today's business environment and how it has changed over the past ten years.
2. Inform participants of various technological communication tools presently available.
3. Highlight the advantages/disadvantages of these communication technologies.
4. Demonstrate:
   - Videoconferencing
   - Teleconferencing
   - Data Conferencing
   - GroupSystems
   - Internet resources
5. Inform participants of various technological communication tools that are in development.
6. Discuss Internet resources available to participants.
7. Discuss how using high-speed communication in today's business environment can give a firm a competitive advantage in the global marketplace.

Job 12

Here is an update on recent progress of the Minneapolis Branch.

Seminar Bookings

We are fully booked through April and May. Additional communication specialists are desperately needed if we are going to expand into other states in our region. Most of our current bookings are in Minnesota, Iowa, and Wisconsin. We will be presenting in Illinois for the first time in May. I anticipate this will lead to additional bookings that we won't be able to accommodate. This is a problem that I enjoy having. Michigan, Indiana, and Ohio provide ample opportunities for expansion, when resources are made available.

New Seminar

A lot of progress has been made on the new seminar we are developing, "Technology in the Workplace" (see attachment for seminar objectives). Our branch will be ready to preview the seminar at our annual meeting. Not only will the seminar be a great addition to our seminar offerings, but also I believe HPJ can use it to communicate better internally. I will present my ideas when I preview the seminar. The seminar covers:

- Videoconferencing
- Teleconferencing

(continued on next page)

- Data conferencing
- GroupSystems
- Internet resources

Graphic Designer

A graphic artist has been hired to design all of the materials for the new seminar. He will design promotional items as well as content-related items. Currently he is working on the manual cover and divider pages. These items will be coordinated with the emblems used in the slide show portion of the presentation, along with name tags, promotional paraphernalia, and business cards. This should give our seminar a more professional appearance. If it works as well as I think it is going to, we will have the designer work on materials for our existing seminars to add the "professional" look.

Job 13

HPJ   From the desk of
Helen St. Claire

Format the text as an unbound report with footnotes (shown at bottom of attached copy). The report will be a handout for the "Listen Up!" seminar.

June 12   HSC

LISTEN UP!

According to Raymond McNulty, "Everyone who expects to succeed in life should realize that success only will come if you give careful consideration to other people."[1] To accomplish this, you must be an excellent listener. One of the most critical skills that an individual acquires is the ability to listen. Studies indicate that a person spends 70 percent to 80 percent of his or her time communicating, of which 45% is spent listening. Nixon and West give the following breakdown for the average individual of an time spent as communicating.[2]

- Writing 9%
- Reading 16%
- Speaking 30%
- Listening 45%

Since almost half of the time spent communicating is spent listening (and we listen at only 25 percent efficiency)[3], it is important to overcome any obstacles that obstruct our ability to listen and to learn new ways to improve our listening ability.

Barriers to Listening

Anything that interferes with our ability to listen is classified as a barrier to listening. These Barriers that obstruct our ability to listen can be divided into two basic categories--external and internal barriers.

(continued on next page)

Internal barriers. Internal barriers are those that deal with the mental or psychological aspects of listening. The perception of the importance of the message, the emotional state, and the tuning in and out of the speaker by the listener are examples of internal barriers.

External Barriers. External barriers are barriers other than those that deal with the mental and psychological makeup of the listener that tend to keep the listener from devoting full attention to what is being said. Telephone interruptions, uninvited visitors, noise, and the physical environment are examples of external barriers.

Ways to Improve Listening

Barriers to listening can be overcome. However, it does take a sincere effort on the part of the listener. Neher and Waite suggest the following ways to improve listening skills.[4]

- Be aware of the barriers that are especially troublesome for you. Listening difficulties are individualistic. Developing awareness is an important step in overcoming such barriers.

- Listen as though you will have to paraphrase what is being said. Listen for ideas rather than for facts.

- Expect to work at listening. Work at overcoming distractions, such as the speaker's delivery or nonverbal mannerisms.

- Concentrate on summarizing the presentation as you listen. If possible, think of additional supporting material that would fit with the point that the speaker is making. Avoid trying to refute the speaker. Try not to be turned off by remarks you disagree with.

[1]H. Dan O'Hair, James S. O'Rourke IV, and Mary John O'Hair, *Business Communication: A Framework for Success* (Cincinnati: South-Western Publishing, 2001), p. 211.

[2]Judy C. Nixon and Judy F. West, "Listening--The New Competency," *The Balance Sheet* (January/February 1989), pp. 27-29.

[3]Mary Ellen Guffey, *Business Communication* (Cincinnati: Thomson South-Western, 2006), p. 75.

[4]William W. Neher and David H. Waite, *The Business and Professional Communicator* (Needham Heights, MA: Allyn and Bacon, 1993), p. 28.

HPJ

From the desk of
Helen St. Claire

Here is the company organization chart we have on file (CD-HPJ-JOB14). Some of the information is missing or outdated. Each branch's website contains the most up-to-date information. Print a copy of the file; then verify the information against that on the website. Mark the changes on the printed copy, and then make the changes to the master file. Change the date to today's date, June 12.

June 12   HSC

HPJ

From the desk of
Helen St. Claire

Prepare (don't send) this message as an e-mail to the communication specialists in the Minneapolis branch from Erika Thomas. You will need to get the e-mail addresses from their Web page. **New Communication Specialist** is the subject.

June 12   HSC

Stewart Peters will be joining our branch as a Communication Specialist on Monday, July 15.

Stewart grew up in New York, where he completed an undergraduate degree in organizational communication at New York University. He recently completed his master's degree at the University of Minnesota.

Stewart's thesis dealt with interpersonal conflict in the corporate environment. Since we intend to develop a seminar in this area, he will be able to make an immediate contribution.

Please welcome Stewart to HPJ and our branch when he arrives on the 15th.

HPJ COMMUNICATION SPECIALISTS

Organization Chart

January 2, 20--

Natasha S. Parker
President & CEO
Minneapolis

New York **Serena DeCosta** Branch Manager	Dallas **Jamal Carter** Branch Manager	Minneapolis **Erika Thomas** Branch Manager	Denver **Steven Powell** Branch Manager	San Francisco Branch Manager

Communication Specialists	Communication Specialists	Communication Specialists	Communication Specialists	Communication Specialists
▪ Fernando Alou ▪ David Ashley ▪ Betty Morneau ▪ Rae Poquette	▪ Virginia Black ▪ Jan Polacheck ▪ Jason Redford ▪	▪ Stephon Gray ▪ William Cody ▪ Tracy Gibbons ▪ Carlos Ryan	▪ Ron Van Horn ▪ Ann Ammari ▪	▪ Kay Logan ▪ Beau McCain ▪ Ed Thomasson ▪ Syd Wright

Job 16

I've started an electronic slide presentation for the annual meeting (CD-HPJ-Job16). Please insert Slides 2–8. I've attached sketches of Slides 2, 3, and 4. Slides 5–8 will be similar to Slide 4, showing a description of each of the new seminars. Get the information for the slides from the New Seminar Descriptions table (Job 7) you formatted earlier.

June 12   HSC

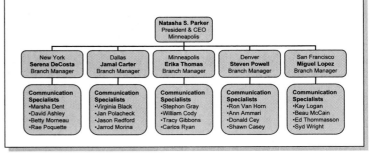

Slide 2

New Seminars

- *Business Etiquette: You Cannot Not Communicate!*
- *Gender Communication: "He Says, She Says"*
- *International Communication*
- *Listen Up!*
- *Technology in the Workplace*

Slide 3

Business Etiquette:
You Cannot Not Communicate!

- *If business etiquette is important to you, don't miss this seminar. Learn what's acceptable—and what's not—in formal business settings.*

Slide 4

UNIT 9

LESSONS 1–5

Enhancing Correspondence Skills

Conditioning Practice

Before you begin the lessons, key each line twice.

alphabet	1	To what extent was Kazu involved with my project before quitting?
figures	2	A van with License No. B928-754 is parked in Space 103 in Lot 16.
speed	3	To my dismay, the official kept the fox by the dog in the kennel.
gwam	1'	1 | 2 | 3 | 4 | 5 | 6 | 7 | 8 | 9 | 10 | 11 | 12 | 13

LESSON 1 WORD PROCESSING 5

OBJECTIVES

- To learn to change fonts and case.
- To learn to find and replace text.

Learn: Change Fonts

font
typeface
styles
effects

The **font** is the type, or letters, in which a document is printed. A font consists of the *typeface*, *style*, *size*, and *effect*. The **typeface** is the design of the letters. Examples include Times New Roman, Courier New, and Arial. Font **styles** include bold and italic, with which you are familiar. Font size is measured in *points* (such as 10 point and 16 point). A point is about 1/72 of an inch. Fonts measured in points are *scalable*; that is, they can be printed in almost any size. An effect may be added to give text a special look. **Effects**, such as shadow, emboss, small caps, and outline, are best when used infrequently. The font features may be used before or after text is keyed to change font, size, and/or effect. In *Microsoft Word*, font features can be changed through the Font dialog box, shown in Figure CA9-1. The number and size of fonts available depend on the software and printer used.

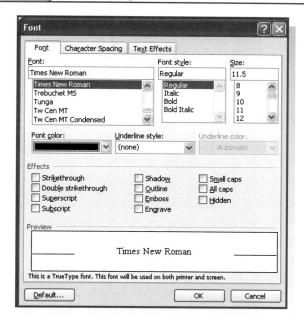

Exercise 1A

Change Fonts

1. Read the information about changing fonts. Open a new word processing document and key lines 1–5 as directed.

---

1. Key this line using Courier font, size 10 pt. Use bold style on the last word.
2. Key this line using Times New Roman, size 12 pt. Use italic style on the font name.
3. Key this line using Arial, 14 pt. Apply bold and italic to the font name.
4. Key this line in Comic Sans MS, 18 pt. Apply bold style and outline effect to the font name.
5. Key this line using the font, size, style, and effect of your choice.

---

2. Save as *CA9-1A*. Close the file.

Learn: Change Case

Use the **Change Case** feature to change capitalization. For example, the Sentence Case option capitalizes the first letter of the first word. The lowercase option changes all selected text to lowercase; the UPPERCASE option changes selected text to all capitals. The Title Case option capitalizes the first letter in each word of the selected text. The Toggle Case option reverses the case of selected text. The different Change Case options are shown in the Change Case dialog box (see Figure CA9-2).

Change Case

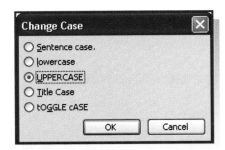

Exercise 1B

Change Case

1. Read the information on the previous page about changing case. Open a new word processing document and key lines 1–5 exactly as shown.

---

1. CHANGE THIS LINE OF TEXT TO SENTENCE CASE.
2. CHANGE THIS LINE OF TEXT TO LOWERCASE.
3. Change this line of text to uppercase.
4. Change this line of text to title case.
5. CHANGE THIS LINE OF TEXT WITH TOGGLE CASE.

---

2. Select and change each line as directed in the line.
3. Save as *CA9-1B*. Close the file.

Learn: Find and Replace

Find

Replace

The **Find** feature is used to locate a specified keystroke, word, or phrase in a document. You can refine this feature to find only occurrences that match the specified case; to find only whole words containing the specified text; to find all forms of a specified word; and to find specified text involving the asterisk (*) and question mark (?) as wildcard (unspecified) characters. The **Replace** feature also finds a specified keystroke, word, or phrase and then replaces it with another keystroke, word, or phrase. All occurrences of the specified text can be replaced at one time, or replacements can be made individually (selectively). The Find and Replace dialog box is shown in Figure CA9-3.

Figure CA9-3   Find and Replace Dialog Box

Find and Replace Text

1. Read the information about finding and replacing text. Open a new word processing document and key the paragraph shown below.

> An individual has to pay a number of assessments. FICA assessments are the assessments that support the social security system and are subtracted from your pay each month. Federal income assessments are also subtracted from your check each month. Assessments that are not subtracted from your check each month include property assessments and sales assessments.

2. Find and count each occurrence of *are* and *each month*.

3. Replace all occurrences of these words: *assessments* with *taxes, subtracted* with *deducted, month* with *pay period*.

4. Save as *CA9-1C*. Close the file.

LESSON 2   LETTERS, MEMOS, AND E-MAIL

OBJECTIVES

> To review block letter format and letter parts.
> To review memos and e-mail formats.

Exercise 2A

Personal-Business Letter

1. Key the personal-business letter shown below in block format using Times New Roman, 14 point.

> 207 Brainard Road | Hartford, CT 06114-2207 | Current date | Mr. Justin A. Alaron | Brighton Life Insurance Co. | I-84 & Rt. 322 | Milldale, CT 06467-9371 | Dear Mr. Alaron
>
> As a senior at Milldale High School, I participate in the **Shadow Experience Program** (SEP). The enclosed resume indicates my career objective: to become an actuary for a large insurance company.
>
> SEP encourages students to "shadow" a person who is working in their planned career field. I would like to shadow you to see firsthand what an actuary does. I can spend one or two days with you at your office during the coming month.
>
> Please send your written response to me so that I can present it to Ms. Michelle Kish, SEP Coordinator. Thank you.
>
> Sincerely | Ms. Valerie E. Lopez | SEP Member | Enclosure | c Ms. Michelle Kish

2. Bold the name of the program in paragraph 1.

Formatting Note: Place a copy notation (c) at the left margin a double space below the preceding letter part.

3. Address an envelope with a return address.

4. Save as *CA9-2A.* Close the file.

Exercise 2B
E-Mail

1. Key the e-mail message shown below.

2. Send it to your instructor with a copy to a classmate. *Note:* If you do not use e-mail, key as a memo to **Carolyn V. Pucevich, Dean** from **Mary B. Tunno, President.** Send a copy to **Arlene Romeo, Vice President.** Use the current date.

SUBJECT: MATHEMATICAL REASONING SKILLS TASK FORCE

A meeting to discuss the formation of a Mathematical Reasoning Skills Task Force has been arranged for Tuesday, April 21, in my office at 2:30 p.m. Vice President Arlene Romeo will join us. Purposes of the meeting are to finalize the project description and identify faculty and advisory committee members who might join the task force.

---

3. Save as CA9-2B. Close the file.

Exercise 2C
Memo

1. Key the memo shown below, using 14-point Times New Roman.

TO: Dr. Diana Patsiga, Statistics | FROM: Mary B. Tunno, President | DATE: May 25, 20-- | SUBJECT: MATHEMATICAL REASONING SKILLS TASK FORCE

After discussions with members of the Presidential Planning Council, I believe that Sundy Junior College should carefully review the curriculum for developing mathematical reasoning skills.

To do so, I am establishing a task force composed of faculty from various disciplines and my planning council. Dean Carolyn Pucevich will chair the task force.

The primary charge to the task force is this: to determine what mathematical content is to be learned and applied in required general education courses, including required math courses.

If you are interested in serving on this task force, please attend an informational meeting on June 2 at 2:30 p.m. in Board Room C.

xx

---

2. Save as *CA9-2C;* then close the file.

Business Letter

1. Key the business letter shown below in block format using open punctuation and a 12-point font.

   Formatting Note: Key a blind copy (bc) notation at the left margin a double space below the preceding letter part—but not on the original letter.

(Current date) | Mr. Harry R. Dobish | Vice President of Operations | Highmark Biochemistry Laboratories, Inc. | 9180 Wayzata Boulevard | Minneapolis, MN 55440-9180 | Dear Mr. Dobish

I've met several times with the biochemistry laboratory technicians and research biochemists who work in the four Madison laboratories. We've identified the renovations needed to meet proposed safety and access regulations and the equipment that should be purchased for Highmark to maintain "world-class" facilities.

I'll have your architect prepare preliminary drawings to show proposed changes to the facilities. Also, I'll meet with a biochemistry salesperson from Hunter Science Equipment to prepare an equipment cost estimate.

When the drawings and estimate are available, I'll schedule an appointment with you.

Sincerely | Mudi A. Mutubu, Consultant | MM:xx | bc Sandra Gimbel, Project Manager | Your staff is very receptive to change and eager to assist management with these important changes.

---

2. Save as *CA9-2D*. Close the file.

Learn: Insert Tables in Documents

Format an inserted table even with the left and right margin of the document or centered between them. Leave one blank line above the first line and below the last line of an inserted table. Gridlines may be used or omitted.

Exercise 2E

Memo with Inserted Table

1. Read the information above about inserting tables.
2. Prepare the memo shown on the following page to **Helen Opher** from **Joshua Franklin** using the current date and **VISITATION REQUEST** as the subject line. Insert the table as directed.

Students from the Pre-Engineering Club at George Westinghouse High School will be touring the plant next Friday according to this schedule.

(**Insert the table in** *CD-CA9-2E* **here**.)

Please arrange for them to see the corporate history video in Homestead Auditorium at 10:15 a.m.

Ms. Rosita Rivetti, the lead electrical engineer with the 750 CHIP TEAM, will meet you and the students at the auditorium at 11 a.m. She will speak to them briefly and then lead them on a tour of the Cyber VII assembly line.

The students plan to leave at 12:45 p.m. Will you escort them from the cafeteria to their bus? Thank you.

JF:xx

3. Save as *CA9-2E*. Close the file.

LESSON 3   MODIFIED BLOCK LETTERS

OBJECTIVES

 To learn modified block letter format.
 To learn mixed punctuation.

Learn: Modified Block Letter Format, Punctuation Styles, and Letter Parts

Modified block format. Modified block format is a variation of block format. (See model, Figure CA9-4.) When modified block format is used, the date and the closing lines (complimentary close, writer's name, and writer's title) begin at or near the horizontal center of the page instead of at the left margin. The tab nearest to center may be used to place the date and closing lines (usually 3"). The paragraphs of a letter in modified block format may be indented 0.5", or they may be blocked at the left margin.

Mailing and addressee notations. Mailing notations (such as REGISTERED, CERTIFIED, or FACSIMILE) and addressee notations (such as CONFIDENTIAL) may be included on a letter as well as the envelope. Key either type of notation in ALL CAPS a double space below the date; double space below the notation to key the first line of the letter address. On the envelope, key a mailing notation below the stamp, about 0.5" above the envelope address. Key an addressee notation at the left margin a double space below the return address. (See model, Figure CA9-4.)

Attention line. Use an attention line to specify a department or job title (*Attention Human Resources Manager*) when the name of a specific person is not available. Key it as the first line of the letter address; use *Ladies and Gentlemen* as the salutation. (See model, Figure CA9-4.)

Open or mixed punctuation. Open or mixed punctuation may be used with block or modified block letter format. You have used open punctuation, which has no punctuation mark after the salutation or complimentary close. Mixed punctuation uses a colon (:) after the salutation and a comma (,) after the complimentary close. (See model, Figure CA9-4.)

Subject line. A subject line (optional) may be keyed in ALL CAPS or caps and lowercase a double space below the salutation. Leave one blank line above and below a subject line. (See model, Figure CA9-4.)

Postscript. A postscript is an optional message added to a letter as the last item on the page. A postscript may be used to emphasize information in the body or to add a personal message to a business letter. Key postscripts a double space below reference initials or Attachment/Enclosure notation or Copy notation if one is used. Block or indent a postscript to match paragraphs in the body. Omit the postscript abbreviation (P.S.). (See model, Figure CA9-4.)

Exercise 3A
Modified Block Letter 1

1. Study the format guides presented above and the model letter displayed in Figure CA9-4 on the following page.
2. Key the letter in Figure CA9-4, using an 11-point font.
3. Use the Print Preview feature to check the format.
4. Save as *CA9-3A*.

Exercise 3B
Modified Block Letter 2

1. Open *CA9-3A* and make these changes:
   a. Delete the subject line and mailing notation.
   b. Change the letter address to:
      Attention Office Manager
      Family Practice Associates
      875 Kenilworth Avenue
      Indianapolis, IN 46246-0087
   c. Use open punctuation.
   d. Indent the first line of each paragraph 0.5".
   e. Revise paragraph 2 by deleting the left and right parenthesis and "is used in this example" and adding "has" after "punctuation" in the first sentence.
   f. Revise paragraph 3 by deleting "as shown here."
   g. Use a 10-point font size.
2. Save as *CA9-3B*.

Online Resources
See Bonus Exercise 3C and 3D
on Modified Block Letters at
www.c21key.bonus-exercises.
swlearning.com.

Approximately 2" TM
or Center Vertically

Date   September 15, 20--
                                                                    ↓ 2

Mailing   FACSIMILE
notation   ↓ 2

Attention line in   Attention Training and Development Department
letter address   Science Technologies
                  3368 Bay Path Road
                  Miami, FL 33160-3368
                                     ↓ 2

Salutation   Ladies and Gentlemen:
                                   ↓ 2

Subject line   MODIFIED BLOCK FORMAT
                                     ↓ 2

Body   This letter is arranged in modified block format. In this letter format the date and closing lines
        (complimentary close, name of the writer, and the writer's title) begin at or near horizontal
        center. In block format all letter parts begin at the left margin.
                                                                       ↓ 2

Default   Mixed punctuation (a colon after the salutation and a comma after the complimentary close) is   Default
or 1" LM   used in this example. Open punctuation (no mark after the salutation or complimentary close)   or 1" RM
           may be used with the modified block format if you prefer.
                                                                 ↓ 2

        The first line of each paragraph may be blocked as shown here or indented one-half inch. If
        paragraphs are indented, the optional subject line may be indented or centered. If paragraphs
        are blocked at the left margin, the subject line is blocked, too.
                                                                      ↓ 2

Complimentary   Sincerely yours,
close   ↓ 4

Writer   Derek Alan
Writer's title   Manager
                                                  ↓ 2

Reference   DA:tj
initials   ↓ 2

Enclosure   Enclosure
notation   ↓ 2

Copy notation   c Kimberly Rodriquez-Duarte
                                           ↓ 2

Postscript   A block format letter is enclosed so that you can compare the two formats. As you can see,
              either format presents an attractive appearance.

At least 1" BM

OBJECTIVE

To practice modified block letter format.

Exercise 4A

Modified Block Letter 1 (Rough Draft)

1. Key the letter below in modified block format using a 12-point font and indented paragraphs.

May 25, 20-- | Dr. Fouad A. Shia | 212 Seventh St. | Bangor, ME 04401-4447

Dear Dr. Shia:

Thank you for conducting the actuarial forcasts seminar four the administrative support staff at Bank Mart last week.

I have reviewed the enclosed results of the evalaution completed by the participants. Without exception all the participants ranked each of your topics as important to there needs. The topic pertaining to probability recieved the higher ranking.

You should also know that all most all participants rated you're presentation style and materials as very good or excellent. Most of the administrative support people staff involved stated they wanted you back for another seminar within the near future.

Yours sincerely, | Ms. Susan L. Delpiore | Training and Development | xx | Enclosure | c Mr. L. James Walter | Vice President, Operations

2. Save as *CA9-4A*.

Exercise 4B

Modified Block Letter 2 (Embedded Errors)

1. Open *CD-CA9-4B* and make these changes:
   a. Delete paragraph indentions and use open punctuation.
   b. Use **Sincerely yours** as the complimentary close.
   c. Add *Gold* before *Instant Access* in paragraph 1.
   d. Change all occurrences of *automatic teller* to *ATM*.
2. Correct the 12 unmarked errors in the letter body.
3. Save as *CA9-4B*.

Exercise 4C

Modified Block Letter 3 (Embedded Errors)

1. Open *CD-CA9-4C* and make these changes:
   a. *First* to *second* in paragraph 1.
   b. All occurrences of *pamphlet* to *brochure*.
   c. *Monday* in last line to *Friday*.
   d. *Public relations* in paragraph 2 to *The Public Relations Department*.
   e. Format to modified block.
   f. Correct 12 unmarked errors.
2. Save as *CA9-4C*.

LESSON 5 — LETTERS FROM FORM PARAGRAPHS

OBJECTIVE

To learn how to prepare letters from form paragraphs.

Learn: Form Letters

A **form letter** is a standard message sent to more than one addressee. Form letters (or form paragraphs that can be combined to create varying letters) may be stored as macros and played back when needed. Thus each letter is an original, though created from stored text.

Exercise 5A

Create Letters from Form Paragraphs

1. Review the Form Letter section on the previous page. Review the Macro feature (Unit 3, page 39).

2. Record each paragraph below as a macro, using a 12-point font. Define each paragraph with a letter (A–H).

A

Congratulations! You have been accepted into the School of Arts and Sciences at Duncan College for the semester that begins in September. Your major will be [major name].

B

Congratulations. You have been accepted conditionally into the School of Engineering at Duncan College for the semester that begins in September. Your major will be [major name].

C

You should schedule a placement examination to determine your beginning mathematics and English courses at Duncan. Choose a date and time from those listed on the enclosed card and return the card.

D

The courses you have completed, the grades you have earned, and your class rank indicate that you are eligible for a Presidential Scholarship. This is an academic scholarship awarded without regard to financial need to six outstanding freshmen. To be considered, you must schedule an interview with faculty. The interview dates and times are listed on the enclosed card. Indicate your first three choices and return the card as soon as possible.

E

To reserve your spot in the September freshman class, you need to remit a $50 deposit. This deposit will be deducted from your tuition and fees for the first semester.

F

To reserve your spot in the September freshman class and the dormitory, you need to remit a $150 deposit. This deposit will be deducted from your tuition, fees, and room and board charges for the first semester.

(continued on next page)

G

We are glad that you chose Duncan College. We are committed to offering quality education in and out of the classroom.

H

Sincerely,

Gerri D. Rhodes
President

GDR:xx

Online Resources

See Bonus Exercise 6A on Modified Block letters and 6B on E-Mail at www.c21key.bonus-exercises.swlearning.com.

3. Use the Macro feature and the information in the table below to create Letters 1–4.

   a. Use modified block format, indented paragraphs, and mixed punctuation.

   b. Insert the current date and the salutation. Add an enclosure notation if needed.

4. Save each letter as indicated in the table.

Letter 1	Letter 2
Address:	Address:
Ms. Tonya Meinert	**Mr. Monte Swauger**
12306 Hicks Road	**101 La Costa Street**
Hudson, FL 34669-3708	**Melbourne Beach, FL 32951-3480**
Paragraphs: A, E, G, and H	Paragraphs: B, C, F, G, and H
Major: **Biology**	Major: **Mechanical Engineering**
Save as *CA9-5A-Letter1*	Save as *CA9-5A-Letter2*
Letter 3	**Letter 4**
Address:	Address:
Ms. Jodie Cresmonauski	**Ms. Kelli Pardini**
1621 Flagler Avenue	**598 S. Sundance Drive**
Jacksonville, FL 32207-3119	**Lake Mary, FL 32746-6355**
Paragraphs: B, D, E, G, and H	Paragraphs: A, C, D, F, G, and H
Major: **Electrical Engineering**	Major: **Mathematics**
Save as *CA9-5A-Letter3*	Save as *CA9-5A-Letter4*

INTERNET ACTIVITY

Explore space at the National Aeronautics and Space Administration.

1. Access NASA's home page through http://www.c21key.swlearning.com/plus/links.html.

2. Explore links that interest you.

3. Write a letter to a friend describing what you located. Use the letter format of your choice and supply all letter parts.

4. Print one or two pages from the website that relate to your letter to enclose with it.

Advanced Word Processing

UNIT 10

LESSONS 1–5

Improving Report Formatting Skills

Conditioning Practice

Before you begin the lessons, key each line twice.

alphabet	1	Jake will buy very good quality zinc from experts at the auction.
fig/sym	2	Al's gas bill was $89.35 (-6%); his office bill was $40.17 (-2%).
speed	3	Nancy may go with me to visit them by the cornfield and big lake.

gwam	1'	1	2	3	4	5	6	7	8	9	10	11	12	13

LESSON ① WORD PROCESSING 6

OBJECTIVES

> To learn outline numbered lists and increase and decrease indents.
> To learn to insert headers and footers, page numbers, paragraph borders, and clip art.

Learn: Outline Numbered Lists and Increase and Decrease Indent

Outline Numbered feature. Outlines, useful for planning and organizing reports, occasionally appear in a finished document—so readers can see the report structure. Unless otherwise directed, use one of the styles in the Outline Numbered word processing feature to show different topic levels. The margins and line spacing for an outline should match the report body. This feature labels each point with a number, letter, and/or symbol, depending on the numbered list style chosen. In *Microsoft Word*, the Bullets and Numbering dialog box is used to create outlines; see Figure CA10-1.

Increase and Decrease Indent feature. The Increase Indent or Decrease Indent feature is used to format the desired outline levels. The Outline Numbered feature can be activated before text is keyed or applied to selected text after it has

Increase Indent or Decrease Indent

been keyed. In either method, you need not key the numbers, letters, or symbols used to label each point—as indents are increased or decreased, the software adjusts the labels automatically. The Increase and Decrease indent buttons on the Formatting toolbar are shown in Figure CA10-2.

 Figure CA10-1 Bullets and Numbering Dialog Box

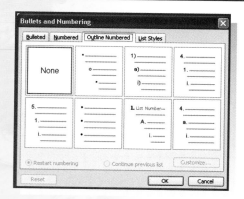

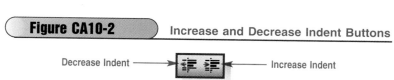 **Figure CA10-2** Increase and Decrease Indent Buttons

Decrease Indent ———→ ┃ ┃ ←——— Increase Indent

Exercise 1A

Outline Numbered Lists and Increase and Decrease Indent

1. Open a blank word processing document and key the outline text (not the level numbers or letters).

2. Use the Outline Numbered feature and Increase or Decrease Indent buttons to format the levels.

1) Breakfast
  a) Cereal
    i) Rice
    ii) Skim Milk
    iii) No Sugar
  b) Toast
    i) Jam
    ii) Butter
  c) Orange Juice
2) Lunch
  a) Sandwich
    i) Wheat Bun
    ii) Meat
    iii) Cheese
    iv) Mustard
  b) Chicken Soup
  c) Apple

3. Save as *CA10-1A*. Close the file.

Learn: Header and Footer

A header or footer is text (such as a chapter title, date, filename, or name of a person or company) or a graphic (a company logo, for example) printed in the top margin (header) or bottom margin (footer) of a page. Reports—especially long ones—often contain headers and/or footers. Page numbers are often included in a header or footer. The header or footer may be invisible as you key the report but will show when you use View and when you print. The Header and Footer toolbar is shown in Figure CA10-3.

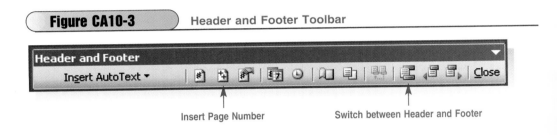

Figure CA10-3 Header and Footer Toolbar

Insert Page Number   Switch between Header and Footer

Exercise 1B

Header and Footer

1. Open *CD-CA10-1B* and insert the text below as a header (name ends at the right margin):

   Summerville High School   A History Report by Barry Gertsner

2. Insert the text below as a footer (page number ends at the right margin).

   December 20--   Page #

3. View the pages to see the header and footer.

4. Delete the header.

5. In the footer, insert the school name at the left and center the date, using 14-point font.

6. Save as *CA10-1B*.

Learn: Border Feature

Use the Border feature to add a border to any or all sides of a page, paragraph, or column, as well as a table or cell within a table. Many line styles and colors are available. In addition, page border options include small graphics (pictures). Borders not only enhance appearance; they also can make text easier to read by emphasizing certain passages. Borders are most effective when used sparingly, however. The Borders and Shading dialog box, shown in Figure CA10-4, controls the use of borders.

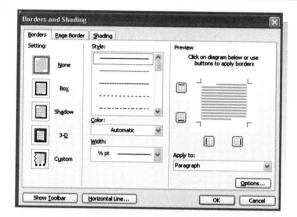

Exercise 1C

Page and Paragraph Borders

1. Open *CD-CA10-1C* and put borders around the third and fourth paragraphs.

2. Save as *CA10-1C-Part1*.

3. Change each of the borders around paragraphs 3 and 4 to a shadow border.

4. Save as *CA10-1C-Part2*.

5. Add a page border in the line style of your choice.

6. Save as *CA10-1C-Part3*.

Learn: Clip Art

Using the Clip Art feature, you can insert drawings and photographs, even sounds and video clips, into documents. You can select from a collection of clip art files provided with your word processing software or from files you add to the clip art files. To insert a clip art file, select Picture from the Insert menu; then select Clip Art. See Figure CA10-5.

Most word processing programs have a Search feature to help you locate the right clip art for your document. An example of the clip art Search feature is shown in Figure CA10-6.

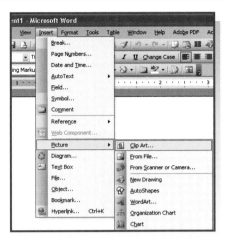

Exercise 1D

Insert Clip Art

1. Open *CD-CA10-1D*.
2. From Clip Art, select a picture that represents a construction worker or one of the building trades named in the paragraph.
3. Insert the picture into the middle of paragraph 2, wrapping text around it.
4. Select a picture of a building from Clip Art.
5. Insert the picture into the middle of paragraph 3, wrapping text around it.
6. Save as *CA10-1D*.

Online Resources

See Bonus Exercise 1E on Report Numbered Lists and 1F on Borders and Clip Art at
www.c21key.bonus-exercises.
swlearning.com.

LESSON 2   MLA-STYLE REPORTS AND OUTLINES

OBJECTIVES

⊙ To format an outline.
⊙ To format reports in MLA style.

Outline

1. Prepare the outline below double spaced, using the Outline Numbered list feature.

Earth's Nearest Neighbor in Space

1) Introduction
   a) Moon's size
   b) Moon's reflection
   c) Moon's atmosphere
2) Moon's Surface
   a) Lowlands (called *maria*) and highlands
   b) Craters
      i) Ray craters
      ii) Secondary craters
3) Moon's Composition
   a) Soil
      i) Color is dark gray to brownish gray
      ii) Consists of ground-up rock and bits of glass
      iii) Depth of soil varies
   b) Rocks
      i) Minerals in the rock
      ii) Basalt and breccia rocks
4) Moon's Orbit
   a) Time to revolve around Earth
   b) Shape of its orbit
   c) Phases of the moon
      i) New moon
      ii) First quarter
      iii) Full moon
      iv) Last quarter
5) Eclipses
   a) Lunar eclipse
   b) Solar eclipse
6) Tides
   a) Caused by the moon's gravity
   b) Frequency of daily high and low tides

2. Save as *CA10-2A*.

Learn: MLA Style

The **Modern Language Association (MLA)** style is often used to document and format students' papers. The MLA documentation method, called *parenthetical reference*, is similar to the textual citation method. MLA reports have these distinctive format features (shown in Figures CA10-7, 10-8, and 10-9 on the following two pages):

Margins. On all pages, the top, bottom, left, and right margins are 1".

Header and page number. A header contains the page number; the writer's last name may be included. The header is right-aligned. Every page is numbered, including the first.

Line spacing. The entire report is double-spaced, including long quotations, bulleted and numbered items, tables, and works cited.

Report identification. The writer's name, instructor's name, course title, and date (day/month/year style) are keyed double-spaced on separate lines at the left margin on page 1.

Report title. The title is centered a double space below the date in title case. The body begins a double space below the title.

Indentations and long quotations. The first line of each paragraph is indented 0.5" (or at the first default tab setting). Long quotations (four or more lines) are indented 1" (or at the second default tab setting) from the left margin.

Inserted tables. Insert a table as near as possible to the text that it illustrates. Key a number (*Table 1*) and caption (title) above the table left-aligned in title case. Double-space above the table number, below the last line (or source note), and between lines within the table. Hide table gridlines. Adjust table width to fit within the left and right margins.

Works cited (references). Key the works cited on a separate page, using the same margins and header as the report body. Center *Works Cited* in title case at the top margin. A double space below the title, list the references in alphabetical order by authors' last names (or by title when a work has no author). Double-space the list and use hanging indent.

Binding. Staple or clip all pages of the report at the top-left corner.

Exercise 2B

MLA-Style Report

1. Read the MLA-style format guides presented above.
2. Key the MLA-style report and Works Cited page as shown in Figures CA10-7, 10-8, and 10-9 on the following two pages.
3. Save as *CA10-2B*.

1" TM

DS I.D.
Information

James Henderson

Professor Lewis

HC101 Composition

15 February 20--
↓ 2

Career Planning ↓ 2

Indent ¶ 0.5"
and DS ¶s

Career planning is an important, ongoing process. It is important because the career you choose

will affect your quality of life.

One important step in career planning is to define your career goals.

Indent long
quotes 1" from
LM and DS

> Whatever your present plans for employment or further education, you should
>
> consider your long-term career goals. You might wonder why someone who is
>
> considering a first job should be thinking beyond that job. Thinking ahead may
>
> help you choose a first job that is closely related to long-term interests. . . . With a
>
> career goal in mind, you can evaluate beginning job offers in relation to that goal.

1" LM and RM

> (Oliverio, Pasewark, and White 528)

1" LM and RM

Another useful step in career planning is to develop a personal profile of your skills, interests, and

values.

An analysis of your skills is likely to reveal that you have many different kinds: (1) functional

skills that determine how well you manage time, communicate, and motivate people; (2) adaptive skills

that determine your efficiency, flexibility, reliability, and enthusiasm; and (3) technical skills such as

keyboarding, computer, and language skills that are required for many jobs.

Values are "principles that guide a person's life" (Fulton-Calkins and Stulz 543), and you should

identify them early so that you can pursue a career that will improve your chances to acquire them.

Values include the importance you place on family, security, wealth, prestige, creativity, power, and

independence.

At least 1" BM

(continued on next page)

1" TM

Interests are best described as activities you like and enthusiastically pursue. By listing and analyzing your interests, you should be able to identify a desirable work environment. For example, your list is likely to reveal if you like to work with things or people, work alone or with others, lead or follow others, or be indoors or outdoors.

1" TM

Works Cited ↓ 2

Fulton-Calkins, Patsy and Karin M. Stulz. *Procedures & Theory for Administrative*

Hanging indent with 0.5" ———▶ *Professionals*. 5th ed. Cincinnati: South-Western, 2004.
indentation

Oliverio, Mary Ellen, William R. Pasewark, and Bonnie R. White. *The Office: Procedures and*

Technology. 4th ed. Cincinnati: South-Western, 2003.

⊙ To practice MLA-style report formatting skills.
⊙ To insert a table in an MLA-style report.

Exercise ▼ 3A

MLA-Style Report 1

1. Key the report shown below in MLA style.
2. Insert a header that contains your last name and the page number.
3. Insert the following report identification:
   - Your name
   - Your instructor's name
   - The course title
   - The current date (day/month/year)

A Need to Know Metrics

Today's students need to learn two systems of measurement--the metric system, which is used throughout the world, and the English or customary system, which is the most-used system in the United States)

Rationale for the Instruction   (Dietz and Southam 446).

DS entire report.

Metrics instruction must be included in the curriculum of our nation's schools because all people must understand the metric system to function in today's society. Metrics are everywhere! Automobile engines; soft drink containers; nutrition information listed on food packages; jean and film sizes; and most of the nuts, bolts, and screws used to assemble products imported to the United States is an example of a common item that is measured in a metric units.

Students must complete a series of learning activities that will enable them to do these activities:

1. Read, write, and pronounce the basic metric measures for length, weight, and capacity.

2. Add, subtract, multiply, and divide metric measurements.

3. Convert from one metric unit to another.

4. Solve problems that use metric measurements.

5. Convert commonly used metric measures to English measures and vice versa.

Instructional Strategies

To accomplish the learning goals, a variety of learning aids, such as charts, oral and written exercises, and word problems, can and should be used extensively in the learning process. A chart is

(continued on next page)

an excellent learning resource that can be used to accomplish many of the objectives.

Table 1 is an example of how basic metric units of length can be presented in visual form (The World Almanac 1999). A similar chart for weight and capacity could be developed.

(Insert the table in *CD-82B-TBL* here. Then hide the gridlines.)

The table can be used several ways to accomplish the instructional objectives.

1. The first column can be used for an oral exercise in which students pronounce each unit of measurement.

2. The second column can be used to show students the abbreviations for metric units, which are always shown in lowercase letters and (w/o) punctuation.

3. The third column can be used to explain that the meter is the basic unit used for measuring length and that other units are parts or multiples of a meter. The table lists the units of measurement from the smallest to the largest.

4. The third column can also be used to show students how to convert from one metric unit to another. Moving the decimal point in the meter measurement to the left converts it to smaller units; moving the decimal point to the right converts it to larger units.

5. The last column of the table can be used to establish the relationship between selected metric and English measurement units.

Summary

The metric system of measurement must be taught along with the English system. Metrics can be presented in an understandable manner if the teacher establishes goals and uses good examples, illustrations, and applications. The table in this report can be used easily to enhance learning.

4. Eliminate any widow/orphan lines and keep side headings with the text that follows them.

5. Prepare the Works Cited page using the references on *CD-CA10-3A-MLA*.

6. Save as *CA10-3A*.

Exercise 3B

MLA-Style Report 2

1. Format the report below in MLA style, correcting the unmarked errors (about 12).

2. Insert your last name and the page number as a header.

3. Insert the following report identification:
   - Your name
   - Your instructor's name
   - The course title
   - The current date

(continued on next page)

The Importance of Saving Money

Open savings account early, financial planners say, so you get into the habit of saving. Later, you may chose higher-yielding and higher-risk investments such as stocks and bonds; but opening an savings account (in your teens or earlier) is a critical first step to a secure future.

A good financial plan is one that makes you feel good now in anticipation of what your will be able to do with your savings in the future.

One of the best ways to save is to have money deducted from earnings before receiving you're paycheck. The idea is this: You wont miss what you dont receive.

Experts agree that saving is simpler when your set financial goals. The goals may relate to a major purchase like a house or car, a college education for yourself or some one else, or retirement.

By saving regularly and allowing the interest to accumulate, you earn interest on the original investment *and* on the interest earned. This is known as *compounding*, and it is a important part of any savings plan.

Besides helping you reach goals for the future, saving also helps the economy, as you savings increase money flow. Thus, your savings may help build a house or school or office building that, in turn, helps other industry's prosper.

4. Save as *CA10-3B*.

LESSON 4 MLA-STYLE REPORTS

OBJECTIVE

⊘ To practice MLA-style report formatting skills.

Exercise 4A

MLA-Style Report 1

1. Key the following report in MLA style.

2. Insert a header that has your last name and the page number.

3. Insert the following report identification:

- Your name
- Your instructor's name
- The course title
- The current date

Mathematics

Most high school students study several mathematics. In college, they complete math courses, some of which prepare them to study even more kinds of mathematics. You may think of math as one subject; in fact, there are many mathematics. This report describes 7 kinds.

(continued on next page)

Arithmetic

DS *ary* Arithmetic is ~~the first~~ branch of mathematics that you ~~study~~ studied in element and middle school. It deals with the study of numbers and
the use of the four fundamental processes:

- Addition
- Subtraction
- Multiplication
- Division

Arithmetic is every day math. You use it in your daily personal
affairs, and ~~it~~ arithmetic is the basis for most other branches of mathematics.

Algebra

DS Algebra is used widely to solve problem in business, industry, and science *s* by using symbols, such as x and y, to represent
unknown values (Algebra). The power of algebra is that it enables
us to create, write, and rewrite problem-solving formulas. Without algebra, we would not have many of the items we use on a daily
basis: television, radio, telephone, microwave oven, etc.

Geometry

Geometry is the branch of mathematics that deals with shapes. More
specifically, geometry is the study of relations, properties, and measurements of
solids, surfaces, lines, and angles (Geometry). It is most useful in building or
measuring things. Architects, astronomers, construction engineers, navigators,
and surveyors are just a few professionals who rely on geometry.

Trigonometry

Trigonometry is mathematics that deals with triangular measurements. Plane
trigonometry computes the relationships between the sides of triangles on level
surfaces called planes. Spherical trigonometry studies the triangles on the surface of a sphere.

Calculus

Calculus is high-level mathematics dealing with rates of change. It has many
practical applications in engineering, physics, and other branches of science.
Using calculus, we understand and explain how water flows, the sun shines, the
wind blows, and the planets cycle through the heavens. Differential calculus
determines the rate at which an object's speed changes. Integral calculus determines the object's speed when the rate of change is known.

Probability

Probability is the study of the likelihood of an event's occurrence. It is useful in
predicting the outcomes of future events. Probability originated from the study
of games of chance. It is now used for other purposes, including to (1) control
the flow of traffic through a highway system; (2) predict the number of accidents
people of various ages will have; (3) estimate the spread of rumors; (4) predict
the outcome of elections; and (5) predict the rate of return in risky investments.

Statistics

Statistics is the branch of mathematics that helps mathematicians organize and
find meaning in data.

Anyone who listens to the radio, watches television, and reads books,
newspapers, and magazines cannot help but be aware of statistics, which
is the science of collecting, analyzing, presenting and interpreting data.

(continued on next page)

Statistics appear in the claims of advertisers, . . . in cost-of-living indexes, and in reports of business trends and cycles. (Statistics)

Works Cited

"Algebra." *Encylopaedia Britannica.* 2003. Encylopaedia Britannica Online. http://search.eb.com/eb/article?eu=120643 (accessed October 14, 2003).

"Calculus." Britannica Student Encyclopedia. 2003. Encylopaedia Britannica Online. http://search.eb.com/eb/article?eu=295242 (accessed October 14, 2003).

"Geometry." Britannica Student Encyclopedia. 2003. Encylopaedia Britannica Online. http://search.eb.com/eb/article?eu=296426 (accessed October 14, 2003).

"Statistics." Britannica Student Encyclopedia. 2003. Encylopaedia Britannica Online. http://search.eb.com/eb/article?eu=299352 (accessed October 14, 2003).

4. Eliminate any widow or orphan lines, and keep all headings with the text that follows them.

5. Save as *CA10-4A.*

Exercise 4B

MLA-Style Report 2

1. Open file *CD-CA10-4B* and format it in MLA style.

2. Change all occurrences of *unit* to *department* and *teachers* to *instructors.*

3. The report contains 20 errors in capitalization, grammar, punctuation, word choice, etc. Correct them.

4. Reverse the order of the Advisory Boards and Awards and Recognition sections.

5. Save as *CA10-4B.*

LESSON 5 · NEWS RELEASES AND MEETING MINUTES

OBJECTIVES

⊙ To format summary meeting minutes.
⊙ To format a news release.

Learn: Meeting Minutes

Format meeting minutes as an unbound report, but single-space the body. Insert a double-space above and below items or paragraphs. Number each item of business summarized in the minutes.

Exercise 5A

Meeting Minutes

1. Study the meeting minutes format guide above, and then format the meeting minutes on the following page.

WOODWARD HIGH SCHOOL BIOLOGY CLUB

March 2, 20-- Meeting Minutes

Participants: All officers, committee chairs, and faculty sponsor attended.

Recorder of minutes: Jerry Finley, Secretary.

1. President Marcie Holmquist called the meeting to order at 2:45 p.m.

2. Written reports from the following officers and committee chairs were distributed, discussed, and approved or accepted (copies are retained by the secretary):

   Vice President/Membership Committee Chair—Accepted
   Treasurer—Approved
   Secretary—February meeting minutes were approved
   Fundraising—Accepted
   Community Service—Accepted

3. This unfinished business was acted upon:

   A. Approved candy sale to begin May 1.
   B. Approved that the Biology Club care for one mile of State Route 163 as part of the community's Adopt-A-Highway Program.
   C. Tabled the recommendation that the Club help support an international student, pending receipt of additional information.

4. This new business was discussed and acted upon:

   A. President Holmquist appointed nominating committee (Sissy Erwin, Roberta Shaw, and Jim Vance).
   B. Approved officers to attend regional leadership conference at Great Valley Resort and Conference Center on April 12.

5. The next meeting is April 3 at 2:45 p.m. in Room 103. The meeting was adjourned at 3:35 p.m.

   2. Save as *CA10-5A*.

Exercise 5B

Meeting Minutes

1. Prepare the meeting minutes below.

2. Center the page number in the footer.

COMPUTER SCIENCE
ADVISORY COMMITTEE MEETING MINUTES

November 15, 20--

Committee members present: Robert Dry-Kenich, Deborah Edington, Amy Lovetro, Ray Meucci, Rosemary Radmanich, Kenneth Ryave, Kim Van Aken, and Leo Yazzani.

School employees present: Mary Amaral, Drew Bowen, Larry Kaufmann, Fred Niklas, Carla Nilson, and Margaret Palmero.

Recorder of minutes: Joseph Gloss.

1. Amy Lovetro, committee chair, called the meeting to order at 11:15 a.m. and welcomed all to the meeting. Ms. Lovetro introduced Kim Van Aken, Hermanie Engineering, as a new member.

(continued on next page)

2. The minutes from the May 14 meeting were read and approved.

3. Mr. Fred Niklas reported:

A. At least 125 students are presently enrolled in the computer science programs. Dunlap High has the most with 25 and West High has the least with 7.

B. Of the 53 health occupation students who were graduated last June, 28 are employed in a computer-related field, 15 have gone on to higher education, 3 entered the military, 5 are employed in unrelated fields, and 2 are unemployed.

4. Unfinished business included passing a motion to recommend that Eastway AVTS students charter a Computer Science Student Organization and that Mary Amaral be appointed sponsor. Each committee member agreed to work closely with the students and the faculty sponsor.

5. New business included passing motions to support these three recommendations:

A. All committee members be invited to participate in the AVTS's career fair.

B. Two members of the committee (Deborah Edington and Kenneth Ryave) be appointed to the AVTS's Strategic Planning Committee.

C. The advisory committee chair be appointed to the AVTS's School-to-Work Transition Committee.

6. The formal meeting was adjourned at 12:35 p.m., and the committee members and school personnel moved to Gessey Dining Room for lunch and informal conversation.

7. The next meeting is scheduled for May 15 at 11:15 a.m.

   3. Save as *CA10-5B*.

Learn: News Release

News releases are formatted as unbound reports with these additional guides. On page 1, key in a bold, 14-point font News Release at the top left and For Release: . . . at the top right margin. On the line below (single space), key Contact: . . . at the right margin. Double-space; begin the news release body. Key the body single-spaced with a double space between paragraphs. Center the symbols ### a double space below the last line.

News Release

1. Read the News Release format guide above, and then format the text below as a news release.

News Release   **For Release: Upon Receipt**
                                         Contact: Guy Madison

     LORAIN, OH, March 24, 20--. Three East Lorain County High School students, members of the ELCHS Science Club, have been invited to exhibit their projects at the Eastern Ohio Academy for Science Fair on April 21-24. The fair will be held in the Stern Exhibit Hall at the Erie Civic Center.

     Susan Marks, Juanita Perez, and John Lavic earned this honor by placing first in their respective categories at the Lorain County Academy for Science Fair on March 15. Marks competed in microbiology, Perez in chemistry, and Lavic in physical science. Ms. Kelly Wyatt, ELCHS physics teacher, is the club's sponsor.

###

---

2. Save as *CA10-5C*.

Online Resources

See Bonus Exercises 6A-6E on
Unbound and Bound Reports at
www.c21key.bonus-
exercises.swlearning.com.

INTERNET **ACTIVITY**

1. Access the National Air and Space Museum at http://www.c21key.swlearning.com/plus/links.html.
2. Find answers to the following questions:
   a. How long and how far did Orville Wright fly during the Kitty Hawk's first flight (12/17/1903)? How much did the Kitty Hawk weigh?
   b. What was the name of the Apollo 11 Command Module (first manned flight to land on the moon)? How much did Apollo 11 weigh?
   c. How many miles did the Breitling Orbiter 3 Gondola fly during the first nonstop balloon flight around the world (March 1999)? How much did the gondola weigh?
3. Key your answers in sentence form and print them.

Communication & Math Skills 3

Number Expression

1. Study each of the eight rules shown below.

a. Key the *Learn* line(s) beneath each rule, noting how the rule is applied.

b. Key the *Apply* line(s), expressing numbers correctly.

Number Expression

Rule 1: Spell a number that begins a sentence even when other numbers in the sentence are shown in figures.

Learn 1 Twelve of the new shrubs have died; 48 are doing quite well.

Apply 2 14 musicians have paid their dues, but 89 have not done so.

Rule 2: Use figures for numbers above ten, and for numbers from one to ten when they are used with numbers above ten.

Learn 3 She ordered 8 word processors, 14 computers, and 4 printers.

Apply 4 Did he say they need ten or 14 sets of Z18 and Z19 diskettes?

Rule 3: Use figures to express date and time (unless followed by o'clock).

Learn 5 He will arrive on Paygo Flight 418 at 9:48 a.m. on March 14.

Apply 6 Exhibitors must be in Ivy Hall at eight forty a.m. on May one.

Rule 4: Use figures for house numbers except house number One.

Learn 7 My home is at 8 Vernon Drive; my office, at One Weber Plaza.

Apply 8 The Nelsons moved from 4059 Pyle Avenue to 1 Maple Circle.

Rule 5: Use figures to express measures and weights.

Learn 9 Glenda Redford is 5 ft. 4 in. tall and weighs 118 lbs. 9 oz.

Apply 10 This carton measures one ft. by nine in. and weighs five lbs.

Rule 6: Use figures for numbers following nouns.

Learn 11 Review Rules 1 to 18 in Chapter 5, pages 149 and 150, today.

Apply 12 Case 1849 is reviewed in Volume five, pages nine and ten.

Rule 7: Spell (and capitalize) names of small-numbered streets (ten and under).

Learn 13 I walked several blocks along Third Avenue to 54th Street.

Apply 14 At 7th Street she took a taxi to the theater on 43d Avenue.

Rule 8: Spell indefinite numbers.

Learn 15 Joe owns one acre of Parcel A; that is almost fifty percent.
Learn 16 Nearly seventy members voted; that is nearly a fourth.

Apply 17 Over 20 percent of the students auditioned for the play.
Apply 18 Just under 1/2 of the voters cast ballots for the best musician.

2. Key Proofread & Correct, expressing numbers correctly. Then follow the steps below.

  a. Check answers.

b. Using the rule number at the left of each line, study the rule relating to each error you made.

c. Rekey each incorrect line, expressing numbers correctly.

Proofread & Correct

Rules

1	1	20 members have already voted, but 15 have yet to do so.
2	2	Only twelve of the dancers are here; six have not returned.
3	3	Do you know if the eight fifteen Klondike flight is on time?
3, 4	4	We should be a 1 Brooks Road no later than eleven thirty a.m.
5	5	This oriental mural measures eight ft. by 10 ft.
5	6	The box of books is two ft. square and weighs six lbs. eight oz.
6	7	Have you read pages 45 to 62 of Chapter two that he assigned?
7	8	She usually rides the bus from 6th Street to 1st Avenue.
8	9	Nearly 1/2 of the cast is here; that is about 15.
8	10	A late fee of over 15 percent is charged after the 30th day.

3. Save as *CS3-ACT1*.

ACTIVITY 2   Reading

1. Open *CD-CS3-ACT2*.

2. Read the document; close the file.
3. Key answers to the questions below.

4. Save as *CS3-ACT2*.

1. Will at least one member of the cast not return for the next season?
2. Has a studio been contracted to produce the show for next season?
3. Does each cast member earn the same amount per episode?
4. Is the television show a news magazine or comedy?
5. How many seasons has the show been aired, not counting next season?
6. Do all cast members' contracts expire at the same time?
7. What did the cast do three years ago to get raises?

ACTIVITY 3   Composing

1. Read the quotations below relating to positive thinking.

2. Choose one and make notes of what the quotation means to you.

3. Key a paragraph or two indicating what the quotation means to you and why you believe it would be (or would not be) a good motto for your own behavior.

4. Proofread, revise, and correct.
5. Save as *CS3-ACT3*.

Attributed to Helen Keller, American author and lecturer, blind and deaf at the age of two.

Keep your face to the sunshine and you cannot see the shadow.

Attributed to Edward Everett Hale, American author and chaplain of the U.S. Senate who wrote *The Man Without a Country*.

  Look up and not down;
  Look forward and not back;
  Look out and not in;
  Lend a Hand.

ACTIVITY 4   Math: Working with Decimals, Fractions, and Percents

1. Open *CD-CS3-ACT4* and print.the file

2. Solve the problems as directed in the file.

3. Submit your answers.

UNIT *11*

LESSONS 1–5
Processing Worksheets

Conditioning Practice

Before you begin the lessons, key each line twice.

alphabet	1	Many plaques were just the right sizes for various duck exhibits.
fig/sym	2	The ski outfit costs $358.41 (20% off), and she has only $297.60.
speed	3	Claudia did lay the world map and rifle by the end of the mantle.

gwam 1' | 1 | 2 | 3 | 4 | 5 | 6 | 7 | 8 | 9 | 10 | 11 | 12 | 13 |

LESSON ① SPREADSHEETS, WORKBOOKS, AND WORKSHEETS

OBJECTIVES

⊙ To learn about spreadsheets, workbooks, and worksheets.
⊙ To enter data, move around in a worksheet, and print a worksheet.

Learn: Spreadsheet Software

Spreadsheet software. Spreadsheet software is a computer program used to record, report, and analyze information, especially information that relates to numbers. Many different types of employees in business, education, and government use spreadsheet software in a variety of ways. Spreadsheet software is especially useful when you need to make repetitive calculations accurately, quickly, and easily. It works equally well with simple and complex calculations.

Numbers can be added, subtracted, multiplied, and divided in a worksheet, and formulas are used to perform calculations quickly and accurately. Additionally, charts can be constructed to present the worksheet information graphically.

One big advantage of spreadsheet software is that when a number is changed, all related "answers" are automatically recalculated. For example, you can use spreadsheet software to quickly calculate how money saved today will grow at various interest rates over various periods of time by changing the values for the rate and time.

Exercise 1A

Access Spreadsheet Software

1. Study the information about spreadsheet software on the previous page.

2. Open your spreadsheet software and refer to the blank document on the screen and to Figure CA11-1 as you learn about worksheets and workbooks in the next sections.

Learn: Worksheets and Workbooks

Worksheet. A worksheet is one spreadsheet computer file—it is where you enter information.

Workbook. A workbook contains one or more worksheets, usually related. When spreadsheet software is opened, a worksheet will appear on the screen. Other worksheets in the workbook appear as **sheet tabs** at the bottom of the screen (see Figure CA11-1). If needed, additional worksheets can be inserted into the workbook.

sheet tabs

Figure CA11-1   Worksheet Screen

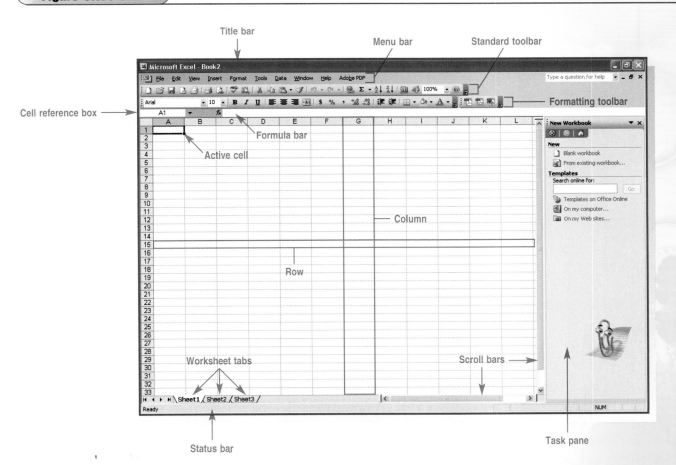

Workbooks and Worksheets

1. Read the information on worksheets and workbooks on the previous page and then refer to your monitor and Figure CA11-1 to answer these questions:

   a. How many workbooks are displayed on your monitor? in CA11-1?

   b. How many worksheets can be accessed in this workbook? in CA11-1?

2. Compare your answers with a classmate's answers.

Learn: The Basic Parts of a Worksheet

Cells. A worksheet contains cells where information is keyed. The cells are arranged in rows and columns.

Columns. Columns run vertically in a worksheet. Each column has a heading (letters from A to Z, AA to AZ, etc.) running left to right across the worksheet.

Rows. Rows run horizontally in a worksheet. Each row has a heading (a number) running up and down the left side of the worksheet.

Exercise 1C

Worksheet Parts

1. Read the information on cells, columns, and rows above and then refer to your monitor and Figure CA11-1 to answer these questions:

   a. How many worksheet columns are displayed on your monitor? in CA11-1?

   b. How many worksheet rows are displayed on your screen? in CA11-1?

2. Compare your answers with a classmate's answers.

Learn: The Basic Parts of a Worksheet Screen

Title bar. This bar displays the application and current worksheet name.

Menu bar. This bar contains the drop-down menu commands.

Standard toolbar and Formatting toolbar. These toolbars provide easy access to frequently used commands.

Cell reference box. This box identifies the active cell by the letter of the column and the number of the row that it intersects. The cell reference box also identifies the range of cells being selected.

Formula bar. This bar displays the contents of the active cell and is used to create or edit text or values.

Active cell. This cell is highlighted with a thick border. When active, it stores information that is keyed in the cell.

Columns. Columns are identified by **letters** that run horizontally.

Rows. Rows are identified by **numbers** that run vertically.

Worksheet tabs. These tabs identify the active worksheet in the workbook.

Status bar. This bar indicates various items of information such as SCROLL LOCK, NUM LOCK, or CAPS LOCK when active.

Scroll bars. These bars are use to move horizontally or vertically within a worksheet.

Exercise 1D

Worksheet Window Parts

1. Read the definitions of the worksheet parts above and refer to your monitor and Figure CA11-1 to locate the various parts.
2. Close the spreadsheet software.
3. Open word processing file *CD-CA11-1D* and complete the activity.
4. Save as *CA11-1D*.

Learn: Moving Around in a Worksheet

Information is entered in the **active cell** of a worksheet. The active cell is the cell with the thick border around it (see Figure CA11-2). Cells can be activated with the mouse, the arrow keys, or keyboard shortcuts.

    To activate a cell with the mouse, move the pointer to the desired cell and click the mouse.

    To move the active cell one or more cells to the left, right, up, or down, use the arrow keys.

    To move the active cell from one spot to another quickly, use the keyboard shortcuts. For example, to make the first cell in a row active, tap HOME; to activate cell A1, press CTRL + HOME; to move the active cell up one page, tap PgUp, etc.

Figure CA11-2   Active Cell

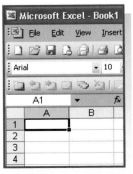

Exercise 1E

Move Around in a Worksheet

1. Read the information on the previous page and refer to the active cell illustration in Figure CA11-2.
2. Learn how to move around in a worksheet by opening a new blank worksheet and completing the following steps:
   a. Use the mouse to make cell G4 active.
   b. Use the mouse to make cell B24 active.
   c. Use the mouse to make cell A12 active.
   d. Use the arrow keys to make cell D11 active.
   e. Use the arrow keys to make cell F30 active.
   f. Use the arrow keys to make cell P30 active.
   g. Use PgDn and arrow keys to make J100 active.
   h. Use PgUp and arrow keys to make L40 active.
   i. Press CTRL + HOME to make cell A1 active.

Learn: Labels and Values

Data entered into a cell is automatically assigned either a label or value status. Data that is to be used in calculations must be entered as a value, since labels cannot be used in calculations.

When only numbers are entered into a cell, the value status is assigned and the data are right-aligned. When letters and/or symbols (with or without numbers) are entered into a cell, the label status is assigned and the data are left-aligned. Numbers that *will not be used* in calculations (such as house or room numbers, years, course or invoice numbers, etc.) can be entered as labels by preceding the cell entry with an apostrophe.

Exercise 1F

Labels and Values

1. Read the information about labels and values above and refer to the worksheet illustration in Figure CA11-3.
2. Complete the following steps to key labels and values.
   a. Key the following names as labels, each in a separate cell, in column A, beginning with row 1: Mary, Henry, Pablo, Susan, Helen, John, James, Paul, and Sandy.
   b. Key the following numbers as values, each in a separate cell, in row 15, beginning with column A: 135790, 673455, 439021, 90888, 569021, 102938, 547612, 102938, and 601925.
   c. Key the following invoice numbers as labels, each in a separate cell, in column I, beginning with row 11: 514620, 687691, and 432987.
   d. Check that data keyed as labels are left-aligned and data keyed as values are right-aligned.
3. Save as *CA11-1F* and close the worksheet.

Figure CA11-3　Worksheet Data

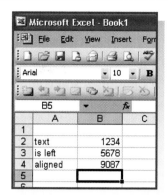

Learn: Printing Gridlines and Column and Row Headings

Gridlines and row and column headings may or may not be printed on a worksheet. If the workbook is set to *not print* gridlines and/or row and column headings, you must select the desired features if they are to be printed (see Figure CA11-4).

If the workbook is set to *print* gridlines and/or row and column headings, you must choose not to print any or all of these features if they are not to be printed.

Exercise　1G

Print Gridlines and Column and Row Headings

1. Read the information above about printing (or not printing) gridlines and row and column headings. Study the information in Figure CA11-4.

Figure CA11-4　Print Gridlines and Row and Column Headings

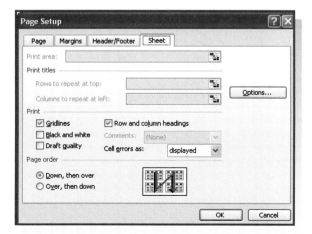

2. Open *CD-CA11-1G* and use Print Preview to determine if the worksheet will be printed with gridlines and column/row headings.

3. Change the default setting as follows:

   a. If the worksheet *does not* have gridlines and column/row headings, specify that they print and then print the worksheet.

   b. If the worksheet *has* gridlines and column/row headings, specify that they not print and then print the worksheet.

4. Save as *CA11-1G*.

Exercise 1H

Key a Worksheet

1. Open a new blank worksheet. Key the worksheet data shown below.

	A	B	C	D	E	F
1	MONTH	JOHN	MARY	LUIZ	PEDRO	SARA
2	January	5567	6623	7359	4986	6902
3	February	2457	7654	3569	2093	6432
4	March	6930	3096	5792	4607	7908
5	April	4783	6212	4390	5934	5402
6	May	5042	5092	4500	9453	5321
7	June	5430	6098	5781	5009	6023

2. Print the worksheet with gridlines and column and row headings.

3. Save as *CA11-1H*. Close the worksheet.

Exercise 1I

Key a Worksheet

1. Open a new blank worksheet. Key the worksheet data shown below.

	A	B	C	D	E
1	PLAYER	SINGLES	DOUBLES	TRIPLES	HOMERS
2	Bosco	65	13	3	1
3	Elliot	54	14	8	4
4	Horan	58	19	10	5
5	Huang	64	22	9	14
6	Myers	52	21	4	9
7	Pasco	49	14	3	4
8	Cordero	25	7	2	2
9	Paulie	27	2	4	0

2. Print the worksheet without gridlines or column/row headings.

3. Save as *CA11-1I*. Close the worksheet.

LESSON ② EDITING WORKSHEETS

⊙ To select a range of cells and edit, clear, copy, and move information in a worksheet.

Learn: The Edit Feature

The Edit feature enables you to change information already entered in a cell. To edit, highlight (activate) the appropriate cell and click the formula bar to make the needed changes there. Alternatively, you can highlight the cell and tap the Edit function key (F2) and then make the changes in the active cell.

Either way, cell contents are edited by selecting the text to be changed and then using the **Insert**, **Delete**, **Typeover**, and **Backspace** features as you would with word processing software.

If the entire contents of a cell are to be changed, it is more efficient to activate the desired cell and then key the correct information. The new information will replace the old information.

Insert
Delete
Typeover
Backspace

Exercise 2A

Edit Cell Content

1. Read the information above about editing cell content. Open *CD-CA11-2A*.

2. **Edit** existing cell content to what is given below:

   A1: **charge**   B1: **care**   C1: **butler**   D1: **compost**
   A2: **whether**   B2: **flew**   C2: **except**   D2: **personal**

3. **Change** the cell contents to what is given below:

   A4: **54321**   B4: **20202**   C4: **four**   D4: **shirt**
   A5: **98765**   B5: **stars**   C5: **herd**   D5: **college**

4. **Edit or change** the cell contents to what is given below:

   A7: **4567**   B7: **Jeanne**   C7: **Kristine**   D7: **8614**
   A8: **Dormont**   B8: **Sandra**   C8: **Hutton**   D8: **Blue**

5. Save as *CA11-2A*. Close the worksheet.

Learn: The Clear and Delete Commands

Most spreadsheet software has a Clear command that enables you to clear the contents *or* format of a cell *or both* without shifting the surrounding cells to replace the cell you cleared.

The Delete command (not the DELETE key) deletes the contents *and* format of the cell, and surrounding cells are shifted to replace the deleted cell.

Exercise 2B

Clear and Delete Cell Content and Format

1. Learn to clear cell contents and formats. Open *CD-CA11-2B* and specify that gridlines and row and column headings are to be printed.

2. Make these changes without having surrounding cells shift:

   a. Clear contents in cells B2, C4, D6, E8, and F10.

   b. Clear format (bold) in cells B4, B6, D4, D8, F6, and F8.

   c. Clear contents and formats in cells B8, B10, D2, D5, F2, and F4.

3. Delete cell B3 and have cells C3 through F3 shift to the left.

4. Delete cell C5 and have cells C6 through C10 shift up.

5. Key Susan in cell F4.

6. Save as *CA11-2B*. Close the worksheet.

Learn: Selecting a Range of Cells

A range of cells may be selected to perform an operation (move, copy, cut, clear, format, print, etc.) on more than one cell at a time. A range is identified by the cell in the upper-left corner and the cell in the lower-right corner, usually separated by a colon (for example, A5:C10). To select a range of cells, highlight the cell in one corner. Hold down the left mouse button and drag to the cell in the opposite corner. The number of rows and columns in the range is typically shown in the Cell Reference box as you drag the mouse. See Figure CA11-5.

Figure CA11-5   Range of Cells

Cell Reference box →

Cell range highlighted

Exercise 2C

Select a Range of Cells

1. Read the information above about cell ranges. Open *CD-CA11-2C*.

2. Select the range of cells B1:F1 and bold the text in the cells.

3. Select the range of cells A1:F6 and print the text in the cells.

4. Save as *CA11-2C*. Close the worksheet.

Learn: Cut, Copy, and Move Text

The contents of a cell or range of cells can be cut, copied, and moved to save time and improve accuracy. Select the cell or range of cells to be cut, copied, or moved;

select the operation (Cut or Copy); select the cell (or first cell in the range) where the information is to be copied or moved; and finally, click Paste to copy or move the information.

Exercise 2D

Cut, Copy, and Move Text

1. Read the information about cut, copy, and move. Open CD-CA11-2D.
2. Clear the contents of cells B6:F6.
3. Move the data in cells in B2:F3 to a range beginning in cell B11.
4. Copy the data in cells in A2:A10 to a range beginning in cell A11.
5. Copy the data in cells in A1:F1 to a range beginning in cell A20.
6. Copy C5 to C6, E5 to E6, B4 to D3, and F4 to F3.
7. Move D12 to B3, C12 to E3, B12 to D6, and F11 to B6.
8. Save as *CA11-2D*. Close the worksheet.

Exercise 2E

Key Worksheet Data

1. Open a new blank worksheet. Key the worksheet data shown below, and then print with gridlines and row and column headings.

	A	B	C	D	E
1	BUDGET				
2	ITEM	BUDGET	JAN	FEB	MAR
3					
4	Rent	400			
5	Electric	44	46	43	42
6	Oil	110	115	90	72
7	Water	20		60	
8	Sewage	22			67
9	Telephone	35	32	38	45
10	Cable TV	35			
11	Insurance	80	120		95
12	Food	315	305	302	325
13	Clothing	75	60	90	55
14	Leisure	75	55	80	60
15	Personal	90	90	85	100
16	Auto Loan	425			
17	Auto Exp.	80	80	95	110
18	Savings	185			

2. Save as *CA11-2E*. Keep the file open for the next exercise.

Edit Worksheet Data

1. Use the file CA11-2E from the previous exercise to make the following changes:

   a. Edit cell A1 to read: BUDGET AND MONTHLY EXPENSES

   b. Move row 18 to row 3.

   c. Copy column B to column F.

   d. Clear rows 16 and 17.

   e. Edit cell E15 to read 95.

   f. Copy B3 to C3:E3 and B4 to C4:E4.

   g. Copy B10 to C10:E10.

2. Print without gridlines and row and column headings.

3. Save as *CA11-2F*. Close the worksheet.

Key Worksheet Data

1. Open a new blank worksheet. Key the worksheet data shown below. Use the Copy feature as much as possible.

	A	B	C	D	E	F	G
1	NAME	QUIZ 1	QUIZ 2	QUIZ 3	QUIZ 4	QUIZ 5	QUIZ 6
2	JOE	90	90	90	100	90	90
3	MARY	90	90	90	80	90	90
4	PAUL	100	100	100	100	100	100
5	CARL	100	80	90	100	90	90
6	SUE	90	100	100	100	100	80
7	TWILA	90	90	90	80	80	80

2. Print with gridlines and row and column headings.

3. Save as *CA11-2G*. Close the worksheet.

LESSON 3 — WORKSHEET FORMATTING

OBJECTIVE

⊙ To format cell contents, adjust column width, and insert/delete columns and rows.

Learn: Change Column Widths

Often cells have content that varies greatly in width or entries that exceed the default width of a column. When the cell entry exceeds the width of the column, a series of number signs (#) appear in the column. To display the entire cell entry, the width must be changed to fit the longest entry in that column.

Exercise 3A

Modifying Column Width

1. Read the information about changing column widths. Open CD-CA11-3A and edit cell D1 so *Wednesday* is spelled out.
2. Resize the columns so each is as wide as its longest entry.
3. Save as *CA11-3A*. Close the file.

Exercise 3B

Modifying Column Width

1. Open *CD-CA11-3B* and designate that gridlines and column and row headings should print.
2. Adjust the width of each column so it is as wide as the longest entry in the column.
3. Save as *CA11-3B*. Close the file.

Learn: Insert and Delete Rows and Columns

Rows and columns can be inserted and deleted. One or more rows or columns can be inserted at a time.

   Columns may be added at the left or within worksheets; rows may be added at the top or within worksheets.

Exercise 3C

Insert and Delete Rows and Columns

1. Read the information above about inserting and deleting rows and columns. Open *CD-CA11-3C* and insert two rows at the top.
2. Insert one column between Monday and Tuesday, one column between Tuesday and Wednesday, and two columns between Wednesday and Thursday. Delete the Friday column.
3. Key Murphy in cells D2 and I2; Shandry in cells C2, E2, and G2; and Lawler in cell H2.
4. Key Monday in C3, Tuesday in E3, and Wednesday in F3:H3.
5. Insert a row between 2 p.m. and 3 p.m. and key 2:30 p.m. in cell A11.
6. Insert three rows between 3 p.m. and 4 p.m.; and key 3:15 p.m. in A13, 3:30 p.m. in A14, and 3:45 p.m. in A15.
7. Clear contents of cells B3:I3.
8. Adjust all column widths to fit the cell contents.
9. Key APPOINTMENT SCHEDULE in cell A1.
10. Save as *CA11-3C*. Close the worksheet.

Learn: Format Numbers

When numbers are keyed into a worksheet, spreadsheet software formats them as General, the default format. If another format (Currency, Percentage, numbers with commas or a fixed number of decimal places, Date, etc.) is preferred, the number(s) can be formatted accordingly. The chart below provides information about commonly used number formats.

Format	Description	Example
General	The default; displays number as keyed	2010.503
Number	Displays number with a fixed number of decimal places	2010.50
Currency	Displays number with $, two default decimal places, and comma separators	$2,010.50
Accounting	Same as currency except $ sign and decimal point are aligned vertically in the column	$ 2,010.50
Percentage	Multiplies number by 100 and displays number and two default decimal places with percent sign	201050.30%
Date	Provides a list of date formats that can be selected to format the day and month, with or without the year and time	1/2 Jan-02 January 2, 2006, etc.
Special	Provides a list to format number as Zip Code, Zip Code + 4, telephone number, or Social Security Number	12345 12345-6789 (123) 456-7890 123-45-6789

Exercise 3D

Format Numbers

1. Read the information above about formatting numbers. Open CD-CA11-3D.

2. Format cells A1:A7 using Number format, two decimal places, and no comma separators.

3. Format cells B1:B7 using Currency format with two decimal places.

4. Format cells C1:C7 using Accounting format with two decimal places.

5. Format cells D1:D7 using Percentage format with two decimal places.

6. Copy D1:D7 to E1:E7 and apply Percentage format with no decimal places.

7. Format cells A9:D9 using Special, Type: Phone Number.

8. Format cells A10:D10 using Special, Type: Social Security Number.

9. Format cells A11:D11 using Date, Type: March 14, 2001.

10. Adjust column widths to fit longest entry.

11. Save as CA11-3D. Close the worksheet.

Learn: Format Cells

The contents of cells (both numbers and text) can be formatted in much the same way as text is formatted using word processing software. The **font** and **font style**, **size**, **color**, and **effect**, and **underline** can be selected and applied to a cell, a cell range, or one or more rows and/or columns. An illustration of the Format Cells dialog box appears in Figure CA11-6.

Cells, rows, and/or columns can be shaded or can have borders, and cell entries can be aligned left or right or centered.

| Figure CA11-6 | Format Cells Dialog Box |

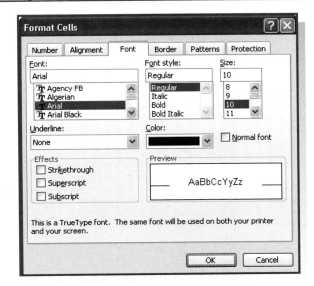

Exercise 3E
Format Cell Contents

1. Read the information above about formatting cell contents and refer to Figure CA11-6. Open *CD-CA11-3E*.

2. Format row 1 in Arial 14-point font using bold and a green font color.

3. Format cells A2:F10 in Arial 12-point font.

4. Format cell ranges B2:B10, D2:D10, and F2:F10 in a brown font color and shade these cell ranges with a tan color.

5. Format cells A2:A10 in italic and a red font color. Shade this range using a rose color.

6. Format cells C2:C10 and E2:E10 in a dark blue font. Shade these ranges in a light blue color.

7. Key Wednesday in cell D1.

8. Key [1] in superscript position to the right of *Hector* in cell C10.

9. Double underline *Bonita* in cell D7.

10. Adjust column width to fit contents, and center-align all cells.

11. Save as *CA11-3E*. Close the worksheet.

Exercise 3F

Key a Worksheet

	A	B	C
1	COURSE	PERIOD	ROOM
2	Applied Mathematics I	1	134-E
3	Consumer Economics	2	114-S
4	Sophomore English	3	210-E
5	Physical Education	4	Gym-N
6	Computer Applications	6	104-S
7	Principles of Technology	7	101-W
8	World Cultures	8	205-S

1. Open a new blank worksheet. Key the worksheet data shown at left.

2. Insert a row between rows 5 and 6; key Lunch in A6, 5 in B6, and Cafeteria in C6.

3. Use a red font for rows 2, 4, 6, and 8 and a green font for rows 3, 5, 7 and 9.

4. Adjust the column widths to fit the contents.

5. Center-align cells B2:B9.

6. Insert a row at the top and key BILL WAVERLY'S SCHEDULE in cell A1.

7. Use a 14-point, dark blue Arial font in rows 1 and 2; Arial 12 point for all others.

8. Shade rows 1 and 2 using a light blue color and insert a thick single-line border around cells A3:C10.

9. Save as *CA11-3F*. Close the worksheet.

Online Resources

See Bonus Exercises 3G and 3H on Keying a Worksheet at www.c21key.bonus-exercises.swlearning.com.

LESSON 4 — WORKSHEETS WITH FORMULAS AND FUNCTIONS

OBJECTIVE

 To perform worksheet calculations using formulas and functions.

Learn: Formulas

Spreadsheet software can add, subtract, multiply, and divide numbers keyed into the cells. To perform calculations, activate the cell in which the results of the calculation are to appear, and then enter a formula in the formula bar. Formulas typically begin with an equals sign (=).

The spreadsheet software interprets the formula, following this order of operations: (1) Calculations inside parentheses are performed first before those outside parentheses. (2) Multiplication and division are performed next in the order that they occur in the formula. (3) Addition and subtraction are performed last in their order of occurrence. Figure CA11-7 shows a formula being entered in a worksheet.

Figure CA11-7 Worksheet Formula

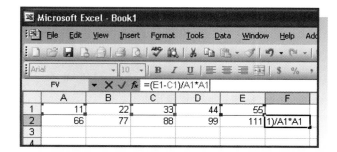

Formulas

1. Read the information on the previous page about using formulas and refer to Figure CA11-7.

2. Open *CD-CA11-4A* and enter these formulas in the specified cell.

   a. A1+B1 in cell A3

   b. D2-C1+B2 in cell B4

   c. A1*B2+E1-D2 in cell C5

   d. C2*B1/C2+A2-B2 in cell D6

   e. (C1+D2)+(D1/A1)+E2 in cell E7

   f. (D1+A1*B2)-(E2/C2-B1*A1)+E1 in cell F8

   g. In cell G9, write and enter a formula to add cells C2, D1, and E2; divide that answer by cell B1; and then subtract cell D2.

3. Format the answers for steps 1a–1g above as *Currency* with two decimal places.

4. Save as *CA11-4A*. Close the file.

Learn: Functions

Spreadsheet software has built-in predefined formulas called functions. Functions have three parts: an equals sign to signal the beginning of the mathematical operation; the function name (SUM, COUNT, etc.) to identify the operation; and an **argument** (usually the cell range) that defines the numbers to be used in the calculation. Figure CA11-8 on the following page shows a function being entered in a worksheet.

 Commonly used functions, their meaning, and examples are given in the chart below.

argument

Function	Meaning	Examples
SUM	Adds the numbers in specified cells	=SUM(A1:A10) adds cells A1 through A10 =SUM(A1,A10) adds cells A1 and A10
AVERAGE	Averages all values in specified cells	=AVERAGE(A1:A10) averages cells A1 through A10 =AVERAGE(A1,A10) averages cells A1 and A10
COUNT	Counts the number of cells that contain numbers in specified cells	=COUNT(A1:A10) counts cells A1 through A10 =COUNT(A1,A10) counts cells A1 and A10
MIN	Identifies and prints the smallest number in specified cells	=MIN(A1:A10) finds smallest number in cells A1 through A10 =MIN(A1,A10) finds smallest number in cells A1 and A10
MAX	Identifies and prints the largest number in specified cells	=MAX(A1:A10) finds largest number in cells A1 through A10 =MAX(A1,A10) finds largest number in cells A1 and A10

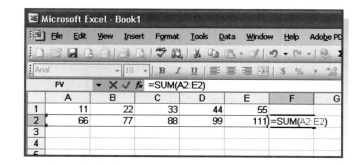

Exercise 4B

Functions

1. Read the information on the previous page about functions, and refer to Figure CA11-8. Open *CD-CA11-4B*.

2. Use the SUM function to add the numbers in cells A1:F1 and cells A2:F2, placing the answers in column G; add the numbers in cells A1:A6 and cells B1:B6, placing the answers in row 7.

3. Use the AVERAGE function to average the numbers in cells A3:F3 and cells A4:F4, placing the answers in column G; average the numbers in cells C1:C6 and cells D1:D6, placing the answers in row 7.

4. In cell G5, use the MIN function to find the lowest number in cells A5:F5; in cell E7, display the lowest number in cells E1:E6.

5. In cell G6, use the MAX function to find the highest number in cells A6:F6; in cell F7, display the highest number in cells F1:F6.

6. Format all numbers as *Accounting* with no decimal places, and print gridlines and column/row headings.

7. Save as *CA11-4B*. Close the file.

Exercise 4C

Key a Worksheet

1. Open a new blank worksheet. Key the worksheet data shown on the following page.

2. Enter a formula in column F (cells F1:F10) to calculate the individual batting averages (Hits/At Bats) to three decimal places.

3. In row 10 (cells B10:E10), use the SUM function to calculate the team totals.

4. In row 11 (cells B11:F11), use the MIN function to calculate the team lows.

5. In row 12 (cells B12:F12), use the MAX function to calculate the team highs.

6. Use color, shading, and borders as desired.

7. Adjust column 1 width to fit cell contents.

8. In cell A13, key BASEBALL TEAM STATISTICS, using a 14-point font.

9. Save as *CA11-4C*. Keep the file open for use in the next exercise.

	A	B	C	D	E	F
1	PLAYER	AT BATS	HITS	HOMERS	RBI	AVG
2	Roberto Orlando	700	225	23	45	
3	Bill York	423	134	2	14	
4	Ernie Hack	590	176	15	35	
5	Joe Dimperio	805	256	33	102	
6	Jose Carlos	476	175	12	31	
7	Hector Avila	365	75	2	5	
8	George Barnes	402	99	16	45	
9	Harry Bell	575	158	17	55	
10	TOTAL					
11	MINIMUM					
12	MAXIMUM					

Exercise 4D

Edit a Worksheet

1. Using *CA11-4C* from the previous exercise, insert the rows below at the right after Harry Bell. Delete the Carlos row.

PLAYER	AT BATS	HITS	HOMERS	RBI
Pat Ortega	25	8	1	2
Brett Peterson	45	14	3	7

2. Save as *CA11-4D*. Close the file.

Exercise 4E

Key a Worksheet

1. Open *CD-CA11-4E*.

2. Use the information below to construct formulas/functions in the column/row indicated or to perform the stated action.

   a. Col E=col C amount * 2

   b. Col F=col B * col C amounts

   c. Col G=col D * col E amounts

   d. Col H=col F + col G amounts

   e. Row 13: SUM(row 4:row 12)

   f. Clear the contents in cells C13 and E13.

   g. Row 14: AVERAGE(row 4:row12); two decimal places

3. Adjust column widths.

4. In cell A16, key RADIOLOGY PAYROLL.

5. Use formatting and shading as desired.

6. Save as *CA11-4E*. Close the file.

OBJECTIVE

⊘ To prepare embedded column, bar, and pie charts using worksheet information.

Learn: Charts

column
bar
line
pie
chart sheet
embedded chart

Spreadsheet software provides options to create a variety of charts including **column**, **bar**, **line**, and **pie** charts. Usually, charts can be created as (1) a **chart sheet** that appears as a separate worksheet, or (2) an **embedded chart** that appears as an object within a worksheet.

In this lesson you will create embedded column, bar, and pie charts using the chart parts described below.

Titles
Axes
category axis
value axis
Data points

Titles—headings that identify chart contents and axes.

Axes—the **category axis**, sometimes called the *x-axis*, is used to plot categories of data. The **value axis**, usually the *y-axis*, is used to plot values associated with the categories of data.

Data points—the bars, columns, or pie slices that represent the numerical data in the chart.

Data labels
Gridlines
Legend

Data labels—numbers or words that identify values displayed in the chart.

Gridlines—lines through a chart that identify intervals on the axes.

Legend—a key (usually with different colors or patterns) used to identify the chart's data categories.

Exercise 5A

Column Chart

1. Read the information above about charts. Open *CD-CA11-5A* and create an embedded column chart with x-axis and y-axis gridlines, data labels as values, and a legend (see the column chart below in Figure CA11-9).

2. Use ACME DEPARTMENT STORE February Report as the chart title.

3. Save as *CA11-5A*. Close the file.

Figure CA11-9   Column Chart

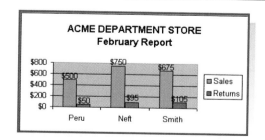

Exercise **5B**

Bar Chart

1. Open *CD-CA11-5B* and create an embedded bar chart with y-axis gridlines, axis titles, and a legend (see the bar chart in Figure CA11-10).

2. Key Class for the x-axis title and Number of Students for the y-axis title. Use ENROLLMENT REPORT as the chart title.

3. Save as *CA11-5B*. Close the file.

Figure CA11-10   Bar Chart

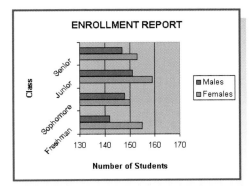

Exercise **5C**

Pie Chart

1. Open *CD-CA11-5C* and create an embedded pie chart displaying a legend and data labels in percentages (see the pie chart below in Figure CA11-11).

2. Use MAJOR MONTHLY EXPENSES as the chart title.

3. Save as *CA11-5C*. Close the file.

Figure CA11-11   Pie Chart

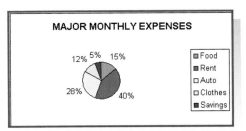

Exercise 5D

Bar Chart

1. Open a new blank worksheet. Key the data shown below.

	A	B	C
1	Month	In Patient	Out Patient
2	APRIL	350	725
3	MAY	365	752
4	JUNE	290	645

2. Create a bar chart, using PATIENT REPORT as the title.

3. Show axis titles, data labels as values, and a legend. Use Month and Number of Patients for the axis titles.

4. Save as *CA11-5D*. Close the file.

Exercise 5E

Column Chart

1. Open a new blank worksheet. Key the data shown below.

	A	B	C
1		THIS	LAST
2	CLASS	YEAR	YEAR
3	Seniors	132	89
4	Juniors	154	144
5	Sophomores	66	54
6	Freshmen	12	18

2. Create a column chart, using PROM ATTENDANCE as the title.

3. Show axes titles and legend, but no data labels. Key Students for the x-axis title, and Number Attending for the y-axis title.

4. Save as *CA11-5E*. Close the file.

UNIT 12

LESSONS 1–3

Improving Worksheet Skills

Conditioning Practice

Before you begin the lessons, key each line twice.

alphabet	1	Jim avoids fizzling fireworks because they often explode quickly.
fig/sym	2	Runner #3019-A was first (49' 35"); runner #687-D was last (62').
speed	3	Nancy works in the big cornfield down by the lake with the docks.

gwam 1' | 1 | 2 | 3 | 4 | 5 | 6 | 7 | 8 | 9 | 10 | 11 | 12 | 13 |

LESSON 1 FUTURE VALUE AND PRESENT VALUE FUNCTIONS

OBJECTIVES

 To learn to use the future value function (FV).

> To learn to use the present value function (PV).

Learn: Future Value Function (FV)

The future value function is a financial function that is used to calculate the amount that an investment or a series of constant, regular investments will be worth at a future date. The future value function is based on projecting that the investment(s) will grow at a constant interest rate. For example, the future value function will answer this question: What will the $5,000 I have invested be worth in 20 years if it earns 6 percent interest during the 20 years? Likewise, the future value function will answer this same question if $100 were added monthly to the $5,000 during the 20-year period.

Excel names this function FV and its syntax is =FV(Rate,Nper,Pmt,Pv,Type).

Fv is the amount the investment will be worth at a future date.

Rate is the interest rate for each investment period.

Nper is the total number of investment periods.

Pmt is the amount of the investment made each period; the amount cannot change over the life of the investment and the amounts must be invested at regular periods. Pmt can be omitted if investments are not added to the original investment. If Pmt is omitted, a Pv argument must be included.

Pv is the present value—the amount the investment is worth today. This argument can be omitted if there is not an amount invested before the constant, regular investments are made.

Type is the value 0 or 1. It indicates when the investments are made. The default value of 0 means that the investment amounts are made at the end of the investment period(s). Key a 1 for Type if the investment amounts are made at the beginning of the investment period(s).

Note: Investment amounts, such as Pmt and Pv, are entered in the formula as negative numbers since they represent money paid. Fv is represented by a positive number since it is money received.

Function Arguments

Figure CA12-1 shows the **Function Arguments** dialog box for the FV function for the following investment: $1,000 is invested and $50 will be added monthly for the next three years. The investments are projected to earn 6 percent interest. The Type default value of 0 is used since the money will be invested at the end of each month.

The Rate is keyed as 6%/12 to convert the annual interest rate to a monthly rate to agree with the monthly investment amounts that are planned. The Nper is 12*3 to indicate that 12 monthly payments will be made during each of the three years. The Pmt is -50 to indicate the constant, regular investment amount; the minus sign indicates that it is money paid. The Pv is -1000 since that is the beginning investment amount. It too represents money paid and is therefore entered as a negative number. Since the default value of 0 for Type is accepted, nothing is keyed. The formula result is given near the bottom of the dialog box.

> **Figure CA12-1**   Function Arguments for Future Value

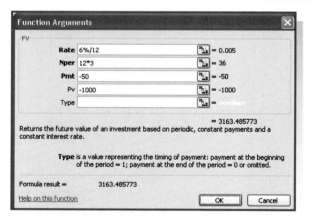

Exercise 1A

Calculate Future Value Using the FV Function

1. Read information above and on the previous page about future value. Open a blank worksheet and key Future Values in cell A1 and adjust the column width to fit the contents.

2. Make cell A2 active. Use the FV function to calculate the future value of the investment described in the section above; that is, an original investment of $1,000 to which $50 monthly investments will be made during the next three years. It is projected that 6 percent interest will be earned. Accept the default value for Type.

3. Make cell A3 active. Use the FV function to enter a future value of $30,000 that is invested today and expected to earn 8 percent interest each year for the next ten years. No additional investments are planned. Accept the default value for Type.

4. Check your answers. Save the worksheet as CA12-1A and close it.

Learn: Present Value Function (PV)

The present value function can be used to determine the amount you need to invest so you will have a desired amount at a future date. For example, if you need to have $40,000 for college in five years, what single amount (present value) must you invest now if your investment is likely to earn 8 percent interest each year?

Excel names this function PV and its syntax is =PV(Rate,Nper,Pmt,Fv,Type).

Pv is today's value (the present value) of the amount that is desired at a future date.

Rate is the interest rate for each investment period.

Nper is the total number of investment periods.

Pmt is omitted when additional investments are not made during the life of the investment.

Fv is the future value—the amount that is desired in the future.

Type is the value 0 or 1, depending on when investments are made. The default value of 0 is used when the investment is made at the end of the period. A Type value of 1 is used when the investment is made at the beginning of the period.

Figure CA12-2 shows the Function Arguments dialog box for the PV function for the following scenario: What amount do I need to invest today to have $1,000 in two years if the investment is likely to earn 7% interest each year? Accept the default value of 0 for Type.

The Rate is keyed as 7%. Nper is 2 to indicate the length of the investment. Pmt is left blank since no additional investments are to be made. Fv is 1000 since that is the desired amount at the end of two years. Since the default value of 0 is accepted, nothing is keyed for Type. Pv is a negative number since it represents the amount of money that needs to be invested (spent).

Figure CA12-2   **Function Arguments for Present Value**

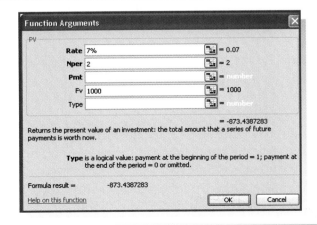

Exercise 1B

Calculate Present Value Using the PV Function

1. Read the information on the previous page about present value. Open a blank worksheet and key Present Values in cell A1 and adjust the column width to fit the contents.

2. Make cell A2 active. Use the PV function to calculate the amount of money to be invested today so $25,000 will be available in ten years. The investment is likely to earn 10 percent interest annually. No additional investments will be made during the ten years. Accept the default value for Type.

3. Make cell A3 active. Use the PV function to determine how much I must invest now to have $1,000,000 at the end of 20 years if the investment is likely to earn 9 percent annually during the life of the investment. Accept the default value for Type.

4. Check your answers. Save the worksheet as *CA12-1B* and close it.

Exercise 1C

Apply the FV and PV Functions

1. Open *CD-CA12-1C* and calculate the future value or present value for each scenario. Record your answers in column B.

2. Check your answers. Save the worksheet as *CA12-1C* and close.

LESSON 2 — PAYMENT FUNCTION

OBJECTIVES

⊙ To learn to use the payment function (PMT) to calculate loan payments.
⊙ To learn to use the payment function (PMT) to calculate saving deposits.

Learn: Payment Function (PMT) and Loans

The payment function is a financial function that can be used to calculate the payments for a loan that has constant and equal payments and a fixed interest rate. To use this function, the interest rate, the number of payments, and the amount of the loan must be known.

The function is named PMT and its syntax is =PMT(Rate, Nper, Pv, Fv, Type).
Rate is the interest rate for each payment period.
Nper is the total number of payments, and Pv is the amount (present value) of the loan.

Fv and *Type* are optional arguments. If a value is not entered for Fv, *Excel* assigns a value of 0 to indicate that the entire loan will be paid off when the last payment is made. If a value is not entered for Type, *Excel* assigns a value of 0, which means that the payments are made at the end of each payment period. If the payment is made at the beginning of the payment period, a 1 should be entered for Type.

When the PMT is calculated, *Excel* assigns a negative value to it to show that the value represents money spent.

Note: You can key the values for the arguments or cell references for the arguments in the dialog box.

Figure CA12-3 shows the Function Arguments dialog box for the PMT function for a $1,000 loan at 6 percent. The borrower is required to make equal monthly payments at the end of the payment period for two years. The Rate is 6%/12 to convert the annual interest rate to a monthly rate since payments are made monthly. The Nper is 12*2 to indicate the loan has 12 payments for each of two years. The Pv is 1000—the amount of the loan. Since the loan will be paid off in full at the end of two years, the default value of 0 is accepted and nothing is keyed for Fv. Since payments are made at the end of the payment period, the default value of 0 for Type is accepted and nothing is keyed. The monthly payment (PMT) is indicated as a negative number beneath the last argument.

Figure CA12-3   **Payment Function Arguments for a Loan**

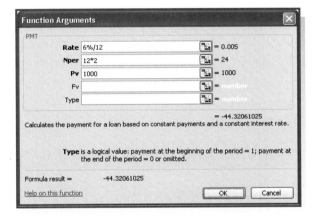

Exercise **2A**

Calculate Loan Payment Using PMT Function

1. Read the information above about loan payments. Open a blank worksheet and key Plan A Monthly Payment in cell A1.

2. Adjust the width of column A to fit the contents.

3. Make cell B1 active. Use the PMT function to enter the monthly payment for the following loan in cell B1: A three-year $15,000 loan at 5.5 percent that will be repaid in full by making equal monthly payments. Accept the default values for Fv and Type.

4. Key Plan B Monthly Payment in cell A2:

5. Make cell B2 active. Use the PMT function to enter the monthly payment for the following loan in cell B2: A two-year $15,000 loan at 4.75 percent that will be repaid in full by making equal monthly payments. Accept the default values for Fv and Type.

6. Save as *CA12-2A*. Close the file.

Learn: Payment Function (PMT) and Investing

The PMT function can also be used to calculate how much you need to invest regularly to have a specified amount of money at the end of a specified time. For example, how much do you need to invest each month to have $8,000 after four years if the investment will earn 3.5 percent interest annually?

When you use the PMT function for this purpose, the Rate is the interest rate for each investment period, Nper is the total number of investments, and Pv is 0 since you are starting out with no investment. Fv is 8000, the amount you want to have after four years. Type is 0 or 1. If investments are made at the end of each period, accept the default value of 0. If investments are made at the beginning of each period, key 1 for Type.

Figure CA12-4 shows the Function Arguments dialog box and entries for the investment plan that will be worth $8,000 in four years.

The Rate is 3.5%/12 to convert the annual interest rate to a monthly rate, since investments are made monthly. The Nper is 12*4 to indicate there are 12 investments for each of 4 years. The Pv is 0 since there is no investment before the first monthly deposit is made. Key 8000 for Fv to specify the amount desired in four years. Since investments are made at the end of the investment period, the default value of 0 for Type is accepted and nothing is keyed. The formula result is given near the bottom of the dialog box. It is indicated as a negative number since it represents money spent.

Figure CA12-4 — Payment Function Arguments for Saving

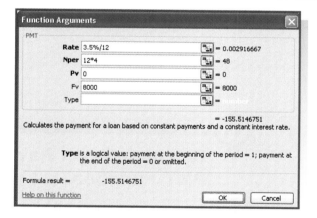

Exercise 2B

Calculate Investments Using PMT Function and Interest Earned

1. Read the information above about the payment function. Open a blank worksheet and add the following information: Key Plan in cell A1, Investment in cell B1, Total Investments in cell C1, and Interest Earned in cell D1. Key Plan A in cell A2.

2. Adjust the width of the columns to fit the contents.

3. Make cell B2 active. Use the PMT function to enter the monthly invest-ment required to have $5,000 at the end of six years. The annual interest rate is 5.5 percent. Accept the default value for Type.

4. Key Plan B in cell A3.

5. Make cell B3 active. Use the PMT function to enter the quarterly invest-ment required to have $5,000 at the end of 6 years. The annual interest rate is 5.5 percent. Accept the default values for Type.

6. In column C, calculate the total amount of the investments over the six-year period for each plan.

7. In column D, calculate the amount of interest each investment plan earned. *Note:* Since column C has negative values, you will need to add C2 and D2 to 5000 to find the interest. Therefore, the formula in cell D2 will be =5000+C2.

8. Shade cell C2 or C3 to identify the plan that earned the most interest.

9. Save as *CA12-2B*. Close the file.

Exercise 2C

Apply the PMT Function

1. Open *CD-CA12-2C* and make these calculations:
   a. In row 8, calculate the total number of payments for each loan.
   b. In row 9, use the PMT function to calculate the payment amount for each loan.
   c. In row 10, calculate the total amount for all payments for each loan.
   d. In row 11, calculate the total interest charged for each loan. *Note:* The values in rows 9, 10, and 11 will be negative values.

2. Format the worksheet to make it attractive and easy to read.

3. Save as *CA12-2C*. Close the file.

4. Open *CD-CA12-2D* and make these calculations:
   a. In row 8, calculate the total number of investments for each plan.
   b. In row 9, use the PMT function to calculate the amount of each in-vestment for each plan.
   c. In row 10, calculate the total of all investments for each plan.
   d. In row 11, calculate the total interest earned for each investment plan. *Note:* The values in rows 9 and 10 will be negative values.

5. Format the worksheet to make it attractive and easy to read.

6. Save as *CA12-2D*. Close the file.

OBJECTIVE

⊙ To learn to use spreadsheet templates to prepare worksheets.

Learn: Spreadsheet Templates

General

When you open a new worksheet, *Excel* displays the default template. It has settings for column width, row height, font, font size, font color, etc. already determined for you. *Excel* names this template **General**. *Excel* offers other templates for you to create frequently used spreadsheet documents like invoices, expense reports, balance sheets, loan amortizations, etc. With Excel, you access these templates by selecting New from the File menu and then clicking On my computer from the New Workbook Task Pane that appears on the right side of your monitor. The General template (the default worksheet) is in the General tab in the Templates dialog box. The templates for this lesson can be opened by selecting the Spreadsheet Solutions tab as shown in Figure CA12-5 and double-clicking the desired template icon.

Figure CA12-5 Spreadsheet Solutions Tab in the Templates Dialog Box

Exercise 3A

Use the Sales Invoice Template

1. Read the information above about spreadsheet templates. Open the Sales Invoice template and key the information that is shown on the following page. *Notes:* Use the Arrow and Tab keys and/or mouse to move within the template the same way you move around in other worksheets. Key the information in the appropriate cells, accepting all the default settings and the information in the boxes that appear. Numbers will be formatted automatically and the amounts in the Total column will be calculated automatically.

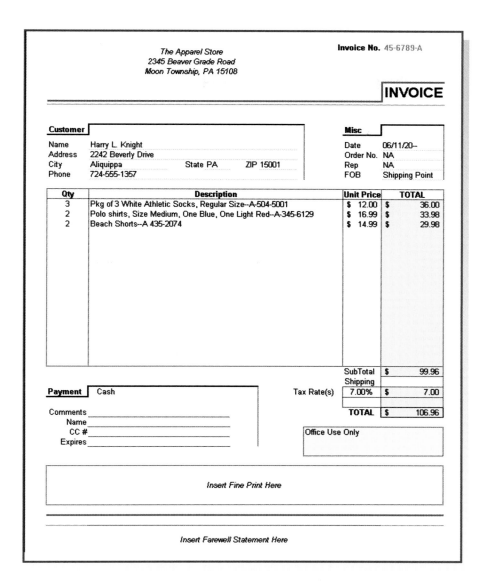

The Apparel Store
2345 Beaver Grade Road
Moon Township, PA 15108

Invoice No. 45-6789-A

INVOICE

Customer

Name	Harry L. Knight
Address	2242 Beverly Drive
City	Aliquippa State PA ZIP 15001
Phone	724-555-1357

Misc

Date	06/11/20--
Order No.	NA
Rep	NA
FOB	Shipping Point

Qty	Description	Unit Price	TOTAL
3	Pkg of 3 White Athletic Socks, Regular Size--A-504-5001	$ 12.00	$ 36.00
2	Polo shirts, Size Medium, One Blue, One Light Red--A-345-6129	$ 16.99	$ 33.98
2	Beach Shorts--A 435-2074	$ 14.99	$ 29.98

	SubTotal	$ 99.96
	Shipping	
Tax Rate(s) 7.00%		$ 7.00
	TOTAL	$ 106.96

Payment   Cash

Comments _____
Name _____
CC # _____
Expires _____

Office Use Only

Insert Fine Print Here

Insert Farewell Statement Here

2. Save the worksheet as *C12-3A*. Close the file.

Exercise   3B

Use the Loan Calculator Template

1. Open the Loan Amortization template and key the following information in the appropriate cells in the Enter Values area of the worksheet to calculate the answers in the Loan Summary area.

1	**Loan Calculator**			
2				
5	**Enter Values**		**Loan Summary**	
6	Loan Amount	$ 15,000.00	Scheduled Payment	$ 215.55
7	Annual Interest Rate	5.50 %	Scheduled Number of Payments	84
8	Loan Period in Years	7	Actual Number of Payments	84
9	Number of Payments Per Year	12	Total Early Payments	$ -
10	Start Date of Loan	7/1/2005	Total Interest	$ 3,106.25
11	Optional Extra Payments			
12				
13	**Lender Name:** ABC LOAN, INC.			

2. Save as *CA12-3B* and print page 1 of the amortization schedule. Close the file.

Communication & Math Skills 4

Pronoun Agreement

1. Study each of the four rules shown below.

   a. Key the *Learn* lines beneath each rule, noting how the rule is applied.

   b. Key the *Apply* lines, choosing correct pronouns.

Pronoun Agreement

Rule 1: A personal pronoun (*I, we, you, he, she, it, their*, etc.) agrees in **person** (first, second, or third) with the noun or other pronoun it represents.

Learn   1   We can win the game if we all give each play our best effort.
(1st person)

Learn   2   You may practice dancing only after you finish all your homework.
(2nd person)

Learn   3   Andrea said that she will drive her car to the antique mall.
(3rd person)

Apply   4   Those who saw the exhibit said that (he, she, they) were impressed.
Apply   5   After you run for a few days, (my, your) muscles will be less sore.
Apply   6   Before I take the test, I want to review (our, my) class notes.

Rule 2: A personal pronoun agrees in gender (feminine, masculine, or neuter) with the noun or other pronoun it represents.

Learn   7   Miss Kimoto will give her talk after the art exhibit. (feminine)
Learn   8   The small boat lost its way in the dense fog. (neuter)

Apply   9   Each winner will get a corsage as she receives (her, its) award.
Apply 10   The ball circled the rim before (he, it) dropped through the hoop.

Rule 3: A personal pronoun agrees in number (singular or plural) with the noun or other pronoun it represents.

Learn 11   Celine drove her new car to Del Rio, Texas, last week. (singular)
Learn 12   The club officers made careful plans for their next meeting. (plural)

Apply 13   All workers must submit (his, their) vacation requests.
Apply 14   The sloop lost (its, their) headsail in the windstorm.

Rule 4: A personal pronoun that represents a collective noun (team, committee, family, etc.) may be singular or plural, depending on the meaning of the collective noun.

Learn 15   Our men's soccer team played its fifth game today. (acting as a unit)
Learn 16   The drill team took their positions on the field. (acting individually)

Apply 17   The jury will render (its, their) verdict at 1:30 today.
Apply 18   The Social Committee had presented (its, their) written reports.

2. Key Proofread & Correct, using correct pronouns.

   a. Check your answers.

   b. Using the rule number at the left of each line, study the rule relating to each error you made.

   c. Rekey each incorrect line, using correct pronouns.

Proofread & Correct

Rules
2   1   Suzy knew that (he, she, they) should read more novels.
3   2   People who entered the contest say (he, she, they) are confident.
3   3   As soon as art class is over, I like to transcribe (our, my) notes.

2,3 4 Mrs. Kelso gave (her, his, their) lecture in Royce Hall.
2 5 The yacht moved slowly around (her, his, its) anchor.
1 6 As you practice the lines, (his, your) confidence increases.
1 7 I played my new clarinet in (my, their, your) last recital.
3 8 The editors planned quickly for (its, their) next newsletter.
4 9 The women's volleyball team won (its, their) tenth game today.
4 10 Our family will take (its, their) annual trip in August.

3. Save as *CS4-ACT1*.

ACTIVITY 2   Listening

1. Open *CD-CS4-ACT2*.

2. Listen to the weather forecast and take notes. Then close the file.

3. Key answers to the questions below.
4. Save as *CS4-ACT2*.

1. What were the high and low temperatures for today?
2. What are the predicted high and low temperatures for Tuesday?
3. Is it likely to rain tomorrow?
4. How many days are likely to have rain in the five-day forecast?
5. What is the highest temperature predicted in the five-day forecast?
6. What is the lowest temperature predicted in the five-day forecast?

ACTIVITY 3   Write to Learn

1. Using word processing or voice recognition software, write a paragraph explaining the meaning of *spreadsheet*, *workbook*, and *worksheet*.

2. Write a second paragraph explaining how you format numbers as currency or percentage.

3. Save as *CS4-ACT3*.

ACTIVITY 4   Composing

1. Read the paragraph below and decide whether the student's action was right or wrong (legally, ethically, or morally). Decide if stealing for any reason can be justified.

2. Compose a paragraph stating your views and giving your reasons.
3. Revise, proofread, and correct your paragraph.

4. Key the paragraph below as paragraph 1; key your corrected paragraph as paragraph 2.
5. Save as *CS4-ACT4*.

A student sees a designer jacket on a bench in the locker room. No one seems to be around. The student tries it on; it looks great. He likes it and wants it. He reasons that if the owner can afford an expensive jacket, he can afford another one. So quickly the student puts it in his gym bag and walks away.

ACTIVITY 5   Math: Finding the Part of a Whole

1. Open *CD-CS4-ACT5* and print the file.

2. Solve the problems as directed in the file.

3. Submit your answers.

Skill BUILDER 3

Reading/Keying Response Patterns

1. Key each line three times (slowly, faster, top speed).
2. Key two 1' timings on lines 7–9; determine *gwam* on each timing.

Emphasize quick finger reaches, wrists low and relaxed.

balanced-hand words

1 is by do if go he so us to me of jam row rug she bus air but city
2 both also busy held duck dial form make rush sick soap when towns
3 visit widow theme title ivory proxy quake shape amend burnt chair

Emphasize high-speed phrase responses.

balanced-hand phrases

4 He owns it | make the signs | paid the man | go to work | if they fix the
5 Go to the | they may make | to the problem | with the sign | and the maps
6 With the city | the eighth neighbor | social problem | the big ornament

Emphasize high-speed, word-level response; quick spacing.

balanced-hand sentences

7 Pamela paid the man by the city dock for the six bushels of corn.
8 Keith may keep the food for the fish by the big antique fishbowl.
9 The haughty girls paid for their own gowns for the island social.

gwam 1' | 1 | 2 | 3 | 4 | 5 | 6 | 7 | 8 | 9 | 10 | 11 | 12 | 13 |

Techniques: Figures

1. Set 0.5" side margins.
2. Clear all tabs; then set tabs 2", 4", and 6" from the left margin.
3. Key the lines slowly, tabbing from column to column.
4. Take three 3' timings. Try to key more characters on each timing.

Keep eyes on copy.

gwam 3'

630-47-3800	11/13/04	(419) 223-3499	$ 738.99	3
469-30-2187	05/29/89	(719) 408-7766	$2,492.00	6
557-61-1209	03/29/91	(630) 340-7854	$6,783.25	9
578-93-9320	12/28/90	(826) 740-3726	$ 67.30	12
739-23-1056	04/16/89	(912) 673-3554	$4,289.98	15
931-78-2130	09/10/85	(419) 549-9678	$8,967.14	18

Timed Writings

1. Key two 1' timings on each ¶; determine *gwam*.
2. Key two 2' timings on ¶s 1–2 combined; determine *gwam*.

A all letters used (MicroPace)

gwam 2'

Respect your newspaper deliveryperson. He or she may   6
become one of the next great statesmen. One of the first jobs   12
Benjamin Franklin had was that of delivering newspapers. Later   19
in life he was recognized for his work in many diverse areas.   25

It was natural for him to become a printer and an author.   31
Benjamin Franklin is also known for his accomplishments as a   37
scientist and a philosopher. Additionally, he is quite well   43
known for his work as a diplomat and for his efforts during and   50
after the American Revolution. You combine all this and you   56
have one of the greatest statesmen of our country.   61

UNIT 13

LESSONS 1–3

Assessing Document Formatting Skills

Conditioning Practice

Before you begin the lessons, key each line twice.

alphabet	1	Extensive painting of the gazebo was quickly completed by Jerome.
figures	2	At least 456 of the 3,987 jobs were cut before November 18, 2005.
speed	3	Janel and I may go to the island to dismantle the bicycle shanty.

gwam 1' | 1 | 2 | 3 | 4 | 5 | 6 | 7 | 8 | 9 | 10 | 11 | 12 | 13 |

LESSON ASSESS CORRESPONDENCE PROCESSING SKILLS

OBJECTIVE

> To assess letter, memo, and e-mail formatting skills.

Exercise 1A

Two Business Letters

1. Key the letter content shown below.
2. Use modified block format, open punctuation, and no paragraph indentations.

June 9, 20-- | Mrs. Vera L. Bowden | 3491 Rose Street | Minneapolis, MN 55441-5781 | Dear Mrs. Bowden | SUBJECT: YOUR DONATION

What a pleasant surprise it was to find your $50 donation to Beta Xi in my mail this morning. I think it is great that you thought of Beta Xi and decided to help members of your local chapter serve those who are less fortunate.

Your contribution will be used to purchase food and clothing for young children in our community as part of Community Day. As you know, Beta Xi, Minnesota Epsilon Chapter, conducts a fall drive to support this event.

(continued on next page)

I have heard about the success you are having in microbiology. Perhaps you would return to speak to our Beta Xi members? Please let me know if you can.

Yours truly | Miss Amelia R. Carter | Beta Xi Sponsor | xx | Enclosure | c Thomas Turnball, Treasurer | A receipt is enclosed since your contribution is tax deductible.

3. Save as *CA13-1A-Letter1.*

4. Change *CA13-1A-Letter1* to block format with mixed punctuation.

5. Delete the subject line.

6. Save as *CA13-1A-Letter2.*

Exercise 1B

E-Mail

1. Key the e-mail message shown below. (*Note:* If you don't use e-mail software, format as a memo using the information below and the current date.)

2. Send the message to your instructor. Attach the file *CD-CA13-1B.*

3. Send one classmate a Cc and send another classmate a Bcc.

SUBJECT: CAREER INTEREST

My report about health-care management--one of my career interests--is attached. I will be ready to give a two-minute presentation (with three to five slides) in class next Tuesday.

In the meantime, I have an appointment with my vocational guidance counselor, Mr. Duncan. Also, since my mother is a health-care manager at Richland County Hospital, I'm going to talk with her some more about her work.

4. Save as *CA13-1B.*

Exercise 1C

Two-Page Memo

1. Key the content below as a two-page memo.

2. Insert the *CD-CA13-1C* file where indicated.

TO: Dorothy A. McIlvain, Dean, Semak College of Arts and Sciences | FROM: Jim R. Tedrow, Head, Faculty Committee on Freshman Qualifications | DATE: June 15, 20-- | SUBJECT: SCHOOL OF ARTS AND SCIENCES FRESHMAN MATH SKILLS

At a recent meeting of the Faculty Committee on Freshman Qualifications, the Enrollment Management representative reported that freshmen entering the Semak College of Arts and Sciences (SCAS) this year have higher average SAT math scores than the freshmen who entered SCAS in each of the past five years.

(continued on next page)

Much discussion centered on the significance of the increase, and we finally decided to compare the math placement records for these same freshmen over the same time period. By doing this, the committee believes it can determine if students are being placed into higher-level math courses as a result of the increase in scores.

This study revealed the course placements (by percent and number) that are reported below. *(Insert CD-CA13-1C here.)*

A comparison of the course placements reveals a steady decline in the percent and number of students needing to enter MATH 100 Pre-College Algebra and a steady increase in the percent and number of students entering MATH 180 College Algebra and MATH 250 Calculus I. This finding supports the contention that as SAT math scores increase, students will begin their college studies in higher-level courses.

This comparison will be reported to Dr. Theodore R. Ostrom, head of the Mathematics Department in SCAS. He and his faculty will then know that more and more arts and sciences students are enrolling in higher-level math courses and that the number needing MATH 100 is decreasing.

I will e-mail the comparison to all SCAS faculty so that they, too, will be aware of the increasing mathematical ability of the students entering SCAS programs.

Perhaps you would like to share this information with the dean of the School of Education since it provides further evidence of success in the education reform movement.

3. Save as *CA13-1C.*

LESSON ② ASSESS REPORT FORMATTING SKILLS

OBJECTIVE

 To assess outline, report, minutes, and newsletter formatting skills.

Exercise ②A

Outline Numbered List

1. Key the outline numbered list shown below.

LEADERSHIP SEMINAR PROGRESS REPORT

1) Introduction
2) Seminar presenter
   a) Selection--Jackson & Associates selected
   b) Reason--Jackson & Associates' definition of leadership
3) Seminar development
   a) Meeting #1--Review content of previous seminars
   b) Meeting #2--Decide content of seminars
4) Seminar dates and locations
   a) October 15--Coultersville
   b) October 22--North Irwin

(continued on next page)

  c) October 29--Port Washington
  d) November 5--Portersburg
 5) Seminar content
  a) Leadership characteristics
   i) Social and environmental responsibility
   ii) International awareness
   iii) Honesty and consistency
  b) Leadership styles--from autocratic to democratic

2. Save as *CA13-2A.*

Exercise 2B

Minutes

1.   Key the minutes as shown below.

GREENWOOD HIGH SCHOOL SCIENCE CLUB

May 15, 20--, Meeting Minutes

All officers, committee heads, and 15 members were present. Sponsor Terry L. Gronbacher was present.

1. President Dee McClinton called the meeting to order at 2:25 p.m.

2. Secretary Sue Smedley read the minutes, which were accepted.

3. Treasurer LaVerne Blatt distributed the April 30 balance sheet and income statement and reported a balance of $1,056. The treasurer's report was approved by unanimous vote.

4. Victor Block, fundraising committee chair, reported that $376.09 was raised from the windsock sale.

5. Under unfinished business, President McClinton reported that the school science fair will have 150 exhibits. Awards will be given to first-, second-, and third-place winners by grade level. Engineers from Greenwood Laboratories will serve as judges and assist in presenting the awards.

6. Under new business, the Club approved the purchase of a microscope as the Science Club's gift to the Greenwood High School Science Department. The microscope will be presented to the Greenwood Board of Education at its June meeting.

7. The meeting ended at 3:35 p.m.

---

2. Save as *CA13-2B.*

Exercise 2C

MLA Report and Title Page

1. Key the content shown on the following page in MLA Report format. Use Kirk Robey as student's name, Ms. Li Pak as instructor's name, Computer Literacy as course name, and June 25, 20-- as the date.

The Internet

Anyone using computers for school, business, or personal use knows the difficulty of keeping up with changing technology. Computer users are demanding that microprocessors become faster and easier to use in order to keep up with the many applications used today. Just when users thought they were catching up, the Internet became popular.

Defining the Internet

Networks have changed the way people communicate. Each day, transactions are sent across high-speed connections to computers all over the world via the Internet. A working definition of the Internet follows:

The Internet is an international "network of networks" comprised of government, academic, and business-related networks that allow people at diverse locations around the world to communicate through electronic mail, to transfer files back and forth, and to log on to remote computer facilities. (Odgers and Keeling 289)

Connecting to the Internet

You must have a device called a modem to link your computer to other computers through telephone or cable lines (Fulton-Calkins and Stulz 181). With some connections, you need to have an account name and password to access the Internet; with others, you may be connected directly to the Internet and need only to click the Internet icon on your computer's desktop.

If you are using the Internet at school or work, the organization is paying a fee for doing so. If you want to access the Internet on your home computer, you will need to subscribe to a commercial Internet service provider (often referred to as an ISP). Most of these providers charge a monthly fee.

Using the Internet

Once you have access to the Internet, you will find many uses for it (Oliverio, Pasewark, and White 98). You will want to establish an e-mail account so you can send electronic messages to your friends and relatives who are also connected to the Internet. You can also use e-mail to send word processing, spreadsheet, database, and presentation files, including pictures, to others.

In addition to e-mail, the Internet has many other useful applications. Common uses include:

- Retrieving information by using search engines or directories that enable you to search massive databases.

- Using bulletin boards to read and post messages related to topics of interest to you and others.

2. Add this bulleted item at the end of the report:
   - Designing and posting a Web page to provide to other Internet users information about yourself, your family, a club or organization, or a business.

3. Place these works cited on a separate page:

Fulton-Calkins, Patsy and Karin M. Stulz. *Procedures & Theory for Administrative Professionals*, 5th ed. Cincinnati: South-Western, 2004.

Odgers, Pattie and B. Lewis Keeling. *Administrative Office Management*, 12th ed. Cincinnati: South-Western Educational Publishing, 2000.

Oliverio, Mary Ellen, William R. Pasewark, and Bonnie R. White. *The Office: Procedures and Technology*, 4th ed. Cincinnati: South-Western, 2003.

4. Save as *CA13-2C-Report*.

5. Use the information from the report, your school name, and clip art and/or border art to prepare a title page for the report.

6. Save the title page as *CA13-2C-Title*.

LESSON 3 — ASSESS WORKSHEET PROCESSING SKILLS

OBJECTIVE

⊙ To assess worksheet processing skills.

Exercise 3A

Worksheets and Charts

1. Key the worksheet shown below. Format numbers with thousands separator, as appropriate.

	A	B	C	D	E	F	G	H	I	J
1	Item	1996	2000	% +/-	2002	% +/-	2004	% +/-	2006	% +/-
2	Aluminum cans	206	112		204		285		280	
3	Cardboard	1114	812		923		2054		2229	
4	Steel cans	192	133		338		226		174	
5	Clear glass	466	483		406		222		164	
6	Mixed glass	158	152		11		142		31	
7	Green glass	0	38		88		5		31	
8	Brown glass	0	28		87		2		32	
9	Magazines	0	0		75		169		221	
10	Newsprint	294	376		282		321		389	
11	Mixed paper	0	0		29		20		141	
12	Office paper	30	251		37		88		331	
13	Phone books	0	6		9		31		0	
14	Leaf/yard waste	2152	838		1000		550		663	
15	Total Tons									

2. In row 15, calculate the Total Tons for each year.

3. In columns D, F, H, and J, calculate the percent of change (no decimal places) from year to year.

4. Add a column K with a heading, and calculate the yearly average for each item (to one decimal place).

5. Add the main title: Harris County Recycling Statistics (in tons).

6. You decide other formatting features.

7. Save as *CA13-3A*.

Exercise 3B
Column Chart

1. Open *CD-CA13-3B.*

2. Create a column chart to show the amount of trash produced by six countries. Use Top Six Trash-Producing Nations as the title, and show axis titles and gridlines.

3. Save as *CA13-3B*.

Exercise 3C
Pie Chart

1. Open *CD-CA13-3C.*

2. Create a pie chart to show the percent of items that are recycled in Banter County. Use Banter County Recycling Statistics as the title, show percents as data labels, and show a legend.

3. Save as *CA13-3C*.

Exercise 3D
Worksheet

1. Key the worksheet shown below. Format numbers with thousands separator as appropriate.

	A	B	C	D	E	F	G	H
1								Tons of
2								Recycled
3					Revenue	Revenue	Tons of	Materials
4				Recycling	per	per	Recycled	Per
5	Year	Population	Homes	Revenues	Person	Home	Materials	Home
6	2001	10607	3650	$304429			729.6	
7	2002	10738	3703	$355678			743.4	
8	2003	10869	3748	$355211			869.5	
9	2004	10986	3793	$336746			943.1	
10	2005	11102	4041	$347891			972.5	

2. Calculate the amounts in E, F, and H.

3. Format dollar amounts to include cents in columns D, E, and F.

4. Format column H to three decimal places.

5. Add **Borough of Eastdale Recycling Statistics** as the title.

6. You decide all other formatting features.

7. Save as *CA13-3D*.

Exercise 3E

Financial Functions

1. Use the future value function to determine what a current $8,000 investment earning 6 percent interest will be worth in ten years if no additional investments are made.

2. Use the present value function to determine what amount needs to be invested today at 6 percent interest to have $13,000 in five years.

3. Use the payment function to determine how much the monthly payments will be to pay off a $10,000 loan at 6 percent interest for eight years. The payments are made at the beginning of the month.

4. If your instructor directs, save the functions in a file called *CA13-3E*.

Exercise 3F

Spreadsheet Templates

1. Open the Sales Invoice template.

2. Key the information shown below and then apply a 6 percent tax to compute the total. There are no shipping charges.

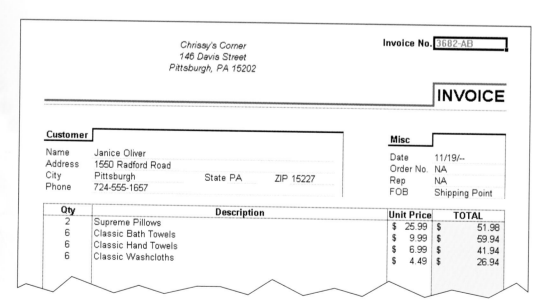

3. Save as *CA13-3F*.

Integrated Workplace Simulation

JOBS 1-15

TSEA: A Science Conference

Conditioning Practice

Key each line twice.

alphabet	1	Zelda was quite naive to pack two big boxes with just fresh yams.
figures	2	Flight 4365 will leave Runway 28L at 10 p.m. with 297 passengers.
speed	3	Mandi kept the emblem and shamrock in the fir box in the cubicle.

gwam | 1' | 1 | 2 | 3 | 4 | 5 | 6 | 7 | 8 | 9 | 10 | 11 | 12 | 13 |

OBJECTIVES

⊙ To demonstrate your ability to integrate your knowledge and skills.

⊙ To demonstrate your ability to solve problems and make correct decisions.

Work Assignment

Assume that you are participating in a school-based work program for Ms. Yvonne Porterfield, a high school biology teacher. Ms. Porterfield is serving as conference director for the Tri-County Science Education Association's Conference that will be held at the Russell Hotel in Charlotte, NC, in June.

Another teacher, Mr. James Herriott, is serving as Exhibits Chair for the conference. You will work for him as well, but Ms. Porterfield will give his work to you.

As an administrative specialist, your main duty is to process documents needed for the conference.

You completed a job orientation that focused on policies, procedures, and routines Ms. Porterfield wants you to follow. To help you further, she wrote these guidelines for you:

Correspondence. Center all letters vertically in modified block format with mixed punctuation and paragraph indentations. I do not use *Ms.* before my name in the closing lines of letters. Use *Conference Director* as my title. Supply an appropriate salutation and complimentary close; use your reference initials; and include enclosure and copy notations as needed.

Tables and worksheets. Print gridlines and change and adjust column widths and row heights to appropriate sizes. Choose all other formatting features to make tables and worksheets easy to read and attractive.

Reports. Format reports as unbound and number all pages except the first. Begin and end tables at the margins.

Other.

- Be alert to and correct errors in capitalization, punctuation, spelling, and word usage.
- If a formatting guide or direction is not given, use your knowledge and judgment to complete the task.
- Unless otherwise directed, use the current date and print one copy of each job.

Name all files you create with *TSEAJ-* and the job number (*TSEAJ-1*, *TSEAJ-2*, etc.). If a job involves more than one document, add *a, b, c,* etc., to the filename. Existing files have *CD* as a prefix.

Job 1

From the desk of
Yvonne Porterfield

Mr. Herriott wants you to add these exhibitors to the list in CD-TSEAJ-1. Sort them in alpha order by company. Print: 2 for the TSEA president and UP.

yp

Adante Technologies, Tara Olen, 8539 Monroe Road, Charlotte 28212-7525, 704-555-0110, 1

Compulink, Anne Crevar, 5018 Sunset Road, Charlotte 28269-2749, 704-555-0156, 1

CT Science Laboratories, Bill Hughes, 5212 W. Highway 74, Monroe 28110-8458, 704-555-0131, 1

DFA Labs, Ed White, 820 Tyvola Road, Ste. 100, Charlotte 28217-3534, 704-555-0107, 1

MTI, Sidorn Huynh, 227 Franklin Avenue., Concord 28025-4908, 704-555-0145, 1

MAR WIN School Supplies, Martha Winter, 700 Hanover Drive, Concord 28027-7827, 704-555-0121, 1

Job 2

From the desk of
Yvonne Porterfield

Find the monthly payment for the loan Mr. Herriott describes in this note.

yp

Yvonne,

We need to buy a laptop and printer that prints, scans, and copies. I suggest we borrow the $2,500 we need from the credit union. We can get a two-year loan at 6% and make monthly payments at the beginning of each month. Please have the administrative specialist determine the monthly payment. I think we have enough in the budget, but I want to be sure before I go to the credit union. Thanks.

Jim

Job 3

CAI Books
Russ Alarmi
4002 Concord Highway
Monroe 28110-8233
704-555-0119

Adobe Systems
Joyce Farno
6701 Carmel Road, Ste. 203
Charlotte 28226-0200
704-555-0149

Toor Publishers
Karen Fernandez
9812 Rockwood Road,
Charlotte 28215-8555
704-555-0198

Liberty Press
Vera Green
3601 Rose Lake Drive
Charlotte 28217-2813
704-555-0159

FirstPlus Experiments
Ralph McNash
525077 Center Drive, Ste. 150
Charlotte 28226-0705
704-555-0191

Integra Biology
John Petroni
5795 Gettysburg Drive
Concord 28027-8855
704-555-0167

Job 4

1 The Tri-County Science Education Association's Sixth Annual Conference is scheduled for June 14, 15, and 16 at the Russell Hotel in Charlotte; and you are invited to exhibit your products and services once again.

2 Do you want to exhibit your products and services at a conference that attracts 300+ science teachers in the Charlotte area? If so, you should reserve exhibit space at the Tri-County Science Education Association's Sixth Annual Conference, scheduled for June 14, 15, and 16 at the Russell Hotel in Charlotte.

3 If you respond within 30 days, we can reserve the same space you had last year. If you prefer another location, please review the locations on the enclosed floor plan and identify your first three choices. We will assign your new location after the 30-day period.

4 To reserve a prime location in the exhibit hall, review the enclosed floor plan and select your first three choices. We will assign exhibit space in the order in which the requests are received. Past exhibitors are given preference for a 30-day period.

5 The cost of reserving one space is $250; two spaces, $450; and three spaces, $600. A $100 deposit is required when the space is reserved, and full payment must be received no later than May 15. Exhibitors not paying by May 15 run the risk of losing their space.

(continued on next page)

6 This year's cost for reserving one space is $250; two spaces, $450; and three spaces, $600. Your cost will be reduced since you have exhibited at the conference for four or more years. Your discount is $50 for one space, $75 for two spaces, and $100 for three. A $100 deposit is required when the space is reserved, and full payment must be received no later than May 15. Exhibitors not paying by May 15 run the risk of losing their space.

7 The Association hopes you will return to our conference so that 300+ science teachers in the Charlotte area can learn firsthand about your science education products and services.

8 TSEA's officers and conference leaders hope you will decide to exhibit at this conference. Over three hundred science teachers in the Charlotte area will be able to speak with your representative and learn how your products and services will help them improve learning.

9 Fill out and return the enclosed exhibitor's registration form soon so that you get the location you prefer. Thank you.

Job 5

From the desk of
Yvonne Porterfield

Prepare this letter for my signature, please.

YP

Mr. Carlos Bautista, Sales Manager, Russell Hotel, 222 E. 3d Street, Charlotte, NC 28202-0222

This letter is to confirm a meeting that Mr. James Herriott and I have with you next Friday afternoon at the Russell Hotel.

The primary purpose of the meeting is to tour areas of the hotel that will be used for sessions, exhibits, dining, and registration at the TSEA Tri-County Science Education Conference that is scheduled for June 14-16, 20--.

In the session rooms, we need to see different various seating arrangements and determine what AV audiovisual and other aids speakers can use. We will need access to the Web Internet in at least two three of the rooms. Also, we need to discuss security issues relating to the exhibit area and discuss the electrical service to each exhibit space.

James and I will meat you in your office next Friday at 3:30 p.m.

Job 6

TO: Nancy Hyduk

SUBJECT: INFO FOR THE GOLF OUTING

Harry Spahr, the golf pro at Twin Lakes Golf Course, called with the information you've been waiting for to prepare for the golf outing and cookout.

TSEA can have a shotgun start at 11:20 a.m. on June 14. Up to 72 golfers can participate in the outing. The cost for each golfer is $65 for green and cart fees. Left- and right-handed clubs can be rented for an additional $10. Those attending the cookout (hot dogs, three cold salads, and soft drinks) at 4:30 p.m. are to pay $10.

Mr. Spahr believes he has given me all the information you requested. If not, he said for you to call him at 704-555-0124, or you can e-mail him at <u>hspahr@twinlakes.com</u>.

Job 7

GOLF OUTING AND COOKOUT REGISTRATIONS

Name	Fees	Rental	Cookout	Total Cost	Deposit	Amount Due
John Doe	65	10	10		50	
Jane Doe			10		0	
Jim Doe	65				40	

Add rows at the bottom to calculate totals and count the entries for columns B-F.

Job 8

SS all H s;
DS between

TSEA Conference Board

Participants: R. Acosta, M. Coughenour, J. Herriott, N. Hyduk, Y. Porterfield, C. Taylor

Recorder of minutes: J. Herriott

1. **Call to order:**   Conference Director Yvonne Porterfield called the meeting to order at 4:15 p.m. at the Russell Hotel.

2. **Committee reports: Program.**   R. Acosta ~~reported that~~ ~~he~~ has prepared the Call for Papers that will be

(continued on next page)

From the desk of
Yvonne Porterfield

I drafted a news release. Open CD-TSEAJ-9 and prepare a final copy for me. It is for immediate release and I am the contact person. Proofread carefully because I didn't.

YP

From the desk of
Yvonne Porterfield

Using your favorite Internet search engine, try to find museums in the 28208 ZIP Code area. If you find some, list the names, addresses, telephone numbers, and hours; or simply print the Web pages. I need to give this information to Connie Taylor.

YP

mailed to all members within a week. In addition, he has contacted two publishing houses to sponsor key note speakers for the general sessions.

Registration. M. Coughenour has designed the registration form, and it will be included in the next newsletter ~~as well as~~ *and* the special conference mailing ~~that will be sent.~~ She ~~stated she~~ needed assistance ~~with~~ getting teachers to work the registration table during the conference.

Exhibits. J. Herriott ~~reported that he~~ is gathering data on past exhibitors and ~~is~~ identifying prospective exhibitors.

Hospitality. C. Taylor had nothing to report this time.

Special events. N. Hyduk is planning to have the golf outing at Twin Lakes Golf Course. She hopes to have confirmation in a *few* ~~matter of~~ days.

3. **Unfinished business:** Y. Porterfield ~~stated that she~~ set a meeting with Russell Hotel personnel and ~~that~~ she and J. Herriott will meet with them soon. Other committee chairs ~~are invited to the meeting. If they~~ need ing specific information about hotel facilities and services are to tell Y. Porterfield within ten days.

4. **New business:** Security for the exhibits area was discussed ~~and it was decided to request~~ *will be requested* funding to post a security guard during all hours the exhibits *Closed* are ~~not open~~ to ~~the~~ conference participants.

Committee chairs are to submit ~~a~~ final request for funds ~~that they need~~ at the next meeting so that Y. Porterfield can present a final budget to the TSEA Executive Board for approval.

5. **Next meeting:** The next meeting date was not set *but* all agreed that a *would be* Tuesday ~~was~~ best. Y. Porterfield will set the date and notify each Conference Board member.

Job 11

Person's name, ZIP Code, and school name. Record the $50 registration fee and the amount paid for one or both of the two special workshops that cost $30 each. Record the $25 fee for the June 14 banquet and the $15 fee for the June 15 luncheon if paid. Also, record the total amount each registrant paid.

We need to know the number of persons paying each of the fees above. Likewise, record the total amount of money received for each of these events that require payment.

By the way, insert three or four fictitious names and fees paid so we can verify the accuracy of your calculations; format the worksheet so it is attractive and easy to read.

Job 12

SECOND TSEA CONFERENCE BOARD PROGRESS REPORT — 14-pt. bold

12-pt. bold — (Yvonne Porterfield, Conference Director)

Satisfactory progress is being made in all areas as the Conference Board continues to make all the arrangements for the Sixth Annual TSEA Conference, that is scheduled at the Russell Hotel (Charlotte) from June 14-16. through June

Conference Board — 12-pt. bold

The Conference Board has met monthly since it was appointed shortly after last year's conference ended. There has been one change in the makeup of the board: Connie Taylor replaced Janice Pearson, who had to relinquished her position as Hospitality Chair due to illness in her family.

Program

The Program Committee has designed the entire program for the 3-day conference and has mailed a Call for Papers to all TSEA members. To date, 15 papers have been received come in. Reviewers are deciding if the

(continued on next page)

papers

~~content is~~ are appropriate for conference presentations.

Within the next two months, the Program Committee plans

to have ~~presenters~~ speakers for all concurrent and general

sessions confirmed. Two publishing ~~houses~~ companies have been

asked to sponsor the two general session speakers. ~~If~~

~~they agree to do this,~~ As sponsors they will pay ~~for~~ the speakers'

travel and lodging expenses and provide a generous

honorarium. In return for this ~~contribution~~ support, each

publishers will receive prominent, public recognition.

~~for their significant contribution.~~

Exhibitors

   The Conference Board members, led by Jim Herriott,
Exhibits Chair, are making an ~~concerted~~ effort to
increase conference revenues by increasing the number of
exhibit spaces sold. They are doing this in two ways:

* Increase the number of exhibitors.
* Increasing the number of tables exhibitors buy.

   The following chart indicates how revenue may be
increased by more than $2,500 if we attract four new exhibitors averaging
two tables each, retain all exhibitors from last year,
persuade last year's exhibitor's to purchase 7
additional spaces, and make ~~there is~~ no change in the
exhibit fee per table.

make rows higher

REVENUE FROM EXHIBITS					
Last Year			This Year		
Vendors	Tables	Revenue	Vendors	Tables	Revenue
7	1	$1,750	4	1	$1,000
5	2	$2,250	11	2	$4,950
2	3	$1,200	3	3	$1,800
14		$5,200	18		$7,750

(continued on next page)

Registration

The conference registration form has been designed and will be included with the next TSEA newsletter ~~that is mailed~~. Additionally, a separate ~~mailing that contains~~ flyer announcing conference highlights and registration procedures will be ~~sent~~ mailed to all science teachers in the Tri-County area, by May 1. The early-bird registration fee ~~will be offered~~ approved at our last meeting apply to all who register before June 5. Efforts are underway to recruit teachers to staff the registration tables throughout the conference.

Special Events

The popular conference golf outing will be held on June 14 at the Twin Lakes Golf Club, prior to the first general session at 7 p.m. Up to 72 golfers can be accommodated. The customary cookout will begin at 4:30 p.m. and all Executive Board members are encouraged to attend. The cost has increased only slightly--from $73 last year to $75 this year.

Hospitality

I will ~~be working very~~ closely with Connie Taylor ~~during the~~ next week to bring her up-to-date with what Janice Pearson ~~had~~ arranged. With that information, Connie will be able to finalize all of the gifts and information we need to ~~provide our conference~~ give to participants.

Conclusion

The Conference Board that you appointed is an excellent one. The members are very responsible, eager to work, knowledgeable, and cooperative. Their goals are to provide an excellent conference at a reasonable price and to generate income for TSEA. I will have ~~each~~ ~~committee's~~ the Conference Board's final budget and estimated conference revenues for your review and action at ~~the~~ our next meeting.

Job 13

TSEA GOLF OUTING

Announcement and Registration Form

The TSEA 18-hole golf outing will be held on June 14 at the well-known Twin Lakes Golf Course. A shotgun start is scheduled at 11:20 a.m. Plan to be at the course no latter than 10:45 a.m. Round-trip transportation from the Russell Hotel will be provided.

The cost for the outing is $65 for green and cart fees. The cookout at 4:30 p.m. is $10. The outing will end in time for you too be at the TSEA opening general session at 7:30 p.m.

If you plan to participate complete the form below and return it by June 5 to:

Nancy Hyduk
East Lake Middle School
9600 Southern Pines Boulevard
Charlotte, NC 28273-5520

Job 14

Insert TRI-COUNTY SCIENCE EDUCATION ASSOCIATION, 6030 Jones Drive, Charlotte, NC 28287-6030 as the company information. Use the current date and list M. Winter as the Rep. Invoice MAR WIN for:

Qty	Description	Unit Price
1	Exhibit space at TSEA Conference at Russell Hotel	$ 250.00
1	8 foot table with blue apron	$ 40.00
3	Electrical outlets with extension cords	$ 15.00

There is a 7.5% sales tax.

Job 15

From the desk of
Yvonne Porterfield

Prepare a slide presentation from the information at the right. Unless otherwise specified, use an appropriate title and slide layout. Use appropriate clip art in the last slide and at least one of the other slides. When done, apply a design template that is attractive and easy to read.

YP

Slide 1--Use a title slide with **Conference Board Report** as the title and my name and TSEA title as the subtitle.

Slide 2--Names of conference board members and their principal assignments: Rich Acosta, Call for Papers; Marsha Coughenour, Registration; James Herriott, Exhibits; Connie Taylor, Hospitality; Nancy Hyduk, Special Events

Slide 3--Show the number of registrations:

Members pre-registered = 102
Members registering on-site = 11
Exhibitor registrants = 21
Guests = 14
Total attending = 148

Slide 4--Insert this table with **Revenue from Exhibitors** as the title.

No. of Exhibitors	Tables	Revenue
4	1	$1,000
9	2	$4,050
3	3	$1,800

Slide 5--Insert this information below using a pie chart. Use **Presenters** as the title. Use Percentage to identify the Data Labels.

Middle School	High School	College
5	8	12

Slide 6--Insert this information with **Golf Outing & Cookout** as the title. Select an appropriate slide layout and insert appropriate clip art.

Number of golfers = 36
Number of males = 22
Number of females = 14
Number attending cookout = 46
Number of golfers = 30
Others = 16

UNIT 15

LESSONS 1–5

Extending Spreadsheet Skills

Conditioning Practice

Before you begin the lessons, key each line twice.

alphabet	1	Myra's expensive black racquet is just a wrong size for children.
figures	2	Order 97-341 for 20 Series 568 storm windows was faxed on May 25.
speed	3	Claudia saw my hand signal to go right when she got to the field.

gwam 1' | 1 | 2 | 3 | 4 | 5 | 6 | 7 | 8 | 9 | 10 | 11 | 12 | 13 |

LESSON 1 FORMAT CELLS AND COLUMNS

OBJECTIVE

 To merge cells, wrap and indent text in cells, and specify column widths.

Learn: Merge Cells

As with cells in a word processing table, cells within a worksheet can be merged with adjacent cells. The text within the merged cells can be center-, left-, or right-aligned horizontally and top-, bottom-, or center-aligned vertically. This is useful for centering worksheet titles and entering column and row entries that span more than one column or row.

The illustration in Figure CA15-1 shows a title centered within cells A1:G1. It also shows column and row headings and entries that span multiple columns or rows.

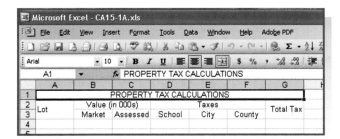

 Exercise **1A**

Merge Cells

1. Read the information about merging cells. Open a new worksheet and complete the following steps:

   a. Center-align **PROPERTY TAX CALCULATIONS** in cells A1:G1 (merge cells).

   b. Center-align **Value (in 000s)** in cells B2:C2 and **Taxes** in D2:F2.

   c. Left-align and vertically center **Lot** in cells A2:A3. Right-align and vertically center **Total Tax** in G2:G3.

   d. Center-align **Market** in B3; **Assessed** in C3; **School** in D3; **City** in E3; and **County** in F3.

2. Print the worksheet with gridlines and row and column headings.

3. Save as *CA15-1A*. Close the file.

Learn: Wrap Text in Cells

Text that is too long for a cell will extend into the adjacent cell if the cell to the right is empty. If the cell to the right is not empty, the text that does not fit will not display. You can choose to have the text wrap within the cell's width in the same way sentences are wrapped in a word processing document. The row height will adjust as shown in Figure CA15-2.

Figure CA15-2 Text Wrap In Cells

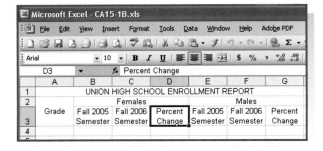

Wrap Text in Cells

1. Read the information on the previous page about wrapping text in a cell. Open a new worksheet and complete the following steps:

   a. Center-align **UNION HIGH SCHOOL ENROLLMENT REPORT** in cells A1:G1 (merge cells).

   b. Center-align **Females** in cells B2:D2 and **Males** in cells E2:G2.

   c. Center-align and vertically center **Grade** in A2:A3.

   d. Using wrap, center-align **Fall 2005 Semester** in cell B3 and again in cell E3; **Fall 2006 Semester** in cell C3 and again in F3; and **Percent Change** in cells D3 and G3.

2. Print the worksheet with gridlines and row and column headings.

3. Save as *CA15-1B*. Close the file.

Learn: Indent Text Feature

Use the Indent Text feature to help distinguish categories or set text apart within cells. The amount of the indent can be increased or decreased by clicking the proper Indent button on the Formatting toolbar or changing the indent setting in the Format Cells dialog box. Figure CA15-3 displays the various indenting styles.

Figure CA15-3   Indent Text Feature

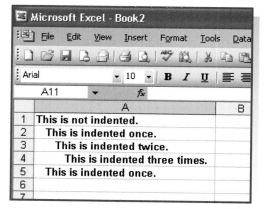

Indent Text

1. Read the above information about indenting text within a cell. Key the worksheet show below using the following formatting features:

   a. Indent column A rows 2, 5, and 8 once.

   b. Indent column A rows 3, 4, 6, 7, 9, and 10 twice.

   c. Indent column A row 11 three times.

   d. Format numbers as Accounting with dollar signs and no cents.

   e. Bold as shown.

   f. Use AutoFit to set column widths to widest entry.

2. Print the worksheet with gridlines and row and column headings.

Distributions to shareholders	Amount
From net investment income	
Class A	$ 43,523
Class B	$ 10,325
In excess of net investment income	
Class A	$ 2,354
Class B	$ 574
From return on capital	
Class A	$ 2,765
Class B	$ 750
Total distributions	$ 60,291

3. Save as *CA15-1C*. Close the file.

Learn: Set Column Width

By default, column widths typically display about eight spaces. You have used AutoFit to resize a column to the width of the longest entry in the column. Another method is to specify an exact number of spaces in the Column Width dialog box. More than one column can be resized to the same width simultaneously if they are selected.

The illustration displayed in Figure CA15-4 indicates the number of spaces specified in each column.

Figure CA15-4   **Column Width Shown In Spaces**

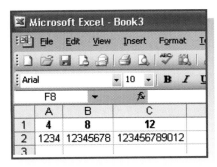

Exercise 1D
Specify Column Width

1. Read the above information about resizing column widths. Key the worksheet shown on the following page using the following formatting features:

   a. Specify column A width to be 15; column B to be 20; and columns C and D to be 10.

   b. Merge cells in A1:D1 and then A2:D2 and right-align text.

   c. Wrap text in cells C3 and D3.

   d. Right-align and vertically center the column headings.

   e. Left-align entries in columns A and B.

   f. Format numbers in columns C and D as Currency, right-aligned.

   g. Use bold and shading as desired.

PORTFOLIO SUMMARY
(In Millions of Dollars)

Property Name	Property Description	Property Cost	Present Value
EXS Tower	10-story office building	7.65	8.24
Marion Mall	retail shopping mall	7.54	8.34
Silver Cove	retail shopping center	6.98	7.92
Redbank Plaza	professional building	5.78	6.02
Reisser Building	8-story office building	5.67	5.78
Reading Mill	retail shopping mall	5.58	5.97
Landmark Park	industrial warehouse	4.53	4.91
Market Arena	distribution center	3.31	3.75

2. Print the worksheet without gridlines or row and column headings.

3. Save as *CA15-1D*. Close the file.

Exercise 1E

Application

1. Key the worksheet as shown below using the following calculations and formatting features:

   a. Calculate the sum in empty shaded cells D8, D13, D17, and D18.

   b. Using the Present Value for each industry and the Total Portfolio Value as the base, calculate the percent in empty shaded cells B8, B13, and B17.

   c. Format numbers in column B as percents with two decimal places, column C with a thousands separator, and column D as currency with no cents.

   d. Right-align all numbers.

MXP COMMON STOCK FUND December 31, 20--			
Industry and Company	**Percent of Portfolio**	**Shares**	**Present Value**
Aerospace			
Fleet Company		4627	205601
Textran		748	37607
Kite Technologies		1312	69459
Total Aerospace			
Energy			
HPNGCO Electric		1701	103855
Gertin Corp		7362	395719
SH Oil		6333	348722
Total Energy			
Real Estate			
The Troyer Company		2151	45324
Suburban Malls, Inc.		6446	164791
Total Real Estate			
Total Portfolio Value			

2. Save as *CA15-1E*. Close the file.

LESSON ② PAGE PRINT AND SETUP

OBJECTIVES

⊛ To use Print Preview and print in landscape orientation.

⊛ To change margins, center and scale worksheets, and insert headers and footers.

Learn: Landscape Orientation

Most documents, including letters, memos, reports, tables, and forms, are printed in portrait orientation, or across the width of the paper (the 8.5" side of paper that is 8.5" by 11"). Many worksheets are wider than 8.5"; these can be printed in landscape orientation, which prints across the length of the paper (the 11" side of 8.5" by 11" paper). Figure CA15-5 shows the Landscape option selected in the Page Setup dialog box.

Figure CA15-5 Page Setup Dialog Box

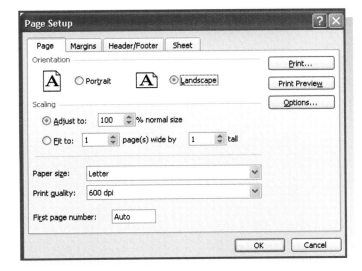

Exercise 2A

Landscape Orientation

1. Open data file *CD-CA15-2A*. Read about Landscape Orientation above.

2. Print the worksheet in landscape orientation.

3. Save as *CA15-2A*. Close the file.

Learn: Arrange Worksheets

To arrange worksheets attractively on a page, you can: 1) change the top, bottom, and side margins; 2) have the spreadsheet software center the worksheet horizontally and/or vertically; and 3) scale the worksheet to print on one page. These changes are made within the Page Setup dialog box, as displayed in Figure CA15-6.

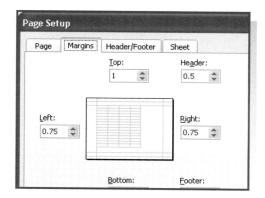

Exercise 2B

Change Margins and Center and Scale Worksheets

1. Read the information about arranging worksheets on a page.
2. Open data file *CD-CA15-2B*; change the side margins to 1.125" and the top and bottom margins to 3". Print the worksheet in landscape orientation without gridlines or headings. Save as *CA15-2B-WS1*. Close the file.
3. Open *CD-CA15-2B*; center the worksheet vertically and horizontally. Print in landscape orientation with gridlines and headings. Save as *CA15-2B-WS2*. Close the file.
4. Open *CD-CA15-2B*, scale the worksheet to fit on one page in portrait orientation, center it vertically and horizontally, and print it without gridlines or headings. Save as *CA15-2B-WS3*. Close the file.

Learn: When to Preview a Worksheet

A worksheet should be previewed before it is printed to make sure it is arranged on the page as desired. If it is not, adjustments can be made to the worksheet before it is printed. These adjustments include changing margins, centering the worksheet, or scaling the worksheet to the desired size. See Figure CA15-7.

Figure CA15-7   Print Preview

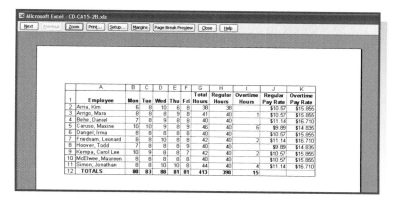

Exercise 2C

Print Preview

1. Open *CD-CA15-2C*. Read about Print Preview on the previous page.

2. Review the worksheet to see the numbers of columns it has, paying particular attention to the names of the columns near the right.

3. Select **Print Preview**. If the worksheet doesn't fit on one page in landscape orientation, scale it to one page and then center it horizontally and vertically.

4. Use Print Preview as many times as needed to ensure the entire worksheet is arranged correctly, and then print it with gridlines and column and row headings.

5. Save as *CA15-2C*. Close the file.

Learn: Use Headers and Footers

Worksheets can contain headers and footers in much the same way as word processing documents can. You can select predefined headers/footers from the spreadsheet software or you can create custom headers/footers. Special codes can be entered in the header/footer to print the date, time, page number, filename, etc. The font, font style, and font size can also be specified. In addition, the header/footer may be left-, center-, or right-aligned. Header and footer options are specified on the Page Setup dialog box as displayed in Figure CA15-8.

Figure CA15-8   Headers and Footers

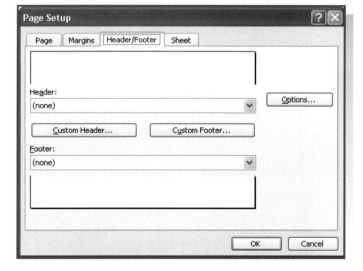

Exercise 2D

Headers and Footers

1. Open *CD-CA15-2D*. Read the information on the previous page about headers and footers.

2. Using Arial 14-point bold font, insert the filename as a right-aligned header and your name and date as a centered custom footer. (*Tip:* The header/footer font does not change automatically when font changes are made in the worksheet.)

3. Preview the worksheet. Print it without gridlines or column/row headings when it is arranged attractively on one page.

4. Save as *CA15-2D*. Close the file.

Exercise 2E

Application

1. Key the worksheet shown below, making these changes:

   a. Specify all column widths at 12.

   b. Format numbers as Currency with no cents.

   c. Insert an 8-character column between C and D and a similar column at the right of the last column, using appropriate shading.

   d. Use Percent Change for the new column headings (wrap the text) and shade appropriately.

   e. Calculate totals and percent of change (use Percent to one decimal place).

   f. Center the Division headings to span the appropriate columns.

JENNCO MONTHLY SALES REPORT					
	Northern Division			**Southern Division**	
		Same Month			**Same Month**
	This	**Last**		**This**	**Last**
Office	**Month**	**Year**	**Office**	**Month**	**Year**
Boston	1540000	1444975	Atlanta	1653450	1582625
Baltimore	1562675	1375755	Dallas	1345870	1467050
Cleveland	2143750	2307450	Mobile	1873525	1852840
Chicago	1957500	2010730	Memphis	2769200	2652810
Boise	780560	755050	Omaha	2459550	2234800
Seattle	2289570	2185525	San Diego	3000540	2750750
Totals			Totals		

220 **Part 1** Unit 15: Extending Spreadsheet Skills

2. Print in landscape orientation, centered on the page with your name as a right-aligned header and today's date as a left- aligned footer, both in 18-point font.

3. Save as *CA15-2E*. Close the file.

LESSON 3 PROOFREAD AND PRINT

> To set a print area, set page breaks, and check spelling.

Learn: Set a Print Area

By default, most spreadsheet software prints all the information in a worksheet. If you need to print only a portion of a worksheet (one or more pages, one cell, or a range of cells), you can specify to have only that portion print.

Exercise 3A

Set Print Area

1. Open *CD-CA15-3A*. Read the information above about setting a print area.

2. Select cells in the range A1:E12 and then print just those cells.

3. Specify and then print only the second page of the worksheet.

Learn: Set Page Breaks

When you are working with multiple-page worksheets, a feature in spreadsheet software will insert page breaks the same as word processing software inserts breaks in multiple-page documents. The default page breaks can be moved so the worksheet information will appear on the correct page.

Exercise 3B

Set Page Breaks

1. Open *CD-CA15-3A* used in the last exercise, if it is not already open. Read the information above about setting page breaks.

2. Verify that the file contains three seating charts.

3 Adjust the page breaks so that one chart is printed per page.

4. Print only the first seating chart. Show gridlines, use portrait orientation, and center horizontally and vertically on the page.

5. Save as *CA15-3B*. Close the file.

Learn: Check Spelling in a Worksheet

Spreadsheet software checks spelling in much the same way as word processing software does. Words are checked for correct spelling but not for context. Numbers are not checked at all. It is therefore important that *you proofread* all words and numbers for accuracy and context after the checker has been used. Proper names should be checked carefully, since the spell dictionary does not contain many proper names. (See Figure CA15-9.)

Figure CA15-9   Spelling Dialog Box

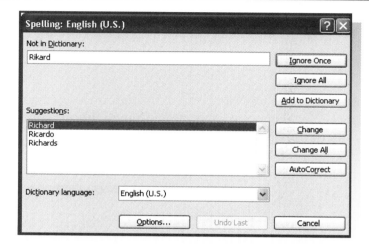

Exercise 3C

Check Spelling

1. Read about checking spelling above. Open *CD-CA15-3C*.
2. Use the spell checker to help proofread and correct errors in the worksheet.
3. Save as *CA15-3C*. Close the file.

Exercise 3D

Application

1. Open a new worksheet and complete the following steps to create a two-day planner.
   a. Specify column A width at 7; column B width at 50.
   b. Merge cells A1 and B1 and key Daily Planner for _____ (left-aligned) in the merged cell.
   c. In column A, key the time in one-hour intervals in every fourth cell. Start with 8 a.m. in cell A2 and end with 7 p.m. in cell A46.
   d. In column B, merge every four rows together. The first four cells to be merged are B2:B5 and the last are B46:49.

e. Make a copy of this planner by copying the cells in the range A1:B49 to a new area beginning with cell A50.

f. Key and left-align your name as a header and the page number as a footer.

g. Insert a page break so each copy of the daily planner will print on a separate page.

h. Center the worksheet on the page, and then print the second page with gridlines.

2. Save as *CA15-3D*. Close the file.

Exercise 3E

Application

1. Key the worksheet shown below (wrap and indent text as shown) making the following changes:

a. Calculate the correct number to be inserted at each set of question marks. The Ending Cash Balance becomes the Opening Cash Balance for the next quarter.

b. Key ROARING SPRINGS GOLF CLUB as a centered heading in 18-point bold font and your name and date as a left-aligned footer.

PROJECTED CASH FLOW FOR 20--

	January to March	April to June	July to September	October to December
Cash Receipts				
Gross Cash Receipts	9500	11000	19000	6550
Returns	445	555	935	305
Net Cash Receipts	???	???	???	???
Cash Disbursements				
Expenses				
Operating Expenses	2335	2357	2390	2240
Other Expenses	150	400	500	300
Cash Disbursements	???	???	???	???
Net Cash Flow				
Opening Cash Balance	9606	???	???	???
Net Cash Receipts	???	???	???	???
Cash Disbursements	???	???	???	???
Ending Cash Balance	???	???	???	???

2. You decide all other formatting features.

3. Check spelling and preview before printing.

4. Save as *CA15-3E*. Close the file.

⊙ To use Fill, rotate text in column headings, and change row heights.

⊙ To rename, format, and reposition worksheet tabs, select print area, set page breaks, and check spelling.

Learn: Use Fill

Information can be quickly copied to adjacent cells by using the Fill feature. This feature can be used to enter a series of days (Monday, Tuesday, Wednesday, . . .), months (Jan, Feb, Mar, . . .), years (2002, 2003, 2004, . . .) consecutive numbers (100, 102, 103, . . .), or numbers in intervals (2, 4, 6, 8, . . . or 2, 4, 8, 16, . . .) in adjacent cells.

Exercise 4A

Fill

1. Read about using Fill above. Open a new worksheet.

2. Key FILL in cell A1 and then use Fill to copy it to cells A2:A15.

3. Use Fill Right to copy cell A5 to B5:J5.

4. Key Monday in C7 and use Fill to enter the days in cells C8:C18.

5. Key 1850 in cell B1 and use Fill to enter the years through 1858 in the cells to the right of B1.

6. Key Jan in E7 and use Fill to enter the months through Dec below E7.

7. Key 1 in F7 and use Fill to enter numbers 2–12 below F7.

8. Key 100 in H7 and use Fill to enter numbers in intervals of 5 to 150 below H7.

9. Use Fill to enter each power of 2 from 2 to 1,024 beginning in A19 and moving right.

10. Print the worksheet with gridlines and column and row headings on one page, using a left margin of 1.25" and top margin of 3".

11. Save as *CA15-4A*. Close the file.

Learn: Rotate Text

When column headings are considerably longer than the information in the columns, the column headings can be rotated to save space. (See Figure CA15-10.)

Exercise 4B

Rotate Text

1. Read the previous information about rotating text.
2. Key the two worksheets shown below. Rotate the text in the column headings at 45° in the first worksheet and 60 in the second.
3. Save as *CA15-4B-WS1* and *CA15-4B-WS2*. Close the files.

Student	Monday	Tuesday	Wednesday	Thursday	Friday
Jim	Present	Present	Present	Present	Present
Harry	Absent	Absent	Absent	Present	Present

Month	Albert	Mary Ann	Roberto	Yin Chi	Zeb
Sep	1	0	0	0	1
Oct	0	0	0	0	0
Nov	1	1	0	2	0
Dec	1	0	0	1	3
Jan	1	0	0	0	0
Feb	0	0	0	0	1

Learn: Change Row Height

You can specify the height of rows just as you can specify the width of columns. The height of rows is specified in points (72 points equal 1"). You can make the height larger or smaller·than the default setting. The illustration shown in Figure CA15-11 shows rows of varying heights.

	A
1	12.75 points (the default)
2	36 points (1/2 inch)
3	10 points
4	24 points
5	
6	
7	

Exercise 4C

Change Row Height

1. Read the previous information about changing row height. Open a new worksheet.

2. Specify row 1 to be 18 points and key your name in cell A1.

3. Specify row 2 to be 36 points and key your course name in cell A2.

4. Specify row 3 to be 54 points and key your school name in cell A3.

5. Specify row 4 to be 72 points and key today's date in cell A4.

6. Use AutoFit to adjust the column width to fit the longest entry.

7. Print the worksheet (centered with gridlines). Check the row height—row 1= .25"; row 2=.5"; row 3=.75"; row 4=1".

8. Save as *CA15-4C*. Close the file.

Learn: Use Sheet Tabs

Sheet tabs (at the bottom of the worksheet) are for each worksheet in a workbook. By default, workbooks usually contain three sheet tabs (sheet 1, sheet 2, and sheet 3)—one for each of the worksheets. Sheet tabs can be renamed, added or deleted, repositioned (that is, moved from first to third, third to second, etc.), or colored. See Figures CA15-12 and CA15-13.

Figure CA15-12   Sheet Tab

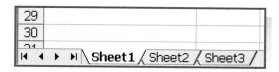

Figure CA15-13   Renamed Sheet Tab

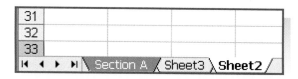

Exercise 4D
Sheet Tabs

1. Read the previous information about sheet tabs. Open a new worksheet.
2. Rename sheet 1 Section A, sheet 2 Section D, and sheet 3 Section C.
3. Insert a new sheet tab between Section A and Section D sheet tabs. Rename the sheet tab Section B.
4. Reposition sheet tabs so they are in alpha order with Section A being the first sheet tab.
5. Apply a different color to each sheet tab.
6. Save as *CA15-4D*. Close the file.

Exercise 4E
Application

1. Open *CD-CA15-4E* and complete the following steps:
   a. In column B, use Fill to complete assigning consecutive payroll numbers (127–134).
   b. Rotate text in column headings at least 70°.
   c. Make rows 2 through 9 0.5" high.
   d. Format column C numbers as social security numbers.
   e. Display column D numbers as dates in the March 14, 2001 format.
   f. Display column E numbers as telephone numbers.
   g. Apply a thick, red border around all cells in the range A2:G9.
   h. Rename sheet 1 Employee Data and Sheet 2 Payroll. Color each tab.
   i. Delete sheet 3 tab.
2. Save as *CA15-4E*. Close the file.

Exercise 4F
Application

1. Complete the steps below to create an answer sheet.
   a. Specify height of rows 1–27 at 0.25" (18 points) and row 28 at 54 points.
   b. Specify the following widths: column A and C at 4; column B and D at 10; column E at 2; and column F at 50
   c. Merge cells A1 to F1 and key ANSWER SHEET, centered in 16-point bold font.
   d. Key Item in cells A2 and C2 and Answer in cells B2 and D2. Center the headings.
   e. In cell F2, key SHORT ANSWER RESPONSES, centered.

f. Merge the following cells: F3 to F10; F11 to F18; F19 to F27; and E2 to E28.

g. Merge cells A28 to D28 and key Student Name, centered horizontally and top-aligned. Key Subject and Period in cell F28 with the same alignment.

h. Use Fill to enter numbers 1–25 in column A cells A3 to A27 and 26–50 in column C cells C3 to C27.

i. Center horizontally and top-align ANSWER 1, ANSWER 2, and ANSWER 3 in the three large merged cell areas in column F, with ANSWER 1 being in the first merged cell.

j. Center the worksheet on the page, and print with gridlines.

2. Save as *CA15-4F*. Close the file.

LESSON ⑤ FREEZE, HIDE, REPEAT, AND SORT

OBJECTIVES

⊙ To freeze and hide columns and rows.
⊙ To sort worksheet information alphabetically and numerically.

Learn: Freeze a Worksheet

Often an entire worksheet cannot be seen on the screen because as you scroll through the worksheet, the information in the column and row headings disappears from the screen. You can freeze the column and row headings so they remain visible as you scroll to other parts of the worksheet. In the illustration in Figure CA15-14, row 1 was frozen and rows 2–49 disappeared from the screen as the user scrolled to row 50.

Rows and columns can be unfrozen when that feature is no longer needed.

Figure CA15-14   Freeze a Worksheet

Microsoft Excel - CD-CA15-5B.xls

	A	B	C TICKET NO.	D DATE RECEIVED	E CHECK NO.
1	LAST	FIRST			
50	BIDDLE	CLAIRE	149	9/15	2596
51	SEJVAR	HENRY	150	9/16	9524
52	SEJVAR	LOIS	151	9/16	9524
53	NEVIN	GREG	152	9/16	1282
54	NEVIN	PAULA	153	9/16	1282

Exercise 5A

Freeze

1. Open the data file *CD-CA15-5A*. Read about freezing column and row headings above.

2. Freeze row 1, and then scroll through the worksheet. Notice that the column headings remain visible.

3. Unfreeze row 1 and close.

Learn: Use the Hide Feature

Rows and columns can be temporarily hidden to enable you to view only those parts of a worksheet that you want to see or print.

Rows and columns can be unhidden when you need to see or print them.

The illustration in Figure CA15-15 shows that columns C, D, E, and G and rows 6–9 have been temporarily hidden from view.

Figure CA15-15   Hidden Columns In a Worksheet

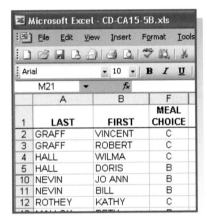

Exercise 5B

Hide

1. Open the data file *CD-CA15-5B*. Read about hiding rows and columns above.

2. Hide columns C, D, E, and G and rows 8, 9, 10, and 11.

3. Unhide columns B, C, D, and E.

4. Hide columns C, D, and E.

5. Print page 1 of the worksheet.

6. Save as *CA15-5B*. Close the file.

Learn: Repeat Row and Column Headings

As worksheets expand to two or more pages, it is very helpful to repeat the row and/or column headings on each page to make the second page and subsequent pages easier to read. (See Figure CA15-16.)

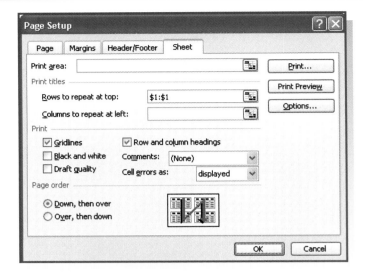

Exercise 5C

Repeat Rows and Columns

1. Open the data file *CD-CA15-5C*. Read about repeating rows and columns above.

2. Print the worksheet, repeating the column headings in row 1 on each page.

3. Save as *CA15-5C*. Close the file.

Learn: Sort a Worksheet

Information in a worksheet can be sorted in much the same manner as information in tables is sorted with word processing software. Sorting reorganizes data to place it in an order that is more meaningful. You can sort in ascending order (A–Z or lowest number to highest number) or descending order (the reverse of ascending). You can sort on information in one column or two or three columns, as shown in Figure CA15-17.

It is always best to rename and save the worksheet before doing the sort to retain the information in its original order.

Figure CA15-17   Sort Dialog Box

Exercise 5D

Sort

1. Open the data file *CD-CA15-5D* and save as *CA15-5D*. Read the previous information about sorting.

2. Sort the information in *CA15-5D* by Date Received (earliest first). Print the first 12 rows that include data for 9/10. Save as *CA15-5D-WS1*.

3. Open *CA15-5D* and sort the information by Last Name and then First Name, both in ascending alphabetical order. Freeze row 1 and hide columns E and G. Print rows 35–54. Save as *CA15-5D-WS2*.

4. Open *CA15-5D* and sort the list by Meal Choice (descending), then Last Name (ascending), and then First Name (ascending). Hide column G. Print the last five C and first five B meals. Save as *CA15-5D-WS3*.

5. Open *CA15-5D* and sort the information by Ticket No. (descending) and then Last and First Names (ascending). Hide columns F and G. Print page one of the worksheet. Save as *CA15-5D-WS4*. Close the file.

Exercise 5E

Application

1. Open the data file *CD-CA15-5E*.
2. Hide columns B–G.
3. Sort by Gross Pay in ascending order.
4. Use your name as a right-aligned header and today's date as a right-aligned footer.
5. Print the worksheet with gridlines and row and column headings, scaled to fit on one page with 2" side margins and centered vertically.
6. Save as *CA15-5E*. Close the file.

Exercise 5F

Application

1. Open *CA15-1D* from Exercise 1D.
2. Key this data into the worksheet:
   Morris Towers, 5-story office building, $4.56, $4.86

Online Resources

See Bonus Exercises 5G, 6A, and 6B on Spreadsheet Applications at www.c21key.bonus-exercises.swlearning.com.

3. Hide column C and sort by present value (ascending). Save as *CA15-5F-WS1* and print the worksheet.
4. Unhide column C, hide column D, and sort by Property Cost (descending) and then by property name (ascending). Save as *CA15-5F-WS2* and print the worksheet.
5. Unhide column D, hide column B, and sort by property name (ascending). Save as *CA15-5F-WS3* and print the worksheet. Close the file.

UNIT *16*

LESSONS 1–5

Enhancing/Integrating Spreadsheet Skills

Conditioning Practice

Before you begin the lessons, key each line twice.

alphabet 1 Packy thought Dom's long joke about the next quiz was very funny.

figures 2 The listing on June 9, 2005, had 87 cars, 41 vans, and 36 trucks.

speed 3 Eight was the divisor for half the problems Nancy did on the bus.

gwam 1' | 1 | 2 | 3 | 4 | 5 | 6 | 7 | 8 | 9 | 10 | 11 | 12 | 13 |

LESSON ① REFERENCE CELLS AND USE FUNCTIONS AND AUTOFORMAT

OBJECTIVES

 To use relative, absolute, and mixed cell references.
 To apply autoformats.

Learn: Cell References

You have learned that spreadsheet software copies a formula across a row or up or down a column. It also adjusts the formula copied into the new cells to reflect its new address and the address of other cells used in the formula.

relative cell referencing

When formulas are copied in this manner, the software is using **relative cell referencing**. That is, the copy of the cell is related to its new address. For example, if cell D1 contains the formula =B1+C1, when this formula is copied to E2, it changes automatically to =C2+D2. Since E2 is down one row and one column over, the cells in the formula are also down one row and one column over from the cells in the original formula.

absolute cell referencing

Sometimes you will not want to change a formula to reflect its new address when copying across a row or up or down a column. In these instances, you will use **absolute cell referencing**. Absolute cell referencing is used by keying a $ sign before the column and row reference in the cell address that is not to change. For example, if you want to divide all the numbers in column B by a number that is in A1, you would make A1 an absolute cell address by keying a $ before the A and a $ before the 1 ($A$1).

A **mixed cell reference** is one that maintains a reference to a specific row or column but not to both. For example, D$1 is a mixed cell reference. The reference to column D is relative, and the reference to row 1 is absolute. When copied to another cell, the reference to column D will change, but the reference to row 1 will remain the same.

Cell reference	Example
Relative	=A1+B1+C1
Absolute	=$A$1+$B+$1+$C
Mixed	=$A1+B1+$C$1

Exercise 1A

Cell References

1. Read the information about cell references. Key this worksheet.

	A	B	C	D	E	F	G
1				Cell Referencing			
2	Numbers			Relative	Absolute	Mixed	Mixed
3	1	2	3				
4	4	5	6				
5	7	8	9				
6	10	11	12				
7	13	14	15				

2. In cell D3, key =A3+B3+C3 and then copy to cells D4:D7. Notice that the formula added the numbers in columns A–C across each row since relative cell referencing was used.

3. In cell E3, key =$A$3+$B$3+$C$3 and then copy to cells E4:E7. Notice that the formula added the numbers in columns A, B, and C across the same row (row 3) since absolute cell referencing was used for the row.

4. In cell F3, key =A$3+B$3+C3 and then copy to cells F4:F7. Notice that the formula always added the numbers in columns A and B, row 3, to each value in column C as the formula was copied to each row.

5. Copy cell F3 to cell G3 and then copy cell G3 to cells G4:G7. In cells G3:G7, notice that the A changed to B and B changed to C in each cell reference in column G since the A and B are relative references. The $3 remained the same in each row in column G since it is an absolute reference. Since C3 is a relative reference, it changed to D3 when copied to cell G3, and then the number changed each time it was copied to a new row in column G.

6. Save as *CA16-1A*.

Application

1. Key this worksheet, supplying the totals (*TOT*) in column I and row 16.

	A	B	C	D	E	F	G	H	I	J
1	**CANDY BAR SALES BY HOMEROOM**									
2	ROOM	MON	TUE	WED	THU	FRI	SAT	SUN	TOT	$REV
3	101	23	45	32	66	66	72	23		
4	103	45	65	82	45	45	56	33		
5	105	45	23	10	75	75	63	77		
6	107	34	23	15	34	56	45	23		
7	109	23	35	46	53	53	49	66		
8	111	22	33	55	88	88	46	23		
9	113	24	57	80	76	76	62	54		
10	115	23	56	80	55	55	65	29		
11	117	78	67	56	46	61	33	60		
12	119	35	65	73	59	92	47	59		
13	121	44	56	71	48	98	32	45		
14	123	35	58	56	59	84	15	38		
15	TOT									
16	CANDY BAR PRICE									
17	$1.25									

2. Specify column A width at 6, B–I at 5, and J at 9.
3. Make all rows 0.25" high.
4. Calculate the total revenue (*REV*) in column J by multiplying column I values by cell A17. Format column J as Currency with two decimal places.
5. Add a nine-character column at the right with the heading % of REV.
6. Calculate each room's percent of the total revenue (cell I16) and display it in the % of REV column. Format it as Percentage with two decimal places.
7. Save as *CA16-1B*.

Learn: AutoFormat

Like most word processing software, spreadsheet software also includes a built-in collection of cell formats that you can quickly apply to a range of cells. The format elements include font size, alignments, borders, numbers, etc. All or some of the elements in the autoformat can be applied. Autoformats can also be removed if desired.

AutoFormat

1. Open *CD-CA16-1C*. Read the information about AutoFormat.

2. Apply various autoformats. If available, apply these:
   - Classic 3
   - Colorful 3
   - List 3
   - 3D Effects

   (If not available, choose four other autoformats.)

3. Save the file as *CA16-1C* with the autoformat you believe is most attractive.

Application

1. Key the worksheet shown below, calculating the % of Net Revenues for each item (use two decimal places).

   Learning Tip: % of Net Revenue = *Value in column B/C2*.

Jones Electric

	12/31/2002	% of Net Revenues
Revenues	$2,257,650	
Returns and Allowances	$ 1,568	
Net Revenues	$2,256,082	
Cost of Goods Sold		
Beginning Inventory	$ 125,612	
Purchases	$ 834,972	
Cost of Goods Available for Sale	$ 960,584	
Ending Inventory	$ 126,829	
Cost of Goods Sold	$ 833,755	
Gross Profit	$1,422,327	
Expenses	$1,165,750	
Net Profit	$ 256,577	

2. Apply an appropriate autoformat. If an appropriate one cannot be applied, format your worksheet using accounting rules (underlines) as shown.

3. Print centered on the page.

4. Save as *CA16-1D*.

OBJECTIVE

 To answer "what if" questions and use the IF function and conditional formatting.

Exercise 2A

Prepare To Learn

1. Key this worksheet.

DETERMINATION OF SALES QUOTA		
1.05 =Company Goal		
Salesperson	Quota This Year	Quota Next Year
Juan Avia	$250,000	
Mary Abelsen	$240,000	
Thomas Willit	$268,000	
Un Chin	$252,000	
Henry Quinez	$220,000	
Marty Merry	$172,000	

2. Calculate Next Year's Quota by multiplying column B values by cell A1.
3. You decide all formatting features.
4. Save as *CA16-2A*.

Learn: "What If" Questions

An advantage of spreadsheet software is its ability to show the effects on all cells of a change in one cell. For example, in the worksheet in Exercise 2A, you determined next year's quota for each salesperson if the company were to make the new quotas 1.05 (105%) of this year's quota. By changing the 1.05 in cell A2 to other numbers representing other possible changes, the effect of the change on the quotas for all salespersons can be computed at once.

Exercise 2B

"What If" Questions

1. Read the above information about "what if" questions.
2. Using *CA16-2A* from the last exercise, answer the following three "what if" questions:
   a. What if the goal is decreased to 95 percent of this year's quota?
   b. What if the goal is increased to 105.5 percent of this year's quota?
   c. What if the goal is increased to 110 percent of this year's quota?

3. Print the worksheet after each question, unless directed to do otherwise.

4. Save the final worksheet as *CA16-2B*.

Learn: IF Function

The IF function compares the contents of two cells. Conditions that contain logical operators (listed in the box below) provide the basis for the comparison. For example, an instructor could use the following IF function (see formula bar in Figure CA16-1) to determine whether a student passed or failed a course.

Figure CA16-1   IF Function

E2		▼	f_x =IF(D2>60, "Pass","Fail")		
	A	B	C	D	E	F

	A	B	C	D	E	F
1	Name	Quiz 1	Quiz 2	Average	Pass/Fail	
2	Joe	89	84	86.5	Pass	
3	Maria	55	62	58.5	Fail	
4	Chu	94	98	96	Pass	
5	Abdul	78	74	76	Pass	

The IF function shown in Figure CA16-1 involves three arguments. The first is the comparison of the scores in column B to the criteria (a score that is greater than [>] 60 in the example). The second argument is the text or value ("Pass" in the example) that is to be displayed if the comparison is true. The third is the text or value ("Fail") that is to be displayed if the comparison is false.

As illustrated, the arguments of the IF function are keyed inside parentheses and are separated from each other with commas. If text is to be displayed for argument 2 or 3, the text should be keyed inside quotation marks. Quotes are not keyed if values are to be displayed.

Exercise   2C

IF Function

1. Read the above information about the IF function.

2. Create a worksheet using IF functions as directed and these logical operators:

Logical Operators

= (value of two cells are *equal*)
< (value of one cell is *less than* the other)
> (value of one cell is *greater than* the other)
<= (value of one cell is *less than* or *equal* to the other)
>= (value of one cell is *greater than* or *equal* to the other)
<> (values are *unequal*)

---

a. Key 25 in cell A1 and 35 in cell B1. In cell C1, key an IF function that prints EQUAL if A1=B1 or UNEQUAL if A1 and B1 are unequal.

b. In cell D1, key an IF function that prints HELP if the sum of A1+B1 is less than 75 and NO HELP if the sum is 75 or greater.

c. In cell A3, key 679805; in cell B3, 354098; in cell C3, 350507. In cell D3, key an IF function that prints EQUAL if A3-B3=C3 and UN-EQUAL if A3-B3 does not equal C3.

d. In cell A5, key 11; 22 in cell B5; 33 in cell C5; 44 in cell D5. In cell E5, key an IF function that prints 1–149 if the sum of A5:D5 is less than 150 and 150+ if the sum of A5:D5 is greater than 150.

3. Print the worksheet with gridlines and row and column headings.

4. Save as *CA16-2C*.

Exercise 2D
Application

1. Key this worksheet.

	A	B	C	D	E	F	G
1	GRADE BOOK						
2	NAME	TEST 1	TEST 2	TEST 3	TEST 4	AVG	NEEDS TUTORING
3	ABEL	78	85	72	78		
4	BOGGS	64	66	71	73		
5	CARR	78	82	86	75		
6	FRYZ	90	93	88	86		
7	GOOD	95	82	86	92		
8	MILLS	71	75	73	76		
9	POPE	62	71	73	66		
10	SIA	75	76	81	71		
11	TODD	66	65	50	61		
12	WILLS	75	64	75	70		
13	ZEON	81	74	65	60		

2. In column F, calculate average score to nearest whole number.

3. In column G, key an IF function that compares the scores in column F to a score of 75. If the score is less than 75, print **TUTORING** in column G. If it is 75 or more, print nothing.

4. You decide all formatting features.

5. Save as *CA16-2D*.

Learn: Conditional Formatting

Conditional formatting enables you to have formatting features appear in a cell only when data in the cell meet specified conditions. For example, your teacher can apply conditional formatting to change the font color, font style, cell shading, borders, etc. to quickly identify students who have low and/or high scores on a test.

Conditional formats remain until they are deleted. Also, revisions that cause cell data to meet the specified condition will display the conditional formats, and revisions that cause cell data to not meet the specified condition will not display the conditional formats.

Exercise 2E

Conditional Formatting

1. Open *CD-CA16-2E*. Read the information about conditional formatting.

2. Apply conditional formatting so that all test scores above 93 are displayed in bold, white font in cells with dark gray shading.

3. Apply conditional formatting so that all test scores below 70 are displayed in bold, white font in cells with light gray shading.

4. Save as *CA16-2E*.

Exercise 2F

Application

1. Open *CD-CA16-2F*.

2. Apply conditional formatting so that the girls who have a time of 101.65 or greater in the 100 Yard Butterfly have their times displayed in cells that are shaded dark gray with a bold, white font.

3. Apply conditional formatting so that the boys who have 400.35 or more points in the diving competition are displayed in cells that have conditional formatting that you choose.

4. Add a column named *States* at the right of the girls' times and the boys' points. Write IF statements in column E to have States print in column E for each girl who has a time less than or equal to 101.65 and for each boy whose points are greater than or equal to 400.35.

5. Save as *CA16-2F*.

LESSON 3 — INTEGRATE WORKSHEETS AND WORD PROCESSING DOCUMENTS

OBJECTIVE

 To learn to copy and link a worksheet to a word processing document.

Learn: Copying a Worksheet into a Word Processing Document

Frequently, text and numbers are copied from a worksheet into a word processing document to avoid rekeying the information. When a worksheet is copied into a word processing document, it appears as a table that can be formatted as needed using the word processing table formatting features.

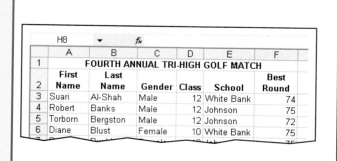

H8

	A	B	C	D	E	F
1	FOURTH ANNUAL TRI-HIGH GOLF MATCH					
2	First Name	Last Name	Gender	Class	School	Best Round
3	Suari	Al-Shah	Male	12	White Bank	74
4	Robert	Banks	Male	12	Johnson	75
5	Torborn	Bergston	Male	12	Johnson	72
6	Diane	Blust	Female	10	White Bank	75

TO: Athletic Directors at Ford, Johnson, and White Bank High Schools

FROM: District 3 Interscholastic Athletic Office

DATE: *Current Date*

SUBJECT: TRI-HIGH GOLF MATCH PARTICIPANTS

Here's the official roster of the golfers who will be participating in the upcoming Tri-High Golf Match at Rolling Hills Golf Course. Additions to the roster cannot be made at this time.

FOURTH ANNUAL TRI-HIGH GOLF MATCH					
First Name	Last Name	Gender	Class	School	Best Round
Suari	Al-Shah	Male	12	White Bank	74
Robert	Banks	Male	12	Johnson	75
Torborn	Bergston	Male	12	Johnson	72

Exercise 3A

Copy a Worksheet into a Word Processing Document

1. Open the word processing document *CD-CA16-3A-WP*. Read the information above and on the previous page about copying worksheets.

2. Open the worksheet *CD-CA16-3A-WS* and save it as *CA16-3A-S*. (*Note:* A file that is to become a source copy for an activity will be saved with a filename that ends in "S." For example, the source file for this activity is named *CA16-3A-S*.)

3. Copy the worksheet into the document, placing it about a double space below the last line of the memo body. Leave about one blank line after the table, and then key your initials.

4. Center the table between the left and right margins with gridlines. Format the table in Times New Roman, using font sizes that will keep the memo to one page. You decide other formatting features.

5. Save as *CA16-3A-WP*.

Learn: How to Link Data

Oftentimes, data in a worksheet that has been copied into a word processing document is routinely updated. To eliminate the need to rekey the word processing document and copy the worksheet each time the data is updated, a link between the word processing document and the worksheet can be created.

Paste Special

With linking, data changed on the source file (worksheet) is automatically updated in the destination file (word processing document). The **Paste Special** command is used to establish this link.

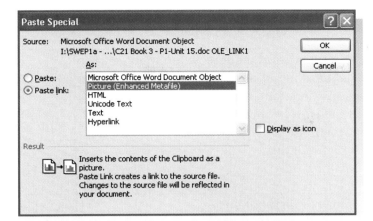

Exercise 3B

Link Data

1. Open the word processing document *CD-CA16-3B-WP*. Read the information above and on the previous page about linking data.

2. Open the worksheet *CD-CA16-3B-WS* and save it as *CA16-3B-S*.

3. Use Paste Special to paste the worksheet into the document to link the worksheet and word processing document.

4. Place the table a double space below the last line of the memo body. Leave about one blank line after the table, and then key your initials.

5. Center between the left and right margins with gridlines. You decide other formatting features.

6. Save as *CA16-3B-WP*.

Exercise 3C

Update a File

1. Open *CA16-3B-S* used in the previous exercise and change the numbers to those given on the following page. *Note:* After you key the new numbers in the source file (*CA16-3B-S*), the destination file (*CA16-3B-WP*) will be updated when you open it since the Manual Update command has not been selected.

Increase in net assets	
Operations	
Net investment income	$ 415,676
Net realized gain	$ 3,297,811
Change in net unrealized appreciation (depreciation)	$ 2,877,590
Net increase in net assets resulting from operations	$ 6,591,077
Distributions to shareholders	
From net investment income	$ (399,456)
From net realized gain	$ (2,195,315)
Total distributions	$ (2,594,771)
Share transactions	
Net proceeds from sales of shares	$ 897,120
Reinvestment of distributions	$ 2,987,407
Cost of shares redeemed	$ 10,976,866
Net increase in net assets resulting from share transactions	$ 897,120
Total increase in net assets	$ 10,082,968
Net assets	
Beginning of period	$ 48,595,195
End of period	$ 58,678,163

2. Save the changes to *CA16-3B-S*.

3. Open *CA16-3B-WP* and note that the numbers in the financial report have been updated automatically.

4. Save as *CA16-3C-WP*.

Exercise Application

1. Open the word processing file *CD-CA16-3D-WP* and save it as *CA16-3D-WP*.

2. Create the worksheet (*CA16-3D-S*) from the data given below and copy it into *CA16-3D-WP* between the paragraphs.

Business	Address	Points	Amount
Avenue Deli	309 Franklin Avenue	92	$15,000
Ford's Newsstand	302 Franklin Avenue	88	$15,000
Hannon Shoes	415 Shefield Avenue	86	$10,000
Unger Appliances	525 Station Street	83	$10,000
Best Food Market	311 Franklin Avenue	76	$ 5,000
Avenue Restaurant	376 Franklin Avenue	76	$ 5,000

3. Save as *CA16-3D-WP*.

Exercise 3E

Application

1. Open the word processing file *CD-CA16-3E-WP* and save it as *CA16-3E-WP*.

2. Open the worksheet *CD-CA16-3E-WS* and save it as *CA16-3E-S*.

3. Delete values in the worksheet file *CA16-3E-S* for Last Year; move values for This Year to Last Year; and move the values for Next Year to This Year.

4. Key these new numbers for Next Year from left to right, formatting as necessary:

   6    $68,217   104 $47,248   15 $49,017

5. Save *CA16-3E-S* changes. Open, update, and save *CA16-3E-WP* changes.

LESSON 4 INTEGRATE WORKSHEETS WITH WORD PROCESSING AND THE INTERNET

OBJECTIVES

 ⊘ To convert word processing documents to worksheets.
⊘ To use worksheets as Web pages.

Learn: Converting a Word Processing Document to a Worksheet

Data from a word processing table can be converted to a worksheet, and then calculations can be performed on the data. If the word processing document is a table or data separated by tabs, it will be copied to separate cells in the worksheet; otherwise, the information will be copied into the highlighted cell of the worksheet.

Exercise 4A

Convert Word Processing Document to Worksheet

1. Read the information above about converting word processing document to a worksheet.

2. Open the word processing document *CD-CA16-4A* and copy it into a blank worksheet.

3. Add a column at the right with Total Hits as the heading; add a row at the bottom with Totals as an indented row heading.

4. Perform the calculations in the added column and row.

5. Adjust font size, row height, and column width as needed to improve the appearance.

6. Save as *CA16-4A*.

Application

1. Key and then save this table as a word processing file named *CA16-4B-WP*. Copy the table into a blank worksheet.

APRIL PAY SCHEDULE			
Salesperson	Sales	Commission	Salary
Frederick Adams	$1,856	$464	$600
Janice Brown	$2,235	$558	$625
Carlos Cruz	$1,975	$493	$600
Enrico Duarte	$1,857	$464	$575
Lisa Ford	$1,785	$446	$600
Marian Mosley	$2,145	$536	$650
Jerry Roberts	$2,098	$524	$600
Leona Williams	$1,674	$418	$575

2. Add Bonus and Total columns at the right of the worksheet.

3. Calculate bonuses: Bonuses are 25 percent of the salary if the sales are more than $1,900. If not, no bonus is earned.

4. Total each salesperson's pay for April.

5. Add an indented Totals row at the bottom, and calculate a total for each column.

6. Format the worksheet to make it attractive.

7. Save as *CA16-4B-WS*.

Learn: Viewing Worksheets on the Web

Worksheets can be saved as HTML (HyperText Markup Language) files to be viewed with a Web browser and then posted on the Internet, if desired.

In this activity you will:

1. Open a worksheet.
2. Use a browser to preview the worksheet.
3. Revise the worksheet, if changes are needed.
4. Save the worksheet as an HTML file.
5. View the worksheet in a browser.
6. Print it from the browser.

Figure CA16-4 shows dialog box options for saving a worksheet in HTML format. Figure CA16-5 shows the Open dialog box of *Internet Explorer*.

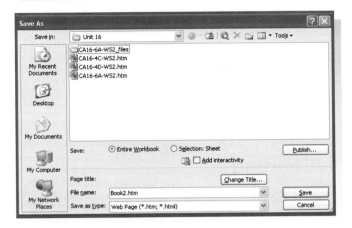

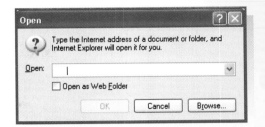

Exercise 4C

View Worksheets on the Web

1. Read the information above and on the previous page about viewing worksheets on the Web.

2. Open the worksheet *CD-CA16-4C-WS* and save it as *CA16-4C-WS1*.

3. Preview the worksheet in a browser to see if any revisions need to be made to improve the worksheet's appearance as a Web page.

4. Close the browser, return to the worksheet, and make the changes, if any.

5. Save the worksheet as a Web page named *CA16-4C-WS2*.

6. Launch your browser and open *CA16-4C-WS2*.

7. From your browser, print *CA16-4C-WS2*.

Exercise 4D

Application

1. Open *CD-CA16-4D-WS* and save it as *CA16-4D-WS1*.

2. Preview the worksheet as a Web page and make any needed changes.

3. Save the worksheet as a Web page file named *CA16-4D-WS2*.

4. Launch a browser, open *CA16-4D-WS2* with the browser, view, and then print it from the browser.

OBJECTIVE

 To create a line chart and chart sheet, use 3-D effects, and edit charts.

Exercise 5A

Charting

1. Open *CD-CA16-5A-WS1* and create a bar chart with chart and axis titles and gridlines. Enlarge the chart as needed to make it easy to read. Save as *CA16-5A-WS1*.

2. Open *CD-CA16-5A-WS2* and create a column chart with chart and axis titles, gridlines, and legend. Enlarge the chart as needed to make it easy to read. Save as *CA16-5A-WS2*.

3. Open *CD-CA16-5A-WS3* and create a pie chart with chart title, legend, and data labels showing %. Enlarge the chart as needed to make it easy to read. Save as *CA16-5A-WS3*.

Learn: Line Charts

Spreadsheet software has several chart types in addition to the bar, column, and pie chart. In this activity, you will create a line chart. Line charts are similar to column charts except the columns are replaced by points joined by a line.

The illustration in Figure CA16-6 shows a line chart with data series for three persons.

Figure CA16-6   Line Chart

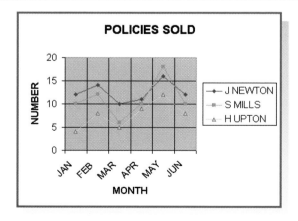

Line Chart

1. Read the information about line charts.
2. Open *CD-CA16-5B* and create an embedded line chart with a chart title, axis title, gridlines, and a legend.
3. Size the chart as needed.
4. Save as *CA16-5B*.

Learn: 3-D Effects

Many spreadsheet charts can be created with 3D-effects. The illustration in Figure CA16-7 is a column chart with 3-D effects. You can also select 3-D effects for pie, bar, and line charts.

Figure CA16-7   Column Chart with 3d Effects

3D Effects

1. Read the information above about 3D effects.
2. Open *CD-CA16-5C* and create an embedded 3-D column chart with a chart title and gridlines.
3. Size the chart as needed.
4. Save as *CA16-5C*.

Learn: Chart Sheet

Charts can be created and displayed two ways—as an embedded object or as a new chart sheet. Charts created previously have been created and displayed as embedded objects. That is, the chart is placed within the worksheet so the chart and data can be viewed at the same time.

   In this activity, charts will be created and placed in a new chart sheet. The chart sheet is a separate sheet in the workbook. You can access the chart sheet by clicking on the chart tab to the left of the worksheet tab near the bottom of the worksheet.

Chart sheets are saved when the worksheet is saved. You can use the default name(s) assigned or give each chart sheet a specific name. Several charts can be prepared from a worksheet if chart sheets are used. (See Figure CA16-8.)

Figure CA16-8   Chart Wizard Dialog Box

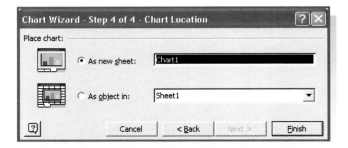

Exercise 5D

Chart Sheet

1. Read the information above and on the previous page about chart sheets.

2. Open *CD-CA16-5D* and create a pie chart with 3D-effects and display the chart on a chart sheet.

3. Save as *CA16-5D*.

Learn: Edit Charts

Charts can be edited. For example, subtitles can be added, the font size and style can be changed, and the color of the bars, columns, lines, etc., can be changed. You can even switch from one type of chart to another without starting over.

Exercise 5E

Edit Charts

1. Read the above information about editing charts. Open *CA16-5A-WS1* from Exercise 5A.

2. Add Auto Outlet, Inc. as a subtitle; change the title and subtitle to a bright red 14-point font.

3. Change axes titles to a bright red font.

4. Make chart bars black, the chart background bright red to match titles, and the axis values bold.

5. Change the bar chart to a column chart.

6. Place the chart on a chart sheet, and if needed, change the alignment of the axis titles to horizontal.

7. Print the chart sheet.

8. Save as *CA16-5E*.

Exercise 5F

Application

1. Key this worksheet and then create a 3-D column chart with a title and legend, and place it on a chart sheet.

THE AMERICAN EAGLE FUND		
INVESTMENT	**MARKET VALUE**	**COST**
Common stocks	$1,954,983	$1,321,964
Long-term bonds	$945,000	$1,004,351
Short-term bonds	$236,982	$212,956
Preferred stocks	$1,345,925	$1,232,007

Online Resources

See Bonus Exercises 6A-6E on Spreadsheets at www.c21key.bonus-exercises.swlearning.com.

2. Add For Period Ending December 31, 20-- as a subtitle; make the bars two different shades of brown, and the background a light green.

3. Decide other formatting features, and then print the chart sheet.

4. Save as CA16-5F.

Communicating for Success

Human Relations—Cultural Diversity

Wherever you work, you will interact with coworkers and customers who differ from you in age, sex, physical ability, and culture. America's workforce is becoming more diverse and its markets more global. One employee skill that employers are on the lookout for is multicultural experience. Companies want employees who are open to other cultures' values and who can work well with people from different cultures.

The chart below appeared in Mitra Toosi's article, "Labor Force Projections to 2012: The Graying of the U.S. Workforce," *Monthly Labor Review Online*, February 2004, Vol. 127, No. 2. (20 April 2005) http://stats.bls.gov/opub/mlr/2004/02/art3exc.htm.

U.S. LABOR FORCE				
Group A	1980	1990	2000	2010
White, non-Hispanic	87.2	85.0	83.2	80.3
Black	10.3	11.1	11.8	12.2
Asian and other	2.5	4.0	5.6	7.5
Group B				
Women	43.3	45.4	46.6	47.5
Men	56.7	54.6	53.4	52.5
Group C				
Hispanic	6.1	8.9	12.4	14.7
Other than Hispanic	93.9	91.1	87.6	85.3

In a group, discuss these questions: What are some implications of the decreasing number of white non-Hispanics in the workplace? of the increasing number of women? Can you explain the slow increase in the percentage of blacks compared to the percentage of Hispanics?

UNIT *17*

LESSONS 1–2
Increasing Worksheet Skills

Conditioning Practice

Before you begin the lessons, key each line twice.

alphabet	1	If Marge has extra help, the jigsaw puzzle can be solved quickly.
fig/sym	2	A & W Co. used P.O. #708-A to buy 125 chairs (#94-63) @ 25 each.
speed	3	The shamrock ornament is an automatic memento for the busy girls.

gwam 1' | 1 | 2 | 3 | 4 | 5 | 6 | 7 | 8 | 9 | 10 | 11 | 12 | 13 |

LESSON ① AUTOFILTER

OBJECTIVE

⊙ To learn to filter a list by using AutoFilter.

Learn: AutoFilter

You can use the AutoFilter feature to display some of the rows of a worksheet. When you filter a list, you hide the rows that contain information you do not want to view. Unlike sorting (which you learned earlier), filtering does not rearrange the rows. Filtering only temporarily hides the rows you do not want to see. For example, if you have a worksheet that contains batting statistics of all players on the team, you can use AutoFilter to hide all but the ten batters with the highest batting averages very quickly. Figure CA17-1 shows a team's ten players with the highest averages when AutoFilter was used to hide the statistics of all other players on the team.

Filters are applied by pointing to Filter on the Data menu and then clicking Auto-Filter. Click the arrow next to the column heading in the column that contains the information you want to filter (see Figure CA17-2) and then make your selection from the options provided.

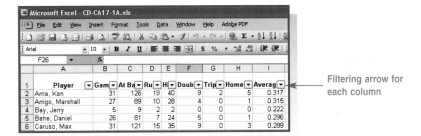

Filtering arrow for each column

Figure CA17-2   Click the Arrow in the Column That Contains the Criteria to Be Filtered

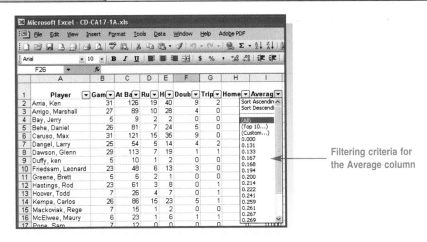

Filtering criteria for the Average column

The options include:

Specific criteria in the list. Click the specific item, e.g., a specific average if you want to display all players hitting at that average.

Top 10 or bottom 10. Click (**Top 10. . .**) if you want the top 10 or bottom 10 items from a column. Use the drop-down lists to make your choices.

Custom criteria. Click (**Custom. . .**) to customize the criteria. For example, to locate players who have played 10 to 20 games, enter the criteria in the Custom AutoFilter dialog box as shown in Figure CA17-3.

A filter can be removed by clicking the arrow next to the column used for the filter and clicking All in the list of filter criteria. The filtering arrow in the columns can be removed by clicking on AutoFilter in the Data menu.

Figure CA17-3   Custom AutoFilter Dialog Box to Filter Players Playing 10 to 20 Games

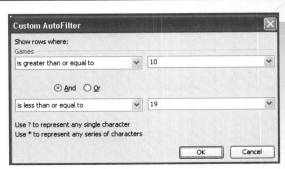

Exercise 1A

Use AutoFilter

1. Read the information about AutoFilter on pages 250 and 251 and then open *CD-CA17-1A*.

2. Use AutoFilter to identify the players who have the top ten batting averages.

3. Save as *CA17-1A-Top*, but do not close the file.

4. Remove the filter.

5. Use AutoFilter to identify the five players who have the least number of At Bats. Save the filtered list as *CA17-1A-Bottom*; do not close the file. Remove the filter.

6. Use AutoFilter to identify the players who have played at least ten games. Save the filtered list as *CA17-1A-Games*; do not close the file. Remove the filter.

7. Use AutoFilter to identify the players whose average is at least .200 but not .300 or higher. Save the filtered list as *CA17-1A-Hitters*. Remove the filter. Close the file.

Exercise 1B

Apply What You Have Learned

1. Open CD-CA17-1B.

2. Filter the Best Round column so only the golfers with scores of 75 or below are displayed. Save this filtered list as *CA17-1B-75*. Remove the filter.

3. Filter the School column so only male golfers from Ford and White Bank are displayed. *Hint:* Filter the Gender column for Male and then the School column for Ford and White Bank.

4. Sort the filtered list so the Best Round scores are arranged in ascending order. Save this filtered and sorted list as *CA17-1B-Sort*. Remove the filters.

5. Filter the columns so only the 12th grade males from Johnson school are displayed. Sort the names in ascending alphabetic order. Save as *CA17-1B-Johnson*. Remove the filters. Close the file.

LESSON 2 — CREATE AND APPLY STYLES

OBJECTIVE

⊙ To learn to create and apply styles.

Learn: Create and Apply Styles

A style is a combination of formatting characteristics, such as font (style, size, color, etc.), alignment, border, and shading that have been named and stored as a set. When the style is applied, all formatting instructions saved in that style are applied at once.

Create a style by selecting Style from the Format menu. In the Style dialog box (see Figure CA17-4), assign a name to the style in the Style name box area. Click the Modify button to display the Format Cells dialog box (see Figure CA17-5). Choose the desired options in the Number, Alignment, Font, Border, Patterns, and/or Protection tabs and then click OK to return to the Style dialog box. Click Add to store the style. Click Close to return to the worksheet.

Figure CA17-4 Style Dialog Box   **Figure CA17-5** Format Cells Dialog Box

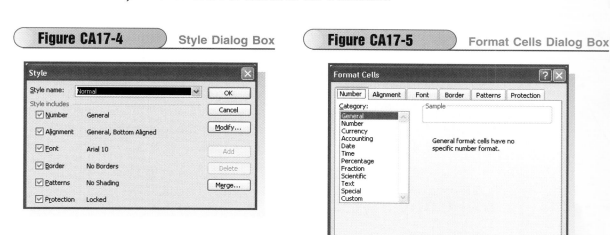

To apply a style that is stored, select the cells you want to format, select Style from the Format menu, select the desired style from the drop down list in the Style name box, and click OK to return to the worksheet (see Figure CA17-6). *Note:* If cells are selected before a style is created, the style will be applied to the selected cells when OK is clicked.

Figure CA17-6 Select a Stored Style from the Style Name Box

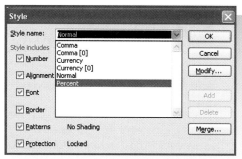

Exercise 2A

Create and Apply a Style

1. Open *CD-CA17-2A*. Read the information above and on the previous page about creating and applying styles.

2. Create a style named **Title** and apply it to row 1. The style should have the following formats: Text centered horizontally and vertically in the

cells; use Arial, Bold, 22 point, and blue for the font; use a thick solid blue line Outline border; and use a 12.5% gray shaded pattern.

3. Create a style named **Subtitle** and apply it to row 2. The style should have the following formats: Text centered horizontally and vertically in the cells; use Arial, Bold Italic, 16 point, and blue for the font; use a thick solid blue line Outline border; and use a 6.25% gray shaded pattern.

4. Create a style named **Heading** and apply it to all cells in row 3. The style should have the following formats: Text centered horizontally and bottom aligned in the cells; use Wrap Text, use Arial, Bold, 10 point, and blue for the font; and use a thick solid blue line Outline border.

5. Create a style named **Total** and apply it to all cells in row 14. The style should have the following formats: Text right and bottom aligned in the cells; use Arial, Bold, 10 point, and blue for the font; and use a thick solid blue line border at the top of the cells.

6. Save the worksheet as *CA17-2A-Payroll* and keep it open.

Learn: Copy Styles

Styles are saved with the workbook where they are created. To use these styles in a different workbook, you must copy them from the workbook where they were created to the other workbook.

To copy styles from one workbook to another:

1. Open the workbook that contains the styles you want to copy.
2. Open the workbook you want the styles copied to.
3. Click the **Format** menu, select **Style**, and then click **Merge**. In the Merge styles from box, click the worksheet that contains the styles you want to copy; then click **OK**.
4. To apply the desired style, select the cells to be formatted; then click the desired style in the Style name list in the Style dialog box. Click **OK**.

Copy and Apply Styles

1. Read the information above about copying styles. Open *CA17-2A-Payroll*, if it is not already open.
2. Open *CD-CA17-2B*.
3. Copy the styles in the *CA17-2A-Payroll* worksheet to the CD-CA17-2B worksheet.
4. Apply the **Title** style to row 1; apply the **Subtitle** style to row 2; apply the **Heading** style to cells in row 3; and apply the **Total** style to row 14.
5. Save *CD-CA17-2B* as *CA17-2B-Payroll* and close *CA17-2A-Payroll*.

Learn: Delete Styles

If desired, you can delete styles that you have created. To delete a style, select Style from the format menu. Select the style to be deleted in the Style name box, and then click Delete. Click OK to return to the worksheet.

Exercise 2C

Delete a Style

1. Read the information about deleting styles. Open *CA17-2B-Payroll*, if it is not already open.
2. Delete the **Total** style.
3. Save as *CA17-2C-Payroll*. Close the file.

Exercise 2D

Apply What You Have Learned

1. Open *CD-CA17-2D* and complete the following steps.
2. Key the information below at the end of the worksheet.

	A	B	C	D	E
1	Locasto	Caroline	1/1/06	Instructor	$36,700
2	McCall	Warren	1/1/06	Instructor	$35,000
3	Perozzi	Louis	1/1/06	Associate	$55,550
4	Ragenman	Vera	1/1/06	Assistant	$37,650
5	Tory	John	6/1/06	Associate	$57,800
6	Wang	Cho	6/1/06	Instructor	$34,500
7	Zalice	Melanie	6/1/06	Instructor	$36,900
8	Cakowski	James	6/1/06	Assistant	$39,600

3. Sort the worksheet in ascending order by last name and then first name.
4. Create a style named **Title** and apply it to row 1. The style should have the following formats: Text centered horizontally and vertically in the row, use Arial Black, 20 point, blue for the font, use a thick solid blue line Outline border, and a light blue shade.
5. Create a style named **Column** and apply it to row 2. The style should have the same formats as the Title style but use a 14-point font.
6. Adjust the widths of the columns to fit the widest entries. Save the worksheet as *CA17-2D-FACULTY*. Do not close the worksheet.
7. Filter the list for the five professors with the highest salaries. Save the filtered list worksheet as *CA17-2D-PROF*. Remove the filters.
8. Filter the list for faculty with salaries from $90,000 up to but not including $100,000. Delete the **Title** and **Column** styles. Center-align rows 1 and 2. Save the filtered list as *CA17-2D-RANGE*.
9. Open *CA17-2D-FACULTY* and sort the faculty by salary (highest to lowest), and then in alphabetic order by last name and then first name.
10. In cell D155, key Total Salary. In cell D156, key Average Salary.
11. In cell E155, compute the total salary for all faculty. In cell E156, compute the average salary for all faculty.
12. Apply the **Column** style to cells D155:E156.
13. Use Page Setup so the worksheet prints with row 2 at the top of each page and with gridlines.
14. Save the file as *CA17-2D-Sort* and close it.

Communication & Math Skills 5

1. Study each of the six rules shown below.

a. Key the *Learn* line(s) beneath each rule, noting how the rule is applied.

b. Key the *Apply* line(s), choosing correct verbs.

Subject/Verb Agreement

Rule 1: Use a singular verb with a singular subject (noun or pronoun); use a plural verb with a plural subject and with a compound subject (two nouns or pronouns joined by and).

Learn	1	The speaker was delayed at the airport for over thirty minutes.
Learn	2	The musicians are all here, and they are getting restless.
Learn	3	You and your assistant are to join us for lunch.
Apply	4	The member of the chorus (is, are) to introduce the speaker.
Apply	5	Dr. Cho (was, were) to give the lecture, but he (is, are) ill.
Apply	6	Mrs. Samoa and her son (is, are) to be at the craft show.

Rule 2: Use the plural verb do not or don't with pronoun subjects I, we, you, and they as well as with plural nouns; use the singular verb does not or doesn't with pronouns he, she, and it as well as with singular nouns.

Learn	7	I do not find this report believable; you don't either.
Learn	8	If she doesn't accept our offer, we don't have to raise it.
Apply	9	They (doesn't, don't) discount, so I (doesn't, don't) shop there.
Apply	10	Jo and he (doesn't, don't) ski; they (doesn't, don't) plan to go.

Rule 3: Use singular verbs with indefinite pronouns (each, every, any, either, neither, one, etc.) and with all and some used as subjects if their modifiers are singular (but use plural verbs with all and some if their modifiers are plural).

Learn	11	Each of these girls has an important role in the class play.
Learn	12	Some of the new paint is already cracking and peeling.
Learn	13	All of the dancers are to be paid for the special performance.
Apply	14	Neither of them (is, are) well enough to sing today.
Apply	15	Some of the juice (is, are) sweet; some (is, are) quite tart.
Apply	16	Every girl and boy (is, are) sure to benefit from this lecture.

Rule 4: Use a singular verb with a singular subject that is separated from the verb by the phrase as well as or in addition to; use a plural verb with a plural subject so separated.

Learn	17	The letter, in addition to the report, has to be revised.
Learn	18	The shirts, as well as the dress, have to be pressed again.
Apply	19	The vocalist, as well as the pianist, (was, were) applauded.
Apply	20	Two managers, in addition to the president, (is, are) to attend.

Rule 5: Use a singular verb if number is used as the subject and is preceded by the; use a plural verb if number is the subject and is preceded by a.

Learn	21	A number of them have already voted, but the number is small.
Apply	22	The number of jobs (is, are) low; a number of us (has, have) applied.

Rule 6: Use a singular verb with singular subjects linked by or or nor, but if one subject is singular and the other is plural, the verb agrees with the nearer subject.

Learn	23	Neither Ms. Moss nor Mr. Katz was invited to speak.
Learn	24	Either the manager or his assistants are to participate.
Apply	25	If neither he nor they (go, goes), either you or she (has, have) to.

2. Key Proofread & Correct, using correct verbs.

  a. Check your answers.

b. Using the rule number at the left of each line, study the rule relating to each error you made.

c. Rekey each incorrect line, using correct verbs.

Proofread & Correct

Rules

1	1	Sandra and Rich (is, are) running for band secretary.
1	2	They (has, have) to score high on the SAT to enter that college.
2	3	You (doesn't, don't) think keyboarding is important.
2	4	Why (doesn't, don't) she take the test for advanced placement?
3	5	Neither of the candidates (meet, meets) the performance criteria.
3	6	One of your art students (is, are) likely to win the prize.
5	7	The number of people against the proposal (is, are) quite small.
4	8	The manager, as well as his assistant, (is, are) to attend.
6	9	Neither the teacher nor her students (is, are) here.
3	10	All the meat (is, are) spoiled, but some items (is, are) okay.

3. Save as *CS5-ACT1*.

ACTIVITY 2   Reading

1. Open *CD-CS5-ACT2*.
2. Read the document; close the file.

3. Key answers to the questions below, using complete sentences.

4. Save as *CS5-ACT2*.

1. What kinds of positions are being filled?
2. What is the minimum number of hours each employee must work each week?
3. Is weekend work available?
4. What kind of service is being offered to those who have to care for elderly people?
5. Is the pay based solely on performance?
6. When are the openings available?
7. Does everyone work during the day?
8. How can you submit a resume?

ACTIVITY 3   Composing

1. Study the quotations below. Consider the relationship between honesty and truth.
2. Compose a paragraph to show your understanding of honesty and truth.

3. Compose a second paragraph to describe an incident in which honesty and truth *should* prevail but don't in real life.

4. Proofread, revise, and correct.
5. Save as *CS5-ACT3*.

Honesty's the best policy.
--Cervantes

Piety requires us to honor truth above our friends.
--Aristotle

To be honest . . . here is a task for all that a man has of fortitude.
--Robert Louis Stevenson

The dignity of truth is lost with protesting.
--Ben Jonson

ACTIVITY 4   Math: Finding What Percent One Number Is of Another

1. Open *CD-CS5-ACT4* and print the file.

2. Solve the problems as directed in the file.

3. Submit your answers.

UNIT 18

LESSONS 1–6
Using Desktop Publishing

Conditioning Practice

Before you begin the lessons, key each line twice.

alphabet	1	Zack told Peg to be quiet and enjoy the first extra cowboy movie.
fig/sym	2	Ho's expenses are taxi--$59; airline--$260; car--$37 (148 miles).
speed	3	Claudia is to land the giant dirigible by the busy downtown mall.

gwam | 1' | 1 | 2 | 3 | 4 | 5 | 6 | 7 | 8 | 9 | 10 | 11 | 12 | 13 |

LESSON 1 DEVELOP DESKTOP PUBLISHING SKILLS

OBJECTIVES

 To use word art, 3-D effects, text boxes, Auto Shapes, shaded paragraphs, drop caps, and the Columns feature.

 To learn to wrap text around graphics, justify text, and insert watermarks.

Learn: Word Art

word art gallery

You can change text into a graphic object by using word art. Most word processors have a **word art gallery** that contains predefined styles such as curved and stretched text as shown in Figure CA18-1. After you choose a style, the word art is inserted into your document as an object that you can edit by using a Drawing toolbar. Use the toolbar to change the object's color, size, alignment, shape, direction, or spacing. You can also select how text is to be wrapped around the object or select another style. See Figure CA18-1.

Figure CA18-1 Word Art

Exercise 1A

Word Art

1. Read the information about word art.

2. Open a new document and use word art to insert your first and last name across the top of the page. Center-align your name; size, shape, and format it as you want.

3. In the same document, use word art to insert the name of your school or school mascot across the bottom of the page. Center the text; size, shape, and format it as you want, using one or more of your school colors.

4. Save as *CA18-1A*.

Learn: 3-D Effects

You can also enhance word art by applying 3-D effects to it. See the illustration of word art with 3-D effects shown in Figure CA18-2.

Figure CA18-2 3-D Effects

Exercise 1B

3-D Effects

1. Read the information above about 3-D effects.

2. Open a new document. Use word art to insert your first and last name near the center of the page.

3. Use the Word Art toolbar to format your name as you wish.

4. Choose a 3-D effect and apply it to your name.

5. Save as *CA18-1B*.

Learn: Text Boxes

Text boxes are frequently used for labels or callouts in a document. Once a text box is inserted in a document, you can format, resize, and move it as you would a graphic object.

You can change the border style or delete the border. Text that is keyed within the text box can be formatted just as regular text is formatted. (See Figure CA18-3.)

Figure CA18-3 Text Box

This is a shaded text box that illustrates reverse type (white letters on dark background).

Text Boxes

1. Read about text boxes on the previous page.

2. Open a new document. Insert a text box that is about 1" high x 2" wide and is horizontally centered near the top margin of the page. Key the following information in the text box, using 12-point Arial italicized font, and then resize the text box to fit the text.

This text box uses Arial 12-point italicized font for the letters.

3. Near the vertical center of the page, horizontally center a second text box that is about 1" high x 2" wide. Shade the text box with a dark color and remove the border. Using center alignment and white 12-point Arial font, key the following copy in the text box. Resize the text box to fit the text.

This is centered text in a shaded text box that has no border.

4. Near the bottom of the page, insert a text box and key your first and last name, your school name, and the date inside the box on three lines. Format the text box and text as you choose.

5. Save as *CA18-1C*.

Learn: Auto Shapes

Word processors have a variety of shapes (stars, banners, callouts, arrows, circles, boxes, flowchart symbols, etc.) that you can add to a document. Once added, these shapes can be manipulated and formatted like other graphic objects. Figure CA18-4 shows a star that has been inserted, sized, shaped, and shaded. Text has been added, and the outside border and text have been colored blue.

Figure CA18-4   Auto Shapes

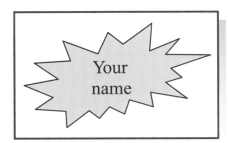

Exercise 1D
Auto Shapes

1. Read about auto shapes.

2. Open a new document. Select a star shape from those available with your software. Make the star approximately 4" wide, center it on the page, and insert your name using a large, bold font for the text. Save as *CA18-1D-A*.

3. Open a new document. Select a shape of your choice from those available with your software. Size it appropriately, key your school name as text, shade the object, remove its border, and make other formatting changes you think appropriate. Save as *CA18-1D-B*.

Learn: Shaded Paragraphs

Like objects, paragraphs can be shaded to focus the reader's attention on their contents. The illustration below shows a shaded paragraph.

> This is an example of a paragraph that has been shaded. Readers are more apt to pay attention to its contents.

Exercise 1E
Shaded Paragraphs

1. Open *CD-CA18-1E*. Read about shaded paragraphs above.

2. Using light colors, shade each paragraph differently.

3. Save as *CA18-1E*.

Learn: Wrapping Text Around Graphics

You can choose how text is to appear near a graphic. Text near a graphic object can be wrapped (positioned) so it is above and below the object only, surrounds the object, or appears to be keyed behind or in front of the object.

In this example, the word processing operator has selected the option that places the text around the object. Other options are available and can be tried to give the desired result.

Exercise 1F
Wrap Text Around Graphics

1. Open *CD-CA18-1E*. Read about wrapping text above.

2. Choose a shape or clip art image (approx 1" high) to insert in the middle of each paragraph. Wrap the text tightly around the object in the first paragraph; above and below the object in the second paragraph; and squarely around the object in the third paragraph.

3. Save as *CA18-1F*.

Learn: Justify

Throughout earlier activities, you have center-, left-, and right-aligned text. Another way to align text is to **justify** (or **full justify**) it. When text is justified, the left and right margins are aligned evenly. The word processing software inserts extra spaces between words so that each line ends even with the right margin.

This and the preceding paragraph are justified—the text is aligned at both the left and right margins (except for the last line of the paragraph). Justified text is used in newspaper-style columns to make reading easier.

Exercise 1G
Justify

1. Open *CD-CA18-1E*. Read the above information about justifying text.
2. Justify the text in each of the three paragraphs.
3. Save as *CA18-1G*.

Learn: Drop Cap

You can format paragraphs to begin with a large initial capital letter that takes up one or more vertical lines of regular text. Drop caps are objects that can be formatted and sized. Two drop cap formats are usually available. One capitalizes the first letter of the first word in the paragraph with a large dropped capital letter and then wraps the text around the drop cap. The second creates a dropped capital letter, but places it in the margin beginning at the first line.

Exercise 1H
Drop Cap

1. Open *CD-CA18-1H*. Read about drop caps above.
2. Format paragraph 1 with a drop cap with text wrapped around it.
3. Format paragraph 2 with a drop cap that is placed in the left margin.
4. Format paragraph 3 the same as paragraph 1, but drop the cap only two lines and change the cap to Arial font.
5. Save as *CA18-1H*.

Learn: Columns

Except for tables, the documents you have created have had a single column of text that extended from the left margin to the right margin.

Multiple-column documents, such as pamphlets, leaflets, brochures, and newsletters, use the Columns feature to divide a document into two or more vertical columns that are placed side by side on a page. The columns may be of equal or unequal width.

As you key, text fills the length of a column before moving to the next column to the right.

Exercise 11

Columns

1. Read the information about columns.

2. Key the text below using a 4" top margin, 4" bottom margin, and three columns of equal width.

CAREER FAIR

The Annual Career Fair will be held May 15 from 9 a.m. to 12:30 p.m. in Gymnasium A. A list of the 20 employers who will attend will be published next week. The employers represent many different areas that hire scientists, technicians, and engineers within the environmental field. Therefore, there will be a variety of career opportunities for our students to explore.

All junior and senior students are urged to attend and speak to as many of the employers as possible. To ensure that students speak to many employers, they will need to obtain signatures of the employers they visit and give the signatures to the Career Fair Coordinator when they leave the gymnasium.

It is important that students dress and act appropriately during the Career Fair. Standard or casual business dress is suggested. Students should have up-to-date resumes to distribute. Also, students should use correct grammar and speak clearly without using slang to improve their chances of making a favorable first impression.

---

3. Save as *CA18-1I.*

Learn: Changing the Number and Width of Columns

The number and width of columns can be changed using the Columns feature. The changes can be made before or after keying the text, and both the number and width of columns can vary on a page. Typically, you can select from several preset formats, or you can design a specific format you need.

Exercise 1J

Changing the Number and Width of Columns

1. Read the above information about changing the number and widths of columns.

2. Open *CA18-1I* used in the last exercise and reformat the text into two columns of equal width. Save as *CA18-1J-A.*

3. Reformat *CA18-1J-A* by deleting the last sentence, centering the title in a single column, and formatting the text into three columns of equal width below the title. Save as *CA18-1J-B.*

Learn: Balancing Column Lengths

Oftentimes, columns need to be balanced (equal or nearly equal in length). The desired balance can be achieved by inserting column breaks as needed.

Exercise 1K
Balanced Column Lengths

1. Read about balancing column widths above.
2. Open *CD-CA18-1K* and reformat the document into two columns of equal width.
3. Balance the columns so they are equal in length. Save as *CA18-1K-A*.
4. Reformat *CA18-1K-A* into a three-column document with balanced length, making certain to leave no widow/orphan lines. Save as *CA18-1K-B*.

Learn: Inserting Vertical Lines Between Columns

If desired, vertical lines can be placed between columns to enhance the appearance of the document. The lines can be inserted before or after keying the document.

Exercise 1L
Vertical Lines Between Columns

1. Read about vertical lines above.
2. Open *CA18-1J-B* and add vertical lines between the columns. Save as *CA18-1L-A*.
3. Reformat *CA18-1J-B* using two columns of unequal width with a vertical line between the columns. Use hyphenation. Save as *CA18-1L-B*.

Learn: Watermarks

A watermark is any text or graphic that, when printed, appears in light print behind the document's text. For example, your school's mascot may appear as a watermark on the school newspaper or stationery. A watermark stating *draft* or *confidential* is often added to letters or memos.

Exercise 1M
Watermarks

1. Read about watermarks above.
2. Open *CA18-1L-A* and add the word **CONFIDENTIAL** as a diagonal watermark.
3. Save as *CA18-1M*.

⊙ To learn document design principles.
⊙ To prepare one-column flyers using shapes, word art, 3-D effects, and text boxes.

Learn: Document Design Principles

Beginning with this lesson, you will use desktop publishing to design documents. You will have many opportunities to use advanced word processing features to format several kinds of documents. You can give your documents a professional appearance and make them easy to read and understand by following these basic document design guidelines.

Font size. Use 12-point font size for most of the text in a document since it is a notably readable size, preferred by most readers. A font that is too small strains the reader's eye and makes the document look crammed and difficult to read. A font that is too large uses more space than is necessary and causes readers to read slowly (letter by letter rather than whole words and phrases). Headlines, headings, titles, etc. in printed items such as flyers, posters, announcements, brochures, advertisements, and newsletters may be in a large font to capture the reader's attention.

Fonts. Use one font (Arial, Times New Roman, Comic Sans MS, etc.) in a document. The variety of sizes and the available variations (styles and effects) within the font provide for sufficient emphasis and contrast.

Underlining and ALL CAPS. Use **bold**, *italic*, and variations in font size rather than underlining and ALL CAPS to emphasize text. Underlining and ALL CAPS, especially in large blocks of text, can make words harder to read.

Typographic elements. Use boxes, borders, bullets, special characters, etc. in consistent styles and sizes throughout a document to improve overall appearance.

Lists. Use numbers and/or letters in outlines to show different levels and when sequencing, cross-referencing, and quantity are important. If listing alone is the goal, bullets (or appropriate special characters) are sufficient.

Side margins. Use margins of 1" to 2". Long lines tend to tire the eye quickly, and short lines cause the eye to jump back and forth too often. The use of a few long or short lines in a document is not likely to cause readers problems, however.

Justification. With normal-length lines, use a ragged right margin. Varying the line endings of normal-length lines is easier to read than justified text, where the lines end evenly and there is inconsistent spacing between words. Justified text is permissible in documents like newsletters that use shorter-length lines in narrow columns.

White space. Use white space in the margins to keep a document from looking crowded. Use white space between document parts to inform the reader where one part ends and another part begins.

Emphasis. Use **bold**, *italic*, and effects (<u>underlining</u>, shadow, outline, emboss, engrave, SMALL CAPS, etc.) in small amounts to call attention to some parts of a document. Avoid overusing one technique or using too many different techniques in a document. When too many parts of a document are emphasized, no one part will seem especially important. When too many different techniques are used, the document will appear cluttered.

Color. Use color to enhance the message or appearance of the document. Generally, use dark shades of color for font and lighter shades of color for highlights and fills. Select contrasting font colors to improve readability when different colors are used near each other.

Graphics. Place graphics (clip art, pictures, charts, shapes, text boxes, etc.) near the text they enhance or as close as possible to their references in the text. Keep the size of the graphic in proportion to the text, column width, and space available.

Exercise 2A

Flyer 1

1. Read the document design principles above and on the previous page.
2. Using the information below, prepare a one-page flyer, using word art, 3-D effects, small caps, shaded text boxes, and auto shapes. You decide the size, shape, color, and placement of all information.

5K Run or Walk

Join RT Alumni
on
Saturday, August 14, 20--
at 9 a.m.
in East Park

$12 ENTRANCE FEE INCLUDES T-SHIRT, PRIZES, AND REFRESHMENTS
CALL (422) 555-0192 TO REGISTER

PRIZES WILL BE AWARDED TO TOP THREE MEN AND WOMEN FINISHERS IN THREE AGE GROUPS

See our website at <u>http:www. pphs org/5k</u>

3. Save as *CA18-2A*.

Exercise   2B

Flyer 2

1. Using the information below, design a flyer, using word art, 3-D effects, shaded text boxes, and auto shapes. You decide all other formatting features.

Event:	The Dangers of Drinking and Driving
Sponsored by:	Students Against DUI
When:	Friday, May 3, at 3:30 p.m.
Where:	Gymnasium B, Welton High School
Cost:	Free admission with school ID card
Guest speaker:	Sgt. Terry Hollinsworth State Trooper Welton South Barracks
Main feature:	Students will use a simulator to observe the effects of DUI.

2. Save as *CA18-2B*.

Exercise   2C

Flyer 3

1. Using the information below, design a flyer, including an excuse form as part of the flyer. You decide all formatting features.

Sponsoring instructor:	Mrs. Porterfield
When:	Wednesday, October 3, Periods 1, 2, 5, 6, and 7
Where:	Classroom 222
Guest speaker:	Dr. Ida Meinert Nutritionist, Blair Hospital
Topic:	Recognizing Eating Disorders
Excuse form:	Space for student's name, name and period of the class to be missed, name of teacher whose class will be missed, and signature of teacher granting permission.

2. Save as *CA18-2C*.

Flyer 4

1. Using the information below, design a flyer your instructor can use to inform others of the value of the course in which you are using this textbook. You decide all formatting features.

---

1. Key the name of the course.

2. Identify some course activities you enjoy.

3. Describe the important things you have learned.

4. Specify reasons why others should take this course.

5. Identify the hardware and software that you use.

6. Explain how this course helps you in other classes or at work.

---

2. Save as *CA18-2C*.

LESSON 3 CREATE COLUMN DOCUMENTS

OBJECTIVE ⊙ To prepare documents using columns, text boxes, shaded paragraphs, justified lines, and drop caps.

Exercise **3A**

Announcement

1. Key the text below, formatting it into two columns of equal width.

Calendar of Events
Week of February 2

Monday, February 2
FUNDAMENTALS OF PRESENTATION SOFTWARE (Repeated on Wednesday)
9-10 a.m., Room 609
Participants learn to make overhead transparencies, speaker's notes, and handouts using Adam Pro View.

RECRUITING TOP-NOTCH TALENT
12 noon-3:30 p.m., Room 1543
Recruiting strategy session covers the hospital's latest methods for attracting top-notch applicants.

(continued on next page)

Westbrook Chamber of Commerce Meeting
1-2:30 p.m., Executive Dining Room, 6th Floor
Westbrook Hospital is hosting this luncheon to announce the renovation project and explain its impact on local business and industry.

Tuesday, February 3

Intranet Technology
4:30-5:30 p.m., Room 610
Gives employees hands-on training in using Westbrook's intranet to improve communications and work flow.

Fundamentals of Adam Word Eze
5-7 p.m., Room 609
Participants learn to prepare documents that include graphics, clip art, text boxes, and shading, using Adam Word Eze.

Wednesday, February 4

Fundamentals of Presentation Software (Repeat from Monday)
9-11 a.m., Room 609
Participants learn to make overhead transparencies, speaker's notes, and handouts using Adam Pro View.

Health Resources on the Web (Repeated on Thursday)
3:30-5 p.m., Room 610
Provides an overview of quality health resources on the Internet and how to locate them by using Westbrook Hospital's Library System Web page.

Thursday, February 5

Calculating and Charting with Spreadsheet Software
1-3 p.m., Room 609
Participants learn to use formulas and charts using Adam Data Pro software.

Health Resources on the Web (Repeat from Wednesday)
3:30-5 p.m., Room 610
Provides an overview of quality health resources on the Internet and how to locate them by using Westbrook Hospital's Library System Web page.

2. Insert appropriate clip art at the top of the first column. Make it about 1" high and surround it with a border.

3. Center the title and subtitle in the first column using a 20-point bold font.

4. Using light gray, shade each day and date.

5. Format the names of events as shown (small caps, bold). Single-space them and double-space between events and above and below the dates.

6. Use a two-line drop cap for the first word in each course description.

7. Justify and hyphenate text.

8. Save as *CA18-3A*.

1. Key the two articles below, formatting them in three equal-width columns.

Basic Life Support Renewal Courses

The School of Nursing at North Hills Hospital will hold its annual basic life support (BLS) renewal courses in March. The courses are open to all staff.

Staff members whose jobs require them to hold a valid BLS completion card must attend a renewal course every two years, according to American Heart Association guidelines. Heart Saver Plus (adult) and Health Care Provider (adult, infant, and child) BLS renewal courses will be offered.

Renewal courses will be held Monday through Friday, March 15 through March 19, and March 22 through March 26, from 7 a.m. to 8 p.m. Renewal courses also will be held Saturday, March 20, from 7 a.m. to 2 p.m. All courses will be held in Wilkins Hall, Room 135.

Staff should allow 60 to 90 minutes to complete the renewal course. To receive a BLS renewal, staff will be required to complete a written test and demonstrate their BLS skills. The renewal course is open to anyone who is due to take a renewal course, even if it is not required for his or her job.

Science Judges Sought

An additional 25 judges with expertise in science and an interest in children are needed for the 61st annual North Hills Science and Engineering Fair. The competition will be held from 8 a.m. to 1 p.m. March 31 at the North Hills Science Center.

Jeffrey Sidora, science fair coordinator, said 60 judges are needed to examine exhibits created by 150 students from 6 area schools. The judges should have technical backgrounds, such as master's degrees in biology, chemistry, physics, computer science, mathematics, engineering, robotics, medicine, microbiology, earth science, or environment.

The judges have to be willing to make a time commitment from 8 a.m. to 1 p.m. Lunch will be provided. At the fair, students in grades 6 through 12 compete for the best science and engineering projects in their age brackets.

2. Use 16-point bold for titles.
3. Shade the second paragraph in the first article, using light gray.
4. Insert the text box and tip shown on the following page between the articles. Format the text box without a border and use reverse type.

5. Justify and hyphenate the text.

6. Save as *CA18-3B*.

LESSON 4 CREATE NEWSLETTERS

OBJECTIVE

> To prepare a document with balanced columns, a different number of columns on a page, and a watermark.

Exercise 4A

Newsletter

1. Format the text below with two equal columns, using these formatting guidelines:

   a. Single-space paragraphs and double-space between paragraphs.

   b. Use 12-point font for the body of the newsletter.

   c. Place title and publication information so they span both columns.

   d. Use word art to create the title; use a 10-point font for the publication information.

   e. Change the paragraph indent (tab stop) to 0.25". Justify and hyphenate the text.

   f. Single-space the *Patient Praises* in an unshaded text box; double-space between comments.

   g. Add shading to the paragraph headings.

   h. Place a **DRAFT** watermark behind the columns.

   i. Balance the columns on the last page, if needed.

WHAT'S UP!

Vol. 6, No. 6   June, 20--

Satisfaction Survey Established

Upton General Hospital has established patient satisfaction as a major organizational goal and is committed to establishing a hospital-wide patient satisfaction survey. Patient satisfaction is recognized as a critical business issue and is a mechanism to demonstrate high-quality care and service to employers, insurers, and the community. "Patient satisfaction surveying is an important tool to help us learn more about our patients' expectations," said Freda Banks, RN, DNS, vice president, Nursing. "By understanding their needs better, we can deliver care in ways that are more satisfying to them."

(continued on next page)

The first phase of the patient satisfaction survey process will be implemented in July. Patients in the burn center, in-patient surgery, emergency, and same-day surgery will be surveyed. Preliminary results will be reported to the board of directors and corporate officers at the August board meeting, and then distributed to department heads.

Upton Says Thanks

Upton says thanks to all the steering committee members for their hard work in preparing for and hosting the on-site review by the Joint Review Committee on Accreditation of Healthcare Providers (JRCAHP). All steering committee and subcommittee members are asked to stop by the Arcadia Dining Room between 11 a.m. and 2 p.m. on Friday, June 25, to enjoy soup and salad and discuss the team's oral exit report. Night-shift staff can enjoy bagels and coffee and a similar discussion in the Main Dining Room from 2 a.m. to 3 a.m. on Saturday, June 26. Watch *What's Up!* for the JRCAHP findings.

New Requirements for Ordering CT Scans

Due to recent changes in third-party payer requirements, referring physicians are advised to request all necessary imaging studies when placing orders with the Radiology Department. Radiologists cannot extend the examination coverage or add additional studies.

The abdominal computed tomography (CT) scan is a common order affected by the recent changes. In the past, inclusion of the pelvic region in an abdominal CT scan was common. However, now it is necessary to specifically order an abdomen and pelvis examination if an image of the pelvic region is deemed necessary.

For more information about the new requirements, contact Stephen Antoncic, MD, director, Radiology Department, at Extension 3512 or antoncic@upton.com.

What's Up! with Our Colleagues

Michelle Glatzko, Central Service, presented "Isolation Carts and Universal Precautions as Related to Central Service Technicians" at the fall conference of the Tri-County Central Service Association and was elected secretary.

Maurice Tarli, volunteer coordinator, was elected secretary of the board, Society of Directors of Volunteer Services, Western chapter.

Two staff members, Larry Szerbin, RN, and Ann Tokar, RN, received degrees. Larry completed a bachelor of science in business administration degree with a major in nursing management from Lynn College. Ann earned a master of science degree in long-term health care from Upton University.

Investment Performance

If you participate in the Upton Retirement Program or Supplemental Retirement Annuity plans, daily balances of your accounts can be obtained via the Internet. All you need to do is visit http://www.hiaa.com and establish a PIN. With your social security number and your PIN, you can obtain end-of-day balances at any time. You no longer need to wait for the quarterly reports to see how your money is growing.

Farewell, Rudy

A retirement tea will be held for Rudy Beissel, Environmental Support Services, on Thursday, June 24, from 1:30 p.m. to 3 p.m. in the Jones Conference Center. Rudy is retiring after 35 years with Upton.

Career Track

Lorretta Slobodnick recently was named as an administrative assistant, Medical Records. She reports to Erika Cooper, head, Medical Records. Lorretta earned her associate degree from Upton County Community College and specialized in medical technology. Please welcome her at Extension 1505 or slobodni@upton.com.

Patient Praises

To Susan Getty, nurse: "Thank you for the compassionate and knowledgeable care."—a stroke patient

"Thanks to all who helped nurse me back to health!" —a Unit 15D patient

To Jill Holt, nurse: "Thanks, thanks, thanks! Your skill is appreciated." —a new mom

---

2. Save as *CA18-4A*.

OBJECTIVES
> To prepare a newsletter with three columns.
> To use shaded text boxes with and without borders, word art, clip art, vertical lines, 3-D effects, drop caps, and balanced columns.

Exercise 5A

Newsletter 1 (from Rough Draft)

1. Format the two articles below as a newsletter, using these formatting guidelines:

    a. Arrange in three columns of equal width with vertical lines separating the columns.

    b. The title and publication information should span the columns and be formatted appropriately.

    c. Correct all errors.

    d. Format article headings in a large font size. Use 11-point font for the article copy. Double-space above and below article titles and text boxes.

    e. Use a two-line drop cap for the first word in each article.

    f. Use shaded text boxes with borders as shown below.

    g. Hyphenate and justify the columns.

2. You decide other formatting features.

STRATEGIES FOR SUCCESS
Vol. 6, No. 3 Spring, 20--

Reputation and Choice

Reputation is the image people have of your standards of conduct--your ethical and moral principals. Most people think that a good reputation is needed to succeed in any job; and it is, therefore, one of the most importnat personal assetts you can acquire in your life.

> A bad reputation can result from one misdeed.

A good reputation is a valued asset that requires time, effort, and discipline to develop and projfect. A bad reputation can be a longterm liability established in a short time. It can be a result from just one misdeed and can be a heavay burden to carry throughout life.

It is very important to realize, therefore, that most of youhave an opportunity to develope and protect the reputation you want. You have many

choices tomake that will destroy or enhance the image you want to extnded. The choices are hard; and honestly, loyalty, and dedicatoin are most often involved.

> Choices you make destroy or enhance your reputation.

Learnig About People

Many aspects of a job present challenges to those who strive to do their best in all they do. One of The most critical

(continued on next page)

challenge**s** all workers face is being able to relate we**ll** to the many individuals with whom they ~~have to~~ work. It is common for workers to have dail**y** dealings with bosses, peers, and subordinates. Also, **most** workers will interact with telephone callers and visitors from outside and inside the company **daily**.

> Relating well to others is a critical challenge.

While it is critical to learn all you can about your job and company, it is often just as c**ri**tical to learn about the people with whom you ~~will~~ work and interact. Frequently**,** you can rely upon experienced workers for information that will help you analyze the formal and informal structures of the organization. What you learn may help you determine what an employer expects**, and** likes, or dislikes, and will help you make a good adjustment to your workplace.

> Learn from experienced workers.

3. Save as *CA18-5A*.

Exercise 5B

Newsletter 2

1. Open *CA18-5A* and insert the text below as a third article. Use **Business Ethics** as the article title.

Ethics is a popular topic today. Many businesses that had written codes for ethical practice years ago set them aside and are now going back to them.

The main purpose of a code of ethics is to convey a company's values and business standards to all its workers. An organization is ethical to the extent that each person in it subscribes to and applies the standards. Far more than a list of do's and don'ts for office employees, ethics cuts across all lines of an organization. It involves how coworkers treat one another as well as how current and future customers, suppliers, and the general public are treated by the business.

Every job has an ethical aspect, and every person has values. When an individual's standards are in sync with the employer's, the situation is generally positive for both. If either of them is inclined to "take shortcuts" or "look the other way" now and then, an unhappy employer-employee relationship is likely to develop.

2. Reformat the three columns into two columns.

3. Insert a small graphic relating to people in article 2 and wrap the text around it.

4. Insert the following text box before the last paragraph.

> A code of ethics conveys a company's values and business standards.

5. Reformat all text boxes with reverse type and no borders.

6. Use word art and 3-D effects to redesign the newsletter title.

7. Use hyphenation and justify.

8. Balance columns as needed.

9. Save as *CA18-5B*.

LESSON 6 CREATE ADVERTISEMENTS AND BOOKLETS

OBJECTIVE

⊘ To prepare a four-page program booklet and a one-page advertisement.

Exercise 6A

Advertisement

1. Create a one-page advertisement for a product of your choice, including the following:

   a. Name of the club or business selling the product.

   b. At least three features or advantages of the product.

   c. Where the product can be purchased.

   d. An object that illustrates the product as much as possible.

   e. Word art, auto shapes, clip art, 3-D effects, shading, color, borders, and/or text boxes as desired.

2. Save as *CA18-6A*.

Program Booklet

1. Prepare a program booklet for the High School Honor Society Induction Ceremony, using the following formatting directions.

2. The brochure will be formatted on *two pages*, using 8.5" x 11" paper in landscape orientation (see illustration below):

   • **Page 1** will have the text for the outside back and front covers.

   • **Page 2** will have the text for the inside left page and the inside right page.

Page 1	**Page 2**

Outside Back Cover (5.5" × 8.5")	**Outside Front Cover** (5.5" × 8.5")	**Inside Left Page** (5.5" × 8.5")	**Inside Right Page** (5.5" × 8.5")

One 8.5" × 11" paper in landscape orientation	**One 8.5" × 11" paper in landscape orientation**

3. Set left, right, top, and bottom margins on both pages at 0.5".

4. Select landscape orientation and two pages per sheet.

5. Set columns as follows:

   a. **Outside Back Cover:** two columns, each 2" wide, with 0.5" between them.

   b. **Outside Front Cover:** one 4.5" column.

   c. **Inside Left Page:** one 4.5" column.

   d. **Inside Right Page:** two columns, each 2" wide with 0.5" between them.

6. Key the information that is given for the covers and pages shown on the following page. You decide all other formatting features and graphics that will be inserted.

Outside Back Cover:

a. Key SENIOR MEMBERS as a title that spans both columns.

b. Insert the senior members' names from *CD-CA18-6B* (balance the names in two columns).

Online Resources

See Bonus Exercises 7A and 7B on Creating Advertisements and Newsletters at www.c21key.bonus-exercises.swlearning.com.

Outside Front Cover:

a. Arrange the following information attractively: High School Honor Society, Induction Ceremony, Laurel High School, December 15, 20--, 6:30 p.m.

b. Insert this text in a shaded text box or auto shape:

> **The High School Honor Society inducts students who have achieved academic excellence, displayed good character, demonstrated leadership qualities, and served the school and community.**

Inside Left Page:

After keying the title PROGRAM, insert this information, using dot leaders:

Welcome . . . . Rob Jansante, President
Opening Remarks . . . . Dr. Paul Henry, Principal
Speaker. . . . . Dr. Helen Rapp, Laurel Community College
Induction Ceremony
    Scholarship . . . . Matt Roman, Vice President
    Character. . . . . Jessica Roman, Treasurer
    Leadership . . . . Stephanie Davis, Secretary
    Service . . . . Meghan Johnson, Historian
Pledge . . . . Rob Jansante
Presentation of Certificates . . Rob Jansante and Dr. Paul Henry
Closing . . . . Rob Jansante

All members and guests are invited to a reception in the Library immediately following the Induction Ceremony.

Inside Right Page:

1. Key INDUCTEES as a title that spans both columns.

2. Insert the names of the inductees from *CD-CA18-6B* (balance the names in two columns). Use 1.5 line spacing.

7. Save page 1 as *CA18-6B-P1* and page 2 as *CA18-6B-P2*.

INTERNET ACTIVITY

1. Access the United States Environmental Protection Agency (EPA) website via http://www.c21key.swlearning.com/plus/links.html.

2. Click the link that gives basic information **About EPA** and follow at least one link of interest to you. Then write, using keyboard or speech recognition software, a brief paragraph describing what you have learned.

3. Click on the home page link to **Educational Resources**, select **High School**, and follow at least one link of interest to you. Then key one or more paragraphs describing what you have learned. Print one page from the EPA website relating to the paragraph(s) you wrote.

UNIT 19

Processing Business Correspondence

Conditioning Practice

Before you begin the lessons, key each line twice.

alphabet	1	Avoid fizzling fireworks because they just might explode quickly.
fig/sym	2	He surveyed 3,657 women, 2,980 men, and 1,400 children last June.
speed	3	It may be a big problem if both of the men bid for the dock work.

gwam 1' | 1 | 2 | 3 | 4 | 5 | 6 | 7 | 8 | 9 | 10 | 11 | 12 | 13 |

LESSON ① PROCESS BUSINESS CORRESPONDENCE

OBJECTIVES

> To review block and modified block letter and memo formats.
> To review open and mixed punctuation and basic letter and memo parts.

Exercise 1A

Business Letters and Memos

1. Format the following memo. Add any memo parts that may be missing, correct the marked errors, and find and correct the five embedded errors.

TO: Olu T. Sangoeyhi, Physical Therapy
FROM: William M. Glause, Administrative Services
DATE: May 14, 20-- *Change this and all other occurrences of "brochure" to "pamphlet."*
SUBJECT: PHYSICAL THERAPY BROCHURE

Here is the first draft of the physical theraphy brochure that
has been ~~okayed~~ *authorized* for publication in this years budget. Please ~~check~~ *proofread*
the copy ~~very~~ carefully *and make sure the pictures are correct.*

(continued on next page)

The public relations staff is in the process of getting permission to use each persons picture in the brochure. All permision forms should be completed within the next ⟨10⟩ *sp* days. If there are ~~any~~ changes in the pictures~~, we are using~~, I will see that you get to review ~~all the~~ changes before we go to printing. *new pictures.*

mark your suggested
Please ∧make ~~the necessary~~ changes ~~in the copy~~ and retrun the brochure to me by next Monday.

Enclosure

2. Save as *CA19-1A*.

Exercise 1B

Document 2 (Letter)

1. Create the letter below using block format, open punctuation, and Arial font, 14 point.

> (Current date) | Mr. Max R. Rice | 23 Oak Street | Schiller Park, IL 60176-6932 | Dear Mr. Rice
>
> If the health plan you chose last year has not delivered everything you thought it would, we have some good news for you. Health Plus is now available to you during this open enrollment period.
>
> Health Plus is the area's largest point-of-service plan that combines the managed care features of an HMO with the freedom of choice of a traditional health plan. As the enclosed directory indicates, this plan gives you access to the best doctors and medical facilities in the area.
>
> To enroll, simply complete the enclosed application and return it to your benefits office within 30 days.
>
> Sincerely | Ms. Peg Jerzak | Account Specialist | xx | Enclosure

2. Save as *CA19-1B*.

Exercise 1C

Document 3 (Letter)

1. Format Document 2 (*CA19-1B*) in modified block with open punctuation and no paragraph indentations. Use Times New Roman font, 15 point.

2. Save as *CA19-1C*.

Document 4 (Letter)

1. Create the letter below using modified block format with mixed punctuation and paragraph indentations. Use Century Gothic font, 12 point.

October 2, 20-- | Ms. Paula Kenney | Sterling Medical Supplies | 4259 Rosegarden Road | Long Beach, CA 98766-4259 | Dear Ms. Kenney

Please accept this invitation to participate in East High's Fifth Annual Health Occupations Career Fair that will be held on Thursday, November 17, from 2 to 4 p.m. at East High.

Last year's career fair attracted 26 employers and associations and more than 400 students. The employers represented hospitals, long-term health-care providers, outpatient clinics, medical insurance providers, medical supply and equipment vendors, and large physician practices. In addition, several associations attended to provide students with career information related to the technical areas.

To reserve a table for your company, please fill out and return the enclosed registration form by November 1. We look forward to having you present.

Sincerely | Lawrence R. Aamont | Health Occupations | xx | Enclosure

---

2. Save as *CA19-1D*.

Document 5 (Letter)

1. Format Document 4 (*CA19-1D*) in block format with mixed punctuation. Use Courier New font, 12 point.
2. Save as *CA19-1E*.

Document 6 (Memo)

1. Format the following information in memo format using Times New Roman font, 18 point:

DATE: April 16, 20-- | TO: Harriett Gross | FROM: Helen Otto | SUBJECT: BEST DENTAL CHOICE

A representative from Best Dental Choice will be visiting the Benefits Office on Tuesday, April 25, to explain the advantages of that dental insurance plan.

(continued on next page)

Please arrange your schedule so you can attend the 2 p.m. meeting, during which the Best Dental Choice sales rep will outline the features of the plan and compare the benefits to our present plan.

Please bring one of your assistants who works closely with the dental plan to the meeting.

2. Save as *CA19-1F.*

LESSON 2 PREPARE LETTERS WITH SPECIAL PARTS

OBJECTIVES

> To review letters with special parts.
> To review format features of two-page letters.

Exercise 2A

Letter 1

1. Prepare the letter below using block format, mixed punctuation, and a 14-point font.

   Formatting Cue: When a company name is used in the closing lines, key it as a double space below the complimentary close in ALL CAPS; then quadruple-space to the writer's name.

April 3, 20-- | SPECIAL DELIVERY | Mrs. Carol T. Yao | Director of Human Resources | Franklin Tool & Die Company | 600 E. Lake Street | Addison, IL 60101-3492 | Dear Mrs. Yao: | YOUR REQUEST FOR ADDITIONAL INFORMATION

Thank you for agreeing to give further consideration to making Protect III available to your employees, beginning with the open enrollment period that starts in June.

Protect III has been among the leaders in the health insurance industry for the past 15 years. Our plan is now used by hundreds of thousands of people in Illinois and is accepted by almost every physician, hospital, and pharmacy in your area.

The enclosed materials will provide you with more information about Protect III that should help you prepare the proposal for your vice president. The following materials are included:

❏ "Top Choice Protection" brochure that explains Protect III's key features.

❏ A benefit summary chart that outlines specific benefits.

(continued on next page)

❑ A provider directory that lists all the Illinois primary care physicians and facilities participating in Protect III.

❑ A pharmacy directory that lists the pharmacies your employees can use as part of the Protect III prescription plan.

❑ A chart of monthly fees for the various levels of coverage your employees may choose.

If you have any questions about Protect III features, the provider network, or the fees that will apply to Franklin Tool & Die Company, call me at 1-800-555-0113.

Sincerely | PROTECT III, INC. | Carlos V. Santana | Corporate Account Rep | CVS:xx | Enclosures | Carol, thank you for giving Protect III the opportunity to provide your company's health care benefits. We're looking forward to serving you and your employees.

2. Save as *CA19-2A*.

Exercise 2B

Letter 2

1. Prepare the letter below using modified block, mixed punctuation, paragraph indentations, and Arial font, 12 point.

March 5, 20-- | Attention Human Resources Department | Central Life Assurance, Inc. | 1520 W. Ohio Street | Indianapolis, IN 46222-1578 | Ladies and Gentlemen

The Action Fitness and Exercise Center is offering an introductory membership to employees of area corporations. This membership is for 90 days and costs only $50, the regular monthly membership fee.

During this 90-day trial period, your employees can use the indoor running track, weight-lifting stations, and exercise equipment (including treadmills, stair climbers, and rowing machines).

Your employees can also enroll in any of the aerobics, weight-control, and healthy-eating classes that are offered on a regular basis.

To take advantage of this offer, distribute the enclosed cards to interested employees. These cards can be presented on the first visit.

Sincerely | Ned V. Mowry | President | xx | Enclosure | c Mary Parker, Club Membership Coordinator

2. Save as *CA19-2B*.

Letter 3

1. Format Letter 2 (*CA19-2B*) as a two-page block letter with open punctuation and Times New Roman, 16 point.

2. Add the subject line: TRIAL MEMBERSHIP FOR YOUR EMPLOYEES

3. Bold the name of the fitness center in the body of the letter.

4. Add the center's name as a company name in the closing lines.

5. Save as *CA19-2C*.

Letter 4

1. Prepare the letter below using block format, mixed punctuation, and Tahoma, 12 point.

May 17, 20-- | REGISTERED | Susan T. Kipin, M.D. | 404 E. Washington Street | Indianapolis, IN 46204-8201 | Dear Dr. Kipin | CHANGE IN HAZARDOUS REMOVAL CONTAINERS

The waste removal containers that we have located at your office will be removed on May 30 and replaced with new containers that provide greater safety for your patients, your employees, and you. A brochure showing the container dimensions is enclosed.

Our technician will fasten a container to the wall in each room you designate. Please be certain that your office manager knows the specific locations.

Once the new containers have been installed, TRT technicians will schedule a time when the waste can be removed daily.

Sincerely | Dorothy C. McIntyre | Service Manager | DCM:xx | Enclosure | bc Harry Williams, Technician

---

2. Save as *CA19-2D*.

Letter 5

1. Format Letter 4 (*CA19-2D*) in modified block; use open punctuation, paragraph indentations, and Arial, 12 point.

2. Save as *CA19-2E*.

Exercise 2F

Letter 6

1. Open *CD-CA19-2F* and format the text as a block letter with mixed punctuation.

2. Key the paragraph below as the final paragraph.

   Proofreading Cue: Find and correct the four errors in the file.

> ¶ The association's staff thanks you for supporting this important nonprofit organization. Without contributions from citizens such as you, thousands more men and women would suffer fatal heart attacks each year.

3. Save as *CA19-2F*.

LESSON 3 DEVELOP MAIL MERGE SKILLS

OBJECTIVES

- ⊘ To create a data source file.
- ⊘ To create a main document file.
- ⊘ To use the Mail Merge feature.

Learn: Mail Merge

main document
data source
merged file

Mail Merge is used to combine information from two files into a third file that is created via the merge process. The Merge feature is often used to merge a letter file (**main document**) with a name and address file (**data source**) to create a personalized letter (**merged file**) to each person in the data source file. (See the illustration in Figure CA19-1.)

Figure CA19-1 Mail Merge

This file	*merged with*	this file	*creates*	this file.
Data Source File contains variable information		**Main Document File** contains generic information		**Merged File** contains personalized (variable and generic) information

Exercise 3A

Mail Merge: Letters

1. Read the information about Mail Merge.
2. Open the main document file (*CD-CA19-3A-Main*) and merge it with the data source file (*CD-CA19-3A-Data*).
3. View the three letters in the merged file created by the Mail Merge.
4. Print one of the merged letters.
5. Save as *CA19-3A-Letters.*

Learn: Data Source Files

Data source files contain a **record** for each name in the database. Each record contains **fields** of information about the person, such as her or his title, first name, last name, street address, city, state, postal code, etc.

Word processors insert **field codes** to separate and distinguish fields of information. Word processors insert **end of record codes** in the data source file to separate and distinguish each record that you key into the file.

record

fields

field codes

end of record codes

Exercise 3B

Create a Data Source File

1. Read the above information about data source files. Open a new word processing file.
2. Use the word processing table feature to create a data source file with these three records, each with seven fields.

INFORMATION FOR THE DATA SOURCE FILE			
Field Name	**Record 1**	**Record 2**	**Record 3**
Title	Mr.	Mrs.	Ms.
First Name	Harold	Noreen	Elizabeth
Last Name	Dominicus	Mueller	Theilet
Address Line 1	14820 Conway Road	15037 Clayton Road	1843 Ross Avenue
City	Chesterfield	Chesterfield	St. Louis
State	MO	MO	MO
ZIP Code	63025-1003	63017-8734	63146-5577

3. Save as *CA19-3B-Data.*

Learn: Main Documents

The main document file contains the generic text and format of the document that remain constant in each letter, plus the **field codes**. The field codes are inserted into the main document file where the variable information from the data source is to appear. The merge process will create the **merged file**, containing a personalized letter for each recipient.

After the data source file and main document file have been created, they are ready to be merged. However, if you need to send the letter to just some of the persons (records) in the data source file, you can specify the one(s) you want to receive the letter. Letters will not be created for the records not selected.

Exercise 3C

Create a Main Document

1. Read the information about main documents above and on the previous page.
2. Create the main document shown below, selecting the data source file *CA19-3B-Data* you created in Exercise 3B as needed.

January 15, 20--

<<AddressBlock>>

<<GreetingLine>>

It was a pleasure to meet you last week to discuss your long-term health care needs. As you requested, I have charted the various policy features from three leading insurance providers.

The chart will show the various options each provider extends and the cost for each option. You can select those that meet your needs the best.

I will call you in a week to arrange an appointment so we can discuss this matter thoroughly.

Sincerely,

Katherine Porter
Agent
xx

Enclosure

---

3. Save as *CA19-3C-Main*.

Exercise 3D

Mail Merge: Letters

1. Merge the main document (*CA19-3C-Main*) with the data source (*CA19-3B-Data*) to produce three letters.
2. View the letters in the merged file and print the Dominicus letter.
3. Save as *CA19-3D-Letters*.

Exercise 3E

Mail Merge: Letters To Selected Recipients

1. Using *CA19-3C-Main* and *CA19-3B-Data*, create a letter for each record with *Chesterfield* in the City field.

2. Print the letters.

3. Save as *CA19-3E-Letters*.

Learn: Editing Data Source Files and Mail Merge Applications

You can edit both records and fields in a data source file. For example, you can add records to, delete records from, revise records in, or sort records in an existing data source file. Also, you can add, delete, or revise fields in an existing data source file. Data source files can be word processing, spreadsheet, database, or e-mail files.

Mail Merge can be used for many other tasks. Frequently, envelopes, mailing labels, name badges, and directories are prepared from information in a data source file.

Exercise 3F

Edit Data Source Files

1. Read the above information about editing data source files and Mail Merge applications.

2. Open *CA19-3B-Data* and make the following changes:

   a. In Record 3, change Elizabeth's title to Mrs. and last name to Popelas.

   b. Delete the record for Harold Dominicus and add these two records:

   Dr. Eugene Whitman, 531 Kiefer Road, Ballwin, MO 63025-0531
   Ms. Joyce Royal, 417 Weidman Road, Ballwin, MO 63011-0321

   c. Add two fields (Company and Email) and then insert the company name and e-mail address in each record as indicated below:

   Mueller—Allmor Corporation; mueller@AC.com
   Popelas—Kurtz Consumer Discount; epopelas@kurtz.com
   Whitman—Whitman Family Practice; whitman@wfc.com
   Royal—Better Delivery, Inc.; jroyal2@betdel.com

3. Save as *CA19-3F-Data*.

Exercise 3G

Mail Merge Applications

1. Using all fields except EMail in *CA19-3F-Data* and a main document you create, prepare a large (No. 10) envelope for each record in the data source file. Use your name and home address as the return address.

2. Save as *CA19-3G-Main1* (main document) and *CA19-3G-Env* (envelopes).

3. Using all fields except EMail in *CA19-3F-Data* and a main document you create, prepare a standard mailing label for each record in the file.

4. Save as *CA19-3G-Main2* (main document) and *CA19-3G-Labels* (labels).

5. Using the First Name, Last Name, Company, and City fields in *CA19-3F-Data* and a main document you create, prepare an attractive name badge for each record in the data source file.

6. Save as *CA19-3G-Main3* (main document) and *CA19-3G-Badges* (name badges).

7. Using the Last Name, First Name, and EMail fields in *CA19-3F-Data* and a main document you create, prepare an e-mail directory for each record in the data source file. Insert a comma between the Last Name and First Name fields. List the last names in alpha order; align the names at the left margin. Align the e-mail addresses at the right margin using a right dot leader tab.

8. Save as *CA19-3G-Main4* (main document) and *CA19-3G-Dir* (directory).

LESSON ④ USE MAIL MERGE

OBJECTIVES

⊘ To create a data source file.
⊘ To use Mail Merge to create letters.

Exercise 4A

Data Source File

1. Create a data source file using the 20 records shown below. Use the column headings as field names.

Title	First Name	Last Name	Address Line 1	City	State	ZIP Code
Mr.	Daniel	Raible	13811 Seagoville Road	Dallas	TX	75253-1380
Ms.	Sally	Lysle	3707 S. Peachtree Road	Mesquite	TX	75180-3707
Mrs.	Luz	Ruiz	13105 Timothy Lane	Mesquite	TX	75180-1310
Mrs.	Jane	Alam	1414 Alstadt Street	Hutchins	TX	75141-3792
Mr.	Paul	Regina	11435 Ravenview Road	Dallas	TX	75253-1143

(continued on next page)

Title	First Name	Last Name	Address Line 1	City	State	ZIP Code
Mrs.	Jane	Abbott	3300 LaPrada Drive	Mesquite	TX	75149-3300
Mr.	John	Eaton	P.O. Box 852238	Mesquite	TX	75185-8522
Ms.	Stacey	Bethel	1717 Castle Drive	Garland	TX	75040-1717
Dr.	Jash	Sharik	2021 E. Park Boulevard	Plano	TX	75074-2021
Mr.	Jack	Dunn	4007 Latham Drive	Plano	TX	75023-4000
Mrs.	Helen	Wever	1001 Cuero Drive	Garland	TX	75040-1001
Ms.	Ann	Buck	1919 Senter Road	Irving	TX	75060-1919
Dr.	Tim	Prady	3901 Frisco Avenue	Irving	TX	75061-3900
Ms.	Lois	Poulos	1632 New Market Road	Mesquite	TX	75149-1056
Mr.	Peter	Como	701 W. State Street	Garland	TX	75040-0701
Ms.	Karen	Rolle	1026 F Avenue	Plano	TX	75074-3591
Mr.	Dale	Zeman	4412 Legacy Drive	Plano	TX	75024-4412
Mr.	Yu	Wei	12726 Audelia Road	Dallas	TX	75243-7789
Ms.	Anne	Sige	532 N. Story Road	Irving	TX	75061-0506
Mr.	David	White	3700 Chaha Road	Rowlett	TX	75088-3700

2. Save as *CA19-4A-Data.*

Exercise 4B

Mail Merge: Letters

1. Using the information on the following page, create a main document file (*CA19-4B-Main*) using block letter format with mixed punctuation and merge it with *CA19-4A-Data.*

October 5, 20--

<<AddressBlock>>

<<GreetingLine>>

¶ Thank you for attending the recent open house reception sponsored by the Dallas Area Environmental Health Association. We hope that you enjoyed meeting our expert staff of scientists, physicians, nutritionists, technicians, and others who work on your behalf to improve your quality of life.

¶ Headaches, sinusitis, fatigue, joint aches, and asthma are some of the common ailments that are often caused by our environment. The Dallas Area Environmental Health Association is dedicated to conducting the research that documents the link between the common ailments and the environment so effective treatments can be offered.

¶ <<Title>> <<LastName>>, now that you know more about the Association, we ask you to schedule a 20-minute consultation with one of our staff members to discuss your health concerns. This consultation is free and carries no obligation to use our services. Just call me at 972-555-0119 to schedule a mutually convenient time.

Sincerely, | Margarita L. Jiminez | Director of Services | xx

2. Save merged letters as *CA19-4B-Letters*.

3. Print the Raible and White letters.

LESSON 5 USE MAIL MERGE

OBJECTIVES

- ⊚ To create main document files.
- ⊚ To use Mail Merge to prepare mailing labels, envelopes, a directory, and name badges.

Exercise 5A

Mail Merge: Mailing Labels

1. Prepare a standard mailing label for each record in the data source file *CA19-4A-Data*.   Save the main document file as *CA19-5A-Main* and the merged document file as *CA19-5A-Labels*.

2. Print the mailing labels.

Exercise **5B**

Mail Merge: Envelopes

1. Prepare a No. 10 envelope for each record in the data source file *CA19-4A-Data* that has *Plano* in the City field. Use your name and address as the return address. Save the main document file as *CA19-5B-Main* and the merged document as *CA19-5B-Env.*

2. Print the envelopes.

Exercise **5C**

Edit a Data Source File

1. Open data source file *CA19-4A-Data.*

2. Add these records:

Field Name	Record 1	Record 2	Record 3
Title	Mrs.	Ms.	Mrs.
First Name	Judy	Janet	Clara
Last Name	Nguyen	Durkay	Shultz
Address Line 1	404 S. Watson Street	800 Austin Street	475 W. Oates Road
City	Seagoville	Garland	Garland
State	TX	TX	TX
Zip Code	75159-9901	75040-8000	75043-4752

Field Name	Record 4	Record 5	Record 6
Title	Ms.	Mrs.	Ms.
First Name	Nyla	Lori	Diana
Last Name	Schnurr	O'Dea	Olech
Address Line 1	801 W. Kearney Street	350 S. Belt Line Road	12726 Audelia Road
City	Mesquite	Mesquite	Dallas
State	TX	TX	TX
Zip Code	75149-0801	75185-3150	75243-8899

Field Name	Record 7	Record 8	Record 9
Title	Mrs.	Mr.	Mrs.
First Name	Tara	Dean	Sandy
Last Name	Koget	Korch	Cougar
Address Line 1	2256 Arapaho Road	1400 W. Arapaho Road	1700 W. Kingsley Road
City	Garland	Richardson	Garland
State	TX	TX	TX
Zip Code	75044-2256	75080-5569	75041-6612

Lesson 5 Use Mail Merge   *291*

3. Delete the records for Mr. Daniel Raible, Ms. Stacy Bethel, and Mrs. Helen Wever.

4. Make these changes to other existing records:

   a. Change Sally Lysle's last name to Beam.

   b. Change Jack Dunn's address to 1606 School Road, Carrolton, TX 75006-4471.

   c. Change Ms. Anne Sige's last name to Holtus and her address to 718 N. Bagley Street, Dallas, TX 72511-0718.

   d. Delete all records that have *Irving, Hutchins, Rowlett,* or *Plano* in the City field.

5. Save as *CA19-5C-Data.*

Exercise 5D
Mailing Labels

1. Prepare a standard mailing label for each record in *CA19-5C-Data* that has *Garland* or *Mesquite* in the City field. Sort the labels by City.

2. Save the main document file as *CA19-5D-Main* and the labels as *CA19-5D-Labels.*

3. Print the mailing labels.

Exercise 5E
Directory

1. Prepare a directory listing all records in *CA19-5C-Data* by City and then in alphabetical order by Last Name within City:

   • Left-align last and first names and set a dot leader right tab at the 6" position to position the city.

   • Include a heading CITY DIRECTORY, center-aligned before the directory listing.

2. Save the main document file as *CA19-5E-Main* and the directory as *CA19-5E-Dir.*

3. Print the directory.

Exercise 5F
Name Badges

1. Prepare a name badge for each record in *CA19-5C-Data* that has *Garland* or *Mesquite* in the *City* field and *Ms.* in the Title field.

2. Sort the badges in alphabetical order by last name.

3. Horizontally center the fields below on two lines; double-space between the lines:

Title, First Name, & Last Name

City

4. Use a large font to make the badges easier to read.

5. Save the main document file as *CA19-5F-Main* and the badges as *CA19-5F-Badges*.

6. Print the name badges.

Online Resources

See Bonus Exercises 6A-6C on Mail Merge at www.c21key.bonus-exercises.swlearning.com.

Exercise is very important to maintaining a healthy body and mind. People exercise to lose weight, get in shape and stay in shape, reduce stress, improve overall health, increase muscular strength, recover from an illness or injury, etc.

Maybe you know what you want to accomplish through exercise, but don't know where to start. This activity requires you to search the Internet to find information about a method of exercise that interests you. For example, you may want to search the broad topic *exercise* and then follow links that interest you. Or you may want to narrow your search by selecting a few exercise routines that are of particular interest to you and searching for them—e.g., aerobics, bodybuilding, climbing, cycling, martial arts, running, swimming, walking, yoga, etc.

INTERNET ACTIVITY

1. Read the two paragraphs at the left.

2. Perform a search on an exercise topic of your choice and then compose (either at the keyboard or using speech recognition software) two or three paragraphs describing what you learned.

3. Print one or two pages from an Internet site that relate to what you wrote.

www.c21key.swlearning.com

UNIT 20

LESSONS 1–2
Creating a Business Plan

Before you begin the lessons, key each line twice.

alphabet	1	Zeke opened jam jars quickly but avoided ruining the waxed floor.
fig/sym	2	I wrote checks 398-430 and 432-457 in July and 458-461 in August.
speed	3	Jane may work with the girls to make the ritual for the sorority.

gwam 1' | 1 | 2 | 3 | 4 | 5 | 6 | 7 | 8 | 9 | 10 | 11 | 12 | 13 |

LESSON ① LEARN ADVANCED WORD PROCESSING FEATURES

OBJECTIVES

⊘ To learn the Split Window, Go To, Word Count, and Send to features.
⊘ To reveal formatting marks and set styles.

Learn: The Split Window Feature

Often it is helpful to be able to see two parts of a document that do not appear in the same window. The Split Window feature is used to display a document in two panes, each with its own scroll bars to help you move around in each pane (see Figure CA20-1). If needed, the panes can be resized.

This feature can be used when you copy or move text between parts of a long document or when you need to see text that is not visible in the window where you are keying.

Exercise 1A

Split Window

1. Read about split windows above.
2. Open *CD-CA20-1A* and split the window.
3. In the lower pane, find *Questions*.

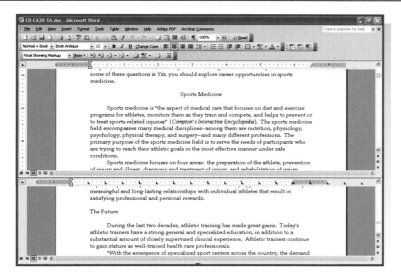

4. Move through the text in the top pane to find the answers to the five questions that appear in the bottom pane, and key your answers in the space between the questions.

5. Move the questions and your answers to the top of page 1 and print page 1.

6. Save as *CA20-1A*.

Learn: The Go To Feature

A quick way to move to a certain page or point in a long document is to use the Go To command. This command can be used to go directly to a specific footnote or endnote, for example. The Go To feature is displayed in Figure CA20-2.

Figure CA20-2 Go To Feature

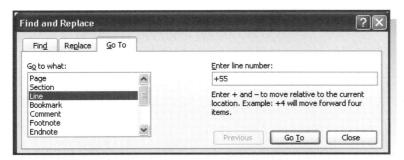

Exercise 1B

Go To

1. Open *CD-CA20-1B* and split the window.

2. Read about the Go To feature above.

3. In the lower pane, find *Questions*.

4. Answer the questions by using Go To to move through the text in the top pane.

5. Print the page with the questions and your answers.

6. Save as *CA20-1B*.

Learn: Show ¶

Word processing documents contain invisible formatting marks that can be displayed by using the Show ¶ command. Commonly used marks are:

   ¶ to show a new line,

   → to show a tab,

   • to show a space between words.

   Being able to see the formatting marks is helpful when editing a document or solving formatting problems. The formatting marks do not print. (See Figure CA20-3.)

Figure CA20-3   **Formatting Marks Revealed**

```
¶
¶
The·¶·mark·indicates·there·are¶
two·blank·lines·above·this¶
text·and·that·ENTER·was·struck¶
at·the·end·of·each·line.¶
The  →   indicates·that·the  →  TAB¶
key·was·struck·after·the·two·occurrences¶
of·the·work·THE·in·line·5.··The·dots¶
indicate···the·number·of·spaces¶
between·INDICATE·and·THE·in¶
line·8.¶
```

Exercise 1C

Show ¶

1. Key the text below, using single spacing and bullets as shown.

You can incorporate fitness into your daily routine by doing these three activities:

   • Walk up stairs for one minute each day instead of taking the elevator. Within a year you should be a pound lighter without changing any other habits.

   • Walk the dog, don't just watch the dog walk. In a nutshell—get moving!

   • Perform at least 30 minutes of moderate activity each day. If necessary, do the 30 minutes in 10-minute intervals.

2. Read about the Show ¶ feature on the previous page.

3. Show the formatting marks for the text you keyed and refer to them to answer these questions below the text you keyed:

   a. How many times was Enter tapped?

   b. How many tabs appear in the copy?

   c. How many times was the Space Bar tapped twice before keying a character?

4. Save as *CA20-1C*.

Learn: Styles

A style is a predefined set of formatting options that has been named and saved so it can be used again to save time and add consistency to a document.

When a style is applied (used), many formatting commands are applied at one time. For example, a style for a report heading may include commands for centering and using a 16-point bold font in Arial. All four formatting commands would be applied when the style is applied.

Paragraph styles apply to the entire paragraph, and character styles apply only to text selected in the paragraph.

Existing styles can be used, existing styles can be modified and then used, or new styles can be created and then used.

Figure CA20-4   Styles

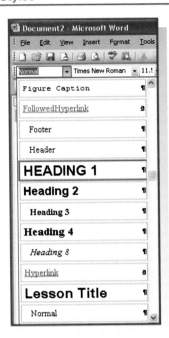

1. Read the information about styles on the previous page. Key the four headings shown below two times.

Career Opportunities in Sports Medicine **(Heading 1 style)**

Sports Medicine **(Heading 2 style)**

Focus **(Heading 3 style)**

Practitioners **(Heading 3 style)**

---

2. **Apply Existing Styles:**
   - Use **Heading 1** style on the first and fifth headings.
   - Use **Heading 2** style on the second and sixth headings.
   - Use **Heading 3** style on the third, fourth, seventh, and eighth headings.

3. **Modify Existing Styles:**
   - Modify **Heading 1** style so it is in ALL CAPS and then apply it to the first heading.
   - Modify **Heading 2** style so it is bold not italic, and apply it to the second heading.

   Formatting Note: When Heading 1 and 2 styles are modified, the heading style used in lines 5 and 6 is changed to match the modified style in the 1st and 2nd headings.

4. **Create New Styles:**
   - Key the paragraph below, and then create and apply a style that uses a red, 11-point Arial font, right-aligned.

Have you given serious thought to the kind of work you want to do when you are graduated from high school? Do you enjoy helping people with their problems, working on a person-to-person basis?

   - Key the paragraph below and apply the style you just created.

Athletic trainers must have basic knowledge and competencies in a variety of different specialty areas within the sports medicine field.

---

5. Save as *CA20-1D*.

Learn: Word Count

The Word Count feature shown in Figure CA20-5 is used to count the number of words within a document or a specific section of the document. This same command usually provides the number of characters, lines, paragraphs, and pages within the document.

Figure CA20-5   Word Count Dialog Box

Exercise 1E
Word Count

1. Open *CD-CA20-1E.* Read about word count above.
2. Using Word Count, key the answers to these questions:
    a. How many words are in the document?
    b. How many lines are in the document?
    c. How many pages are in the document?
    d. How many words are in the first two paragraphs of the Sports Medicine section?
    e. How many characters (with spaces) are in the second line of the first paragraph?
    f. How many lines are in the first four paragraphs of the Duties and Responsibilities section?
3. Save as *CA20-1E.*

Learn: Send To

Outlines created using Styles in word processing software can be sent to presentation software to make slides that can be used in a presentation (see Figure CA20-6).

Text formatted using Heading 1 style becomes the title of a new slide, text in Heading 2 style becomes first-level bullets on the slide, and text in Heading 3 style becomes second-level bullets on the slide, and so on.

In this section, you will create a word processing document and then send it to presentation software. Default settings will be used to format the slides. Later, you will learn how to change the format of the text and the slides.

Exercise 1F

Send To

1. Key the text, using default tab settings and Heading 1 style for first-level text, Heading 2 style for second-level text, and Heading 3 style for third-level text.

Career Opportunities in Sports Medicine **(first level)**
Sports Medicine
    Focus **(second level)**
    Practitioners
Athletic Trainers
    Places of Employment
        Sports Teams **(third level)**
        Clinics
        Others
    Professional Relationships
Requirements
    Education
    Internships
    Continuing Education

---

2. Save as *CA20-1F-WP*.
3. Read about the Send To feature above.
4. Send the document to your presentation software.
5. View the outline and slides in the presentation software.
6. Print the four slides (as handouts, six to a page, if possible).
7. Save as *CA20-1F-PP*.

LESSON ② CREATE A BUSINESS PLAN

⊙ To prepare a long report with a title page, table of contents, and appendices.

⊙ To demonstrate your ability to integrate your knowledge and skills.

Learn: What Is a Business Plan?

A business plan is a blueprint for a company. Developing a business plan helps entrepreneurs take an objective, critical look at a business. A well-written plan communicates the company's ideas and message to lenders, investors, and employees. A written business plan also is a management tool that helps measure the performance of the business.

The key elements of a business plan are:

1. A **market analysis** that defines the market and specifies the strategies to be used to achieve the revenues.
2. An **action plan** to guide the implementation of the strategies.
3. **Financial projections** that show the expected results.

market analysis

action plan
financial projections

Exercise 2A

Business Plan

1. Read the information above about business plans.
2. Open *CD-CA20-BUSPLN* and preview the business plan quickly to familiarize yourself with its content, organization, and length.
3. Check for inconsistencies in spacing, paragraph indentations, and for spelling errors. Key a list of the errors you find. Save as *CA20-2A*.
4. Correct the errors you found.
5. Save as *CA20-BUSPLAN*.

Learn: Formatting a Business Plan

Margins. The business plan is to be bound at the left; therefore, use a 1.5" left margin and a 1" right margin. Use a default or 1" top and bottom margin on all pages except the first (the first page has a 2" top margin).

Page numbering and header. A header with the company name followed by the words *Business Plan* blocked at the left margin and the page number flush with the right margin is keyed in 12-point font on all pages of the report body and appendices except the first page of the report body.

Line spacing and font. The entire report is double spaced using 12-point Times New Roman font unless otherwise directed.

Text. Paragraphs and single-line bulleted lists should have at least two lines (or bullets) at the bottom of the page and carry over at least two lines to the next page. Headings and at least two lines of text should be kept together. Footnotes should be the same typeface and font size as the text. Tables should not be split between pages. The report body should be left-aligned and hyphenated.

Heading styles. Use these heading styles in the body of this business plan.

Level 1—centered, ALL CAPS, bold, 16-point Times New Roman font, double spaced

Level 2—left-aligned, ALL CAPS, bold, 14-point Times New Roman font, double spaced

Level 3—left-aligned, small caps, bold, 12-point Times New Roman font, double spaced

Table of contents. Include TABLE OF CONTENTS as a centered heading in ALL CAPS, 16-point font, and 2" from top. Then double-space before listing Level 1, 2, and 3 report headings, including Appendices A and B.

Key Level 1 headings in ALL CAPS, blocked at the left margin. Indent Level 2 headings 0.5" and key in initial caps. Indent Level 3 headings 1" and key in initial caps.

Double-space above and below all Level 1 and 2 headings. Single-space Level 3 headings.

Key the page number (with leaders) for each heading at the right margin.

Use small Roman numerals (i, ii) centered in a footer to number the table of contents pages.

Exercise 2B
Business Plan

1. If needed, open *CA20-BUSPLAN* and then read above how this business plan is to be formatted.

2. Using the formatting information, set margins and create styles for Level 1, 2, and 3 headings in the business plan.

3. Apply the heading styles throughout the report. Headings appear in the draft as follows:

   - Level 1 headings—centered initial caps
   - Level 2 headings—left-aligned with initial caps and underlined
   - Level 3 headings—left-aligned with initial caps

4. Double-space the entire report; use a 2" top margin on page 1.

5. Print pages 1 and 9 of the business plan.

6. Save as *CA20-BUSPLN*.

Exercise 2C
Business Plan

1. Open *CA20-BUSPLN* and key the text on the following page after the first paragraph of the business plan.

Mission Statement

The *mission* of Casa Di Italia is to serve and sell hi-quality Italian foods at moderate prices in a friendly, ~~family type~~ *healthy* atmosphere that offers, ~~good~~ *superior* service to customers.

Vision Statement

Within 5 years, Casa Di Italia ~~hopes to~~ *will* be recognized as one of the top 5 moderately priced Italian restaurants in the Brenthall area.

2. Apply an appropriate style to headings.

   Proofreading Alert: The rough-draft copy contains one embedded error; correct it as you process the copy.

3. Print page 1.

4. Save as *CA20-BUSPLN*.

Exercise 2D

Business Plan

1. Open *CA20-BUSPLN* and insert the text below and on the following page before the side heading *Baldwin Hills Growth*.

   Proofreading Alert: The rough-draft copy contains two embedded errors. Proofread your work carefully, checking to make sure all errors have been corrected.

Industry Analysis

Casa Di Italia ~~will be~~ *is* part of an industry that has established itself as an integral part of an American lifestyle. More than 45% of today's food dollar is spent away from home and almost 1/2 *half* of all adults are restaurant patrons on a typical day. Children*, teenagers,* and young adults are more familiar with restaurants and knew cuisines than ever before and are increasing their restaurant ~~visits~~ *spending*. The same is true for the baby boomers and members of the older generations who have been

(continued on next page)

empowered by strong ~~growth~~ *economic* growth and gains in income.

<u>National Growth</u>

The restaurant industry enjoyed (9) *sp* consecutive years of real sales growth as they entered the new century. Sales in 2003 were calculated at $426 billion and are expected to increase *steadily* to $577 billion by 2010, an increase of 35(%) *sp* in seven years. ~~Eat-in~~ *Full-service* restaurants accounted for ~~more than~~ *about* two-thirds or $297 billion of the ~~United States~~ 2003 sales. Using the same ratio, *full-service* restaurants ~~should~~ *will* account for about $388 billion of the industry sales in 2010.

2. Apply appropriate styles to headings.

3. Insert a reference for footnote #1 at the end of the first paragraph, and key the following footnote using the same font typeface and size as the text in the business plan:

   [1]National data used in the business plan are from the National Restaurant Association obtained at http://www.restaurant.org/research in November 2003.

   Note: Do not be concerned if the footnote "splits" between two pages. You will make adjustments as necessary in a later activity.

4. Print the page(s) on which the *Industry Analysis* and *National Growth* sections appear.

5. Save as *CA20-BUSPLN*.

Exercise 2E

Business Plan

1. Open CA20-BUSPLN and insert the text below and on the following page after paragraph 2 of the *Baldwin Hills Growth* section.

Casa Di Italia will develop a strong presence in the Baldwin Hills area by serving high-quality, healthy Italian entrees at moderate prices and providing superior service. The competitive advantage will be strengthened by the *award-winning* chef ~~that~~ *who*

(continued on next page)

has agreed to work at Casa Di Italia, and the specialty retail ~~area that will provide quality products.~~

Target Market

Casa Di Italia target's a variety of people, but for the most part they have these characteristics:

(change to bulleted list)

1. Located in the Baldwin Hills area
2. Make buying decisions based on quality, service, and convenience
3. Part of the middle to upper socioeconomic group
4. Between the ages of 25 and 70
5. Married or dating couples

The *census* data for the ~~the~~ Young County shows the following characteristics for the population in ~~our~~ *the restaurant's* primary service area:

- ❏ 57% of the population is between the ages 25 and 69
- ❏ 75% or more households have an annual income of $45,000 or higher
- ❏ 49% of the population is married
- ❏ Italian heritage is the third-highest ethnic group in Young *County*
- ❏ 17% of the families *are* working married couples with children at home
- ❏ 13% of the families are working married couples with no children at home
- ❏ 20% of the households are single *is* and living ~~at home~~ alone

2. Insert Market Share as a Level 1 heading, and apply appropriate styles to other headings.
3. Select a character for bulleted items. Apply it to the bullets in this insert and other bulleted items in the business plan.

   Proofreading Alert: The rough-draft copy contains one embedded error. Proofread your work carefully, checking to make sure all errors have been corrected.
4. Print the page(s) on which this inserted text appears.
5. Save as *CA20-BUSPLN.*

Exercise 2F

Business Plan

1. Open *CA20-BUSPLN*.

2. Move the *Management Structure* section to make it the last section in *Management and Organization*.

3. Print the page(s) on which the *Management Structure* section appears.

4. Save as *CA20-BUSPLN*.

Exercise 2G

Appendix A

1. Open *CA20-BUSPLN*.

2. Insert a page break at the end of the business plan.

3. On the new page, key Appendix A 2" from the top as a Level 1 heading and then double space.

4. Key the comment card shown below so that it will fit on a 4" x 6" card. You decide the layout of the card and the font size, style, color, etc. If desired, use word art and/or other graphics you select.

Dear Customer:

Your opinions are very important to the owners and employees of Casa Di Italia. Will you, therefore, take a moment to complete this card? Thank you.

Michelle Calvini and Rachel Costanzo, Owners

Rate the quality of the food:

Superior		Adequate		Poor
5	4	3	2	1

Rate the quality of the service:

Superior		Adequate		Poor
5	4	3	2	1

Please tell us what we did that pleased or did not please you: _____

_____

_____

---

5. Print Appendix A.

6. Save as *CA20-BUSPLN*.

Business Plan

1. Open *CA20-BUSPLN*.
2. Key this text after the *Target Market* section.

   Proofreading Alert: The rough-draft copy contains embedded errors. Proofread your work carefully, checking to make sure all errors have been corrected.

Direct Competition

Casa Di Italia will face strong competition from area restaurants, especially Italian restaurants, and specialty food stores. There is won store specializing in Italian foods within 2 miles of our location. Only on-street parking is available to its customers. There are 6 Italian restaurants within a 5-mile radius of Casa Di Italia. Four of these are well established and two have opened within the past 2 years. Spot checks during peak dining hours reveal that all but one is attracting customers in adequate or large numbers. Four of the restaurants offer free parking in a restaurant lot, one offers valet parking only, and one has only on-street parking available. One restaurants serves high-priced meals, four serve moderately priced meals, and one offers low-priced meals. None of these restaurants has a specialty food store housed within the restaurant. Four restaurants take reservations, one has call-ahead seating, and one does not take reservations in any form.
The 6 nearby Italian restaurants and their distance from Casa Di Italia are given below.

The Italian Warehouse--2.5 miles to the east

The Pepper Garden--1.3 miles to the northeast

Mike's Pasta House--1.6 miles to the west

Carbonara Ristorante--5 miles to the north

Calabro's--3.6 miles to the southwest

Sestilli's Restaurant--4.3 miles to the northwest

bulleted list

3. Print the page(s) on which this text appears.
4. Save as *CA20-BUSPLN*.

Exercise 2I

Business Plan

1. Open *CA20-BUSPLN*.

2. Insert this table so it appears after the word *assumptions:* in the *Financials* section.

Quarter	Customers Each Day	Revenues Per Customer	Total Revenues
September 15 to December 14	140	$20	$252,000
December 15 to March 14	150	$20	$270,000
March 15 to June 14	155	$20	$279,000
June 15 to September 14	130	$20	$234,000

3. Print the page on which the table appears.

4. Save as *CA20-BUSPLN*.

Exercise 2J

Appendix B

1. Key the worksheet.

	QTR 1 9/15-12/14	QTR 2 12/15-3/14	QTR 3 3/15-6/14	QTR 4 6/15-9/14
Revenue	$252,000	$270,000	$279,000	$234,000
Cost of sales	$ 93,240	$ 99,900	$103,230	$ 86,580
Gross profit	$158,760	$170,100	$175,770	$147,420
Expenses				
Salaries and wages	$ 68,040	$ 68,040	$ 68,040	$ 68,040
Employee benefits	$ 13,860	$ 13,860	$ 13,860	$ 13,860
Direct operating expenses	$ 12,600	$ 13,500	$ 13,950	$ 11,700
Marketing	$ 6,300	$ 6,750	$ 6,975	$ 5,850
Energy and utility service	$ 10,080	$ 10,800	$ 11,160	$ 9,360
Administrative and general	$ 9,576	$ 10,260	$ 10,602	$ 8,892
Repairs and maintenance	$ 5,040	$ 5,400	$ 5,580	$ 4,680
Building costs	$ 15,624	$ 15,624	$ 15,624	$ 15,624
Total expenses	$141,120	$144,234	$145,791	$138,006
Net income	$ 17,640	$ 25,866	$ 29,979	$ 9,414

2. Key the following headings in column F:

cell F1: YEAR 1

cell F2: 9/15-9/14

3. Calculate the yearly totals in cells F3:F15.

4. Print the worksheet and save the file as *CA20-2J-WS* to be used as Appendix B.

Exercise 2K

Appendix B

1. Open *CA20-BUSPLN* and create a new page at the end for Appendix B.

2. Key Appendix B as a Level 1 heading 2" from the top of the page.

3. About 0.5" below the title, insert *CA20-2J-WS* and center it horizontally between the left and right margin settings.

4. Print Appendix B.

5. Save as *CA20-BUSPLN*.

Exercise 2L

Business Plan

1. Open *CA20-BUSPLN*. Spell-check and proofread the entire document.

2. Hyphenate the document.

3. If needed, make adjustments so the footnote appears on the correct page, paragraphs and bullets are divided correctly, headings are kept with text correctly, and tables are not split between pages.

4. Insert a header on all pages except page 1. Refer to the format guides on pages 301–302 of this unit.

5. Print pages 1–5, 12, 15, and 19–21 unless directed otherwise.

6. Save as *CA20-BUSPLN*.

Exercise 2M

Title Page

1. Key Casa Di Italia at the top of the title page.

2. Near the center of the page (about 5" from the top), key Business Plan on one line and Michelle Calvini and Rachel Costanzo, Owners on the next line.

3. About 8" from the top, key 881 McCabe Road, Baldwin Hills, PA 15238-0937, 412-555-0112, and http://www.casadiitalia.com on four lines at the bottom.

4. Use word art, clip art, font effects, borders, and/or shading to make the title page attractive, adjusting vertical spacing as needed.

5. Save as *CA20-2M-TP*.

Exercise 2N

Table of Contents

1. Use the formatting information on page 302 of this unit to create a table of contents using the headings below.
2. If the page numbers given do not agree with those in your document, use your page numbers.

(continued on next page)

3. Save as *CA20-2N-TC*.

Exercise 20

Outline and Presentation

1. Use the three levels of headings in the table of contents (Exercise 2N) to prepare an outline numbered list using your word processing software.

2. Send the outline numbered list to presentation software to prepare slides for use in an oral presentation.

3. Insert the title CASA DI ITALIA BUSINESS PLAN at the beginning of the presentation.

4. Print the slides as a handout, with six slides on a page.

5. Save as *CA20-2O-ONL* and *CA20-2O-PP*.

UNIT 21

LESSONS 1–3

Workgroups and Collaboration

Conditioning Practice

Before you begin the lessons, key each line twice.

alphabet	1	Jimmy wants seven pens and extra clips in a kit for the big quiz.
fig/sym	2	I sold 54 advertisements for $6,738 between 9/12/05 and 12/19/06.
speed	3	A goal of the proficient tutor is to quantify the right problems.

gwam 1' | 1 | 2 | 3 | 4 | 5 | 6 | 7 | 8 | 9 | 10 | 11 | 12 | 13 |

LESSON 1 COMMENTS AND TRACK CHANGES IN WORD PROCESSING DOCUMENTS

OBJECTIVES

⊙ To display and print tracked changes and comments.
⊙ To edit a document online by tracking changes.
⊙ To accept or reject tracked changes and delete comments of a reviewer.

Learn: Track Changes

In Part 1, Unit 2 you learned to insert comments that appear in color-coded, shaded balloons in the margin of a document. This Comment feature facilitates collaborative writing.

Another tool that facilitates online editing and review by other persons is the Track Changes feature. When the Track Changes feature is active, each insertion, deletion, or formatting change you make while editing a document is tracked. A mark is inserted where changes are made or comments inserted. You can choose to show insertions underlined in the document and deletions and format changes in color-coded balloons in the margin area (see illustration below in Figure CA21-1), or the opposite—deletions with strikethroughs in the document and insertions and format changes in balloons.

The changes and comments are visible in color-coded text and balloons in Print Layout View and Web Layout View. If more than one person tracked changes or inserted comments in a document, each person's changes and comments appear in a

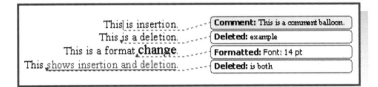

different color. A document can be printed with or without the tracked changes and comments by making the desired choice before printing.

To track changes while editing, you must activate the Track Changes feature. When this feature is activated, a Reviewing toolbar (see below in Figure CA21-2) will be displayed and TRK will appear in the status bar in bold.

Use Print Layout View to see the changes that you make while editing. If desired, the Track Changes features can be deactivated while preparing a document.

Figure CA21-2 Reviewing Toolbar

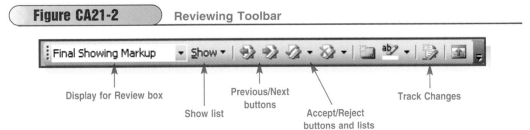

Exercise 1A

Display and Print Tracked Changes and Comments

1. Read about the Track Changes features above.
2. Open *CD-CA21-1A* and display the tracked changes and comment.
3. Read the content of the file.
4. Print the document with the tracked changes and comments.
5. Print the document without the tracked changes and comments.
6. Compare the two documents. Close the file.

Exercise 1B

Track Changes

1. Open *CD-CA21-1B* and use Track Changes to indicate the changes in steps a through g below.

   a. Center-align the heading in bold, 14-point font.

   b. Insert **suggested** before *revisions* in line 1.

   c. In paragraph 1, line 5, add an s to *other* and delete *people*.

    d. In paragraph 2, line 2, insert **in a document** after *displayed*.

    e. In paragraph 2, line 5, replace *use* with **activate and deactivate**.

    f. Bold each occurrence of *Track Changes*.

    g. Insert this comment at the end of the last line: **I think we need to mention that students will accept and reject changes in Activity 3**.

2. Print the document with the tracked changes and without the tracked changes.

3. Save as *CA21-1B*.

Learn: Accept and Reject Tracked Changes

You can accept or reject tracked changes and comments by reviewing each item in sequence or accepting or rejecting all changes and comments. Rejecting all changes at once will also delete all comments at once. Use the buttons on the Reviewing toolbar to accept or reject individual or all tracked changes or comments (see Figure CA21-3).

Figure CA21-3   Reviewing Toolbar Buttons

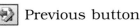 Previous button

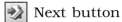 Next button

 Accept Change button/list

 Reject Change/Delete Comment button/list

Exercise 1C

Accept and Reject Tracked Changes

1. Read about accepting and rejecting tracked changes above.

2. Open *CD-CA21-1C* and accept and reject individual tracked changes and comments as directed in steps a through k below.

    a. Accept the formatting change for the top margin.

    b. Read and then delete the comment at the end of the title.

    c. Accept the *or Reject* deletion in paragraph 1.

    d. Reject the *individually* deletion paragraph 1.

    e. Accept the *much* deletion paragraph 2.

    f. Accept the *tracked* insertion paragraph 2.

    g. Accept the *drop down* insertion in paragraph 3

    h. Accept the *color-coded* deletion in paragraph 5.

    i. Reject the *drop down* deletion in paragraph 5.

j. Accept the suggestion in the comment at the end of paragraph 5, delete the comment, deactivate the Track Changes feature, and then make the suggested formatting change.

k. Print without tracked changes and comments.

3. Save as *CA21-1C*.

Exercise 1D

Application: Track Changes

1. Open *CD-CA21-1D*.

2. Use the Track Changes feature to edit (correct errors) and arrange the letter in block format with mixed punctuation.

3. Save as *CA21-1D*.

Exercise 1E

Application: Accept/Reject Tracked Changes

1. Exchange *CA21-1D* files with a classmate.

2. Open your classmate's file.

3. Accept or reject the changes your classmate made to the letter.

4. Save as *CA21-1E* and return it to your classmate so he/she can see the changes you accepted and rejected.

LESSON 2 COMPARE AND MERGE WORD PROCESSING DOCUMENTS

OBJECTIVE

> To write collaboratively by comparing and merging versions of documents that were edited by multiple reviewers.

Learn: Compare and Merge Documents

Copies of a word processing file can be sent to several different reviewers when a document is being written collaboratively. The file is usually sent to each reviewer via e-mail or posted on the Internet, intranet, or ftp site.

Each reviewer uses the Track Changes feature to edit the document and insert comments. Reviewers then return their version of the file to the author. When files from all reviewers have been received, the author can use word processing software to Compare and Merge the documents into a new or current document. Once the documents are merged, the author can accept or reject changes and delete comments as desired to prepare the final document.

Merge Documents

1. Read about comparing and merging documents on the previous page.
2. Open *CD-CA21-2A* and save it as *CA21-2A-ORIG*. This is the document that will be used for merging the changes.
3. Activate the Compare and Merge feature.
4. Open *CD-CA21-2A-REV1*, which contains the changes suggested by Reviewer 1. Merge it into the current document, *CA21-2A-ORIG*.
5. Open *CD-CA21-2A-REV2*, which contains the changes suggested by Reviewer 2. Merge it into the current document, *CA21-2A-ORIG*.
6. Accept each change individually, except reject duplicate changes as needed to make the final copy correct.
7. Proofread and correct any errors. Print the document without showing the markups.
8. Save as *CA21-2A-FINAL*.

Exercise 2B

Writing Collaboratively

1. Open a new word processing document and compose a letter to a friend asking him or her to join you and your family on a summer vacation. Provide information about the vacation location, the days you will leave and return, who is going, where you will stay, and the planned activities. Tell your friend that your family will pay for all travel, food, lodging, and admittance fees. Give him or her a date by which to decide if he or she is going. Name and save the file.
2. Give the word processing file to two or three classmates for them to edit using the Track Changes feature. Ask them to save their file with their initials added to your filename.
3. Retrieve the files from your reviewers and then merge their changes and comments into your original file.
4. Accept or reject the changes your reviewers suggested and save and rename your file.

LESSON 3 COMMENTS IN WORKSHEETS

OBJECTIVES

⊙ To insert and delete comments in a worksheet.
⊙ To resize, move, edit, format, and print comments.
⊙ To display and hide comments and their indicators.

Learn: Insert Worksheet Comments

A comment is a note attached to a cell in a worksheet that can be used as a reminder to yourself or to provide feedback to or from other users. Comments are separate from the cell content. They are identified by a user name so that you can tell who keyed each comment. This is especially important when a worksheet is shared and edited by others.

By default, comments have an indicator in the upper-right corner of the cell in which it was inserted. The user's name and space to key the comment appear in a box. The box is connected to its cell with a line and arrow. In Figure CA21-4 below, the red triangle in cell A5 is the indicator, a black arrow and short line connects the comment box to the cell A5, and the user's name is Coach. The text of the comment is below the user's name.

Figure CA21-4   Worksheet Comment

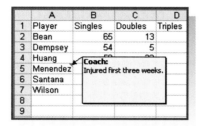

Exercise   3A

Insert Worksheet Comments

1. Open *CD-CA21-3A*. Read about inserting worksheet comments above.

2. Complete steps a through c, using the default settings for box location and size and user name. Verify that an indicator appears in the cells with the comments and that there is an arrow and line connecting the box and cell.

    a. In cell A5, insert this comment: **Injured first three weeks**.

    b. In cell D7, insert this comment: **Was thrown out at 3rd base twice**.

    c. In cell E4, insert this comment: **Includes two inside-the-park homers**.

3. Save as *CA21-3A*.

Learn: Print Worksheet Comments

By default, comment boxes are not printed when the worksheet is printed. To display them with the printed worksheet, select the appropriate option in the Page Setup dialog box (see Figure CA21-5).

Figure CA21-5   Page Setup Dialog Box

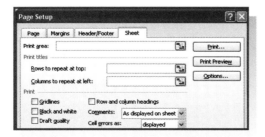

Printing Worksheet Comment Boxes

1. Open *CA21-3A* if it is not already open. Read about printing worksheet comments on the previous page.

2. Print *CA21-3A* with comment boxes using As displayed on sheet option.

3. Print *CA21-3A* with comment boxes using At end of sheet option.

4. Print *CA21-3A* without the comment boxes.

Learn: Resize and Move Worksheet Comment Boxes

Comment boxes can be resized to fit the content in them, and they can be moved from their default locations to elsewhere on the worksheet. To resize a comment box, click its border and then drag the resizing handles until the desired size is reached. To move the comment box, click and drag its border to the desired location when the four-arrow pointer appears.

The comment box in Figure CA21-6 has been resized and moved from its default location. The border has been clicked to reveal the eight resizing handles used to move the comment.

Figure CA21-6 Comment Box

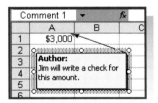

Exercise 3C

Resize and Move Worksheet Comment Boxes

1. Open *CA21-3A* if it is not already open. Read about resizing and moving worksheet comment boxes above.

2. Complete steps a through h below.

   Learning Cue: The user's name in the comment box can be changed by selecting it and keying another user's name.

   a. Reduce the height of the comment box for cell A5 to fit the contents.

   b. Reduce the width of the comment box for cell D7 so *3rd base* appears on the second line with *twice,* and then reduce the height to fit the contents.

   c. Reduce the height of the comment box for cell E4 to fit the contents.

   d. Move the cell A5 comment box so its upper-left corner is aligned with the left edge of column A about .25" below row 7.

e. Move the cell D7 comment box to the right of the comment box for cell A5. Align its top with the top of cell A5 comment box.

   f. Move the cell E4 comment box to the right of the comment box for cell D7. Align its top with the tops of the other two comment boxes.

   g. Change the user's name from *Coach* to **Mr. Bolton**.

   h. Print the worksheet with gridlines, column and row headings, and comments as they are displayed on the worksheet.

3. Save as *CA21-3C*.

Learn: Format Worksheet Comments

The text font, font style, size, color, effects, etc. within a comment box can be changed by selecting the text to be changed and then choosing appropriate options from the Font dialog box. The comment box background color and border color, thickness, and shape can be changed much like you use word processing software to format text boxes.

Exercise **3D**

Format Worksheet Comments

1. Open *CA21-3A*. Read about formatting worksheet comments above.

2. Complete steps a through f below.

   Learning Cue: To access the *Excel* Format Comment dialog box, click in the comment box and then click the border when the resizing handles are visible.

   a. Change the user's name to **Coach Nueva** in all comment boxes.

   b. Change font attributes of the comment text to 10-point, red, Comic Sans MS in all comment boxes.

   c. Change the background color of all comments to a light blue.

   d. Change the border of each comment box to a dashed, dark red, 3-point line.

   e. Resize and move the boxes so each is fully visible.

   f. Print the worksheet displaying the comments as shown.

3. Save as *CA21-3D*.

Learn: Display and Hide Worksheet Comments

By default, worksheet comments and their indicators are displayed on worksheets. By clicking on the Tools menu and using selections in the *Excel* Options dialog, the comments or the comments and their indicators can be hidden. When only the comment is hidden, it can be read by moving the pointer over the cell that contains an indicator. The example in Figure CA21-7 shows that the Comments indicator only radio button has been chosen from the View tab of the Options dialog box.

   Hidden comments and indicators can be displayed by clicking on the View menu and selecting Comments.

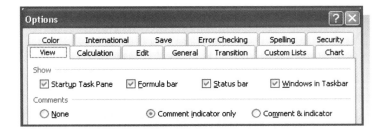

Exercise 3E

Display and Hide Worksheet Comments

1. Open *CD-CA21-1A*. Read about displaying and hiding worksheet comments above and on the previous page.
2. Hide the comment boxes but display their indicators.
3. Hide the comment boxes and their indicators.
4. Display the comment boxes and their indicators.
5. Keep the file open for the next exercise.

Learn: Delete Worksheet Comments

One or more comments can be deleted from a worksheet by selecting the cells that have the comments to be deleted and then deleting their comments by clicking on the *Excel* Edit/Clear menu and selecting Comments.

To select cells quickly, use the Go To command on the Edit menu, click Special, click Comments, and then click OK. Then delete the comments by using the Edit/Clear/Comments command. (See Figure CA21-8.)

Figure CA21-8 Edit Menu

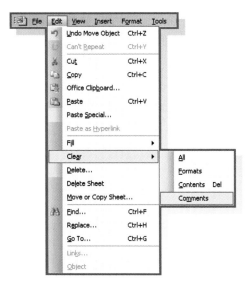

Exercise 3F

Delete Worksheet Comments

1. Open *CD-CA21-1A*. Read about deleting worksheet comments on the previous page.

2. Delete the first comment and then print *CD-CA21-1A* with the remaining comments displayed on the page. Save as *CA21-3F-1*.

3. Open *CD-CA21-1A* and delete all comments at once and then print the worksheet.

4. Save as *CA21-3F-2*.

Exercise 3G

Application: Worksheet with Comments

1. Key the worksheet below.

2. Add a column at the right and compute each student's average.

3. Add a row at the bottom and compute each test and the overall average.

4. You decide all formatting features to make the worksheet attractive and easy to read.

GRADE BOOK				
NAME	TEST 1	TEST 2	TEST 3	TEST 4
ABEL	78	85	72	78
BOGGS	64	66	71	73
CARR	78	82	86	75
FRYZ	90	93	88	86
GOOD	95	82	86	92
HOI	66	85	76	78
LOPEZ	88	80	94	93
MILLS	71	75	73	76
POPE	62	71	73	66
PUSTARI	75	75	71	73
ROSARIO	91	82	88	78
SIA	75	76	81	71
TODD	66	65	50	61
ULM	58	66	76	74
VERI	81	75	85	75
WILLS	75	64	75	70
ZEON	81	74	65	60

5. Insert these comments in the cell indicated. Use Mrs. Kite as the user's name:
   - B7: Volunteered for peer tutoring.
   - C4: Did not attend tutoring.
   - C8: Came to three tutoring sessions.
   - B11: Absent two days before exam.
   - D15: Absent three days during week before exam.
   - D19: Stopped attending tutoring.
   - F15: Reported as ineligible for interscholastic athletics.
6. Resize each comment box to fit its contents.
7. Format all comments the same—do not use the default font, font color, background color, and border.
8. Delete the comment in cell B11.
9. Move each comment so it is visible and does not hide any cell entry.
10. Print the worksheet comments using the As displayed on sheet option.
11. Save as *CA21-3G-1*.
12. Print the worksheet with comments using the At end of sheet option.
13. Save as *CA21-3G-2*.

UNIT 22

LESSONS 1–2

Assessing Advanced Word Processing, Spreadsheet, and Desktop Publishing Skills

Conditioning Practice

Before you begin the lessons, key each line twice.

alphabet 1 Zelda will judge quickly and pay them for excellent book reviews.

fig/sym 2 A loan (#397-4) was made on 5/1/2005 for $68,000 at a rate of 6%.

speed 3 The official paid the men for the handiwork they did on the dock.

gwam 1' | 1 | 2 | 3 | 4 | 5 | 6 | 7 | 8 | 9 | 10 | 11 | 12 | 13 |

LESSON ① ASSESS ADVANCED SPREADSHEET/ WORKSHEET PROCESSING SKILLS

OBJECTIVE

 To assess worksheet processing skills.

Exercise 1A

Worksheet

1. Open *CD-CA22-1A-WKS1* and make these changes:

   a. Change column A to 20 spaces and all other columns to 10 spaces and wrap text in the cells as needed.

   b. Rotate the headings in row 2 45 degrees upward.

   c. Format the numbers as currency with no decimal places.

   d. Change rows 3 through 9 to 26 points and change row 1 to 30 points.

   e. Merge cells A1:G1 and format the text centered in 20-point bold font.

   f. Change the name of Sheet 1 to Portfolio. Delete the Sheet 2 and Sheet 3 tabs.

    g. Add this as a footer: Portfolio Six-Month Performance

    h. Sort the worksheet alphabetically by fund name in ascending order.

    i. Check spelling of the worksheet entries.

    j. Print the worksheet centered horizontally and vertically in landscape orientation.

2. Save as *CA22-1A-WKS1*.

Exercise 1B

Spreadheet and Word Processing

1. Open *CD-CA22-1B-WKS1* and save it as *CA22-1B-WKS1* and then do the following:

    a. Calculate Next Year's Goal in column C by multiplying column B values by cell A2.

    b. Apply conditional formatting in column C so that all cells with salesperson's goals equal to or greater than $260,000 appear in gold font color.

    c. In column D, calculate what percent each salesperson's goal is of next year's total goal. Format the answer as a percent with one decimal place.

    d. Apply an autoformat that makes the worksheet attractive and easy to read. Save the worksheet.

    e. Open *CD-CA22-1B-WP1* (word processing document) and save it as *CA22-1B-WP1*.

    f. Copy *CA22-1B-WKS1* into *CA22-1B-WP1* so the worksheet and wp document are linked. Place the worksheet between the paragraphs so it is horizontally centered. Save the memo file as *CA22-1B-WP1* and close it.

    g. Open *CA22-1B-WKS1* and change the value in cell A2 to 1.09.

    h. Open *CA22-1B-WP1* to update the file with the new goals. Save this document as *CA22-1B-WP2*, print it, and close it.

    i. Open *CA22-1B-WKS1* and create a pie, bar, or column chart with 3D-effects that shows each salesperson's percent of next year's goal. Format the chart to make it attractive and easy to interpret. Display the chart on a chart sheet.

2. Using the Save As Web Page feature, save the worksheet and chart with the name *CA22-1B-WEB*. From your browser, print the chart sheet and the worksheet.

Exercise 1C

Worksheet

1. Open *CD-CA22-1C-WKS1* and make these changes:

   a. Delete the comment in cell A5.

   b. Insert the following comment in cells A7 and A11: E-mail parents about performance. Format it in 12-point Times New Roman bold, red font; resize the box as needed, and display the comments at the bottom of the worksheet.

   c. Create a style named Headings and apply it to rows 1 and 2. The style should have these formats: Text centered horizontally; a bold, blue 12 point font; and a solid blue Outline border around the cells.

   d. Create a style named Grades and apply it to cells B3:G19. The style should have these formats: text centered horizontally and a bold, italic font.

2. Make needed adjustments to the worksheet so the comments are displayed attractively at the bottom of the worksheet. Print the file with the comments displayed. Save the file as *CA22-1C-WKS1*.

3. If needed, open *CA22-1C-WKS1*. Filter the list for all students who earned a B grade. Print the filtered list and save it as *CA22-1C-WKS2*.

LESSON 2

ASSESS ADVANCED WORD PROCESSING AND DESKTOP PUBLISHING SKILLS

OBJECTIVE

> To assess advanced word processing and desktop publishing skills.

Exercise 2A

Newsletter

1. Open *CD-CA22-2A-NEWS* and make these changes:

   a. Format the newsletter with 1" left and right margins arranged in three columns of equal width separated by a vertical line.

   b. Use word art with 3D-effects to format the newsletter name. The newsletter name should span the width of the three columns with a 3-point solid line separating the heading information from the articles.

   c. Use a 14-point bold Arial font style for the article titles (name the style Heading 2 + Not Italic) and 11-point bold Arial font for all other text except the newsletter name.

   d. Hyphenate the titles and articles; justify the articles, but not the titles.

   e. Insert the text on the following page in four shaded text boxes with double-line borders at appropriate places throughout the text.

Text box 1:

> **Recover your containers promptly after collection.**

Text box 2:

> **Where do we get our waste?   About 32% of all household waste comes from packaging.**

Text box 3:

> **Recycling saves money!**
> ❑ **Lowers manufacturing costs for products made from recycled materials**
> ❑ **Avoids costly landfill and incineration fees**
> ❑ **Conserves natural resources**

Text box 4:

> **Costs of recycling include collection, transportation, and processing fees and equipment, container, and labor expenses.**

2. You decide all other formatting features.

3. Balance the columns and print the newsletter.

4. Determine the number of words in the newsletter and write the number in the upper-left corner of the newsletter.

5. Save the newsletter as *CA22-2A-NEWS*.

Exercise 2B

Data Source File

1. Open *CD-CA22-2B-DATA* and make these changes:

   a. Add new fields named Title and Company, and then key the four records below.

Mr. Gerald Bruni Bruni Auto Parts 11184 Greenhaven Drive Navarre, OH 44662-9650	Mrs. Mary Phillip Union Cleaning Co. 123 Marrett Farms Union, OH 45322-3412
Ms. Ruth O'Hara Warren Florists 426 Forest Street Warren, OH 44483-3825	Mr. Henry Lewis Lewis Printing 3140 Beaumont Street Massilon, OH 44647-3140

b. Delete the *Eiber* record.

c. Add the titles and company names for the other records shown below.

Last Name	Title	Company
Adams	Mrs.	Adams Medical Association
Aitken, Albert	Mr.	Compilers Plus
Aitken, Barbara	Mrs.	Database & More
Gioia	Mr.	Four Springs Golf Course
Harris	Mr.	Brite House Electricians
McClintock	Mr.	Banquets Unlimited
Springer	Mrs.	County Motors

d. Sort by postal code in descending order and then alphabetically by last name and then first name.

2. Save the data source file as *CA22-2B-DATA*.

Exercise 2C
Mail Merge

1. Merge *CD-CA22-2C-MAIN* with *CA22-2B-DATA*.

2. Print the last two letters. Save the merged letters as *CA22-2C-LTRS*.

Exercise 2D
Mailing Labels

1. Prepare a standard mailing label for each record in the data source *CA22-2B-DATA*. Save the main document file as *CA22-2D-MAIN* and the merged document file as *CA22-2D-LBLS*.

2. Print the mailing labels.

Exercise 2E
Merge Documents

1. Open *CD-CA22-2E* and save it as *CA22-2E-REV1*.

2. Use the Track Changes feature to make these revisions:

   a. Change *there* to their in line 2, paragraph 1.

   b. Insert daily before *habits* in line 3, paragraph 1.

   c. Hyphenate *one-on-one* in line 1, paragraph 2.

   d. Add and medical appointments to the sentence in paragraph 2.

3. Save the changes.

4. Use the Compare and Merge feature to merge the comments of *CA22-2E-REV1* and *CD-CA22-2E-REV2*.

5. Assume that all the changes are desirable; therefore, accept/reject changes as needed to make the final copy correct.

6. Save as *CA22-2E-FINAL*.

Communication & Math Skills 6

Terminal Punctuation: Period, Question Mark, Exclamation Point

1. Study each of the five rules shown below in the color boxes.

a. Key the *Learn* line(s) beneath each rule, noting how the rule is applied.

b. Key the *Apply* line(s), using correct terminal punctuation.

Terminal punctuation: Period

Rule 1: Use a period at the end of a declarative sentence (a sentence that is not regarded as a question or exclamation).

Learn 1 I wonder why *Phantom of the Opera* has always been so popular.
Apply 2 Fran and I saw *Cats* in London We also saw *Sunset Boulevard*

Rule 2: Use a period at the end of a polite request stated in the form of a question but not intended as one.

Learn 3 Matt, will you please collect the papers at the end of each row.
Apply 4 Will you please call me at 555-0140 to set up an appointment

Terminal punctuation: Question mark

Rule 3: Use a question mark at the end of a sentence intended as a question.

Learn 5 Did you go to the annual flower show in Ault Park this year?
Apply 6 How many medals did the U.S.A. win in the 1996 Summer Games

Rule 4: For emphasis, a question mark may be used after each item in a series of interrogative expressions.

Learn 7 Can we count on wins in gymnastics? in diving? in soccer?
Apply 8 What grade did you get for history for sociology for civics

Terminal punctuation: Exclamation point

Rule 5: Use an exclamation point after emphatic (forceful) exclamations and after phrases and sentences that are clearly exclamatory.

Learn 9 The lady screamed, "Stop that man!"
Learn 10 "Bravo!" many yelled at the end of the Honor America program.

Apply 11 "Yes" her gym coach exclaimed when Kerri stuck the landing.
Apply 12 The burglar stopped when he saw the sign, "Beware, vicious dog"

2. Key *Proofread & Correct*, using correct terminal punctuation.

  a. Check answers.

b. Using the rule number(s) at the left of each line, study the rule relating to each error you made.

c. Rekey each incorrect line, using correct terminal punctuation.

Proofread & Correct

Rules	
5	"Jump" the fireman shouted to the young boy frozen with
1	fear on the window ledge of the burning building "Will you
3	catch me" the young boy cried to the men and women holding a
1,5,1	safety net forty feet below "Into the net" they yelled
	Mustering his courage, the boy jumped safely into the net and
1	then into his mother's outstretched arms

3. Save as *CS6-ACT1*.

ACTIVITY 2   Listening

1. Open sound file *CD-CS6 -ACT2*, which is a set of driving directions.

2. Take notes as you listen to the directions to the Mansfield Soccer Field.

3. Close the sound file.

4. Using your notes, key the directions in sentence form.

5. Save as *CS6-ACT2*.

ACTIVITY 3   Write to Learn

1. Using word processing or voice recognition software, write a paragraph explaining how you would split a window so you can display a document in two panes.

2. Write a second paragraph explaining what a style is and how you can use the Style feature.

3. Save as *CS6-ACT3*.

ACTIVITY 4   Composing

1. Read the paragraph below.

2. Compose a paragraph indicating what you think the results of your poll would be and what your response would be.

3. Proofread, revise, and correct.

4. Save as *CS6-ACT4*.

If you were to take a poll of your classmates, what percent of them would believe that current TV and movie fare glamorizes violence and sex without portraying the negative consequences of immoral behavior? What percent would have the opposite belief?

ACTIVITY 5   Math: Finding the Whole of a Number

1. Open *CD-CS6-ACT5* and print the file.

2. Solve the problems as directed in the file.

3. Submit your answers.

Skill BUILDER 4

Tabulation

1. Set tabs at 1.5", 3", and 4.5" from the left margin.
2. Key the text, using the TAB key to move from column to column.
3. Key three 1' writings.

Alabama Montgomery	Alaska Juneau	Arizona Phoenix	Arkansas Little Rock
California Sacramento	Colorado Denver	Connecticut Hartford	Delaware Dover
Florida Tallahassee	Georgia Atlanta	Hawaii Honolulu	Idaho Boise
Illinois Springfield	Indiana Indianapolis	Iowa Des Moines	Kansas Topeka

Timed Writing

1. Take a 1' writing.
2. Add 5 *wam* to the rate attained in step 1.
3. Take four 1' writings, trying to achieve the rate set in step 2.

A all letters used (MicroPace)

gwam 1'

A basic knowledge of parliamentary procedure is an excellent 12

skill to acquire. Those who possess this skill will be able to 25

put it to use in any organization they belong to that conducts 38

meetings based on parliamentary law. A meeting that is run by 50

this procedure will be conducted in a proper and very orderly 63

fashion. Just as important, the rights of each member of the 75

group are protected at all times. 82

gwam 1' | 1 | 2 | 3 | 4 | 5 | 6 | 7 | 8 | 9 | 10 | 11 | 12 | 13 |

Reading/Keying Response Patterns

Key each line 3 times (slowly, faster, top speed).

Goal: To reduce time interval between keystrokes (read ahead to anticipate stroking pattern).

Emphasize curved, upright fingers; finger action keystroking.

1 car no cat inn fat ink ear beg verb sea lip oil tea pull see milk
2 acre pool rest link base lily seat lion vase noun dear junk barge

Emphasize independent finger action; stationary hands.

3 at my best|in my career|best dessert|my bad debts|my exact grades
4 only rebate|in my opinion|we deserve better|minimum grade average

Emphasize continuity; finger action with fingers close to keys.

5 Ada agreed on a minimum oil target after a decrease in oil taxes.
6 In my opinion, Edward Freeberg agreed on a greater water reserve.

gwam 1' | 1 | 2 | 3 | 4 | 5 | 6 | 7 | 8 | 9 | 10 | 11 | 12 | 13 |

UNIT 23

LESSONS 1–3

Creating Advanced Electronic Presentations

Conditioning Practice

Before you begin the lessons, key each line twice.

alphabet 1 Carl asked to be given just a week to reply to the tax quiz form.

fig/sym 2 Rooms 268 and 397 were cleaned for the 10:45 meetings last night.

speed 3 Nancy may go to the big social at the giant chapel on the island.

gwam 1' | 1 | 2 | 3 | 4 | 5 | 6 | 7 | 8 | 9 | 10 | 11 | 12 | 13 |

LESSON 1 LEARN MICROSOFT PRODUCER

OBJECTIVES
⊘ To learn about *Producer's* capabilities by viewing a presentation created with *Producer.*
⊘ To learn the basic features of *Producer.*

Learn: What Is Producer?

Microsoft Producer software allows you to create high-level presentations that combine audio, video, text, and still images. With *Producer* you can capture, import, organize, and synchronize these different types of media to develop very sophisticated presentations.

Once produced, the presentation can be delivered in a variety of ways, including CDs, the Internet, and e-service providers' sites. If a company has its own intranet, the presentations can be made available to company employees throughout the world via the intranet. The presentations that are produced with this type of software are being used not only in the business environment but in the educational environment as well.

View Presentation

1. Open and view the *Producer* file: *Mike and Nicole Presentation.htm.*

2. As you view the presentation, notice how the video clips are synchronized with the *PowerPoint* slides to give a professional-looking presentation.

Learn: Key Features of Producer Software

Now that you know what *Producer* is capable of doing, let's learn the key features of the software so that you will be able to create a presentation using *Producer* software. Let's start by having you open the *Producer* software and discussing the key features. Since you are not going to be creating a presentation at this time, click Cancel on the dialog box that appears on the screen asking how you want to create your presentation.

You should be familiar with many of the commands on the *Producer* menu bar and toolbar; they are the same as those you used in other Microsoft programs. However, there are some new features that you will need to know in order to use *Producer*.

Beneath the toolbar are three tabs—the Media tab, the Table of Contents tab, and the Preview Presentation tab. Since you have not yet created a presentation using *Producer*, the screens you view will not have any files and will be different than the illustrations shown in this lesson.

Media Tab

The Media tab pane shows the folders of the different types of media that can be imported or recorded in *Producer*. When video is imported, it will automatically be placed in the Video folder. When slides are imported, they will automatically be placed in the Slides folder.

Figure CA23-1 illustrates what the Media tab pane looks like for the presentation you viewed earlier. When the presentation you viewed was produced, it was saved in a file called *Mike and Nicole Presentation*. Notice the six video files that are shown beneath the *Video* folder and the seven slide files that are shown beneath the *Slides* folder. These are the video and slide files that were imported and used to produce the presentation that you viewed at the beginning of this lesson.

The middle of the Media tab pane shows the files for the folder that has been clicked (video files). Double-clicking on one of the picture icons (video files) activates the file and allows you to preview the video file in the black screen at the far right of the pane.

You can view the content of the other folders in the same way. Simply click on the folder and the files will appear in the middle of the pane.

Table of Contents Tab

The Table of Contents in *Producer* is much like the table of contents of a textbook; it provides information about what is included in the presentation. Clicking on an entry in the Table of Contents automatically takes you to that part of the presentation. The Table of Contents pane for the presentation you just observed is shown in Figure CA23-2.

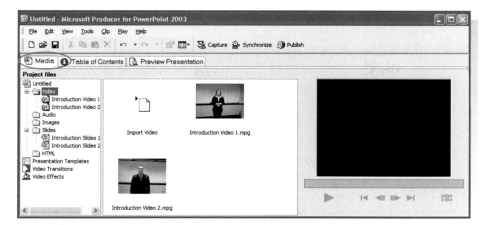

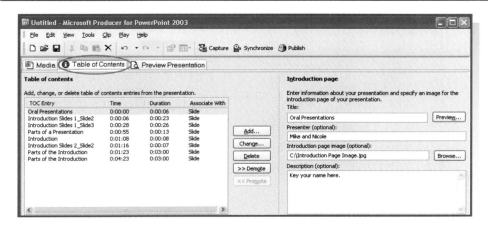

An entry appears for each slide that is included in the presentation. These entries are automatically placed in the Table of Contents as each *PowerPoint* file is imported into the presentation. There will be an entry for each slide of each file that is imported. If there is text on the slide, the entry will be the first line of text on the slide. If there are only graphics on the slide, the entry will be the name of the file and the number of the slide in the file. For example, the first entry in the Table of Contents is *Oral Presentation* and the second entry is *Slides for the Introduction for Nicole_Slide 2* (see Figures CA23-3 and CA23-4 below).

Figure CA23-3   Slide 1 of Table of Contents (*Oral Presentations*)

Figure CA23-4   Slide 2 of Table of Contents (*Slides for the Introduction for Nicole_Slide 2*)

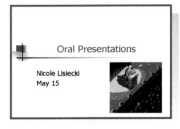

The right-hand portion of the Table of Contents pane displays the information that is included on the Introduction page of the presentation. Information such as the title, name of the presenter(s), introduction page image, and description of the presentation can be included on this page. Once the information is keyed and/or imported, it can be viewed by clicking the Preview button. Figure CA23-5 shows the introduction page created for the presentation you viewed at the beginning of this lesson. The length of the presentation is also shown on the introduction page. The length is automatically calculated and entered.

Notice that the title of the presentation (*Oral Presentations*) appears at the top of the screen; a graphic, if included, is placed in the middle of the screen; and the presenters' names are placed beneath the graphic. The length of the presentation is placed at the bottom of the screen at the left margin.

Figure CA23-5   Introduction Page

Preview Presentations Tab

The Preview Presentation Tab pane (Figure CA23-6) can be used to preview the presentation by using the playback buttons located beneath the video portion of the pane on the left-hand side. The function of each playback button is shown in Figure CA23-7.

Figure CA23-6   Preview Presentation Tab

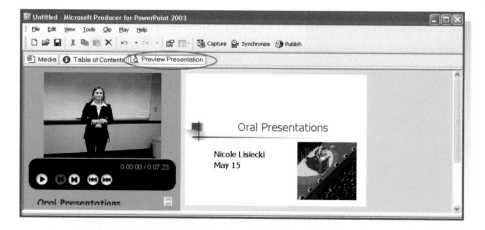

Playback Buttons

The Play/Pause button starts and stops the video clip. The (◄) button takes the presentation back to the point where the previous slide is first displayed. The (►) button advances the presentation to the point where the next slide is displayed. Each time you click on the (◄◄) button, you are rewinding the presentation by 10 seconds. To go forward in the presentation by 10 seconds, click the (►►) button. Each time you click it, it will advance the presentation by 10 seconds.

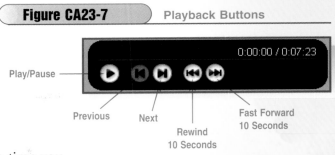

Figure CA23-7   Playback Buttons

Play/Pause

Previous   Next   Rewind 10 Seconds   Fast Forward 10 Seconds

0:00:00 / 0:07:23

Timeline

The bottom portion of the Producer pane is where the timeline is shown. There are four parts to the timeline—the timeline tools, the timeline display, the timeline tracks, and the hide timeline feature. The parts of the timeline are labeled in Figure CA23-8.

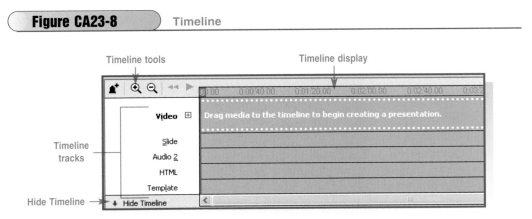

Figure CA23-8   Timeline

Timeline tools

Timeline display

Timeline tracks

Video

Slide
Audio 2
HTML
Template

Drag media to the timeline to begin creating a presentation.

Hide Timeline → ↓ Hide Timeline

Timeline Tools

There are five timeline tools that are included in the timeline portion of the screen. The tools with their corresponding icons are shown below along with a brief description of their function.

🔹	Timeline snaps	The timeline snaps tool is used to synchronize two different types of files so they play at the same time. For example, if you want to have a slide appear at the same time a video file appears, a timeline snap can be inserted at the beginning of the video file. You can then click and drag the slide to snap to the same point on the timeline.
🔍	Timeline zoom in	The timeline zoom in feature allows you to see the files on the timeline in greater detail. Zooming in decreases the amount of time displayed on the timeline.
🔍	Timeline zoom out	The timeline zoom out feature does just the opposite. It decreases the detail of each file and increases the amount of time displayed on the timeline.
◄◄	Timeline rewind	The timeline rewind tool takes the playback point to the beginning of the timeline.
►	Timeline play/pause	The timeline play/pause starts and stops the playback of the files on the timeline.

Timeline Display

The timeline display shows the time in hours, minutes, and seconds (H:M:S). It can be used to determine the length of each file in the presentation as well as the approximate length of the entire presentation. For example, Figure CA23-9 shows that the first file on the timeline took 1 minute and 7.47 seconds.

Figure CA23-9 Timeline Display

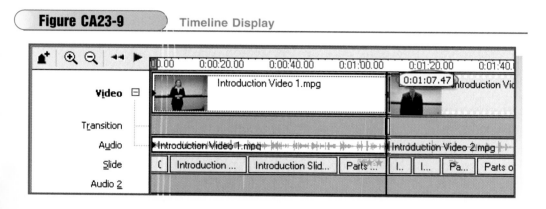

Timeline Tracks

The timeline tracks portion of *Producer* allows you to work with a variety of different types of files. There are separate tracks for:

- Video
- Audio
- Audio 2
- Templates
- Transitions
- Slides
- HTML

In the presentation you viewed there were video, audio, slide, and template files included. These are shown in Figure CA23-10.

Figure CA23-10 Timeline Tracks

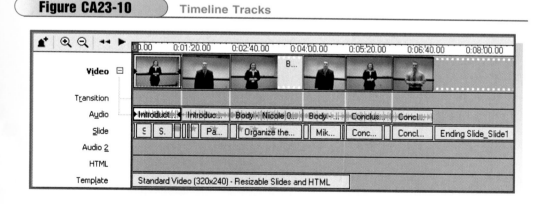

By using the zoom in feature, you will be able to see the files in greater detail. Notice as the zoom feature is used the filename is also shown; see Figure CA23-11. This is helpful for working with the files that you include in the project.

Figure CA23-11 Zoom In on Timeline Tracks

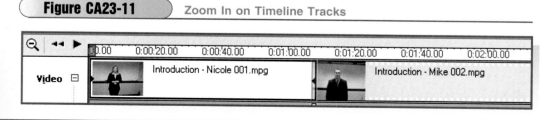

Hide Timeline

The hide timeline feature allows you to take the timeline off the screen. When you click on this feature, the timeline is no longer displayed; the size of the top portion of the screen is increased to fill the screen. This is particularly useful when you are using the Preview Presentation tab. When the timeline is hidden, the size of the slides increases and you are able to see more of the table of contents that appears beneath the video.

These are the basic features you will use in the next lesson as you develop a presentation using *Producer*.

LESSON ② LEARN MICROSOFT PRODUCER

OBJECTIVE

⊙ To create a presentation using *Producer*.

Learn: New Presentation Wizard

The New Presentation Wizard is a feature of *Producer* that will walk you through the step-by-step process of importing files to create a presentation. The files you import into *Producer* may be files created by someone else or files created by you. The Wizard is very helpful as you learn *Producer*.

Exercise 2A

Create a Presentation

Creating a presentation using *Producer* is quite easy. Let's recreate the first part of the presentation on giving an oral presentation that you viewed in Lesson 1 by using the New Presentation Wizard and following the steps shown below:

1. Open *Producer*.
2. Select **Use the New Presentation Wizard** and click **OK** (Figure CA23-12). If *Producer* is already open, select **New Presentation Wizard** from the File menu.

Figure CA23-12 — Use the New Presentation Wizard

Figure CA23-13 — Welcome to the New Presentation Wizard

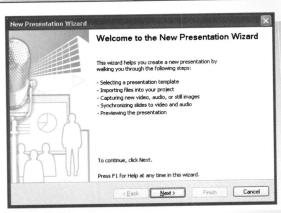

3. When the *Welcome to the New Presentation Wizard* screen comes up, click **Next** (Figure CA23-13).

4. When the *Presentation Template* screen comes up, select **Default** and click **Next** (Figure CA23-14).

Figure CA23-14 Presentation Template

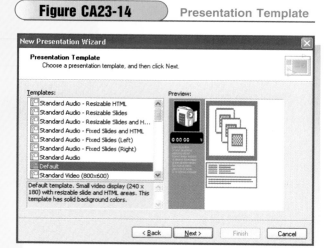

Figure CA23-15 Choose a Presentation Scheme

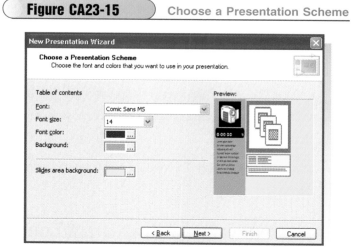

5. When the *Choose a Presentation Scheme* screen appears, use the drop-down menus to select the following (Figure CA23-15):

Font: **Comic Sans MS**
Font size: **14**
Font color: **Black**
Background: **Light green**
Slides area background: **Light yellow**

After making the changes shown above, click **Next**.

Note: Making the changes will give the presentation a different look from the one you viewed in Lesson 1.

If you don't like the color scheme, click **<Back** and select new colors.

6. When the *Presentation Information* screen appears, key the information as shown in Figure CA23-16 for the Title, Presenter, and Description.

Figure CA23-16 Presentation Information

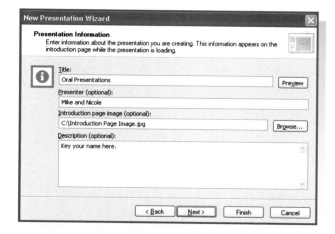

Use the Browse button to locate and insert the *Introduction Page Image* file. After clicking on the Browse button, locate the folder containing the file you want to insert. Once you open the folder, click on the file you want to insert (*Introduction Page Image.jpg*) and click **Open** in the lower-right corner of the screen. When you are finished keying and importing the file, click **Next**.

Introduction Page Image.jpg

7. On the *Import slides and Still Images* screen (Figure CA23-17), use **Browse** to locate and insert the two *PowerPoint* files (*Introduction Slides 1.ppt* and *Introduction Slides 2.ppt*).

   To do this:

   a. Click the **Browse** button.

   b. Locate the folder containing the desired file (*Introduction Slides 1.ppt*).

   c. Click on the file (*Introduction Slides 1.ppt*).

   d. Click **Open**.

   e. Click the **Browse** button again.

   f. Click on the second file (*Introduction Slides 2.ppt*).

   g. Click **Open**.

   h. Click **Next**.

Figure CA23-17   Import Slides and Still Images

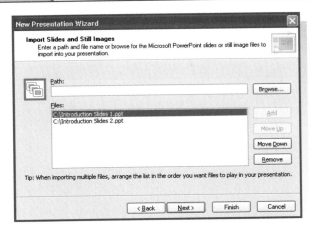

8. On the *Import or Capture Audio and Video* screen (Figure CA23-18), use **Browse** to locate and insert the two video files (*Introduction Video 1.mpg* and *Introduction Video 2.mpg*). Use the same procedure for inserting these files as you did for inserting files in Step 7.

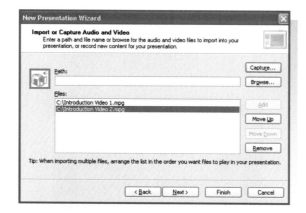

When you are finished inserting the files, click **Next**.

9. On the *Synchronize Presentation* screen (Figure CA23-19), select **Yes** and click **Next**.

Figure CA23-19   Synchronize Presentation

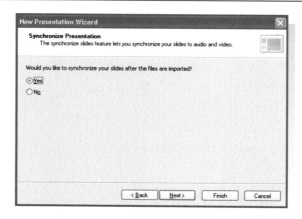

10. On the *Complete Presentation* screen (Figure CA23-20), click **Finish**.

Figure CA23-20   Complete Presentation

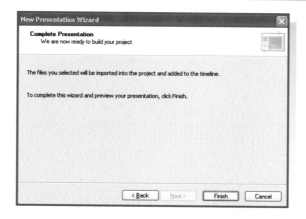

You are now ready to learn how to synchronize the media. Keep the file open for the next exercise.

Learn: Synchronize Media

After the files have been imported into the presentation, the synchronize feature of *Producer* lets you coordinate the playing of the audio and video files with *Power-Point* slides and still images. For example, if the video clip is of a speaker talking about five different video games, still images of each game could be made to appear as the speaker is talking about each of the five games.

When the files finish loading, your screen should look like Figure CA23-21. The Synchronize Slides page appears automatically when you click **Finish** in the last screen of the Wizard. You can also get the Synchronize Slides page to appear by clicking on Tools on the menu bar and selecting Synchronize.

Figure CA23-21   Synchronize Slides

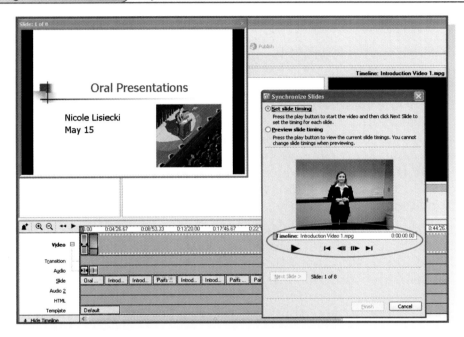

Notice the area that is circled in red and shown below. You will need to understand the function of each of the circled items in order to synchronize the *Power-Point* slides that you inserted in the file with the video files.

Figure CA23-22   Synchronize Buttons

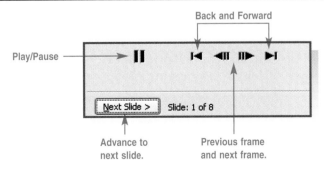

When you click on ▶, the audio file will start. Once you start playing the file, you can click the arrow again to stop playing the file. The arrow will change to the parallel bars shown in Figure CA23-22.

1. A script of the audio file is shown below. Read through the script in preparation for synchronizing the files. Red arrows (▼) have been placed in the script at each location where a slide should be advanced.

Script for Presentation

How do you think people responded when asked what their greatest fear was? ▼ Interestingly enough, two of their responses were the fear of speaking in public and the fear of death. They ranked the fear of public speaking higher than the fear of death. I guess that means that people would rather die than get up before a group of people and give a presentation. ▼ Hi, my name is Nicole Lisiecki, and today, I'll be talking with you about giving a good oral presentation. I'll be sharing with you some of what I've learned about giving an oral presentation while attending college. During the past four years I've been a student at the University of Wisconsin-Eau Claire. During that time I've had many opportunities to give presentations in classes as well as organizations that I've belonged to. ▼ Today I'll be talking with you about the three parts of a good presentation. These parts include: The Introduction ▼ The Body, ▼ and The Summary or Conclusion. ▼ So, let's get started. ▼

You have just seen and heard the delivery of the first part of a presentation—the introduction. ▼ My name is Mike Axon, and I'll be discussing the introduction. A good introduction accomplishes three things. First, ▼ the introduction should capture the audience's attention. ▼ Nicole did this by asking a question. "How do you think people responded when asked what their greatest fear was?" ▼ Secondly, the introduction should establish the speaker's credibility. Another word for credibility is believability. Why are you up there giving the presentation rather than the person that's sitting next to you? Nicole established her credibility by briefly talking about the many presentations that she has given while attending UW-Eau Claire. ▼ And thirdly, the speaker introduces their topic and previews what they are going to be talking about next. Nicole did this by stating, "Today, I'll be talking with you about the three parts of a good presentation. These parts include: The Introduction, The Body, and The Summary or Conclusion." Now let's go back and hear the body of Nicole's presentation.

---

2. Now you are ready to synchronize the *PowerPoint* slides with the video files. Click on the Play button. Follow along with the narrative. When you come to a red arrow, click on the **Next Slide** button to synchronize the *PowerPoint* slides with the video file. When you have inserted the last slide, click **Finish**.

3. Now you are ready to preview the presentation. Click on the **Play/Pause** button beneath the video clip. If you have completed the steps correctly, your slides should now be synchronized with your video. Remember that you can click on **Hide Timeline** to show the presentation on the entire screen. Keep the file open for the next exercise.

Learn: Video Transitions

Video transitions can be used between video files to enhance your presentation. A transition is a passage from one video file to another video file. Rather than have one file end and the next one begin, a transition can be added, which gives the presentation a more professional appearance.

Exercise 2C
Add Transitions

Let's now add a transition between the video files of Nicole and Mike by completing the following steps.

1. Click the **Media** tab.
2. Click **Video Transitions**, which is located under the file folders on the Media tab. (See Figure CA23-23.)
3. On the timeline, locate the playback indicator between the two video files. The easiest way to do this is by clicking on the second picture on the timeline (see Figure CA23-24).

Figure CA23-23 Video Transitions

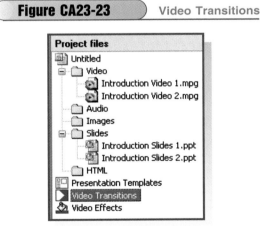

Figure CA23-24 Playback Indicator

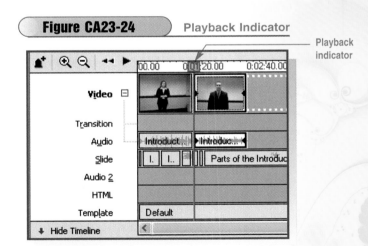

4. Click the desired transition effect. For this one, let's go with **Circle**, **Out** (see Figure CA23-25).
5. On the menu bar, click **Clip** and then click **Add To Timeline**.
6. Use the Preview Presentation tab to view the transition. You can view only that portion of the presentation by placing the playback indictor near the end of the first video file and playing from that point.
7. Save the file as *CA23-2C*.

Now you are ready to publish your presentation. You will learn to publish a presentation in the next lesson.

LESSON ③ LEARN TO PUBLISH A PRODUCER FILE

OBJECTIVE

⊙ To publish a presentation using *Producer.*

Learn: Publishing Your Presentation

Generally, you create a presentation to communicate a message to others. *Producer* lets you communicate your message (presentation) to others in a variety of ways. You can make a copy of your presentation available on a CD, on a network, or on a Web server. Or you can simply make it available on your computer and use a data projector to show the presentation to a large audience.

In order to make your presentation available to others using any of these means of distribution, you will need to learn how to publish your presentation. This is quite simple to do using the **Publish Wizard**. The Publish Wizard takes you through a step-by-step publishing process.

Publish Wizard

Exercise ③A

Publish a Presentation

Let's publish the presentation you created in Lesson 2 by using the Publish Wizard. Follow these steps:

1. Create a new folder for publishing your presentation. Name the folder **Unit 23**. You will use this folder in Step 5.

2. Open *CA23-2C,* the file you created in the last lesson.

3. Click the **Publish** button on the toolbar.

4. When the *Select a Playback Site* appears on the screen, select **My Computer** and click **Next**. (See Figure CA23-26.)

Notice that this option allows you to publish the presentation on your computer or to a CD. The other options available are to publish the presentation to *My Network Places* or to a *Web Server.*

5. When the *Publishing Destination* screen appears (Figure CA23-27), key **CA23-3A-Your Name** for the filename; use the **Browse** feature to locate the folder where you want to publish the files (Unit 23). Then click **Next**.

6. When the *Presentation Information* screen comes up (Figure CA23-28), key in the following information.

   Title: Oral Presentations
   Presenter: Mike and Nicole

   Introduction Page Image: *Introduction Page Image.jpg*. Use the **Browse** feature to locate the file. After locating the file, click on it and then click Open.

   Description: Key your name
   Click **Next**.

7. When the *Publish Settings* screen appears (Figure CA23-29), click on **Use suggested settings** and then click **Next**.

8. When the *Publish Your Presentation* screen appears, click **Next** to begin publishing your presentation. The screen shown in Figure CA23-30 will appear. It will take a few minutes to complete this step.

9. On the *Presentation Preview* screen (Figure CA23-31), click on the medium that is available on your computer for playback. Wait until the next screen appears—it will take a few seconds.

Figure CA23-30 Publish Your Presentation

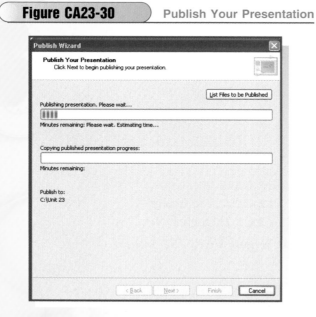

Figure CA23-31 Presentation Preview

Depending on your computer security settings, you may get security messages similar to those shown in Figures CA23-32.

If so, click **Yes** to allow the scripts and Active Content.

Once the title screen appears, click **Play** to view your presentation. When you are done viewing the presentation, close *Microsoft Internet Explorer*.

After the initial viewing of the published file, the file can be viewed again by accessing it through My Computer or by opening it in *Internet Explorer* or another medium that was selected in Step 9.

Figure CA23-32 Security Messages

Communication & Math Skills 7

1. Study each of the six rules described below in the color boxes.

a. Key the *Learn* line(s) beneath each rule, noting how the rule is applied.

b. Key the *Apply* lines, inserting commas correctly.

Internal Punctuation: Comma

Rule 1: Use a comma after (a) introductory phrases or clauses and (b) words in a series.

Learn   1   When you finish keying the report, please give it to Mr. Kent.
Learn   2   We will play the Mets, Expos, and Cubs in our next home stand.

Apply   3   If you attend the play take Mary Jack and Tim with you.
Apply   4   The last exam covered memos simple tables and unbound reports.

Rule 2: Do not use a comma to separate two items treated as a single unit within a series.

Learn   5   Her favorite breakfast was bacon and eggs, muffins, and juice.

Apply   6   My choices are peaches and cream brownies or ice cream.
Apply   7   Trays of fresh fruit nuts and cheese and crackers awaited guests.

Rule 3: Use a comma before short direct quotations.

Learn   8   The man asked, "When does Flight 787 depart?"
Apply   9   Mrs. Ramirez replied "No, the report on patriotism is not finished."
Apply   10   Dr. Feit said "Please make an appointment for next week."

Rule 4: Use a comma before and after a word or words in apposition (words that come together and refer to the same person or thing).

Learn   11   Coleta, the assistant manager, will chair the next meeting.
Apply   12   Greg Mathews a pitcher for the Braves will sign autographs.
Apply   13   The personnel director Marge Wilson will be the presenter.

Rule 5: Use a comma to set off words of direct address (the name of a person spoken to).

Learn   14   I believe, Tom, that you should fly to San Francisco.
Apply   15   Finish this assignment Mary before you start on the next one.
Apply   16   Please call me Erika if I can be of further assistance.

Rule 6: Use a comma to set off nonrestrictive clauses (not necessary to the meaning of the sentence); however, do not use commas to set off restrictive clauses (necessary to the meaning of the sentence).

Learn   17   The manuscript, which I prepared, needs to be revised.
Learn   18   The manuscript that presents voting alternatives is complete.

Apply   19   The movie which won top awards dealt with human rights.
Apply   20   The student who scores highest on the exam will win the award.

2. Key *Proofread & Correct* on the following page, inserting commas correctly.
  a. Check answers.

b. Using the rule number(s) at the left of each line, study the rule relating to each error you made.

c. Rekey each incorrect line, inserting commas correctly.

Proofread & Correct

Rules
1	1	My favorite sports are college football basketball and soccer.
1	2	If you finish your history report before noon please give me a call.
1,2	3	I snacked on milk and cookies granola and some raisins.
3	4	Miss Qwan said "I was born in Taiwan."
4	5	Mr. Sheldon the historian will speak to our students today.
5	6	Why do you persist Kermit in moving your hands to the top row?
6	7	The report which Ted wrote is well organized and informative.
6	8	Only students who use their time wisely are likely to succeed.
3	9	Dr. Sachs said "Take two of these and call me in the morning."
6	10	Yolanda who is from Cuba intends to become a U.S. citizen.

3. Save as *CS7-ACT1*.

ACTIVITY 2 — Reading

1. Open *CD-CS7-ACT2*.
2. Read the document; close the file.

3. Key answers to the questions below, using complete sentences.

4. Save as *CS7-ACT2*.

1. What was the final score of yesterday's soccer match?
2. Was the winning goal scored in the first or second half?
3. Will last year's City League champion be playing in this year's championship match?
4. Will the top-ranked team in the state be playing in this year's championship match?
5. Will the top-ranked team in the city be playing in the championship match?
6. Is the championship game to be played during the day or the evening?
7. Has one or both of the teams playing in the championship match won a City League championship before?

ACTIVITY 3 — Composing

1. Key the paragraph below, correcting word-choice errors. (Every line contains at least one error.)
2. Compose a second paragraph to accomplish these goals:

• Define what respect means to you.
• Identify kinds of behavior that help earn your respect.
• Identify kinds of behavior that cause you to lose respect.

3. Proofread, revise, and correct.
4. Save as *CS7-ACT3*.

That all individuals want others too respect them is not surprising. What is surprising is that sum people think their do respect even when there own behavior has been unacceptable or even illegal. Key two the issue is that we respect others because of certain behavior, rather then in spite of it. Its vital, than, to no that what people due and say determines the level of respect there given buy others. In that regard, than, respect has to be earned; its not hour unquestioned right to demand it. All of you hear and now should begin to chose behaviors that will led others to respect you. Its you're choice.

ACTIVITY 4 — Math: Working with Percents of Change

1. Open *CD-CS7-ACT4* and print the file.

2. Solve the problems as directed in the file.

3. Submit your answers.

UNIT 24

LESSONS 1–8

Database Overview and Developing Database Skills

LESSON 1 DEVELOP DATABASE SKILLS

OBJECTIVES
- ⊗ To create a database.
- ⊗ To create database tables.
- ⊗ To create database forms.
- ⊗ To key information into tables and forms.

Learn: What Is a Database?

A database is an organized collection of information. A few examples of different types of databases include customers' names and addresses, personnel records, sales records, payroll records, inventory records, telephone numbers, and investment records.

Learn: Database Objects

A database may include tables for storing information, queries for drawing information from one or more tables, forms for displaying information, and reports for summarizing and presenting information. Database tables, queries, forms, and reports are called database objects. (See Figure CA24-1 on the following page.)

Learn: Database Tables

Database tables are created by the user in software programs designed for inputting, organizing, and storing database information. The tables are set up to contain

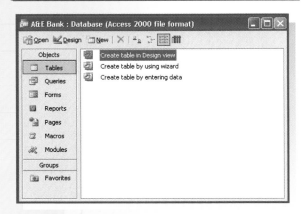

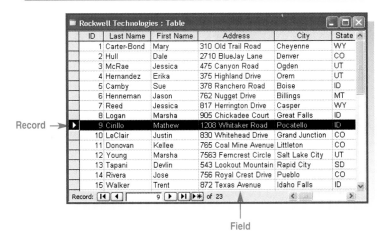

columns and rows of information. In a database table, the columns are called **fields** and the rows are called **records**.

fields
records

The table illustration shown in Figure CA24-2 shows a table that contains five fields—*Last Name*, *First Name*, *Address*, *City*, and *State* (plus the ID number).

Record 9 is highlighted in the illustration and shows the information contained in each of the five fields for one person (Mathew Cirillo). The database table is the foundation from which forms, queries, and reports are created based on the information in the table.

Learn: Define and Sequence Fields of Database Tables

source document

primary key

Fields should be arranged in the same order as the data in the **source document** (paper form from which data is keyed). This sequence reduces the time needed to key the field contents and to maintain the records. The illustration shown in Figure CA24-3 shows the field definition and sequence for the table shown above. The **primary key** shown below is used to identify each record in the table with a number. In this case, a unique ID number would automatically be assigned each sales rep's record. Thus, no two sales reps could be given the same ID number.

Learn: Define Field Properties

The bottom half of the Design View screen, shown in Figure CA24-4, is the area called field properties. This area is used to customize the fields in the database.

Primary
Key

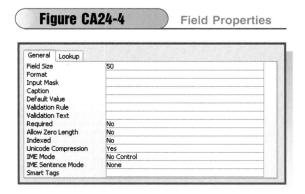

The **Format** field property allows you to display numbers, dates, times, and text in specific ways. For example, if you keyed 1-5-2006 in the field where the Long Date Format had been selected, it would automatically format the date as Thursday, January 05, 2006.

Format

The **Input Mask** controls the data format allowed in the field. For example, if the field is to be used for telephone numbers, an input mask can be used that will automatically insert the parentheses, space, and hyphens in a phone number. When an Input mask is used, the data entry person only keys the numbers. A number such as 7158364877 would automatically appear as (715) 836-4877.

Input Mask

When the field name is not what you want to use in a table or a form, you can use the Caption field property. What you input as the Caption will automatically appear in the designated field rather than the field name.

The **Default Value** field property will automatically insert what is designated as the default value in each record unless something else is imputed. For example, if 95 percent of the customers in a database were from the state of Colorado and only 5 percent were from Wyoming, a default value of "Colorado" could be used. Thus, only when the customer was from Wyoming would you need to input the state.

Default Value

The **Required** field property is used when not having information keyed in the field is unacceptable. For example, if you have a database for contacting individuals via the telephone, you would want to have the phone field required. Once the phone field has been defined as being required, *Access* alerts you that there is no information in the phone field if you try to key a record without recording a phone number.

Required

Learn: Database Forms

Database forms are created from database tables and queries. Forms are used for keying, viewing, and editing data.

Database forms are computerized versions of paper forms, such as a job application or a class registration form. On a printed form, you fill in the blanks with the information that is requested, such as your name and address. In a database form, the blanks in which information is keyed are called **fields**. When the blanks are filled in, the form becomes a **record**. The form illustrated in Figure CA24-5 is Mathew Cirillo's record (Record 9) from the table illustrated in Figure CA24-2.

Depending on the software used, a variety of different form formats are available. Forms may be created manually or by using the software Wizard.

Learn: Database Query

Queries are questions. The Query feature of a database program allows you to ask for specific information to be retrieved from tables that have been created. For example,

Figure CA24-5 Database Form

the query shown in Figures CA24-6 and CA24-7 is based on the table illustration in Figure CA24-2. The query answers the question, *"Which sales reps live in Colorado?"*

When the sales rep table is expanded to include sales, a query could be made requesting all sales reps with sales over $45,000 for July or all sales reps with sales less than $45,000. By using the query feature, you can answer a variety of questions that are based on the information contained in database tables.

Figure CA24-6   Database Query

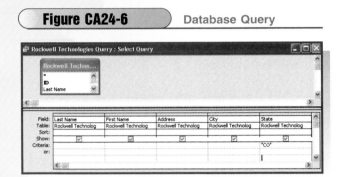

Figure CA24-7   Select Query

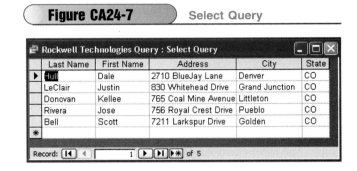

Learn: Database Report

Database reports are created from database tables and queries. Reports are used for organizing, summarizing, and printing information. The easiest way to generate a report is by using the Report Wizard. The Report Wizard provides for grouping and sorting the data, as well as for designing various layouts and styles in which to present the data. Notice in the example report shown in Figure CA24-8 that the sales reps are grouped by state and sorted by last name.

Figure CA24-8   Database Report

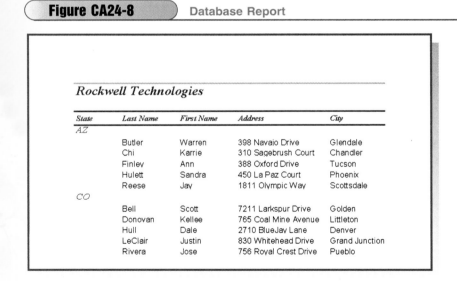

Learn: Modify Database Tables/Forms

When necessary, database tables/forms can be modified. For example, if a new field is needed, it can be added and then the field information for each record can be keyed. Also, it is possible to delete a field. When a field is deleted, *all* the information in that field is deleted.

Learn: What Is Sorting?

The Sort feature controls the sequence, or order, of the records. Information can be sorted in ascending or descending order. Ascending order is from A to Z (alphabetic information) and 0 to 9 (numeric information); descending order is from Z to A and 9 to 0.

Preview

In the databases units, you will have the opportunity to work with databases of several companies. There is **A&E Bank**, whose database contains credit card applicant information. The Software Professionals database contains information about its software. **Rockwell Technologies** has a sales rep database; **Eastwick School of Dance** has a student information database.

Exercise 1A

Adding Records to an Existing Database

1. Copy the *A&E Bank* database (*CD-A&E Bank*) to your data storage area.

2. Open the *A&E Applicants* table file in the *A&E Bank* database you just copied.

3. Key the information contained on the following three card applications into the database table.

A&E Bank Card Application				
Last Name	First	Middle		
Lowell	Cynthia	Sue		
Street Address	City	State	ZIP	Phone
1208 Marietta Street	Asheville	NC	28803-4309	704-564-3874
Birth Date (Month, Day, Year)	Social Security Number		Name of Employer	
03-08-75	342-35-6766		Brickworks	
Address of Employer	City	State	Annual Income	Employer's Phone
3302 Old Toll Road	Asheville	NC	$24,000	704-328-9901

A&E Bank Card Application				
Last Name	First	Middle		
Eisenhower	Andrew	Shane		
Street Address	City	State	ZIP	Phone
302 Featherstone Drive	Greenville	SC	29611-9931	864-232-9301
Birth Date (Month, Day, Year)	Social Security Number		Name of Employer	
07-02-56	382-56-2200		Kirkwood Dental	
Address of Employer	City	State	Annual Income	Employer's Phone
380 Lake Shore Drive	Greenville	SC	$75,000	864-344-8788

(continued on next page)

A&E Bank Card Application

Last Name	First	Middle		
Johnson	Beth	Anne		
Street Address	City	State	ZIP	Phone
3152 Duke Street	Fayetteville	NC	28304-4351	910-188-2211
Birth Date (Month, Day, Year)	Social Security Number		Name of Employer	
04-15-49	520-66-3820		Fenton Motor, Inc.	
Address of Employer	City	State	Annual Income	Employer's Phone
382 Greenbriar Drive	Fayetteville	NC	$22,000	910-168-8399

Exercise 1B

Adding Records to an Existing Database Form File

1. Open the *A&E Applicants* form file in the *A&E Bank* database.
2. Key the information contained on the following three card applications into the database form.
3. Print a copy of the *A&E Applicants* table file in landscape orientation after keying the last record.
4. Save and close the database.

A&E Bank Card Application

Last Name	First	Middle		
White	Carlos	Benito		
Street Address	City	State	ZIP	Phone
9873 Clear Crossing Lane	Charlotte	NC	28112-8309	704-126-1580
Birth Date (Month, Day, Year)	Social Security Number		Name of Employer	
06-20-59	829-23-8729		Charlotte Legal Services	
Address of Employer	City	State	Annual Income	Employer's Phone
390 Dunbar Street	Charlotte	NC	$55,000	704-140-5554

A&E Bank Card Application

Last Name	First	Middle		
Castillo	Mary	J.		
Street Address	City	State	ZIP	Phone
3820 Stonegate Court	Greensboro	NC	27406-8631	910-156-2798
Birth Date (Month, Day, Year)	Social Security Number		Name of Employer	
04-15-57	389-56-9821		Rochelle Gallery	
Address of Employer	City	State	Annual Income	Employer's Phone
310 Sherman Street	Greensboro	NC	$25,500	910-190-1200

A&E Bank Card Application				
Last Name	First	Middle		
Russell	Reed	Martin		
Street Address	City	State	ZIP	Phone
8291 Regency Drive	Charleston	WV	25341-9938	304-129-8292
Birth Date (Month, Day, Year)	Social Security Number		Name of Employer	
12-24-57	389-51-8830		Auto Glass Specialists	
Address of Employer	City	State	Annual Income	Employer's Phone
8392 White Oak Drive	Charleston	WV	$18,000	304-128-7356

LESSON 2 CREATE A DATABASE AND TABLE

OBJECTIVES

⊙ To create a database.
⊙ To create a database table.

Learn: What Is Stored in a Database Table?

Information has always been critical to the successful operation of a business. In today's business environment, more and more information is being stored and accessed through the use of databases. As noted earlier, a database is an organized collection of information (data). The information is stored in tables. A database may contain one table or any number of tables.

The database you worked with in Lesson 1 was a credit card application file that contained information about each applicant. In the remainder of this unit you will be creating and working with several different databases.

Exercise 2A

Create a Database and Table

Lynda Smoltz, the manager of Software Professionals, would like you to create a database for the software products they sell. She would like the database table to include the following field information:

- Stock Number
- Software
- Price
- Beginning Inventory

1. Create a new database using the filename *Software Professionals*.
2. Create a table in Design View.
3. Save the table as *Software Professionals*.

   Learning Tip: See Figure CA24-3 for an example of defining and sequencing fields of a database table.

1. Enter the records given below into the *Software Professionals* database table.

2. Save and close the database table.

	Record 1	Record 2	Record 3
Stock No.:	B929	E246	E786
Software:	Basic Spreadsheets	Computer Geography	Computerized Reading
Price:	$139	$259	$189
Beg. Invt.:	2000	2500	1000
	Record 4	**Record 5**	**Record 6**
Stock No.:	E561	B821	E320
Software:	Creative Bus. Letters	Data Controller	English Enhancement
Price:	$125	$309	$219
Beg. Invt.:	500	500	800
	Record 7	**Record 8**	**Record 9**
Stock No.:	B689	B586	E758
Software:	Financial Advisors	Graphics Designer	Keyboard Composition
Price:	$99	$165	$155
Beg. Invt.:	2500	400	3000
	Record 10	**Record 11**	**Record 12**
Stock No.:	B615	B731	E641
Software:	Language Arts Skills	Quick Key WP	Spelling Mastery
Price:	$139	$75	$139
Beg. Invt.:	1500	2500	2000

LESSON 3 CREATE A DATABASE TABLE

OBJECTIVES

To create a database table.

To add records to a database table.

Exercise 3A

Create a Database and Personnel Table

Paul M. Vermillion, District 13 sales manager for Rockwell Technologies, would like you to create a database containing the names and addresses of all sales representatives in his district. He would like you to use the following field names:

- Last Name
- First Name
- Address
- City
- State

1. Create a new database using the filename *Rockwell Technologies*.
2. Create and save a table in Design View with the filename *Sales Reps – District 13*.

Exercise 3B

Add Records to a Database

1. Enter the records given below into the *Sales Reps – District 13* database table.
2. Save and close the database table.

SALES REPRESENTATIVES				
Last Name	First Name	Address	City	State
Carter	Mary	310 Old Trail Road	Cheyenne	WY
Hull	Dale	2710 BlueJay Lane	Denver	CO
McRae	Jessica	475 Canyon Road	Ogden	UT
Hernandez	Erika	375 Highland Drive	Orem	UT
Camby	Sue	378 Ranchero Road	Boise	ID
Henneman	Jason	762 Nugget Drive	Billings	MT
Reed	Jessica	817 Herrington Drive	Casper	WY
Logan	Marsha	905 Chickadee Court	Great Falls	ID
Cirillo	Mathew	1208 Whitaker Road	Pocatello	ID
LeClair	Justin	830 Whitehead Drive	Grand Junction	CO
Donovan	Kellee	765 Coal Mine Avenue	Littleton	CO
Young	Marsha	7563 Ferncrest Circle	Salt Lake City	UT
Tapani	Devlin	543 Lookout Mountain	Rapid City	SD
Rivera	Jose	756 Royal Crest Drive	Pueblo	CO

OBJECTIVES

⊙ To create a new table in an existing database.

⊙ To add records to a database file.

Exercise ④A

Create a New Table in an Existing Database

The owner of Eastwick School of Dance, Ashley Eastwick, would like you to create another table (*Eastwick Fees*) in the *Eastwick School of Dance* database to keep track of the student fees. She would like you to use the following field names:

- Last Name
- First Name
- Dance Class 1
- Dance Class 2
- Monthly Fees

1. Copy the *Eastwick School of Dance* database (*CD-Eastwick School of Dance*) to your data storage area.

2. Open the *Eastwick School of Dance* database.

3. Create and save a new table using the filename *Eastwick Fees*.

Exercise ④B

Add Records to a Database File

1. Enter the records information given on the following page into the *Eastwick Fees* database table.

2. If the monthly fee is not given, use the following Fee Schedule information to calculate the fee.

	Fee Schedule	
Beginning	**Intermediate**	**Advanced**
Beg. Ballet $28	Inter. Ballet $30	Adv. Ballet $34
Beg. Tap $25	Inter. Tap $29	Adv. Tap $33
Beg. Jazz $27	Inter. Jazz $29	Adv. Jazz $32

3. Save and close the database.

Eastwick School of Dance			
Name	Dance Class 1	Dance Class 2	Monthly Fees
Julie Stewart	Beg. Ballet	Beg. Jazz	$55
Julie Vaughn	Adv. Ballet		$34
Lauren Martin	Beg. Ballet	Beg. Tap	$53
Jacqueline Finley	Inter. Ballet		$30
Angela Garcia	Beg. Jazz	Inter. Ballet	
Kirsten Edmonds	Beg. Tap	Adv. Ballet	
Camille Ramirez	Inter. Tap	Inter. Jazz	$58
Stacy Rice	Inter. Jazz		
Loren Rizzo	Beg. Ballet		$28
Judy Higgins	Beg. Jazz		
Jill Giani	Beg. Ballet		$28
Anne Griffith	Inter. Ballet	Inter. Jazz	$59
Jayne Boyer	Beg. Tap	Beg. Jazz	$52
Diane Bunnell	Inter. Ballet		
Brook Byrns	Beg. Jazz	Inter. Ballet	$57
Alison Koosman	Adv. Ballet	Adv. Jazz	$66
Tasha Lang	Beg. Ballet	Inter. Tap	$57
Kayla Maas	Beg. Tap		$25
Carolyn McDowell	Beg. Ballet		

LESSON ⑤ ADD NEW RECORDS TO UPDATE A DATABASE

OBJECTIVES

⊙ To add new records to a database.

⊙ To update a database table.

Exercise 5A

Add New Records to an Existing Database Table

You can add records to update a database table at any time. Lynda Smoltz provided the information on the following page to be added to the *Software Professionals* database table.

1. Open the *Software Professionals* table in the *Software Professionals* database.
2. Add the records shown below.
3. Save and close the database.

	Record 13	**Record 14**	**Record 15**
Stock No.:	B952	B658	B839
Software:	Tax Assistant	Telephone Directory	Art Gallery
Price:	$129	$119	$249
Beg. Invt.:	5000	5000	1000
	Record 16	**Record 17**	**Record 18**
Stock No.:	B794	B833	E910
Software:	Your Time Manager	Office Layout	Math Tutor
Price:	$69	$129	$59
Beg. Invt.:	2500	500	2000

Exercise 5B

Update a Database Table

Mr. Vermillion would like the information about the additional sales reps listed below added to the *Sales Reps – District 13* table.

1. Open the *Sales Reps – District 13* table (*Rockwell Technologies* database).
2. Add the records shown below to the table.
3. Save and close the database.

SALES REPRESENTATIVES

Last Name	First Name	Address	City	State
Walker	Trent	872 Texas Avenue	Idaho Falls	ID
Wetteland	Cynthia	380 Clearview Drive	Missoula	MT
Chi	Carrie	310 Sagebrush Court	Chandler	AZ
Finley	Ann	388 Oxford Drive	Tucson	AZ
Reese	Jay	330 Shiloh Way	Scottsdale	AZ
Bell	Scott	7211 Larkspur Drive	Golden	CO
Doolittle	Lisa	872 Kingswood Way	Sioux Falls	SD
Butler	Warren	398 Navajo Drive	Glendale	AZ
Hulett	Sandra	450 La Paz Court	Phoenix	AZ

Exercise 5C

Update a Database Table

1. Open the *Eastwick Fees* table (*Eastwick School of Dance* database).
2. Key the records information shown below in the table.
3. Save and close the database after you key the information.

Eastwick School of Dance			
Name	Dance Class 1	Dance Class 2	Monthly Fees
Tarin Chan	Inter. Ballet	Adv. Jazz	$62
Marcia Moreno	Inter. Jazz		$29
Elizabeth Pingel	Beg. Tap		$25
Sonja Phelps	Inter. Jazz	Adv. Tap	$62
Charlotte Ross	Beg. Ballet		$28
Lynda Sackett	Inter. Ballet	Adv. Tap	

Exercise 5D

Update a Database Table

1. Open the *A&E Applicants* table (*A&E Bank* database).
2. Add the following two new bank card applicants to the table.
3. Save and close the database.

A&E Bank Card Application				
Last Name	First	Middle		
Hutton	Grant	K.		
Street Address	City	State	ZIP	Phone
811 Kirkland Lane	Charleston	SC	29401-3311	803-129-5501
Birth Date (Month, Day, Year)	Social Security Number		Name of Employer	
09-08-60	181-32-7002		La Crosse Medical Center	
Address of Employer	City	State	Annual Income	Employer's Phone
760 Briarstone Court	Charleston	SC	$55,000	803-645-2200

A&E Bank Card Application					
Last Name	First	Middle			
Upshaw	*Andrea*	*Jane*			
Street Address	City	State	ZIP		Phone
432 Pennsylvania Avenue	*Columbia*	*SC*	*29204-6634*		*803-837-1329*
Birth Date (Month, Day, Year)	Social Security Number		Name of Employer		
02-07-63	*212-06-8280*		*Timberdale Insurance*		
Address of Employer	City	State	Annual Income		Employer's Phone
671 Wimbledon Court	*Columbia*	*SC*	*$49,500*		*803-674-1734*

LESSON 6 — ADD NEW FIELDS TO A DATABASE TABLE

OBJECTIVE

> To add new fields to a database table.

Exercise 6A

Add New Fields to an Existing Database Table

Database software lets you add additional fields to a database table after you have created it. *Software Professionals* would like you to add the following fields to the table:

- Purchases
- Sales

1. Open the *Software Professionals* database table.
2. Add the fields for Purchases and Sales in the table.

Exercise 6B

Update Records

1. Update the records in the *Software Professionals* database table to include the new information provided on the following page.
2. Print a copy of the revised table.
3. Save and close the database.

	Record 1	Record 2	Record 3
Software:	Basic Spreadsheets	Computer Geography	Computerized Reading
Purchases:	1200	400	500
Sales:	1578	850	674
	Record 4	**Record 5**	**Record 6**
Software:	Creative Bus. Letters	Data Controller	English Enhancement
Purchases:	250	0	1000
Sales:	400	240	1200
	Record 7	**Record 8**	**Record 9**
Software:	Financial Advisors	Graphics Designer	Keyboard Composition
Purchases:	1000	500	1000
Sales:	1987	437	1753
	Record 10	**Record 11**	**Record 12**
Software:	Language Arts Skills	Quick Key WP	Spelling Mastery
Purchases:	500	1000	0
Sales:	759	1378	300
	Record 13	**Record 14**	**Record 15**
Software:	Tax Assistant	Telephone Directory	Art Gallery
Purchases:	0	1000	500
Sales:	980	1873	673
	Record 16	**Record 17**	**Record 18**
Software:	Your Time Manager	Office Layout	Math Tutor
Purchases:	1000	300	0
Sales:	1379	475	39

Exercise 6C

Add New Table Fields and Data

1. Open the *Sales Reps – District 13* table (*Rockwell Technologies* database).

2. Add the fields shown below:
   - Territory
   - ZIP
   - July Sales
   - August Sales

3. Update the records in the database table to include the new information provided below.
4. Print a copy of the revised table in landscape orientation.
5. Save and close the database.

SALES REPRESENTATIVES				
Last Name	Territory	ZIP	July Sales	August Sales
Carter	Wyoming	82001-1837	45,351	37,951
Hull	Colorado	80233-0070	53,739	49,762
McRae	Utah	84404-2835	33,371	38,978
Hernandez	Utah	84057-1572	39,371	40,790
Camby	Idaho	83702-8312	42,173	65,386
Henneman	Montana	59102-6735	17,219	29,737
Reed	Wyoming	82607-9956	53,791	59,349
Logan	Montana	59404-3883	49,712	21,790
Cirillo	Idaho	83202-7523	29,731	37,956
LeClair	Colorado	81503-2270	63,212	40,321
Donovan	Colorado	80123-0091	37,198	45,865
Young	Utah	84118-0111	44,876	56,791
Tapani	South Dakota	57702-9932	59,145	39,645
Rivera	Colorado	81005-8376	55,400	37,751
Walker	Idaho	83402-3326	43,900	44,750
Wetteland	Montana	59803-8388	33,650	40,765
Chi	Arizona	85224-1157	39,750	48,621
Finley	Arizona	85711-5656	19,765	35,765
Reese	Arizona	85268-0012	67,890	45,780
Bell	Colorado	80401-7529	39,200	43,286
Doolittle	South Dakota	57106-7621	64,890	37,102
Butler	Arizona	85302-1300	35,975	46,873
Hulett	Arizona	85023-2766	56,730	46,720

Add New Table Fields and Data

1. Open the *Eastwick Fees* table (*Eastwick School of Dance* database).
2. Add the fields shown below:
   • Sept. Fees
   • Oct. Fees
   • Nov. Fees
   • Dec. Fees
3. Update the records in the database table to include the new information provided below.

Eastwick School of Dance				
Name	**Sept. Fees**	**Oct. Fees**	**Nov. Fees**	**Dec. Fees**
Stewart	55	55	55	
Vaughn				
Martin	53	53		
Finley				
Garcia	57	57		
Edmonds	59	59		
Ramirez	58	58		
Rice				
Rizzo				
Higgins	27			
Giani	28	28		
Griffith	59	59		
Boyer	52	52		
Bunnell				
Byrns	57	57	57	
Koosman	66	66		
Lang				
Maas	25	25	25	
McDowell	28	28		
Chan	62	62		
Moreno	29			
Pingel	25	25		
Phelps	62	62	62	
Ross	28	28		
Sackett	63			

4. Print a copy of the revised table in landscape orientation.

5. Save and close the database.

LESSON (7) EDITING RECORDS

OBJECTIVES

> To move around in a database.
> To edit records in a database.

Learn: Moving Around in a Database

There are several ways to move to a new location on the screen of a database table and a database form. Some methods take more keystrokes than others. The method requiring the fewest keystrokes should be used. Examine the various moves in Figure CA24-9 below.

Figure CA24-9   Insertion Point Moves

INSERTION POINT MOVES—TABLE		INSERTION POINT MOVES—FORM	
To move:	**Keys**	**To move:**	**Keys**
One field left	←	Next field	↓
One field right	→	Previous field	↑
One line up	↑	Top of form	HOME
One line down	↓	Bottom of form	END
Leftmost field	HOME	First record	CTRL + HOME
Rightmost field	END	Last record	CTRL + END
Down one window	**PgDn**	Next record*	**PgDn**
Up one window	**PgUp**	Previous record*	**PgUp**
To first record	CTRL + HOME		
To last record	CTRL + END		

*In case the record has more than one screen, use **CTRL + PgUp (PgDn)**.

Exercise 7A

Move Around in a Database

1. Open the *A&E Applicants* table (from *A&E Bank* database) that you worked with in Exercise 1A, and practice moving through it.

2. Open the *A&E Applicants* forms file (from *A&E Bank* database) that you worked with in Exercise 1B, and practice moving through it. Close without saving.

Learn: Editing Database Records

Editing existing database records is similar to editing word processing documents. Simply move the insertion point to the location where the change is to be made and use the INSERT, DELETE, or BACKSPACE keys to make changes. Larger segments of text may require the use of the Block Text feature to make changes.

Exercise 7B
Editing Records

1. Open the *Software Professionals* database table.
2. Make the changes shown below:
   - Change the price of *Computer Geography* to $279.
   - Change the name of *Creative Business Letters* to Creative Letters.
   - Change the price of *Basic Spreadsheet* to $159.
   - The beginning inventory of *Data Controller* should have been 300.
   - Change the name of *Language Arts Skills* to Language Skills.
3. Save and close the database.

Exercise 7C
Editing Records

1. Open the *Eastwick Fees* database table.
2. Make the changes shown below:
   - *Stacy Rice* is enrolled in Inter. Jazz and Inter. Ballet. (*Be sure to change fees.*)
   - *Byrns* should be spelled Burns.
   - *Tasha Lang* should be Trisha Lang.
   - *Diane Bunnell* is enrolled in Adv. Ballet, not Inter. Make the necessary adjustments.
   - *Lynda Sackett* decided not to take Adv. Tap. Make the necessary adjustments to reflect this change. The September Fees will stay at $63.00; however, change the Monthly Fee to $30.00 to reflect this change for future months.

Exercise 7D
Editing Records

1. Open the *Eastwick Address* database table (*Eastwick School of Dance* database).
2. Make the changes shown below:
   - *Diane Bunnell* has a new address and telephone number.
     380 Innsbruck Drive
     St. Paul, MN 55112-8271
     612-329-7621
   - *Jackqueline Finley's* name should be spelled Jacqueline. Her phone number should be 715-386-6764.

- Make sure you change the spelling of *Brook Byrns* (Burns) and *Tasha Lang* (Trisha).

- Change *Judy Higgins's* mother's name to Ms. Erin Schultz.

- *Kayla Maas* has a new address and telephone number.

  1125 Westbrook Lane
  Minneapolis, MN 55436-2837
  612-348-8211

3. Save and close the database.

Exercise **7E**

Editing Records

1. Open the *Sales Reps – District 13* table (*Rockwell Technologies* database).

2. Make the changes shown below:

- *Carrie Chi's* first name should be spelled Karrie.

- *Jay Reese* has moved; his new address is:

  1811 Olympic Way, N.
  Scottsdale, AZ 85268-8811

- *Devlin Tapani's* July sales were incorrectly recorded. They should have been $49,145.

- The ZIP code for *Jason Henneman* should be 59102-5624.

- *Mary Carter* would like her name recorded as Mary Carter-Bond.

3. Save and close the database.

Exercise **7F**

Editing Records

1. Open the *A&B Applicants* table (from the *A&E Bank* database) to correct data entry errors.

2. Make the changes shown below:

- Ms. *Capers's* first name should be spelled Julie, not Julia.

- *Carol Merritt's* address is 121 Delaware Street.

- Ms. *Ford's* name should have been spelled Glenda, not Glenna.

- Mr. *Guidry's* ZIP Code should be 29601-7474.

- Ms. *Ford's* income should have been $41,000, not $42,000.

3. Save and close the database.

LESSON 8 CREATING DATA SORTS

OBJECTIVES

⊙ To learn to create data sorts.

⊙ To answer questions from data sorts.

Learn: Sorting a Database

The records of tables and forms can be arranged in a specific order by using the **Sort** feature. A sort can be done on one field or on multiple fields.

For example, the Eastwick Address table could be sorted by State in ascending order. A sort using the State field would group all students from Minnesota first, with all students from Wisconsin next. It would not, however, arrange the cities in each state alphabetically. A **multiple sort**, first by State and then by City, would be necessary to accomplish this arrangement.

Learn: Multiple Sorts

The illustration in Figure CA24-10 shows a multiple sort on the *Eastwick Address* file. The file was first sorted (*primary sort*) by State in ascending order. This sort placed all the students with a Minnesota address together and all the students with a Wisconsin address together.

Figure CA24-10   Illustration of a Multiple Sort

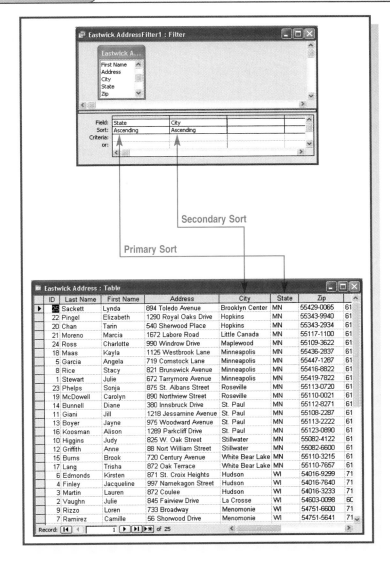

The second sort (*secondary sort*) was by City in ascending order. This sort put all the Minnesota cities in alphabetical order and all the Wisconsin cities in alphabetical order.

Advanced Filter/Sort

Learning Tip: The **Advanced Filter/Sort** feature was used to do the multiple-level sort. This feature provides a way for keying multiple criteria to display selected records. These records match a specified filter and sort.

Exercise 8A

Create Single and Multiple Sorts

1. Open the *A&E Bank Applicants* table file (from the *A&E Bank* database).
2. Perform the sorts outlined below.
3. Print a copy of the multiple sort by State and City.
4. Close the database.

Single Sorts—Ascending Order

1. Last Name
2. City
3. State
4. Zip code
5. Annual Income

Multiple Sort—Ascending Order

1. Primary sort by **State**, secondary sort by **City**.
2. Primary sort by **Last Name**, secondary sort by **First Name**.

Exercise 8B

Sort for Quick Answers

1. Open the *Software Professionals* table.
2. Open *CD-CA24-8B*. Run sorts to answer the questions. Record your answers in the right-hand column.

   Learning Tip: Sorts and queries can be used to arrange information to provide quick answers to questions. (Queries will be taught in a future lesson.)

3. Save as *CA24-8B*.
4. Print a copy of your answers.

Exercise 8C

Sort for Quick Answers

1. Open the *Sales Reps – District 13* table (*Rockwell Technologies* database).

2. Open *CD-CA24-8C*. Run sorts to answer the questions. Record your answers in the right-hand column.

3. Save as *CA24-8C*.

4. Print a copy of your answers.

Exercise 8D

Sort for Quick Answers

1. Open the *Eastwick School of Dance* database.

2. Open *CD-CA24-8D*. Run sorts to answer the questions. Record your answers in the right-hand column.

3. Save as *CA24-8D*.

4. Print a copy of your answers.

UNIT 25

LESSONS 1–3
Enhancing Database Skills

Conditioning Practice

Before you begin the lessons, key each line twice.

alphabet | 1 | Mack Walsh did quite a job to put an extravaganza on before July.

figures | 2 | Only 386 of the 497 students had completed the exam by 12:50 p.m.

speed | 3 | The visitor and I may handle all the problems with the amendment.

gwam | 1' | 1 | 2 | 3 | 4 | 5 | 6 | 7 | 8 | 9 | 10 | 11 | 12 | 13 |

LESSON ① DATABASE FIELD PROPERTIES

OBJECTIVES

To learn the Default Value option.

To learn the Input Mask option.

Exercise 1A

Create a Database

Your younger brother would like you to create a database for his newspaper route. He will use the database for sending thank-you notes to customers, returning customer calls, and preparing route lists for when he has someone else do his route for him.

1. Create a new database using the filename *Newspaper Route*. Create a table in Design View; save the table as *Customer List*.

2. Include the following fields in the database.
   - Last Name
   - First Name
   - Courtesy Title
   - Address
   - City

- State
- ZIP
- Type of Subscription

3. Select an appropriate data type and supply an appropriate description for each field name.

4. Leave the database open for all exercises in this lesson.

Learn: Field Properties—Default Value

You have worked with the Field Name, Data Type, and Description fields in Design View in Unit 24. The bottom half of the Design View screen is the area called *Field Properties*. This area is used to customize the fields in the database. For example, by using the Default Value option, you can make it so that the same information appears in this field for each record that is added to the database. If the city is the same for all the records in a database (as it will be for the database you are currently creating), you can use the default value so the name of the city (*West Palm Beach*) automatically appears rather than your having to key it in for each record. This saves a great deal of time, especially in larger databases. If a few of the records were to require a different city name, only those entries would have to be keyed.

To key a default value in Design View, click the Field Name (*City*) and then click default value and key the text that you want to appear in the field. Repeat the procedure for each field that should have a default value. (See Figure CA25-1.)

Figure CA25-1   Field Properties in Design View

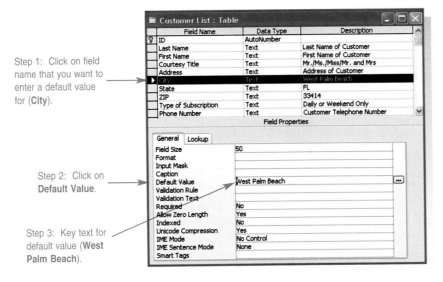

Step 1: Click on field name that you want to enter a default value for (**City**).

Step 2: Click on **Default Value.**

Step 3: Key text for default value (**West Palm Beach**).

Exercise 1B

Field Properties—Default Value

1. In the database that you are creating, key the default values for the following fields:
   - City: West Palm Beach
   - State: FL

- ZIP: 33414
- Type of Subscription: Daily

Note: By setting a default value of *Daily* for *Type of Subscription*, you will only have to key information in this column when the customer subscribes to weekend service rather than daily service. When you tab to the *Type of Subscription* field as you key each record, it will highlight *Daily*. If the record you are keying has Weekend Only service, simply key Weekend; *Daily* will automatically be deleted. If the record you are keying has Daily service, tab to the next column since the column already has *Daily* keyed.

2. After keying the default values, close the Design View Screen and click **Yes** in response to the "Do you want to save changes to the design of table?" prompt.

3. Name the table *Customer List*.

4. Click **Yes** to indicate you want a Primary Key Defined.

Exercise 1C

Add Records to a Database

1. Enter the records given below into the *Newspaper Route* database.

	Record 1	**Record 2**	**Record 3**
Last Name:	Benson	Boone	Brown
First Name:	Blaine	Lindsay	Seth
Courtesy Title:	Mr.	Miss	Mr.
Address:	929 Cherry Lane	535 Azure Lane	601 Bluebell Court
City:	West Palm Beach	West Palm Beach	West Palm Beach
State:	FL	FL	FL
ZIP Code:	33414	33414	33414
Type of Subscription:	Weekend	Daily	Daily
	Record 4	**Record 5**	**Record 6**
Last Name:	Burke	Burrell	Cabrera
First Name:	Stewart	Gavin	Juanita
Courtesy Title:	Mr. and Mrs.	Mr.	Ms.
Address:	450 Azure Lane	635 Bluebell Court	650 Bluebell Court
City:	West Palm Beach	West Palm Beach	West Palm Beach
State:	FL	FL	FL
ZIP Code:	33414	33414	33414
Type of Subscription:	Daily	Weekend	Daily

2. When you are finished keying the data, verify that all customers have daily service except Benson and Burrell.

Exercise 1D

Add a Field to a Database

In Design View, add a field to the database to record customer phone numbers. Use Phone Number for the field name. Key Text for the Data Type. Leave Design View open for the next exercise.

Learn: Field Properties–Input Mask

The Input Mask is another option located in the Field Properties portion of the Design View screen that is used to customize the field. For example if you have telephone numbers in a database, you could create an input mask like (561) ###-#### for the phone number field using the Input Mask feature. When keying information in this field, you only have to key the last seven numbers. The prefix number (561) will automatically be entered for you. The parentheses and the hyphen separating numbers also automatically appear. As you key, the insertion point skips to the place the next number occurs.

The input mask for a phone number will only allow you to key numbers. If you accidentally try to key a letter, it won't accept it and will make a sound, letting you know that you keyed something other than a number.

The procedure for creating an input mask is similar to creating a default value. Click the field (*Phone Number*) you want to create a mask for. Then click Input Mask. To the right of the Input Mask is a button that will start a Wizard to create the input mask; click it. A dialog box appears asking you if you want to save the table now. Click Yes. (See Figure CA25-2.)

Figure CA25-2   Input Mask

Field Properties		
General	Lookup	
Field Size	50	
Format		
Input Mask		... ———— Input Mask Wizard Button
Caption		
Default Value		

The first Wizard dialog box appears (Figure CA25-3); click Phone Number and click Next. When the next dialog box appears, key 561 in place of 999 (Figure CA25-4). Then click the Placeholder character down arrow and select the character to be used in the mask (#), and then click Next. The final screen asks how you would like to store the data. Click With the symbols in the mask, like this. Click Next and then click Finish. Close Design View. Click Yes when asked if you want to save changes to the design of the table.

When you key data, the mask appears as you tab to the column where the input mask has been keyed.

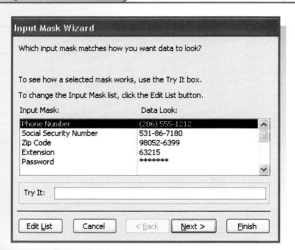

Exercise 1E

Field Properties—Input Mask

After creating an input mask for the telephone number field with 561 for the prefix, open the *Customer List* table. Key the phone numbers shown below for the customers in the database.

When you place the insertion point in the Phone Number field of the table, the Phone Input Mask appears. Key only the last seven numbers of the telephone number. Notice that if the last seven numbers start with a 5, as does the prefix, you have to key 5 twice to get the first number after the prefix to appear. If you move the insertion point down to the next record with the arrow keys after keying the first number, no input mask appears until you key the first number.

	Record 1	**Record 2**	**Record 3**
Last Name:	Benson	Boone	Brown
First Name:	Blaine	Lindsay	Seth
Phone No.:	(561) 333-4827	(561) 547-8291	(561) 382-0295
	Record 4	**Record 5**	**Record 6**
Last Name:	Burke	Burrell	Cabrera
First Name:	Stewart	Gavin	Juanita
Phone No.:	(561) 547-2881	(561) 333-1029	(561) 547-5647

LESSON 2 DATABASE FIELD PROPERTIES

OBJECTIVES

- ⊙ To learn the Required option.
- ⊙ To learn the Format option.
- ⊙ To learn the Caption option.

Learn: Field Properties—Required

Another option in the Field Properties is the Required option. The Required default option is set for *No*. This means that no value has to be keyed in the field. If the default option is changed to *Yes*, *Access* will inform you that that a field requiring a value does not contain one and that you are to key a value in the specified field. *Access* will not let you leave that record until a value has been keyed in the field that has a required setting. For example, if you changed the required value for the *First Name* field to *Yes*, you would get the message shown in Figure CA25-5 below if you tried to leave the record without keying the first name.

Figure CA25-5   Required Field Error Message

Exercise 2A

Field Properties—Required

1. In the *Newspaper Route* database, open Design View and make the First Name field **Required**. (Click the **First Name** field, and then click **Required** and change *No* to **Yes**).

2. Close Design View and try adding the two records shown below to the database without the first name in Record 7.

	Record 7	Record 8
Last Name:	Castilla	Cirillo
First Name:	*Leave Field Blank*	Ryan
Courtesy Title:	Mr.	Mr.
Address:	1057 Cherry Lane	1009 Cherry Lane
City:	West Palm Beach	West Palm Beach
State:	FL	FL
ZIP Code:	33414	33414
Type of Subscription:	Weekend	Daily
Telephone No.	(561) 382-5834	(561) 382-7210

3. Note that the software will not let you go on to Record 8 until you key a first name in Record 7. Key Gordon for the first name in Record 7 and then key Record 8. Did you remember to change *Daily* to Weekend for Mr. Castilla?

Learn: Field Properties—Format

The Format Field Properties option allows you to identify how you want numbers and dates to display. Figure CA25-6 shows the options that are available.

Figure CA25-6   Format Field Properties Options

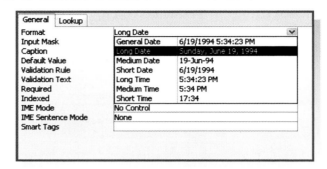

In the illustration, the Long Date has been selected. If you keyed *1-5-2006* in the field where the Long Date option had been selected, *Thursday, January 05, 2006,* would appear. If you keyed *Jan. 5, 2006,* then *Thursday, January 05, 2006,* would still appear. Whatever you key in the field that is in a recognizable format will be displayed in the format that has been selected. Even if you keyed just *Jan. 5,* it would appear as *January 5* with the current year and day of the week.

Exercise 2B

Field Properties—Format

1. In Design View, add two more fields to the *Newspaper Route* database. Use **Stop** for the field name of the first field added and **Restart** as the second field name. Specify **Date/Time** as the Data Type. Leave the *Description* field blank. In the Field Properties, specify **Long Date** for the Format option. To do this, click **Format, Down Arrow, Long Date**.

2. Save the changes to the Design Table and key the Restart and Stop dates shown below for Mr. and Mrs. Burke and Miss Boone. Expand the column width so the entire date is visible in the table.

	Mr. and Mrs. Burke	Miss Boone
Stop:	June 10	June 12
Restart:	June 24	June 19

Learn: Field Properties—Caption

If you want headings that appear in tables, forms, reports, and queries to be different than the Field Names used in the database, the Caption field property can be used. In Design View, simply click the field, then click Caption in the Field Properties section and key the heading that you would like to appear. (See Figure CA25-7.)

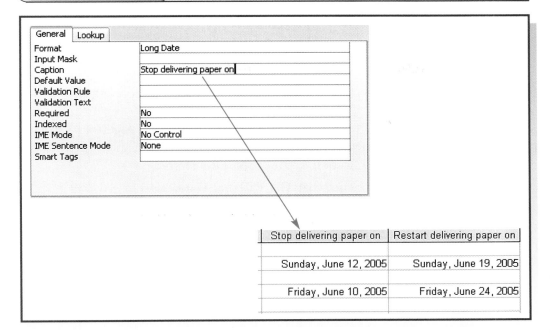

Exercise 2C

Field Properties—Caption

1. In the *Newspaper Route* database, the *Stop* and *Restart* headings are not very descriptive. Make them more descriptive by keying a caption for the *Stop* field of Stop delivering paper on. For the *Restart* field, key a caption of Restart delivering paper on.

2. For the *Type of Subscription* field, key a caption of Daily or Weekend Only Delivery. Close Design View and open the *Customer List* table. Increase the width of the three columns so the entire column headings can be seen.

3. Close your database.

LESSON 3 IMPORT DATA

OBJECTIVES

⊙ To learn how to import data into *Access* from *Excel*.
⊙ To learn how to import data into *Access* from *Word*.

Learn: Import Data from Excel into a New Table

Data created in other applications can be imported into *Access*. The data can be brought in as a new table in *Access* or as part of an existing *Access* table. In this lesson, you will import data from *Excel* and from *Word*.

Exercise 3A

Import Data from Excel into a New Table

You have an *Excel* file (*CD-Algebra I Grades – Section 1.xls*) that has the grades for Section 1 of Algebra I recorded. You would like to import those grades into an *Access* database file.

1. Start by creating a new database; call the new database **Algebra I Grades**. With the new database open, follow the procedures outlined below to import the grades for Section 1 from *Excel* into *Access*:

    a. From the File menu, click **Get External Data**.

    b. Click **Import**. (This will open an Import dialog box. From the dialog box select the file to be imported. In order to view *Excel* files, you will need to change *Files of type* to **Microsoft Excel (*.xls)**.

    c. After selecting the file (*Algebra I Grades – Section 1.xls*), click **Import**. This opens the Import Spreadsheet Wizard.

    d. Click **Next**.

    e. In the next screen, if there is a check mark in the box before *First Row Contains Column Headings*, click **Next**. If it doesn't have a check mark in the box before it, click the box to get the check mark to appear. Then click **Next**.

    f. Click **In a New Table** when it asks where you would like to store your data. Then, click **Next**.

    g. On the next screen, you can specify information about each of the fields you are importing. Notice how it places the column heading in the *Field Name*. If you want to use something else for the field name, you can key it in the Field Name box. Whatever you key in the Field Name box becomes the new column heading. Also note that if you don't want all the columns appearing in the *Excel* spreadsheet, you can highlight the field you don't want to be imported and then click **Do not import field (Skip)** in the Field Options. When you are done specifying information about each field, click **Next**.

    h. For the Primary key screen, click **No primary key**; then click **Next**.

    i. In the next screen there will be a box *For the Import to Table*. Name the table **Section 1** and then click **Finish**.

Exercise 3B

Import Data from Excel to a New Table

Use the same procedure to import the grades for Section 2 (*CD-Algebra I Grades – Section 2.xls*) from *Excel* in a new database table. Name the table *Section 2*.

Exercise 3C

Import Data from Excel into an Existing Table

Now you are going to combine the data from Section 1 and Section 2 into one table When you are finished, you will have three tables in the *Algebra I Grades* database.

1. Do this by importing Section 1 again and calling it *Section 1 and 2 Combined Grades*.

2. Then import Section 2 again, but this time on the screen where it asks where you would like to store your data, click *In an Existing Table*. Then click the down arrow and select **Section 1 and 2 Combined Grades**.

3. Open the *Section 1 and 2 Combined Grades* table and sort the names so that they appear alphabetically by last name starting with A.

4. Close the database.

Exercise 3D

Import Data from a Word Table into an Existing Access Table

1. In the *Newspaper Route Access* database you have a *Customer List* table. It only contains eight of your customers. The information for the rest of your customers was saved in a table in *Word*. The filename is *CD-Customer Information.doc*. Open the *Newspaper Route Access* database and import the *Customer Information* file from *Word* into the *Customer List* table of the *Newspaper Route Access* database so all the customer information is in one place.

2. The process for importing *Word* files is very similar to importing files from *Excel*. However, before importing a *Word* file, it must be saved with an .htm extension. To do this, open the Word document and use the Save As command. In the Save As dialog box, click the **Save as type** down arrow and select **Web Page (*.htm; *.html)** as shown below and then click **Save**.

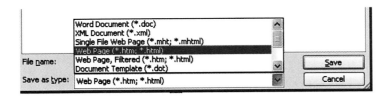

3. Then go through the steps of the Wizard (similar to the Wizard for importing *Excel* files) to import the *Word* file.

4. Print a copy of *Customer List* after importing the *Word* file.

5. Close the database.

UNIT 26

LESSONS 1–6
Expanding Database Skills

Conditioning Practice

Before you begin the lessons, key each line twice.

alphabet 1 An exclusive photo of a mosque by Dr. Kjelstad was quite amazing.

fig/sym 2 They were born on May 22, 1964, July 13, 1975, and June 18, 1980.

speed 3 Gus paid the men for the work they did on the shanty by the lake.

gwam 1' | 1 | 2 | 3 | 4 | 5 | 6 | 7 | 8 | 9 | 10 | 11 | 12 | 13 |

LESSON 1 CREATING QUERIES AND COMPUTED FIELDS

OBJECTIVES

 To execute a query.

To create computed fields in a query.

Learn: What Is a Query?

As discussed earlier, a database is a collection of organized information where answers to many questions can be determined. For example, the *Sales Reps – District 13* table of the *Rockwell Technologies* database can answer questions such as:

- Who are the sales reps from Colorado?
- Who are the sales reps with ZIP Codes starting with 5?
- Which sales reps had July sales of more than $50,000?

To generate answers to these questions, a query to the database must be made. A query is a question structured in a way that the software (database) can understand.

Learn: How to Create a Query

The illustration in Figure CA26-1 was created to help you understand how queries can be used to extract information from a database table.

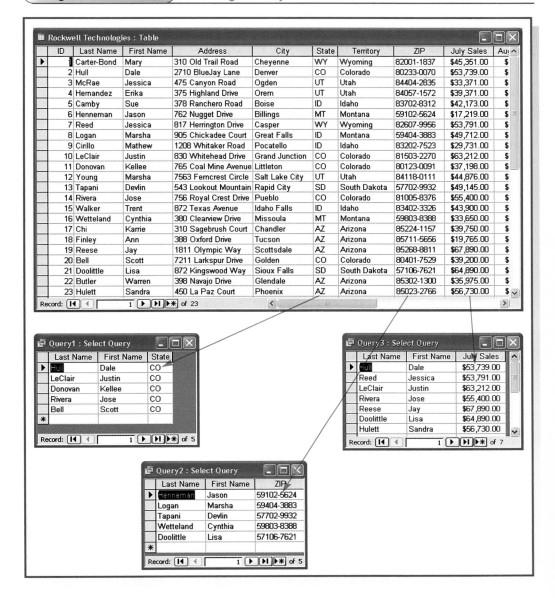

Query 1 was designed to include:

- Last Name

- First Name

- State

The criteria for the state field was set to equal CO, thus extracting only those reps from the state of Colorado.

Query 2 was designed to include:

- Last Name

- First Name

- ZIP

The criteria for the ZIP field was set to be less than 6 (<6), thus extracting only those reps with ZIP codes starting with 5.

Query 3 was designed to include:

- Last Name
- First Name
- July Sales

The criteria for the *July Sales* field was set for greater than $50,000 (>50000), thus extracting only those sales reps with sales of more than $50,000.

The illustration in Figure CA26-2 shows the steps required to run a query. The Queries feature is used to extract and display specific information from a table. The criteria line of the Query Design box is where instructions are given to the software that tells it which information to display. The basic criteria expressions are:

- equal to (=)
- greater than (>)
- less than (<)

In the illustration, ="CO" was used to extract only those sales reps from Colorado. If the criteria had been = "CO" or "AZ," the sales reps from both Colorado and Arizona would have been displayed.

Figure CA26-2 Steps Required to Run a Query

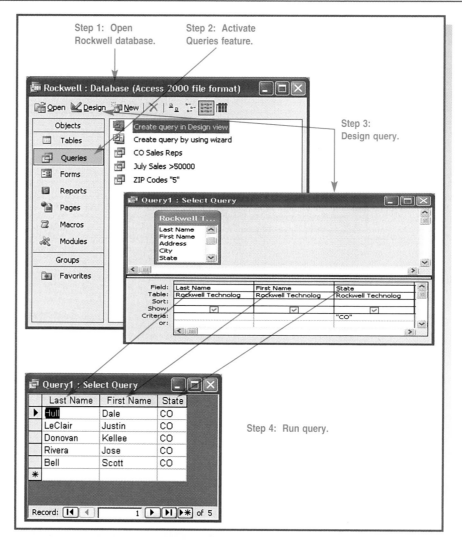

Execute a Query

1. Open *Software Professionals*.
2. Use the Queries feature to answer the questions below.
3. Print the results of each query.

No.	Query	Fields to Include	Criteria
	SOFTWARE PROFESSIONALS		
1	What are the names of the software packages that were designated as "Educational" (Stock No. starting with E)?	Stock Number Software	Like "E*"
2	What software sells for more than $150?	Stock Number Software Price	>150
3	What software sold more than 1,500 units?	Stock Number Software Sales	>1500
4	What software sold less than 500 units?	Stock Number Software Sales	<500

Exercise 1B

Execute a Query

1. Open *Eastwick School of Dance*.
2. Use the Queries feature to answer the questions shown below.
3. Print the results of each query.

No.	Query	Fields to Include	Criteria
	Eastwick School of Dance		
1	What are the names and addresses of the students living in Minneapolis/St. Paul?	First Name Last Name Address State	"Minneapolis" Or "St. Paul"
2	What are the names and addresses of the students living in Wisconsin?	City ZIP	"WI"
3	Which students have not paid their September fees?	Last Name First Name September Fees	Is Null

Execute a Query

1. Open *Rockwell Technologies*.
2. Use the Queries feature to answer the questions below.
3. Print the results of each query.

No.	Query	Fields to Include	Criteria
	ROCKWELL TECHNOLOGIES		
1	What are the names and addresses of our Arizona sales reps?	First Name Last Name Address	"Arizona"
2	What are the names and addresses of our Montana and Wyoming sales reps?	City State ZIP Territory	"Montana" Or "Wyoming"
3	Which sales reps had sales of more than $55,000 during July?	First Name Last Name July Sales	>55000

Learn: Create Computed Fields

Calculations can be done on existing fields by using the Expression Builder in the Forms feature.

In the illustration shown in Figure CA26-3, two additional fields were added to the *Sales Reps – District 13* table of the *Rockwell Technologies* database using the Design feature. The values for these two new fields (*Total Sales* and *Average Monthly Sales*) were automatically calculated by using the Expression Builder to create formulas.

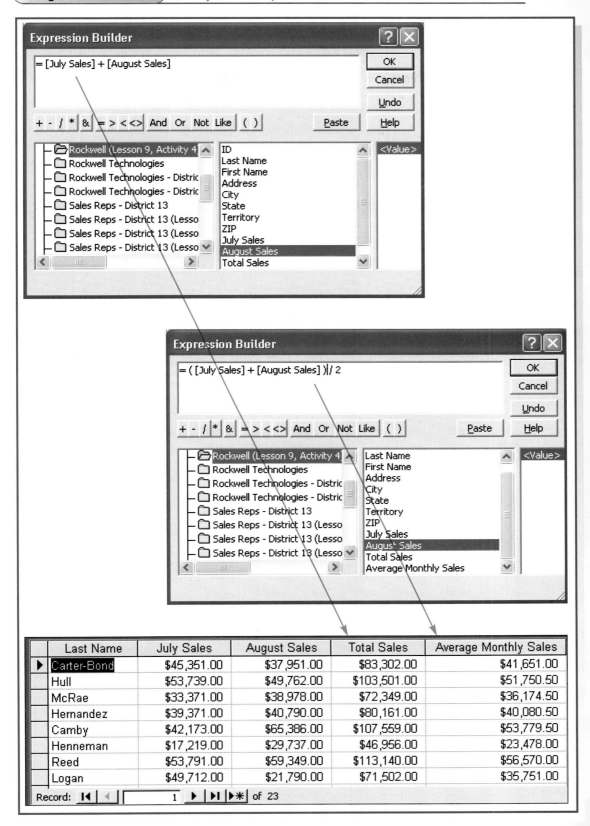

Creating Computed Fields

1. Add a field for **Total Sales** and **Average Monthly Sales** to the *Sales Reps – District 13* table of the *Rockwell Technologies* database.

2. Use the Expression Builder to create formulas to calculate the Total Sales and the Average Monthly Sales.

3. Print a table showing the information requested below.

ROCKWELL TECHNOLOGIES	
The printout should include:	
1.	*Sales Reps' Last Names*
2.	*July Sales*
3.	*August Sales*
4.	*Total Sales*
5.	*Average Monthly Sales*
Formula for Total Sales	*= [July Sales]+[August Sales]*
Formula for Avg. Monthly Sales	*= ([July Sales]+[August Sales])/2*

Creating Computed Fields

1. Add a field for **Total Fees Paid** to the *Eastwick Fees* table of the *Eastwick School of Dance* database.

2. Use the Expression Builder to create a formula to calculate the Total Fees Paid.

3. Print a table showing the information requested below.

Eastwick School of Dance	
The printout should include:	
1.	Students' First Names
2.	Students' Last Names
3.	September Fees
4.	October Fees
5.	November Fees
6.	Total Fees Paid
Formula for Total Fees Paid	=[Sept. Fees]+[Oct. Fees]+[Nov. Fees]

Exercise 1F

Creating Computed Fields

1. Add a field for **Ending Inventory** to the *Software Professionals* table of the *Software Professionals* database.

2. Use the Expression Builder to create a formula to calculate the Ending Inventory.

3. Print a table showing the information requested below.

SOFTWARE PROFESSIONALS	
The printout should include:	
1.	Stock Number
2.	Software Name
3.	Beginning Inventory
4.	Purchases
5.	Sales
6.	Ending Inventory
Formula for Ending Inventory	= [Beginning Inventory]+[Purchases]-[Sales]

LESSON 2 CREATING FORMS

OBJECTIVE

> To use the Wizard feature to create forms.

Learn: Create a Database Form

You can use forms to key or view the information in a database. When using the Forms feature, you have the option of viewing only one record or multiple records at a time. When doing the former, it is easy to key and view data in the clearly labeled fields.

Using the Wizard makes it easy to create well-designed forms. As shown below, the Wizard feature allows you to have all the fields in a database included in the form or only selected fields.

The forms shown in Figures CA26-4, CA26-5, and CA26-6 were created using the Create form by using Wizard feature. The first form includes every field in the *Software Professionals* database. The second form includes only the *Stock Number*, *Software*, and *Ending Inventory* fields. Both forms are in **Columnar** layout. The third form shows the same fields as the second, but in **Tabular** layout, which allows you to view multiple records on the screen at the same time. The first two forms let you view one record at a time on the screen.

Columnar

Tabular

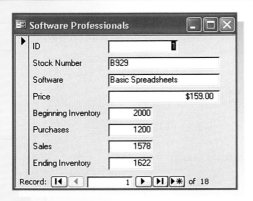

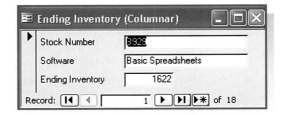

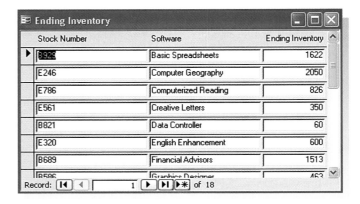

Exercise 2A

Creating Forms

1. Open *Software Professionals*.
2. Create the three form files shown above in Figures CA26-4, CA26-5, and CA26-6 in the database.
3. Use **Columnar** layout and **Standard** style for the first two forms. Title the first form **Software Professionals** and the second form **Ending Inventory (Columnar)**.
4. Use **Tabular** layout and **Standard** style for the third form and title it **Ending Inventory (Tabular)**.

Exercise 2B

Creating Forms

1. Open *A&E Bank*.
2. Create a form in the database with the information requested on the following page.
3. Save as *Applicant's Annual Income*.

A&E Bank	
Form Specifications	
Layout: Columnar Style: SandStone Title: Applicant's Annual Income Sort: Descending Order by Annual Income	Last Name First Name Annual Income

Exercise 2C
Creating Forms

1. Open *Eastwick School of Dance*.
2. Create a form in the database with the information requested below.
3. Save as *Eastwick Student Enrollment*.

Eastwick School of Dance	
Form Specifications	
Layout: Tabular Style: Expedition Title: Eastwick Student Enrollment Sort: Ascending Order by Last Name	Last Name First Name Dance Class 1 Dance Class 2

Exercise 2D
Creating Forms

1. Open *Rockwell Technologies*.
2. Create the forms in the database with the information requested below.
3. Save as *Rockwell Sales for July and August*.

ROCKWELL TECHNOLOGIES	
Form Specifications	
Layout: Tabular *Style: Blends* *Title: Rockwell Sales for July and August* *Sort: Ascending by Last Name*	*Last Name* *First Name* *July Sales* *August Sales*

Creating Forms

1. Open *Rockwell Technologies*.
2. Create the forms in the database with the information requested below.
3. Save as *Sales Reps' Territory*.

ROCKWELL TECHNOLOGIES	
Form Specifications	
Layout: **Justified** *Style:* **Sumi Painting** *Title:* **Sales Reps' Territory** *Sort:* **Ascending by Territory**	*Last Name* *First Name* *Territory*

LESSON ③ COMPOSING REPORTS

OBJECTIVE

⊘ To create database reports.

Learn: Create Reports in a Database

The Report features of the database are used for summarizing, formatting, and printing selected data from the database.

Summarizing: Generally, only a portion of the data contained in a database is needed for a particular application. The Summarizing feature allows for the selection of specific data for inclusion in the report.

Formatting: Formatting can be accomplished automatically using the Wizard feature of the software. The form can be modified by using the Design View feature.

Printing: Once the data has been specified and formatted, professional-looking hard copies can be printed and distributed for information and decision-making purposes. Today, electronic distribution of reports is also quite common.

Three different database reports are illustrated below. The first report (Figure CA26-7) was created using the Create report by using wizard feature. The report was sorted in **Ascending** order by Ending Inventory. The report was formatted in **Tabular** layout with **Portrait** orientation using **Casual style**.

The next report (Figure CA26-8) was created using the Create report by using wizard feature. The report is in **Portrait** orientation with **Justified** layout in **Formal** style. The report is sorted in **Descending** order by Ending Inventory. Only the first six entries of the report are shown.

Ending Inventory

Ending Inventory	Stock Number	Software
60	B821	Data Controller
325	B833	Office Layout
350	E561	Creative Letters
463	B586	Graphics Designer
600	E320	English Enhancement
826	E786	Computerized Reading
827	B839	Art Gallery
1241	B615	Language Skills
1513	B689	Financial Advisors
1622	B929	Basic Spreadsheets
1700	E641	Spelling Mastery
1961	E910	Math Tutor
2050	E246	Computer Geography
2121	B794	Your Time Manager
2122	B731	Quick Key WP
2247	E758	Keyboard Composition
4020	B952	Tax Assistant

Ending Inventory (Justified)

Ending Inventory	Stock Number	Software
4127	B658	Telephone Directory

Ending Inventory	Stock Number	Software
4020	B952	Tax Assistant

Ending Inventory	Stock Number	Software
2247	E758	Keyboard Composition

Ending Inventory	Stock Number	Software
2122	B731	Quick Key WP

Ending Inventory	Stock Number	Software
2121	B794	Your Time Manager

Ending Inventory	Stock Number	Software
2050	E246	Computer Geography

The last report (Figure CA26-9) was created using the Create report by using wizard feature. The report is in **Portrait** orientation with **Columnar** layout in **Bold** style. The report is sorted in **Ascending** order by Ending Inventory. Only the first four entries of the report are shown.

Figure CA26-9

Report In Portrait Orientation, Columnar Layout, Bold Style

Ending Inventory (Columnar)

Ending Inventory	60
Stock Number	B821
Software	Data Controller
Ending Inventory	325
Stock Number	B833
Software	Office Layout
Ending Inventory	350
Stock Number	E561
Software	Creative Letters
Ending Inventory	463
Stock Number	B586
Software	Graphics Designer

Exercise 3A

Creating Reports

1. Open *Software Professionals*.
2. Create reports in the database with the information requested below.
3. Save as *Software Price List* and *Software Sales*.

SOFTWARE PROFESSIONALS		
Report Specifications		
Report 1	Layout: Columnar Style: Bold Title: Software Price List Sort: Ascending by Software	Software Stock Number Name of the Software Price of the Software
Report 2	Layout: Justified Style: Compact Title: Software Sales Sort: Descending by Sales	Software Stock Number Name of the Software Sales

Exercise 3B

Creating Reports

1. Open *Eastwick School of Dance*.
2. Create reports in the database with the information requested below.
3. Save as *Student Address List* and *Student Telephone List*.

Eastwick School of Dance		
Report Specifications		
Report 3	Layout: Tabular Style: Formal Title: Student Address List Sort: Ascending by Last Name	Student's Last Name Student's First Name Address City State ZIP
Report 4	Layout: Tabular Style: Soft Gray Title: Student Telephone List Sort: Ascending by Last Name	Student's Last Name Student's First Name Student's Telephone Number

Exercise 3C

Creating Reports

1. Open *Rockwell Technologies*.
2. Create reports in the database with the information requested below.
3. Save as *July/August Sales* and *July/August Sales by Territory*.

ROCKWELL TECHNOLOGIES		
Report Specifications		
Report 5	*Layout: Tabular* *Style: Corporate* *Title: July/August Sales* *Sort: Descending by Total Sales*	*Sales Rep's Last Name* *Sales Rep's Territory* *Sales Rep's July Sales* *Sales Rep's August Sales* *Sales Rep's Total Sales*
Report 6	*Prepare a sales report with the same information used in Report 5. Group the sales by territory. Use **July/August Sales by Territory** for the report title.*	

OBJECTIVE

⊙ To use the Mail Merge feature.

Learn: Mail Merge

Merge

The **Merge** feature is used to combine information from two sources into one document. It is often used for mail merge, which merges a word processing file (form letter) with a database file.

The database file contains a record for each recipient. Each record contains field(s) of information about the person such as first name, last name, address, city, state, ZIP, etc.

The word processing file contains the text of the document (constant information) plus the field codes and field names (variable information). The field codes and names are positioned in the document where the variable information from the database is to appear. A personalized letter to each recipient is the result of merging the two files.

Figure CA26-10 illustrates how the data file was merged with the word processing file to produce the letter at the bottom of the illustration.

Figure CA26-10 Mail Merge Process

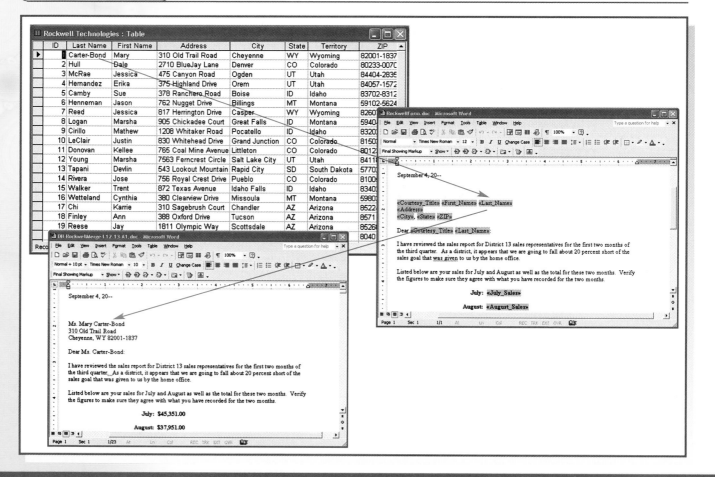

1. Create the form letter shown below to send to the sales reps in the *Rockwell Technologies – District 13* database.

2. Save as *Rockwell Form*.

3. Add a new field to the *Rockwell Technologies – District 13* database with a field name of **Courtesy Title**.

4. Use **Ms.** for all female reps except McRae, Donovan, and Finley. They prefer to use **Mrs.** for their courtesy title. Use **Mr.** for all male reps.

5. Merge and print the letters to Hernandez, Tapani, and Butler.

6. Save as *Rockwell Merge*.

September 4, 20--

«Courtesy_Title» «First_Name» «Last_Name»
«Address»
«City», «State» «ZIP»

Dear «Courtesy_Title» «Last_Name»:

I have reviewed the sales report for District 13 sales representatives for the first two months of the third quarter. As a district, it appears that we are going to fall about 20 percent short of the sales goal that was given to us by the home office.

Listed below are your sales for July and August as well as the total for these two months. Verify the figures to make sure they agree with what you have recorded for the two months.

July:	«July_Sales»
August:	«August_Sales»
Total Sales:	«Total_Sales»

Please make every effort possible during September to reach the goal that was set for your territory last May. It is my understanding that most of the other districts are going to meet or exceed the goals that were given to them.

If I can provide additional assistance to you to help you meet your goal, please contact me.

Sincerely,

Paul M. Vermillion
District Sales Manager

Exercise 4B

Merging Sources

1. Create the form letter shown below to send to the parents of students who have not paid their September dance fees.

2. Save as *Eastwick Form*.

   Tip: Insert necessary fields and data from *Eastwick Fees* into your *Eastwick Address* table. Include a new **Title** field and supply the appropriate courtesy title **Mr.** or **Ms.**

3. Create a query to determine which parents should receive a letter.

4. Merge and print the letters to Finley and Dye.

5. Save as *Eastwick Merge*.

October 15, 20--

«Title» «First_Name_Guardian» «Last_Name_Guardian»
«Address»
«City», «State» «ZIP»

Dear «Title» «Last_Name_Guardian»:

Please check your records to see if you have paid for «First_Name»'s September dance fees. Our records show that we have not received the fees in the amount of «Monthly_Fees». Let us know if our records are incorrect or send the fees with «First_Name» to her next dance class.

I have enjoyed working with «First_Name» this fall. Observing the students' progress from one skill level to the next is always very satisfying to me. The students are looking forward to performing for you at the December recital.

Sincerely,

Ashley Eastwick
Dance Instructor

xx

Exercise 4C

Merging Sources

1. Send the letter on the following page to applicants in the *A&E Bank* database with an income greater than $30,000. Be sure to include an enclosure notation.

2. Save as *A&E Bank Form*.

3. Add a new field, **Courtesy Title**, to the *A&E Bank* database before completing the merge. (Supply the appropriate courtesy title, **Mr.** or **Ms.**, for each applicant.)

4. Merge and print the letters to Eisenhower and Upshaw.

5. Save as *A&E Bank Merge*.

```
October 12, 20--


«Courtesy_Title» «First_Name» «Last_Name»
«Street_Address»
«City», «State» «ZIP»

Dear «Courtesy_Title» «Last_Name»:

Your credit card application with A&E Bank has been approved.  A
copy of our credit card rules and regulations is enclosed.
Please contact us at 800-563-8800 if you have questions after
reviewing the documents.

Your initial line of credit on the card is $5,000.  The limit is
reviewed on a periodic basis and will be increased as warranted.

We are looking forward to serving your credit needs.  When we
can be of further service, please contact us.

Sincerely,


Jason R. Rhyer
Credit Card Department
```

LESSON 5 PREPARING MAILING LABELS AND ENVELOPES

OBJECTIVES

⊘ To prepare mailing labels using the Mail Merge feature.
⊘ To prepare envelopes using the Mail Merge feature.

Learn: Prepare Mailing Labels and Envelopes

Mailing labels and envelopes can be created by using the mailing labels and envelopes features of Mail Merge in conjunction with your database file. Figure CA26-11 shows an example of mailing labels. Figure CA26-12 shows an example of envelopes created with the Mail Merge feature.

Figure CA26-11 — Mailing Labels

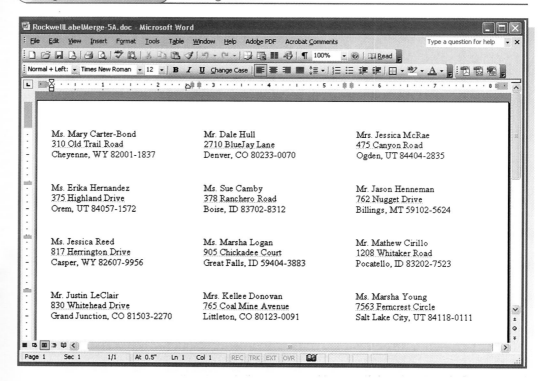

Figure CA26-12 — Envelopes

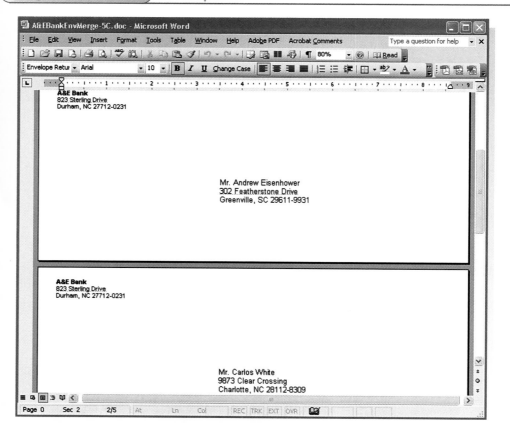

Exercise **5A**

Mailing Labels

1. Create mailing labels (illustrated in Figure CA26-11) for the merge letters generated for *Rockwell Technologies* in Exercise 4A.

2. Use Avery Product No. 5160 labels.

 Exercise **5B**

Mailing Labels

1. Create mailing labels for the merge letters generated for *Eastwick School of Dance* in Exercise 4B.

2. Use Avery Product No. 5160 labels.

 Exercise **5C**

Envelopes

1. Create and print envelopes as illustrated in Figure CA26-12 for the merge letters generated for *A&E Bank* in Exercise 4C.

2. Use Standard Size 10 envelopes and only print envelopes for Eisenhower and Upshaw.

The return address for the bank is:

A&E Bank
823 Sterling Drive
Durham, NC 27712-0231

 LESSON **6** **ASSESSMENT**

OBJECTIVE

⊙ To assess your knowledge of database applications.

 Exercise **6A**

Key Information into Forms

1. Open the *Rockwell Technologies – District 14* form.

2. Key the information shown on the following page into the form.

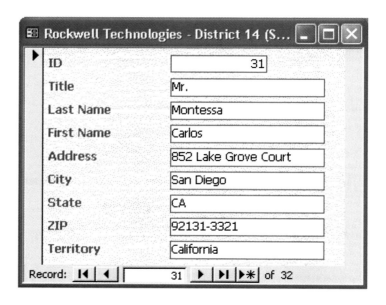

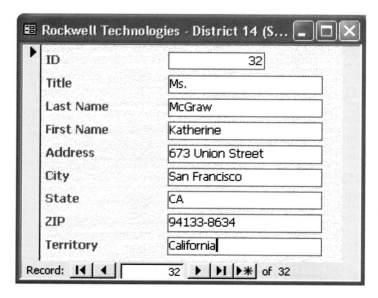

Exercise 6B

Editing Records

1. Make the changes shown below to the records in the *Rockwell Technologies – District 14* table.

   - Change *Winters'* address to 1472 Prescott Street.

   - Change the ZIP Code for *Culver* to 97301-8824.

   - Change *Phillips'* address to 387 Ferguson Avenue, Modesto, 95354-3210.

Add Fields to an Existing Database Table

1. Add the fields shown below to the *Rockwell Technologies – District 14* table.

   - July Sales
   - August Sales
   - Total Sales
   - Average Monthly Sales

2. Key into the table the information shown below.

SALES REPRESENTATIVES		
Last Name	*July Sales*	*August Sales*
Hughes	$55,671	$63,339
Winters	65,882	73,563
Chambers	43,812	54,650
Hanson	50,092	39,751
Yang	27,389	48,762
Zimmer	63,982	58,332
Aguilera	60,010	69,756
Winfield	44,396	58,675
Gonzalez	39,792	57,381
Keller	74,981	47,343
Wilkins	49,201	59,752
Bushlack	70,500	75,306
Lopez	65,730	62,385
Weiss	54,750	34,780
Culver	47,980	58,656
Miller	29,760	39,716
Sherman	80,754	54,354
Bailey	49,753	50,330
Stockton	75,880	82,791
Pizarro	54,900	60,230
Davis I.	39,763	48,655
Rice	65,830	66,385
Gilmore	40,340	37,381
Chi	52,379	59,659

(continued on next page)

SALES REPRESENTATIVES (continued)		
Last Name	July Sales	August Sales
Phillips	38,751	49,763
Taylor	57,925	50,845
Ryan	42,700	49,655
Backwith	68,524	62,566
Davis B.	57,247	62,318
Bolling	42,700	47,930
Montessa	59,650	55,428
McGraw	49,831	54,900

Exercise 6D

Query

1. Run a query on the *Rockwell Technologies – District 14* table to select all the sales reps from California.
2. Include First Name, Last Name, Territory, and July and August Sales.
3. Sort the query by Last Name in ascending order.
4. Print a copy of the query.

Exercise 6E

Computed Fields

1. Create a form file for the *Rockwell Technologies – District 14* table of all the sales reps that shows Last Name, First Name, July Sales, August Sales, Total Sales, and Average Monthly Sales. You will need to create computed fields for the Total Sales and Average Monthly Sales using the Expression Builder.
2. Sort the query by last name in ascending order.
3. Print the form in Datasheet View, landscape orientation.

Exercise 6F

Report

1. Create a report similar to the one shown on the following page for *Rockwell Technologies – District 14*.
2. Include the sales rep's Last Name, First Name, Territory, and August Sales.
3. Group the reps by Territory and sort by August Sales in ascending order.
4. Select an appropriate layout and style.

Rockwell - District 14

Territory	August Sales	Last Name	First Name
California			
	$34,780.00	Weiss	Daniel
	$39,716.00	Miller	Michelle
	$47,343.00	Keller	Loretta
	$49,655.00	Ryan	Terri
	$49,763.00	Phillips	Lori
	$50,845.00	Taylor	Dean
	$54,900.00	McGraw	Katherine
	$55,428.00	Montessa	Carlos
	$57,381.00	Gonzalez	Renae
	$58,332.00	Zimmer	Albert
	$58,675.00	Winfield	Kevin
	$59,659.00	Chi	Xi
	$59,752.00	Wilkins	Brian
	$60,230.00	Pizarro	Jose
	$62,385.00	Lopez	Juan
	$66,385.00	Rice	Donna
	$82,791.00	Stockton	Greg
Nevada			
	$39,751.00	Hanson	Harriet
	$50,330.00	Bailey	Jamal
	$54,650.00	Chambers	Chad

Exercise 6G

Mailing Labels

1. Prepare a set of mailing labels similar to the ones shown below for *District 14* sales reps.

2. Use Avery 5160 labels. Print the labels.

Mr. Justin Hughes
313 Glenwood Drive
Vancouver, WA 98662-1148

Ms. Rose Winters
1472 Prescott Street
Portland, OR 97217-8755

Mr. Chad Chambers
2317 Silver Dollar Avenue
Las Vegas, NV 89102-9964

Mrs. Harriet Hanson
1890 Rancho Verde Drive
Reno, NV 89511-2221

Mrs. Mai Yang
2187 Klamath Street
Salem, OR 97306-9031

Mr. Albert Zimmer
330 Van Ness Avenue
Los Angeles, CA 90020-3341

Mr. Mark Aguilera
388 Boston Lane
Eugene, OR 97402-1133

Mr. Kevin Winfield
820 Calle Roca
Palm Springs, CA 92264-0304

Ms. Renae Gonzalez
101 Brookside Avenue
Oakland, CA 94618-2212

Ms. Loretta Keller
329 Mountain View Court
Orange, CA 92669-9911

Mr. Brian Wilkins
40 Beacon Street
San Francisco, CA 94131-0167

Mr. Michael Bushlack
2387 Noschka Road
Olympia, WA 98502-1190

Prepare the letter shown below for *Rockwell Technologies – District 14* sales reps with August sales greater than $70,000.

September 16, 20--

«Title» «First_Name» «Last_Name»
«Address»
«City», «State» «ZIP»

Dear «Title» «Last_Name»

Congratulations! The sales report I received from your district manager lists your name as one of the three sales representatives in District 14 with sales over $70,000 for the month of August.

August was a very good month for District 14 sales representatives. They averaged over $56,104 of sales during August. This was an increase of approximately 4.3 percent over July and an increase of 7.8 percent over last August. This increase is due in large part to your efforts during the month.

We appreciate your hard work to make this the best year ever at Rockwell Technologies.

Sincerely

Leslie R. Fenwick
President

xx

Communication & Math Skills 8

1. Study each of the six rules below in the color boxes.

  a. Key the *Learn* line(s) beneath each rule, noting how the rule is applied.

  b. Key the *Apply* lines, using commas and colons correctly.

Internal Punctuation: Comma

Rule 1: Use a comma to separate the day from the year and the city from the state.

Learn 1 Lincoln delivered the Gettysburg Address on November 19, 1863.
Learn 2 The convention will be held at Cobo Hall in Detroit, Michigan.
Apply 3 Did you find this table in the March 16 2003, *USA Today*?
Apply 4 Are you on the history panel in San Antonio Texas?

Rule 2: Use a comma to separate two or more parallel adjectives (adjectives that could be separated by the word *and* instead of a comma).

Learn 5 The big, loud bully was ejected after he pushed the official.
Learn 6 Cynthia played a black lacquered grand piano at her concert.
Apply 7 The big powerful car zoomed past the cheering crowd.
Apply 8 A small red fox squeezed through the fence to avoid the hounds.

Rule 3: Use a comma to separate (a) unrelated groups of figures that occur together and (b) whole numbers into groups of three digits each. (*Note:* Policy, year, page, room, telephone, invoice, and most serial numbers are keyed without commas.)

Learn 9 By the year 2005, 1,100 more local students will be enrolled.
Learn 10 The supplies listed on Invoice #274068 are for Room 1953.
Apply 11 During 2004 2050 new graduates entered our job market.
Apply 12 See page 1069 of *Familiar Quotations*, Cat. Card No. 68-15664.

Internal Punctuation: Colon

Rule 4: Use a colon to introduce an enumeration or a listing.

Learn 13 These students are absent: Adam Bux, Todd Cody, and Sue Ott.
Apply 14 Add to the herb list parsley, rosemary, saffron, and thyme.
Apply 15 We must make these desserts a cake, two pies, and cookies.

Rule 5: Use a colon to introduce a question or a quotation.

Learn 16 Here's the real question: Who will pay for the "free" programs?
Learn 17 Who said: "Freedom is nothing else but a chance to be better"?
Apply 18 My question stands Who are we to pass judgment on them?
Apply 19 He quoted Browning "Good, to forgive; Best, to forget."

Rule 6: Use a colon between hours and minutes expressed in figures.

Learn 20 They give two performances: at 2:00 p.m. and at 8:00 p.m.
Apply 21 You have a choice of an 11 15 a.m. or a 2 30 p.m. appointment.
Apply 22 My workday begins at 8 15 a.m. and ends at 5 00 p.m.

2. Key *Proofread & Correct* on the following page, inserting commas and colons correctly.

  a. Check answers.

  b. Using the rule number(s) at the left of each line, study the rule relating to each error you made.

  c. Rekey each incorrect line, inserting commas and colons correctly.

Proofread & Correct

Rules		
1,3	1	The memorial was dedicated on November 13 1999—not 1,999.
1	2	We played in the Hoosier Dome in Indianapolis Indiana.
1	3	I cited an article in the May 8 2003, *Wall Street Journal*.
2	4	Carl sent Diana a dozen bright red, long-stem roses.
2	5	He buys most of his clothes at a store for big tall men.
3	6	Our enrollment for 2004, 1,884; for 2005 2040.
3	7	Where is the request for books and supplies for Room 1,004?
1,3	8	Policy #HP294,873 took effect on September 20 2005.
3	9	Della and Eldon Simms paid $129000 for their new condo.
4	10	Dry cleaning list 1 suit; 2 jackets; 3 pants; 2 sweaters.
5	11	Golden Rule Do unto others as you would have them do unto you.
5	12	I quote Jean Racine "Innocence has nothing to dread."
6	13	Glynda asked me to meet her 2 15 p.m. flight at JFK Airport.
6	14	Ten o'clock in the morning is the same as 10 00 a.m.

3. Save as *CS8-ACT1*.

ACTIVITY 2   Listening

1. You answered a telephone call from George Steward, your father's business associate. Mr Steward asked you to take a message for your father.

2. Open sound file *CD-CS8-ACT2*. As you listen to the message, take notes as needed.

3. Close the sound file.

4. Key the message—in complete sentences—for your father.

5. Save as *CS8-ACT2*.

ACTIVITY 3   Composing

1. Key the paragraph, correcting word-choice errors. (Every line contains at least one error.)

Some people think that because their good at sum sport, music, or other activity, there entitled to respect and forgiveness for anything else they choose to do in the passed. Its not uncommon, than, when such people break the law or violate sum code of conduct, four them to expect such behavior to be overlooked buy those who's job it is to enforce the law or to uphold an established code of conduct. Sum parents, as well as others in hour society, think that a "star's" misbehavior ought too be treated less harshly because of that person's vary impressive "celebrity" status; but all people should be treated equally under and threw the law.

2. Compose a second paragraph to accomplish these goals:
- Express your viewpoint about special treatment of "stars."
- State your view about whether the *same offense/same penalty* concept should apply to everyone alike.

3. Proofread, revise, and correct.

4. Save as *CS8-ACT3*.

ACTIVITY 4   Math: Working with Markups and Discounts

1. Open *CD-CS8-ACT4* and print the file.

2. Solve the problems as directed in the file.

3. Submit your answers.

UNIT 27

LESSONS 1–2

Assessing Database and Advanced Electronic Presentation Skills

Conditioning Practice

Before you begin the lessons, key each line twice.

alphabet	1	Jake Lopez may give a few more racquetball exhibitions in Dallas.
figures	2	Ray quickly found the total of 8.16, 9.43, and 10.25 to be 27.84.
speed	3	Bob's neighbor may dismantle the ancient shanty in the big field.

gwam   1' | 1 | 2 | 3 | 4 | 5 | 6 | 7 | 8 | 9 | 10 | 11 | 12 | 13 |

LESSON 1 DATABASE ASSESSMENT

OBJECTIVE

 To assess database skills.

Exercise 1A

Create a Database File and Table

1. Create a new database using the filename *Jaeger Enterprises*.
2. Create a table in Design View using the filename *Employee Information*.
   The table should include the following fields:
   - First Name
   - Last Name
   - Department
   - Phone Number

3. Include the following field properties in the table:
   - **Required** – *First Name*
   - **Default Value** – For the *Department* field, include a default value of **Sales**
   - **Input Mask** – For the *Phone Number* field, include an input mask of **(318) 487-####**

4. Leave the table open and continue with Exercise 1B.

Exercise 1B

Add New Records to a Database Table

Enter the following records into the *Employee Information* Table:

First Name	Last Name	Department	Phone No.
Julie	Zimmerman	Sales	(318) 487-3107
Dustin	Jones	Sales	(318) 487-4093
Sarah	Jardin	Accounting	(318) 487-3210
Michael	Dombrowski	Marketing	(318) 487-5400
Jason	Harrelson	Finance	(318) 487-2289
Hiroko	Iwata	Management Information	(318) 487-2910
Connie	Hudson	Sales	(318) 487-5671
Tim	Jones	Accounting	(318) 487-3208
Rebecca	Miller	Sales	(318) 487-4932
Adam	Martinez	Sales	(318) 487-1187
Leslie	Scanlon	Marketing	(318) 487-3012
Justin	Jones	Sales	(318) 487-5560
Stacey	Nikolai	Sales	(318) 487-8902
Jack	Nordstrom	Finance	(318) 487-3471

Exercise 1C

Add New Fields to a Database Table

1. Add two new fields to the *Employee Information* table. Use Supervisor and Date Hired for the new field names.

2. For the *Date Hired* field, use the field property long date format so that 6/15/2002 becomes Saturday, June 15, 2002.

3. Key the name of each employee's supervisor and the date that each employee was hired (shown on the following page) in the database table.

4. Enter a caption for the *Date Hired* field: Date of Initial Employment.

Name	Supervisor	Date Hired
J. Zimmerman	McKee	04/15/87
D. Jones	McKee	06/04/00
S. Jardin	Fuller	12/05/79
J. Dombrowski	Chan	09/29/95
J. Harelson	Rodriguez	05/20/05
H. Iwata	Maddux	01/19/89
C. Hudson	McKee	10/03/95
T. Jones	Fuller	01/28/06
R. Miller	McKee	11/12/91
A. Martinez	McKee	03/30/79
L. Scanlon	Chan	08/18/03
J. Jones	McKee	07/02/99
S. Nikolai	McKee	02/07/90
J. Nordstrom	Rodriguez	04/28/81

5. Update the *Employee Information* table to include the employees shown below. They were all hired on June 17, 2005.

First Name	Last Name	Department	Extension	Supervisor
Trevor	Martin	Sales	(318) 487-1521	McKee
Jessica	Van Noy	Finance	(318) 487-6711	Rodriguez
Troy	McMichael	Sales	(318) 487-7220	McKee

6. Save and print a copy of the table.

Exercise 1D

Create a Data Sort

1. Create the data sorts shown below using the *Employee Information* table. Print copies of the table after each sort has been completed.

- Sort the table by employee last name in ascending order
- Sort the table by supervisor in ascending order.

Exercise 1E

Create Queries

1. Create queries to answer the questions below. Include the employee's first and last name, department, and supervisor in each query. Print the results of each query.

   • Which employees have McKee for a supervisor?

   • Which employees have Jones for a last name?

   • Which employees work in the Sales Department?

Exercise 1F

Create a Report

1. Generate a report similar to the one shown below. Complete a primary sort by employee last name in ascending order and a secondary sort by employee first name in ascending order. Title the report Telephone Directory.

Telephone Directory

Last Name	First Name	Phone Number	Department
Dombrowski	Michael	(318) 487-5400	Marketing
Harrelson	Jason	(318) 487-2289	Finance
Hudson	Connie	(318) 487-5671	Sales
Iwata	Hiroko	(318) 487-2910	Management Information
Jardin	Sarah	(318) 487-3210	Accounting
Jones	Dustin	(318) 487-4093	Sales
Jones	Justin	(318) 487-5560	Sales
Jones	Tim	(318) 487-3208	Accounting
Martin	Trevor	(318) 487-1521	Sales
Martinez	Adam	(318) 487-1187	Sales
McMichael	Troy	(318) 487-7220	Sales
Miller	Rebecca	(318) 487-4932	Sales
Nikolai	Stacey	(318) 487-8902	Sales
Nordstrom	Jack	(318) 487-3471	Finance
Scanlon	Leslie	(318) 487-3012	Marketing
Van Noy	Jessica	(318) 487-6711	Sales
Zimmerman	Julie	(318) 487-3107	Sales

2. Generate another report. Group by department. Sort by employee last name in ascending order. Use *Outline 1* for the layout. Use Telephone Directory 2 for the title of the report.

Exercise 1G

Import a Word File

1. Import the *Word* file *CD-Jaeger Employees 2* into the *Employee Information* table. Sort the table by last name in Ascending Order.

2. Print a copy of the table.

OBJECTIVE

 To assess advanced electronic presentation skills.

Exercise 2A

Produce an Electronic Presentation

Use the New Presentation Wizard in *Producer* to create an electronic presentation entitled Presentation Delivery. You will use the files below to create the presentation. Before you begin, preview the files to see what each file contains.

CD-Advance slides script.doc

CD-PowerPoint1.ppt

CD-PowerPoint2.ppt

CD-Erika Slide 1.jpg

CD Erika Slide 2.jpg

CD-Erika Slide 3.jpg

CD-Erika Slide 4.jpg

CD-Erika Slide 5.jpg

CD-Erika Slide 6.jpg

CD-Presentation Delivery Intro.mpg

CD-Presentation Delivery Do's.mpg

CD-Presentation Delivery Don'ts.mpg

CD-Presentation Delivery Ending.mpg

Follow these steps:

1. Open *CD-Advance slides script* and print a copy of the script. Review the script to see where the slides and images need to be synchronized in the video files.

2. Open *Producer;* use the New Presentation Wizard to create the presentation.

3. Use the default for the Presentation Template.

4. For the Presentation Scheme use the following:

   • Font: **Comic Sans MS**

   • Font Size: **14 point**

   • Font Color: **White**

   • Background Color: Select a color to complement the color of the *PowerPoint* slides being used in the presentation.

   • Slide Area Background Color: **White**, or select a color to complement the color of the *PowerPoint* slides being used in the presentation.

5. Use the following Presentation Information to create a title slide that looks like this using *CD-Erika Slide 1.jpg*:

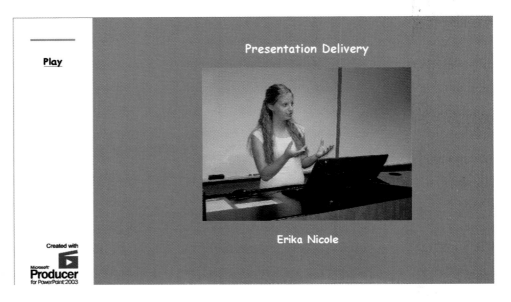

6. Import slides and still images in the following order:

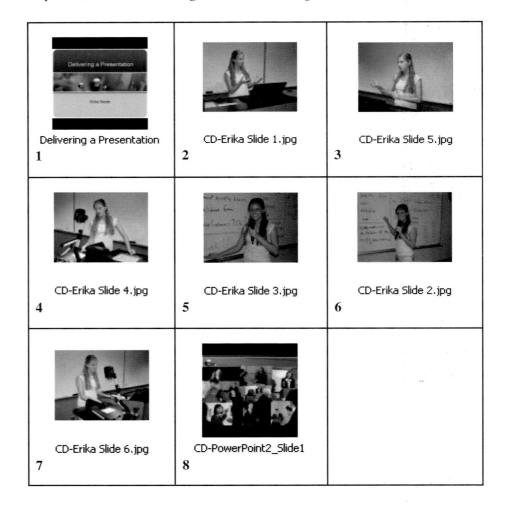

Delivering a Presentation **1**	CD-Erika Slide 1.jpg **2**	CD-Erika Slide 5.jpg **3**
CD-Erika Slide 4.jpg **4**	CD-Erika Slide 3.jpg **5**	CD-Erika Slide 2.jpg **6**
CD-Erika Slide 6.jpg **7**	CD-PowerPoint2_Slide1 **8**	

7. Import video files in the order shown below:

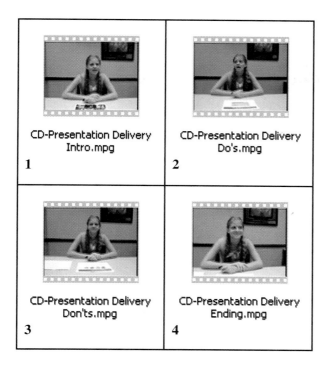

CD-Presentation Delivery
Intro.mpg
1

CD-Presentation Delivery
Do's.mpg
2

CD-Presentation Delivery
Don'ts.mpg
3

CD-Presentation Delivery
Ending.mpg
4

Exercise 2B

Synchronize Video Files and Add Transitions

1. Using the *Advance Slides Script* you printed for 2A, synchronize the video files with the image and slides files. The script is marked with ▼ to show when the slides should be advanced.

2. After the files have been synchronized, insert video transitions of your choice between each of the video files.

3. Save the file as *CA27-2B*.

Exercise 2C

Publish the Presentation

Publish the presentation you created in 2A and 2B using the Publish Wizard. Your instructor will inform you where to publish the presentation. Use *CA27-2C-Your Name* for the filename.

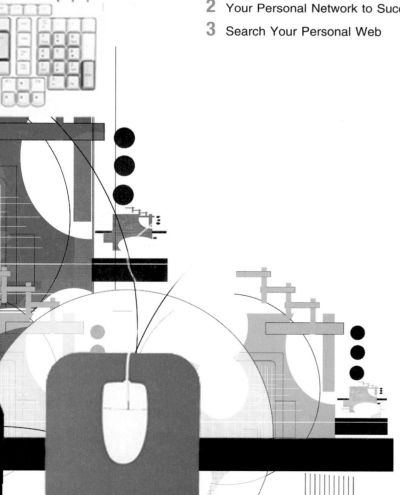

Part 2

UNIT 1

History of Computers and Hardware

Conditioning Practice

Before you begin the lessons, key each line twice.

alphabet	1	Next week Zelda Jacks will become a night supervisor for quality.
figures	2	Scores of 94, 83, 72, 65, and 100 gave Rhonda an average of 82.8.
speed	3	Kay paid the maid for the work she did on the shanty by the lake.

gwam 1' | 1 | 2 | 3 | 4 | 5 | 6 | 7 | 8 | 9 | 10 | 11 | 12 | 13 |

LESSON 1 EARLY HISTORY

OBJECTIVES

- ⊙ To examine the early influence of counting machines.
- ⊙ To study the contributions of Blaise Pascal, Gottfried Wilhelm von Leibniz, Charles Xavier Thomas, and Joseph-Marie Jacquard.
- ⊙ To review the accomplishments of Hermann Hollerith and IBM.
- ⊙ To review the intellectual achievements of Charles Babbage, Ada Byron, and George Boole.

Learn: The Abacus Advantage

People learned early in human history to rely on the inventions that gave them an advantage. Seeking this advantage goes deep into history. Consider fire, the wheel, bronze, iron, steel, the plow, steamships, locomotives, plastics, jet aircraft, and the personal computer. Each invention gave the people that first used it distinct benefits.

abacus

Figure OA1-1 An Abacus

© PHOTODISC GREEN /GETTY IMAGES

One such invention was the **abacus**. In 3,000 B.C., ancient Babylonians in the Middle East made calculations by placing pebbles and drawing lines in sandboxes. In 500 B.C., the abacus improved on this early sandbox design by placing beads on wires in a wooden, rectangular frame (see Figure OA1-1). This rather simple-looking device helped ancient peoples count and tabulate. The modern computer can trace its origins to early mechanical counting devices like the abacus.

Don't Be Blasé About Mechanical Computers

Over time, mechanical counting tools grew more and more sophisticated. **Blaise Pascal** (1623–1662) as an 18-year-old concocted an adding machine to help his father collect taxes. Eventually, he created the **Pascaline**, a sophisticated mechanical calculator (see Figure OA1-2).

Figure OA1-2 The Pascaline

SCIENCE MUSEUM / SCIENCE & SOCIETY PICTURE LIBRARY

In 1671, **Gottfried Wilhelm von Leibniz** (1646–1716)—who also invented calculus in parallel with Sir Isaac Newton—created a mechanical calculator called the **Arithmetickal Engine** that could add, divide, and multiply. Neither the Pascaline nor the Arithmetickal Engine were used extensively. They proved difficult to use or were viewed as mere curiosities. However, they did inspire other inventors like **Charles Xavier Thomas** (1785–1870).

Thomas created a practical mechanical calculator called the **Arithmometer** that could add, subtract, multiply, and divide. (See Figure OA1-3.) This spurred a series of innovations. Soon after, memory functions were added to counting machines. Later, adding machines provided printed copies of the results. This was the forerunner of the receipts we receive today while making purchases at a store. The mechanical calculator was finally a commercial success.

Figure OA1-3 The Arithmometer

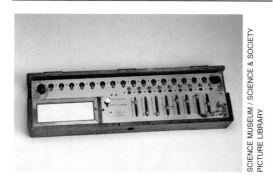

SCIENCE MUSEUM / SCIENCE & SOCIETY PICTURE LIBRARY

Descendents of early adding machines were still popular through the 1970s. Mechanical adding machines were used every day in stores and other businesses, government agencies, scientific labs, and schools. People soon became comfortable having machines do some of their thinking for them.

Helpful Herman Hollerith

Inventors in the 19th century benefited from the work of **Joseph-Marie Jacquard** (1752–1834). Jacquard used a series of punch cards to control the actions of an automatic loom for making cloth. He proved that punch cards had the ability to store input instructions for a mechanical loom to produce colorful patterns and styles of fabric. For an example of a punch card, see Figure OA1-4.

Hermann Hollerith (1860–1929) used Jacquard's punch card idea in combination with an electromechanical machine. His machine could tabulate and store data. In 1890 it was used to count

Figure OA1-4 A Punch Card

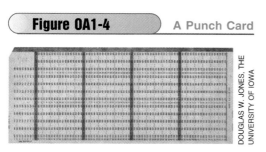

DOUGLAS W. JONES, THE UNIVERSITY OF IOWA

Luddites

The Luddites (1811–1816) in early 19th-century England believed that new technologies, such as the mechanical looms found in a growing number of automated factories, were stealing jobs away from impoverished, small-scale textile workers. They were also angry about the terrible working conditions in the textile factories. Their response was to sabotage the new technologies. The term **Luddite** is now synonymous with someone who opposes technological change.

DOUGLAS W. JONES, THE UNIVERSITY OF IOWA

the United States census, for which every person in the country must be counted with a high degree of accuracy. The previous census had taken nine years to count; Hollerith completed the job in six weeks. Soon, cards were used to store data for government agencies and businesses. Even elections were tabulated with punch cards. Punch cards became indispensable.

Hollerith wasn't finished making history. He took his ideas and technologies and created a company called the Tabulating Machine Co., which later became IBM or International Business Machines. IBM is responsible for many of the advances in computing we enjoy today.

Punch cards were still in widespread use for counting election results until the 2000 presidential election in the United States. The results of the presidential election between Albert Gore and George W. Bush came down to just a few votes in Florida. Flaws and inaccuracies in punch card balloting were revealed. In a very tight election for president, punch cards proved unreliable and fell into disfavor.

LIBRARY OF CONGRESS PRINTS AND PHOTOGRAPHS DIVISION WASHINGTON, D.C. 20540 USA

Difference Engine
Analytical Engine

The Brains of Babbage, Byron, and Boole

Creating mechanical counting devices using punch cards was certainly a huge step forward from the abacus. But before modern digital computers could be invented, theorists like **Charles Babbage** (1791–1871) had to break new scientific ground. Babbage, a mathematics professor at Cambridge University in England, designed what can be called the first "computer."

Babbage's first design was called the **Difference Engine**. It was meant to calculate celestial tables and help navigators. However, work on the engine was never completed. Then, in 1833, Babbage designed a steam-powered **Analytical Engine**. It was designed to run with the aid of punch cards and was programmable.

Another early theorist was **Lady Ada Byron, Countess of Lovelace** (1815–1852). Her father was Lord Byron, one of the greatest romantic poets in history. She became a close friend of Babbage, translated some of his writings, helped promote his work, and created the first theoretical programs to run on Babbage's Analytical Engine. She is widely heralded as the first computer programmer.

© QUEEN'S PRINTER AND CONTROLLER OF HMSO, 2005. UK GOVERNMENT ART COLLECTION.

Lady Byron caught a vision of the future. She understood what all of this theoretical work had the power to create. She predicted that someday, computing machines would serve scientific purposes, produce graphics, compose music, complete everyday practical tasks, and much more. Her forecasts were accurate, but her predictions were also 150 years ahead of their time.

Running Ada Byron's programs, the Babbage steam-powered Analytical Engine would have been the first general use computer. But, just as history was about to be made, the British government suspended Babbage's funding. Nevertheless, Babbage made enough of a splash to radically change people's thinking about the future of computing tools.

George Boole (1815–1864) was another one of the essential early thinkers behind the development of modern computers. Boole realized that only two numbers were needed to complete arithmetical functions, and thus invented the binary system of Boolean algebra. In Boolean terms, mathematical equations can be written as either **true or false**. This can be represented by the numbers **0** and **1**, or alternatively as **on** and **off**. With this system, a way was foreseen to design a brain for a machine. Boolean algebra is both simple and powerful at the same time.

Exercise 1A

How to Build an Abacus

Can you build an abacus of your own and learn how to use it? To accomplish this exercise, you may need to complete the next unit first and learn how to research such interesting questions on the Internet. You will need to find a workable design for an abacus, figure out what materials you would need to make it, and then learn how the device works.

LESSON 2 MAJOR EVENTS IN THE HISTORY OF COMPUTERS

OBJECTIVES

⊙ To study the following major computer events:
  o The era of vacuum tubes
  o The era of the first transistors
  o The era of the integrated circuit
  o The era of the personal computer
  o The era of mobile computing
⊙ To understand the convergence of other technologies with the personal computer

Victory with Vacuum Tubes

While mechanical counting machines certainly paved new ground, it wasn't until World War II that work accelerated on computers that use electric currents to perform calculations. Early electrical computers came about as a by-product of an invention by Bell Telephone Laboratories. Technicians at Bell Labs figured out that they could decrease or increase voltage into vacuum tubes. They used this invention to help build a coast-to-coast phone system.

Vacuum tubes (see Figure OA1-5) started the ball rolling on the first generation of electrical computers. In 1940, **John Atanasoff** (1903–1995), with the help of a graduate student named Clifford Berry, used tubes to create an electric computer with circuits that turned on and off. By applying Boolean algebra, they knew that arithmetical functions could be solved using 0s or 1s by turning tubes on or off.

© AP / WIDE WORLD PHOTOS

© BETTMANN/CORBIS

ENIAC or Electrical Numerical Integrator and Calculator

Soon, Atanasoff and Berry had hundreds of vacuum tubes turning on and off, with each tube completing its part of a calculation.

In 1947, **John P. Eckert** (1908–1980) and **John W. Mauchly** (1907–1980) at the University of Pennsylvania built the **ENIAC** or **Electrical Numerical Integrator and Calculator** (see Figure OA1-6). The ENIAC used nearly 18,000 vacuum tubes and was the size of a room—taking up 1,800 square feet of floor space.

Computers using vacuum tubes were big—occupying entire rooms—were extremely expensive, costing millions of dollars each; and could only perform a few hundred calculations per second. For example, the ENIAC could perform 5,000 addition problems per second. It wasn't quite so fast at division, only completing 38 division problems per second. Changing programs could take weeks, and the ma-

Making Connections

Debugging a Computer

If something goes wrong with a computer, it is often blamed on a "bug." Fixing errors is called "debugging." **Grace Murray Hooper** (1906–1992), a pioneer of the United States Navy's computer efforts, was checking vacuum tubes looking for the cause of an error. She found that a dead moth was causing the problem. She "debugged" the problem, and the computer started to work again. Her famous moth, along with her log of the disruption, is on display at the Smithsonian Institution in Washington, DC.

COURTESY OF THE NAVAL SURFACE WARFARE CENTER, DAHLGREN, VA., 1988.

chine required many hours of general maintenance. The ENIAC, and the other computers of this era such as the Mark 1, generated a lot of heat and required lots of electricity to power the tubes. An urban myth spread saying that every time the ENIAC was turned on, the nearby city of Philadelphia experienced an electrical brownout.

The Transition to Transistors

In 1947, at Bell Labs in Murray Hill, New Jersey, the **transistor** was discovered by three future Nobel Prize recipients: **John Bardeen** (1908–1991), **William Shockley** (1910–1989), and **Walter Brattain** (1902–1987). Their earthshaking discovery marked the next milestone in the development of computers. By comparison to vacuum tubes, transistors were lighter, faster, smaller, and required much less electrical power to perform calculations.

transistor

In 1951, Eckert and Mauchly, who had created the ENIAC a few years earlier, got busy incorporating transistors into a new computer called the **UNIVAC**, or **UNIVersal Automatic Computer**. Interestingly, their first client was the United States Census Bureau, which was always on the lookout for a state-of-the-art way to efficiently count the population. Unable to totally fund the project, the duo joined forces with the Remington-Rand Corporation, which marketed and sold the new computer.

UNIVAC
UNIVersal
Automatic
Computer

The UNIVAC become the first commercially viable computer. Well-funded businesses, universities, governments, and major municipalities could now take advantage of computer technologies. As a publicity stunt, the UNIVAC was used to predict a winner in the 1952 presidential election. Soon, the UNIVAC became both popular and profitable.

Meanwhile, IBM, the company Hermann Hollerith founded, wasn't taking the UNIVAC's challenge to their computing prowess lightly. From 1953 to 1960, IBM introduced its 700 series of computers. The IBM 704, released in 1956, was called the world's first supercomputer. These supercomputers were often called **mainframes**. Smaller versions were called **minicomputers**. In 1960 IBM released the 7090, which instantly became the fastest computer in the world. Then, in 1964, the company introduced the IBM 360, which became *the* standard mainframe computer for businesses, government agencies, schools, and hospitals. The IBM 360 and its descendents made IBM the dominant mainframe and minicomputer manufacturer for the next 20 years. IBM became known as Big Blue, and its stock became a bellwether on the New York Stock Exchange. Many considered owning IBM stock a "sure thing."

mainframes
minicomputers

integrated circuit or **IC**
chips

Learn: The Importance of Integrated Circuits

In 1959, two separate inventors, **Jack Kilby** (1923–2005), of Texas Instruments, and **Robert Noyce** (1927–), cofounder of Intel Corporation, created the **integrated circuit** or **IC**. The IC was the next major step forward in the computer odyssey. See Figure OA1-7.

Before a transistor can work, it needs an accompanying resistor, capacitors, and connective wiring. Kilby and Noyce were able to integrate these various parts, miniaturize them, and place them on silicon wafers made of quartz. The silicon wafers were nicknamed **chips**. Chip-based

COURTESY OF TEXAS INSTRUMENTS

computers with integrated circuits were smaller, faster, and burned a lot less electricity than any previous systems. Kilby would eventually receive 60 patents and became the inventor of the portable, handheld calculator. Noyce was awarded 16 patents and cofounded Intel Corporation, the company that invented the modern microprocessor.

The discovery of the IC was so important that this period in history is often called the Silicon Age. One of the technological centers of the United States, south of San Francisco Bay, was even dubbed Silicon Valley.

The integrated circuit became one of the most prized inventions in the history of mankind. The first IC was the size of a fingernail and held only one transistor. Today, companies are perfecting microprocessors with a billion transistors. More transistors means greater computing power at a reduced cost. According to Jack Kilby:

Figure OA1-7 The First Integrated Circuit

COURTESY OF TEXAS INSTRUMENTS

What we didn't realize then was that the integrated circuit would reduce the cost of electronic functions by a factor of a million to one.[1]

Kilby wasn't alone in his enthusiasm. **Gordon Moore** (1929–), who cofounded Intel with Robert Noyce, predicted in 1965 that the number of components in an integrated circuit would double every few years. This would increase the power of computers exponentially while at the same time reducing their costs. This prediction became known as **Moore's Law.**

Moore's Law

To understand Moore's Law, examine the growth of transistors found in microprocessors over the years. For example, the microprocessor that landed the lunar module on the moon in 1969 had about 5000 transistors. By the year 2000, microprocessors had over 42 million transistors. Now, computers with billions of transistors are being designed for the next generation of computers.

THE GROWTH OF TRANSISTORS		
Year	Transistors	Intel Model
1971	2,250	4004
1972	3,500	8008
1974	6,000	8080
1978	29,000	8086
1982	134,000	286
1985	275,000	386™ processor

(continued on next page)

---

[1]"'Humble giant' Hailed for Inventing Integrated Circuit: Computer Maker Launches Observance of 1958 Development." September 9, 1997, DALLAS (CNN) http://www.cnn.com/TECH/9709/09/chip.inventor/

Year	Transistors	Intel Model
1989	1,180,000	486™ DX processor
1997	7,500,000	Pentium II processor
1999	28 million	Pentium III processor
2000	42 million	Pentium 4 processor
2003	220 million	Early Itanium 2
2005	500 million	Next Generation Itanium 2
2007–2009	Over a billion	

Taking It Personal

The Big Blue mainframe-style computers that dominated the 1960s and 1970s were far from personal. Prices dropped dramatically from the days of the UNIVAC, but computers were still overly expensive, big, bulky, and hard to use. No one ever dreamed of owning a computer of their own—but the space program changed all that.

The Apollo program, which first took astronauts to the moon, needed tiny computers to run its guidance systems. This required inventing small, lightweight computers. That, in turn, ignited the fledgling personal computer industry. Inspired by the space program, computer scientists turned their dreams of small, lightweight, portable computers for everyone into a reality.

Intel Corporation created one of the first miniature microprocessors called the 4004. By 1972, the Intel 4004 was guiding the *Pioneer* spacecraft to Saturn, and the chip went on to make history in other ways.

Using the Intel 4004 chip, Micro Instrumentation and Telemetry Systems (MITS) built the first personal computer and sold it as a hobby kit through science magazines. The **MITS Altair 8800** (see Figure OA1-8) sold for about $700 in 1975. For the money, a computer enthusiast would receive an integrated microprocessor with a central processing unit, memory, and input and output controls. Hobbyists could build the computer at home and complete a few calculations at the end of the experiment. Only a few thousand were ever sold, but the Altair got a lot of people buzzing around the idea of mass-producing personal computers for the average person.

MITS Altair 8800

In 1975, **Bill Gates** (1955–) and **Paul Allen** (1953–) started a little company called Microsoft and began by writing software for the MIPS Altair 8800. Microsoft quickly gained a reputation for programming usable software.

Figure OA1-8 The MITS Altair

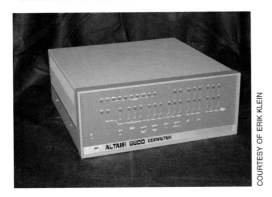

Learn: The Birth of the Desktop PC

Another team of pioneers, **Steve Wozniak** (1950–) and **Steve Jobs** (1955–), thought they could create a mass-market personal computer that was small enough to sit on someone's desk at work or at home. They started with the Apple I computer (1976), which they built with their own hands using readily available components. The project met with limited but encouraging success. When they later released the Apple II (1977), they had created the first affordable and usable desktop computer. The Apple II was as influential in the late 1970s as the UNIVAC had been in the 1950s or the IBM 360 series was in the 1960s. See Figure OA 1-9.

Figure OA1-9 — **Early Apple Computer**

COURTESY OF ERIK KLEIN

But the 1980s would belong to Big Blue. Not to be outdone by Apple Computer Corporation, IBM designed its first personal desktop computer, called the IBM PC, using a new Intel microprocessor, the 8088 (see Figure OA1-10).

In 1981, IBM went to tiny Microsoft looking for an operating system for its first desktop computer. As a result, Microsoft's operating system, called MS DOS, would soon run the overwhelming majority of the world's personal computers.

IBM coined the acronym PC for *personal computer* in a series of TV commercials. In a few short years, hundreds of thousands of IBM's desktops running Microsoft's operation system were sold. The era of the personal desktop computer was in full swing.

text interface

Figure OA1-10 — **IBM PC**

COURTESY OF ERIK KLEIN

Both the Apple II and the IBM PC used a **text interface**. There was no mouse, no digital pen, and no speech recognition. The primary input tool was a keyboard. For example, to execute commands, users had to press a series of keystrokes, such as [Shift] [F7] [Enter] to print a document. Users pressed the following series of keys just to open a popular word processing program of that time.

C: [Enter]

CD WP [Enter]

WP [Enter]

Nevertheless, people found computers useful for spreadsheets, numerical calculations, and word processing. Computers began to show up on desks in businesses, government agencies, libraries, university dormitories, and in a growing number of homes.

Computers Go GUI

Between 1983 and 1986, Apple created another first by designing a line of desktop computers with a **GUI** (pronounced *gooie*) interface called **Macintosh** or simply **Mac** for short. GUI is short for **graphical user interface**. Drawing upon research at the Xerox **Palo Alto Research Center (PARC)**, Apple created a new operating system (Apple OS) for its line of Mac desktop computers. In the process, they popularized a new way of working with computers.

Instead of typing hard-to-remember text commands, GUI software was activated simply by moving and clicking a device called a mouse. The mouse was invented

Macintosh

Mac

graphical user interface

Palo Alto Research Center (PARC)

by **Douglas Engelbart** (1925–) while working at the Stanford Research Institute. It got its name because of a long cord attached to it that looked something like a tail. Commands would be activated by clicking a mouse button on graphical icons on the screen.

A GUI interface made computers much easier to use and became so compelling that Microsoft released its own GUI operating system called Windows in 1985. By 1995, over 90 percent of the PCs worldwide were running Microsoft's GUI Windows operating system.

Learn: The Power of Mobile Computers

While a tremendous improvement over mainframe computers for the average person, desktop computers still left a lot to be desired. Computers continued to evolve, and a new generation of mobile computers came into vogue. Smaller, sleeker computer designs were introduced to the market.

The first portable computer was introduced in 1983 by Compaq Computer Corporation and weighed over 30 pounds. These early portables evolved into laptops, ultralight portables, tablet PCs, handheld computers, pocket PCs, and smart phones. Today's powerhouse computers are much smaller, use less energy, are far more powerful, and weigh a fraction of earlier computers. Many mobile computers use a digital pen or stylus as input tools instead of a mouse or even a keyboard.

COMPARING THE WEIGHT OF COMPUTERS

Name of Computer	Decade	Weight
ENIAC	1940s	Over 30 tons
Early Compaq and IBM "portable" computers	1980s	33 pounds
Tablet PC	2000s	3 pounds
Palm OS and Pocket PC	2000s	3 ounces

The first financially successful handheld computer was the Palm Pilot, introduced in 1996 by PalmSource. The Palm Pilot was a **personal digital assistant** or **PDA**. Its small size and portability made it a popular tool for businesspeople who needed to carry personal planning and contact information with them wherever they traveled. PDAs continued to grow in power and became so popular that many of their best features were integrated into cell phone technologies. The marriage of PDA and cell phone produced what is often called a **smart phone**. The smart phone provides the best of both technologies in a single device. A smart phone or handheld computer that you may be using today has more computing power than the ENIAC, the UNIVAC, and the first Apple II and IBM PC computers.

As computers became smaller, the space available for full-sized keyboards started to disappear. One answer to this problem was invented simultaneously by both Dragon Systems and IBM in 1997. Both companies released their first **Continuous Speech Recognition (CSR)** software in the same year, which in turn

personal digital assistant
PDA

smart phone

Continuous Speech Recognition (CSR)

Speech User Interface (SUI)

created the **Speech User Interface (SUI)**. (See Part 3 Unit 2.) The first CSR applications allowed handicapped users hands-free use of their PCs.

Speech technologies require fast computers in order to process human speech successfully. Therefore, speech software continually improved in direct proportion to increases in CPU power, as predicated by Moore's Law. As a result of the exponential increase in the number of transistors on today's CPUs, trained CSR users today can voice-type accurately between 100 and 200 words per minute.

The magic of Moore's Law continues to lead to other interesting new technologies, designs, and uses for today's chips. Many are predicting that future computers may be as small as a button on a shirt. Some say a computer can be built into someone's sunglasses. This branch of computer science is called **wearable tech**.

wearable tech

We've certainly progressed a long way from the abacus. But wherever the electronic computer revolution continues to lead us, it will certainly create new and different ways of working and learning. The key, however, is not how small or how powerful computers become, but how well you put these tools to good use. Learning how to use your computer tools effectively will give you an advantage in your academic, professional, and personal life. You will be able to achieve new goals and reach new levels of educational excellence and professional success.

Making Connections

It's Bigger Than Computers

This unit traced the history of the modern computer. However, computers are just one aspect of a much bigger story. Consider these other astonishing inventions:

- Networks and the Internet
- The telephone
- The digital pen
- Printing
- Television
- Photography and film
- Copiers and scanners
- Speech recognition and language translation technologies
- Electronic gaming
- Satellites and GPS technologies
- Security and surveillance systems
- Digital music and video technologies

Each of these technologies has merged with computers to create new tools that work in exciting ways. These hybrid technologies are often called **Digital Communication Tools** or **DigiTools**. As computers and other technologies merge together, new labor-saving devices and new ways of working are invented.

Keep your eyes on the technologies in this list. You are sure to encounter each one of them at some point in your academic and professional pursuits.

Early Computing History

In preparation for exercises in units to come, answer the following short answer questions using either *Microsoft OneNote or Microsoft Word*. Use this table listing important computer pioneers to help you answer the questions.

Blaise Pascal	Gottfried Wilhelm von Leibniz	Charles Xavier Thomas
Joseph-Marie Jacquard	Charles Babbage	Ada Byron
George Boole	John Atanasoff	John P. Eckert
John W. Mauchly	Grace Murray Hooper	John Bardeen
William Shockley	Walter Brattain	Herman Hollerith
Jack Kilby	Robert Noyce	Gordon Moore
Steve Wozniak	Steve Jobs	Bill Gates
Paul Allen	Douglas Engelbart	

1. Do you know what each of the 23 computer pioneers listed in this chapter accomplished? Review the list in the table above. Open *Microsoft Word* or *Microsoft OneNote* and jot a note about the contributions of each. Try to record this from memory without reviewing the unit, then go back and double-check your answers.

2. From your reading of this unit, which computer pioneer listed in the table above do you consider the most important contributor to the rise of the computing machine?

3. At least three of the history-making inventors discussed in this unit were awarded the Nobel Prize for the development of the transistor. Who were they?

4. If you had the ability to go back in time to award the Nobel Prize for science to any of the other 23 computer pioneers listed in the table above, which would receive the prize?

5. Which person in the table above would you most like to research and learn more about? Briefly explain why you picked the person you've selected.

6. In your opinion, what is the most important single event in the history of the computer? Defend your assertion in a few short statements.

7. What do you believe to be the most important computer-related invention in the last 10 years? Defend your answer in a few brief written statements.

8. Save your answers in a *Word* file named *OA1-2A*. (*Microsoft OneNote* saves automatically.)

Ranking Technology

1. Using *Microsoft Excel*, or the Tables feature in *Microsoft Word*, create the following spreadsheet/table and rank the following computer-related technologies in four ways:

   a. The most often used and widely used technologies

   b. The most important technologies in the development of society

   c. The technologies that demonstrate the greatest growth potential in the future

   d. The technologies that you believe are providing the greatest profit for technology companies worldwide

2. Rank each of these technologies from 1 to 12, with 12 being the most important or providing the greatest potential, and 1 indicating the technology with the least potential or ability to grow. There are no right or wrong answers.

3. Save your table or spreadsheet as *OA1-2B*.

	A. Most often and widely used	B. Most important to society	C. Greatest growth potential	D. Most profitable technologies	Total score
Networking and Internet					
Telephone					
Pencil and pen					
Printing					
Television					
Photography and film					
Copiers and scanning					
Speech recognition and translation					
Electronic gaming					
Satellites and GPS					
Security and surveillance					
Digital music and video					

Exercise 2C

Improving Technology

1. Open either *Microsoft Word* or *Microsoft OneNote* and answer the following questions in a short, rough-draft essay of approximately 500 words.

    • You have been around technology your entire life. Which technologies do you think are frustrating and need improvement or change? In what ways would you improve these technologies? How would you suggest that computer engineers make them better, easier to use, and more efficient?

2. Save your rough draft for a future exercise. Name your Word file *OA1-2C*. (*Microsoft OneNote* saves automatically.)

Exercise 2D

The Future of Technology

Record the answers to these questions using *Microsoft Word* or *Microsoft OneNote*.

1. Predict the future of computers. Will they ever become wearable devices that people talk to and hardly think about?

2. We have many new computerized tools to choose from, but do we use them effectively? In your opinion, what can people do to get more out of their DigiTools or digital communication tools?

3. Save your answers in a *Word* file named *OA1-2D*. (*Microsoft OneNote* saves automatically.)

UNIT 2

LESSONS 1–3
Your Personal Network to Success

Conditioning Practice

Before you begin the lessons, key each line twice.

alphabet 1 Vicki expects to query a dozen boys and girls for the major show.

fig/sym 2 Ramon Jones & Company's fax number was changed to (835) 109-2647.

speed 3 If the tug slams the dock, it may make a big problem for the men.

gwam 1' | 1 | 2 | 3 | 4 | 5 | 6 | 7 | 8 | 9 | 10 | 11 | 12 | 13 |

LESSON 1 — A HISTORY OF THE NET AND NETWORKING

OBJECTIVES

> To learn about networking and why networks are important.
> To understand what the Internet it is used for.
> To trace the history of the Internet beginning with the first electronic networks: the telegraph, the telephone, ARPANET, NSFNET, and NREN.
> To plot the rapid growth of the Internet.
> To go online using an URL to locate specific information.

Expand Your Reach Around the Globe

Before computers, if someone said they were *networking* they were busy improving their interpersonal relationships. The goals of interpersonal networking are to learn, expand one's opportunities, improve oneself, and to reach out to others with similar interests. Soon after the first mainframe computers came into use, computer technicians began linking them together for the same reasons. A computer **network** is created whenever two or more digital devices are linked to share information. A network can be fashioned by connecting just a few, or a few thousand, computers together. When computers are interconnected, technology users can reach around the globe and find others with similar interests, expand their opportunities, and learn new things online.

 The ultimate achievement in digital networking is the Internet. The **Internet** is an unfathomably big, global system connecting hundreds of millions of smaller net-

network

Internet

works, as seen in Figure OA2-1. As such, the Internet is often described as "The Network of Networks."

Computers Connect to Network Hosts/Servers That Connect to the Internet

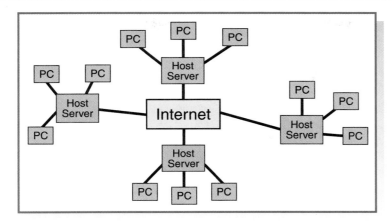

The word *Internet* is often shortened to the **Net**. People use the Net to:

Net

- View files or pages of information on almost any topic imaginable
- Read e-mail, send instant messages, make phone calls, or videoconference
- Research and access information from a variety of sources
- Purchase items
- Download software and software updates
- Manage money through online banking, investing, or financial research
- Download music, movies, and multimedia
- Play online games

This unit will trace the history of the Internet, explain how it works, and teach you how to use it for research purposes: to learn, expand your opportunities, and to reach out to others no matter where they may live in the world.

Learn: Pre-Internet Electronic Communications Networks

The first electronic communications network, the telegraph, was perfected in 1837. Its inventor, Samuel F. B. Morse (1791–1872), used electromagnets to send and receive clicks from one telegraph operator to another at the rate of about 10 wpm. The length of time between the clicks was important in understanding Morse code, a system of short and long clicks used to transmit letters of the alphabet. Soon, telegraph lines were spreading across the globe. Where once it took weeks or even months to send a letter, the telegraph could transmit a message as fast as it took for the telegrapher to key in the letters.

Telegraphers were considered highly skilled and were well paid. Just knowing Morse code could land someone a great job. Often, the safety of thousands depended on knowing Morse code. When the Titanic hit an iceberg, Jack Phillips, the wireless operator on board, sent out a distress signal in Morse code to any ships nearby that could hear it. Mr. Phillips sent the traditional distress code letters, CQD (—.—.   — —.—   —..), which meant "listen, we are in distress." Then he

HULTON ARCIVE/GETTY IMAGES

followed it up with a new code being implemented because it was easier for operators in stressful situations to enter. The code was SOS (. . . — — — . . .). Sadly, the wireless operator on a ship less than 20 miles away was asleep and didn't hear the plea for help. After the Titanic, an urban legend sprang up saying that SOS meant "Save Our Souls."

The SOS signal, popularized by the Titanic disaster, saved many lives thereafter. As late as 1980, the ship Prinsendam burst into flames in the Gulf of Alaska. For some reason, satellite communications failed, but Morse code continued to work. The distress signal was heard as far away as New Zealand. Ships responded and lives were saved. Take a few seconds in the next exercise and try your hand at Morse code.

Communicating for Success

A Heroic Blink of the Eye

Jeremiah Andrew Denton (1924–) was a Navy pilot, shot down over Vietnam on July 18, 1965. He spent nearly eight years as a prisoner of war, much of it in the infamous Hanoi Hilton, where he was tortured repeatedly. At one point, he was dragged before television cameras and made to "confess," presumably condemning his country. Denton thwarted the plot by blinking out the word "torture" in Morse code. After gaining his freedom, Denton went on to become the United States Senator for the state of Alabama.

Exercise 1A

The Clicks and Clacks of Morse Code

1. Review this table containing Morse code.

A .—	B — . . .	C —.—.	D —..	E .
F .. —.	G — —.	H	I ..	J .— — —
K —.—	L .—..	M — —	N —.	O — — —
P .— —.	Q — —.—	R .—.	S . . .	T —
U ..—	V . . . —	W .— —	X —..—	Y —.— —
Z — —..				

2. Decipher the first electronic message ever sent by Samuel Morse.

.— —   . . . .   .—   —

. . . .   .—   —   . . . .

— —.   — — —   —..

.— —   .—.   — — —   ..—   — —.   . . . .   —   ?

3. Translate the following message in Morse code:

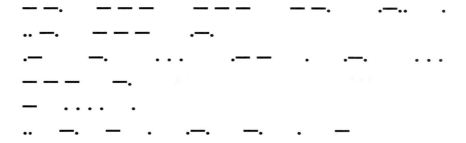

The Telephone

The next step in the progression of communications networks was the telephone, which Alexander Graham Bell (1847–1922) invented on March 10, 1876. The first phone conversation with his assistant, Mr. Watson, was much less dramatic than the message sent by Samuel Morris over the first telegraph line. He simply said, "Mr. Watson, come here, I want you." Nonetheless, his words reverberated around the globe in anticipation of a time, soon to come, when anyone would be able to talk to a person in another country by dialing the number and saying hello.

Telephone lines followed the path of the telegraph and soon stretched to the far corners of the earth. The world-wide telephone grid, like the Internet, is a network of networks working together. For example, a person can call from a California Pacific Bell payphone or use a Cingular wireless network and talk with a friend in London, England over the British Telecom phone system. In this example, multiple telephone networks work together to complete one conversation.

The worldwide telephone networks provided much of the necessary **infrastructure** needed to construct the early Internet. The word *infrastructure* refers to things like roads, railroads, water systems, telecommunications links, and similar systems that allow our modern society to function properly. The Internet was able to grow quickly because a vibrant communications infrastructure had already been built through the telephone networks.

infrastructure

Learn: ARPANET

The direct digital forerunner of today's Internet was the 1960s research project called the **ARPANET** or **Advanced Research Projects Agency Network**. The ARPANET was born out of both scientific and military research needs. Its main purpose was to maintain communications in case something, such as nuclear war or a natural disaster, destroyed large sections of the communications infrastructure. In theory, if any computer or part of the ARPANET ever went down (say from enemy attack), the ARPANET had the ability to reroute computer information down different network paths, insuring that at least part of the computer network would remain alive. ARPANET research helped make the current Internet very durable. In fact, the Internet is nearly impossible to shut down. Even when some governments have tried to block Internet use, someone is usually able to figure out a way around the obstacles.

ARPANET or **Advanced Research Projects Agency Network**

Creating the Current Internet

National Science
Foundation or NSF

In the mid-1980s, the **National Science Foundation** or **NSF** funded six supercomputers for scientific research. The computers were located in Princeton, New Jersey; San Diego, California; Champaign, Illinois; Pittsburgh, Pennsylvania; Ithaca, New York; and Boulder, Colorado.

backbone
NSFNET

Since there were only a few supercomputers, it was decided that scientists living in other parts of the country should be allowed to log in to the supercomputer centers remotely. To accomplish this remote access, a communications network **backbone** was created. In 1986, the NSF created its backbone by funding the **NSFNET**. The infrastructure for the first Internet backbone was a system of high-speed phone lines carrying digital computer data instead of voice traffic. The backbone first connected the six supercomputer sites to each other. Later, the ARPANET was brought into the new system.

National Research
and Education
Network or NREN

In 1991, Senator Albert Gore (1948–) greatly expanded the new Internet when he proposed the High Performance Computing and Communications Act. The new law supported the **National Research and Education Network** or **NREN**. Soon afterwards, colleges and universities from all over the country hooked to the backbone. The National Aeronautics and Space Administration (NASA), the Department of Energy (DOE), and other government agencies soon hooked up as well. Later, American secondary and elementary schools were encouraged to join the new system and the modern Internet was born.

Plotting the Growth of the Internet

Internet Service
Provider or ISP

host

server

Your Internet begins with your PC, connects to an **Internet Service Provider** or **ISP**, and expands to hundreds of millions of networks and computers around the globe. Before you can go online, you must connect to the Net through a **host** computer provided by an ISP. The term **server** is also used to describe these essential computers. Strictly speaking, a computer is a host/server only if users can log in from a personal computer and use its online resources. For example:

- A host/server in Texas may allow you to download reports on crash test ratings for popular automobiles.

- A host/server in Florida may allow you to research a paper for a Science course.

- A host/server in Ottawa may allow you to join a discussion about a favorite hobby or sports team.

Counting the number of Internet hosts is a good way to track the rapid growth of the Internet. There were fewer than 300 hosts on the Internet in 1982. The Internet grew quickly. In the early part of 2001, the Internet passed 100 million hosts with over 350 million users and was growing at a rate of nearly 50 percent each year. And its spectacular growth continues. In the next exercise you will get a chance to plot its growth.

Going Online

It is next to impossible to avoid using the Internet these days. You probably know all about it. However, if you are a bit rusty, the next exercise will review a few basics you must remember.

The most common way to connect to the Internet is by using a piece of software called a browser. There are many competitive browsers including *Internet Explorer, Netscape, Firefox, Opera,* and *Safari,* to name just a few. Most of these browsers have very similar pieces and parts, as explained in Exercise 1B.

Exercise 1B

Launch Your Browser

1. Start **Internet Explorer** or another browser.

2. Memorize the following parts and features of *Internet Explorer* shown in Figure OA2-2. (*Note:* The features will be very similar in most other browsers.)

Figure OA 2-2   Memorize Your Browser's Tools

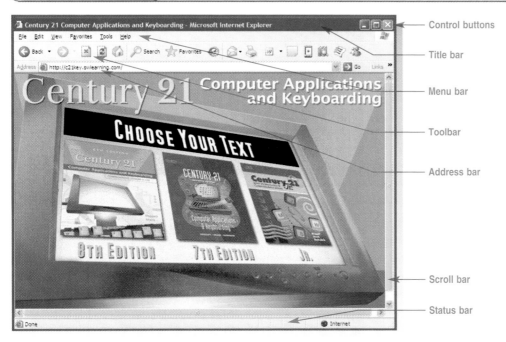

Internet TiP

Internet Explorer can be opened by clicking its browser icon on the desktop, clicking its browser icon on the Windows taskbar, choosing **Start** and selecting **Internet**, or following the traditional path, **Start, All Programs, Internet Explorer**. With Dragon NaturallySpeaking you can simply say, **START INTERNET EXPLORER**, and the application will spring into action.

3. Examine the toolbar in more detail. Memorize the names of the buttons and review what they do in the table below.

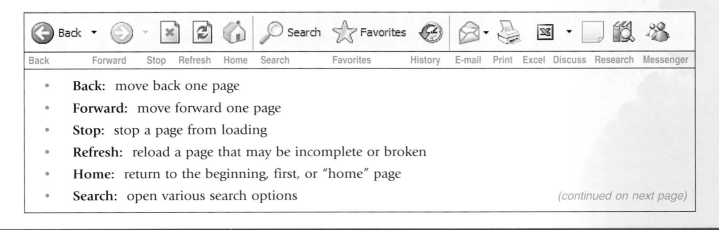

- **Back:** move back one page
- **Forward:** move forward one page
- **Stop:** stop a page from loading
- **Refresh:** reload a page that may be incomplete or broken
- **Home:** return to the beginning, first, or "home" page
- **Search:** open various search options

(continued on next page)

Back	Forward	Stop	Refresh	Home	Search	Favorites	History	E-mail	Print	Excel	Discuss	Research	Messenger

- **Favorites:** return to a page that has been marked as a favorite or "bookmarked" for convenient retrieval
- **History:** view a running history of the pages that have been visited
- **E-mail:** open the default e-mail program
- **Print:** print the current page
- **Excel:** edit data using *Microsoft Excel*
- **Discuss:** view various discussion groups
- **Research:** open the Research task pane
- **Messenger:** open Microsoft's Instant Messenger application for online chats

Uniform Resource Locator or URL

Internet TiP

URLs are case sensitive, which means that every capital and lowercase letter must be entered exactly. Also, every period (.) and every forward slash (/) must be keyed precisely as written. Finally, you won't find any spaces in an URL. Sometimes, an underscore (_) is used to create the illusion of a space.

Finding Your Exact Needle in a Billion Haystacks

A browser can locate a single page of information from the billions of pages of information that exist on the Web. It does so by following a path leading to a *file*, also referred to as a *page*, on an Internet host. The path is defined by the **Uniform Resource Locator** or **URL**. The secret behind the success of Internet browsers is found in how URLs work.

An URL can be entered into an *Address* bar of a Web browser. Let's analyze the following URL and see if you can decipher its path.

www.c21key.swlearning.com/plus/student/downloads.html

www.c21key.swlearning.com	/plus	/student	/downloads.html
Domain name directing the web browser to look for a host called c21key.swlearning.com	A folder on the host computer	A subfolder on the host computer	The name of a file or "page" of information

Exercise 1C

Find and Use a Specific Page

1. Open your browser and click the **Address** box. The current address will be highlighted. If it is not, click and drag over the address to select it.

2. In the **Address** box, key www.c21key.swlearning.com/student/downloads.html. Choose the link for **Reading 3**.

3. Click the **Go** button to the right of the Address box or tap the ENTER key. The characters *http://* will be automatically added to the beginning of the address. A Digital Reading will appear, similar to Figure OA2-3.

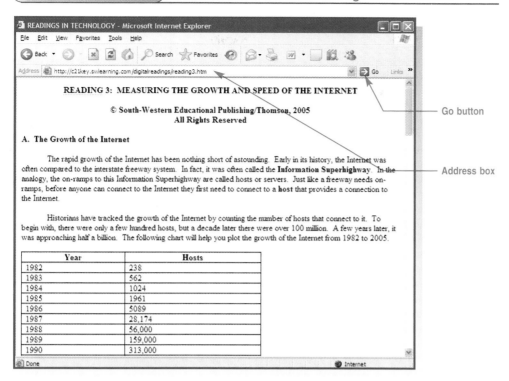

4. Read the first portion of *Reading 3, Part A. The Growth of the Internet.*

5. Copy and paste the information in *Part A. The Growth of the Internet* directly to either a *Microsoft Word* or *Microsoft OneNote* page. (Note: If you have already learned to use *Microsoft OneNote*, drag and drop this data from this page to a OneNote page for easy off-line reference. If you don't know how to use *OneNote*, complete this exercise in *Microsoft Word*.)

6. Include the URL to the information you have downloaded in your notes. (*Note: OneNote* will automatically reference the URL for you. *Word* users will need to manually copy and paste the URL from the browser's Address window. Recording the URL will come in very handy when accurate citations are required.)

7. Using *Microsoft Excel* and the data in the table you just retrieved, create a bar chart graphing the explosive growth of the Internet from 1982 to 2005. To simplify the task, only graph the odd-numbered years: 83, 85, 87, 89, 91, 93, 95, 97, 99, 01, 03, and 05. Save your *Excel* spreadsheet and graph as *Internet Growth.*

8. Copy and paste your *Excel* spreadsheet graph to either your *OneNote* or *Word* page where you saved your downloaded information in step 5.

9. Save your notes and its accompanying graph as *Digital Reading 3.* (*Note: OneNote* users, use *Digital Reading 3* as the title of your page. *OneNote* files are saved automatically.)

> To learn how TCP/IP, IP numbers, domain names, and DNS servers route information along network paths.
> To learn the meaning of top-level domain names.
> To examine the role of Tim Berners-Lee in the creation of the World Wide Web.
> To use a variety of Web browser features and buttons.
> To use hyperlinks to find information on the Web.
> To use online resources to research the relative speed of an Internet connection.
> To learn about older Web technologies that have been incorporated into the Web.
> To view the HTML source of a Web document.

client/server

IP address

IP

Internet Protocol

packet

TCP or **Transfer Control Protocol**

domain name

DNS (Domain Name System)

Instant Message

Vint Cerf (1943–) lead the development team that created TCP/IP. As such he has been called the "Father of the Internet." In the late 1960s, Cerf's team invented the tools that made the ARPANET possible, linking four research universities: UCLA, University of Utah, Stanford, and UC Santa Barbara.

© AP / WIDE WORLD PHOTOS

Learn: Transmission Control Protocol/Internet Protocol

Remembering domain, folder, and file names is relatively easy to do—for humans, that is. But computers don't communicate in words; they communicate in numbers. This lesson will explain how computers convert URLs into a numeric language they can understand.

The Internet works on the **client/server** system, with the server being an Internet host/server and the client being the Internet software used by the individual computer user. To understand how the system works, imagine that the Net is like a large Italian restaurant. Each table in the restaurant is assigned a number so the restaurant's hosts and servers can get the correct meals to the many clients they serve.

Each Internet computer is also assigned a number, which is called an IP number or **IP address**. **IP** is shorthand for **Internet Protocol**. A protocol is an agreed-upon way that computers are required to communicate over networks.

A typical IP number includes four sets of numbers with dots or periods between them and looks something like this: 158.91.46.218. Each set of numbers can go as high as 254 or as low as 1. Every Internet host, server, and active computer must be assigned its own unique number to avoid confusion.

Assigning an IP address is a little bit like assigning a number to a table at our large Italian restaurant. The numbering scheme ensures the correct meal gets to the proper table. On the Internet, the term **packet** is used to describe the bits and bytes of information sent over the Net. In this example, the packets are akin to the food arriving from the restaurant's kitchen.

To help keep track of all of the packets, **TCP** or **Transfer Control Protocol** is used. If a packet does not arrive, or is broken into unintelligible pieces, TCP asks the host to send the file again. TCP works like a restaurant waiter, writing down the order and making sure it gets from the kitchen to the proper table in perfect condition.

Computers speak in numbers, so IP addresses are a natural way for them to keep things organized. However, people have an extremely difficult time remembering IP numbers, so they are converted into user-friendly names. Let's face it; it's a lot easier to remember www.microsoft.com than a number like 158.91.46.218.

A name like www.microsoft.com is called a **domain name**. Domain names are converted to IP numbers by specially designed **DNS (Domain Name System)** servers that match names to their assigned IP numbers and whisk the request along its path to the customer for which it is intended. Just over a dozen DNS servers are required to make all of these conversions. As soon as additional domain names are added to the Internet, the DNS servers are updated, usually within 24 hours, so information can flow effortlessly around the world.

You can find information on just about anything online. For example, in the next exercise, read about things you must know in order to buy a personal computer capable of Net travels. As you visit the site, look carefully at the status bar and see if you notice the domain names turning into IP numbers in front of your eyes!

Making Connections

Top-Level Domain Names

Internet domain names carry extensions called **top-level domain names**, abbreviated to the acronym **TLD**. You can tell much about the content of the website by examining top-level domain names. For example:

.mil = military domain
.edu = educational domain
.com = commercial domain
.org = organizational domain
.biz = business domain
.gov = governmental domain
.net = network provider domain
.name = individual domains
.museum = for museums
.jobs = for employment sites
.travel = for travel and related entertainment sites
.us, .mx, .uk, .ca, .sa, and .tv = examples of country codes for the United States, Mexico, the United Kingdom, Canada, Saudi Arabia, and Tuvalu.

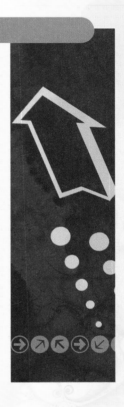

Exercise 2A

How to Pick a Computer

1. Open your browser and click the **Address** box. Key www.c21key. swlearning.com/plus/student/downloads.html and click **Go** or tap ENTER.

2. Read *Reading 1 Assessing Your Technology Needs*, and answer the following questions in either *Microsoft OneNote or Microsoft Word*.

   a. Do you need a top-of-the-line, state-of-the-art computer to use the Internet?

   b. What do you need if you want mobile access to the Internet?

   c. What is a needs assessment, and why would a business or government agency conduct one?

   d. What is price/performance, and how does it apply to computers?

   e. How can you stay informed about changes and improvements in technology?

Internet TiP

The instant you click GO, glance at the status bar and see if you can see the domain names turn into IP numbers.

3. *Optional:* Scroll to the bottom of Reading 1 and complete *Activity 1 Ask Those Who Know*.

4. Save your work either in *Microsoft Word* or with *Microsoft OneNote* as *Digital Reading 1*.

Tim Berners-Lee

You may be wondering, "Who came up with all of these URLs and Web pages anyway?" It really boils down to one key figure: Tim Berners-Lee (1955–).

Tim Berners-Lee, an Englishman working as a computer programmer at the European Particle Physics Laboratory (CERN), engineered a revolution in mass-media communication. He called his invention the World Wide Web, also known as WWW, W3, or the Web. (Anything with four names has to be good!) His goal was to allow people to publish documents, and from their documents create links to almost any other related resource, "Be it personal, local or global, be it a draft or highly polished.[1]"

The World Wide Web was designed, first and foremost, as a tool to aid scientific research. Tim Berners-Lee wanted to create a system that would allow information sharing and interpersonal networking among scientists. Berners-Lee accomplished this through the creation of **hypertext links** or **hyperlinks**.

hypertext links or
hyperlinks

The convenience of hyperlinks made the World Wide Web a nearly instant success among scientists trying to share research information over the clunky networks of the early 1990s. One of the fundamentals of science is the importance of citing sources from other scientific publications supporting scientific findings. On Berners-Lee's Web, active, clickable links could be created from one scientific paper to any other related research publication found anywhere in the world. (See Figure OA2-4.)

Figure OA 2-4   Berners-Lee Started the W3 Consortium to Coordinate the Web's Growth

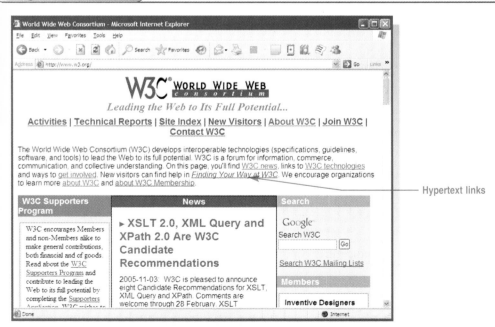

Hypertext links

---

[1]Tim Berners-Lee, "The World Wide Web: A Very Short Personal History," World Wide Web Consortium, http://www.W3.org/People/Berners-Lee/ShortHistory.HTML (accessed June 1, 2005).

Hypertext words are marked in some way. Most often they are underlined as seen in Figure OA2-4, but they can also appear in a different color, or show up as graphics. When you select the hyperlink, you will jump automatically to another selection of text. The new text may be located in:

- Any spot in the current document
- Another document on the local World Wide Web host
- Any Web document on any remote host anywhere in the world

Hypertext is a bit like hyperspace in *Star Wars*. Choose any link and suddenly you are transported from one document to another in the blink of an eye. (See Figure OA2-5.) You can jump from a Web page in your hometown to a computer in Hong Kong, Paris, or Kenya in an instant.

Figure OA2-5 Hyperlinks Can Be Created To Any Page on the Web

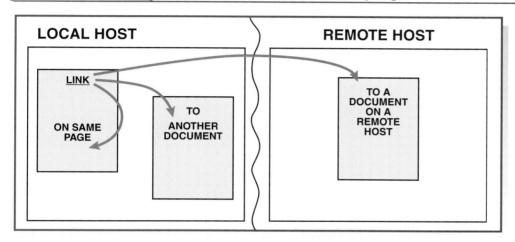

Exercise 2B

Hyperlinking Around to Test Your Speed

1. Return to a familiar page, only this time use hyperlinks to get there. Key the following URL into your Web browser's address window and choose **Go** or tap ENTER:

   www.c21key.swlearning.com/plus/student/downloads.html

2. Choose the hypertext link that says:

   READING 3: <u>MEASURING THE GROWTH AND SPEED OF THE INTERNET</u>

3. Choose the next hypertext link that says:

   B. <u>Assessing the Speed of a Net Connection</u>

4. Read section B. *Assessing the Speed of an Internet Connection*. When you are finished reading, choose the **Back** button to return to the index.

5. Open either your *Microsoft OneNote* or your *Microsoft Word Digital Reading 3* file and answer the following question at the end of the document:

   Without looking back at the article you just read, to the best of your memory, what do the following mean?

a. b
b. B
c. Kb
d. KB
e. Mb
f. MB
g. Gb
h. GB

6. Click the **Forward** button several times to return to your article. Double-check your answers from step 5 and make sure you have an accurate definition of the technical terms.

7. Click the **Back** button a few times and take the next section of the quiz without looking. Record your answers. (*Note:* Click the **Forward** button to double-check your answers *after* you make your initial guess.)

   Without looking back at the article you just read, to the best of your memory, what do the following mean?

   a. bps
   b. Kbps
   c. KBps
   d. Mbps
   e. MBps
   f. Gbps
   g. GBps

8. Click your **History** button. When the *History* pane opens, choose the link that says **READINGS IN TECHNOLOGY**. You will be taken back to the index.

9. Choose the following links in the following order:

   • READING 3: <u>MEASURING THE GROWTH AND SPEED OF THE INTERNET</u>

   • C. <u>Connection Methods and Their Relative Bandwidth</u>

10. Read section C. *Connection Methods and Their Relative Bandwidth*. Then investigate the type of connection you must use to connect to your ISP. You may need to ask your local system administrator directly for this information. Also, ask what the connection speed of your Internet connection happens to be as measured in bps. (If this information is unavailable to you, you may be able to guess based on what you learn in the online readings.)

11. Finally, test the speed of your connection by completing the experiment explained in *Activity 4 Time It for Yourself*. Locate the experiment by following these links. Go to:

    • http://www.c21key.swlearning.com/plus/student/downloads.html

    • READING 3: <u>MEASURING THE GROWTH AND SPEED OF THE INTERNET</u>

    • Activity 4 <u>Time It for Yourself</u>

12. Record the results of your experiment. Compare the results in bps with the speed given to you in step 9 by your ISP. Do they match up? Are

you able to download at the speed suggested by your system administrator, or is your actual performance more or less than reported? Is your connection slower or faster than expected?

13. Resave your work in your *Digital Reading 3* file.

What Makes the World Wide Web Go 'Round

To complete his dream of a user-friendly and interconnected Web of information, Tim Berners-Lee invented two new technologies:

1. **Hypertext Transfer Protocol** or **HTTP** is a communications structure that simplifies the writing of addresses or URLs. HTTP knows how to search the Web for the exact address indicated and will automatically call up the file or page to be viewed.

2. **Hypertext Markup Language** or **HTML** consists of a series of tags or markings that format a document so that it can be viewed by a software client called a browser.

Hypertext Transfer Protocol or **HTTP**

Hypertext Markup Language or **HTML**

After creating the technologies behind the Web, Tim Berners-Lee and his cohorts at CERN did something unexpected: *They released the entire system online for free.* As a result, the Web caught on like a wildfire. Its success spelled doom for many older, competitive Internet technologies that can be read about in the text box called *The Triumph of the Web.*

Communicating for Success

The Triumph of the Web

Between 1989, when Tim Berners-Lee first envisioned the Web, and 1995, when the World Wide Web became wildly popular, the Internet was made up of many separate and distinct systems and protocols. In fact, there were many competitive systems that could have dominated the online world. However, most of these competitors failed under the crush of the Web's success. Some of the more important tools were simply absorbed into the Web browser. Here's just a sampling:

Gopher: Named for the Golden Gophers of the University of Minnesota, Gopher allowed users to burrow through lists and layers of computer menus until they found the specific file they were looking for. In 1994, there were more Gopher servers than Web hosts. Today, scant mention of Gopher exists.

File Transfer Protocol or **FTP:** Efficient system for transferring files from computers to host/servers and back again. The technology has been built into most Web browsers.

Telnet: Before the Web, Telnet was the preferred way to log into and use a distant host computer, such as a supercomputer. The need for Telnet technologies waned under the crush of the World Wide Web.

(continued on next page)

E-mail: Allows users to receive and send memos and attachments around the world with an Internet address. E-mail is alive and well and can be accessed through a Web browser or through separate e-mail client software. (See Lesson 3.)

USENET Newsgroups: Newsgroups were once available for almost any topic imaginable. Tens of thousands of discussion groups were set up under the old USENET system, providing a viable way for people to consult with others of similar interests. Most discussion groups evolved and are now available via Web technologies.

Internet Relay Chat or IRC: The forerunner of today's Instant Messaging or IM and videoconferencing software, IRC allowed users to chat with text, voice, or even video over the Internet. Most of these technologies can now be launched from within a Web browser.

Exercise 2C

See The Source of the Web's Success

1. Click the **History** button in your Internet browser. When the *History* pane opens, choose the link that says **READINGS IN TECHNOLOGY**. You will be taken back to the index.

2. Add this page to your Favorites list by clicking the **Favorites** button and choosing **Add to Favorites** (or by using a similar command in an alternative Web browser).

3. View the HTML source code found in this digital reading. Do so by choosing **View**, **Source** or similar command in an alternative Web browser. This will reveal the hidden HTML tags, as seen in Figure OA2-6.

Figure OA2-6 View HTML Code as Designed by Tim Berners-Lee and Others

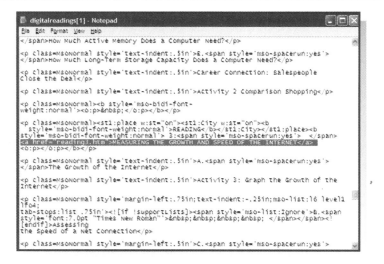

4. Notice the segment of code highlighted in Figure 2-6. It reads, *<a href="reading3.htm">MEASURING THE GROWTH AND SPEED OF THE INTERNET</a>*. This is the segment of HTML code that actually creates a hypertext link. Notice that reading3.htm is referenced so the browser knows exactly where to go to retrieve the requested information.

5. Visit the website of the World Wide Web Consortium, established by Tim Berners-Lee to serve as a clearinghouse for ideas to improve the World Wide Web and to serve as a guardian of the standards upon which it is based. Key the following URL:

   www.w3.org

6. Add this page to your Favorites list. And as long as you are just visiting, click a few links and learn more about how the W3 consortium works to promote the Web.

LESSON ③ THE HISTORY AND USE OF E-MAIL

OBJECTIVES
- ⊘ To study how e-mail came to be.
- ⊘ To dissect how e-mail addresses are configured.
- ⊘ To locate popular e-mail hosts.
- ⊘ To learn how e-mail messages are formatted.
- ⊘ To learn how to use TO, CC, BC, Subject, Send, Attachment, and other e-mail features.

Rewind to the History of E-mail

E-mail preceded the World Wide Web, so we need to rewind our history of the Internet back to 1971. While working as an engineer on the Department of Defense ARPANET project, Ray Tomlinson (1941–) successfully tested the first use of e-mail.

His invention was an outgrowth of a program used on early supercomputers called SNDMSG (SeND MeSsaGe), which technicians could use to leave messages for their colleagues working on the same supercomputer. Tomlinson's innovation was to figure out a way to send messages between networks. He calculated that network usernames could serve as a prefix, a network domain name as a suffix, and the two names could be separated by the *at sign* (@). The table dissects this e-mail address: *Melissa_Kim@corpview.com*

Melissa_Kim	**@**	**corpview.com**
A network e-mail username. E-mail usernames are not case-sensitive and can be written in a variety of ways such as: Mkim, melissakim, kimmelissa	At sign separating the username from the domain name	A domain name or the name of a known network host on the Internet

E-mail is a speedy, relatively informal way of communicating. An e-mail message can be delivered almost anywhere in the world in a matter of seconds. For most people, e-mail has now replaced letter writing.

Instant Message

With e-mail, every e-mail username on a network must be unique, or different, from all other names. There can only be one Melissa_Kim@corpview.com; however, there can be other Melissa_Kim usernames on other networks, such as Melissa_Kim@swep.com or Melissa_Kim@ubi-sw.com.

E-mail TiP

Spaces are never used in an e-mail address. An underscore (_) or a period (.) is sometimes used to separate parts of the username.

To use e-mail, you must first have an e-mail account. This will give you an e-mail address as explained above. Your Internet service provider may provide e-mail service. Most e-mail can also be sent and received using Web-based e-mail clients.

Exercise 3A

Find an E-mail Address to Call Your Own

1. Investigate three e-mail programs available on the Web. You may substitute another of your favorite online e-mail websites if you wish. Pick three e-mail providers from among the following URLs or use additional e-mail providers you already know about.

   www.gmail.com or gmail.google.com

   www.hotmail.com

   mail.yahoo.com

   mail.excite.com

2. Which of your three, if any, would you recommend to another person? Are there any fees? Restrictions? What should someone know about these services before joining up?

3. Work with your local administrator or go online to find your own e-mail account. If you cannot obtain an account from your local administrator or ISP, apply for one of the free e-mail services provided online.

Learn: E-mail Formatting Guidelines

Few technologies provide such an opportunity to foster interpersonal networking quite like e-mail. Friends, colleagues, and business associates use it to stay in touch, keep informed, and tell each other of career opportunities. E-mail allows you to reach out to others in a personal way no matter where they may be in the world. Typically, e-mail includes:

- the e-mail address of the person (or persons) receiving the message
- your e-mail address as the sender
- the date the e-mail message was sent
- the subject of the message
- the body or text of the message (increasingly, e-mail messages can also be sent with attachments, multimedia, pictures, video, or even sound)

These features are marked in Figure OA2-7.

The e-mail address of the person receiving the message is keyed into the **TO** box. If you wish other persons to receive a copy of the e-mail, even though the message is not primarily intended for them, you can place their e-mail addresses in the **CC** (Complimentary Copy) box. The CC feature allows everyone to see who receive copies of the message. If you want someone to receive a copy of the message without anyone else knowing they received it, use the **BC** (Blind Copy) feature.

Always key a subject in the **Subject** box. The Subject line serves as a title for the content of the message. Many people will not bother to read e-mail messages with-

E-mail Tip

When a message is sent to more than one person, separate the e-mail addresses with a comma (,) or semicolon (;) and a space. This can vary depending on the e-mail client you use.

TO

CC

BC
Subject

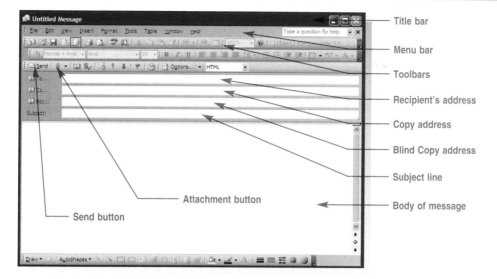

out a Subject line. Subject lines are usually keyed using initial capital letters. Here are some additional tips:

*   E-mail messages are usually single-spaced.

*   Normally, a 10-12 point font is used.

*   E-mail messages are usually block style with default margins.

*   Minimal formatting is required for e-mail messages.

*   Double spacing between paragraphs is a must.

*   All text aligns flush with the left margin.

Exercise

Send an E-mail Message

1. Prove to your instructor that you have completed earlier exercises. Open your answers for *Digital Reading 1* in either *Microsoft Word* or *Microsoft OneNote*.

2. Open a new e-mail message and enter the following information:

    *   In the TO box, key the address of your instructor.

    *   In the Subject box, key Reading 1 Answers.

3. Begin the body of e-mail message with the following text:

    Dear [title and name of instructor],

    Here are my answers for Digital Reading 1.

4. Copy your answers for *Digital Reading 1* from either *Microsoft Word* or *OneNote* and paste them into your e-mail message.

5. Enter a complimentary close to conclude your message. For example:

    Sincerely,

    [your name]

6. Click the **Send** button to send your message.

Instant
Message

Files such as *Word* or *OneNote* documents, spreadsheets, pictures, sound files, or even presentations, can be attached to an e-mail message and opened after the e-mail message itself has been opened and read.

Learn: Managing E-mail

Inbox
Outbox
Sent

Mail coming to you is stored in an **Inbox**. Mail that is written but has yet to be sent is stored in an **Outbox**. Mail you have sent is stored in the **Sent** box. Once you start sending and receiving e-mail, messages can accumulate. You will need to manage the messages to keep your boxes from overflowing. After you have read your messages, you have many options. You can:

- Reply to the sender
- Reply to all of the people in the TO, FROM, and CC fields
- Forward the message to another person
- Attach documents to the reply or forwarded message
- Delete the message
- Save the message

Practice some of these skills in the next exercise.

Exercise 3C

Extend Your E-mail Skills

1. Share your *Digital Reading 3* notes with other students. Learn the e-mail addresses of at least two or three other students.

2. Open a new mail message and enter the following information:
   - In the TO box, key the addresses of those you are networking with.
   - In the Subject box, key Reading 3 Notes.

3. Begin the body of the e-mail message with the following text:

   Hello,

   Here are my notes for Digital Reading 3.

   Sincerely,
   [your name]

4. Choose the **Attachment** feature of your e-mail program. Browse to your notes that you collected for online *Digital Reading 3*. Attach your *Microsoft Word* or *OneNote* file.

5. Click the **Send** button to send your message.

6. You should have also received several copies of notes for *Digital Reading 3* from other students. Create a separate folder for these notes and store them in that subfolder.

7. After you have finished with this course, make sure you delete all of these messages and attachments after you no longer need them.

E-mail
TiP

Did you know that if you're using *Microsoft Word* or *Microsoft OneNote*, you can simply click the E-mail button and it will launch an e-mail client so you can send whatever notes or document you're working on directly to colleagues?

Exercise 3D

Evaluate Internet Pioneers

1. In Unit 1, you studied 23 computer pioneers. This unit introduced you to another half-dozen digital communication pioneers. Use this table to help answer the following questions:

Samuel F. B. Morse	Alexander Graham Bell	Albert Gore
Tim Berners-Lee	Ray Tomlinson	Vint Cerf

a. What have each of the technology pioneers accomplished?

b. From your reading of this unit, which computer pioneer listed above do you consider to be the most important contributor to the rise of the interconnected networking world?

c. In your view, how do the accomplishments of this list of Internet pioneers compare with the 23 computer pioneers in Unit 1? Are they more or less important? Would you award any one of the six the Nobel Prize? If so, why?

d. In your opinion, what is the most important single event in the history of the Internet? Defend your assertion in a few short statements.

e. Previously, in Unit 1, Exercise 2A, you chose one of the 23 early computer pioneers for study later in Unit 3. Would you like to substitute one of the six Internet pioneers in this list for that name? You will begin your research on this individual at the beginning of the next unit.

2. Save your answers in a *Microsoft Word* file named *Internet Pioneers* or complete your work in *Microsoft OneNote*, which saved automatically.

Exercise 3E

How to Judge a Computer

1. Click your **Favorites** button. When the *Favorites* pane opens, search back and choose the link that says **READINGS IN TECHNOLOGY**. You will be taken to the index.

2. Choose the following link:

READING 2: MEASURING COMPUTER PERFORMANCE

3. Read the entire reading and answer the following questions posed in the text using either *Microsoft Word* or *Microsoft OneNote*.

a. How is the power of a CPU gauged?

b. How is the speed of a CPU measured?

c. How is computer memory measured?

d. How much active memory does a computer need?

e. How much long-term storage capacity does a computer need?

4. After answering the questions, complete *Activity 2 Comparison Shopping* found at the end of the article. Use the hypertext links at the end of the activity to visit several computer manufacturers. These links will help you do your comparison shopping for a dynamite computer that will serve your needs both online and in your academic or professional life.

5. Save all of your work as *Digital Reading 2*. E-mail a copy of your work to your instructor as an attachment.

Communication & Math Skills 9

1. Study each of the six rules shown below in the color boxes.

  a. Key the *Learn* line beneath each rule, noting how the rule is applied.

  b. Key the *Apply* lines, using semicolons and underlines correctly.

Internal Punctuation: Semicolon

Rule 1: Use a semicolon to separate two or more independent clauses in a compound sentence when the conjunction is omitted.

Learn	1	Ms. Willis is a superb manager; she can really motivate workers.
Apply	2	His dad is a corporate lawyer his law degree is from Columbia.
Apply	3	Orin is at the Air Force Academy Margo is at the Naval Academy.

Rule 2: Use a semicolon to separate independent clauses when they are joined by a conjunctive adverb (*however, therefore, consequently*, etc.).

Learn	4	Patricia lives in Minneapolis; however, she works in St. Paul.
Apply	5	No discounts are available now consequently, I'll buy in July.
Apply	6	I work mornings therefore, I prefer an afternoon interview.

Rule 3: Use a semicolon to separate a series of phrases or clauses (especially if they contain commas) that are introduced by a colon).

Learn	7	Al spoke in these cities: Denver, CO; Erie, PA; and Troy, NY.
Apply	8	Overdue accounts follow: Ayn, 30 da. Lowe, 60 da. Shu, 90 da.
Apply	9	I paid these amounts: April, $375 May, $250 and June, $195.

Rule 4: Place the semicolon outside the closing quotation mark. (A period and a comma are placed inside the closing quotation mark.)

Learn	10	Miss Trent spoke about "leaders"; Mr. Sanyo, about "followers."
Apply	11	The coach said, "Do your very best" Paula said, "I'll try"
Apply	12	He said, "It's your own fault" she said, "With your help"

Internal Punctuation: Underline

Rule 5: Use an underline to indicate titles of books and names of magazines and newspapers. (Titles may be keyed in ALL CAPS or italic without the underline.)

Learn	13	The <u>World Almanac</u> lists <u>Reader's Digest</u> as the top seller.
Apply	14	I read the review of Runaway Jury in the New York Times.
Apply	15	He quoted from an article in Newsweek or the Chicago Sun-Times.

Rule 6: Use an underline to call attention to words or phrases (or use quotation marks). *Note:* Use a continuous underline (see line 13 above) unless each word is to be considered separately as shown below. Do not underline punctuation marks (commas, for example) between separately underlined words.

Learn	16	Students often use <u>then</u> for <u>than</u> and <u>its</u> for <u>it's</u>.
Apply	17	I had to select the correct word from their, there, and they're.
Apply	18	He emphasized that we should stand up, speak up, then sit down.

2. Key *Proofread & Correct*, using semicolons and underlines correctly.

  a. Check answers.

  b. Using the rule number(s) at the left of each line, study the rule relating to each error you made.

  c. Rekey each incorrect line, using semicolons and underlines correctly.

Proofread & Correct

Rules

1 1 Ms. Barbour is a great coach she is honest and fair.
1 2 Joe Chin won a scholastic award Bill Ott, an athletic one.
1 3 Maxine works from 4 to 7 p.m. she studies after 8:30 p.m.
3 4 The cities are as follows: Ames, IA Provo, UT and Waco, TX.
2 5 The play starts at 8 therefore, you should be ready by 7:30.
3 6 They hired 11 new workers in 2002 6, in 2003 and 8, in 2004.
1,4 7 Troy said, "You can do it" Janelle said, "You're kidding."
1,4 8 Rona sang "Colors of the Wind" Cory sang "Power of the Dream."
5 9 TV Guide ranks No. 2 according to Information Please Almanac.
6 10 "Why," she asked, "can't people use affect and effect properly?"

3. Save as *CS9-ACT1*.

ACTIVITY 2   Listening

1. Open *CD-CS9-ACT2*. It contains three mental math problems.

2. Each problem starts with a number, followed by several addition and subtraction steps. Key or handwrite the new answer after each step, *but* compute the answer mentally.

3. Record the last answer for each problem.

4. After the third problem, close the sound file.

5. Save as *CS9-ACT2*.

ACTIVITY 3   Write to Learn

1. Using word processing or voice recognition software, write a paragraph explaining the rules of netiquette you follow when preparing e-mail messages.

2. Write a second paragraph explaining what you can do to protect yourself from identity theft.

3. Save as *CS9-ACT3*.

ACTIVITY 4   Composing

1. Key the paragraph below, correcting punctuation and word-choice errors.

2. Compose a second paragraph, including this information:
  • The level of your self-image: high, low, or in-between.
  • Factors that make your self-esteem what it is.
  • Factors you think could improve your self-esteem.
  • Plans you have to raise your self-esteem.

3. Proofread, revise, and correct.

4. Save as *CS9-ACT4*.

Narcissus, a mythical young man saw his image reflected in a pool of water fell in love with his image, and starved to death admiring himself. Unlike Narcissus, our self-esteem or self-image should come not threw mirror reflections but buy analysis of what we are--inside. Farther, it is dependent upon weather others who's opinions we value see us as strong or week, good or bad positive or negative. No one is perfect, of course; but those, who develop a positive self-image, wait the factors that affect others views of them and work to improve those factors. Its time to start.

ACTIVITY 5   Math: Working with Simple Interest

1. Open *CD-CS9-ACT5* and print the file.

2. Solve the problems as directed in the file.

3. Submit your answers.

UNIT 3

Conditioning Practice

Before you begin the lessons, key each line twice.

alphabet 1 Jaxie amazed the partial crowd by kicking five quick field goals.

figures 2 Call 555.375.4698 by May 27 to set the 10 a.m. meeting with Sara.

speed 3 Their visit may end the problems and make the firm a tidy profit.

gwam 1' | 1 | 2 | 3 | 4 | 5 | 6 | 7 | 8 | 9 | 10 | 11 | 12 | 13 |

LESSON 1 THE BROWSER WARS

OBJECTIVES

- To explore the history of the Web's GUI interface.
- To discover the history of the Browser Wars.
- To research and take notes on your browser's capabilities and features.
- To research and take notes about alternative Web browsers.
- To write an article comparing three competitive Web browsers.

What, No Pictures?

The first widely used Web browser, called *Lynx*, offered no pictures and no multimedia. Only a few people actually used it. It displayed plain old text files—which was all well and good if you were a scientist at CERN and wanted to share documents on particle physics research—but it wasn't very exciting to most people.

For the average person, the early Web was a cold, forbidding, even boring place. The Web needed to become user-friendly and it needed pictures—lots of pictures. After all, computer users had grown used to the graphical interfaces provided by Microsoft Windows and Apple OS. If it had not developed a GUI interface, the Web would have forever remained in obscurity.

Colorful Mosaic

National Center for Supercomputing Applications, or **NCSA**

The solution to the GUI dilemma came from a group of computer science students at the **National Center for Supercomputing Applications**, or **NCSA**. The NCSA is located deep in the heart of the University of Illinois in Urbana-Champaign. Between 1992 and 1994, these students designed the **Mosaic** browser. *Mosaic* forever changed the way people used the Internet, and it generated widespread enthusiasm about going online.

The lead student programmer of the first *Mosaic* client was **Marc Andreessen** (1971–). His *Mosaic* software defined the basic user-friendly GUI interface we still see in browsers today: with the **Back** button, **Forward** button, **Reload** or **Refresh** button, **Home** button, and **Print** button. (See Figure OA3-1.)

With the invention of *Mosaic*, graphics could be displayed and even turned into hyperlinks.

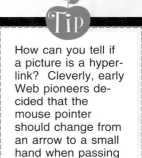

The Web was suddenly a lot more interesting to everyone, but especially to the business community. A multimedia-based Web provided an exciting way to showcase products, advertise, and to extend the image of their brands.

Mosaic was given away free starting in March 1993. Over 2 million copies of *Mosaic* were downloaded in its first year. However, the vision of a free Internet was soon to change on the eve of the Browser Wars.

The Browser Wars Episode I

In early 1994, Marc Andreessen graduated from the University of Illinois and traveled to Silicon Valley, where he took a job programming for a company in Palo Alto, California. Out of the blue, he received an e-mail from **Jim Clarke** (1944–). Clarke was a former Stanford University professor who founded a company called Silicon Graphics and wanted to reinvest his money. Within minutes a reply came and a meeting was set up for the next morning at the Cafe Verona, where the duo would begin making plans for a new company to be called **Netscape Communications Corp**.

Clarke and Andreessen determined it was feasible to create a better browser that could outdo *Mosaic*. The two men flew back to Illinois and hired a few of Andreessen's programming buddies from the University. Each moved to California and started working around the clock. The code name for their new browser was **Mozilla**, the *Mosaic* killer. Time was of the essence because *Mosaic* was rapidly gaining popularity. They had to get Mozilla out into the market quickly.

A few months later, in December 1994, they officially released version 1 of a browser they

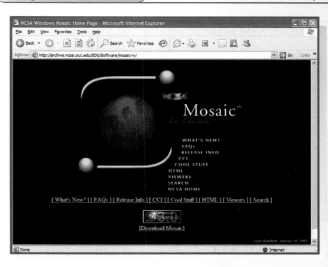

Mosaic

Netscape Communications Corp

Mozilla

TIP

How can you tell if a picture is a hyperlink? Cleverly, early Web pioneers decided that the mouse pointer should change from an arrow to a small hand when passing over a hyperlink.

Figure OA3-2 The first *Netscape* Welcome page

Netscape

named **Netscape**. (See Figure OA3-2.) It was an instant success. It was faster than *Mosaic* and handled graphics much more effectively. It was simply a better browser.

By the end of 1995, *Netscape* had literally swept *Mosaic* from the Internet landscape, commanding over 90 percent of the browser market.

When Netscape Communications Corp. went public in August of 1995, Netscape's stock jumped to $75 per share, making the *Netscape* browser's programmers instant millionaires. Jim Clarke was worth $544 million for his investment. Andreessen was worth a cool $58 million. A few years after graduating from college, Andreessen had become an Internet legend.

From College Campuses to Private Businesses

Graduating students added fuel to the fire of *Netscape* mania. After leaving school, they missed the convenience of the Internet and wanted continued access. They missed their e-mail, and they loved using *Netscape* to do what came to be called **surfing** or exploring the Web. Many new companies began meeting this new demand and provided access to the Internet for a fee.

surfing

To serve the needs of this growing base of customers, Internet service providers (ISPs) grew up like wildfire. A few even became household names: America Online, EarthLink, CompuServe, Prodigy, People PC, Netcom, NetZero, and Delphi. Other major companies like MCI, Comcast, AT&T, Apple Computer Corp., and Microsoft soon joined in. A new way of interacting and communicating on a global basis was created, and a new ISP industry was born.

Exercise 1A

ID Your Personal Browser

1. Open your Web browser.

2. After your welcome page appears, float your mouse or pen pointer over each graphic. Notice the arrow turning to a hand when it passes over hyperlinks. Also, glance at the status bar and you will see the URL to which the link has been assigned. (*Note:* You will learn to create these links in Unit 6.)

3. Choose the **Help** button from the menu bar.

4. Choose the **About** link (such as **About Internet Explorer**).

Figure OA3-3

Look For the Name, Version, and Copyright of Your Browser

5. In your notes, record the name of your browser and its version number (usually a number like 5.0, 6.0, or 7.0) as seen in Figure OA3-3.

6. Look for the copyright date. Record in your notes the year your browser was first copyrighted.

7. What else can you learn about your browser and its history? Make a few notes. (For instance, looking at Figure OA3-3, you can see that *Internet Explorer* was based on the original NCSA *Mosaic*. How did this come about? Stay tuned for *Browser Wars Episode II*.)

8. Close the **About** window and return to your browser's main screen.

9. Join with a team of classmates to learn seven new skills or techniques for using your Web browser more effectively. Here are a few hints: Choose the **Help** menu. You will be presented with a variety of options. Choose those you think will be most helpful. For example, plow through the **Contents and Index**, attempt the **Online Support**, or try the **Tip Of The Day**.

10. Record your team's seven findings individually in your notes for later use.

The Browser Wars: Episode II

Netscape, having dispatched *Mosaic* quickly, was now in for the fight of its life against Microsoft. Bill Gates, the President and CEO of Microsoft, was not about to let the Internet slip away. On December 7, 1995—ironically, on the 54th anniversary of the attack on Pearl Harbor—Gates declared that Microsoft was turning its full energies toward the Internet. He announced that Microsoft would give a free copy of a Microsoft browser to every Windows user.

The University of Illinois had assigned *Mosaic*'s commercial rights to Spyglass, Inc., who licensed *Mosaic* to other companies for a fee. To get a jump start on a browser of their own, Microsoft licensed *Mosaic* through Spyglass. Thus began one of the most innovative periods in Internet history.

Literally hundreds of Microsoft programmers started improving the *Mosaic* application. Microsoft called its new and improved browser **Internet Explorer** or **IE**. Microsoft released its first version of *IE* in 1995. At that time, *IE* was appreciably behind Netscape, which controlled over 90% of the browser market.

Internet Explorer or **IE**

Netscape, in an effort to stay ahead of Microsoft, released one new advance after another. New releases with cutting-edge innovations from Netscape hit the market every few months. Microsoft responded. And while the first few versions of *IE* weren't very good, by version 3 Microsoft's *IE* was becoming more capable and exciting to use. Then, in 1996, a dramatic shift was recorded in the popularity of *IE*, as seen in Table 3-1.

Stunningly, the tables were turning in favor of Microsoft who, about a year later, dominated the browser market, eventually growing to more than a 90 percent share. Netscape's stock price and market share began falling. By 2002, Netscape's share had dipped below 4 percent and it continued to fall even further.

| Table 3-1 | The Turning Point in the Browser Wars | |

Month	Netscape Navigator	Microsoft Internet Explorer
May 1996	83.2%	7.0%
June 1996	78.2%	8.3%
July 1996	72.6%	15.8%
August 1996	62.7%	29.1%

Source: http://www.netvalley.com/intvalweb.html

The Browser Wars Episode III

With Netscape out of the race, the competition that had fueled such wonderful innovations came to an end for many years. But the World Wide Web is a resilient place. In search of a better browser, other companies have made inroads. New competitors to *IE*—*Firefox, Opera, Safari,* and a resurrected version of *Netscape*—have picked up the battle. By the summer of 2005, these browsers have nibbled into Microsoft's dominance, as seen in Table 3-2.

Table 3-2		Browser Market Share as of June 7, 2005
Internet Explorer	88.6%	The market leader, a copy of *Internet Explorer (IE)* ships with each copy of Windows.
Firefox	6.7%	Created by the Mozilla Organization. Fifty million copies were downloaded in its first six months.
Netscape	1.8%	Created a tabbed interface that has made it an effective information organizer.
Opera	.5%	Added a new tabbed interface and was first to build in voice-command features.
Safari	Unknown	Apple Computer Corp. browser for Apple OS.

Source: *PC Magazine*, June 7, 2005, http://www.pcmag.com.

There is no better place to learn about changes in Web technologies than on the Web itself. Complete the following exercise and learn about some of these alternative browsers, their features, and what they do well. After you complete your research, write an article called "Browser Wars Episode III," comparing the browsers for a high-tech magazine. Assume the role of a high-tech technology reviewer or critic.

Exercise 1B

Browser Wars Article

1. Open your Web browser.
2. Visit two websites for competitive browsers. Choose two that are different from the one you are using today (as identified in Exercise 1A). Use the following URLs to guide your search for information about two alternative browsers.

   - http://www.microsoft.com/windows/ie or www.microsoft.com/ie
   - http://www.mozilla.org or www.mozilla.org/products/firefox/
   - http://www.opera.com
   - http://www.netscape.com or browser.netscape.com
   - http://www.apple.com/safari

3. Take notes and record your thoughts on the following questions concerning the two alternative browsers you have selected to research:

   a. What do the developers claim are the major strengths of their browsers?

   b. What differences can you see from the pictures and explanations that are provided between your browser and the alternatives?

   c. What arguments are given that support choosing one browser over another?

   d. Are any of these alternative browsers able to work on small PDAs and handheld computers?

   e. Do any of these browsers offer voice-activated controls or speech-recognition support? Can you use any of these browsers just by talking to them?

   f. How important is security in the promotional materials about the alternative browsers you have chosen to review? What security features do they promote?

4. Continue to scour the Web looking for tutorials, online training, and tips and tricks on how to use these alternative browsers effectively. Record a list of these helpful resources in your notes.

5. Do you have the latest version of your current browser? You identified your version number in Exercise 1A. Go to the website supporting your browser and see if there is an available upgrade to a newer version. Record whether or not an update is available, as well as how it can be downloaded, in your notes.

6. Using your notes to guide your writing, write an article in Microsoft Word as if you were a reviewer for a high-tech magazine. In your article, compare your browser with the two alternatives you have studied. You must include the following elements in the article:

   • Use a 1- to 5-star ranking system (with 5 being the highest possible score) to rank the browsers. Each of the three browsers must have a different star ranking.

   • Create and insert a table in your report comparing the features of the three browsers.

   • Include some tips and tricks on how to use these browsers effectively.

   • Explain to your readers how to obtain a copy of each browser. Include the URLs to the websites where these updates and alternative browsers can be located. (*Note:* Do not download and install a browser or an update to your current browser without the permission of your system administrator.)

   • In the conclusion, state your opinion as to which browser is the most effective.

7. Save your article as *OA3-1B*.

- ⊙ To learn how to navigate an online directory.
- ⊙ To review a history of search engines.
- ⊙ To narrow down an Internet search based on keywords.
- ⊙ To study phrase searching, stemming, and the negation of insignificant words.
- ⊙ To use a spreadsheet to track the effectiveness of various search strategies.
- ⊙ To apply new ways to search for books, definitions, street addresses, weather and airport conditions.
- ⊙ To learn new ways to query images, discussion groups, news items, e-commerce, and local events.
- ⊙ To study advanced search and personal preference options at Google.
- ⊙ To use online sources to improve your knowledge and to prepare a *PowerPoint* presentation on search engines.

Finding Information of Value

The excitement created by the World Wide Web generated one of the Internet's biggest dilemmas: an overwhelming number of Web pages and online resources. Let's face it: there are billions of pages that are absolutely of no use to you! It's quite natural to wonder, "How do I sift through all of the junk and isolate only the important information I need?" There are two primary solutions:

- Directories
- Search engines

Directories

directory

By 1994, **Yahoo!** had became the first wildly popular **directory** or "Table of Contents for the Web." Yahoo! was the brainchild of **David Filo** (1966–) and **Jerry Yang** (1968–), two Ph.D. candidates in the Electrical Engineering department at Stanford University. What started out as a hobby grew into a mega-million-dollar Internet business. Yahoo! remains a very popular, full-service search site.

Creating directories is painstaking work. However, after they are created, accessing a Web directory is as easy as selecting general topics and narrowing down the search by choosing among the subtopics that appear. Give it a try at Yahoo!, the original home of the first famous directory.

Exercise 2A

Direct Me to Your Web Directory

1. As a team, open your Web browser and visit http://www.yahoo.com.

2. As Yahoo! opens, look at its central list of general topics. The most popular general topics are on the Welcome page, as marked in Figure OA3-4. To see the supporting subtopics, click any of the general topic links. (*Note:* You can click on **All Y! Services** to see a full list of general topics.)

3. Choose the **Finance** topic from the Yahoo! directory topic list.

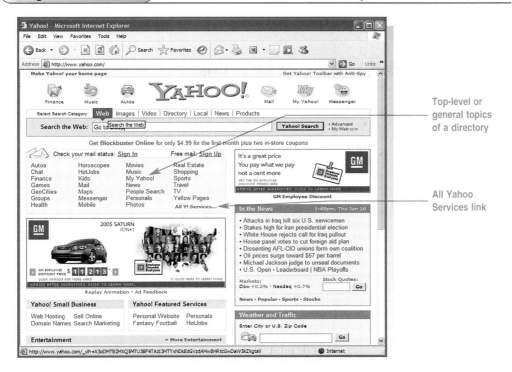

4. As you come to the Financial section, notice the many subtopics listed on the page. Some appear as graphics. Others appear as hypertext links. Consult with your team. Assign each team member a different Financial subtopic, such as: *Mutual Funds, Bill Pay, Banking, Loans, Insurance, Planning, Taxes, Mortgage Center, Mortgage Calculators, Dow, NASDAQ, S&P 500,* or one of the news items. (See Figure OA3-5.)

5. Individually research the financial subtopic you have chosen. Don't forget to take notes!

Figure OA3-5   Choose a Subtopic on Which to Report

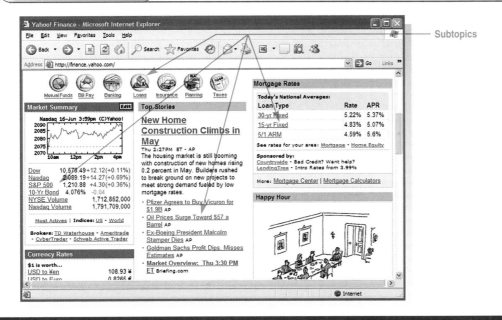

6. Based on your notes, individually create a 7- to 10-slide *PowerPoint* presentation explaining what you have learned. Save it as *OA3-2A*.

7. Deliver your *PowerPoint* show to your team members; then listen to what they have to present about the financial topics they have uncovered in Yahoo's directory.

Search Engines

It soon became apparent that organizing the entire Web by hand using directories was completely impractical. The Web had become so large that it was virtually impossible to catalog everything. Even the directory at Yahoo! quickly became so big and cumbersome that it also required a search capability. The Web was rescued from information overload by search engines. Table 3-3 briefly reviews some of the significant steps forward in the history of search engines.

Table 3-3   A Chronology of Search Engine History

Name	Year	Accomplishment	Web Address
WebCrawler	1994	Began "crawling" over Web pages and indexing their content. Developed at the University of Washington.	http://www.webcrawler.com
Lycos	1994	By 1996 had indexed over 60 million Web pages. Developed at Carnegie Mellon University.	http://www.lycos.com
AltaVista	1994	First search tool to allow natural queries.	http://www.altavista.com
Yahoo!	1994	Not to be left out, Yahoo quickly added a search capability.	http://www.yahoo.com
Hotbot	1996	Greatly improved the cataloging of pages. Designed at Cal Berkeley.	http://www.hotbot.com
Ask Jeeves	1997	Pioneered natural language processing tools that made searching more natural and user-friendly.	http://www.ask.com or http://www.askjeeves.com
Google	1998	Used the concept of implied value of inbound links to create the most popular search site as of 2003. Catalogs and ranks billions of sites.	http://www.google.com
MSN search	1998	Constantly working to compete with Google, MSN continually acquires and creates tools to improve its searching software.	http://www.msn.com

First Search

Each search engine employs different technologies that they feel give them a competitive advantage. Each has its own special rules and peculiarities. To simplify our examples, we will use Google as our search tool throughout this series of exercises.

query

Each time you conduct a search, you are conducting a **query**, which is a type of question the search engine is asked to resolve. All search tools use some sort of filtering logic to satisfy your query based on the **keyword**(s) you enter. Early search tools used Boolean logic (see *Boolean Operators* on page 469), but since then, search systems like Google have added other filtering criteria that lead to even more productive searches. (See *Why Google Is Grinning* on page 466.)

keyword

Answers to a query are called **results**. A keyword search can produce a list of hundreds of thousands, if not millions, of results. Notice that keywords in Google queries do not need to be capitalized. Here are a few examples of acceptable keywords:

results

- hawaii
- oahu
- north shore

Communicating for Success

Sponsored Versus Statistical Links

Most of the major search engines provide two types of links: **sponsored** and **statistical**. The statistical links are derived by searching the Web and finding the best possible matches to the search query. However, companies that wish to pay an advertising fee can sponsor links that will automatically appear when certain combinations of search words are entered. Sponsored links are essentially advertisements. They are a source of revenue for the search tool provider and help companies like Google pay their bills. Most search tools clearly mark the difference between sponsored and statistical links. However, with some search engines you'll need to look closely to notice the difference.

Exercise 2B

Narrow Down Your Keyword Queries

1. Launch your browser and go to http://www.google.com.

2. Key the word hawaii in the search window and tap ENTER or click the **Google Search** button, as shown in Figure OA3-6.

3. In your notes, record the number of results you received, as seen in Figure OA3-7. It probably numbers in the millions.

4. Scroll down through and review the variety of results that have been returned. Notice that they can encompass any Hawaii-related topic. For example:

   - *Schools in Hawaii*
   - *Hawaii State Government*
   - *Vacations in Hawaii*
   - *Scheduled road repairs on the Leeward side of Hawaii*

Figure OA3-6 A Simple One-Word Google Search

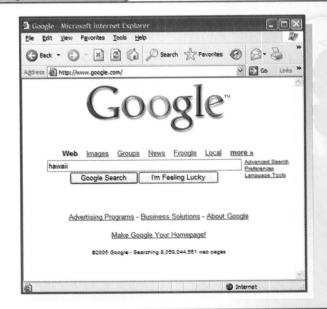

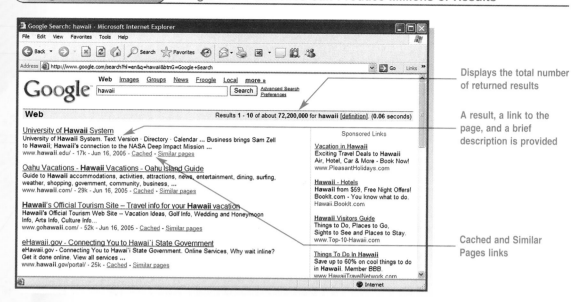

Displays the total number of returned results

A result, a link to the page, and a brief description is provided

Cached and Similar Pages links

Figure OA3-8   **Narrow Down Your Search With Multiple Words**

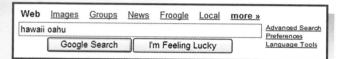

5. Now narrow down the search geographically by entering the search words hawaii oahu and tapping ENTER or clicking the **Google Search** button. In your notes, record how many results you received for just a single Hawaiian island. (See Figure OA3-8.)

6. Now key hawaii oahu north shore to narrow your search further to include only information about a stretch of beachfront along the north coast of Oahu. Record how many results you received in your notes.

TIP

Next to each result in Google there is a **Cached** link. This is a snapshot of the Web page that Google stores for emergencies. If a website is unavailable for some reason, you can always click the Cached link for a copy.

stemming

Phrase Searching, Stemming, and Insignificant Words

In the next exercise you will search for a big wave surfing contest held in Oahu. Imagine that you can only recall the most vague details about the surfing competition, but you do recall that it is held on the North Shore and it involves surfing very, very big waves.

As you surf the Net searching for information, remember some of these important Google tips.

- Search engines like Google have **stemming** features that find the stem of a word like *surf* and include related words with different endings or tenses in the search, such as *surfs*, *surfing*, and *surfed*. If you key the word *waves*, it will also search for *wave*. If you key the word **shore**, it will also look for *shores*. The keyword *vacationing* will also result in hits for *vacations* and *vacation*.

- If you use multiple words, such as *north shore big wave*, you will receive a list of results that correlates with all four words. But the correlation may be random. For example, you may be taken to a Web article that talks about a **big** *Art Festival in* **northern** *Canada on the* **shores** *of a lake that is attended by* **waves** *of enthusiastic fans.* This may not be at all what you are looking for.

- You can turn individual words into phrases by using quotation marks; for example, "**north shore.**" This is called **phrase searching**. The quotation

phrase searching

marks force a search for the exact sequence of words enclosed within the marks.

© PHOTODISC GREEN/GETTY IMAGES

- Google throws out small or insignificant words such as *and*, *I*, *it*, *the*, *or*, or single digits such as *1* or *7*. This helps speed searching along, so don't bother entering them.

- If a normally insignificant word is absolutely essential to the success of a search, put a + directly in front of it preceded by a space; for example, **+1**.

Exercise 2C

Explore Phrase Searching

1. Visit http://www.google.com.

2. Key the words north shore and record the number of results received in your notes.

3. Focus the search by adding two more keywords. Enter: north shore big wave. Record how many results came from your query.

4. Key the words within quotation marks: "north shore" "big wave". Record how many results came from your query.

5. Did Google return results that talk about the **Big Wave Invitational** competition held on the North Shore? If so, to whom is this competition dedicated? Does the competition have a nickname based on this legendary surfer? Record your answers in your notes.

6. Choose the **Similar Results** links next to one of the links that discusses the Big Wave Invitational. Notice that pages with a high correlation to the page you just selected are revealed. Use this technique when you want to dig deeper into a topic. In your notes, copy the top three results that appeared after you chose the Similar Results link.

> **TIP**
>
> The *I'm Feeling Lucky* option on Google will take you directly to Google's most relevant website result for your query.

Exercise 2D

Tabulate Your Successful Searches

1. Open *Microsoft Excel* and tabulate from your notes the following data, as seen in Figure OA3-9.

Figure OA3-9   Create a Spreadsheet

KEYWORDS	RESULTS	REDUCTION	
Exercise 2B			
hawaii	7,230,000		
hawaii oahu	230,000	7,000,000	=B3–B4
hawaii oahu north shore	39,000	7,191,000	=B3–B5
Exercise 2C			
north shore	222,000		
north shore big wave	187,000	35,000	=B8–B9
"north shore" "big wave"	1,250	220,750	=B8–B10

2. Format the spreadsheet as follows:

- Uppercase, bold, and center the titles/labels in row 1.
- Enter subtitles/labels for Exercises 2B and 2C. Bold each subtitle.
- Below each subtitle/label, enter the keywords used to reduce the number of results from the queries, as seen in column A in Figure OA3-8.
- Enter the results recorded in your notes for each query in column B.
- Enter subtraction formulas in column C under the *Reduction* label.
- Highlight the areas from cells A3–C5 and A8–C10 in different colors.
- Format numbers with no decimals, and use a comma as the thousands separator.
- Resize the column widths to display all of the data within each column.

3. Save your work as *OA3-2D*.

Making Connections

Why Google Is Grinning

Sergey Brin (1974–), of Moscow, Russia, and **Larry Page** (1975–), of East Lansing, Michigan, teamed up to create a better way to search called Google. By 2003, Google had become the preeminent online search engine. Their creation became so important that it became a verb, as in "I'm googling," or "Just google it."

While many parts of the core Google search technologies remain secret, it is known that Google classifies the relevance of the sites it returns as its top results by how many other sites link to it. This creates some very effective search queries, placing the most relevant results at the top of the list. Also, at a time when most search portals were packing as many links, advertisements, graphics, and pop ups as possible onto their busy Welcome pages, Google kept a very simple, uncluttered, and inviting interface that people appreciate. (See Figure OA3-10.)

But, in the end, it's the effective search results that Google yields that make it the most popular search tool in history. Google is constantly cataloging and caching billions of Web pages and provides innovative ways for users to sift though the trivial to find the valuable pages they seek. Needless to say, this has Googlers smiling.

Fun, Intuitive Ways to Search

At one time, Web searchers needed to learn Boolean operators to search successfully. Now, searches are much less complicated and more intuitive. In this next exercise, you will get the chance to try some of these fun new search techniques. In the next exercise you will:

1. Search for the types of *books* you'd like to read, by keying:

- **books about surfing**
- **books about hawaii**

2. Query for a definition by keying *define* and the word you want. If you want a list of possible definitions, use the operator *define:* followed by the word without a space. For example:

   - **define: surfing**

3. Search for a street map by entering the address along with the city and state, or substitute the ZIP Code for the city and state. For example:

   - **66005 haleiwa rd haleiwa hi**
   - **66005 haleiwa rd 96712**

4. Query a stock quote by keying the appropriate ticker symbol for the company or mutual fund you are inquiring about. For example:

   - **MSFT**
   - **IBM**
   - **APPL**

5. Conduct queries to find the weather in a city or at any airport by using its airport code or the name of the city, as seen in these examples:

   - **hnl airport**
   - **weather haleiwa**

6. Imagine you are looking for great places to eat in Oahu, but simply do not feel like Italian food. You can exclude Italian restaurants from the search by attaching the negative operator (-) preceded by a space:

   - **restaurants -italian**
   - **oahu restaurants -mexican**

7. Pose queries in the form of natural questions such as:

   - **What is the population of hawaii?**
   - **Who is king kameamea?**

Exercise 2E

Try Some Intuitive Search Queries

1. Go to http://www.google.com.

2. Search for the following books:

   - books about surfing
   - books about hawaii

3. Conduct a search for the types of books you like to read. List the top three results in your notes.

4. Find a map for the following location on the North Shore of Oahu. (*Note:* Near this address are found some of the most helpful surfing shops on the island. This is also the original home of Hawaiian Shaved Ice!)

   - 66005 haleiwa rd haleiwa hi

   or

   - 66005 haleiwa rd 96712

5. Use the zoom control to move out from the location until you see the entire island of Oahu.

6. Use your street address and ZIP Code to find a map that zooms in on your street.

7. Conduct a query to find the current stock price for Microsoft, IBM, and Apple. Use the following ticker symbols. Record the current price of each in your notes.
   - MSFT
   - IBM
   - AAPL

8. Find the weather at the Honolulu Airport, and then locate the weather conditions in Haleiwa, on the North Shore. Record the current conditions.
   - hnl airport
   - weather haleiwa

9. Find a list of great restaurants in Oahu, but exclude Italian food. Record the three top results in your notes. Key:
   - oahu restaurants -Italian

10. Find a list of restaurants in your area but exclude fast food restaurants. How complete a list did you obtain?

11. Use a natural question to find answers to the following queries. Record the answer to each question in your notes:
    - What is the population of hawaii?
    - Who is king kameamea?

12. For practice, ask a couple of natural questions of your own. Record your questions and answers in your notes.

Be Frugal with Google

Modern search engines like Google provide all sorts of powerful tips and tricks that can help you find exactly what you are looking for in the most efficient way possible. In the next exercise, search for new ways to query information. For example, what's the best way to find a movie listing for a theater in your local area? Is there any way to track a package you have mailed cross country? Can you translate a Spanish language Web page into English? How can you use Google to answer a math problem?

Get with your team, surf to the next exercise, and see what you can learn about advanced search techniques at Google. Also learn about setting personal preferences and localizing searches. There are more resources than you can possibly imagine emanating from the very simple welcome screen seen in Figure OA3-10.

Figure OA3-10

Team Up to Learn More About Google's Advanced Searches

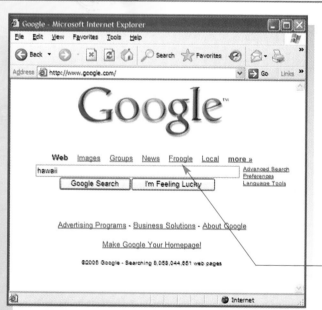

Investigate links to Images, Groups, Froogle, Local, Advanced Search, and more.

Exercise 2F

Advanced Search Tools

1. Go to http://www.google.com.

2. As a team, research the best way to do the following:
   - How can you search for local movie listings?
   - How can you track a package you have sent across the country?
   - How can you translate a Web page you came across written in a foreign language?
   - How can you use your search tool to find an answer to a difficult math problem?

3. Divide up this list and learn what can be accomplished at the following links:
   - Images
   - Groups
   - News
   - Froogle
   - Local
   - More

Making Connections

Boolean Operators

Early search engines filtered their search results with Boolean operators, based on Boolean principles invented by George Boole in the 19th century. In a Boolean search, operators are used to filter results based on a YES or NO ranking system. Just as add (+), subtract (-), multiply (*), and divide (/) are primary operators of arithmetic, AND, OR, and NOT are the primary Boolean operators.

The AND operator instructed the search engine to search for all documents containing two or more keywords; for example, *cats AND dogs*. Some search tools used the plus symbol (+) as the AND operator. However, most search tools, like Google, simply assume the AND operator, rendering it largely unnecessary.

The OR operator instructed a search to find documents containing either keyword specified. If *cats OR dogs* were entered in the search box, all documents containing either word would appear. This operator has also fallen out of general use. In Google, for example, the word is simply omitted and has no impact on a search.

The NOT operator excludes documents containing a defined keyword, such as *lions not bears*. Google still allows this operator. If you put a - in front of any word, pages containing that keyword will be excluded from the results.

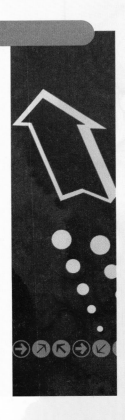

Evaluate More Internet Pioneers

1. In Unit 1, you studied a list of 23 computer pioneers. In Unit 2 you studied 6 more. This unit introduced you to a half dozen new Net legends. Use the table to help answer the following questions about each:

Marc Andreessen	Jim Clarke	David Filo
Jerry Yang	Sergey Brin	Larry Page

   a. What has each of the Web pioneers accomplished?

   b. From your reading of this unit, which computer pioneer listed above do you consider to be the most important contributor to the success of the World Wide Web?

   c. In your view, how do the accomplishments of this list of Internet pioneers compare with the 23 computer pioneers in Unit 1 and the 6 in Unit 2? Are they more or less important? Would you award any one of the six candidates above the Nobel Prize? If so, why?

   d. In your opinion, what is the most important single event in the history of the Browser Wars? Defend your assertion in a few short statements.

   e. Previously, in Unit 1, you chose one of the 23 early computer pioneers for study. You had a chance to substitute 1 of the 6 Internet pioneers for that name in Unit 2. Now, you have one last chance to substitute your selection with any one of the six new Web candidates listed above. Do you want to make a change? Record your final choice now!

2. Save your answers in a *Microsoft Word* file named *OA3-2G*, or complete your work in *Microsoft OneNote*, which saves automatically.

Exercise **2H**

Evaluate More Internet Legends

1. At the end of Exercise 2G you made a final choice as to your most interesting technology leader out of 35 possible choices. Research your choice online using a search tool. Gather all the relevant information you will need to complete a report on this leader. (*Note: Microsoft OneNote* is ideally suited to collect the information you require from your Web searches.)

2. Prepare a report to the following specifications:
   - Use the unbound report format you learned in Part 1 Unit 10.
   - The report must be a minimum of three pages.
   - Include a minimum of three references and a separate reference page at the end of your report.
   - Create a cover page for your report.
   - Use a 12-point Times New Roman font.
   - Include at least one graphic.
   - Include at least one table.

3. Save your report as *OA3-2H*.

Exercise 21

Evaluate Alternative Search Engines

1. As a team, choose two alternative search engines other than Google as identified in the next table. (*Note:* You may also substitute other search engines of your choice for this assignment.)

Name	Web Address
WebCrawler	http://www.webcrawler.com
Lycos	http://www.lycos.com
AltaVista	http://www.altavista.com
Yahoo!	http://www.yahoo.com
Hotbot	http://www.hotbot.com
Ask Jeeves	http://www.ask.com or http://www.askjeeves.com
Google	http://www.google.com
MSN search	http://www.msn.com

2. Research your alternative search engine choices. Conduct the same in-depth research of the features of your search engine selections as you did in Exercise 2F for the Google search engine.

3. Scour their respective websites looking for tips and tricks on how to use these alternative search engines effectively. Record a list of these helpful resources in your notes.

4. Using your notes to guide you, prepare a *PowerPoint* show as a team explaining the strengths and weaknesses, pluses and minuses of the three search engines that you have researched. Include the following elements in the presentation:

   - Use a 1- to 5-star ranking system (with 5 being the highest possible score) to rank the search engines, just as you did for Web browsers. Each of the three search engines must have a different star ranking.

   - Create and insert a table in your *PowerPoint* show comparing the features of the three search engines.

   - Include some tips and tricks on how to use these search engines effectively.

   - Explain to your audience how to locate the search tools.

   - In the conclusion, state your opinion as to which search engine your team recommends as the most effective, and explain your position in a bulleted list.

5. Save your article as *OA3-2I*.

UNIT 4

Ethics, Netiquette, and Our Digital Society

Conditioning Practice

Before you begin the lessons, key each line twice.

alphabet	1	Sixty glazed rolls with jam were quickly baked and provided free.
figures	2	Ted was born 1/7/42, Mel was born 3/2/86, and I was born 5/18/90.
speed	3	The auditor cut by half the giant goal of the sorority endowment.

gwam 1' | 1 | 2 | 3 | 4 | 5 | 6 | 7 | 8 | 9 | 10 | 11 | 12 | 13 |

LESSON ① THE DIGITAL WAYS OF DOING THINGS

OBJECTIVES

- ⊙ To explore how everyday life has changed in our digital age.
- ⊙ To discover how banking and finance have changed as a result of e-commerce.
- ⊙ To research how travel and tourism have changed as a result of e-commerce.
- ⊙ To study how online shopping and auction sites have changed how people buy and sell products.
- ⊙ To investigate how the auto industry has changed as a result of online digital information systems.
- ⊙ To study the history of recorded music.
- ⊙ To report on changes in a selected e-commerce industry.

Doing Things Differently

Many things work differently than they did before *Mosaic*, *Netscape*, and *IE* first battled it out for control of the online world. The inventions and software created during the Browser Wars generated an untold number of new ideas, creativity, jobs, and business opportunities. The Browser Wars changed how our society works and functions. Even some of the most routine tasks imaginable underwent change. For instance, before the Browser Wars, everyone paid their yearly taxes by mailing paper copies of their tax forms and personal checks to the government in stamped envelopes. Today, most people submit their taxes online—click, submit, and done!

The Net has changed many everyday things, including the way people communicate, shop, and do business. During the Browser Wars, the hyphenated letter **e-** (for electronic) was added to the lexicon. It started with **e-mail**, then along came **e-commerce**, which is literally doing business on the Web. Some e-commerce sites are now household names like **eBay** (the popular online auction site) and **Amazon**

e-mail
e-commerce
eBay
Amazon

(the first major online retailer). Large, medium-sized, and small businesses alike quickly learned that websites are a vital part of their e-business operations. Take a closer look at a few changes wrought by e-commerce in Table 4-1.

Table 4-1   Four E-Commerce Categories

Banking and Finance	*Before the Web, banking was done in bank buildings and bills were paid with handwritten checks.* Now, banks, credit unions, investment brokers, and financial institutions of all kinds are online. You can invest, save, pay bills, check your balances, transfer funds, or obtain financial advice using the Net. WellsFargo.com, Schwab.com, and WallStreetJournal.com are just three of the tens of thousands of financial websites available to you.
Travel and Tourism	*Before the Web, booking a vacation meant driving to a travel agency and sitting down personally with a travel agent.* Now, e-travel is a multibillion-dollar Internet sector with new brands as popular as Expedia.com, Travelocity.com, and Orbitz.com. Every airline, car rental agency, and hotel chain you care to name have websites to lure customers in the lucrative travel market. Want to book a trip, flight, car, or hotel? You will likely book it online.
Online Shopping	*Before the Web, if you needed to buy something, you drove to a local store or ordered it from a mail-order catalog.* Now, nearly everything can be bought and sold online, including: • Books from Amazon.com or BarnesandNoble.com • Clothes or new flip-flops for a vacation from Net stores like JCPenney.com, WalMart.com, or Target.com • HDTVs and digital cameras from e-stores like BestBuy.com or CompUSA.com • Accessories for an iPod at Apple.com or a new MP3 player from Sony.com or Samsung.com • Computers from Dell.com, Toshiba.com, HP.com, or Gateway.com
Online Automotive Information	*Before the Web, it was much harder to find detailed information about new and used cars. Car buying choices were limited to what people saw on their local car lots. Information about these vehicles was limited to what the local dealer chose to share, placing the prospective car buyer at a disadvantage.* Online automotive shoppers today can check the maintenance and collision history of any vehicle through its **Vehicle Identification Number** or **VIN** number, and they can go online to learn about new automobiles on such sites as GM.com, Ford.com, Toyota.com, or VW.com.
Online Music and Movies	Read *A Century of Recorded Sound* to learn more about how the music and movie industries have changed as a result of evolving technologies. Also, complete Lesson 2 and discuss various ethical issues raised by the use of digital file sharing and music swapping technologies.

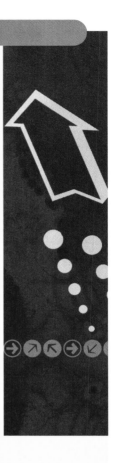

A Century of Recorded Sound

The history of recorded music spans just over a century. It began when Thomas Edison (**1847–1931**) first recorded the words from the song "Mary Had a Little Lamb" on a tinfoil cylinder on August 12, 1877. A short while later, vinyl records were sharing music the world over. Early recordings often sounded scratchy and distant by today's digital standards, but the hand-cranked Victrolas allowed hundreds of millions of people to hear the world's greatest artists and symphonies in the four corners of the earth.

Hand-cranked turntables soon gave way to electronic stereo systems. Record sales exploded, and the money that was generated created the lucrative and powerful recorded music industry. Recorded sound merged with movies in 1927 when Al Jolson (1899–1954) starred in the first "talking" picture, a musical called *The Jazz Singer*. Jolson, one of the most popular recording idols of his era, is considered to have been the first superstar.

The jarring of the road made it impossible to play vinyl records on turntables in automobiles, so the 8-track tape was invented. An 8-track was a bulky tape-filled cartridge that would loop continuously through an entire recorded album. But the 8-tracks were soon squeezed out by cassette tapes, which were much smaller and more practical. The cassette format made new products possible. For instance, the Sony Walkman, a portable cassette player, became a huge hit among teenagers who wanted to listen to their music wherever they chose to go.

While solving the problem of listening to music in a car or on the go, cassette tapes created a problem for the powerful recording industry. Music could easily be recopied to tape using the popular boom boxes of the '70s and '80s. Some said such recopying was nothing less than piracy, while others called it a personal freedom. In the famous Betamax case (so named for a less-than-profitable Sony video recording technology), the Supreme Court ruled that incidental copying of a tape or the copying of music from the radio for personal use was legal or "fair use." As a result, cassette tapes for recording both music and video became legal and popular.

The quality of a recording will degrade, or get worse, when making a copy of a copy using cassette tapes. In search of ever-improving digital storage mediums, CDs were developed. Previous recorded mediums like cassettes were analog technologies, recording the actual sound waves themselves. CDs allow digital input, where sound is converted into the zeros and ones of the digital age. With digital technologies, every copy is exactly the same as the original. This fact marked a big improvement in recorded video and audio quality.

However, digital CDs and DVDs have a drawback. Namely, the surface of CDs scratch easily, making them unusable. **Ripping** (the process of creating backup copies of CDs on a personal computer) became popular, if not downright essential in preventing the music from being lost in the event of a scratched or misplaced CD. CD "burners" became vital PC tools for most computer users.

(continued on next page)

The **iPod** took the next step in the progression of recorded sound. One hundred twenty-five years after Edison first recorded "Mary Had a Little Lamb" on a tinfoil cylinder, the iPod was created by Apple Computer Corp., becoming the most successful digital music recording device ever, even surpassing the eminently popular Sony Walkman used by an earlier generation. Thousands of songs can be ripped and downloaded to an iPod from a PC or an online file-sharing music site. IPods and similar MP3 players don't scratch, will store thousands of songs, and can always be synchronized and backed up on a personal computer. The iPod caught on like no other and the world of music and video reproduction would never be quite the same again.

With so much music ripped and stored on the hard drives of PCs, it would only take the invention of a peer-to-peer file-sharing tool, like Napster, to reignite the controversy over the reproduction of copyrighted music and video. (See Lesson 2.)

Exercise 1A

Research a Vacation Online

1. Using a search tool, find and visit three online reservation and travel services.

2. Use one of the online travel services to plan a weeklong vacation to a destination that interests you. Your vacation destination can be as extreme as scuba diving off the Grand Banks of Australia or as everyday as a visit to Disneyland. Plan your weeklong adventure online and determine the cost of such a trip.

3. Price roughly the same vacation using two other online travel services. (The hotels may be different or you may be traveling on different airlines, but the level of accommodations and flight times should be equivalent.) Save the comparative information and pricing provided by the three Web-based travel services.

4. Interview a travel agent or someone who remembers using a travel agency and find out how travel planning and the travel industry have changed since the Net became popular in 1995. Prepare for your interview by creating questions that will help you to learn more about how vacationing and booking travel changed after 1995. Ask such questions as:

   • Is service in the travel industry better now than it was the past?

   • Are travelers getting better travel bargains today as a result of the Web?

   • Are there more or fewer jobs in travel agencies today than there were 20 years ago?

   • What other positive or negative changes have occurred in the travel industry?

Exercise 1B

Comparison Shop Online

1. List three products you will need to take with you on the vacation you researched in Exercise 1A. You can research any relevant products, such as a digital camera, a surfboard, or SCUBA gear.

2. Go online to three separate e-commerce sites and price out the three products you listed in step 1. Take notes on price, quality, availability, and shipping times.

3. Has shopping changed much since the Web hit the popular scene in 1995? Interview an older person and inquire about such changes. Prepare for your interview by defining questions such as:

   - Do you shop online?

   - Do you enjoy online shopping, and do you find it a convenience?

   - What are the disadvantages and advantages of online shopping?

   - What do you think of eBay-like auction sites?

Exercise 1C

Research a New or Used Vehicle Online

1. Find the VIN number from your car or the car of a family member. (*Note:* The VIN is found on a little metal plate just under the windshield on the driver's side of the vehicle.)

2. Research this car online. You can start with Google or find other car-related websites. What can you learn about this vehicle for free online by using its VIN number? What additional information may be purchased online about the car? Record this information in your notes.

3. Visit the online websites for three major automobile manufacturers. Research one automobile from each manufacturer in the same class. For example: small economy car, hybrid, utility truck, SUV.

4. Capture notes about each vehicle in the same class, comparing at least a half-dozen essential features such as fuel mileage, warranty, and safety information.

5. Interview an elderly person and find out how purchasing a car was different before the Browser Wars in 1995.

   - How have people changed the way they research and buy vehicles since the Internet?

   - Are car buyers getting better deals today as the result of technology?

   - Are the autos of today better as a result of all the onboard computers they now have?

   - How do online wireless services like OnStar benefit car owners?

Exercise 1D

Research Online Banking

1. Using your search tool, locate the website for a local bank or credit union with which you or your family does business. Take notes on the types of the online services that are offered.

2. Do a search for online banks or credit unions. List two additional banks or credit unions that offer online services. Take notes as you compare the online services for the three banks or credit unions you have identified in steps 1 and 2.

3. Learn how customers can access their bank accounts remotely for your three banks or credit unions. For example, is it difficult for customers to access their accounts when traveling abroad or vacationing far from home?

4. Interview an older person about how banking has changed since 1995. Keep notes! Prepare for your interview by devising such questions as:

   • How have things changed when it comes to people's banking habits?

   • Are people better money managers and wealthier today as a result of new ways to manage their finances?

   • People mostly used checks in the past, now they mainly use credit and debit cards. Has this been a good change?

   • What other positive and negative changes have occurred in the financial industry due to the Net?

Exercise 1E

Report on E-Life

1. Each member of your team has researched four separate topics related to e-commerce in Exercises 1A, 1B, 1C, and 1D. Have each team member choose one of the following topics on which to report in more detail:

   Online Banking and Finance   Online Shopping

   Online Travel and Tourism   Online Vehicle Resources

2. After the topics have been divided, meet with each team member on your selected topic. Obtain a copy of their notes and talk to them about what they learned as they researched your assigned topic. Capture what they learned in their interviews with older people about how things were different in this market sector before the Net's rise in 1995. Incorporate what they have learned into your report.

3. Use *PowerPoint* to prepare your presentation. Begin by recounting what older people have said about how things have changed since 1995. Then go into detail about what you've learned regarding the research you conducted in the previous four exercises. Don't forget to compare the research from you and your teammates.

4. Present your report to your team members or to a larger group as assigned.

1. This is going to be a race that will pit you against your team members. As a group, pick a popular name brand product. Then each of you will have five minutes to find the best online price for this product. There are many e-commerce sites as well as auction sites that can be queried. Ready, set, go!

LESSON ② NEW E-ETHICS FOR AN ONLINE SOCIETY

OBJECTIVES

- ⊙ To explore the ethical use of computers and the Internet.
- ⊙ To review the meaning of copyright.
- ⊙ To evaluate the issue of plagiarism.
- ⊙ To learn how online sources must be cited.
- ⊙ To review how online sources must be formatted.
- ⊙ To explore the ethics and legal ramifications of file sharing.

The Ethical Use of Computers

Computers and the Internet can be used for many wonderful purposes, but they can also be used for unethical activities. Some use computers to find cures for serious illnesses, organize food drives for victims of natural disasters, or raise money for charitable causes. Still others use them for criminal behavior.

ethics

The use of computers should be governed by **ethics**, the moral principles that govern human interaction. Computers don't possess ethics. No machine can. They can only do what we ask them to do. In every case, humans must make the ethical decisions regarding what a computer and the Net will be used for, whether it is for good or for ill.

Making Connections

Acceptable Use Policies

To clarify the ethical boundaries of the new online world, organizations that maintain access to Internet accounts for their clients, students, or employees often institute Acceptable Use Policies or AUPs to prevent abuse and to protect all of their computer users. Acceptable use policies follow a very familiar pattern and usually include the following bullet points:

- Never disclose a password to another person.
- Never allow others to use your computer account without the express permission of a superior.
- Never use a computer to lie, distort, harass, or offend other people.
- Only use a computer and the Net for official purposes.
- Do not forward suspicious e-mail or files.
- Do not download copyrighted material or steal files.
- Log out of your computer at the end of each day.

Many people use technologies without ever considering their ethical use. And there are often many confusing legal points of view regarding legal uses of new technologies. It can be difficult, without research and discussion, to know with certainty where the courts stand on certain legal matters.

Learn: Copyright Issues

People or companies that create works that are new, useful, and potentially profitable may be granted a **copyright** for those works. A copyright is a form of protection granted by the United States and other governments for **intellectual property**. Works created through the intellectual creativity of a person or business—such as books, articles, software, music, plays, movie scripts, and artwork—are considered intellectual property and can be copyrighted. Copyrighted material may carry the © symbol. However, you should assume that materials may be copyrighted even if you do not see this symbol.

Copyright laws govern how copyrighted works may be used legally. As a general rule, you may not use copyrighted material unless you have the owner's permission. However, you may be able to use a small portion of the copyrighted work for educational purposes. The rule that relates to this type of use is called the **fair use doctrine**.

copyright
intellectual property

fair use doctrine

Learn: Avoiding Plagiarism

However, the fair use doctrine does not apply to plagiarism. Plagiarism is an all-too-common online activity that is clearly unethical. Plagiarism is the unauthorized use of someone else's words, ideas, music, or writing without acknowledgment. When you use someone else's material in your document, you must give that person credit for his or her work. It's considered a serious breach of netiquette—besides being unethical, unprofessional, and possibly illegal—to quote online work that's not your own without citing it. Plagiarism is best explained with examples:

- Copying text, graphics, music, video, or other content
- Paraphrasing without referencing the source
- Buying a research paper online and presenting it as your own
- Having others prepare your work

Finding a report on the Internet that just fits your assignment and turning it in with your name as the author is plagiarism. Plagiarism in academic work may result in serious punishment.

Much of the information found on Web pages online is copyrighted. This means that it may be illegal to reprint, post, download, and republish without permission. For example, suppose you see a great picture on a website. You decide to download the picture and display it on the desktop of your computer. You also send the graphic to friends. If the picture has been copyrighted, you may be breaking the law by copying and sharing it without the owner's permission.

Learn: Citing Electronic Sources

If you take a quote or information from online sources, you must create a proper citation. There are many different style guides governing how citations should be written. Most include the following pieces of information in this order:

- Author's name
- Title of work
- Book title, publication, magazine, or title of Web page (as it appears in the title bar of your browser) underlined or italicized
- The page number (section number or identifying feature) if applicable
- The date
- The electronic address or URL, such as http://www.corpview.org

The citation is formatted as follows:

- Begin the first line at the left margin and indent all the following lines in the citation.
- Use periods, not commas, to separate parts of the citation.[1]

You won't always be able to find *all* the information suggested. List as much as you can. View some example citations by reading the box entitled *Online Citation Formats*.

Internet TiP

Look for copyright statements and links such as legal notices on the websites you visit. These notices will help you determine whether the material is legally protected or not.

Communicating for Success

Online Citation Formats

Professional Web Page
The Nebraska Writer's Project. Ed. Ben Rand. Nebraska State University. http://www.nstate.edu/writer/.

Corporate Web Page
Corporate View Welcome Page. Corporate View. http://www.corpview.com.

Personal Web Page
Barksdale, Karl. Web page. Downloaded: 1 July 2005. http://www.karlbarksdale.com.

Online Magazine Article, Blog, or Webzine
Rutter, Michael. "Catching Lake Trout." *Outdoor Life*. http://www.outdoorlife.com.

Article in an Online Database
"Impressionism." *Britannic Online*. Vers. 99.1.1 May. *Encyclopaedia Britannica*. 29 May 1999. http://www.eb.com.

E-mail
Barksdale, Karl. Amazon River Pollution Tests. 22 May 2005. kbarksdale@corpview.com.

An Ethical Debate: Is File Sharing Wrong?

A popular activity among college students at the turn of the twenty-first century was downloading "free" music from various **file sharing** sites. A debate ensued as to

file sharing

---

[1]Karl Barksdale and Michael Rutter. Corporate View. Citing Electronic Sources. Downloaded August 1, 2005. www.corpview.com.

whether this activity was a crime or an exciting new way of distributing music, videos, and other entertainment content.

The ethical and legal debate started simply enough. At age 19, **Shawn Fanning (1980–)**, a freshman at Northeastern University, invented a new way to share music that would totally revolutionize music distribution and turn the traditional music recording industry on its ear.

Working alone and nearly nonstop, Fanning created **Napster**, which allowed people to use **peer-to-peer** (P2P) networking to share their computers' music and video collections online. With peer-to-peer technologies, people can download and swap music and video files effortlessly and virtually without cost. Like Andreessen and Berners-Lee before him, Fanning had broken the mold, changed the prevailing way of doing things, and became an overnight Internet legend.

Napster
peer-to-peer

Soon, Shawn Fanning had the entire music industry breathing down his neck. Legal pressure shut Napster down, but not before 32 million users from all over the world were sharing and swapping files. Other file-sharing sites instantly emerged to replace Napster, such as Kazaa, Morpheus, Grokster, LimeWire, and others. File sharing music and video became more popular than ever.

Recording Industry Association of America or **RIAA**

The **Recording Industry Association of America** or **RIAA** clamed peer-to-peer file sharing was an infringement of copyright laws. The RIAA protects copyrighted music on behalf of musicians, artists, and the recording companies. When CD sales began to decline at the start of the twenty-first century, the RIAA blamed file sharing and took Grokster and thousands of individuals to court. After a few years of legal wrangling, the Supreme Court made its decision. You'll get a chance to research and examine the issue of file sharing and the Court's decision in the next exercise.

Instant Message

Shawn Fanning's nickname was Napster, which described the state of his hair underneath his trademark baseball cap. Today, Napster.com is a legitimate file-sharing site.

Making Connections

MP3

MP3 is an audio compression standard created by the **Moving Picture Experts Group** or **MPEG**, which is a subcommittee of the **ISO** or **International Organization for Standardization**. This same group has created standards for video compression as well.

The magic of MP3 is that rather large audio files can be compressed or shrunk down in size without sacrificing the quality of the audio. The small size makes MP3 an ideal format for sharing music over peer-to-peer networks. Audio files compressed according to the standard are dubbed MP3s. In fact, the acronym MP3 has become synonymous with music files downloaded from the Net. People can listen to MP3s on their computers or on portable MP3 players.

Metro-Goldwyn-Mayer vs. Grokster

1. Analyze the following paragraph. Isolate key words that will allow you to use Google or some other search tool to research the controversy related to peer-to-peer file sharing.

   In June 2005, the Supreme Court issued a unanimous decision on the issue of peer-to-peer file sharing. At question was whether or not file-sharing sites, such as Grokster and Morpheus, can be held responsible when students use their software to download and listen to music from a friend's computer. The Recording Industry Association of America (RIAA) spent four years arguing the case through the court system. The landmark case was called Metro-Goldwyn-Mayer vs. Grokster.

2. Using *Microsoft OneNote* or *Microsoft Word*, collect information on the famous case. Find arguments that help explain Grokster's opinions about peer-to-peer file sharing and arguments that help explain the viewpoint of Metro-Goldwyn-Mayer and the RIAA on the subject.

3. Find out how the courts ruled on the case. What were some of the highlights of the Supreme Court's decisions and opinions? Record this information in your notes.

4. For background information, read about hearings held by Senator Orrin Hatch on the file-sharing issue in 2000. Testimony was taken from none other than Shawn Fanning himself. Open *CD-Fanning.doc* and get the inside scoop on what drove him to do what he did.

5. Imagine you have been called to testify at another round of Senate hearings on the issue of peer-to-peer file sharing. To get ready for the hearing, prepare a written copy of your testimony in advance using an unbound report format. Write your testimony in the form of a persuasive essay, either supporting or dissenting from the Supreme Court's decisions on the topic of peer-to-peer file sharing. Your essay should be approximately 3,000 words in length and should be supported by arguments from actual court cases, congressional hearings, or other informed sources. Here's a possible question to help you think about your opening thesis statement:

   "Is it ethical or not for individuals to share music, graphics, photos, and video over the Net?"

6. Include properly written and edited citations in your written public testimony.

Exercise 2B

Debate the Ethics of File Sharing

Research and prepare a debate on both sides of the file-sharing issue. Assign half of your team to represent the RIAA and the other side to represent students arguing the rights of consumers. Include in your debate some of the following issues:

- Is peer-to-peer technology illegal or unethical to use? Are there any acceptable or legal reasons to use peer-to-peer file sharing technologies?

- How do copyright laws protect artists and musicians?

- If you buy a CD that becomes scratched and unusable after a day or two, would it be unethical to download the exact same music and transfer it to your iPod over a peer-to-peer network?

- Is it unethical to buy a CD of popular music and lend it to a friend?

- Is it unethical to make a backup copy of all of your music on your personal computer?

- Is it unethical to allow a friend to listen to your music that has been backed up on your personal computer?

- Is it unethical if your friend accesses your computer over the Internet from a distant location and listens to the music on your PC?

- Is it unethical to broadcast music from your PC over the Internet or to Podcast a reading from a popular book to an iPod or computer for others to hear?

- If you purchased music, can you decide what to do with it?

- Do you have to pay for the same music more than once? Say you purchased a Beatles album in the 1960s or '70s on vinyl and then purchased the same album again five years later on cassette tape, and again five years later on CD. That CD has since been warped by the sun and doesn't play. Is it unethical to download a copy of that same music from the peer-to-peer network over the Internet to your PC and transfer that music to your iPod or MP3 player?

Exercise 2C

Search For File-Sharing Sites

1. As a team, go online and find a half dozen legally compliant file-sharing and music and video download sites.

2. As a team, discuss the pluses and minuses, the benefits and disadvantages associated with each site discovered in step 1.

3. As a team, vote and rank the sites in order of preference from the first to the last. Discuss why one site rose above the rest in terms of its popularity within the group.

OBJECTIVES

- ⊘ To define libel, slander, aspersion, harassment, and defamation.
- ⊘ To evaluate First Amendment protections in regard to the use of new technologies.
- ⊘ To review e-mail and instant messaging guidelines.
- ⊘ To study the role of online netiquette.

The First Amendment vs. Libel, Slander, Aspersion, Harassment, and Defamation

libel
slander
aspersion
harassment
defamation

The Web continues to develop new technologies for sharing digital communication. With each new creation, old ethical issues resurface and need to be reevaluated, reinvented, or reinforced. Ethical principles regarding **libel**, **slander**, **aspersion**, **harassment**, and **defamation**—long applied to print and broadcast journalism—must be reconsidered.

E-mail was one of the first new technologies to bring up these ethical issues. Sometimes people say things in an e-mail message that they regret later. The same is true for instant messaging on a computer and text messages from cell phones, which allow instantaneous responses between people online. E-mail, text messages, and instant messages have been available for years, so rules have been established for their ethical use. (Read *E-mail, Text Messaging, and IM Guidelines* on the next page.)

E-mail is usually stored on a server and can be retrieved months, years, even decades later. Oftentimes, old e-mail messages are subpoenaed by courts in order to help law enforcement determine if crimes have been committed.

blog
Weblog
blogger
blogosphere

A relatively new form of communication is called a **blog**. The origin of the word is from the term **Weblog**, which is an online personal journal or log. Someone who keeps a blog is called a **blogger**. The world of blogs is called the **blogosphere**.

The first blogs started as personal weblogs or journals written by individuals. Bloggers typically update their blogs daily or weekly. Because blogs are considered personal journals, bloggers tend to write what they think and bring their opinions to the forefront for all to read.

podcasting

Similar to blogging is a relatively new phenomena called **podcasting**. Podcasts are audio transmissions. Because podcasts are audio files, they can be downloaded through peer-to-peer technologies the way MP3 music files can so listeners may hear a favorite podcast whenever they feel like it. Individuals can create podcasts of their own or subscribe to the podcasts of others. Podcasting is an outgrowth of the peer-to-peer technologies pioneered by Shawn Fanning.

The First Amendment to the U.S. Constitution guarantees freedom of speech, but as you will explore in the future activity, are there areas where bloggers, podcasters, e-mailers, and instant messengers may go too far and actually break laws? While each of these Net technologies—e-mail, instant messaging, blogging, and podcasting to name a few—are positive tools expanding free speech, they can also resurrect traditional legal and ethical issues related to *libel*, *slander*, *harassment*, *defamation*, and *aspersion*.

E-Mail, Text Messaging, and IM Guidelines

Follow these guidelines for writing e-mail, sending text messages, or using your instant messaging software (IM) on your computer:

• Be courteous to others in your messages.
• Keep your messages short and to the point, but include all the needed information.
• Place the most important points of the message in the first few words or lines of text.
• Do not use ALL CAPITAL LETTERS for whole words. Using ALL CAPS is viewed as shouting at the reader and is considered rude. Use bold or italic text instead of ALL CAPITAL LETTERS.
• Proofread your messages before you send them.
• Do not send private or personal information.
• Remember that e-mail and instant messages are not private forms of communication. Always assume that someone besides the person to whom you're writing may see the message.
• Do not forward inappropriate or private correspondence.

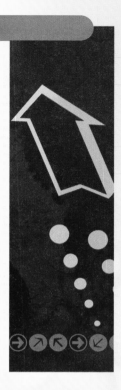

Learn: Netiquette

There wouldn't be problems with libel, slander, aspersion, defamation, or harassment if Web users would mind their manners. When communicating online—via voice, video, graphics, or text—apply the rules of polite behavior to whatever situation you're in. On the Internet, these implied rules of behavior are called **netiquette**. The word is formed by merging the words **etiquette** (the requirements for proper social behavior) and **Net**.

netiquette

To be an effective online communicator, you must learn the nuances of netiquette. Some rules are a bit obscure, such as the non-use of UPPERCASE letters in e-mail, text messages, and instant messages. Uppercase letters imply shouting, agitation, passion, or extreme excitement. You wouldn't answer your cell phone and start shouting at someone. This would be considered beyond the pale of acceptable behavior. The use of uppercase words can be used to add EMPHASIS, but their use must be carefully planned, if they are to be used at all.

Often, particularly in e-mail and other text messaging formats, humor sometimes comes across with a big thud. Some humor relies on facial expressions, body language, and verbal inflections to project the witticism, cheeky comment, cynicism, or sarcasm. All are difficult to achieve in a text format. Therefore, **emoticons** and abbreviations are used to signal those inflections, such as :-) to mean a smile or <grin> to signal humor or sarcasm, or LOL to mean *laughing out loud*.

emoticons

Many communication conflicts are the result of unedited messages. People should proofread and review their e-mail, instant messages, blogs, and podcasts to make sure they are grammatically correct and ethically appropriate. Sometimes, after a bit of reflection, effective communicators will revise what they wish to share with others. Careful editing is the highest form of netiquette.

Exercise 3A

Legal Definitions

1. Use your Internet search tools to define the following legal terms:
   - libel
   - slander
   - aspersion
   - defamation
   - defamatory statements
   - harassment

2. Which term or terms above do not apply to a blogger?

3. Which term or terms do not apply to a podcast?

4. Which term or terms do not apply to e-mail?

5. Imagine you're working for a company and amending the acceptable use policy or AUP. As a team, write a one-paragraph explanation for each of the unethical behaviors listed in step 1. Attempt to explain to employees why libel, slander, aspersion, defamation, defamatory statements, and harassment cannot be tolerated in the workplace.

Exercise 3B

First Amendment Protections

1. Using a search tool, locate a copy of the First Amendment to the Constitution of the United States. Read and review it.

2. As a group, address the following question:

   While libel, slander, aspersion, defamation, and harassment are clearly out of bounds, what First Amendment protections do bloggers and podcasters have in regard to freedom of speech?

3. Research the question posed in step 2, looking for citable sources on the topic of freedom of speech as it relates to blogging and podcasting.

4. Have each member of the team prepare individual position papers, of roughly 1,500 words, on the topic.

5. Debate within the group various position papers explaining freedom of speech in regard to the use of these new technologies.

Exercise 3C

Search for Acronyms and Emoticons

1. As a team, do an Internet search for acronyms and emoticons that can be helpful when instant messaging, text messaging, in e-mail, or for online blogs. For example:
   - Laughing out Loud = LOL
   - By the Way = BTW

- Just Kidding = JK
- :-)
- :-(

2. As a team, prepare an outline or a table containing at least 25 emoticons and acronyms for rapid and polite communication. You can use the five examples in step 1, which means you only have 20 to go! Good luck.

Communication & Math Skills 10

1. Study each of the six rules shown below in the color boxes.

a. Key the *Learn* line(s) beneath each rule, noting how the rule is applied.

b. Key the *Apply* lines, using apostrophes correctly.

Internal Punctuation: Apostrophe

Rule 1: Use an apostrophe as a symbol to represent feet or minutes. (Quotation marks may be used to signify inches or seconds.)

Learn   1   Floyd bought twenty-four 2" x 4" x 12' studs for the new deck.
Learn   2   Shawnelle scored the 3-pointer with only 1' 18" left to go.
Apply   3   The new computer lab at my school is 18 ft. 6 in. x 30 ft.
Apply   4   The students were told to print 3 min. writings on 8.5 in. x 11 in. paper.

Rule 2: Use an apostrophe as a symbol to indicate the omission of letters or figures (as in contractions).

Learn   5   Didn't you enjoy the "Spirit of '76" segment of the pageant?
Apply   6   I dont know why he doesnt take advantage of our new terms.
Apply   7   Last years reunion combined the classes of 97, 98, and 99.

Rule 3: Use an apostrophe plus *s* (*'s*) to form the plural of most figures, letters, and words used as words rather than for their meaning *(6's, A's, five's)*. In stock quotations and to refer to decades or centuries, form the plural of figures by adding s only.

Learn   8   She studied hard and earned A's throughout the 1990s.
Learn   9   I sold Century As and 4s and bought Cosco 45s.
Apply 10   Correct the outline by changing the As, Bs, and Cs to CAPS.
Apply 11   My broker urged that I buy Apache 76's in the 1980's.

Rule 4: To show possession, use an apostrophe plus s after (1) a singular noun and (2) a plural noun that does not end in *s*.

Learn 12   Jerrod's store had a great sale on men's and women's apparel.
Apply 13   Ritas class ring was lost under the stands in the schools gym.
Apply 14   Our back-to-school sale on childrens clothes is in progress.

Rule 5: To show possession, use an apostrophe plus *s* (*'s*) after a proper name of one syllable that ends in *s*.

Learn 15   Jon Hess's next art exhibit will be held at the Aronoff Center.
Apply 16   Rena Haas new play will premiere at the Emery Theater.
Apply 17   Jo Parks ACT scores were superb; Ed Sims SAT scores, mediocre.

Rule 6: To show possession, use only an apostrophe after (1) plural nouns ending in s and (2) a proper name of more than one syllable that ends in *s* or *z*.

Learn 18   The girls' new coach will visit at the Duclos' home next week.
Apply 19   The new shipment of ladies sportswear will arrive on Friday.
Apply 20   Lt. Santos plan for the officers annual ball was outstanding.

2. Key *Proofread & Correct*, using apostrophes correctly.
   a. Check answers.

b. Using the rule number(s) at the left of each line, study the rule relating to each error you made.

c. Rekey each incorrect line, using apostrophes correctly.

Proofread & Correct

Rules

1	1	Jay Corbin played 12 min. 30 sec.; Jack Odom, 26 min. 20 sec.
1	2	My desk is 3 ft. x 5 ft. 6 in.; the credenza is 2 ft. x 6 ft.
2	3	Didnt O'Brien prepare a sales comparison for 98 and 99?
3	4	Major changes in technology occurred in the 1980's and 1990s.
3	5	Dr. Knox gave mostly As and Bs, but he gave a few Cs and Ds.
2,4	6	Didnt you go to the big sale on childrens items?
5	7	Tess escort gave her a wrist corsage of exquisite violets.
6	8	The boys and girls teams appreciated Dr. Morris compliments.
6	9	Do you know whether the ladies swim coach is in her office?
2,6	10	Didnt you ask if the cast is set for Miss Winters new play?

3. Save as *CS10-ACT1*.

ACTIVITY 2   Composing

1. Read the case of the "extra change."

2. Considering the comments and suggestions, compose a paragraph to indicate what you would do in this situation, identifying how and why you made your choice.

3. Proofread, revise, and correct.

4. Save as *CS10-ACT2*.

You and your friends have arranged to go to dinner together before separating for other activities: a ball game, a movie, a "mixer." To pay for the dinner, you have collected money from each friend.

The restaurant is upscale, the food very good, and the service excellent. Your server has been friendly and has quickly met all your needs. Your server has not rushed you to finish, so you and your friends have enjoyed conversation and laughter long after the meal ended.

When it is time to go, you ask your server for the check and pay it. When you receive your change and are leaving a tip, you notice that your change is $10 more than you should have received.

A discussion takes place among the six of you regarding this error. Various comments and suggestions are made:

1. Keep the money; the server will never know to whom he gave the extra change.

2. Are you lucky! This never happens to me.

3. You have to return the money. If you don't, the server will have to make up the loss of money at the end of the evening.

Several thoughts go through your mind as you listen to the comments of your friends. You know it would be great to have ten extra dollars to share with your friends. What will my friends think if I return the money, or if I keep it? The server has been very pleasant and has worked hard this evening. If I keep the money, is it right to make the server pay for the error? How would I want to be treated if I made the same mistake at my job?

ACTIVITY 3   Math: Working with Measures of Central Tendency

1. Open *CD-CS10-ACT3* and print the file.

2. Solve the problems as directed in the file.

3. Submit your answers.

UNIT 5

LESSON 1
Online Privacy and Safety

Conditioning Practice

Before you begin the lessons, key each line twice.

alphabet 1 Wixie plans to study my notes just before taking the civics quiz.

fig/sym 2 Our soccer league had 4,129 boys and 3,587 girls playing in 2006.

speed 3 The busy field hand kept the fox in a big pen to keep it in sight.

gwam 1' | 1 | 2 | 3 | 4 | 5 | 6 | 7 | 8 | 9 | 10 | 11 | 12 | 13 |

LESSON 1 FIGHTING ONLINE CRIME

OBJECTIVES

- ⊙ To study cyber crimes and scams.
- ⊙ To learn ways that hackers, phishers, and identity thieves operate.
- ⊙ To Research viruses, spyware, firewalls, and other potential online security solutions.
- ⊙ To learn how to protect yourself from identity theft and other online crime.
- ⊙ To examine various software solutions to protect computer data.

Clearly a Crime

While the Internet and e-commerce created new opportunities for business, it also opened up new ways for criminals to cheat consumers. Cyber-criminals can cheat victims around the globe. The CEO of a Nebraska-based online business described this **scam**, or con game, that almost cost the company thousands of dollars.

scam

Instant Message

A scammer gains the confidence of someone in order to steal from them.

A vacationing Kansas couple, Frank and Fran, took a cruise from Seattle to Alaska. A member of the crew stole their credit card number after they used their card to pay for meals and souvenirs. The stolen number was quickly e-mailed over the Net to criminals in another hemisphere. The cyber-criminals then scoured websites from all over the world looking for products that could be purchased online and shipped quickly using the stolen credit card number. Speed was essential. The ill-gotten card number had to be used quickly before Frank and Fran returned home and caught on to the problem. The products purchased with the stolen credit card number could be sold for a profit on the black market.

The scammers contacted and gained the confidence of the Nebraska-based e-business, fooling them into believing they represented a legitimate import-export business. Orders were placed against the card for thousands of dollars. But a sales manager in Nebraska was suspicious and blocked the order at the last second, stopping shipment in Hong Kong, the last transit point before the ill-gotten goods arrived at their final destination. She checked with the bank and found that the owners, Frank and Fran, lived in neighboring Kansas, not in a country on the other side of the planet. The case was turned over to law enforcement who informed Fran and Frank of the scam.

The story of Fran and Frank had a happy ending and may seem like an isolated incident. Far from it. According to *USA Today*, small businesses have been hit hard by Internet scams. Far too many report tens of thousands of dollars of fraudulent charges. And the problem is getting worse.[1] Security breaches have compromised millions of credit card numbers.

hacker

For example, *CNN/Money* reported on June 20, 2005, that over 40 million credit card accounts were compromised by a **hacker**. A hacker accesses computers and networks without proper permission. The criminal gained access to the computers of a Tucson, Arizona company that processes credit card transactions for businesses and banks. In total, 13.9 million MasterCard and 22 million Visa accounts were compromised by the hacker's **virus**, which is a form of malicious computer code. This particular virus was designed to search out certain types of credit card transactions and steal vital information.[2]

PHOTODISC RED / GETTY IMAGES

virus

Computer-related crime can take many forms. For example, malicious computer viruses can hijack information, destroy digital data, shut down computers, or disrupt entire computer networks. Any computer that has received a virus is said to be **infected**. Some viruses can steal e-mail names from your computer without you even knowing about it, and hit your friends, colleagues, and coworkers with unwanted viruses and **spam** (unwanted and unsolicited advertising).

infected

spam

Individuals, governments, schools, and businesses all can become victims of high-tech crime. As the story of Fran and Frank illustrates, everyone must be careful to protect their private information. Even charitable organizations must take care. During the hurricane Katrina disaster, criminals posing as representatives of the American Red Cross created and sent fake e-mail messages with links to web sites that looked exactly like the real thing. As outrageous as it sounds, many well-meaning people were conned into giving their credit card numbers and other personal information to these criminals. Sadly, their donations never arrived to help people in need.

In the sections to follow, you will learn more about protecting yourself and the organizations you work with against criminal activity.

Learn: Identity Theft

Sometimes a criminal may take more than a credit card number or a few e-mail addresses. He or she may steal a person's entire identity! The criminals will find out

---

[1]John Schwartz, "Credit Card Fraud Hits Small Online Merchants Hard," *USA Today*, June 28, 2005.
[2]Jeanne Sahadi, "40M Credit Cards Hacked," *CNN/Money*, June 20, 2005, downloaded from http://money.cnn.com/2005/06/17/news/master_card/.

identity theft

credit report

spyware

firewalls

> The U.S. Federal Trade Commission and other government and private financial institutions provide resources to help victims of identity theft.

as much as they possibly can about a victim. They may be able to acquire bank account numbers, social security numbers, job information, loan information, family information, and spending records. Personal information may also come from stolen purses or wallets. Information can also be derived by stealing mail from trash cans!

Once a criminal has this type of information, he or she can pretend to be the victim. This is called **identity theft**. Money may be moved out of the victim's bank account, purchases made on their credit cards, loans taken out using the victim's name, and charges made on calling cards. Vacations, cars, and other expensive items may be charged to the victim.

When bills are not paid, the overdue accounts are reported on the victim's **credit report**. Credit reports keep track of a person's financial history and award them a score which is used to predict a person's financial integrity and ability to pay debts. A positive credit report is necessary in order to take out a loan or to make a major purchase. The victim may then be turned down for loans or not hired for jobs because of a negative credit report. The victim may not know at first what is happening or that a credit report has gone negative.

Matters can go from bad to worse. An identity thief may give the victim's name to the police during an arrest. If the person is released from police custody but does not show up for a court date, an arrest warrant may be issued for the victim!

Millions of Americans have been victims of identity theft. Businesses and victims have lost billions of dollars due to this type of crime. To reduce the chance of becoming a victim, read and follow the *Ten Rules to Help Avoid Identity Theft*.

	TEN RULES TO HELP AVOID IDENTITY THEFT
1.	Avoid giving out personal information on the phone, through the mail, or over the Internet unless the company is reputable and provides guaranteed service warranties and consumer protection. Never give out financial information like credit card, social security, or account numbers unless you know exactly with whom you're doing business.
2.	Use strong passwords on credit card, bank, and phone accounts. Never share your ATM PIN or your passwords for your bank accounts, Internet service provider, or other Internet access point.
3.	Ask about information security procedures in your workplace and security measures provided by your Internet service provider.
4.	Install software to protect your data. For example, install any security updates to your e-mail and Web browser software. Use virus and **spyware** protection software and other tools, such as **firewalls**, to protect personal information. A firewall can include a combination of hardware and software security tools to block and filter out intrusions made by a hacker. Spyware can be installed on a computer by a hacker to gather data about the computer user.
5.	Secure personal information in the home and office. Shred charge receipts, credit records, checks, bank statements, invoices, and bills before they are thrown away. Shred any documents that may contain personal account and credit card information.
6.	Keep your social security card, driver's license, and passport in a safe place.
7.	Protect access to home computers and guard against computer viruses and hackers.

(continued on next page)

	TEN RULES TO HELP AVOID IDENTITY THEFT (continued)
8.	Notify your bank or credit union of any suspicious e-mail messages, text messages, or phone calls asking you to verify financial information.
9.	Make sure your bank or credit union and companies with which you do business have privacy policies that they enforce. Make sure they use **encryption**, which is a set of software security tools that converts information to secure, unbreakable code.
10.	Order an annual copy of your credit report in order to look for any potential problems.

encryption

Exercise 1A

Learn How to Obtain a Credit Report

1. A friend of yours is concerned about her credit. The other day, she had trouble qualifying for a loan. She is worried about identity theft. Prepare an e-mail to your friend explaining how she can check her credit report online. Prepare to write your message by researching the following:

   - Visit the FTC site at http://www.consumer.gov/idtheft/ and read what they suggest to do if you suspect identity theft. Take notes on what you learn, and include the main points in your e-mail.

   - Visit the FTC site that will guide you to more information about obtaining free credit reports at http://www.ftc.gov/bcp/conline/pubs/credit/freereports.htm.

   - Visit an industry site that can help you learn more about viewing your credit report on a yearly basis: point your Web browser to http://www.annualcreditreport.com.

   - In your e-mail, explain that there are three major credit card reporting agencies. Visit each and learn how your friend can obtain credit reports from each of them. Include a breakdown of costs and the services they provide.

     - http://www.Equifax.com
     - http://www.Experian.com
     - http://www.TransUnion.com

2. Prepare an e-mail message based on what you have learned and recorded in your notes.

Exercise 1B

Press Release on Bank Precautions

1. In Unit 4 Exercise 1D, *Research Online Banking*, you used a search tool to locate three banks or credit unions offering online services. Revisit each bank or credit union and learn what each may or may not provide in the way of assistance for victims of identity theft.

2. Prepare a two-page press release addressing the issue of identity left. Present your press release as if you were the Identity Theft Officer of the MoneyView First Bank & Trust.

3. Review the proper formatting of a press release as shown in Part 1 Unit 10. Use this format to guide the formatting of your press release. Your press release should fit comfortably on two single-spaced pages.

4. Save and print a copy of your press release.

Going Phishing?

phishing

Criminals are using increasingly sophisticated ways to steal identities. One scam is called **phishing**. Criminals may mock up an e-mail message, complete with company logos and seemingly proper information, to fool some customers into thinking the e-mail is legitimate. Criminals out phishing are only looking for a few victims to take their bait.

Here is an example of an actual phish that was sent out over the Net through e-mail. We have removed the name of the bank because they are also victims of this scam.

Dear [name of bank] customer,

Fraudulent activity has been registered on your account. Please visit the following webpage [http://www.linktofakewebsite.com].

Once you have confirmed your account records you will be able to continue using your [name of bank] Internet Banking account.

Copyright © 2005 [name of bank]. All Rights Reserved
[name of bank] Bank, Member FDIC.

online-banking-representative@name_of_bank.com

Phishers have become more and more creative. One infamous phish proclaimed that someone's personal Internet account was about to expire due to a credit card reporting error. Unless the victim clicked a hypertext link, then entered and verified their personal information, their Internet service would be cut off within 24 hours! Naïve Internet users would take the bait, hand over all of their personal information, and then have to deal with the consequences of identity theft. For more examples, read *Famous Online Scams*.

Communicating for Success

Famous Online Scams

Here's a collection of some of the most common and famous online scams:

- An e-mail arrives, usually from the "legal representative" of a former prince of an African nation or a rich oil magnate from Russia. Having suffered political turmoil and discrimination in their country, they are looking for a partner to help them transfer millions of dollars from bank accounts in

(continued on next page)

Switzerland or the Cayman Islands to the country in which you live. All they need is someone they can trust — like you, along with your account number and a few thousand dollars — to complete the paperwork and make the process legal. If you help them, so the scam goes, you will receive a percentage of the total assets or a commission worth hundreds or thousand or even millions of dollars.

- An e-mail arrives advertising popular prescription drugs from Canada, Mexico, or the European Union at a discount. Money is spent but no drugs arrive.
- A message offers super savings on the most popular software at drastically discounted prices. The software is pirated, if it exists at all.
- A website offers pre-release copies of an upcoming popular video game at a discount to "preferred customers." The software is pirated or is an earlier version of the software.
- An offer is made for a special pre-release copy or online version of an upcoming popular novel, such as the next installment of the *Harry Potter* series. No such book exists, and your money quickly disappears.
- An offer advertises popular consumer products such as computers, cell phones, or MP3 players. After the first payment, old junk components are shipped. The shipment is just a stall tactic that will allow you to track the shipment over several days or weeks. In the meantime, the criminals are packing their bags and moving away, much to your dismay.
- An announcement proclaims you the winner of a large sum of money. To collect your earnings, all you have to do is download an attachment to the mail message, complete the form, and mail it in. By clicking on the attachment, you download a virus that scours your computer for personal data.

Protect Yourself

Most people online are honest and trustworthy. They have no intention of harming or cheating you in any way. However, don't be naïve. There are also people online who *will* cheat or harm you. For this reason, computer users must consider their personal security, even safety.

After all, when you meet someone on the Internet, you only have their word about who they are and who they represent. For instance, you probably cannot see this person, so they can say they are 18 or 19 when in reality they can be 14, 45, or 104 years old. How would you ever know?

People online often assume imaginary identities — sometimes for fun but sometimes for malicious intent. Someone may say they are a woman when they are really a man. A person may pretend to be interested in the things that interest you in order to gain your trust. The person's real motive may be to deceive, scam, or harm you.

To protect yourself, never give your full name, personal address, phone number, school address, or other private information to individuals you do not know personally. We can't emphasize this strongly enough. For example, never send your picture to someone you meet online that you do not know. Never agree to a face-to-face meeting with a person you have met online unless you have taken the time to run a security check on this person and have friends, peers, and parents present when you meet. Never meet a stranger in private. Don't take a chance with your personal privacy.

Exercise 1C

Group Discussion on Scams

1. Meet with your group and discuss spam, viruses, phishes, scams, and illegal activity associated with the online world. What experience has each team member had with scams, phishes, and other illegal online activities? Have they heard any urban legends (a fictitious story that sounds true) about Internet fraud that proved to be false? Have they heard any true stories that can be researched and validated about ways people have been scammed and cheated?

Exercise 1D

Searching Online For Problem-Solving Solutions

1. Visit two of the largest and most popular software security companies online. As you do so, take notes on the current virus threats and learn what services the companies offer for virus protection, spyware protection, firewalls, and spam blockers.

   • http://www.norton.com
   • http://www.mcafee.com/us/

2. Using Google or some other search tool, find websites for other virus protection services and companies. Take notes on what you find. For people without a lot of money, are there free or inexpensive software security solutions? How many of the sites would you trust with your computer's data?

3. There are many terms used to describe fraudulent activity and Internet attacks on networks and personal computers. If you don't already know the meaning of the following terms, look them up online:

Adware	Phishing
Backdoor	Spam
Cookies	Spyware
Encryption	Virus
Hacker	Web bugs
Malware	Worm
Zombie PC	

4. Prepare a briefing in the form of a press release assuming the role of a network administrator informing your network's users of the various threats to their data. Explain how they should protect themselves from malicious attacks to their digital data.

Corporate Responsibility

Companies have a responsibility to secure the privacy of their customers. To assist in this, many companies post a privacy policy on their websites. A privacy policy states how personal data will be stored, used, and deleted. Links such as *Privacy Statement* or *Privacy Policy* are often shown at the bottom of a site's welcome page. The first part of a typical privacy statement may read like this example, taken from http://www.thomson.com:

> This Privacy Statement relates solely to the online information collection and use practices of our website located at www.thomson.com (this "Web Site"), and not to any subdomains of this Web Site. We recognize that many visitors and users of this Web Site are concerned about the information they provide to us, and how we treat that information. This Privacy Statement, which may be updated from time to time, has been developed to address those concerns.

> **TIP**
>
> The manufacturers of Web browsers offer secure data connections. After a secure data connection is made, you will see a little icon in the shape of a lock on the status bar of your browser. Look for it the next time you're online!

Exercise 1E

Privacy Statements

1. Visit one of the popular online e-commerce sites and review the privacy and security policies. For example, how does eBay.com or Amazon.com plan to protect your private data? Read an e-commerce site's privacy policy to see if you approve of how your data may and may not be used and how it will be protected.

2. Prepare a short, three-minute verbal presentation reviewing the privacy and personal security policies of your selected e-commerce site.

Communicating for Success

E-Harassment

Online harassment is a crime. In the workplace as well as in schools, people are obligated to cultivate an atmosphere where harassment is not tolerated. The same is true for the online community. Harassment of any kind, especially regarding race, color, religion, sex, national origin, age, or disability, will not be tolerated and may be grounds for immediate dismissal on the job, possible expulsion from school, and exclusion from using the services of an Internet service provider.

Unlawful harassment is characterized by unwelcome or unsolicited verbal or physical conduct which creates an intimidating, hostile, or offensive environment. Harassment in the form of e-mail messages, text messages, podcasts, or blogs is still harassment and must be dealt with appropriately. Harassment must be reported immediately to supervisors, human resource personnel, or Internet service providers so the verbal or physical conduct can be investigated fairly.

Companies and schools are required to investigate each allegation of harassment promptly and to act accordingly. No retaliation for making or pursuing a complaint will occur. To the extent possible, all complaints and related information should remain confidential.

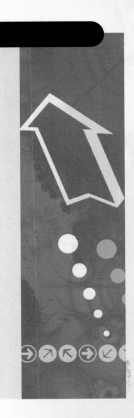

Internet Crime Investigation

1. Imagine that you are an investigative reporter doing a radio report on Internet crime. Search the Net looking for famous online crimes that would be of interest to your listeners.

2. Prepare a script to be read on the air detailing the issue of Internet crime and how people can protect themselves from harm. Use the Internet to research your sources to make sure that you don't include urban legends or other myths. Focus on real, substantiated crimes that people have encountered in the online world.

Critical Thinking/ Decision Making

Ethics: The Right Thing to Do

Imagine yourself in this situation: In a grocery store, you see your best friend putting items under her coat. What do you do? Deciding what to do in ethical situations isn't always easy. What is a good way to make an ethical decision?

1. Get the facts. Learn as much as possible about the situation before jumping to a conclusion. Make an intelligent decision rather than an emotional one.

2. Don't let assumptions get in the way of the facts. As the actor and comedian Will Rogers said, "It isn't what we don't know that gives us trouble[;] it's what we know that ain't so." You don't like it when people make assumptions about you. Make sure your judgment isn't colored by preconceptions or stereotypes.

3. Consider the consequences for everyone. Try to see the situation from the point of view of each party involved. What is each person or group likely to lose or gain as a result of your decision?

4. Consider your personal values. Apply your own beliefs and standards to the problem.

5. Make your decision.

Key a paragraph telling how you would use the five-step process to make a decision to handle the situation described above. Form a group with some other students and discuss an ethical issue in your community. Make sure everyone contributes. Did everyone in the group agree? In an e-mail to your teacher, briefly explain the issue your group chose and state your point of view. Include your reasons. Always present your viewpoint in a professional and respectful manner.

Communication & Math Skills 11

1. Study each of the six rules shown below in the color boxes.

a. Key the *Learn* line(s) beneath each rule, noting how the rule is applied.

b. Key the *Apply* lines, using quotation marks and hyphens correctly.

Internal Punctuation: Quotation Marks

Rule 1: Use quotation marks to enclose direct quotations. *Note:* When a question mark applies to the entire sentence, place it outside the quotation marks.

Learn 1   Professor Dye asked, "Are you spending the summer in Europe?"
Learn 2   Was it Emerson who said, "To have a friend is to be one"?
Apply 3   Marcella asked, May I borrow your class notes from yesterday?
Apply 4   Did John Donne say, No man is an island, entire of itself?

Rule 2: Use quotation marks to enclose titles of articles, poems, songs, television programs, and unpublished works, such as theses and dissertations.

Learn 5   Kari read aloud the poem "Fog" from Sandburg's <u>Selected Poems</u>.
Apply 6   The song Getting to Know You is reviewed in my recent article, Top Ten.
Apply 7   The title of his term paper is Computer Software for Grade 4.

Rule 3: Use quotation marks to enclose special words or phrases used for emphasis or for coined words (words not in dictionary usage).

Learn 8   My problem: I have "limited resources" and "unlimited wants."
Apply 9   His talk was filled with phrases like ah and you know.
Apply 10   She said that the words phony and braggart describe him.

Rule 4: Use a single quotation mark (the apostrophe) to indicate a quotation within a quotation (including titles and words as indicated in Rules 2 and 3, above).

Learn 11   I wrote, "We must have, as Tillich said, 'the courage to be.'"
Apply 12   I said, "As Milton wrote, he is 'sober, steadfast, and demure."
Apply 13   I say, "Don't lie, for Swift said, facts are stubborn things."

Internal Punctuation: Hyphen

Rule 5: Use a hyphen to join compound numbers from twenty-one to ninety-nine that are keyed as words.

Learn 14   Sixty-seven students met in the gym; about twenty-seven wore the uniform.
Apply 15   Thirty five guests attended Anita's twenty-first birthday party.
Apply 16   Thirty four delegates went to the national convention.

Rule 6: Use a hyphen to join compound adjectives preceding a noun they modify as a unit.

Learn 17   End-of-term grades will be posted outside the classroom.
Apply 18   The most up to date fashions are featured in the store window.
Apply 19   Their new computer programs feature state of the art graphics.

2. Key *Proofread & Correct*, using quotation marks and hyphens correctly.

a. Check answers.

b. Using the rule number(s) at the left of each line, study the rule relating to each error you made.

c. Rekey each incorrect line, using quotation marks and hyphens correctly.

Proofread & Correct

1   1   The coach asked, How many of you practiced during the summer?

1   2   Didn't Browne say, "There is no road or ready way to virtue?"

2   3   Do you and your sister regularly watch National Geographic on TV?

2   4   My mom's column, Speak Up, appears in the local newspaper.

3   5   You have trouble deciding when to use accept and except.

1,4   6   I said, I must take, as Frost wrote, 'the road less traveled.

5   7   Jae boasted, "I'm almost twenty one; you're thirty two."

6   8   My older self confident cousin sells life insurance door to door.

6   9   The hard working outfitter readied our canoe faster than I expected.

6   10   Over the counter sales showed a great increase last month.

3. Save as *CS11-ACT1*.

ACTIVITY 2   Preparing to Speak

1. You have been selected to introduce a speaker, Douglas H. Ruckert, to your class. His resume appears in the file *CD-CS11-ACT2*. The introduction is to be 30" to 1'. The audience is your classmates.

2. Review the resume and decide which points you will include in your introduction.

3. Key an outline of these points.

4. If time and resources permit, record your speech in a sound file.

5. Save the outline as *CS11-ACT2* and the sound file as *CS11-ACT2-SOUND*.

ACTIVITY 3   Write to Learn

1. Using word processing or voice recognition software, write a paragraph explaining how to print one page from a website.

2. Write a second paragraph explaining how to change the background of a Web page.

3. Save as *CS11-ACT3*.

ACTIVITY 4   Reading

1. Open *CD-CS11-ACT4*.

2. Read the document; close the file.

3. Key answers to the questions, using complete sentences.

4. Save as *CS11-ACT4*.

1. What service does WebGate provide?

2. What is the amount of the most recent acquisition?

3. Was WebGate founded more than five years ago?

4. In what states does WebGate do business?

5. In what state does the most recent acquisition do business?

6. Have all acquisitions been financed by a Charlotte bank?

7. About how many customers does WebGate serve?

ACTIVITY 5   Math: Working with Probability

1. Open *CD-CS11-ACT5* and print the file.

2. Solve the problems as directed in the file.

3. Submit your answers.

Part 3

UNIT 1

Conditioning Practice

Before you begin the lessons, key each line twice.

alphabet 1 Quent packed an extra big jar of very zesty wild apples for them.

figures 2 I tried this equation: $7(12X + 140) + 5(X - 6) = 3(X + 50) - 98$.

speed 3 The ensign works with the busy official to right the big problem.

gwam	1'	1	2	3	4	5	6	7	8	9	10	11	12	13

LESSON 1 MOBILE COMPUTING

OBJECTIVES

- To explore mobile computing.
- To learn about handtyping hardware.
- To discover handtyping software.
- To practice hovering.
- To substitute mouse movements with digital pen movements.

Computers on the Go

There are some jobs that require people to be on the move, constantly interacting with others. For instance, Hilary is a salesperson. She travels around her state to meet with clients three or four days a week. She needs a mobile computer she can take with her wherever she may be. A big, heavy, desktop computer simply will not do.

Mari, a university student, finds it tiring to sit at a desktop computer studying for hours on end. Sometimes she likes to take her schoolwork to her favorite café or sit under a shady tree and complete her work away from her dormitory or the library.

Sometimes, professionals like Cory feel like taking their work home with them and getting out of the office for a change. He needs a computer that he can use to **telecommute**

telecommute—a common term for working at home—between his corporate office and his home. Cory also has to travel a great deal in his job, bouncing from London to New York to Hong Kong several times a year. He needs a compact, fully powered computer that can travel with him around the world.

An entirely new generation of lightweight, mobile, and powerful PCs have been created for people like Hilary, Cory, and Mari. These include tablet PCs, personal digital assistants or PDAs, and smart phones. (Learn about PDAs and smart phones in Appendix A.)

Handtyping Hardware

One of the remaining constraints to truly mobile computing is the dependence some users have on the keyboard and mouse. Recently, exciting and effective alternatives have been created:

- Handwriting recognition using a digital pen.
- Speech recognition using a wireless or USB headset.
- Projected keyboards using a laser projection system.

Speech recognition will be covered in Part 3 Unit 2. This unit will focus on handwriting recognition and the **digital pen** as an essential alternative input tool for computer users.

digital pen

A digital pen has an unlimited supply of digital ink and can only write on special computer screens and handwriting boards attached to personal computers. Digital pens can be used for both **handtyping** and **inking**. On-screen handtyping and inking will help improve your hand-eye coordination.

handtyping
inking

- Handtyping converts your handwritten words into typed text just as if you typed it on a keyboard. At the end of this lesson, you should be handtyping with ease.
- Using a digital pen to draw, doodle, and sketch, or to write in your own handwriting, is called inking. You'll have fun handwriting and sketching with your digital pen.

With luck, you will be able to try inking and handtyping on a **tablet PC**, as seen in Figure IT1-1. A tablet PC is a radical new computer designed specifically for handwritten, handtyped, and speech recognition input. A tablet PC is part of a growing family of smaller, lighter, and more powerful computers built for mobile users.

tablet PC

Thousands of new applications have been created for these exciting new technologies. For instance, take a look at Mari in Figure IT1-2. She is using *Microsoft OneNote* for notetaking. She isn't huddled over a keyboard typing away, but is tak-

| **Figure IT1-1** | Tablets Provide Radical New Designs for Mobile Computers | **Figure IT1-2** | Digital Notetaking Can Be Like Writing on Paper |

© AP / WIDE WORLD PHOTOS

© SUNNY PHOTOGRAPHY.COM / ALAMY

A Wacom Handwriting Tablet Allows Handwriting Recognition on Desktop and Laptop PCs

© COURTESY OF WACOM TECHNOLOGY CORP.

ing notes as naturally and as comfortably as if she were writing on a yellow pad of note paper. Because Mari is using a tablet PC, she can write her notes directly on the glass surface of the computer's monitor.

If you don't have a Tablet PC, you can still use handwriting recognition and a digital pen with a traditional desktop or laptop PC by adding a Wacom handwriting board, as pictured in Figure IT1-3. Using a Wacom board is a great way to learn and practice one of the most important new computer literacy skills—penmanship. That's right; penmanship has now become an essential computer literacy skill, a skill with which everyone must become proficient in order to be effective with future technologies.

Handwriting Recognition Software

Computer scientists have worked for years to perfect handwriting recognition. Today, many professionals and students alike are benefiting from these breakthroughs. Inking and handtyping can be subdivided into five separate categories of software tools. In this next section, you can preview each category before beginning.

Instant Message

Typically, people can handtype at approximately 20–30 *wpm*. Accuracy depends on the quality of one's penmanship. With handtyping tools, good penmanship is always rewarded!

- Handtyping tools
- Character-by-character (or Graffiti) handtyping tools
- Tappable keyboards
- Handwriting/inking tools
- Drawing/inking tools

Figure IT1-4

Turn Your Handwriting Into Typing

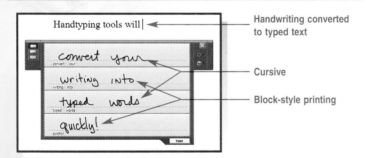

Handwriting converted to typed text

Cursive

Block-style printing

Handtyping Tools

Handtyping tools will allow you to convert your handwriting into typed text. This is done in a couple of ways. On a tablet PC, you can select your handwritten sentences and have your cursive or printed writing converted into typed words after you've written them.

More typically, however, you will use an Input Panel tool called Writing Pad to enter your handwritten words. The words are inserted as typed text into a document. Both block-style printing and cursive styles are recognized, as seen in Figure IT1-4.

Figure IT1-5

Letter-by-Letter DigiTools Are Popular for Editing

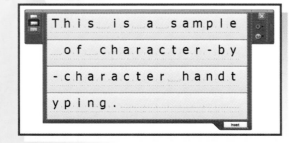

Character-by-Character (*or Graffiti*) *Handtyping Tools*

Some people feel more comfortable writing one letter at a time. Individual letter-based or character-by-character software tools are often called Graffiti. Graffiti is very popular on

PDAs and is also helpful for editing and handtyping on tablet PCs and Wacom boards. If you just need to change a letter or two in a word or need to make a precise edit, you can't beat this DigiTool. (See Figure IT1-5.)

Tappable Keyboards

Tappable keyboard software is often used to enter passwords, edit text, or insert special characters or symbols. Also called virtual keyboards, tappable keyboards are not a very fast means to handtype, but when a keyboard isn't handy, the tappable method is available. Tappable keyboards are also important tools on PDAs. (See Figure IT1-6.)

Figure IT1-6   Tappable Keyboards Come in Handy for Special Characters and Editing

Handwriting/Inking Tools

Inking tools allow you to take notes or sign documents in your own handwriting. They also allow you to mark up an existing "typed" document with corrective marks or notations. (See Figure IT1-7.)

Ink/Drawing Tools

Drawing tools have been part of the desktop computing experience since the very beginning of the PC age. Artists have long known that digital pens allow them more control and precision over their work. But even if you lack the talent of Leonardo da Vinci, you can still use the drawing tools to doodle, sketch, plan, and brainstorm—using pictures instead of words to explain your ideas and creativity. (See Figure IT1-8.)

For example, before creating a *PowerPoint* presentation, you may need to create a storyboard with thumbnail sketches of what each slide should communicate.

Office versus Windows/Tablet PC Handwriting Software

There are now many versions of Microsoft's handwriting recognition software: some newer and some older. They work in similar ways. Nevertheless, there are enough differences that the instructions for *Office* and Windows/tablet PC versions of the software have been divided at key points during this unit. The instructions you follow will depend on the software and hardware tools you are using. Follow the instructions that best fit your version of handwriting and skip the rest, as explained in Table 1-1.

Figure IT1-7   Take Notes, Sign Documents, or Make Corrections Using Ink Technologies

Paper too short. Need More information for an A.

B+

A BRIEF HISTORY OF THE PEN

By Mari Rosales

Handwriting recognition is one of the most impressive inventions in the short history of personal computers. However, would anyone have thought about making a digital pen if the ~~normal~~ pen hadn't been invented in the first place?
^ ink

Early pens were often made from the tips of bird feathers sharpened with a knife. The tips would be dipped in ink. Only a few words could be scratched out before the tips ran out of ink and they had to be dipped into an ink bottle again. Feathers were soon replaced with metal-tipped pens that didn't need to be sharpened.

The Fountain Pen

Constantly dipping into an ink bottle became too much trouble for a New York businessman, ~~named~~ **Lewis Waterman,** who invented the first workable fountain pen **in 1884**. Earlier attempts at such a pen didn't work very well and were just downright messy, with ink flowing unevenly across the paper. The new fountain pen used capillary action to feed ink to the tip of the pen, which flowed out smoothly and evenly. Many pages could be written before the ink reservoir inside the pen had to be refilled.

Figure IT1-8   Drawing Tools Have Become Easier to Use

Table 1-1 Software Comparison Chart

Use **Microsoft Office Instructions** if:	Use **Microsoft Windows/Tablet PC Instructions** if:
You are using a desktop or laptop PC and are running Microsoft Office XP or Microsoft Office 2003 handwriting recognition tools.	*You have a tablet PC running Microsoft Windows XP Tablet PC Edition or Microsoft Windows Vista.*
 © COURTESY OF WACOM TECHNOLOGY CORP. You will probably be using a Wacom handwriting board and a digital pen to accomplish this task. In the absence of a Wacom board, you can substitute a mouse but with limited efficiency.	Your task will be much easier because you can write directly on the screen of the PC. You'll also  © GETTY IMAGES be able to use some advanced handwriting recognition features unavailable on desktop PCs, laptop PCs, smart phones, and PDAs.

Hover Before You Touch Down

pen pointer

You must learn to hover your digital pen over your Tablet PC screen or Wacom handwriting board. Hover 1/4" above the surface to move the mouse pointer, which has been aptly renamed the **pen pointer**. The pen pointer will change shape depending on the object it is hovering over. It may be an arrow, a vertical bar, an hourglass, a multisided arrow, a hand, or a pen. Common pen pointer shapes are seen in Figure IT1-9.

There are two separate hardware devices you can use with your digital pen. Mastering the hovering skill is essential for both tools, albeit there are significant differences in how the two tools respond. See Table 1-2 to learn the differences before continuing to the next exercise.

Figure IT1-9 Common Pen Pointer Shapes

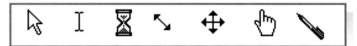

Table 1-2 How to Hover

Microsoft Office Instructions	Microsoft Windows/Tablet PC
Notice the rectangle drawn in the middle of the Wacom handwriting board/tablet. This rectangle represents your computer screen and the outer limit of where the pen may hover. You must hover 1/4" above the surface of the board/tablet within the rectangle.	On a tablet PC, hover the pen pointer to every corner and part of your screen's desktop by sliding your digital pen 1/4" above the surface of the glass.
Your pen pointer may stop moving when the pen's tip reaches the edge of the rectangle. Lift your pen 2" off the surface of the board, bring your hand back to the middle of the rectangle, and then continue pushing the pen pointer into the four corners of the Windows desktop.	

Exercise 1A

Happy Hovering

Combined Office and Microsoft Windows/Tablet PC Instructions

1. Before beginning, review these pen tips:

   • Hold your digital pen normally, but slightly more upright than you would a normal number 2 pencil or a ballpoint pen. (Many incorrectly grip the pen in the middle or as if they were holding a stick!)

   • Keep your fingers curved.

   • Don't grip the pen too tightly.

   • Don't press down hard with your pen or you may damage the surface of a tablet PC's screen, a Wacom board, or the tip of your digital pen.

2. Hover 1/4" from the surface of your board or tablet. Observe the pen pointer as you move your digital pen around the screen's desktop in a slow circle. (Read Table 1-2 for more information.)

3. Hover your digital pen and move the pen pointer to the four corners of your Windows desktop. Move the pen pointer to the:

   • Top right corner of the screen

   • Bottom left corner of the screen

   • Top left corner of the screen

   • Bottom right corner of the screen

   Then return to the center of the screen.

> **Tip**
>
> You can rest your hand lightly on the surface of a tablet PC or on a Wacom handwriting board.

> **Instant Message**
>
> It helps to focus your gaze on the pen pointer rather than on the tip of your digital pen.

Tap, Double Tap, Touch and Drag

Practice the various pen movements that replace mouse movements. You'll need to tap, double tap, and touch and drag instead of clicking. These movements are explained in Table 1-3.

In the next exercise, practice opening applications and using the Minimize, Maximize, Restore, and Resize functions with a digital pen instead of a mouse.

Table 1-3 Comparing Pen and Mouse Movements

Pen Movement	Mouse Movement
Tap	click
double tap	double click
touch and drag	click and drag

Exercise 1B

Open, Close, and Manipulate Microsoft Word

1. Hover down to your **Start** menu button and tap on it with a single quick and steady tap.

2. Hover up to **(All) Programs** and tap that option.

3. Hover to your *Microsoft Office* folder, open it, and open *Microsoft Word*. Hover and tap as needed.

4. To expand the *Microsoft Word* window to its maximum size, tap the **Maximize** button. (See Figure IT1-10.)

Figure IT1-10 The Restore and Maximize Buttons

Restore ⟶   ⟵ Maximize

5. To restore *Microsoft Word* to a smaller window, tap the **Restore** button seen in Figure IT1-10.

6. Touch and drag the **resize** handle, located in the bottom left corner of the restored window, to change the size of the window. (See Figure IT1-11.)

Figure IT1-11 The Resize Handle

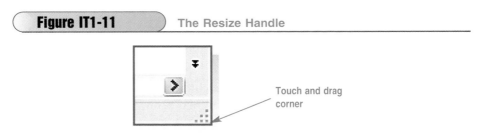

Touch and drag corner

7. To minimize *Microsoft Word* so that it appears on the Start menu taskbar, tap the **Minimize** button. (See Figure IT1-12.)

Figure IT1-12 The Minimize Button

8. To restore *Microsoft Word* and have it appear once again on the desktop, tap the **Microsoft Word icon** on the taskbar. (See Figure IT1-13.)

Figure IT1-13 The Minimized Document in the Taskbar

Tap the *Word* document button

9. To close *Microsoft Word*, tap the **Close** button. (See Figure IT1-14.)

Figure IT1-14 The Close Button

10. Return to step 2 and redo the maximize, minimize, restore, and resizing techniques, repeating the above steps with the following applications.
    - *Paint*
    - *Microsoft PowerPoint*
    - *Microsoft Excel*

Instant Message

Take a few extra minutes to draw or paint in *Microsoft Paint* using your digital pen.

LESSON (2) HANDTYPING AND THE INPUT PANEL

- ⊙ To compare Windows tablet PC to *Microsoft Office* handwriting DigiTools.
- ⊙ To find your handwriting recognition tools.
- ⊙ To manipulate the Language bar or Input Panel.
- ⊙ To practice handtyping with printed characters.
- ⊙ To practice handtyping with cursive characters.

You're Only a Tap Away

With Microsoft's latest handwriting software you're only one tap away from all of the digital input tools described in Lesson 1. In the next lessons, you'll get a chance to try each one of them. But first, you must locate your tools. Follow the instructions that most closely match your version of Microsoft's handwriting software.

Exercise 2A

Find and Manipulate Your Handwriting Tools

Instructions appear for both *Microsoft Office* handwriting recognition and tablet PC users. Follow the instructions that best fit your handwriting software.

Microsoft Office Instructions

For *Microsoft Office* versions of handwriting recognition, you will use the Language bar as seen in Figure IT1-16. The Language bar is a DigiTool that contains both speech and handwriting recognition commands and options.

1. Open *Microsoft Word*. If handwriting recognition has already been installed properly on your PC, you will see the Language bar as shown in Figure IT1-16. If you don't see the Language bar, tap **Tools**, **Speech**, as seen in Figure IT1-15. (*Note:* Your software may want to install speech recognition at this time. Choose **Cancel** and then **OK** to prevent this as you will not be needing speech recognition until the next unit.)

Figure IT1-15 Open the Language Bar in *Microsoft Word*

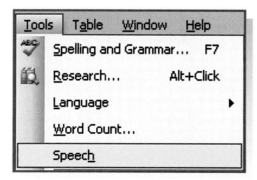

2. When the Microphone has been turned off, the Language bar will appear in its collapsed state, as shown in Figure IT1-16. If the speech recognition microphone is on, the Language bar will be expanded and will have additional buttons. Since you will not use speech recognition at this time, click or tap the **Microphone** button to turn speech recognition off and return the Language bar to its collapsed state.

Figure IT1-16   The Language Bar Provides Access to Handwriting Tools

3. Tap the **Minimize** button, shown in Figure IT1-16, to send the Language bar to the taskbar.

4. When the Language bar is on the taskbar, it will look similar to Figure IT1-17. Choose the **Restore** button to bring the Language bar back to the desktop.

Figure IT1-17   The Minimized Language Bar on the Taskbar

5. Tap the **Handwriting** button on the Language bar. Choose **Writing Pad**. The Writing Pad will open, as shown in Figure IT1-18.

Figure IT1-18   Writing Pad

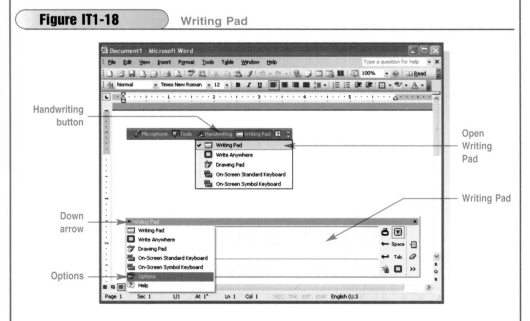

Turn Off Automatic Recognition. *Microsoft Office* handwriting recognition has an important setting called automatic recognition. This option inserts text automatically into a document after a short pause. However, most people find this option frustrating at first because it doesn't allow time to correct mistakes. Turning off Automatic recognition will allow you to control the pace of your handwriting and to erase errors.

6. Tap the down arrow on the Writing Pad title bar and choose **Options**. (See Figure IT1-18.)

7. Tap the **Common** tab as marked in Figure IT1-19. Remove the check mark next to **Automatic recognition**. Tap **OK** to return to Writing Pad.

Figure IT1-19 Uncheck Automatic Recognition in the Handwriting Options Dialog Box

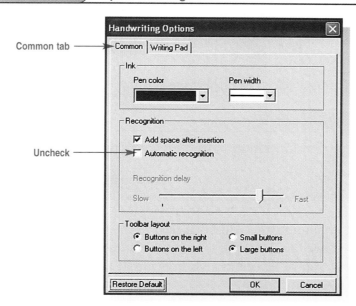

8. Close Writing Pad by tapping the **Close** button on the title bar in the upper-right corner of Writing Pad.

9. Tap the **Handwriting** button on the Language bar. Choose **Drawing Pad**. The Drawing Pad will open. Use this tool for making and inserting simple drawings into your documents. Close Writing Pad by tapping the **Close** button.

10. Tap the **Handwriting** button on the Language bar and choose the **On-screen keyboard** button. One of the tappable keyboard options will appear. Close your tappable keyboard by tapping the **Close** button.

Microsoft Windows/Tablet PC Instructions

1. If the Tablet PC Input Panel can't be seen, tap the **Tablet PC Input Panel** (TIP) button next to the Start button. (See Figure IT1-20.)

Figure IT1-20 The Tablet PC Input Panel Button

2. Tap the **Character Pad** button to display the character-by-character input feature. (See Figure IT1-21.)

Figure IT1-21 The Character Pad

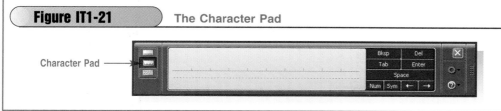

3. Tap the **Keyboard** button to display the On-Screen Keyboard. (See Figure IT1-22.)

Figure IT1-22   The On-Screen Keyboard

Keyboard button

4. Tap the **Writing Pad** tab to display the Writing Pad. (See Figure IT1-23.)

Figure IT1-23   The Writing Pad

Writing Pad button

Close button

5. The Windows Input Panel can be docked to the top or the bottom of the screen or allowed to float. Choose the **Tools and Options** button and select **Dock at Top of Screen** as seen in Figure IT1-24.

Figure IT1-24   Dock the Input Panel at the Top of the Screen

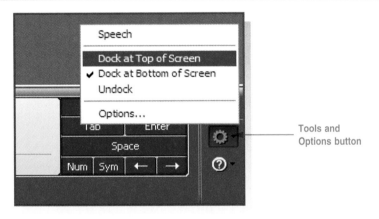

Tools and Options button

6. Choose the **Tools and Options** button and select **Dock at Bottom of Screen**.

7. Open *Microsoft Word* first. Then choose **Tools and Options** button and select **Undock**.

8. Hover 1/4" over the surface of *Microsoft Word*. Look for the small **Input Panel icon** that looks like a tappable keyboard with a little pen over it, as seen in Figure IT1-25. Tap on the icon to open the Input Panel.

Figure IT1-25   Hover and Tap to See the Input Panel Icon

9. Choose the **Tools and Options** button and select **Dock at Bottom of Screen**. (*Note:* If the Tablet PC Input Panel can't be seen, tap the **Tablet PC Input Panel** button next to the Start button to reveal the Input Panel again.)

10. To hide the Tablet Input Panel completely, tap the **Tablet PC Input Panel** button next to the Start button or click the **Close** box in the top right corner of the Input Panel.

Note: With a tablet **PC**, change the orientation of your screen from portrait to landscape mode by pressing the orientation buttons on the side of the monitor, as explained in your owner's manual; or by opening the Tablet and Pen Settings Control Panel and changing the orientation of the screen. (See Figure IT1-26.)

Figure IT1-26　　Screen Orientations

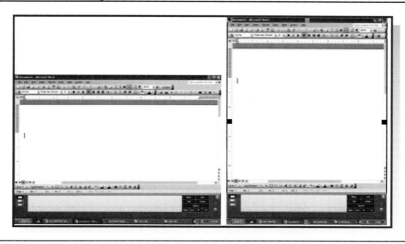

Writing with Style

Microsoft analyzed hundreds of thousands of handwriting samples in order to discover the most common writing styles. As a result, Writing Pad can understand several styles of handwriting:

- Vertical printing
- Slanted printing
- Vertical cursive
- Slanted cursive

In Figure IT1-27, see how both block style and a cursive sentences have been converted into typed text.

Figure IT1-27　　Both Printing and Cursive Are Recognized

Lazlo Biro created the ballpoint pen!
Lazlo Biro created the ballpoint pen!

Lewis Waterman created the fountain pen!
Lewis Waterman created the fountain pen!

Penmanship Matters

If you write clearly, chances are the software will understand your writing. With handtyping tools, penmanship matters! Skills you may not have thought about since you were a kid in elementary school will quickly be brought to mind.

The key to successful handtyping accuracy is to write clearly. What handwriting recognition software cannot recognize is sloppy writing or words that are incomplete or semi-scribbled. Try using your best block-style printing and cursive styles to see if they are accurate for you. As you practice, you will find that your handwriting will gradually improve.

You should be able to clip along handtyping at approximately 15 to 30 *wpm*—but don't worry about handtyping speed; focus only on handwriting clarity. Handtype each word carefully and remember these additional hints:

- Separate words by at least 1/2" of blank space.
- Enter punctuation marks immediately after a word.
- Do not try to write too many words on a line. One or two words is sufficient.
- When you have finished writing, send the text by tapping the appropriate command.
- Write slightly larger than you normally would on paper.
- It isn't always necessary to dot your i's or cross your t's, but doing so can help improve recognition accuracy.

Block-Style Printing

Start by practicing your best block-style printed letters. Over the years, you may have developed your own handwriting style. You are welcome to try your style and see how it works. However, you may be more accurate if you use the same printing or block style you learned in elementary school. Table 1-4 will remind you how to form the traditional block letters taught in the elementary grades.

Table 1-4	Printed Characters

a b c d e f g h i j k l m n o p q r s t u v w x y z
A B C D E F G H I J K L M N O P Q R S T U V W X Y Z

Exercise 2B

Practice Printing

Instructions appear for both *Microsoft Office* handwriting recognition and tablet PC users. Follow the instructions that best fit your handwriting software.

Microsoft Office Instructions

1. Open *Microsoft Word*, the Language bar, and the **Writing Pad** tool.
2. Tap the **Text** button seen in Figure IT1-28 and skip to step 3 below the Windows/Tablet PC Instructions.

Figure IT1-28 — Write Using Printed Characters

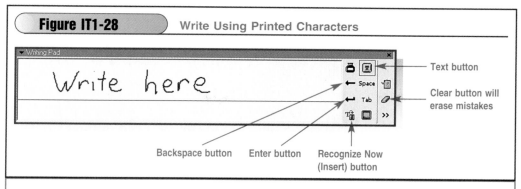

Text button

Clear button will erase mistakes

Backspace button   Enter button   Recognize Now (Insert) button

Windows/Tablet PC Instructions

1. Open *Microsoft Word.* Open the **TIP**.

2. Tap the **Writing Pad** button as seen in Figure IT1-29, and then jump to step 3 below.

Figure IT1-29 — Write on a Tablet PC TIP with Printed Characters

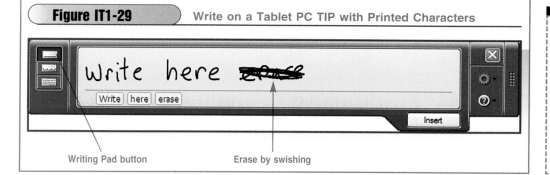

Writing Pad button   Erase by swishing

Combined Office and Windows/Tablet PC Instructions

3. Print the words Accuracy matters! above the line in Writing Pad as shown in Figures IT1-28 and IT1-29. (If your handwriting is sloppy, erase mistakes as explained in the Tips before inadvertently inserting them into your document.)

4. Choose the **Insert** button (Windows/tablet PC) or the **Recognize Now** button (*Office*) to insert the text into your document.

5. Replace the word *Accuracy* with the word Penmanship. Touch and drag over the word *Accuracy* in your document as seen in Figure IT1-30. Tap the BACKSPACE button to erase the word. Position your insertion point (flashing line) in front of the word *matters*. In Writing Pad, write the word Penmanship and choose the **Insert** or **Recognize Now** button. Your sentence should now read *Penmanship matters!*

Figure IT1-30 — Substitute the Word

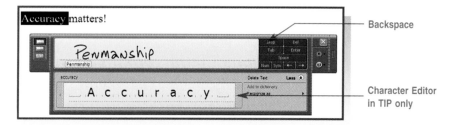

Backspace

Character Editor in TIP only

6. Replace the word *matters* with the word counts. Your sentence should now read *Penmanship counts!*

7. Position your insertion point after the exclamation point (!). Tap ENTER twice to create a double space.

8. Handtype the following sentence. Only write a few words on each line. When you see the |, tap the **Insert** or **Recognize Now** button to send that word or phrase; then continue writing the next two or three words of the sentence.

Handwriting | recognition | is one of | the great | inventions | in the history | of computing.

9. Tap the ENTER button twice after you complete the sentence.

10. Make the following changes to your sentence:
    - Replace the word *great* with the words most important.
    - Between the words *of computing*, insert the word personal so the phrase reads *of personal computing*.

11. Touch and drag over the entire sentence, and then tap the BACKSPACE button to erase it.

Instant Message

If your words bunch and crunch together and you need to add a space, tap your insertion point between the words and tap the Space button. If more spaces appear than are needed, use the BACKSPACE button to delete them.

Handtype with Cursive Characters

Cursive is a faster, smoother way to write. In this next exercise, use cursive to handtype. If you are a bit rusty, review the characters in Table 1-5.

Table 1-5 Cursive Characters

a b c d e f g h i j k l m n o p q r s t u v w x y z
A B C D E F G H I J K L M N O P Q R S T U V W X Y Z

Exercise **2C**

Practice Cursive in Writing Pad

Office and Windows/Tablet PC Instructions Combined

Instant Message

Leave about 1/2" of space between words.

1. Start *Word* and open Writing Pad. Write the sentences below using cursive letters. Remember to write just a few words at a time. Then tap the **Insert** or **Recognize Now** button to place the text in your document. Use the ENTER key to leave one blank line between sentences.

Using a | digital pen | takes a | bit of | practice.

Tapping | with a | digital pen | can be | faster than | clicking with | a mouse.

2. Now try four more sentences using cursive letters. Decide for yourself how many words to place on each individual line before you send or insert the text.

Do you know the history of the pen?

The fountain pen was a big improvement over writing with ink and feathers!

The ballpoint pen is less messy, less expensive, and less trouble than a fountain pen.

It is completely true; a digital pen works best on tablets or handwriting boards.

3. Save your work as *Exercise IT1-2C* and exit your document. If possible, try saving by tapping with a digital pen instead of clicking your mouse. If you can, use the tappable keyboard to name the file.

Exercise 2D
Handtype with Writing Pad

Office and Windows/Tablet PC Instructions Combined

1. Start *Word* and open Writing Pad again. Start with a new, blank document and handtype the two paragraphs below. Use either cursive or printed writing styles, whichever works best for you.

Handwriting recognition is one of the most impressive inventions in the short history of personal computers. However, would anyone have thought about making a digital pen if the normal pen hadn't been invented in the first place?

Early pens were often made from the tips of bird feathers sharpened with a knife. The tips would be dipped in ink. Only a few words could be scratched out before the tips ran out of ink and they had to be dipped into an ink bottle again. Feathers were soon replaced with metal-tipped pens that didn't need to be sharpened.

2. Correct any mistakes using your digital pen as much as possible. Save the document as *The History of Pens*.

LESSON 3 CORRECTING, EDITING, AND FORMATTING DOCUMENTS

OBJECTIVES

- To correct mistakes before they are inserted as text.
- To use the character editor to correct mistakes on a tablet PC.
- To practice making corrections and edits to existing text.
- To create a heading with a tappable keyboard and the Caps Lock option.
- To format a report using tappable keyboard shortcuts.

Correction Techniques

There are two places to make corrections:

- In Writing Pad before mistakes are inserted into a document.
- In an existing document.

Clearly, it's better to catch mistakes before they enter your document. But sometimes changes need to be made after the fact. For example, you may be writing and decide to reword a sentence. Such editing utilizes the same correction techniques used to correct a misrecognition. Recent improvements in handwriting recognition provide clever new ways to make edits and catch mistakes. Learn more about two of these techniques.

Technique 1: Swish or Clear the Mistake

As you learned in the *Tips* in the previous lesson, if you are using *Office* handwriting, tap the Clear button to erase any misrecognized words in Writing Pad. If you are using a tablet PC and Windows handwriting recognition, quickly swish back and forth three or four times across a word with your digital pen to erase a mistake. (See Figure IT1-28 for *Office* handwriting recognition and Figure IT1-29 for Windows/tablet PC handwriting recognition.)

Technique 2: Use the Correction List

If you select a mistaken word and open the correction list, a variety of alternatives will appear. Pick the correct option from the list, as seen in Figure IT1-31 for *Microsoft Office* and Figure IT1-32 for Windows/tablet PC handwriting software.

Office Instructions

1. Select the mistaken word.

2. Choose the **Correction** button.

3. Pick the correct word from the list.

4. If the word does not appear in the list, rewrite the word, and insert it.

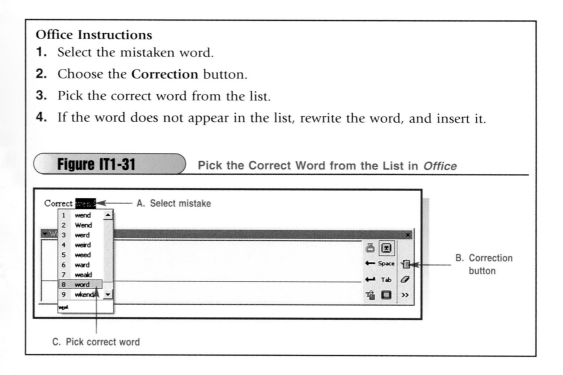

Figure IT1-31   Pick the Correct Word from the List in *Office*

Windows/Tablet PC Instructions

1. Use the TIP in the undocked mode.

2. Select the mistaken word.

3. Pick the correct word from the correction list if it appears.

4. If the word does not appear in the list, use the character recognizer to correct the mistake.

Figure IT1-32 | Pick the Correct Word from the List in the TIP in Undocked Mode

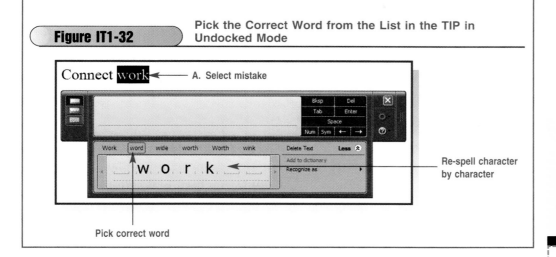

With Windows handwriting recognition on a tablet PC, making changes never requires the keyboard. Editing, however, is easier for most in the **undocked** mode. After you have switched to undocked mode, simply select the misrecognition. A list will appear along with a character-by-character input screen. If the correct alternative appears in the list, choose the alternative. If it doesn't, simply enter the correct letters one at a time. (See Figure IT1-32.)

Practice these error correction techniques as you complete handtyping your report on the history of the pen.

> **TIP**
>
> If you have a word or name that is not in the common English dictionary, you can tap the Add to Dictionary option. Adding the word to the dictionary will increase the likelihood that it can be hand-typed correctly.

Exercise 3A

Add to a Report

Office and Windows/Tablet PC Instructions Combined

1. Open "The History of Pens" report you started in Exercise 2D.

2. Add the following two paragraphs to the bottom of your report. Be sure to correct each and every mistake using the techniques described at the beginning of this lesson.

Constantly dipping into an ink bottle became too much trouble for a New York businessman, who invented the first workable fountain pen. Earlier attempts at such a pen didn't work very well and were just downright messy, with ink flowing unevenly across the paper. The new fountain pen used capillary action to feed ink to the tip of the pen, which flowed out smoothly and evenly. Many pages could be written before the ink reservoir inside the pen had to be refilled.

The ballpoint pen, however, quickly replaced the fountain pen after its invention. It was invented by a Hungarian journalist who grew tired of constantly refilling his fountain pen. Also, even the best fountain pens could still be very messy if a spill occurred while refilling the pen with ink. Spilling was a huge problem for pilots and flight crews flying at high altitude. During World War II, the British Royal Air Force used ballpoint pens to solve this problem. Soon the ballpoint pen was flying high and became the dominant pen used today.

3. Resave your combined paragraphs as *The History of Pens.*

Keyboard- and Mouse-Free Formatting

You can do anything with a digital pen that you used to do with both the keyboard and mouse combined. It's two DigiTools in one. However, it will take a little practice to learn how to format and do all the things you used to do with the mouse and keyboard. In this exercise, you will format your report on the history of pens in *Microsoft Word* without your keyboard and mouse.

One of the things that people like about keyboards are the shortcut or combination keystrokes that accomplish certain tasks very quickly. Fortunately, you can accomplish the same tasks with a tappable keyboard. For example, if you tap the Caps Lock key, every letter you touch will be capitalized. If you select text and tap the Control (CTRL) key followed by the b, then a selection of text will be bolded. Review Table 1-6 for a more complete list of tappable keyboard shortcuts.

Table 1-6 Tappable Keyboard Shortcuts

Command	Action
Caps button	Makes every subsequent letter a capital letter
CTRL + b	Applies bold format
CTRL + i	Applies italic format
CTRL + u	Applies underline format
CTRL + x	Cuts selected text
CTRL + c	Copies selected text
CTRL + v	Pastes copied or cut text

Exercise 3B

Using Tappable Shortcuts

Office and Windows/Tablet PC Instructions Combined

1. Start *Microsoft Word* and open the tappable keyboard.

   - In Office, choose the **Handwriting** button on the Language bar and select **On Screen-Keyboard**.

   - In Windows/tablet PC, open the **Tablet Input Panel (TIP)** and choose the **On-Screen keyboard** button. (See Figure IT1-22.)

2. Reopen your report called *The History of Pens*.

3. Position your insertion point at the top of your document. Tap the ENTER key four times to create a quadruple space at the top of your report so you can enter a title. Use the arrow keys on your handwriting software to move up four spaces.

4. Tap the CAPS button to reveal capital letters. Tap in the following title for your report. Tap the Space Bar button to leave a space between words.

In *Office* handwriting recognition, tap the >> button to reveal the arrow keys.

A BRIEF HISTORY OF THE PEN

5. Tap the CAPS button again to return to the On-screen Standard keyboard.

6. Using the tappable keyboard, select the heading and then tap the **Center** button in *Microsoft Word*.

7. Select the heading again and press **CTRL + b** combination to bold the heading.

8. Using either the tappable keyboard or the character-by-character input method described at the beginning of this lesson, make the following edits to improve the historical accuracy of your report. The improvements are marked in bold in Figure IT1-33.

   - Add **named Lewis Waterman**, and **in 1884** to the first sentence in the third paragraph so it reads, *Constantly dipping into an ink bottle became too much trouble for a New York businessman,* **named Lewis Waterman,** *who invented the first workable fountain pen* **in 1884**.

   - Add **in 1838** and **Laszlo Biro**, to the sentences in the fourth paragraph so it reads, *The ballpoint pen, however, quickly replaced the fountain pen after its invention* **in 1938**. *It was invented by* **Laszlo Biro**, *a Hungarian journalist who grew tired of constantly refilling his fountain pen.*

   - Create a side head called **The Fountain Pen** just above the paragraph about Lewis Waterman's invention.

   - Create another side heading called **The Ballpoint Pen** just above the paragraph about Laszlo Biro's invention.

   - Use the **CTRL + i** and the **CTRL + b** shortcuts to bold and italicize both side headings.

9. Key two spaces below the last paragraph and then Key By <Your Name> either with the tappable keyboard or with the character-by-character input tools.

Some digital pens have right and left click-equivalent buttons on the side of their pens. Try clicking these buttons while you are hovering using your thumb.

10. Select **By <Your Name>** by touching and dragging over your name. Then press **CTRL + x** to cut the text. Using your digital pen, scroll to the top of your document, and then on the third line, just below the title, press **CTRL + v** to paste your name.

11. Center and bold your name. Add two extra spaces after your name, as seen in Figure IT1-33.

12. Position your insertion point at the beginning of each paragraph, and tap the **TAB** button to indent each paragraph 1/2" from the left margin.

13. Using the handtyping input method of your choice, key the final or concluding paragraph to your report, as seen in Figure IT1-33.

Figure IT1-33　　Your Final Handtyped and Formatted Report

A BRIEF HISTORY OF THE PEN

By <Your Name>

Handwriting recognition is one of the most impressive inventions in the short history of personal computers. However, would anyone have thought about making a digital pen if the normal pen hadn't been invented in the first place?

Early pens were often made from the tips of bird feathers sharpened with a knife. The tips would be dipped in ink. Only a few words could be scratched out before the tips ran out of ink and they had to be dipped into an ink bottle again. Feathers were soon replaced with metal-tipped pens that didn't need to be sharpened.

The Fountain Pen

Constantly dipping into an ink bottle became too much trouble for a New York businessman, **named Lewis Waterman,** who invented the first workable fountain pen **in 1884**. Earlier attempts at such a pen didn't work very well and were just downright messy, with ink flowing unevenly across the paper. The new fountain pen used capillary action to feed ink to the tip of the pen, which flowed out smoothly and evenly. Many pages could be written before the ink reservoir inside the pen had to be refilled.

The Ballpoint Pen

The ballpoint pen, however, quickly replaced the fountain pen after its invention **in 1938**. It was invented by **Laszlo Biro,** a Hungarian journalist who grew tired of constantly refilling his fountain pen. Also, even the best fountain pens could still be very messy if a spill occurred while refilling the pen with ink. Spilling was a huge problem for pilots and flight crews flying at high altitude. During World War II, the British Royal Air Force used ballpoint pens to solve this problem. Soon the ballpoint pen was flying high and became the dominant pen used today.

Waterman and Biro made the pen a common tool that nearly everyone depends upon for basic communication and notetaking needs. It is only natural then that digital pens should emerge, transferring the feel and function of a pen to the use of personal computers. The evolution of the pen makes one wonder if the digital pen will one day replace ballpoint pens, just as the ballpoint pen replaced the fountain pen which, in turn, replaced feather pens.

Ink Annotating

Do you remember your English instructor poring over your essays and marking them up with a red ink pen? (Sometimes it was a green pen, but mainly it was red.) She or he would mark mistakes, show you where edits could be made, and leave comments all over the paper on how to improve your writing. This part of the editing process is often called **annotating**. Now, with tablet PC tools, annotating on computers makes sense; and the ink is digital, never runs out, and can be made with almost any color. (See Figure IT1-34.)

annotating

For example, if you turn in an essay via e-mail, your instructor can pull it up on the tablet PC's screen, annotate it just as if they were marking edits on paper, and e-mail it right back to you. No extra printed pages and no inky mess. Digital annotating is becoming extremely popular in distance education courses.

Disclaimer: The Ink Annotations feature is only available in *Office 2003* or higher and can only be installed on tablet PC computers fitted with the proper digital pen technologies. You may not be able to complete this activity if you do not have the proper software and hardware. However, read through the steps regardless so you know how the feature is used, and you'll be prepared to apply ink annotations once you upgrade your computer system.

Exercise 3C

Annotating and Editing with Ink

Windows/Tablet PC Instructions Only

1. Reopen *Microsoft Word* and your report called *The History of Pens*.
2. In *Word*, choose **Insert, Ink Annotations**, as seen in Figure IT1-34 on the following page.
3. Choose the down arrow next to the **Pen** icon and choose the **Red Felt Tip Pen** option. (See Figure IT1-34.)
4. Choose the **Line Color** option and choose a lovely shade of green, as seen in Figure IT1-35 on the following page.
5. Make all of the corrective marks shown in Figure IT1-36. Use the eraser if you make mistakes.
6. Switch back to a red felt tip pen and add all of the comments and the grade as seen in Figure IT1-36 on page 525.
7. When finished, tap the **Stop Inking** button and close the Ink Annotations toolbar.

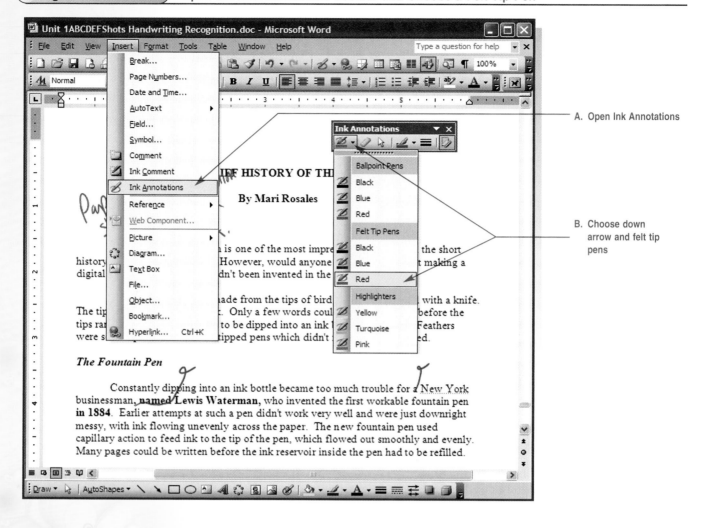

A. Open Ink Annotations

B. Choose down arrow and felt tip pens

Figure IT1-35   Change Your Felt Tip Pen Color to Green

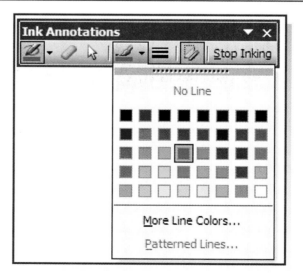

(handwritten: Paper too short. Need More information for an A.)

A BRIEF HISTORY OF THE PEN

By Mari Rosales

(handwritten: B+)

Handwriting recognition is one of the most impressive inventions in the short history of personal computers. However, would anyone have thought about making a digital pen if the normal pen hadn't been invented in the first place?

Early pens were *(handwritten: ^ ink)* often made from the tips of bird feathers sharpened with a knife. The tips would be dipped in ink. Only a few words could be scratched out before the tips ran out of ink and they had to be dipped into an ink bottle again. Feathers were soon replaced with metal-tipped pens that didn't need to be sharpened.

The Fountain Pen

Constantly dipping into an ink bottle became too much trouble for a New York businessman, named Lewis Waterman, who invented the first workable fountain pen **in 1884**. Earlier attempts at such a pen didn't work very well and were just downright messy, with ink flowing unevenly across the paper. The new fountain pen used capillary action to feed ink to the tip of the pen, which flowed out smoothly and evenly. Many pages could be written before the ink reservoir inside the pen had to be refilled.

The Ballpoint Pen

The ballpoint pen, however, quickly replaced the fountain pen after its invention **in 1938**. It was invented by **Laszlo Biro,** a Hungarian journalist who grew tired of constantly refilling his fountain pen. Also, even the best fountain pens could still be very messy if a spill occurred while refilling the pen with ink. Spilling was a huge problem for pilots and flight crews flying at high altitude. During World War II, the British Royal Air Force used ballpoint pens to solve this problem. Soon the ballpoint pen was flying high and became the dominant pen used today.

(handwritten: Conclusion   Add side head)

Waterman and Biro made the pen a common tool that nearly everyone depends upon for basic communication and notetaking needs. It is only natural then that digital pens should emerge, transferring the feel and function of a pen to the use of personal computers. The evolution of the pen makes one wonder if the digital pen will one day replace ballpoint pens, just as the ballpoint pen replaced the fountain pen which, in turn, replaced feather pens. *(handwritten: Do not Bold)*

(handwritten: very interesting)

Drawing with Ink

Digital ink is great for sketches and drawings. Windows/tablet PC users can use ink annotation tools to draw in their documents. For those using *Microsoft Office* hand-writing recognition, there is a special tool called Drawing Pad that allows sketches to be inserted into a document.

Using Drawing Pad

Tablet PC users, use the Ink Annotation tools to complete this exercise. *Office* users, review the *Office* instructions below.

Office Instructions

1. Open a new, blank document in *Microsoft Word* and open the Language bar.

2. Choose the **Handwriting** button and choose **Drawing Pad**.

3. Start by drawing a simple diagram, like a sketch of the horse seen in Figure IT1-37.

Feature IT1-37 Use Drawing Pad to Create Sketch Art

Instant Message

Open Writing Pad's Options to change the color and width of your pen.

TIP

Tap the Clear or Eraser button to erase all of your drawing. If you want to remove just the last line you have drawn, simply tap on the Remove Last Stroke button.

UNIT 1

LESSONS 1–3

Assessing Handtyping and Formatting Skills

LESSON (1) **ASSESS HOVERING SKILLS AND HAND-EYE COORDINATION**

OBJECTIVES

⊙ To assess digital pen use.
⊙ To assess hand-eye coordination skills.

Exercise **1A**

Hover for Answers

1. Using your digital pen, open *Microsoft Word*, *Internet Explorer*, and other applications as needed to complete this exercise. Hover over various parts of the Windows interface. Observe when each of the different pen pointer shapes in Figure IT1-38 appear.

Figure IT1-38   Find These Mouse Pointers

2. Use your handtyping skills to explain what each of these shapes indicates as it passes over an object in the Windows operating system. Record your answers in either *Microsoft OneNote* or *Microsoft Word*. Save your brief explanations in a file called **Pen Pointers** or name your *OneNote* page by the same name.

Exercise **1B**

Solve Math Problems with a Pen

1. Using your digital pen, open your Windows Calculator by hovering down to the Start button and choosing **Start, (All) Programs, Accessories, Calculator**.

2. Using only your pen, tap out the answers to these mathematical problems.

Addition Problems	Subtraction Problems	Multiplication Problems	Division Problems
4 + 4 =	27 − 14 =	3 x 5 =	6 / 307 =
54 + 46 + 65 =	56 − 38 =	28 x 13 =	32 / 7,332 =
606 + 445 + 504 =	807 − 234 -65 =	(67 x 13) x 2 =	31.2 / 5,409 =

3. Save your answers in a *Microsoft Word* file called **Math Problems** or record them on a *OneNote* page of the same name.

LESSON 2 ASSESS PENMANSHIP AND INPUT PANEL SKILLS

OBJECTIVES

⊙ To assess penmanship with handtyping using block-style printing.
⊙ To assess penmanship with cursive handtyping.
⊙ To assess the use of tappable keyboard and/or character-by-character input tools.

Exercise 2A

Handtype with Block-Style Printing

1. Open your report on *The History of Pens*. It's time to work toward an A+. You need to include new information. Just after the paragraph on Laszlo Biro, and just before your concluding paragraph, handtype the following paragraph using block-style printed letters.

   Most of us take the ballpoint pen for granted: You can find one almost anywhere; they normally always work; and if they quit working, a replacement can be purchased for a few quarters.

2. Resave your file on *The History of Pens* and, if time permits, leave it open for the next exercise.

Exercise 2B

Handtyping with Cursive

1. Repen your report on *The History of Pens* if necessary. Right after the paragraph you just entered using block-style printing, add another paragraph, but this time use only cursive-style writing.

   However, a workable ballpoint pen was not easy to invent. Previous ballpoint pens used the popular India ink of the day, which would puddle and smudge. Fortunately, Laszlo had the help of his brother George Biro. As luck would have it, George was a chemist who set about making a special ink that would flow smoothly and dry immediately.

The ballpoint pen also requires a small ball, usually made of copper, steel, or tungsten, approximately .5 mm in size. The ball is held inside a socket. As the ball rotates across the paper, the specialized ink stored in a small tube behind the socket is propelled by gravity to flow over the ball and onto the paper in carefully controlled amounts so it dries instantly.

2. Resave your file on *The History of Pens*, and if time permits, leave it open for the next exercise.

Exercise 2C

Use Character-by-Character Tools and/or The Tappable Keyboard

1. Repen your report on *The History of Pens* if necessary. Right after the paragraph you just entered using cursive-style printing, add another paragraph; but this time use the tappable keyboard and the character-by-character input tools if they're available to you.

   Today, BIC is the leading manufacturer of ballpoint pens. The company was founded by Marcel Bich, who dropped the letter h from his company's name. BIC introduced its first ballpoint pen in December 1950, after receiving patent rights from Laszlo Biro. Today, BIC ships 22 million products each day around the world.

2. Resave your file on *The History of Pens* and, if time permits, leave it open for the next exercise.

LESSON 3 ASSESS EDITING AND FORMATTING

OBJECTIVE
 To assess formatting and editing using a digital pen.

Exercise 3A

Make Corrections

1. Reopen your report on *The History of Pens* if necessary. Using Figure IT1-36 as a guide, make the corrections illustrated in green ink using only your digital pen and handwriting tools.

2. Add a new side heading just before the concluding paragraph called **Conclusion**.

3. If you have a tablet PC, erase all of the comments marked in red and the corrections marked in green using the **Eraser** button found on the Ink Annotations toolbar.

4. Resave your file on *The History of Pens* and, if time permits, leave it open for the next exercise.

Change Formatting

1. Reopen your report on *The History of Pens* if necessary. Using your digital pen and formatting features in *Microsoft Word,* make the following changes to your document.

   a. Double-space each paragraph in the document. (Do not allow quadruple spacing between paragraphs. They should also be double-spaced.)

   b. Change the font style for the entire document to Arial.

   c. Increase the font size of the main title or heading to 14 points.

   d. Remove your name from its current position and place it into the top right corner of a header.

   e. Insert a page number in the bottom center of the document.

   f. Change the color of the entire report to a nice, vibrant blue.

2. Resave your file on *The History of Pens*.

UNIT 2

LESSONS 1–2
Speech Recognition

Conditioning Practice

Before you begin the lessons, key each line twice.

alphabet	1	Beth Vegas excluded quick jaunts to the town zoo from many plans.
fig/sym	2	Kaitlin renewed Policies #23-4598 (truck) and #65-9107-44 (auto).
speed	3	The man is to visit the widow when he works by the mall downtown.

gwam | 1' | 1 | 2 | 3 | 4 | 5 | 6 | 7 | 8 | 9 | 10 | 11 | 12 | 13 |

LESSON 1 UP AND RUNNING

OBJECTIVES

- ⊙ To adjust your microphone.
- ⊙ To create your speech user file.
- ⊙ To view the tutorial.
- ⊙ To read a training story.
- ⊙ To adjust your audio settings.
- ⊙ To manipulate your speech recognition toolbar.
- ⊙ To learn about avoiding injuries.

Voice-It!

Running a computer by talking to it is an amazing experience. With the latest **speech recognition (SR)** software—like *Microsoft Windows Vista SR* or ScanSoft's *Dragon NaturallySpeaking*—you can do everything by talking that you can do with a mouse or digital pen. It's as easy as substituting clicks or taps with voice commands.

And with SR, your writing is no longer limited by your keyboarding speed or the pace of your pencil across a notepad. You *can* think, talk, and **voice-write** at the same time. Soon you'll be **voice-typing** sentences and paragraphs at the speed of speech—between 100 and 200 words per minute.

Hands-free computing is now a reality for millions of computer users. This is a major step forward for those who want or need it. For example, Karla suffers with carpal tunnel syndrome in both hands and has a case of trigger finger in her right

speech recognition (SR)

voice-write
voice-typing

repetitive stress injuries (RSIs)

© PHOTODISC RED / GETTY IMAGES

Instant Message

Older versions of SR, such as *Microsoft Office XP* and *Office 2003 SR*, offer only limited computer commands, lower dictation accuracy, and limited performance. These SR applications are not recommended for those who need hands-free computing. However, they can provide a nice break from typing.

noise cancellation headset

hand. These painful **repetitive stress injuries (RSIs)** have stolen the strength from her hands and prevent her right hand from closing properly. She has chosen to stop typing and uses speech recognition to complete her computer work.

Gustaf suffered a devastating spinal injury while cliff diving as a young man of 18, leaving him a quadriplegic. He's able to use hands-free computing to get the most out of his technology tools.

Even for those without the serious injuries Karla and Gustaf face, SR is proving to be a powerful tool to help prevent keyboard-related injuries while dramatically increasing productivity at the same time. SR can increase your productivity both on the job and in your academic pursuits. By using speech you'll become more efficient, you'll be more employable, and you'll probably enjoy writing and computing much, much more. And it won't take you very long to master the basic skills, either.

Consistency Matters

Speech recognition software loves consistency. If you speak clearly and consistently, your speech software will reward you with improved accuracy and performance. But first, you should give your software a chance to perform at its best by teaching it to understand your voice patterns, your accent, your unique way of talking. This requires:

- Adjusting your microphone
- Viewing the tutorial
- Reading a short training story

Read the next few sections carefully for tips and hints about how to complete these tasks successfully.

A Poor-Quality Headset Will Never Do

Speech recognition requires the use of a high-quality **noise cancellation headset** microphone. These microphones are designed specifically for speech recognition and cancel out the background noises around you. This way, SR software can focus on just the words you say. Three commonly used headsets are described in detail in Table 2-1.

Table 2-1   COMPARING HEADSETS

Analog		Typically the least expensive models, analog headsets plug directly into the sound card on your desktop, laptop, or tablet PC.
		(continued on next page)

Table 2-1   COMPARING HEADSETS (continued)

| USB | 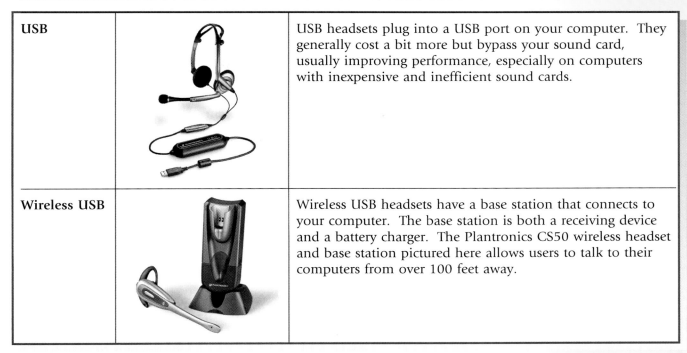 | USB headsets plug into a USB port on your computer. They generally cost a bit more but bypass your sound card, usually improving performance, especially on computers with inexpensive and inefficient sound cards. |
| Wireless USB | | Wireless USB headsets have a base station that connects to your computer. The base station is both a receiving device and a battery charger. The Plantronics CS50 wireless headset and base station pictured here allows users to talk to their computers from over 100 feet away. |

© 2005 HEADSET PHOTOS COURTESY PLANTRONICS, INC.

Adjust Your Microphone Position

The consistency principle applies to how you wear your headset. If you place your headset in the proper position every time you use your speech software, your CSR system will give you greater reliability.

Be careful as you handle your headset's arm, which is called a **boom**. The microphone is located at the end of the boom and is usually covered by a sponge called a **windscreen**. Review the other important parts of a typical headset in Figure IT2-1.

boom

windscreen

Figure IT2-1   The Parts of a Headset

Headband

Boom

Earpiece/speaker

Windscreen

Mute button and volume control

Digital signal processor (DSP)

USB connector

Most booms come down from the headband about three-quarters of the way, but no further. Decide on which side of your mouth you want the microphone to rest. Bring the boom down carefully to that side. Less expensive headsets often have a wire boom. Be careful that this wire does not bend outward, forcing the microphone away from your mouth. Usually there is a dot, the word *voice*, or some other mark to indicate which side holds the listening portion of the microphone. Face that mark toward your mouth. Complete Exercise 1A to learn more about proper headset care and consistent positioning.

Exercise 1A

Position Your Headset

1. Make sure your headset is plugged into the proper ports on your computer. (See Table 2-1 Comparing Headsets.) If your headset has a mute button, make sure it is turned to the On position.

2. Consistently place the windscreen covering the microphone in the proper position. Follow this rule of thumb: Place the microphone's windscreen at least a thumb's width away, or about 1/2" from your lower lip. (See Figure IT2-2.) This same rule applies for headsets without windscreens.

3. Don't touch the microphone windscreen with your hands or mouth. This can pull your headset out of position and can create static electricity or unintentional sounds, causing extra words to appear in your document.

Figure IT2-2   Position Your Microphone Consistently

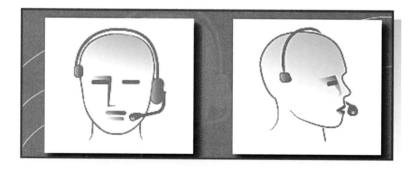

About Your User File

The first time you use speech recognition, you will be required to create an SR user file. As you log into your SR system and identify yourself, your software will begin creating this personal **speech user file** just for you.

Your user file will be different from every other person's voice file on the planet. As you learn to use SR, your user file will grow and learn along with you. It will learn how you speak and how you say things, and will hone in on the unique words and pronunciations you like to use.

Complete Tutorials

Each software program has a tutorial to help you get started with the software. With *Microsoft Vista*, you will participate in the tutorial first before starting. With

Dragon NaturallySpeaking, IBM ViaVoice, Office XP, and *Office 2003*, the tutorial comes after you read your initial training story. Either way, take the time to learn as much as you can from any tutorials that are available to you. (See Figure IT2-3.)

(See Figure IT2-3.)

Figure IT2-3   Complete Any Tutorials as They Appear

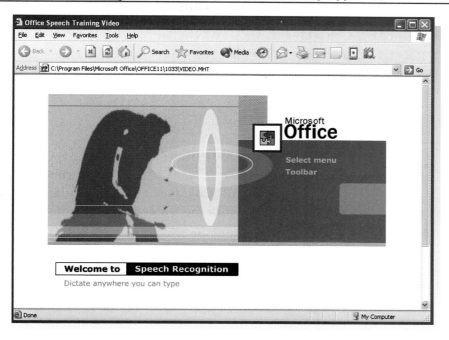

Complete Training Stories

You will want your speech software to voice-type the sentences you speak with the highest level of accuracy possible. With older speech recognition programs, like *Office XP* and *2003*, reading training stories can be a time-consuming task. The user must read multiple stories in order to achieve an acceptable level of accuracy.

With modern SR, reading a training story may be optional to start with. With *Microsoft Vista*, for example, if you complete the tutorial described earlier, you may not be required to read a training story right off the bat. As you participate in the tutorial, the software is automatically recording how you speak and making the necessary adaptations to accommodate your manner of speaking.

Nevertheless, we recommend that you do read a training story or two. Readings are short and can radically improve overall accuracy and performance. Because accuracy is the name of the game, you should read additional training scripts. (See Exercise 1B.) As you read, the computer will listen to how you say things. After all, no two people speak alike! The software wants to understand how *you* speak so it can improve its accuracy based on your speech patterns.

A sloppy, inconsistent reading of the story may result in decreased accuracy. As you read:

- Imagine you are reading aloud to a small group of people.
- Don't rush, but keep up a normal, consistent pace.
- Don't exaggerate or be overly theatrical.
- Be consistent. Read in the way you intend to talk to the computer in the future.

With that background, let's begin!

Complete Training and Tutorials

Follow the step-by-step instructions for the enrollment training and tutorials provided by your software. We are presenting step-by-step instructions for several speech recognition programs: *Microsoft Office XP* and *2003* (in the areas surrounded by a blue border), and *Dragon NaturallySpeaking 7* and *8* (in the areas surrounded by a red border). The instructions for your software may vary depending on which SR version your computer is running. Follow the instructions that most closely match your software.

Complete Training and Tutorials

Microsoft Office	Dragon NaturallySpeaking

Microsoft Office

1. Open *Microsoft Word* and the **Language bar** (see Part 3 Unit 1 Exercise 1C).

2. Turn the **Microphone** on. If you haven't trained your user file, your SR software will walk you through the process. If training doesn't immediately start, choose the **Tools** button on the Language bar and then select **Training** as seen in Figure IT2-4. (*Note:* Read *Office Troubleshooting Tips* if the training doesn't start.)

Figure IT2-4 Complete the Training

3. The software will instruct you to adjust your microphone settings. Adjust your headset as explained in Exercise 1A, and then choose **Next** to continue. Follow the instructions on the screen to adjust your microphone volume settings.

4. Continue following the instructions until you come to the Voice Training wizard. Here you'll be asked to read a story aloud. As you read, words will become highlighted or grayed out behind you. If you need to take a break, choose **Pause**. If you have trouble with a word, choose **Skip Word**. (See Figure IT2-5.)

Dragon NaturallySpeaking

1. Start *Dragon NaturallySpeaking* by choosing **Start, All Programs, Dragon NaturallySpeaking** or click the **Dragon** icon on your desktop.

2. Depending on which user you are, follow the instructions that apply to you:
   - **First User:** Simply follow the steps that appear on the screen. Jump to step 3 for additional tips.
   - **Second User:** Choose the **NaturallySpeaking** button on the DragonBar, and then choose **Manage Users**. Choose **New** from the Manage Users dialog box.
   - **Third or Later User:** Choose **New** from the Open Users dialog box.

3. In the New User Wizard, key your name and choose the **Next** button. (See Figure IT2-6.)

Figure IT2-6 Enter Your Name

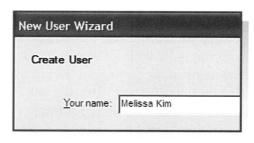

4. Follow the on-screen instructions and choose your user headset configuration and adjust the audio settings of your headset. After the quality check, you should receive a passing score, as seen in Figure IT2-7. Choose **Next** to continue. (*Note:* If you received a failing score, troubleshoot your headset microphone before continuing.)

Figure IT2-5 — Read a Training Story

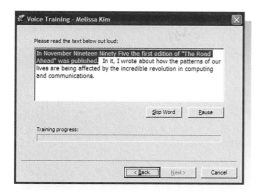

5. At the end of the training you will be asked if you want to finish or read additional stories. If time permits, read more training stories and scripts.

6. After you finish reading, your software will open to a short online tutorial. If this tutorial has been installed on your PC, listen to all of the advice it gives you.

Office Troubleshooting Tip

If you are unable to create a new user file as explained above, choose **Tools, Options** from the Language bar. Then, after the Speech Input Settings window opens, choose the **Advanced Speech** button. In the Speech Properties window, choose **New**, key your name, and follow the instructions carefully on the screen.

Figure IT2-7 — Achieve a Passing Score

Speech-to-noise ratio: 21
Audio quality check: PASSED

5. Your software will ask you to read several sentences and then choose a story to read. Choose **Talking to Your Computer**, the first story on the list, or **Stories Written by Children**, which appears further down the list.

6. As you read, wait for the little yellow arrow to appear. *Read one sentence at a time until the words begin graying out behind you.* If you need to take a break, choose **Pause**. If you have trouble with a word, choose **Skip Word**. (See Figure IT2-8.)

Figure IT2-8 — Wait for the Yellow Arrow Before Speaking

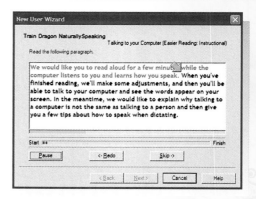

7. After you finish reading, click **OK** and your voice pattern will be analyzed.

8. The few additional screens will follow. One screen will ask to analyze all of your written documents. At this early stage you may wish to skip having your documents analyzed and continue directly to the tutorial. If your tutorial is available, view it before continuing.

Protect Your Wrist and Your Voice

One of the benefits of using speech recognition software is that it reduces your risk of developing serious Carpal Tunnel Syndrome (CTS) in your wrists and other repetitive stress and strain injuries (RSIs). RSIs can afflict your hands, arms, elbows, or shoulders. These injuries are often painful and can reduce your ability to use your hands normally. RSIs have a variety of causes such as video gaming and instant messaging, but a contributing factor can be excessive and repetitive typing and mouse-clicking.

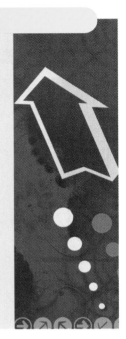

A great way to reduce computer-related RSIs is to voice-type with your SR software. However, voice-typing may place an added strain on your vocal cords! Keep a water bottle handy and take constant sips. Take frequent breaks from talking. Also, raise your chin slightly when dictating. Don't let repetitive vocal cord injuries replace other RSIs!

Speech Toolbars

Before you continue, analyze Figures IT2-9 and IT2-10. The figures display two different speech recognition toolbars: the *Microsoft Office SR* Language bar (Figure IT2-9) and the ScanSoft *Dragon NaturallySpeaking* DragonBar (Figure IT2-10). Your speech toolbar is the control center for SR activities. Think of it as an operating system for your speech interface. You will use your SR toolbar to turn your microphone on and off, adjust your speech recognition settings, locate your user name, and troubleshoot your system.

For example, your speech toolbar can help you make sure you have chosen your user profile. You must ALWAYS use your speech user file! If you accidentally choose another person's user file, your accuracy will plummet. Figure IT2-9 demonstrates how to double-check to see if your user profile has been opened in *Microsoft Office*. It is as simple as choosing the Tools button and then the Current User option.

Instant Message

The *Microsoft Office SR* Language bar is the same bar you learned to use in the handwriting recognition unit. If you need help remembering how to manipulate the Language bar, repeat *Unit 1 Exercise 1C*.

Figure IT2-9   The Expanded *Microsoft Office* Language Bar

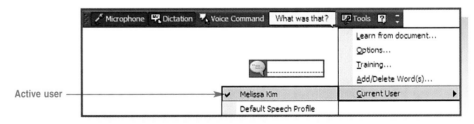

chevron

In Figure IT2-10, you can also see if you are the active user by choosing the two down arrows, called a **chevron**, on the top right side of the DragonBar. If your name appears, you're ready to go! If it doesn't appear, choose the **NaturallySpeaking** button, **Open User**, and choose your name.

Figure IT2-10   The *Dragon NaturallySpeaking* DragonBar

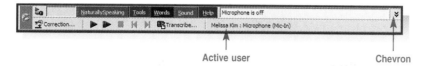

Active user   Chevron

Use Your SR Toolbar to Troubleshoot Your Microphone

Here is another example of how valuable your SR toolbar can be. Your voice file automatically remembers your audio settings from session to session. However, you should readjust your audio settings if one of the following occurs:

- Your background noise or acoustic conditions change.
- There is a noticeable decline in your recognition accuracy.
- Another person has used the speech recognition system before you on your computer.

To troubleshoot your microphone, follow the steps in Exercise 1C for your specific software.

Exercise 1C

Troubleshoot Current User and Microphone Settings

1. Make sure your microphone headset is plugged in properly. If you have a mute button, make sure the microphone has not been muted by mistake.

2. Continue to follow the instructions that best fit your SR software.

Troubleshoot Current User and Microphone Settings

Microsoft Office	Dragon NaturallySpeaking
3. Verify that you are the active user by choosing the **Tools** button and then **Current User**. If your name has a check mark by it, continue to step 4. If not, choose your name. (*Note:* If you are the only person using SR under your login name, your file may be called *Default Speech Profile*.)	3. Verify that you are the active user by choosing the **chevron** on the far right corner of the DragonBar.
4. From the Language bar, select **Tools, Options**. Then, after the Speech Input Settings window opens, choose the **Advanced Speech** button. In the Speech Properties window, choose the **Configure Microphone** button.	4. Open *Dragon NaturallySpeaking* and click **Tools, Accuracy Center**, and **Check Your Audio Settings**.
5. Read and follow the instructions. Tap the **Next** button to continue from screen to screen.	5. Read and follow the instructions. Tap the **Next** button to continue from screen to screen. You must receive a passing score. If you don't, you will need to troubleshoot your system further.

Conquer Your SR Toolbar

To use your speech recognition software effectively, you must first conquer your speech recognition toolbar. SR toolbars can appear in different ways and in different places on the screen. Review Table 2-2 to learn more about how to display your toolbar. Soon, you will find the toolbar display that best fits your own style and needs.

> ### Table 2-2   Manipulate Your SR Toolbar
>
> ### Microsoft Office
> 1. Open *Microsoft Word*. You should see the Language bar in its collapsed state as shown in Figure IT2-11. You should also see the Microphone button.
>
> > #### Figure IT2-11   The Collapsed Language Bar
> >
> >
>
> 2. Click or tap the **Microphone** button to view the expanded Language bar as shown in Figure IT2-12. Notice that two new buttons are added to the SR toolbar. They are called *Dictation* and *Voice Command*.
>
> > #### Figure IT2-12   The Expanded Language Bar [callouts:, Mode]
> >
> >
> >
> > Floating speech balloon
> > Dictation button
> > Voice Command button
>
> 3. Collapse the Language bar again and turn off the microphone by clicking or tapping on the **Microphone** button one more time.
>
> ### Dragon NaturallySpeaking
> 1. You can display the DragonBar in several different ways by clicking the **Dragon** icon in the top left corner of the DragonBar. For beginners, it is best to leave the system in the **Docked to Top** mode until you complete this unit. Later, you may choose the mode you prefer from the drop-down menu seen in Figure IT2-13.
>
> ### Troubleshooting Tip
>
> If you accidentally get stuck in **Tray Icon Only** mode, right-click on Dragon's red microphone found on the Windows taskbar at the bottom of your screen. Choose **Restore Previous DragonBar Mode**.
>
> *(continued on next page)*

Instant Message

In Lesson 2, you'll learn how to switch between Dictation mode and Voice Command mode. Dictation mode is used for voice-typing, and Voice Command mode is used to give commands to *Office* applications.

Table 2-2 Manipulate Your SR Toolbar (continued)

Figure IT2-13 Choose the Dragon Icon to Change the DragonBar Display Mode

About DragonBar modes. The DragonBar menu allows you to switch between various dictation modes. Like *Office SR*, *Dragon* can work in Command and Dictation only modes, but most choose to use both modes together in combination, which is called **Normal Mode**. Make sure Normal Mode is always selected as seen in Figure IT2-14 unless specifically instructed to switch to another mode.

Figure IT2-14 Make Sure You Are in Normal Mode

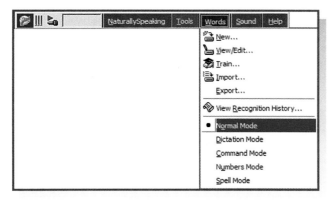

OBJECTIVES

- ⊙ To speak voice commands.
- ⊙ To dictate words clearly.
- ⊙ To clear your screen with your voice.
- ⊙ To use the cut and paste voice commands.
- ⊙ To say line and paragraph commands.
- ⊙ To speak essential punctuation.
- ⊙ To navigate a document with voice commands.
- ⊙ To use voice commands in dialog boxes.
- ⊙ To save documents via voice.

Clear as a Bell

To achieve success with speech recognition you must speak clearly—as clear as a bell—so the computer knows exactly what you're trying to voice-write. It does no good to mumble, scream, shout, yell, or whisper. You must speak in a normal tone of voice—the voice you would use to explain something important to an instructor or a coworker.

You will need to practice enunciating words, commands, and punctuation. Practice speaking smoothly and consistently. When you speak, follow these rules:

- Say each word, command, and punctuation mark clearly.
- Speak in a normal tone of voice. Your software will work best when you speak naturally and consistently.
- Do not worry if your words fail to appear immediately as you say them. Your software will catch up to you soon enough.

Speak Commands Clearly

Speech recognition software interprets silence as a clue that a command is about to be spoken. If you are <silent> for a half second before you say a command, the software will execute the command. (See Table 2-3.)

Table 2-3   Rules for Saying Commands

Rule	Sample
Be totally silent before saying commands. (*Note:* It also helps to be silent after saying a command, too.)	Say . . . **<silence> New Paragraph**
When several words are part of a command, say it as a phrase, not as separate words. Don't stop in the middle of a multiword command.	Do not say . . . **New <silence> Paragraph**
Say each word in the command clearly. Don't rush or slur commands or leave sounds out.	Do not say . . . **<silence> Newparagra . . .**
Don't shout and don't whisper commands. Use a normal tone of voice.	Do not say . . . **<silence> NEW PARAGRAPH!**

Exercise 2A

Speak Microphone Commands Clearly

Start your speech recognition software and open your speech user file.

Speak Microphone Commands Clearly

Microsoft Office

1. Start *Microsoft Word* and click or tap **Microphone**, expanding the Language bar.

2. Switch to Voice Command mode by saying: <silence> Voice Command (*Note:* You may also click or tap the **Voice Command** button as seen in Figure IT2-15.)

| Figure IT2-15 | Switch to Voice Command Mode |

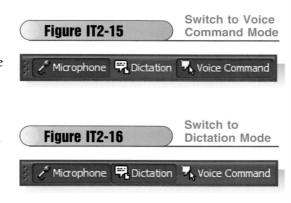

3. Switch to Dictation mode by saying: <silence> Dictation. (*Note:* You may also click or tap the **Dictation** button as seen in Figure IT2-16.)

| Figure IT2-16 | Switch to Dictation Mode |

4. Switch back and forth between Voice Command and Dictation modes several times by repeating steps 2 and 3.

5. Turn your microphone completely off by saying <silence> Microphone or by clicking and tapping the **Microphone** button. (See Figure IT2-17.)

| Figure IT2-17 | Turn off the Microphone |

You will save time in *Office SR* if you dictate all of your text first in Dictation mode before switching to Voice Command mode to format your document and to make corrections.

Dragon NaturallySpeaking

1. Open *NaturallySpeaking* by selecting **Start, (All) Programs, Dragon NaturallySpeaking** or choosing the **Dragon** icon on your desktop. (See Figure IT2-18.)

| Figure IT2-18 | Open Dragon SR |

2. Turn your microphone on by clicking or tapping the **Microphone** icon on the left side of the DragonBar. *Note:* When turned on, the microphone on the DragonBar will pop up and turn green in color. The volume meter box will show yellow, green, or even red as it monitors the sound volume. (See Figure IT2-19.)

| Figure IT2-19 | The Microphone and Volume Meter When Activated |

3. These first few commands will hibernate the microphone (see Figure IT2-20) and wake it back up again. In hibernation mode, the volume meter will turn gray and the microphone icon will fall at a 45° angle and turn yellow.

Figure IT2-20   The Microphone in Hibernation Mode

Practice each of these on/off combinations several times. Remember to be silent before you say each command. Say:

<silence> Stop Listening
<silence> Listen to Me
<silence> Go to Sleep
<silence> Wake Up

4. To turn the microphone completely off, say: <silence> Microphone Off.

5. Turn the microphone on and off again by tapping the plus key (+) on your numeric keypad several times. Watch the microphone spring into action and then shut down again each time you tap +.

Speak Menu Commands Clearly

Speaking menu commands is as easy as saying the menu names, such as, **<silence> File** or **<silence> Edit**. Say the **<silence> Cancel** command to close an open menu.

Exercise **2B**

Speak Menu Commands

Follow the commands that best fit your software.

Speak Microphone Commands Clearly

Microsoft Office SR	Dragon NaturallySpeaking
1. Start *Microsoft Word* and turn on your microphone.	**1.** Look up the name of your shortcut for *Microsoft Word* by clicking or tapping **Start, All Programs.** Open the Microsoft Office folder if necessary, and look for the name of the shortcut. It is usually something like: Microsoft Office Word 2003 or Microsoft Word
2. Switch to Voice Command mode by saying: <silence> Voice Command (you may also click or tap the **Voice Command** button as seen in Figure IT2-15).	
3. Open and close *Microsoft Word*'s menus from the menu bar by saying: <silence> File <silence> Cancel	**2.** Open *NaturallySpeaking*. Then open *Microsoft Word* by saying the

<silence> Edit
<silence> Cancel
<silence> View
<silence> Cancel
<silence> Insert
<silence> Cancel
<silence> Format
<silence> Cancel
<silence> Tools
<silence> Cancel
<silence> Table
<silence> Cancel
<silence> Window
<silence> Cancel
<silence> Help
<silence> Cancel

4. Close *Microsoft Word* completely by saying the following commands in Voice Command mode:

<silence> File
<silence> Exit

5. If you're asked to save, say <silence> No.

6. Turn your microphone completely off by saying **<silence> Microphone** or by clicking or tapping the **Microphone** button.

name of the shortcut preceded by the word **<silence> Start** or **<silence> Open**, such as:

<silence> Start Microsoft Office Word 2003
or
<silence> Start Microsoft Word

3. Open the menus of *Microsoft Word* from the menu bar. Be silent between each command. Say:

<silence> File
<silence> Cancel
<silence> Edit
<silence> Cancel
<silence> View
<silence> Cancel
<silence> Insert
<silence> Cancel
<silence> Format
<silence> Cancel
<silence> Tools
<silence> Cancel
<silence> Table
<silence> Cancel
<silence> Window
<silence> Cancel
<silence> Help
<silence> Cancel

4. Close *Microsoft Word* completely by saying the following commands:

<silence> File
<silence> Exit

5. If you're asked to save, say <silence> No.

6. Turn the microphone completely off by tapping the plus key (+) or by saying:

<silence> Microphone Off

Instant
Message

You can also close an open application by simply saying **Click Close**.

Speak Words Clearly

Everyone makes mistakes in the beginning! Don't worry about correcting mistakes when you practice your pronunciation in this lesson. You will learn to correct mistakes in Lesson 3. Until then, practice speaking clearly, continuously, and consistently. Simply enunciate each sentence several times, concentrating on the way you say the words and phrases. Remember these rules:

• Say each word clearly and consistently.

- Speak in phrases and full sentences, NOT in individual words. For example, say **This is important**, not **This . . . is . . . important.**

- Don't break words into syllables. For instance, say **popcorn**, not **pop corn**.

- Say each sound in the word and don't run words together. Say **candy bar**, not **canybar**.

- Don't speak too fast. Don't speak too slowly. Speak at a speed that is just right for you!

- Don't shout and don't whisper. Don't let your speaking volume fall off toward the end of the sentence. Speak consistently.

Exercise 2C
Say Your First Dialogue

1. Open *Microsoft Word* and your speech recognition software. Turn the microphone on. (*Microsoft Office* users say Dictation or click on the **Dictation** button.) Say the following dialogue, remembering to say the periods:

   Talk to your computer Period. Speak normally and say each word clearly Period. Don't shout and don't whisper Period. Do not stop in the middle of a sentence Period. Practice speaking clearly Period.

2. Turn your microphone off and analyze your mistakes. Some speakers run words together or speak too quickly, which causes unnecessary errors. For example, many say *innamiddleof* instead of saying *in the middle of*. Other people speak too slowly and break words apart such as *mid . . . dle* instead of *middle*. Speak at a normal pace.

3. Try the paragraph again, concentrating on the sound or the pronunciation of any word you may have missed the first time. Don't forget to say Period every time you see a (.).

   Talk to your computer. Speak normally and say each word clearly. Don't shout and don't whisper. Do not stop in the middle of a sentence. Practice speaking clearly.

4. Turn off your microphone and analyze how you spoke. Don't worry about being perfect, you're just getting started. Leave the text on the screen for the next exercise, where you will learn how to delete it with your voice.

Clear the Screen with Your Voice

Erasing all of the text on your screen is an important skill required for many future exercises. Clearing the screen is a simple task with a few well-spoken voice commands.

Delete On-Screen Text

The dialogue you dictated from Exercise 2C should still be on your screen. If not, go back and repeat the dialogue before continuing. Follow the commands for your specific software.

Delete On-Screen Text

Microsoft Office	Dragon NaturallySpeaking
1. Turn your microphone on and make sure *Microsoft Word* is active by clicking or tapping on it.	1. Turn your microphone on and make sure *Microsoft Word* is active by clicking or tapping it.
2. Say the following voice commands: <silence> Voice Command <silence> Edit <silence> Select All <silence> Backspace (*Note:* You may also say <silence> Delete.)	2. Say the following commands: <silence> Select All <silence> Backspace (*Note:* You may also say <silence> Delete That.)

Practice Your Speaking Skills

Enunciation is the art of speaking in a clear and steady way. When it comes to enunciation for SR, like anything else, practice is critical. There are ways to correct mistakes with your voice so that your computer can learn how you speak and avoid making the same mistakes again. However, it doesn't make much sense to train the computer to fix mistakes that you can control by enunciating correctly. Give it a try in this exercise.

Exercise 2E

Practice Speaking and Clearing the Screen

1. Turn your microphone on and make sure *Microsoft Word* is active by clicking or tapping it.

2. Make sure your screen is clear of any unwanted text, and then speak the following dialogue as clearly as you can. Don't forget to say punctuation marks!

   Don't break any speed records when you speak to your computer. Speaking fast will cause you to run words together. Speaking slowly can also cause problems. If you speak very fast or very slowly, the system will have trouble understanding you. Talk at a speed that is just right for you.

3. Turn off your microphone and examine how well you did.

4. Using the skills you learned in Exercise 2D, clear your screen of all text.

5. Turn on your microphone again and try saying the same paragraph from step 2. See if you can improve your accuracy the second time.

6. Clear your screen once again of all text.

Speak Line and Paragraph Commands

The **<silence> New Paragraph** and **<silence> New Line** commands are essential. Saying these commands is like tapping the Enter key on your keyboard. *New Line* causes the insertion point (or flashing line) to jump down to the next line, just as when you tap the Enter key once. New Paragraph is equivalent to tapping the Enter key twice to create a double space.

To make your dictating easier, you can say either of these commands while in Dictation mode in *Microsoft Office SR*, or in Normal Mode in *Dragon NaturallySpeaking*.

Exercise

Speaking Line and Paragraph Commands

Remember these tips before continuing:
- Do not stop in the middle of a sentence.
- Remember to say punctuation marks.
- Be silent before and after saying commands.
- Never hesitate in the middle of a command. For example:
  Say **<silence> New Line**, not **New <silence> Line**.

1. Open *Microsoft Word* and your speech recognition software if they have been closed.

2. Practice the **<silence> New Line** command by saying the command after each of the following sentences. Turn on your microphone and say:

This is a complete sentence.	<silence> New Line
Speak clearly without stopping.	<silence> New Line
Speak in a normal voice.	<silence> New Line

3. Clear your screen and practice the **<silence> New Paragraph** command with the sentences below.

Think about your audience.	<silence> New Paragraph
Evaluate your purpose in writing.	<silence> New Paragraph
Use an appropriate writing style or personality.	<silence> New Paragraph
Don't make your documents very long.	<silence> New Paragraph

4. Clear your screen and continue practicing the **<silence> New Line** and **<silence> New Paragraph** commands. Say the following familiar phrases and create line breaks between them. Don't run words together, as in **Timeflies whenyor' havin' fun**. Do not speak too slowly; say **stopping** instead of **stop...ping**. Remember to say the punctuation mark at the end of each sentence. Dictate:

Time flies when you are having fun.
Don't rock the boat.

Hope springs eternal.
Never have so many owed so much to so few.

Speak clearly without stopping in the middle of your sentences.
Say each sentence clearly.

5. Clear your screen and turn off your microphone.

Speak Punctuation and Move Around Your Document

Some of today's SR software programs allow the software to guess where punctuation marks go in a paragraph. However, there are many rules and many variables governing the placement of punctuation marks, so automatic punctuation features are still a bit unreliable. Therefore, it is still common practice to say the punctuation marks as you need them, giving you more precise control over your writing.

Say punctuation marks clearly. It sometimes helps to pause briefly before and after saying a punctuation mark. Refer to Table 2-1 for hints on how to say the punctuation marks.

Table 2-1   Speak Punctuation

To create a . . .	Say:
.	Period
,	Comma
?	Question Mark
!	Exclamation Point/Mark
:	Colon
;	Semicolon
-- or —	Dash
" "	Open Quote Close Quote

Exercise 2G

Dictating Punctuation Marks

1. Start *Microsoft Word* and your SR software. (*Note:* Clear screen of any text.)

2. Practice dictating punctuation marks by saying the next few sentences. Try each sentence two times, working to improve your enunciation of the words and punctuation marks. Turn on your microphone and say:

Is that your final answer?

Congratulations! You have just won the grand prize.

Do you want to buy a new computer?

I know what you want: red dog, yellow cat, and blue tropical fish.

Don't speak very fast; don't speak very slowly; speak at just the right speed for you.

I think this is going rather well—better than expected!

"By the way," said Thomas, "using speech recognition software is easy."

3. Clear your screen and try saying the following punctuated paragraphs. (*Note:* Say each paragraph in this one-sided conversation before taking a break and reviewing the result. Don't stop in the middle of any sentence.)

May I help you? We have some wonderful items on sale today. Our prices are the best—the very best!

We have popcorn, peanuts, and candy bars of all kinds. We sell oranges, apples, apricots, bananas, plums, and peaches. Do you want any of our fabulous foods?

Why not? What do you mean I'm a pushy salesperson? Leave this establishment immediately! If you don't like apples, you can't stay here.

Goodbye!

4. Clear your screen and dictate the paragraphs in step 3 one more time. Try to improve the way you say any punctuation marks you may have missed the first time. Leave the sentences on the screen for the next exercise.

Moving Around Documents

Instant Message

Words in parentheses are optional, but they can often help with performance.

It's important to be able to move around a document while proofreading, editing, and making corrections. After you become proficient navigating the document by voice, you'll find it faster to use SR to navigate a document rather than using the scroll bar with your mouse or digital pen. When saying multiple word commands, do not pause between each word. Say:

<silence> Move to (the) Beginning of (the) Document

Do not say:

Move to (the) <silence> Beginning of (the) <silence> Document

Exercise 2H

Practice Navigation Commands

1. Make sure that the document you dictated in Exercise 2G appears on your screen. Follow the steps that best apply to your SR software.

Practice Navigation Commands

Microsoft Office	Dragon NaturallySpeaking
2. To move to the top and bottom of a document, say:	2. To move to the top and bottom of a document, say:
<silence> Voice Command	<silence> Go to Top
	<silence> Go to Bottom
<silence> Move to Beginning of Document	<silence> Go to Top
<silence> Move to End of Document	<silence> Go to Bottom
<silence> Move to Beginning of Document	<silence> Move to (the) Beginning of (the) Document
<silence> Move to End of Document	<silence> Move to (the) End of (the) Document
<silence> Move to Beginning of Document	<silence> Move to (the) Beginning of (the) Document

3. Use the following commands to move up and down a document line by line.

<silence> Move to Next Line
<silence> Move to Next Line
<silence> Move to Next Line

<silence> Move to Previous Line
<silence> Move to Previous Line
<silence> Move to Previous Line

<silence> Down Arrow
<silence> Down Arrow
<silence> Up Arrow
<silence> Up Arrow

4. Use the following commands to delete paragraphs. Move your insertion point around and try these commands several times on different paragraphs.

<silence> Select Paragraph
<silence> Backspace (or Delete)

3. Use the following commands to move up and down a document line by line.

<silence> Move Down One Line
<silence> Move Down Three Lines
<silence> Move Up Three Lines
<silence> Move Up One Line

4. Use the following commands to move comfortably between paragraphs and to delete them.

<silence> Move Down One Paragraph
<silence> Move Down Three Paragraphs
<silence> Move Up Three Paragraphs
<silence> Move Up One Paragraph
<silence> Move to (the) End of (the) Paragraph
<silence> Move to (the) Beginning of (the) Paragraph

<silence> Select Paragraph
<silence> Backspace (or Delete That)

5. Select your entire document and then clear the screen of all text before continuing to the next exercise.

Navigate Dialog Boxes and Save Documents

Saving files is obviously essential. To make saving easy, SR programs allow you to say the names of any buttons you want to voice-tap in any dialog box as you see them on the screen. For example, in the Save As dialog box (see Figure IT2-21), you can say <silence> **Save** to tap the Save button, or <silence> **Cancel** to tap the Cancel button.

Figure IT2-21   The Save As Dialog Box

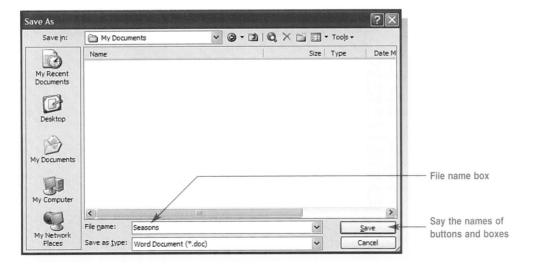

Saving Documents in Dialog Boxes

1. Open your SR software and *Microsoft Word*. Make sure you have a clean document with no extra words appearing on the screen.

2. Dictate the following sentences before you save them. (*Note:* Sometimes abbreviations for state names will appear, like FL for Florida and WA for Washington. That's perfectly acceptable.)

   New York, New York.
   I want to visit New York in the fall.

   Paris, France.
   I love Paris in the spring!

   Tallahassee, Florida.
   My parents live in Tallahassee in the winter.

   Seattle, Washington.
   Seattle is pretty in the summer.

3. Save your document following the instructions for your SR software.

Saving Documents in Dialog Boxes

Microsoft Office	Dragon NaturallySpeaking
4. Save the document with the file-name **Seasons** by saying: <silence> Voice Command <silence> File <silence> Save As 5. Make sure your insertion point is located in the **File name** box and then say: <silence> Dictation <silence> Seasons <silence> Voice Command <silence> Save	4. Save the document with the file-name **Seasons** by saying: <silence> (Click) File <silence> (Click) Save As 5. Make sure your insertion point is located in the **File name** box and then say: <silence> Seasons <silence> (Click) Save

Instant Message

In *Dragon NaturallySpeaking* you can add **<silence> Click** as a trigger word. Words in parentheses like (*Click*) are optional. Use the trigger word if the system seems to hang up a bit on a command.

Online Resources

See Bonus Lesson 3 on Correcting Speech Errors and Bonus Lesson 4 on Special Voice Formatting Solutions at www.c21key.bonus-exercises.swlearning.com.

UNIT 2

LESSONS 1–2

Assessing Speech Recognition Skills

LESSON **ASSESS GENERAL KNOWLEDGE OF SPEECH RECOGNITION**

OBJECTIVE

> To assess the knowledge needed to independently set up an SR system.

Exercise

Explain How to Get an SR System Up and Running

If possible, find someone who has never used speech recognition before and teach them the basic setup and dictation skills. If you can't find such a person willing to help you with this assignment, review with a teammate how to:

- Properly position a speech recognition headset
- Create a user file
- View a tutorial
- Read a training story

- Manipulate the speech recognition toolbar
- Say commands
- Dictate text and voice-type

LESSON **ASSESS ENUNCIATION SKILLS**

OBJECTIVES

> To assess the enunciation of words.
> To assess the enunciation of commands.
> To assess the enunciation of punctuation marks.
> To assess the ability to save a document with voice commands.

Exercise 2A

Enunciate Clearly and use the New Line and Paragraph Commands

1. Open your SR software and *Microsoft Word.* Dictate the following dialogue on a clear screen using the paragraph and line commands to display the list as seen below.

   I want to visit the following North American cities:

Seattle	Boston
Toronto	Denver
Chicago	Baltimore
Atlanta	Mexico City
Dallas	Miami

2. Using voice commands as much as possible, voice-save your file as *Cities.* If time permits, leave the file open for the next exercise.

Exercise 2B

Warmup: Evaluating Speed and Enunciation Accuracy

In traditional keyboarding classes, teachers count every five characters as a word. The formula includes spaces. Chances are, based on this formula, you are already speaking between 100 and 200 *wpm.* A quick way to measure speed is to count the number of characters and divide by five. If you can speak 500 characters in a minute, or 250 characters in 30 seconds, you are speaking faster than 100 *wpm.* Not bad at all!

1. Practice your enunciation skills by dictating the following two paragraphs. Time yourself, but do not focus on speed. Focus on accuracy instead, which is much more important than the speed at which you speak. Say this:

   Who will read your message? It is critical to know your audience. Is it a friend, a business client, or an instructor? Your message must be directed to this audience.

   Always have an exact reader in mind when you write. This is your target audience!

2. Turn off your microphone. Evaluate how many seconds you spent on these paragraphs. If you dictated them in 30 seconds or less, you were over 100 *wpm.* If you manage to say it all in 15 seconds or less, you are over 200 *wpm!* Count how many errors you made.

3. Clear the screen and try the paragraphs one more time, focusing on accuracy. Can you reduce your total number of errors using clear enunciation?

4. Voice-save this file as *Message.*

Communication & Math Skills 12

1. Study each of the five rules shown below in the color boxes.

a. Key the *Learn* line(s) beneath each rule, noting how the rule is applied.

b. Key the *Apply* line(s), using parentheses and dashes correctly.

Internal Punctuation: Parentheses

Rule 1: Use parentheses to enclose parenthetical or explanatory matter and added information. (Commas or dashes may be used instead.)

Learn	1	Vice President Gore (a Democrat) ran for the presidency in 2000.
Learn	2	The contracts (Exhibits C and D) need important revisions.
Apply	3	Sean Duncan the person with highest sales is being honored.
Apply	4	The Sixth Edition 2005 copyright date has been delivered.

Rule 2: Use parentheses to enclose identifying letters or figures of lists within a sentence.

Learn	5	Check for these errors: (1) keying, (2) spelling, and (3) grammar.
Apply	6	The focus group leaders are 1 Ramos, 2 Zahn, and 3 Pyle.
Apply	7	The order of emphasis is 1 technique and 2 speed of motions.

Rule 3: Use parentheses to enclose a name and date used as a reference.

Learn	8	Thousands of us heard the "I Have a Dream" speech (King, 1963).
Apply	9	He cited "The Gettysburg Address" Lincoln, 1863 in his report.
Apply	10	We read *The Old Curiosity Shop* Dickens, 1841 in class.

Internal Punctuation: Dash

Rule 4: Use a dash (two hyphens with no space before or after) to set off clarifying or added information, especially when it interrupts the flow of the sentence.

Learn	11	The skater--in clown's disguise--dazzled with fancy footwork.
Apply	12	Our trade discounts 10%, 15%, and 20% are the best available.
Apply	13	The gown a copy of an Italian original sells for only $150.

Rule 5: Use a dash before the author's name after a poem or quotation.

Learn	14	"All the world's a stage . . . ." --William Shakespeare
Apply	15	"I have taken all knowledge to be my province." Francis Bacon

2. Key Proofread & Correct, using parentheses and dashes correctly.
  a. Check answers.

b. Using the rule number(s) at the left of each line, study the rule relating to each error you made.

c. Rekey each incorrect line, using parentheses and dashes correctly.

Proofread & Correct

Rules

1	1	The appendices Exhibits A and B utilize computer graphics.
2	2	The three areas are 1 ethical, 2 moral, and 3 legal.
2	3	Emphasize: 1 writing, 2 speaking, and 3 listening.

(continued on next page)

3　4　You cited the "Liberty or Death" speech Henry, 1775 twice.

4　5　The payment terms 2/10, n/30 are clearly shown on the invoice.

4　6　The article and I know you're interested is in <u>Newsweek</u>.

5　7　"The finger that turns the dial rules the air."　Will Durant

1　8　The contract reads:　"For the sum of $600 Six Hundred Dollars."

4　9　Albert Camus, as you know a Frenchman was an existentialist.

2　10　Her talk addressed two issues:　A family values and B welfare.

3. Save as *CS12-ACT1*.

ACTIVITY 2　　Listening

1. You have answered a telephone call from Maria MacDonald, who serves as an officer in the alumni association of which your mother is president. She asks you to take a message.

2. Open *CD-CS12-ACT2* and listen to the message, taking notes as needed.

3. Close the file.

4. Using your notes, key a message in sentence form for your mother.

5. Save as *CS12-ACT2*.

ACTIVITY 3　　Write to Learn

1. Using word processing or voice recognition software, write a paragraph explaining the voice recognition commands you can use to move around in a document.

2. Save as *CS12-ACT3*.

ACTIVITY 4　　Preparing to Speak

1. You have been nominated for treasurer of your regional Future Business Leaders of America (FBLA). Now you must make a 1' to 2' speech to the voting delegates from each school in your region.

2. Key an outline of the major points you want to make about yourself and your qualifications for being

treasurer.　Include experiences that show you to be capable, reliable, responsible, and trustworthy.　Examples follow:

- Math, accounting, and other applicable courses you have completed or are taking
- Leadership positions you hold/held in other organizations

- Jobs you hold/held
- Experiences handling money (writing checks, making deposits, following a budget, investing, etc.)

3. If time and resources permit, record your speech in a sound file.

4. Save the outline as *CS12-ACT4* and the sound file as *CS12-ACT4-SOUND*.

ACTIVITY 5　　Math:　Finding Combinations and Probability

1. Open *CD-CS12-ACT5* and print the file.

2. Solve the problems as directed in the file.

3. Submit your answers.

UNIT 3

LESSONS 1–3

Scanning, Photos, and Digital Imaging

alphabet	1	Mrs. Gaznox was quite favorably pleased with the market projects.
fig/sym	2	Book prices increased 17% from 05/09/06 to 08/03/06 in 42 stores.
speed	3	The widow may visit the city to see the robot shape an auto body.

gwam 1' | 1 | 2 | 3 | 4 | 5 | 6 | 7 | 8 | 9 | 10 | 11 | 12 | 13 |

LESSON 1 SCANNING

OBJECTIVES

- ⊙ To learn about imaging technologies.
- ⊙ To learn the digitizing process of the scanner.
- ⊙ To learn the appropriate file formats for scanned images.
- ⊙ To learn how to set up and care for a scanner.
- ⊙ To preview, crop, and scan images.
- ⊙ To adjust scanner settings.

Ready, Set, Scan

Imaging devices are hardware tools that capture images. Fax machines and copy machines are imaging tools. Cameras are also imaging devices. While cameras allow you to snap pictures of nearly anything you can point your lens at, scanners are better for capturing images of

Imaging devices

- printed documents
- magazines pages
- book covers
- printed photos
- drawings or paintings

A scanner captures images and converts them into graphics files. The scanner then passes the images to a personal computer so they can be manipulated by high-end, digital imaging applications such as *Adobe Photoshop®*, *Microsoft Digital Image®*, and *Corel Photo-Paint®*. Scanned images can be used in *Microsoft Word*, *PowerPoint*, or a multitude of other applications.

Many people are now using scanners to preserve old printed historic and family photographs in a digital format. Mari, on a recent trip to visit extended family in England, came across a box of dusty, old, fading, and deteriorating family photos from the 1930s and '40s. Some of these photographs will be used in this unit to demonstrate how preservation is possible with a digital scanner and digital imaging software.

Scanner Setup and Care

There are dozens of scanner makers and hundreds of different models. (See Figure IT3-1.) Each scanner works a little differently. Scanners come with their own software that should be installed before you use them. If you have lost your installation CD, you can usually download a copy of the necessary software from your manufacturer's support website.

Figure IT3-1   Various Types of Scanners

© PRNEWSFOTO/LEXMARK INTERNATIONAL, INC.

© TERRI MILLER/E-VISUAL COMMUNICATIONS, INC.

Instant Message

Be careful using common household cleansers on your flatbed scanner. Some cleaners can scratch the surface of the glass. Scratches can show up on the surface of your digitized images.

Follow the installation instructions that come with your scanner. Make sure you have plugged your scanner into the power outlet and into your PC. And make sure all connections fit snugly.

A scanner takes a picture of everything it sees, so keep your scanner clean. Fingerprints, smudges, dust, or anything else on the surface of the scanner will show up in your image. Before you start any scanning project, follow the manufacturer's instructions to clean the scanner properly.

Steps to Scanning

There are three basic steps to scanning an image:

    A. Position the image.
    B. Preview, adjust, and scan the image.
    C. Save the image.

Position the Image

The first step is to position the image on the scanner itself. If you have a flatbed scanner, place the original face down. Be sure to put the top of the image at the top of the scanning bed in the direction you wish to see it. If your image is too wide to fit the bed, place it sideways.

The way an image is positioned is called its **orientation**. When the long side of the image is at the top, it is in **landscape** orientation. When the short side of the image is at the top, it is in **portrait** orientation. See Figure IT3-2.

Figure IT3-2   Landscape and Portrait Orientations

Portrait

Landscape

Place documents as straight as possible on a scanning bed. Use the ruler or markers found on the side of the scanning bed to help you place your object in the proper position.

If your scanner has a lid, lower it carefully over your image so it doesn't move out of position. The lid will keep your image in place and will also keep the bright light from the scanner's lamp from hurting your eyes.

Preview, Adjust, and Scan the Image

After an image has been scanned, you'll have a chance to preview and adjust the scanned image before you save it. For instance, an image may have been scanned at a slant, which is called **skewed**, or scanned sideways or even upside down. Open the lid, straighten the image, and preview again. (See Figure IT3-3.)

Also, you can preview and adjust the type of image that will be saved. For example, you can scan:

- Color images
- Grayscale images
- Black-and-white images

Figure IT3-3   A Skewed and Rotated Image of an English Monument

Picture Type Options

The color option will result in a color image close to the original. The grayscale option substitutes colors with various shades of gray. The black-and-white option is used for images or text documents without any color. There is also a custom option allowing changes in resolution, brightness, or contrast. Options for picture type are shown in Figure IT3-4.

Look carefully at the preview of your scan. If you don't like what you see, you can always rescan, readjust your scanner's settings, and reposition your image.

Picture type:
- ⦿ Color picture
- ◯ Grayscale picture
- ◯ Black and white picture or text
- ◯ Custom

Save the Image

After an image has been scanned, it can be saved in a variety of file formats. Some common file formats include:

JPEG (.jpg)	The Joint Photographic Experts Group is an organization that created the standards for the JPEG format. This format supports millions of colors and can be compressed. For computer backgrounds and Web graphics, lower resolutions can be used. For printed documents, increasing the resolution is desirable. However, increasing the resolution will increase the file size.
GIF (.gif)	The Graphics Interchange Format (GIF) is a popular format for images used on the Internet. Images in this format are small and compressed. The format is acceptable for cartoons, logos, Web graphics, graphics with transparent areas, and animations.
TIFF (.tif)	The Tagged Image File format (TIFF), also seen as Microsoft Office Document Imaging File, is a high-resolution format. It is commonly used in desktop publishing and print publishing. Resolution can be increased and decreased in this format. It allows black-and-white and grayscale images as well as color images. It is one of the most widely supported file formats.
• BMP (.bmp)	The Bitmap or BMP file format was created by Microsoft and is used widely by *Microsoft Windows* and other *Office* programs.
• PSD (.psd)	The Photoshop or PSD file format is the default standard supported by *Adobe Photoshop*. If you're working with *Photoshop*, this file format will preserve most of the specialized *Photoshop* features.

From earlier lessons you have learned that JPEG and GIF are probably better for Internet images. TIFF and PSD images are probably better for printed documents. BMP images are easy to manipulate in *Microsoft Office* applications. Pick the file format that best fits the specific need you have for your scanned graphic.

You will need to name your saved image. Choose a name that will help you identify the image when you see it later in a list of filenames. Also, choose the proper folder in which to save your images. In *Microsoft Windows*, a good location would be inside the **My Pictures** folder.

Rasters, Bitmaps, and Vectors

Digitizing Images

A scanner creates images through a process called **digitizing**. Digitizing divides an image into tiny squares in a grid pattern. For this discussion, we will call each tiny square a dot. Each dot in the grid is given a mathematical value. This value is then translated into black, white, gray, red, green, blue, yellow, or other colors. The result is a bitmap image that can then be saved in a variety of formats.

The density of the dots determines its resolution. The more dots, the higher the resolution. Resolution is often expressed in **DPI** or **dots per inch**. This is often expressed in the number of rows and columns in the grid, such as 640 x 480 or 1024 x 768.

On a computer screen, grids of dots are displayed by **pixels**, little dots of light that display color on the monitor. The resolution of monitors is measured in **pixels per inch** or **PPI**. Little dots are also used by printers to print photographs or documents. Other imaging technologies such as cameras, scanners, and fax machines convert the images they see into little grids of dots: black-and-white dots, grayscale dots, or color dots. Such bitmapped graphics are also called **raster graphics**. If you **zoom** in closer and closer on a raster or bitmap graphic, the image gives way to the squares or dots of color. (See Figure IT3-5.)

Figure IT3-5 Zoom in on a Raster Graphic

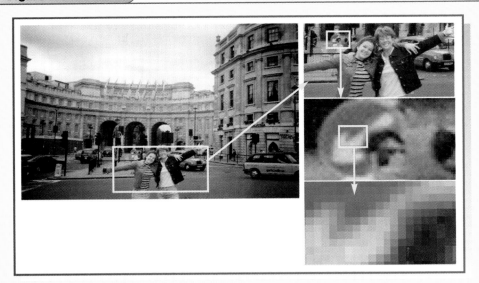

While raster graphics capture little dots as squares of color, **vector graphics** use mathematical formulas to define all of the shapes in an image. Vector graphics are scalable and are perfect for such things as scalable fonts that can grow and shrink based upon what the graphic will be used for. Vector graphics do not display jagged and rough edges when subjected to close scrutiny.

Sunbathing at the Beach in 1930

A poor-quality photo for scanning purposes

Image Selection

When selecting an image to scan, choose the best-quality image available. The better the original, the better the copy. Not all images are great candidates for scanning. Some are too dark and others are too faded. Some lack color or definition. Figure IT3-6 displays a poor candidate for scanning.

Even a poor candidate for scanning, such as the one seen in Figure IT3-6, may be an important family or historical photo. Such photos can be restored using specially designed imaging software. For example, notice how this photograph has been partially restored with just a few simple techniques using *Adobe Photoshop*. (See Figure IT3-7.)

Figure IT3-7

A 75-Year-Old Photograph That Has Been Partially Restored

Scan an Image with Your OS Software

In this first exercise, we'll capture an image using the Windows OS scanning utility. Your specific computer system may require a different set of steps. Consult your system administrator if you have problems scanning. Your computer may have other software that can do the same job, perhaps even more effectively. If you are comfortable using alternative scanning software, by all means, use it.

For the upcoming exercise, choose a photo, magazine page, magazine cover, or some other image that is important to you—something you feel should be preserved in a digital format. In the example found in the exercise, Mari has a snapshot that was taken of her grandparents' home in England—the same home where she found all of the old photographs stuffed in the attic in a dusty old shoebox. She wants to scan the image and preserve it with the older, black-and-white historical photos she is preserving.

Exercise 1A

Figure IT3-8

Open the My Pictures Window

Windows OS Scanning Instructions

1. Place the original face down on the surface of a clean flatbed scanner. Orient your document so it is as straight as possible. If the scanner has a lid, lower it carefully.

2. In Microsoft Windows, click the **Start** button and choose **My Pictures**. See Figure IT3-8.

3. Under Picture Tasks pane, choose **Get pictures from camera or scanner**. See Figure IT3-9.

4. On the Welcome to the Scanner and Camera Wizard window, click or tap **Next**.

5. In the Scanner and Camera Wizard window, select the **Color picture** option as shown in Figure IT3-10. Then click the **Preview** button. The scanner will run its lamp

down the full length of the scanner's glass bed. A small image of your document will show in the preview screen as seen in Figure IT3-10.

Figure IT3-9   Choose Get Pictures from Camera or Scanner

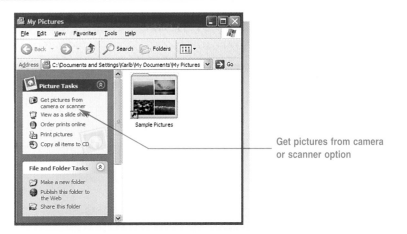

Get pictures from camera or scanner option

Figure IT3-10   Set Your Scanning Preferences

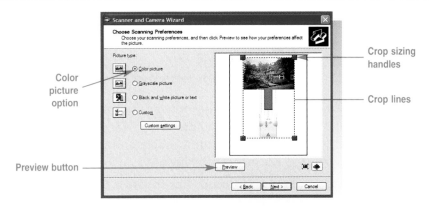

Crop sizing handles

Color picture option

Crop lines

Preview button

6. The Wizard will display crop lines and crop handles around the image as shown in Figure IT3-11. Click or tap and drag inward on one of the crop handles until you have selected only the part of the image you wish to capture.

Figure IT3-11   Crop Your Image by Dragging the Crop Handles

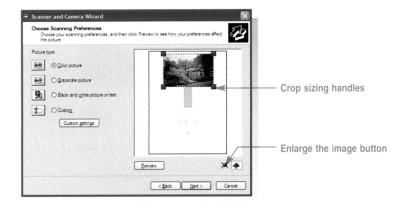

Crop sizing handles

Enlarge the image button

> **TIP**
> If you have more than one scanner or device connected, you may need to set the paper source to Flatbed or to some other scanner setting as directed by the scanner owner's manual. If you are asked, set the page size to Letter.

> **TIP**
> To **crop** means to cut or trim.

7. Click the **Enlarge the image** button to see how the scanned image will look when printed or opened in a photo imaging application such as *Photoshop*. (See Figure IT3-12.) If you need to change the area that has been selected, click the **Show the Entire Image** button. To make a change, click the **Enlarge the image** button again.

8. When you have the image selected, click **Next**. The Picture Name and Destination window will appear.

9. For the name of your picture, key **Practice Scan 1**. Choose **JPG (JPEG image)** for the file format. Save your image in your **My Pictures** folder or the folder where you normally save your work. (See Figure IT3-13.)

Figure IT3-12   Enlarge Your Preview of the Image

Enlarge the image button

Show the entire image button

Figure IT3-13   Name the File and Choose the Image Format

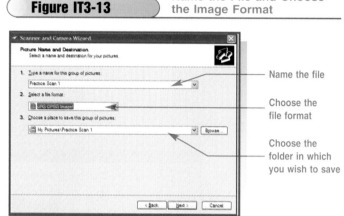

Name the file

Choose the file format

Choose the folder in which you wish to save

10. Click **Next**. The scanner may or may not need to rescan the image, depending on the type of scanner you are using. (See Figure IT3-14.) If a rescan occurs, wait for the operation to finish and then select any options that will allow you to finish the operation.

11. In the next window select **Nothing. I'm finished working with these pictures**.

12. Click **Next** followed by **Finish**. The Wizard will close and return you to the Windows My Documents/My Pictures folder (or the folder to which you save your images). Windows will give you a chance to preview your final image, as seen in Figure IT3-15.

Figure IT3-14   Complete Your Scan

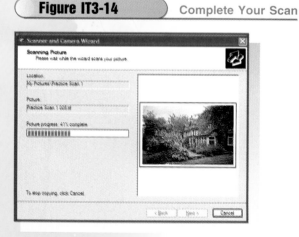

Figure IT3-15   Preview Your Final Image

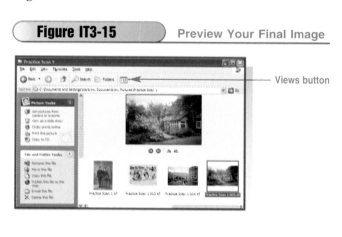

Views button

13. Windows will allow you to preview photos and a variety of ways. Choose the **Views** button down arrow, as seen in Figure IT3-16. Explore each of the following views to see which one best suits your needs: Filmstrip, Thumbnails, Tiles, Icons, List, and Details.

Figure IT3-16

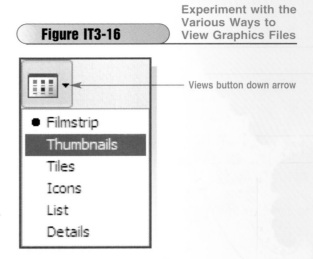

Views button down arrow

Scanning Old Photos with Grayscale

In this section we will experiment with black-and-white and grayscale scanning. Grayscale substitutes color for 256 gradations of gray, from black (0), to pure white (255). Grayscale can turn a color photograph into a black-and-white image or preserve an old-fashioned black-and-white photograph.

 Exercise 1B

Scanning Classic Photos

1. If possible, find an old black-and-white photo or another image of your choice. Our sample is a 70-year-old photograph of British soldiers in North Africa in World War II. The photo needs cropping and digital preservation.

2. Place the original face down on the surface of a clean flatbed scanner. Orient your document so it is as straight as possible. If the scanner has a lid, lower it carefully.

3. As an experiment, choose **Black and white picture or text**. Select **Preview** to view the scan. Scan the photo using the steps learned in Exercise 1A. The scan was probably unsatisfactory. This is because most black-and-white photos are not truly black and white but shades of gray.

4. Try to scan again, this time choosing **Grayscale**. (See Figure IT3-17.) Select **Preview** to view the scan. The image is probably much, much sharper.

5. Crop your photo. In our example, a fifth soldier's face on the far right was accidentally cut in half by the photographer. Instead of showing just half a face, the photo has been cropped to center the four remaining soldiers around the table. Readjust your image on the scanner if necessary, and crop your image to make it more interesting. Choose **Preview** again. When you are satisfied with your preview, select **Scan**.

6. Begin making adjustments to the scanned photograph. Our sample image is somewhat faded and washed out. Select the **Custom** option and click the **Custom Settings** button marked in Figure IT3-18 on the following page.

 **Figure IT3-17**

Preview and Crop a Grayscale Image

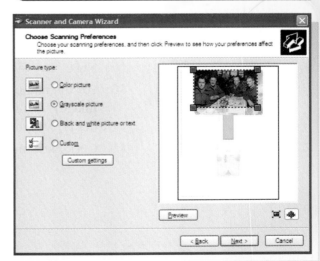

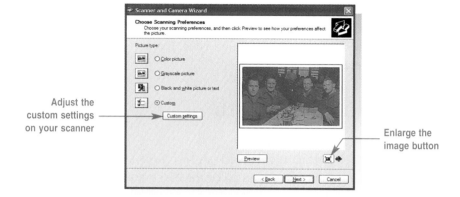

Adjust the
custom settings
on your scanner

Enlarge the
image button

Tip

If you are not satisfied with your brightness and contrast settings, choose the Custom Settings button again, choose Reset, and then try adjusting the contrast and brightness sliders again. Slight changes are probably better than dramatic changes.

7. In our sample image, we will adjust the Brightness and Contrast settings to make the image look much sharper and less faded. In the Properties dialog box, experiment with the **Brightness** and **Contrast** settings for your particular photograph. (See Figure IT3-19.) Choose **OK** to return to your Preview.

8. Click the **Preview** button and preview your scan one more time. (See Figure IT3-20.)

Figure IT3-19   Adjust the Brightness and Contrast of Your Grayscale Image

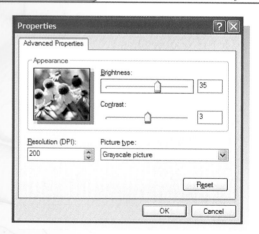

Figure IT3-20   Preview Your Final Image

9. When you have the image previewed and ready for completion, click **Next**. The Picture Name and Destination window will appear.

10. For the name of your picture, key **Practice Scan 2**. Choose **JPG (JPEG image)** for the file format. Save your image in your **My Pictures** folder or the folder where you normally save your work.

11. Click **Next** and finish your scan as you did in Exercise 1A.

LESSON ② DIGITAL CAMERA IMAGES

OBJECTIVES
- ⊙ To learn about the powerful features of today's digital cameras.
- ⊙ To experiment with the settings of a digital camera.
- ⊙ To take pictures with a digital camera.
- ⊙ To download digital images to a PC from a camera.

Click, Click, Click, Click

It seems like everyone has a camera. They either have one in their phone, they are packing a disposable camera, or they have a digital camera. Many full-featured digital cameras will capture both still photos and video.

In the past, all cameras used film. When the shutter opened, light exposed the film, and the image was captured. The film was developed with strong, toxic chemicals and produced extremely high-quality images. When digital cameras first came to market, most people still preferred film photography. Early digital cameras had a hard time competing with the quality of film. Digital cameras were scoffed at because of their terrible resolution, which yielded very poor picture quality.

© PHOTODISC RED/GETTY IMAGES

megapixels

Many Years, Megapixels, and Features Later . . .

Digital cameras quickly improved during the 1990s. Digital camera resolution is measured in **megapixels**. *Mega* means a million, and *pixels* describe those little dots of color explained in Lesson 1. The greater the number of pixels, the higher the resolution. Early digital cameras captured images at a rate of only 1 megapixel or less. At this rate, picture resolution and quality were very poor.

Today, 3, 5, 10, or even higher megapixel cameras are available. Today's 5 and 8 megapixel cameras begin to rival the quality of film photography. (See Table 3-1.)

Table 3-1 Megapixel Picture Sizes

2 megapixel camera . . .	. . . suitable for 5 x 7 photos
3 megapixel camera . . .	. . . suitable for 8 x 10 photos
5 megapixel camera . . .	. . . suitable for 11 x 14 photos
8 megapixel camera . . .	. . . suitable for 13 x 19 photos

LCDs or **liquid crystal displays**
optical zoom
digital zoom

Digital cameras are equipped with **LCDs** or **liquid crystal displays** that let you see the pictures you have taken immediately. This gives you the chance to decide whether a picture is acceptable or if you need to shoot it again. And since digital cameras can hold hundreds of photos, it's always good to take a few backup shots of important subjects.

Many current digital cameras come with two types of zoom. An **optical zoom** physically adjusts the lenses and will close in on a subject without sacrificing quality. The **digital zoom** feature will also zoom in on a subject, but image quality will be sacrificed if the zoom is too "tight" or close, much as zooming in on a raster graphic can cause the image to dissipate. (See Figure IT3-5 on page 561.)

© PRNEWSFOTO/NIKONMERA

Digital cameras can store pictures as image files on memory devices. The number of pictures that can be stored depends on the size of the memory card and the number of megapixels captured in each photo. (See Table 3-2.) Images saved either in the camera's memory or on a memory device can be downloaded to a PC with minimal difficulty.

Table 3-2   Memory Card Capacity

	3 megapixels	5 megapixels	8 megapixels
128 MB memory card	~108 photos	~52 photos	~10 photos
256 MB memory card	~218 photos	~104 photos	~20 photos
512 MB memory card	~436 photos	~209 photos	~40 photos
1 GB memory card	~874 photos	~419 photos	~80 photos

Just like scanners, most digital cameras let you select the file type, quality (comprehension) level, and resolution. Decide what you're going to do with the picture before selecting these settings. If you're going to look at an image on a computer screen, post it on a website, or e-mail it to a friend, keep the file size small. However, capture as many pixels per inch as your camera will permit if you intend to print a large picture in color on expensive photographic paper.

Get to Know Your Camera's Settings

Most digital cameras come with various quality option settings. If you increase the quality of the image, you will increase the pixels, which will give you more flexibility in the size and resolution of the photo you can print. However, higher-quality images will take up more memory and increase file size, as seen in Table 3-2 and Table 3-3.

Table 3-3   Camera Resolution Experiment

Picture #	Quality	Resolution	File Size
1	Good	Low	Small
2	Better	Low	Medium
3	Good	High	Large
4	Best	Low	Large
5	Best	High	Very Large

You will need to experiment with your camera before deciding the quality and resolution settings that will work best in a given photographic session. To do this, take a series of photos of the same subject while changing the camera settings. It may be helpful for you (or your team) to keep a log like the one shown in Table 3-3. The entries in the sample log show the file size getting bigger as the resolution and picture quality improves. The settings on your camera may vary, so your table may look very different from the sample.

Exercise 2A
Experiment with Your Camera

1. Alone or as a team, work through the settings on your digital camera. Investigate the quality settings on your camera and the various resolution options. Your camera may have more or fewer settings depending on its quality, price, and features.

2. Take notes of your experiment in *OneNote* or start *Microsoft Word* and create a table that will accommodate your experiment. Remember that you will be experimenting with three to six photographs of the same subject shot at different quality and resolution levels with varying file sizes. Adjust your table and the number of images you are going to shoot based on your camera's available settings.

3. Look through the viewfinder at the subject you want to photograph. Hold the camera as still as possible and press the shutter button. (*Note:* Don't turn the camera off until it has had time to save the image.)

4. Change the quality and resolution settings and take your next picture. Record the settings in your table. Continue to adjust the quality and resolution settings. Take three to six photographs of the same subject at different settings depending on the features available for your camera.

5. Compile your notes and save them in a file called *Camera Settings*.

Downloading Images to Your PC

There are a few possible ways to download images from a camera to a computer. First, the camera can be attached by a cable directly to the computer. Second, the camera's memory card can be removed and read by a card reader that is built into or attached to a computer. Follow the instructions that come with your particular camera's user manual.

Exercise 2B
Move Your Images to a PC

1. If you're using a cable connection to your camera, plug your cable into your camera and into your USB or FireWire port on your PC. If you are using a card reader, connect it to your PC. Remove the memory card from your camera and insert it into the card reader.

2. Your operating system should automatically sense that you have connected a card reader or camera to your PC and display a screen asking if you want to copy the pictures to your PC. (See Figure IT3-21 on the next page.) (Note: If this fails to happen, choose **Start**, **My Computer**, and open your reader or camera files from the list or open your **My Pictures** file and choose **Get pictures from camera or scanner** as seen in Figure IT3-21.)

Copy Your Pictures
to Your PC

3. Click **OK**. The Scanner and Camera Wizard will begin. Click **Next** on the welcome screen and follow the on-screen instructions.

4. Select your three to six pictures by making sure there's a check mark in each box as shown in Figure IT3-22. Click **Next**.

5. In the Picture Name and Destination window, enter a name for the group of pictures. For example, a good name for our sample group of photos would be **Graduation**.

6. Select a folder in which to save the pictures in the second box. Choose either the **My Pictures** folder or the folder in which you save your work. If you want to select a folder that is not in the drop-down list, use the **Browse** button to find the folder. Click **Next**.

7. Continue following the on-screen instructions. The pictures will be copied to the folder you selected, and the folder will open.

8. Click **View** on the menu bar. Choose **Details**. This will allow you to see the file size of each photograph. Add the file size data as displayed in the Details view to the notes you created in Exercise 2A Experiment with Your Camera. Use this information to complete the data in your **Camera Settings** file.

9. Click **View** on the menu bar. Choose **Thumbnails** to see small images of each picture.

Figure IT3-22 Choose the Images You Wish to Download

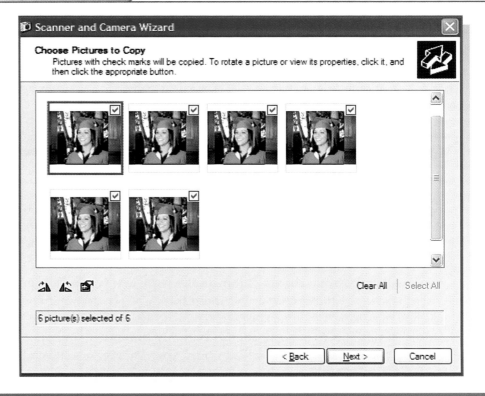

- ⊚ To adjust for brightness, contrast, shadow, highlights, hue (color), saturation, and lightness.
- ⊚ To rotate images.
- ⊚ To crop images
- ⊚ To save in various file formats.
- ⊚ To display a file on a PC desktop.

Improving Images with Imaging Software

After you have downloaded your images successfully to your PC, you can do many things to improve or enhance them using imaging software such as *Adobe Photoshop®*, *Microsoft Digital Image®*, and *Corel Photo-Paint®*. You can also use your photos in other applications:

- In reports created in *Microsoft Word*
- In *PowerPoint* shows
- On Web pages
- In your operating system (for example, as a desktop background)

About *Photoshop*

In Exercises 3A, 3B, and 3C, we will use *Adobe Photoshop* to provide examples of how imaging software can be used to enhance photographs and other images. *Photoshop* is currently the most popular and widely used imaging software. If you do not have access to *Photoshop*, search your Help features to learn how to accomplish these same steps using your particular digital imaging application.

The exercises that follow do not represent an extensive exploration of *Photoshop*. Far from it! Entire professional-level courses are based on the program. However, by manipulating a few features you will soon acquire a feel for how digital imaging software works and how these tools can benefit anyone working with photos, doing photo restoration, and improving graphics.

Note: Over time, *Photoshop* has evolved and changed. In our examples we will include instructions for a recent version of *Photoshop*. In parentheses, we will include instructions for an early version. Look for *Classic Photoshop* for these instructions. However, depending on your version of *Photoshop*, you may need to search your Help files to learn how to accomplish these basic steps.

Manipulating Settings

After you have downloaded an image to your PC, open it in *Photoshop* or in another imaging software application and manipulate it, improving upon the image any way you like. *Photoshop* and its counterparts have thousands of features and millions of settings. In this exercise, we will explore just a few of them.

In Exercise 3A, you'll see a photo taken on a bright, sunny day that has too much overall brightness and diminished contrasts. The shadows and highlights are somewhat washed out. The colors are not vibrant, either. Photos you have taken or images you have scanned may not need the same improvements; nevertheless, try each feature to see the possible changes you can make to your images. You will change settings for

- Brightness
- Contrast
- Shadow
- Highlight
- Hue (Color)
- Saturation
- Lightness

Exercise 3A

Contrasting Colors

1. Open *Photoshop* or other imaging software. Select **File**, **Browse** and browse to any one of your color images you created in either Lesson 1 or Lesson 2. If you don't have a suitable color image, you may need to

   - Scan or shoot a new image to download to your PC.
   - Use the data file called *American Home* provided by your instructor.

2. Click or tap **Image**, **Adjustments**, followed by **Brightness/Contrast** to reveal the Brightness/Contrast dialog box as shown in Figure IT3-23. Make sure the **Preview** box is checked so that you can see a before and after view of your image. (*Classic Photoshop:* Choose **Enhance**, **Brightness/Contrast** followed by **Brightness/Contrast** again, or use your Help files and search for *Brightness* and *Contrast*.)

Figure IT3-23   Adjusting Brightness and Contrast

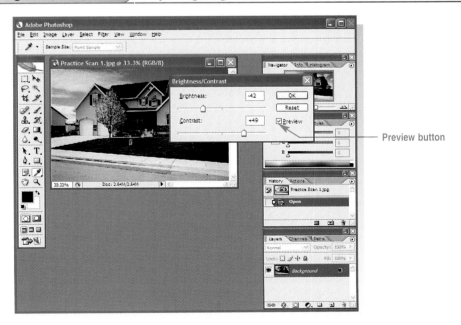

Preview button

3. Slide the **Brightness** slider to the left, and then to the right. The image will get darker and then lighter.

4. Move the Brightness slider back to the middle so that the brightness adjustment (the number next to the slider) is 0.

5. Slide the **Contrast** slider to the left. The image should become lower in contrast and eventually go flat gray. Now slide the **Contrast** slider all the way to the right. The contrast should increase and the image should be more distinct.

6. Click **File** and then **Revert** to make sure you're back to the original image.

Instant Message

As you continue to increase the contrast, some of those areas getting darker reach pure black and some of those getting brighter reach pure white.

7. Click **Image, Adjustments,** followed by **Shadow/Highlights** to reveal the Shadow/Highlights dialog box as shown in Figure IT3-24. Make sure the **Preview** box is checked. (*Classic Photoshop:* Choose **Enhance, Variations** and make shadow and highlight selections based upon personal preferences; then skip to step 10.)

8. Slide the **Shadows** slider slowly to the right and then to the left. The normally lit parts of the image stay the same, but you can see more or less detail in the darker parts of the image.

9. Slide the **Highlight** slider slowly to the right and to the left. (*Note:* In our example, the grass in the foreground becomes slightly darker and less washed out, and then lighter and more washed out. What happens to your image?)

Figure IT3-24 — Shadow/Highlight Dialog Box

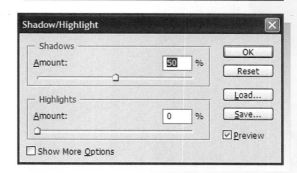

10. Click **Image, Adjustments,** followed by **Hue/ Saturation** to reveal the Hue/Saturation dialog box as shown in Figure IT3-25. Make sure the **Preview** box is checked. (*Classic Photoshop:* Choose **Enhance, Color, Hue/Saturation.**)

11. Slide the **Hue, Saturation,** and **Lightness** sliders slowly to the right and left. Notice the changes that occur.

12. Click **File** and then **Revert** again to make sure you're back to the original image.

Figure IT3-25 — Shadow/Highlight Dialog Box

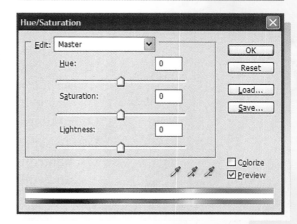

13. Click **Image, Adjustments,** followed by **Color Balance** to reveal the Color Balance dialog box as shown in Figure IT3-26. Again, make sure the **Preview** box is checked. Also, choose **Midtones.** (*Classic Photoshop:* Choose **Enhance, Variations** and make color balance selections based upon personal preferences; then skip to step 15.)

14. Slide the **Cyan/Red, Magenta/Green,** and **Yellow/Blue** sliders slowly to the right and left. Notice the changes.

15. Now that you have experimented with brightness, contrast, shadows, colors, and highlights, adjust the

Figure IT3-26 — Color Balance Dialog Box

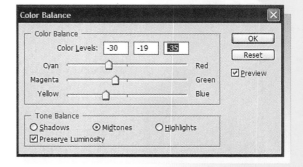

image to your liking. For example, you may only want your shadows to be at 20, or your highlights at 5. You may want to slightly increase or decrease contrast and adjust the brightness to get the most out of your image. Record the settings you chose for your image in the following table in either *Microsoft Word* or *Microsoft OneNote*:

Adjustment Choices 1	
Setting	**Number**
Brightness setting	
Contrast setting	
Shadow setting	
Highlight setting	
Hue setting	
Saturation setting	
Lightness setting	
Cyan/Red	
Magenta/Green	
Yellow/Blue	

16. Save your table in *Microsoft Word* or rename your *OneNote* page *Adjustment Choices 1*. (*Classic Photoshop:* Since some of the settings may not be easily found or applied in your earlier version of *Photoshop*, describe what options you chose and the impact of those selections.)

17. To save your image as *Perfect Picture*, choose an appropriate file format and compression for this picture. Imagine that the home is up for sale and will be displayed on a realtor's website. In *Photoshop*, save the image for the Web by

    a. Choosing **File, Save As**.

    b. Naming the file *Perfect Picture* in the File name box.

    c. Choosing **JPEG** from the format box.

    d. Changing the quality of the photograph to **3** or **Low**.

    e. Tapping or clicking **OK** followed by **Save**.

Rotating Photographs

What happens if you accidentally scan a picture upside down? No worries. *Photoshop* has several ways to rotate the photograph. Practice your rotating skills by selecting a photograph and deliberately placing it upside down in the scanner or shooting your subject with your camera upside down.

In our example, seen in Figure IT3-27, we will scan a picture of a monument to Queen Victoria along the Thames River in London. We can't imagine Queen Victoria will like being upside down for very long!

Figure IT3-27   Even Photographs Scanned Upside Down Can Be Fixed

Instant Message

Chances are, very few of your photographs will be scanned or shot upside down. The importance of learning to rotate is to adjust those small problems created by improper camera angle.

Exercise 3B

Flipping Photos

1. Find a color image and place the original upside down on the surface of the flatbed scanner. (If you don't have an image of your own, choose *Victorian Monument* from the data files. If you are using this file, skip to step 3.)

2. Follow the steps you've learned in previous exercises to scan the image. Readjust and crop your image using the **Preview** mode of your scanner. When you are satisfied with your scan, select **Scan**. (See Figure IT3-28.)

3. Open the image in *Photoshop* or other imaging software.

4. Expand the viewing window (called the **canvas**) so extra space appears around the four sides of the image. (See Figure IT3-29 on the next page.)

5. Choose **Image, Rotate Canvas, 180°**. (See Figure IT3-30 on the next page.)

6. Try choosing **Image, Rotate Canvas**, and **Flip Canvas Horizontal**. This will completely reverse the picture as seen in Figure IT3-31 on the next page. (*Classic Photoshop:* Choose **Image, Rotate, Flip Canvas Horizontal**.)

Figures IT3-28   Scan a Photo Upside Down

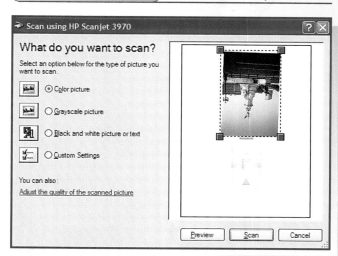

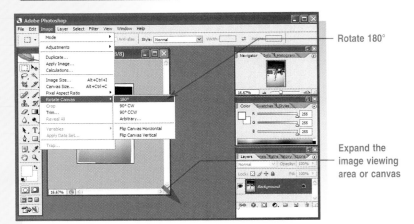

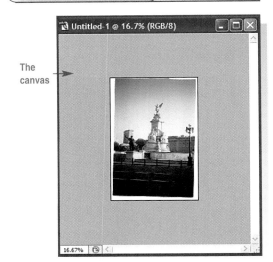

Figure IT3-31 Flip the Image

7. Flip the image horizontally again, back to its original perspective.

8. To save your image as *Flipped Photo*, choose an appropriate file format and compression for this picture. Imagine that the picture of the monument may find its way to a printed report on the history of England, or may even be printed and placed in an 8 x 10 frame sometime in the future. In *Photoshop*, save the image for printing by

   a. Choosing **File**, **Save As**.

   b. Naming the file *Perfect Picture* in the File name box.

   c. Choosing **TIFF** from the format box.

   d. Tapping or clicking **OK** followed by **Save**.

Figure IT3-32 Cropping Images

Cropping Photographs

After you have finished rotating your photograph to your liking, you may wish to crop it in order to capture the most important parts of the image. Take a look at the examples in Figure IT3-32. The first image displays the complete photograph. It is only mildly interesting because there is a great deal of extraneous information in the image. The second image has been cropped to focus on the key parts of the image. The final image is much more dynamic.

Crop It

1. Photos often become much more interesting if the extraneous information is cut out of the image. Use the **Navigator** to zoom in on the central parts of the photograph. Use the scroll bars to position the photograph so that the area you wish to crop is clearly visible. (See Figure IT3-33.)

Figure IT3-33   Prepare the Image for Cropping

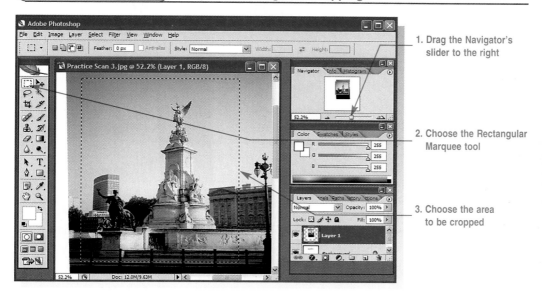

2. Choose the **Rectangular Marquee** tool from the toolbar.
3. Draw a rectangle over the area to be cropped.
4. After you have defined the area to be cropped, choose **Edit, Cut**.
5. Choose **File**, **New**. When the New dialog box appears, key the name **Cropped Image** as seen in Figure IT3-34.
6. Make sure the preset is set to **Clipboard** as seen in Figure IT3-34. Then choose **OK**.

Figure IT3-34   Set the Preset to Clipboard

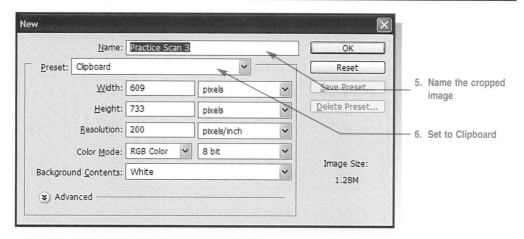

7. A new canvas will then be created. Paste your copied image into the new canvas by selecting **Edit**, **Paste**. (See Figure IT3-35.)

Figure IT3-35   The Cropped Image in a New Canvas

8. Make the proper adjustments to the photograph. Change brightness, colors, contrast, shadows, and highlights. Complete the following chart based on your choices. Upon completion, save your chart or name your *OneNote* page as *Adjustment Choices 2*.

Adjustment Choices 2	
Setting	**Number**
Brightness setting	
Contrast setting	
Shadow setting	
Highlight setting	
Hue setting	
Saturation setting	
Lightness setting	
Cyan/Red	
Magenta/Green	
Yellow/Blue	

9. To save your image as *Cropped Image*, choose an appropriate file format and compression for this picture. Imagine that it will be used in a *Power-Point* show on the history and culture of England, and may later find itself printed in a report. In *Photoshop*, save the image for printing by

   a. Choosing **File**, **Save As**.

   b. Naming the file *Cropped Image* in the File name box.

   c. Choosing **JPEG** from the format box.

   d. Changing the quality of the photograph to **5** or **Medium**.

   e. Tapping or clicking **OK** followed by **Save**.

Displaying an Image on the Desktop

To use your favorite image as a background on your computer's desktop, you will need to save it in a compressed file format such as JPEG, GIF, or BMP. If you have a favorite image that is not saved in a compressed format, review the previous four exercises and save your image in a low-resolution format. For example, a low or 3 JPEG image may do the trick.

Exercise **3D**

Using an Image As a Desktop Background

1. Open an image in *Photoshop* or other imaging software and save it in a low-resolution, compressed file format for display on a computer screen (JPEG, GIF, or BMP).

2. To make an image your desktop background, right-click on your Windows desktop. Choose **Properties** from the pop-up menu.

3. The Display Properties dialog box will appear. Click the **Desktop** tab as shown in Figure IT3-36.

Figure IT3-36 Choose Your Photo as a Desktop Background Image

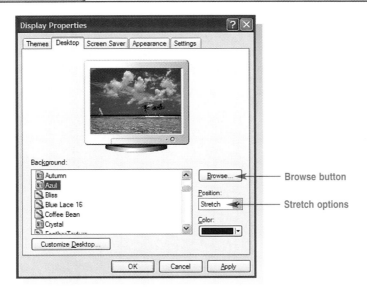

4. Click the **Browse** button. Go to the **My Pictures** folder or the folder where you have stored your images.

5. Select your picture from the background list as shown in Figure IT3-36.

6. Under **Position**, choose the **Stretch** option. Click **Apply**. Click **OK**. Your image should now be your desktop background.

Making Connections

What to Know About Printing Pictures

When printing pictures, your image resolution and quality settings must be higher when compared with images used for Web pages and the Internet. Your picture will only be as good as the image being sent from the computer to the printer.

Also, make sure that the resolution on your printer has been set to the proper setting. For the most part, you will want to choose a higher-quality resolution setting. But be careful; some photos may not be worth the extra cost in terms of ink, expensive photographic paper, and the additional time it takes to print them. If you are printing an important photo, the added expense and time may be worth it.

Also, make sure your ink cartridges are full and aligned properly. Most printers use multiple cartridges and colors to print full-color photos. If one of your colors in your cartridge is near empty, the image will be distorted.

UNIT 3

LESSONS 1–3

Assessing Scanning, Photo, and Imaging Tools Skills

LESSON (1) **ASSESS SCANNING SKILLS**

OBJECTIVES
- ⊙ To assess preservation needs.
- ⊙ To assess the ability to scan in color and grayscale.
- ⊙ To assess the ability to crop a prescanned image.
- ⊙ To assess the knowledge of how to adjust brightness and contrast for a prescanned image.

Exercise **1A**

Assess Preservation Needs

1. Do you or your family have any old photos stuck in dusty shoe boxes? Do a search and find any family photos that need digital preservation.

2. After your search, open *Microsoft Excel* and make the following estimates in a new worksheet called *Photo Restoration Project*:

   • Estimate the number of photos that need preservation. Divide the photos into three groups and estimate how many color, grayscale, and black-and-white images will need scanning.

   • Make an estimate of file size for the average photo in each category.

   • Make a determination using your *Excel* spreadsheet as to how much computer hard drive space may be required to store the historic photos.

3. Scan a sample color and a grayscale photo (if necessary) from your pile of photos that need preservation. Estimate the amount of time it will take to scan, crop, and preserve each of these photo types. Start timing each sample scan from the second you begin sorting and selecting the photograph, to its placement on the scanning bed, through preview, cropping, scanning, saving, and finally removing the photograph from the scanning bed. In your *Excel* spreadsheet, estimate the time it will take to adequately select, place, preview, adjust brightness and contrast if necessary, scan, crop, save, and preserve all of the photos that you have identified.

4. Save your *Excel* worksheet as *Photo Restoration Project*.

Exercise 1B

Assess Scanning Needs for Print Documents

1. Are you currently working on a report, brochure, flyer, or other printed document? Do you have a completed report that you believe would be enhanced by adding a picture, graphic, or other image? If so, find an appropriate subject or existing image and scan or photograph it, download it to your computer, and use it in a printed document. Adjust the brightness and contrast settings if necessary. Be sure to choose the right file format quality, compression, and resolution for a printed document.

LESSON 2 — ASSESS PHOTO INPUT SKILLS

OBJECTIVES

 To assess the ability to take photographs and transfer them from a camera to a personal computer.

 To assess the understanding of how photos can be used in *PowerPoint* presentations.

 To assess the ability to research relevant information online.

Exercise 2A

Conduct a Photo Shoot of Local Historical Interest

1. Locate a digital camera (or obtain a disposable camera that can be developed with an accompanying CD of digital images).

2. Conduct a photo shoot, capturing images of local historical interest. Imagine what someone would like to know and see a hundred years from now about you, where you live, and how you live.

3. Choose an appropriate resolution and quality setting for your photos. (*Hint:* The photos may be used to develop a website of local historical interest in Exercise 3C.)

4. Download your completed photos to your PC.

Exercise 2B

Discover Better Photography Techniques Online

TEAMWORK

1. As a team, use your Internet searching skills to find articles relating to photography. Principally, search for articles that answer the question, "How can someone become a better photographer?"

2. In *Microsoft Word* or *Microsoft OneNote*, key the source information for the articles you have found. Include the names of each article, the website source, the website address, and the date you read the material. Summarize the main points of each article.

3. Practice the skills you have learned, and see if they improve your photographic skills.

4. Summarize what you have learned in a group *PowerPoint* presentation called *What Expert Photographers Know*. Be sure to include samples of what you have learned. This may require taking photos, downloading them to your PC, compressing them appropriately, and using them in your *PowerPoint* presentation.

LESSON 3 ASSESS DIGITAL IMAGING SKILLS

OBJECTIVES

> To assess the ability to improve color images.
> To assess the ability to improve grayscale images.
> To assess the ability to prepare and use images on a website.

Exercise 3A

Make It Look Better!

An English countryside home has been put up for sale. The owner wants to post an advertisement online and needs to provide the realtor with an image suitable for the Web. Using your digital imaging software, such as *Photoshop*, *Digital Image*, or *Photo-Paint*, take on the following project:

1. Open the file called *English Countryside Home* in your digital imaging software.

2. Flip the image horizontally, so the home is facing in the opposite direction.

3. Crop the image so it presents a more dramatic scene.

4. Improve the image by adjusting the brightness, contrast, shadows, highlights, hues/colors, saturation, and lightness of the image.

5. Save your improved image as the *English Home Revitalized*.

Exercise 3B

Grayscale Photo Restoration Project

Using your digital imaging software, take on a restoration of a badly deteriorating, approximately 70-year-old black-and-white photograph. The image you restore will be reprinted on high-quality photographic paper for placement in an 8 x 10 frame. You can use an image of your own or you can choose from three images in the data files.

1. Choose a grayscale photo of your own or one of the following grayscale photos from the data files:

   • *Portrait Soldiers*

   • *Landscape Soldiers*

   • *Day at the Beach*

2. Crop the image so it presents the most dramatic image possible.

3. Improve the image by adjusting the brightness, contrast, shadows, high-lights, saturation, and lightness of the image.

4. Using your **Help** feature, learn how you can improve the photo even further by applying such tools as a clone tool or a spot healing brush. Investigate how these tools may restore scratches, tears, and faded portions of the image.

5. Save your improved image as *Grayscale Photo Revitalized*.

Exercise 3C

Using Digital Images on a Website

1. Create an image gallery website. Choose from one of the following projects:

   - Add your own digital images to the website project you designed and created in the assessment Exercises 1A, 2A, and 3A in Part 2, Unit 6. Find appropriate subjects or existing images, scan or photograph them, and use them on your website.

   - Complete the preservation project planned in Exercise 1A. Scan at least a dozen photos for display on a website in an online photo gallery. Create a website to display these important photos in an attractive and informative way.

   - Take the photos you shot in Exercise 2A and create a website displaying your historical photos in an attractive and informative way in an online photo gallery.

2. Be sure to select the correct graphics file formats and resolution settings required for online images.

3. Make sure you name your Web-based graphics appropriately with no capital letters and spaces.

4. Provide written explanations on your website of each image and why it would be considered of importance or of high interest.

Communication & Math Skills 13

ACTIVITY 1 — Application: Subject/Predicate Agreement

1. Key lines 1–10, selecting the proper verb.

2. Save as *CS13-ACT1*.

1 (Wasn't, Weren't) you aware that the matinee began at 2:30 p.m.?
2 Our senior debate team (has, have) won the city championship.
3 A number of our workers (are, is) to receive proficiency awards.
4 Either the coach or an assistant (are, is) to speak at the assembly.
5 Maria (doesn't, don't) know whether she can attend the beach party.
6 Ms. Yamamoto and her mother (are, is) now American citizens.
7 (Was, Were) the director as well as his assistants at the meeting?
8 The number of applicants for admission (are, is) greater this year.
9 The logic behind their main arguments (elude, eludes) me.
10 It (doesn't, don't) matter to me which of the two is elected.

ACTIVITY 2 — Application: Capitalization and Number Expression

1. Key lines 1–10, capitalizing and expressing numbers correctly.

2. Save as *CS13-ACT2*.

1 "the jury," said the judge, "must reach a unanimous decision."
2 for what percentage of total sales is mrs. rhodes responsible?
3 i need a copy of the <u>dictionary of composers and their music</u>.
4 miss valdez told us to go to room eight of corbett hall.
5 the institute of art is at fifth avenue and irving place.
6 "don't you agree," he asked, "that honesty is the best policy?"
7 is the "tony award show" to be shown on tv on april seventeen?
8 dr. robin j. sousa is to address fbla members in orlando.
9 see page 473 of volume one of <u>encyclopedia americana</u>.
10 here is pbc's check #2749 for $83 (less ten percent discount).

ACTIVITY 3 — Write to Learn

1. Using word processing or voice recognition software, write a paragraph explaining the steps you would take to scan a document into your computer.

2. Save as *CS13-ACT3*.

ACTIVITY 4 — Preparing to Speak

1. You will attend a meeting of a club you joined recently. The members likely will ask you to introduce yourself briefly (about 1' to 2').

2. Prepare an outline of the points you want to include. Suggestions follow:
   - State your name and year in school, and mention your hobbies.
   - Describe your aspirations after graduation.
   - Tell the audience about other things you do or like.

3. If time and resources permit, record your speech in a sound file.

4. Save the outline as *CS13-ACT4* and the sound file as *CS13-ACT4-SOUND*.

ACTIVITY 5 — Math: Applying Math Skills by Using Mental Math

1. Open *CD-CS13-ACT5* and print the file.
2. Solve the problems as directed in the file.

3. Submit your answers.

UNIT 4

Conditioning Practice

Before you begin the lessons, key each line twice.

alphabet 1 Tezz quickly indexed jokes for a public performance he will give.

fig/sym 2 Sales discounts (15%) amount to $134,682, an increase of $21,790.

speed 3 The eight busy men may do the work for us if he pays for the ivy.

gwam 1' | 1 | 2 | 3 | 4 | 5 | 6 | 7 | 8 | 9 | 10 | 11 | 12 | 13 |

A Note to Students and Instructors

This unit will help you learn the Microsoft electronic notetaking software called *OneNote*. If you have learned to use speech and handwriting technologies in the previous units, you can certainly apply what you have learned to *OneNote*.

We have selected Unit 1 Computer History from the beginning of Part 2 to provide a true-to-life example of how to use *OneNote* to boost your studies. Since Unit 1 is a history lesson, there are no prerequisites, so everyone should be able to participate with equal ease. Hopefully, by working through the history chapter, you can see how *OneNote* can enhance your retention of what you are learning.

LESSON ① TAKING NOTE OF *ONENOTE*

OBJECTIVES

- ⊗ To discover electronic notetaking.
- ⊗ To review the *OneNote* interface.
- ⊗ To create a *OneNote* folder.
- ⊗ To create a *OneNote* section.
- ⊗ To create *OneNote* pages.
- ⊗ To create *OneNote* subpages.
- ⊗ To show and hide page titles.
- ⊗ To minimize, maximize, restore, and close *OneNote*.

Studying with *OneNote*

OneNote is, quite simply, an electronic notetaking program. Microsoft designed the program to help you with your studies. *OneNote* allows you to take and organize your notes, search them skillfully, and get the most out of your study time. *OneNote* will help you achieve in this course and any other course you may take in the future.

OneNote has also become a popular business notetaking tool. Salespersons use *OneNote* to keep track of their customers and clients, human resource managers use it to record employee evaluations, and nearly every businessperson can use the software to take notes in meetings.

OneNote is a place to enter, organize, store, study, and search notes. It's like a big storage facility for all of your study and research materials. It's a place to toss all of your notes (quotes, lectures, ideas, excerpts, clips from Web pages, citations, scanned images, photos, graphics, even video clips) until you need them. If there is something you wish to remember, *OneNote* is the place to put it.

The Familiar Parts of *OneNote*

If you are already comfortable working with *Microsoft Word*, *Excel*, or *PowerPoint*, the top portion of *OneNote* will look very familiar to you. If you have never used any of these *Microsoft Office* products before, you're in luck. Once you learn the basic toolbar features in *OneNote*, you'll know how to use them effectively in other *Office* applications, too.

For example, *OneNote* has the same title bar, menu bar, and essential Formatting and Standard toolbars found in other *Microsoft Office* products. Examine the familiar parts of the *Microsoft Office OneNote* interface in Figure IT4-1.

Figure IT4-1   The Organizing Features of *OneNote*

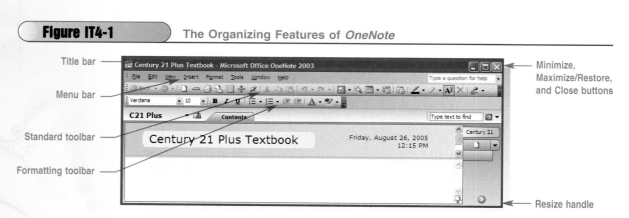

Exercise **1A**

Explore the Familiar Parts of *OneNote*

1. Start *OneNote* by choosing **Start, All Programs, Microsoft Office, Microsoft Office** *OneNote*.

2. Expand *OneNote* to its maximum size by clicking or tapping the **Maximize** button.

3. Restore *OneNote* to a smaller window by tapping the **Restore** button marked in Figure IT4-1. Then click or tap and drag the resizing handle in the bottom corner of *OneNote* to make the *OneNote* window fill about 75 percent of the screen.

4. Minimize *Microsoft OneNote* so that it appears on the Start menu taskbar by clicking or tapping the **Minimize** button. Then restore *OneNote* and have it appear again on the desktop by tapping the **Microsoft OneNote icon** on the taskbar. (See Figure IT4-2.)

5. Click or tap the down arrow at the end of either the Standard or Formatting toolbar and choose **Show Buttons on Two Rows** as shown in Figure IT4-3. (*Note:* Showing the buttons on two rows will allow you to see all of the available tools.)

6. Close *Microsoft OneNote* by choosing the **Close** box on the title bar.

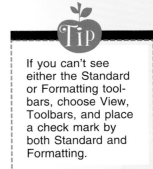

If you can't see either the Standard or Formatting toolbars, choose View, Toolbars, and place a check mark by both Standard and Formatting.

Figure IT4-2 The Minimized Document in the Taskbar

Tap the *OneNote* icon

Figure IT4-3 Display the Formatting and Standard Toolbars on Two Rows

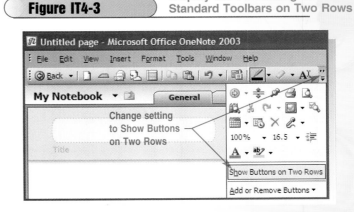

Making Connections

How Unique Is OneNote?

In some ways, *OneNote* works quite a bit differently than other applications you may have used in the past. This unit only scratches the surface of the things you can do with *OneNote*. For example:

- You never have to save in *Microsoft OneNote*! *OneNote* automatically saves notes every 30 seconds or upon exit. This way, you are unlikely to lose track of any notes you take.
- *OneNote* does its best work on mobile tablet PCs, but also works on traditional laptops or even stationary desktop computers.
- You can drag and drop information from the Internet or nearly any Microsoft Windows application into *OneNote*.
- Even if you create thousands upon thousands of note pages for dozens of classes, *OneNote* has the search tools to help you locate and retrieve what you need quickly.
- You can drag and drop text or outlines you have completed in *OneNote* into applications such as *Microsoft Word*, saving the time of having to reenter the text.
- You can record audio and video notes so you can go back later to view and hear what happened in a class or meeting.
- You can e-mail any page of notes to anyone on your e-mail list. In fact, with the correct Internet connection, several people can be working on the same *OneNote* pages simultaneously.

The Unfamiliar Parts of OneNote: Folders, Sections, and Pages

Below the *OneNote* toolbars you will see some very different features from those found in other *Office* applications. Most notably, *OneNote* is organized by tabs, like an everyday school notebook.

Think of each *OneNote* folder as if it were a multisubject notebook. Inside the notebook are section dividers (or tabs) in different colors for different subjects. Between the tabs are numerous notetaking pages. (See Figure IT4-4.)

Figure IT4-4 — A School Notebook with Divider Tabs

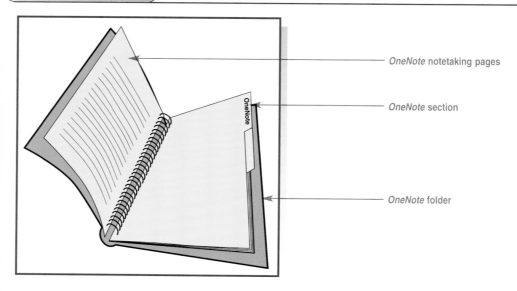

OneNote notetaking pages

OneNote section

OneNote folder

Instant Message

Click on the Type/Selection Tool marked in Figure IT4-5. This will allow you to type in your text with either a keyboard, handtyping software, or speech recognition. Choose that button now, as you will be entering typewritten text for the next several exercises.

folder tab

section tab

Understanding how to create and organize tabs is critical to the OneNote experience. There are four key types of tabs:

- Folder tabs
- Section tabs
- Page tabs
- Subpage tabs

Notice in Figure IT4-5: There are two types of tabs just below the Formatting and Standard toolbars. The first is a **folder tab** and the second is a **section tab**. Think of each section tab as a separate, individual file. Folders help keep sections/files organized, normally by topics; for example, math notes and assignments may be stored in a Math folder, science work in a Science folder, and English course notes in an *English* folder. (In Figure IT4-5, you can see the Century 21 Plus [C21 Plus] folder for this course.)

Remember the following *OneNote* concepts:

- You can create as many new section tabs as you wish inside any folder.
- A section can have as many notetaking pages as you want it to have.
- Each page can also have any number of subpages.
- Every time you create a new page, a date appears in the header area above the *OneNote* notetaking area.

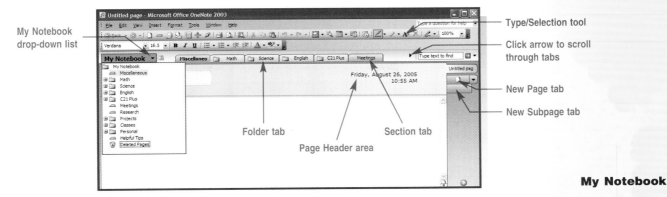

My Notebook drop-down list

Type/Selection tool

Click arrow to scroll through tabs

New Page tab

New Subpage tab

Folder tab

Section tab

Page Header area

My Notebook

- The date and time section of the header records exactly when you began taking notes on that specific page. (See Figure IT4-5.)

Notice the **My Notebook** list in Figure IT4-5. A My Notebook folder is created for every *OneNote* user and placed inside their personal My Documents folder. (Review Exercise 3B in Prerequisites Unit 1.)

If you choose the down arrow next to the My Notebook folder, you can see all of the sections and subsections, folders and subfolders that you have created. (However, the individual pages are still hidden from view until you open a section.) Some sections have been created for you by Microsoft. You can use them, delete them, or ignore them, whatever you choose.

Instant Message

In Exercise 1-B, you'll begin organizing your *OneNote* folders, sections, and note pages for this course of study, using *Part 2, Unit 1* to provide a true-to-life example of how to use *OneNote* to augment your studies.

Exercise 1B

Create Folders and Sections

1. Open *Microsoft OneNote*.
2. To create a new folder, choose **Insert**, **New Folder**. A folder tab will appear with the name *New Folder*. The name will be highlighted as shown in Figure IT4-6.

Instant Message

OneNote sections are organized in folders. These folders are similar to other folders you created on your Windows PC in the Prerequisites unit. Folders are an organizing tool. Inside folders you can create any number of related sections.

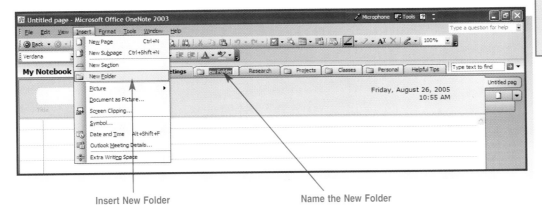

Insert New Folder

Name the New Folder

3. To name the folder, key **C21 Plus**, an abbreviated name for this textbook. (See Figure IT4-7.) Tap ENTER or click and tap in the notetaking area to record the name of the folder.

Figure IT4-7 A Folder Named C21 Plus

Abbreviated names are often used to label tabs

If you tap Enter before keying the new name, you can still rename the folder by right-clicking on the folder name to open the pop-up menu and choosing Rename, as indicated in Figure IT4-8. (*Note:* Tablet PC users, right-click by holding your digital pen directly on the tab's name and then releasing after the ring of dots appears.)

Figure IT4-8 Rename the Folder if Necessary

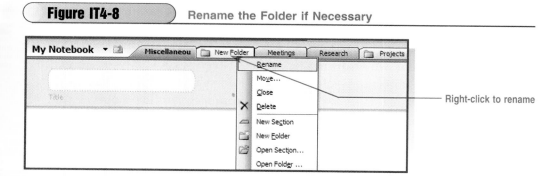

Right-click to rename

4. Click or tap the **C21 Plus** folder tab. You will be greeted by the message shown in Figure IT4-9. Click or tap in the middle of the message on the screen. A new section (or file) will be generated automatically.

Figure IT4-9 Click or Tap the Middle of the Screen's Message to Begin a New Section

Instant Message

Navigation tools are provided just below the Standard and Formatting toolbars. If you click or tap the little folder with the small, green up arrow, you will move up one level in the folder structure. Notice that the name of the current folder always appears above the notetaking area. (See Figure IT4-9.)

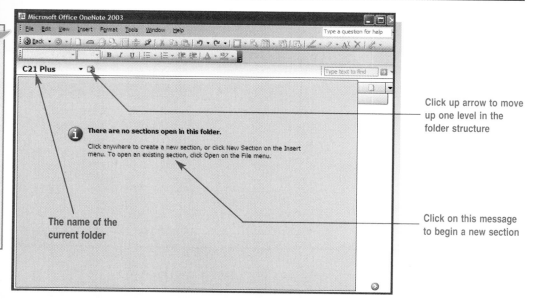

Click up arrow to move up one level in the folder structure

The name of the current folder

Click on this message to begin a new section

5. The name of the new section will be highlighted. Key **Index** and tap ENTER (or click or tap in the notetaking area). The word *Index* will be keyed as the name of the section, as seen in Figure IT4-10.

Figure IT4-10   Change the Name from Index to Contents

6. Oops! A mistake has been made in naming this section. An *Index* is found at the back of a book and indexes detailed topics alphabetically. This section is meant to be a *table of contents*, an overall preview of upcoming sections! Right-click the tab name and choose **Rename** from the pop-up menu. (See Figure IT4-10.) Change the name of this section from *Index* to **Contents**. (See Figure IT4-11.)

7. Click or tap the page header's title box. Key **Century 21 Plus Textbook**, as shown in Figure IT4-11.

Figure IT4-11   Name the Page in the Page Header

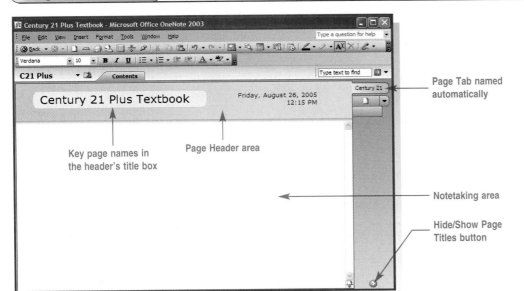

Key page names in the header's title box

Page Header area

Page Tab named automatically

Notetaking area

Hide/Show Page Titles button

Instant Message

The name keyed in the header's title box becomes the name on the page. The first part of that name will appear on the page name tab, as seen in Figure IT4-11.

8. Page tabs can be displayed by number or by header titles. You can change views by clicking the **Hide/Show Page Titles** button in the bottom right of the screen. Click or tap this button several times to see both views. (See Figure IT4-12.)

9. Click the **Hide/Show Page Titles** button again, if needed, to display the full page name titles.

Figure IT4-12   Hide/Show Page Titles Buttons

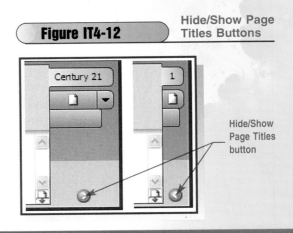

Hide/Show Page Titles button

OBJECTIVES

⊙ To create multiple containers.

⊙ To resize, merge, reorder, and break containers.

⊙ To highlight, bullet, bold, italicize, underline, and color notes.

⊙ To create new folders.

⊙ To make a definitions page.

⊙ To organize outlines using single, double, and triple columns.

⊙ To insert additional notetaking space between existing notes.

Containers: Where and How to Take Notes

containers

Instant Message

The **Show/Hide Rule Lines** button marked in Figure IT4-13 will add or take away rule lines in your notetaking page.

OneNote organizes notes in areas called **containers**. This is an appropriate term. Think of containers as storage units that can contain blocks of text, or a picture, or any other electronic file. Each container can be moved around as needed. In Figure IT4-13, five separate containers were entered into the notetaking area. You can enter notes in a variety of ways.

- Handwrite notes with digital ink.

- Handtype notes with handwriting recognition.

- Key notes on a keyboard.

- Speak notes with speech recognition software.

Figure IT4-13   Inputting Notes into *OneNote*

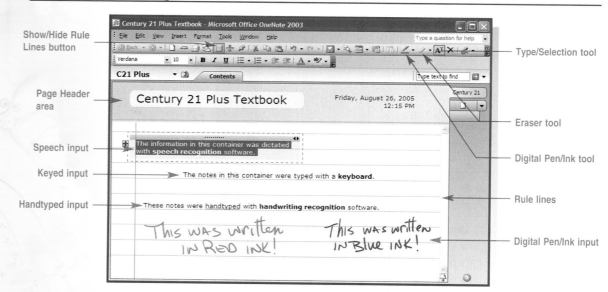

OneNote will allow you to enter notes in any order—even in a random fashion—inside multiple, movable, and resizable containers. This flexibility is very important, especially for those moments when you'll need to write facts and ideas quickly before you forget what's being said!

Reorganizing notes is a simple thing to do. When you click or tap on a container, or move the mouse/pen pointer over a container, a handle (colored bar) appears at the top. This handle allows you to move or resize the container. (See Figure IT4-14.)

Exercise 2A

Create and Manipulate Containers

1. Open *OneNote*. Click or tap the **C21 Plus** folder and then click or tap again the **Contents** section. If necessary, also click or tap the **Century 21 Plus Textbook** page.

2. Select the **Type/Selection Tool** button marked in Figure IT4-14.

3. Click or tap the top left corner of the notetaking area. Enter the word **Prerequisites** as shown in Figure IT4-14.

4. Click or tap in the top right corner of the notetaking area to create a new container, as seen in Figure IT4-14. Enter the following text in the new container:

   Part 1 Computer Applications/Key Concepts

5. Click or tap the bottom left corner of the notetaking area to create a new container. Enter the following text as indicated in Figure IT4-14:

   Part 2 Living Online/Online Applications

6. Click or tap the bottom right corner of the notetaking area. Enter the following text as displayed in Figure IT4-14:

   Part 3 Emerging Input Technologies

7. Click or tap the center of the notetaking area. In a new container, enter the word **Appendices**.

8. You should now have five sets of notes contained in five separate containers. Your screen should appear similar to Figure IT4-14. Click or tap any one of the containers to view the **Container Move** bar, **Resize** handle, and **Paragraph Move** handle marked in Figure IT4-15 on the following page. (*Note:* These will be explained in more detail in the next section.)

9. Close *OneNote* or continue to the next exercise.

Instant Message

You can turn on the rule lines if you find them helpful or turn them off if you find them distracting. To do so, click or tap the Show/Hide Rule Lines button.

Instant Message

You can input typed text with your keyboard, speech recognition, or handtyping software by selecting the Type/Selection Tool button first. Regardless of the input tool you choose, the word will appear as typed text.

Tip

If you make a mistake and need to delete a container, choose the container by tapping on its Container Move bar and choose BACKSPACE or DELETE.

Figure IT4-14   Containers Can Be Randomly Placed on a Page

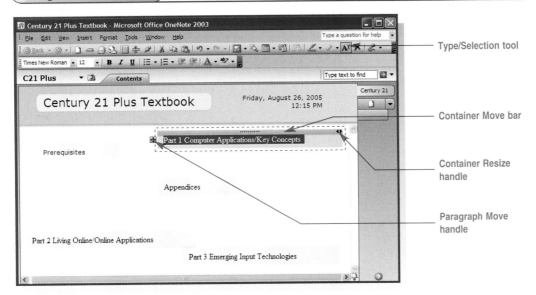

Container Resize handle

Paragraph Move handle

Resizing and Reorganizing Notes

OneNote permits you to reorganize and change your notes after you've created them. You can move, merge, resize, and split *OneNote* containers. You can also delete containers and the notes they hold.

In step 8 of the previous exercise, you clicked or tapped one of the containers. As you did, a move bar appeared above the container that can be used to move the container around the screen. At the far end of the move bar, a double-sided arrow marks the **Container Resize handle**. This handle can be used to make containers as long or as narrow as necessary.

A **Paragraph Move handle** will appear in front of any paragraph. (See Figure IT4-15.) To make the Paragraph Move handle appear, hover over the paragraph with your digital pen or mouse, or even select the paragraph. This four-sided arrow can be used to move a specific paragraph up and down within a container and into or out of another container.

Figure IT4-15   Move and Resize Features for *OneNote* Containers

Exercise 2B

Resize and Merge Containers

1. Open *OneNote*. Click or tap the **C21 Plus** folder, the **Contents** section, and the **Century 21 Plus Textbook** page

2. Click or tap each of the three multiword containers to display the **Container Resize handles**. Shorten each container by 50 percent by grabbing the two-sided arrow and dragging to the left, as seen in Figure IT4-16.

Figure IT4-16   Resize the Three Largest Containers

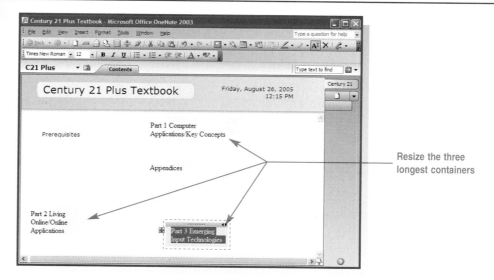

3. Click or tap the container that holds the note, **Part 1 Computer Applications/Key Concepts**. Drag it by its Container Move handle and move it immediately underneath the word *Prerequisites*. (See Figure IT4-17.)

4. Click or tap the move handle for the **Part 2 Living Online/Online Applications** container and drag it underneath *Part 1 Computer Application/Key Concepts*.

5. Click or tap the move handle for the **Part 3 Emerging Input Technologies** container and drag it underneath *Part 2 Living Online/Online Applications*.

6. Click or tap the move handle for the **Appendices** container and drag it underneath *Part 3 Emerging Input Technologies*. Compare what you have done with Figure IT4-17.

7. Expand the newly merged container by grabbing the **Container Resize** handle and dragging it to the right. Your merged container should now look like Figure IT4-18.

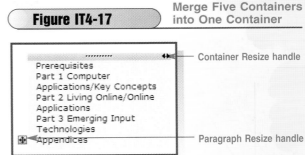

Figure IT4-17

Merge Five Containers into One Container

— Container Resize handle

— Paragraph Resize handle

Figure IT4-18   **Expanding a Single Container**

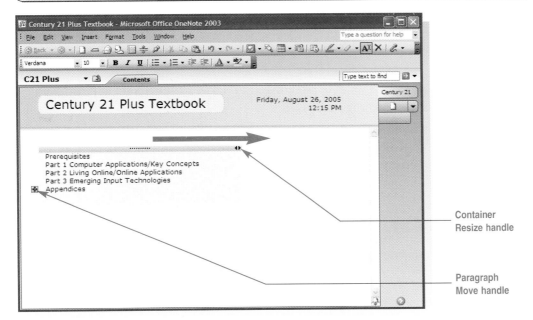

Container Resize handle

Paragraph Move handle

> **Tip**
>
> When merging containers, make sure you push the containers into each other as if you are *snapping* them together. It's a little like pressing toy building blocks together to combine individual blocks into a single object.

Exercise 2C

Break Apart, Highlight, Color, and Bullet Containers

1. Open *OneNote*. Click or tap the **C21 Plus** folder, the **Contents** section, and the **Century 21 Plus Textbook** page.

2. Roll your mouse or hover your digital pen over the word **Appendices** until the Paragraph Move handle with its four-sided arrow appears next to the word *Appendices*. (See Figure IT4-18.) Click or tap and drag the Paragraph Move handle's four-sided arrow down and to the right to break the word *Appendices* into a separate container. (See Figure IT4-19 on the next page.)

3. Continue breaking the merged container apart into five separate containers by dragging each paragraph by its Paragraph Move handle. Drag each paragraph into an empty space on the screen, as seen in Figure IT4-19.

Figure IT4-19   Break the Container Apart Again

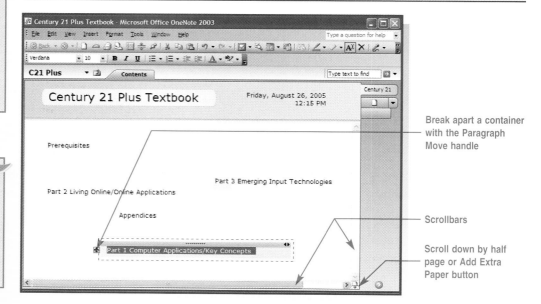

Break apart a container with the Paragraph Move handle

Scrollbars

Scroll down by half page or Add Extra Paper button

4. Merge all five containers back together again so the single container appears as it did in Figure IT4-18.

5. Click or tap the **Container Move bar** for the newly remerged container. This will select its entire contents. Then choose the **Bullets** button from the Formatting toolbar to bullet each item in the list. (Refer to Figure IT4-20.)

Figure IT4-20   Bullet and Highlight Your Notes

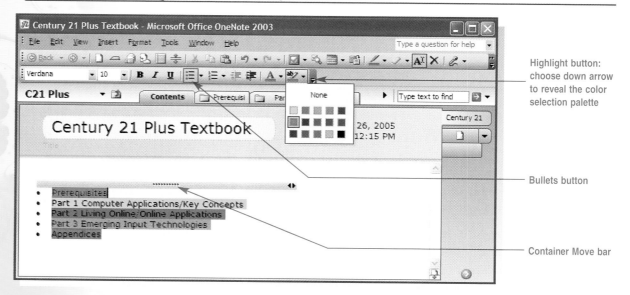

Highlight button: choose down arrow to reveal the color selection palette

Bullets button

Container Move bar

6. Click or tap and drag over each individual paragraph one by one. Using the **Highlight** color selection down arrow, select a different color for each paragraph. Apply the color by tapping on the **Highlight** button marked in Figure IT4-20.

7. Exit *Microsoft OneNote*.

Creating New Folders

Your Contents page lists the five main sections found in this book. Create five new folders representing each of the five major sections, as seen in Figure IT4-21. The names of your folders will match the bulleted list in your Contents page.

Newly created folders are often inserted before older folders. To keep your folders looking sequential, create them in reverse order: **Appendices**, **Part 3**, **Part 2**, **Part 1**, and finally **Prerequisites**.

Figure IT4-21   Creating New Folders

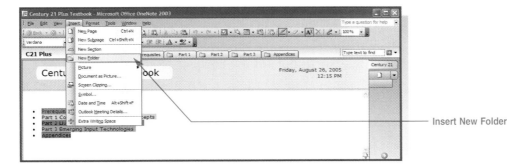

Insert New Folder

Exercise 2D

Organize Your Folders for Century 21 Plus

1. Open *Microsoft OneNote*. Open your **C21 Plus** folder, click or tap your **Contents** section, and make sure the **Century 21 Plus Textbook** page is visible as seen in Figure IT4-21.

2. To create a new folder, choose **Insert**, **New Folder**. Name the folder **Appendices**. (See Figure IT4-21.) Tap ENTER or click or tap the notetaking area to record the name of the folder.

3. Choose **Insert**, **New Folder** again. Name the new folder **Part 3**. (See Figure IT4-21.) Tap ENTER or click or tap the notetaking area to record the name.

4. Make three additional folders with the following names:
   • Create a new folder named **Part 2**.
   • Create another folder named **Part 1**.
   • Create the last folder with the name **Prerequisites**.

Instant
Message

It's a proven fact that color can help you remember important notes. Don't be afraid to make your notes as colorful as you like. In *OneNote*, you can change both the highlight and text/font colors. You can use your digital ink with nearly any pen color imaginable.

TIP

If you tap ENTER before keying the new name, you can still rename the folder by right-clicking on the folder name to open the pop-up menu and choosing Rename. (Tablet PC users, right-click by holding your digital pen directly on the tab's name and then release after the ring of dots appear.)

TIP

If you make a mistake and wish to delete a folder, right-click on the folder name and choose Delete from the pop-up menu. You can also copy, move, and rename folders from this same list.

Keeping Track of Definitions

Most chapters in most textbooks are replete with terms and definitions. These definitions are usually highlighted or placed in bold lettering. *OneNote* is the place to keep track of all of your definitions.

horizontal outlining

In the next exercise, use *OneNote*'s special two-column **horizontal outlining** feature to make sure your definitions stand out from the words they define. To take advantage of this feature, create new containers in precisely the following way:

1. Enter the new term or vocabulary word,
2. Select the TAB key,
3. Enter the definition.

Exercise 2E

Entering Definitions in a Two-Column Outline

1. Open *Microsoft OneNote* if it has been closed. Open your **C21 Plus** folder, click or tap your **Contents** section, and then tap your **Part 2** folder. You will be greeted by the same message seen in Figure IT4-9 in *Exercise A1-B*. Click the middle of the message to start a new section.

2. Name your new section **Unit 1**. Name the first page in that section **Definitions**, as seen in Figure IT4-22.

Figure IT4-22   Create a New Section and Page Inside a New Folder

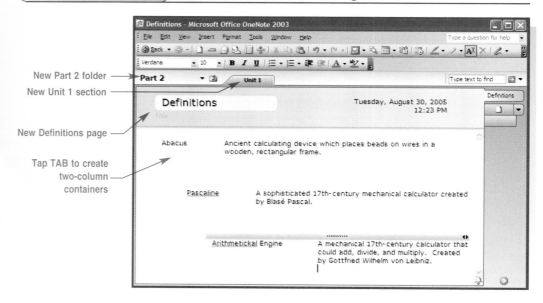

3. The word *abacus* is the first vocabulary word in the *History of Computers and Hardware* unit. Enter this word and its definition by creating a new container in the top left-hand portion of the notetaking area. Enter **Abacus** as seen here and in Figure IT4-22. Tap the TAB key. Then enter the definition as follows:

Abacus   <Tab>   Ancient calculating device that places beads on wires in a wooden, rectangular frame.

4. Create separate containers for the following definitions seen here and in Figure IT4-22:

Pascaline   <Tab>   A sophisticated 17th-century mechanical calculator created by Blaise Pascal.

Arithmetickal Engine   <Tab>   A mechanical 17th-century calculator that could add, divide, and multiply. Created by Gottfried Wilhelm von Leibniz.

5. Merge the three definitions together into one container in alphabetical order, as seen in Figure IT4-23.

Figure IT4-23   Merge the Definitions in Alphabetical Order

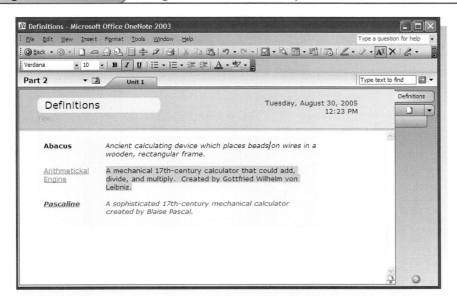

Instant Message

Some words like *Arithmetickal* and *Pascaline* are derived from German and French words. They do not appear in the English dictionary, so *OneNote* thinks it has found a spelling mistake. Supposed spelling mistakes appear with a squiggly red line underneath. You can either ignore the red squiggly line or right-click on the word and choose Ignore from the pop-up spelling list to remove the squiggles.

6. To help you study and remember these definitions, format, highlight, and color your vocabulary terms and definitions in a variety of ways. There are many possible tools to use, as seen in Figure IT4-24. Notes can be bolded, italicized, underlined, or can appear in a different color. They can even be highlighted, numbered, or have their font size and font style changed. Experiment. Decide for yourself how best to use formatting tools.

Figure IT4-24   Tools on the Formatting Toolbar

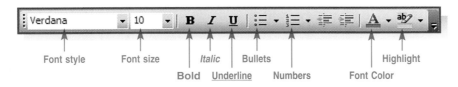

Font style   Font size   *Italic*   Bullets   Highlight
Bold   Underline   Numbers   Font Color

Change Column Width

When using the horizontal outlining feature, you may need to change the width of your columns in order to display all the words properly. Follow the steps in the next exercise.

Resizing Columns in Horizontal Outlines

1. Open *Microsoft OneNote* if it has been closed. Open your **C21 Plus** folder and then tap your **Part 2** folder. Open **Unit 1** and choose the **Definitions** page.

2. To make a column wider or narrower, hover over or tap a definition in the second column with your mouse or digital pen to display the Paragraph Move handle four-sided arrow. (See Figure IT4-25.) Right-click the Paragraph Move handle to open the pop-up menu. Then click **Resize Previous Column** on the shortcut menu.

Figure IT4-25 Resize the Second Column

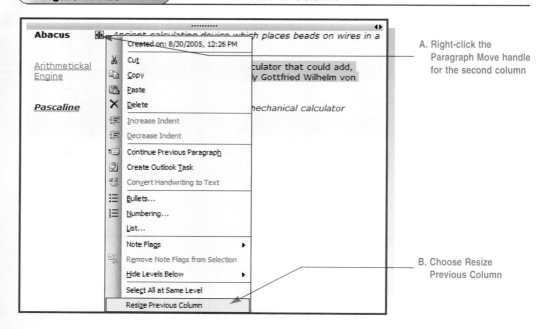

3. Click or tap and drag the Paragraph Move handle to the right until the words *Arithmetickal Engine* appear on a single line. (See Figure IT4-26.)

Figure IT4-26 Drag the Column to the Right

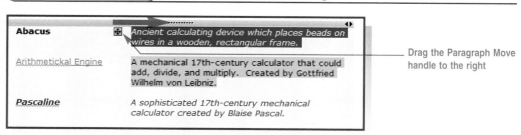

Creating a Chronological History of People

It took many years and thousands of talented people to invent the first personal computer. The groundwork for the modern computer started as early as the abacus, and led invention by invention to our modern microprocessors. Along the way, certain key individuals contributed to the evolution of thinking machines. Create a new *OneNote* page outlining a chronology of these important people.

Instant Message

Display your historical figures in **chronological order**, meaning that the earliest dates appear at the top and the most recent dates at the bottom.

Exercise 2G

Entering Important People and Companies

1. Open your **Part 2** folder in the C21 Plus section by choosing it from the My Notebook list. Choose your **Unit 1** section and your **Definitions** page.

2. Choose the **Insert New Page** button, as indicated in Figure IT4-27.

3. Name your second page as **Famous People**.

Figure IT4-27   Create a New Important People Page

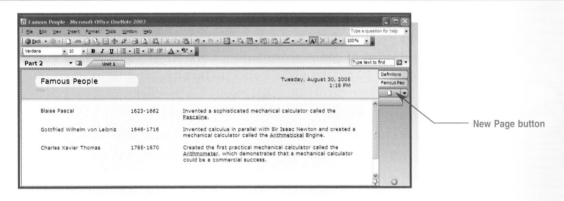

New Page button

4. Create three separate containers with the following information in each. (*Note:* To create the three columns, remember to click the **Tab** key between the names and the dates, and between the dates and the paragraph explaining what these important people accomplished. Use the **Resize Previous Column** feature as explained in the previous exercise to align the three columns.)

Blaise Pascal	1623–1662	Invented a sophisticated mechanical calculator called the Pascaline.
Gottfried Wilhelm von Leibniz	1646–1716	Invented calculus in parallel with Sir Isaac Newton and created a mechanical calculator called the Arithmetickal Engine.
Charles Xavier Thomas	1785–1870	Created the first practical mechanical calculator called the Arithmometer, which demonstrated that a mechanical calculator could be a commercial success.

5. Format, highlight, and color your vocabulary terms and definitions using bold, italic, underline, highlights, or a variety of font colors.

Vertical Outlining

Sometimes, when a list is all that is needed, the best tool to use is a simple vertical outline. Vertical outlines in *OneNote* mimic more traditional outlining styles used in word processing programs such as *Microsoft Word*. Such outlines are divided into levels. The top levels are main topics. Sublevels contain subordinate topics and ideas. Many sublevels can be created as needed.

However, what happens if you suddenly come upon notes that need to be inserted into an existing outline? *OneNote* has a great feature that allows you to insert as much extra writing space as you need between existing notes. Complete the next exercise and see how this feature works.

Exercise 2H

Outline Vertically and Add Paper

1. Open your **Part 2** folder in the C21 Plus section by choosing it from the My Notebook list. Choose your **Unit 1** section and your **Definitions** page. Choose the **Insert New Page** button and create a new page called **Computer Milestones**.

2. Enter this list of computer milestones in a single container, as indicated in Figure IT4-28. Tap ENTER after each entry.

Mechanical Counting Machines	[Enter]
Vacuum Tubes	[Enter]
Transistors	[Enter]
Integrated Circuits	[Enter]
Personal Desktop Computer	[Enter]
GUI Interface	[Enter]
Mobile Computers	[Enter]

3. Choose the **Insert Extra Writing Space** button marked in Figure IT4-28.

Figure IT4-28   Insert Extra Writing Space Between Paragraphs in a Container

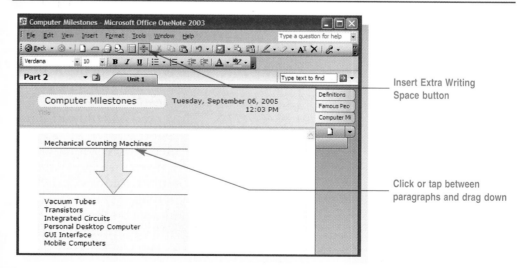

4. Click or tap between the first two paragraphs and drag down 1" to create additional space, as seen in Figure IT4-28.

5. Between the first and second paragraphs, enter the following related information. Use the TAB key to indent the subtopics below the main topic. Use either the down arrow or the ENTER key to move to the next line.

Mechanical Counting Machines
  Abacus
  Pascaline
  Arithmetickal Engine
  Arithmometer
  Punch Card
  Difference Engine
  Analytical Engine
  Ada Byron
  Boolean Algebra

6. When you're finished entering all of the subtopics below *Mechanical Counting Machines*, delete any extra spaces following the list with the Backspace or Delete keys.

7. Repeat steps 3–6 and insert the following information after the *Vacuum Tubes* main heading, as seen in Figure IT4-29.

Vacuum Tubes
  Bell Labs
  Atanasoff and Berry
  ENIAC
  Hooper

Figure IT4-29   Enter Additional Subtopics

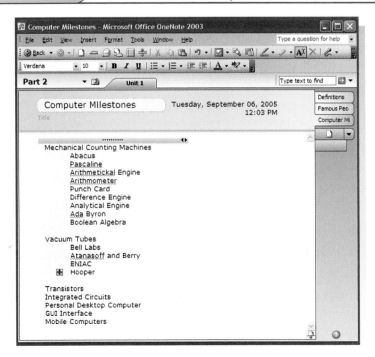

8. Format, highlight, and color your vocabulary terms and definitions using bold, italic, underline, highlights, or a variety of font colors.

Creating Subpages

Sometimes you will want to create pages that are related to other pages. These are called subpages. For example, it wasn't always a famous person creating important digital communication technologies; often it was a corporation that provided the major breakthroughs in the history of computing tools. In the next exercise, create a subpage underneath the *Famous Persons* page that accounts for the accomplishments of several groundbreaking corporations.

In the upcoming exercise, you will create a two-column outline, giving you the names of the major corporations that need to be researched, but not providing you with much information about any of them. Notes that are complete will be colored in blue. Where more research is needed, a notation will be made in red. After you have had a chance to research the companies, you can "get the red out" by inserting notes about each company. Change the color of all completed notes to blue. Such color coding can help remind you of what still needs to be studied.

Exercise 21

Create a Subpage

1. Open your **Part 2** folder in the C21 Plus section by choosing it from the My Notebook list. Choose your **Unit 1** section and your **Famous People** page. Choose the **Insert New Subpage** button (Figure IT4-30) to create a new subpage below the *Famous People* page tab.

2. Don't research the corporations just yet. Create a two-column outline structure to organize your topics of study for each corporation, as seen below. Start by entering the word **Corporations** at the top; then enter the company names, followed by the TAB key, and add your notes and notations as shown here. (Also see Figure IT4-30.)

Corporations

IBM   International Business Machines. Also known as Big Blue. Founded by Herman Hollerith. *Research more . . .*

Bell Labs   *Research this . . .*

PARC   *Research this . . .*

MITS   *Research this . . .*

Apple   *Research this . . .*

Microsoft   *Research this . . .*

3. Format your **Famous People/Corporations** subpage in the following way:
   - Make **Corporations** 14-point bold.
   - Make each company name bold and blue.
   - Italicize any completed notes and make them blue as seen above.
   - Make the *Research more . . .* and *Research this . . .* notations red to remind you that you still have research to complete.
   - As you finish entering notes, color them blue and italicize them.

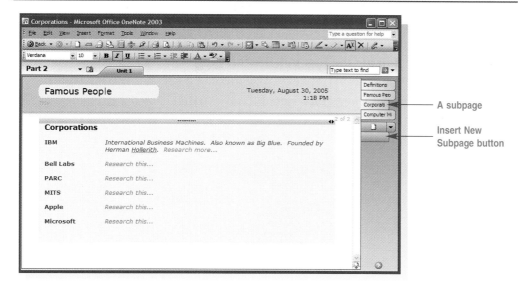

A subpage

Insert New Subpage button

4. Open your textbook to Part 2, Unit 1. Study the many contributions of corporations to the success of today's technologies and add this information to your notes. Take notes, replacing the *Research this . . .* placeholders currently marked in red on your **Part 2/Unit1/Famous People/Corporations** subpage with historical information.

LESSON ONLINE NOTETAKING AND OTHER NOTETAKING EXTRAS

OBJECTIVES

- ⊗ To copy and paste notes from the Internet.
- ⊗ To create handwritten Side Notes.
- ⊗ To convert notes from handwriting to text on tablet PCs.
- ⊗ To draw in your notes.
- ⊗ To move note pages.
- ⊗ To research how to record, flag, e-mail, and delete notes.

Notes from the Internet

The Internet is today's primary source of research information. *OneNote* is designed specifically to gather notes from the Internet. You can cut and paste or drag and drop notes directly from any Web page into *OneNote*. Then *OneNote* does a pretty helpful thing; it automatically references the Web page from which the information was extracted. Later, as you begin creating citations for a report, or if you wish to pass the Web address to a friend or business colleague, you will have the exact website reference you need.

Downloading to *OneNote* is not limited to text. You can download pictures, graphics, charts, and data of all kinds from the Web—as well as from other applications—using copy and paste commands. There are several ways to use copy and paste:

- Choose Edit, Copy/Paste from the menu bar.
- Use the Copy and Paste buttons on the Standard toolbar.
- Drag and drop directly from one application to another.

Download Text and Graphics

1. Click or tap the **C21 Plus** folder; then open the **Appendices** folder for the first time. Name the first new section in this folder **OneNote**. Name the first page **Definitions**. (*Note:* You'll come back to this page later.)

2. Create a second new page called **Ryan's Article** as seen in Figure IT4-31.

Figure IT4-31 Create a New Appendices/*OneNote* Section with Two Pages

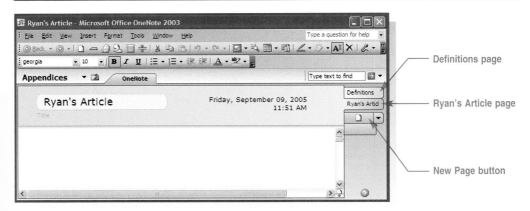

3. Open your Web browser. Enter this Web page address into the Address bar of your browser and tap ENTER:

   http://www.speakingsolutions.com/news/onenote04.asp

4. Resize your browser so that it fits on the left-hand side of the screen and only occupies about one-half to three-quarters of the screen. (See Figure IT4-32.)

5. Open *OneNote* and position the window so that it is on the right-hand side of your screen. Resize the window so that it only covers about one-half to three-quarters of the screen. (See Figure IT4-32.)

6. Select the title and the copyright statement. Then click or touch and drag the text from the Web page onto the *OneNote* page called *Ryan's Article*.

7. Look below the title and copyright statement that you just copied to *OneNote*. You will see a Web page reference showing where the information was taken from. The reference should look something like this:

   Pasted from http://www.speakingsolutions.com/news/onenote04.asp

8. Click or tap on the graphics and accompanying text displayed on the Web page just before the copyright information. Click or touch and drag the graphic from the Internet page onto the *OneNote* page called *Ryan's Article*. (See Figure IT4-32.)

9. Scroll down to the bottom of the *OneNote* page below the graphic. Click or tap the **Add Extra Paper** button (Figure IT4-33) to add additional notetaking area to the bottom of the page.

10. Switch to your Web browser and select only the middle portion of Ryan's article beginning with **Favorite Updates** down to the **Conclusion**. Then choose the **Copy** button from the Standard toolbar of your Web browser. (See Figure IT4-32.)

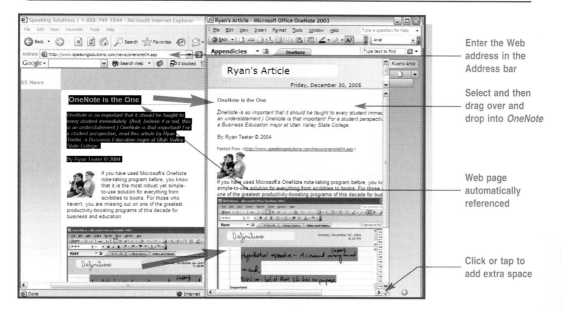

Enter the Web address in the Address bar

Select and then drag over and drop into *OneNote*

Web page automatically referenced

Click or tap to add extra space

Figure IT4-33   Copy and Paste

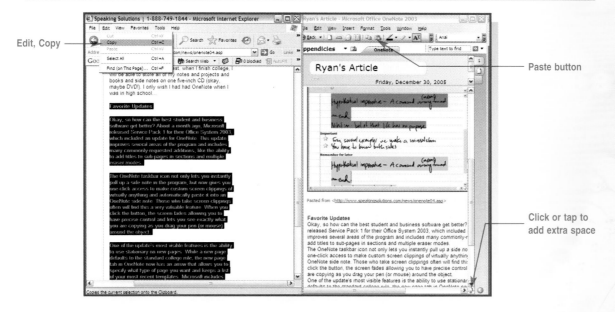

Edit, Copy

Paste button

Click or tap to add extra space

11. Switch to the *OneNote* page called *Ryan's Article*. Click or tap the **Type/Selection Button** if it is not already selected. Click or tap in an area below the graphic you just moved to the Ryan's Article *OneNote* page. Then choose the **Paste** button from the Standard toolbar marked in Figure IT4-32.

Side Notes and Handwritten Notes

Side Notes can be a lifesaver. Imagine being in a situation where you have to start taking notes instantly. What if something important is being said? You may not have time to:

- Click or tap the Start menu
- Open the All Programs folder and the Microsoft Office folder

- Open *OneNote* and wait for it to open
- Find the appropriate folder and section
- Create a new notetaking page
- Begin notetaking

For these emergency situations, Side Notes are the answer.

If you look very closely at the taskbar near the current time, you should see a little N, as indicated in Figure IT4-34. If you click or tap it, a small notetaking window will appear as seen in Figure IT4-35. This will happen in a flash, and you'll be ready to start taking notes instantly.

The Side Notes window will stay on top of all other windows on your screen until you're done with it. And if you maximize it, you will see that this new page of notes is saved in a *Side Notes* section in your My Notebook folder. Each new side notes page that you create is added immediately to the Side Notes section. (See Figure IT4-36.) From this location, you can move these side notes to a more topical folder anywhere inside of *OneNote*.

Exercise 3B

Taking Side Notes

1. Click or tap the **Open New Side Note** button located in the taskbar. The button has a big letter *N* in the middle of it, as shown in Figure IT4-34. (*Note:* You may need to click or tap the arrow in order to display any hidden shortcuts.)

Figure IT4-34 Open Your Side Notes

Click or tap to expand

Click or tap to open a Side Note window

2. If you have a digital pen, select the **Pen** icon and handwrite the following notes as seen in Figure IT4-35. If you don't have a digital pen, click the **Type/Selection** tool and type your notes instead.

Pascal: an early programming language was named after Blaise Pascal.

Figure IT4-35 Enter Side Notes

The Maximize button

The Type/Selection button

Click or tap to add extra space

The Pen button

3. Click or tap the **Maximize** button. All of *OneNote* will appear, as you can see in Figure IT4-36.

Instant Message

Click or tap the Scroll Down by Half Page button to add extra notetaking space, as shown in Figure IT4-36.

Figure IT4-36 Maximize Your Side Notes Window.

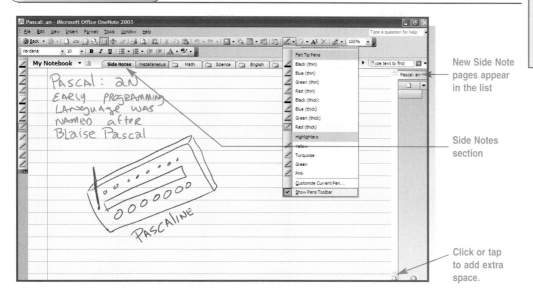

New Side Note pages appear in the list

Side Notes section

Click or tap to add extra space.

4. Again, if you have a digital pen, make a rough sketch of Pascal's Pascaline. A picture of the Pascaline can be found in Part 2, Unit 1.

5. Move the Side Note to a more topically appropriate folder for long-term storage. Right-click on the Side Notes page tab and choose **Move Page to > Another Section** from the pop-up menus. (See Figure IT4-37.)

Tip

If you are using a tablet PC, you can select all of the handwritten text and turn it into typewritten text by simply choosing Tools, Convert Handwriting to Text. If you have a tablet PC, try it! See if your penmanship is good enough to be recognized and converted into typing.

Figure IT4-37 Move the Side Note Pascal Page

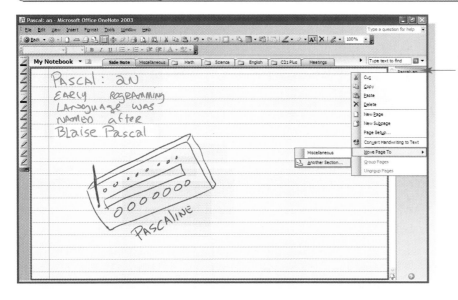

Right-click on the Page tab and choose Move Page to > Another Section

6. When the Move Page To window appears, choose the **Part 2** folder. Choose the **Unit 1** section, as seen in Figure IT4-38 on the next page.

7. In the header, name the page you have moved **Pascal** in the header's title box. (See Figure IT4-39 on the next page.)

Instant Message

To open the Part 2 folder, you may need to click or tap on the + next to the Part 2 folder. This will display the Unit 1 section inside.

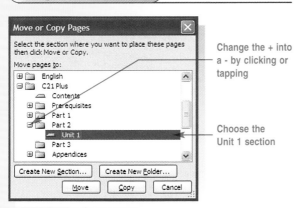

Change the + into a - by clicking or tapping

Choose the Unit 1 section

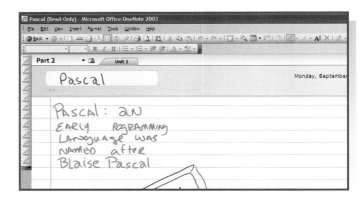

Searching OneNote Notes

If you are a good note taker, what will start out as a puddle of notes will quickly grow into a lake, a bigger lake, and then an ocean of notes. The number of individual note pages will soon exceed all recollection. Despite your best efforts to organize your folders and sections topically, you may not be able to find where certain notes have been placed. Fortunately, *OneNote* has an answer to this enormous problem. *OneNote*'s **Find** feature makes it very easy to pinpoint the exact notes you are looking for.

The Find feature uses search words, much like Internet search engines such as Google, to locate specific tidbits of information. However, in contrast to a Google search, *OneNote*'s Find feature limits its searching to your own notes.

The searches happen quickly. The Find feature will search both typed and handwritten notes, provided you have handwritten them clearly. Then it will display its findings in a list along with hints about the context surrounding the search word. You can simply scroll through the results, as shown in Figure IT4-41, or pick from the list.

Exercise 3C

Using the Find Feature

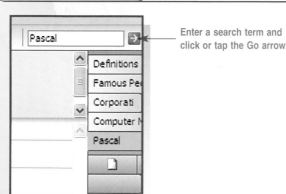

Enter a search term and click or tap the Go arrow

1. Open *OneNote* and click or tap the **C21 Plus** folder.

2. Locate the search entry box just below the Standard and Formatting toolbars and immediately above the page tabs. (See Figure IT4-40.)

3. Enter the word **Pascal** in the text box and click the **Go** arrow beside the box.

4. After the search results have been acquired, choose **View List**, as marked in Figure IT4-41.

5. You now have a choice in how you search the results: you can click or tap the forward and back arrows and move through the selections one by one, or you can scan the list and see if you can pinpoint the exact reference you are looking for. Try both methods and evaluate how they work for future reference.

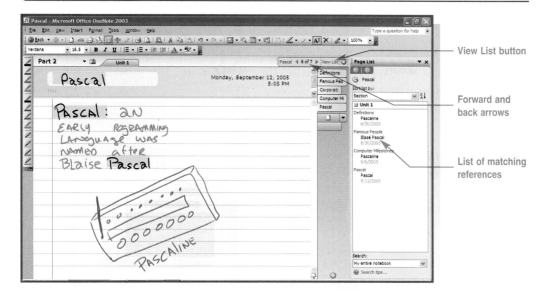

Labels on figure:
- View List button
- Forward and back arrows
- List of matching references

Back Up Your Notes Often

It is important to back up your notes. Wouldn't it be sad to have several years of notes accumulated in your My Notebook folder lost in a computer system crash, never to be seen again? Backing up is simple and essential. If you have questions about how to accomplish this task, review Lesson 3 in the Prerequisites section of this text. Follow these steps:

1. Insert a blank CD or a USB flash drive into your computer.
2. Open your **My Documents** folder in Windows. Scroll through and find your **My Notebook** folder.
3. Copy the **My Notebook** folder to your blank CD window or your flash drive window. When copying to a USB flash drive, the files will be copied automatically on the device. If you have copied your My Notebook folder to a blank CD, choose **Write Files to Disk** to burn the files permanently to a CD.
4. Store your CD or flash drive in a safe place.

Just Scratching the Surface

You are just beginning to learn about all the features available to you in *Microsoft OneNote*. Here are some things you and your teammates can learn how to do together using *OneNote*'s Help feature:

- Flag notes
- Record notes
- E-mail notes
- Share notes

Exercise 3D

Learning More

1. Divide up the four topics above among your teammates.

2. Open *OneNote* and click or tap the **Help** menu. Choose **Microsoft Office OneNote Help** (or tap the F1 shortcut key).

3. Enter your assigned search term, for example, **Flag notes**, and tap the **Go** button. (See Figure IT4-42.)

Figure IT4-42   Enter a Topic

4. Find, open, and study several related topics.

5. Meet with your teammates and demonstrate the techniques you have learned. Teach your teammates in a hands-on way by having them try the new operations for themselves as you talk them through the steps.

UNIT 4

LESSON 1

Assessing OneNote Skills

LESSON (1) **ASSESS GENERAL KNOWLEDGE OF ONENOTE FEATURES AND INTERFACE**

OBJECTIVE

To assess the knowledge needed to set up *OneNote* for improved personal research and study.

Exercise **1A**

Set up OneNote for This Specific Book

Prepare your C21 Plus folder to accommodate each part and unit of this textbook.

1. Open the Table of Contents for this textbook. Notice that the book is divided into Parts and Units.

2. Open *OneNote* and your **C21 Plus** folder.

3. Create a section for each unit found in the text. For example, in Part 1 you will have Unit 1, Unit 2, Unit 3, etc. Make sure the correct number of units are created inside the folder for each part. Create a **Definitions** page for each section. This will be the first page for each unit in the text.

> **TIP**
>
> For each unit you may wish to create a Definitions page in advance, which can serve as a place to store new terms and vocabulary words along with their definitions for each unit.

Exercise **1B**

Set up OneNote for Another Class

1. Choose another course that you are currently taking. How would you organize and prepare *OneNote* for this class? Plan out your *OneNote* organizational structure in advance, and then create a separate *OneNote* folder for the class.

2. Organize the necessary subfolders and sections to accommodate the new course. Keep this new course completely separate from your C21 Plus folder.

OBJECTIVE

⊙ To assess the ability to take and organize notes.

Exercise 2A

Record the Definitions in the History Chapter

1. Open *Microsoft OneNote* if it has been closed. Open your **C21 Plus** folder, and then tap your **Part 2** folder. Open **Unit 1** and choose the **Definitions** page.

2. With *Microsoft OneNote* open, continue reading and studying the *History of Computers and Hardware* unit found in Part 2.

3. Using *OneNote*, add these definitions to your Definitions page. Start by creating each one in its own container and then merge it into the list in its proper place alphabetically. Enter definitions for the following words:

Terms and Definitions for Unit 1 Computer History		
Arithmometer	Mainframe	GUI
Luddites	Minicomputer	Macintosh
Difference Engine	IBM	PARC
Analytical Engine	Integrated circuit	PDA
Boolean algebra	Moore's Law	Smart phone
Vacuum Tubes	MITS Altair 8800	CSR
ENIAC	Apple II	SUI
Bug	PC	Wearable Tech
UNIVAC	Text Interface	DigiTools

Exercise 2B

Complete Notes for the History Chapter

1. Study your textbook or go online to learn more about each of the following technology leaders. Find the dates they were born, when they died, and provide a brief description of the accomplishments of each in your *OneNote C21 Plus/Part 2/Unit 1/Famous People* page.

Famous People Continued for Unit 1 Computer History		
Hermann Hollerith	John P. Eckert	Robert Noyce
Joseph-Marie Jacquard	John W. Mauchly	Gordon Moore
Charles Babbage	Grace Murray Hopper	Bill Gates
Ada Byron	John Bardeen	Paul Allen
George Boole	William Shockley	Steve Wozniak
John Atanasoff	Walter Brattain	Steve Jobs
Clifford Berry	Jack Kilby	Douglas Engelbart

Exercise 2C

Outline Notes on Historic Computer Milestones

1. Study your textbook or go online to learn more about each of the following milestones in computer history. List any related subtopics for each milestone underneath these main headings:

   Transistors
   Integrated Circuits
   Personal Desktop Computer
   GUI Interface
   Mobile Computers

2. Complete the outline you started in your *OneNote C21 Plus/Part 1/Computer Milestones* page.

LESSON ③ ASSESS THE ABILITY TO LEARN NEW SKILLS INDEPENDENTLY

OBJECTIVES
- ⊘ To assess the ability to learn important *OneNote* features independently.
- ⊘ To assess the deletion and restoration of folders and sections.

Exercise 3A

Use Help to Learn How to Delete Unwanted Folders and Sections

You probably have many folders and sections that you do not need. For instance, some folders and sections have been created by the software itself. The creators of the software hoped to anticipate the needs of potential users.

However, these folders and sections may not fit your needs. It is important to clear these out and customize *OneNote* to fit your personal notetaking style.

1. Use *OneNote*'s Help feature to learn how to delete unwanted folders and sections.

2. Search through your My Notebook *OneNote* folder and delete any unnecessary or unwanted folders and sections.

Exercise 3B

Use Help to Learn How to Restore Deleted Folders and Sections

What happens if you accidentally delete a folder or section that you need? They are easily restored. Use your Help feature to learn how to accomplish this task.

1. Use *OneNote*'s Help feature to learn how to restore previously deleted folders and sections.

2. For practice, choose a folder or section and delete it.

3. Using the skills you just acquired in step 1, restore your deleted folder or section back into *OneNote*.

Communication & Math Skills 14

ACTIVITY 1   Application: Commas

1. Key lines 1–10, inserting commas correctly.

2. Save as *CS14-ACT1*.

1 When you get to State Street make a right turn at the light.
2 She will ask Ken you and me to serve on the planning committee.
3 They moved to Las Cruces New Mexico on September 15 2004.
4 Elden be sure to turn off all equipment before you leave.
5 Ms. Rogers said "Keep the insertion point moving steadily."
6 Winona who is our class treasurer couldn't attend the meeting.
7 By the middle of 2003 we had 273 employees; in 2005 318.
8 The probability is that only 1 in 280000 have the same DNA.
9 Dr. Woodburn has a strong pleasant personality.
10 The choir director Elena Spitz is planning a special program.

ACTIVITY 2   Application: Punctuation

1. Key lines 1–10, punctuating each sentence correctly.

2. Save as *CS14-ACT2*.

1 Vanessa Williams sang the quite beautiful Colors of the Wind
2 After you see the film Pocahontas, she said, write a review.
3 Miss Tallchief signed a two year contract as ballet director.
4 Dr. Cho said that 30 second and 1 minute spurts build speed.
5 The dance competition is scheduled for 9 15 a.m. on October 15.
6 My goal is to develop 1 self-confidence and 2 self-esteem.
7 "A textual citation follows the quote." Sanchez, 2005, 273
8 Who, she asked, is your all time favorite country singer?
9 Ms. Ott said: Read Frost's poem The Housekeeper by Monday.
10 Home Improvement was a very popular TV show in the late 1990s.

ACTIVITY 3   Listening

1. Open sound file *CD-CS14-LISTN*, which contains three mental math problems.

2. Each problem starts with a number, followed by several addition, sub- traction, multiplication, and division steps. Key or handwrite the new answer after each step, but com- pute the answer mentally.

3. Record the last answer for each problem.

4. After the third problem, close the sound file.

5. Save as *CS14-ACT3*.

ACTIVITY 4   Math: Applying Math Skills by Using Mental Math

1. Open *CD-CS14-ACT4* and print the file.

2. Solve the problems as directed in the file.

3. Submit your answers.

Appendix A

LESSONS 1–4

PDAs, Smart Phones, and Handheld Computers

LESSON 1 UNLEASH THE POWER OF HANDHELDS

OBJECTIVES
- To discover handheld PDAs and smart phones.
- To investigate handheld operating systems.
- To research the software features of PDAs, handhelds, and smart phones.
- To compare PDA, handhelds, and smart phone makes and models.

Eventually, Good Things Come in Small Packages

In 1965, Gordon Moore proclaimed that the power of microprocessors would double every few years. This doubling effect, called Moore's Law, meant that the calculations once requiring a mainframe computer the size of a house can now be completed by devices that can fit in the palm of your hand. The processors that power today's handheld devices are smaller than a dime.

Making powerful processors smaller than the smallest coin was very difficult and took over 40 years of invention. Many problems had to be overcome. For one thing, powerful computer processors emitted a great deal of heat—so much so that they could literally melt. To keep them cool, the earliest computers were housed in temperature-controlled rooms. Computer technicians dressed in lab coats, in part, to keep warm. Learning to create small yet powerful processors that wouldn't burn a hole in the palm of your hand was one of the greatest design challenges of the late 20th century.

By 1994, small, cool processors with some limited power became available. Jeff Hawkins (1957-) took advantage of these new processors, founded Palm Computing, and invented the PalmPilot. (See Figure A-1.) The PalmPilot was the first truly successful **Personal Digital Assistant** or **PDA**.

Early critics didn't give the PalmPilot much of a chance to succeed. After all, Apple Computer Corp. had given up on its first ground-breaking handheld computer called the Newton. The Newton had many wonderful features, but failed in the marketplace.

Figure A-1 The PalmPilot Started It All

© COURTESY OF PALMONE, INC.

Other handheld computer efforts had failed, too. And desktop PC sales were booming. How could the little, underpowered PalmPilot compete with powerful new PCs?

Despite the critics, by the fall of 1996 the PalmPilot was winning all sorts of awards and gaining recognition. Millions were purchased by busy businesspeople who needed to keep track of contacts, appointments, and other data while traveling.

PDAs of the late 1990s were small, cute, prestigious, and fun—like cell phones are today. Businesspeople with money to spare threw away their paper-based personal planning notebooks and began using handheld PDAs instead. Sales boomed through the end of the 1990s, and pretty soon, many other companies started making handheld devices.

To Every Device, Its Own OS

PDAs are powerful digital communication tools. They carry many different brand names: Tungsten, Zire, Treo, Smart Phone, Palm, PalmPilot, Axim, iPAQ, BlackBerry, or Pocket PC. The many names reflect the many PDA makes, models, and operating systems. Picking the perfect device for your needs can be extremely confusing. Understanding the various operating systems can help eliminate this confusion.

Every PDA and smart phone requires an operating system or OS. Just as with a personal computer, the OS of a handheld is essential to its operation. Three operating systems in widespread use today are explored in Table A-1.

Table A-1

Palm OS http://www.palm.com http://www.palmsource.com	The original PDA operating system created by Palm. This OS first captured the popular imagination in 1996. It is considered by many to be the easiest operating system to learn. A version of its software runs on smart phones. Palm OS is now owned and developed by PalmSource, a subsidiary of ACCESS. The Treo 700w smartphone is Palm's first Windows Mobile device.
RIM OS http://www.rim.com	Runs on the BlackBerry line of handhelds. The acronym RIM comes from *Research In Motion Ltd.*, the name of the Canadian company that created this extremely powerful OS. Originally designed as a fast way to read e-mail on the go, the system has rapidly expanded its capabilities into full PDA and smart phone features.
Windows Mobile for Pocket PC http://www.microsoft.com/windowsmobile	A product of Microsoft Corp., the OS became popular in the late 1990s. Often called just **Pocket PC**, it's a natural fit for anyone familiar with the Windows OS on personal computers. The Pocket PC is fully integrated with *Microsoft Office* computer applications: *Outlook, Word, PowerPoint,* and *Excel.* A smart phone version of the software is also available.

Search for an OS Update

1. Take notes in either *Microsoft Word* or *Microsoft OneNote*. Name your notes file *Handheld Tools*.

2. Open your Web browser and visit each of the websites for the three major OS software makers listed in Table A-1.

3. After visiting the three websites, in your opinion, which site does the best job of selling you on the quality and excitement of their products? In your notes, explain why the company's website you have selected communicates its message more effectively than the other two websites.

4. Continue to scour the website you have selected. Take notes on the new and exciting features and products being promoted on the website. Are there any new technologies that you did not know about or would like to buy for yourself? Record your observations in your notes.

Inventing Increasingly Smarter Devices

Originally, the only thing you could do on a cell phone was tap in a phone number and call somebody. That was it! We now call these devices *dumb phones*.

The PDA boom led to the invention of a host of handheld devices with increased capabilities. Chief among these is the **smart phone**. A smart phone is a cell phone with a powerful processor allowing PDA capabilities to be integrated into its circuits. Virtually every mobile phone sold today has some features once found only in very expensive PDAs.

For instance, it was quickly discovered that smart cell phone users wanted digital cameras, MP3 players, and even video cameras built into their cell phones. And it didn't stop there. Here is a quick list of some of the features that can be found in today's increasingly powerful handheld devices:

- Text messaging
- Voice messaging
- Wireless Internet
- MP3 players
- Digital cameras
- Voice-activated dialing
- Time management tools such as calendars and alarms
- Contacts (names, phone numbers, e-mail addresses, etc.)
- E-mail
- Pocket-sized notetaking software
- Pocket versions of applications like *Microsoft Word*, *PowerPoint*, and *Excel*
- Ring tones
- Games
- Walkie-talkie feature
- Calculator and financial software
- GPS (global positioning system) software
- E-book reading software
- More, more, and much more!

The wants and needs of customers, combined with ever-faster processors and better storage media, have inspired new types of miniature computers to fit everyone's interests, needs, and pocketbooks. Small devices just keep getting smarter and smarter. They also, amazingly, are growing less expensive, and they keep changing in size and shape. Smart phones, PDAs, ultralight laptop PCs, and tablet PCs will continue to evolve and change. The computer devices used today will be radically different in five years. Learning to use the small devices effectively will be an important part of your future, both academically and in your business pursuits.

Exercise A1B

How Smart Is Your Phone?

TEAMWORK

1. Reopen your notes named *Handheld Tools* from Exercise 1A.
2. Team up. Pull out your cell phones and power them up for this exercise. As a team, evaluate which of the cell phones available to your team is the smartest, best, and most powerful.
3. Determine how smart the selected phone is! Prepare a list of all the features found on the cell phone. Scroll through its various menus, applications, and features and list them all. In short order, the list may become extensive. Include everything from the most common features like *contact lists* and *text messaging* to more advanced features such as *voice-dialing* or even a *digital camera* if those features are present on the device.
4. Make a separate list of any features that you wish were also on the device.

Making Connections

Keyboard Alternatives for Tiny Computers

Another barrier to the increasing miniaturization of computers is the common, everyday keyboard. A keyboard large enough for fast, efficient typing by the human hand must be about 4" by 9", making them bulky and restrictive. Much less restrictive input tools had to be invented.

One of the first input tools was a mini-keyboard that operated with your thumbs. Another was a stylus, like a digital pen, that could be used for input. And speech recognition is just now becoming useful in small devices in a limited way. A combination of all of these tools may soon become the logical alternative to keyboards.

But don't count keyboards out quite yet. One of the more interesting possibilities is the virtual or phantom keyboard, which projects a laser image imitating the keyboard on any surface (see Figure A-2). There are some prototypes that can manufacture a keyboard in thin air. Also, for many ultralight tablet PCs and PDAs, consumers can buy docking stations, which allow them a full-size keyboard when they sit down to work at their desks with their handheld devices.

Figure A-2   Alternatives to Traditional Keyboards

© PRNEWSFOTO/MOTOROLA

© CANESTA, INC.

Picking A PDA or Smart Phone

PDAs can be purchased for a pittance, or they can be so expensive that you'll need to take out a loan and make payments. Often, you get what you pay for. The least expensive devices have black-and-white screens and limited functions. That may be all some need; however, most PDAs and smart phones are powerful, colorful devices that require a larger investment. There are seven major considerations when picking a PDA or smart phone:

- Processor
- Memory
- Expansion
- Wireless Conductivity
- Battery Life
- Synchronization
- Applications and Features

- **Processor:** Every PDA and smart phone needs a computer processor. This is the CPU or central processing unit of the device. Obviously, the faster the processor, the better! Processor speed is measured in megahertz or thousands of cycles per second. A 400 MHz processor is faster than a 200 MHz processor, but less powerful than an 800 MHz model. The CPU power and speed is an important measure to consider when buying any PDA, PC, or smart phone.

- **Memory:** PDAs and smart phones store personal information in **Random Access Memory** or **RAM** (also DRAM or SDRAM), and in **ROM** or **Read Only Memory** (also Flash ROM), which is maintained by battery power. If the power is shut off, the data may be lost. Some low-cost handhelds come with 64 MB of RAM. Generally, 128 MB to 256 MB of ROM is considered a minimum for color devices. Every PDA and smart phone comes with its essential software prerecorded safely in ROM. The original OS and applications can be restored from the built-in ROM. You may find yourself wishing you had double, triple, or even quadruple the memory.

- **Expansion:** Because RAM is limited, it's often impossible to store everything you want in a PDA's memory. Extra storage is provided by expansion slots available on most handheld devices. For example, digital cameras have memory cards. Similar storage tools work with PDAs and handheld devices. A slot is just a small space designed to receive a card-like storage device. Make sure any PDA you buy has the ability to add additional storage capacity.

- **Wireless Conductivity:** Smart phones instantly connect to the worldwide telephone networks. However, without the proper software, surfing the Internet may not be possible. Any device you buy should have the ability to connect to the Internet wirelessly and should contain the browser software necessary to view Web pages.

- **Battery Life:** RAM is volatile. If all power is cut off to a PDA or smart phone, much of the device's information will be lost entirely. Good batteries are essential. Most PDAs come with two batteries, a primary battery and a backup. When considering any handheld device, ask about the "battery life" of the device.

Instant Message

If you need to erase all the information on your PDA, you can do a **hard boot**, which will erase all of your data in the RAM of your PDA and allow you to reset its original software from the PDA's ROM. The procedures for doing a hard boot reset can be found in the documentation of your device.

- **Synchronization:** Very few things in the electronic world are as tragic as losing large amounts of personal data due to a device failure or loss of power. Synchronization will back up information from a PDA, smart phone, or other handheld device to a personal computer. Synchronization has the added advantage of making the data available on a PC without having to reenter it. Make sure your synchronization system is available with your device.

- **Applications and Other Features:** Every handheld device comes with a standard set of software programs. Most are designed to perform specific tasks. For example, the calendar application will keep track of your appointments, meetings, and your personal schedule. Make sure all of the important applications you need are available in any handheld device that you may be considering.

Exercise

Pitching a PDA or Smart Phone

1. Have each member of your team visit a different PDA, handheld, or smart phone manufacturer online. Here is a partial list of websites:

   http://www.hp.com
   http://www.dell.com
   http://www.blackberry.com
   http://www.palm.com
   http://www.sonyericsson.com
   http://www.samsung.com

2. Have each team member pick one PDA or smart phone they like the best. Research your choice online as your team members research their choices independently of each other. Return to the group to deliver a "sales pitch" with the goal of trying to sell your PDA or smart phone to the other team members.

3. After all the sales pitches have been delivered, as a group, vote to see which PDA or smart phone comes out on top and is the consensus choice of the group. Take notes regarding your group's final choice. Write a short summary about why your group voted for one PDA or smart phone over the other possible choices in your *Handheld Tools* notes.

LESSON ② SET UP AND VIEW APPLICATIONS

OBJECTIVES
- ⊙ To learn how handheld PDAs and smart phones work.
- ⊙ To view available PDA applications, functions, and features.
- ⊙ To learn the purpose of the Today or Home screen.
- ⊙ To reset time, date, and time zone settings.
- ⊙ To navigate with both stylus and buttons.

Learn: Setting up a PDA

As you examine your PDA, you will notice all sorts of buttons and icons. PDAs generally have hard buttons that you tap with your thumbs or fingers, and soft buttons or icons that appear on the screen. All of these buttons open applications and special features. The PDA seen in Figure A-3 is fairly typical, although some PDAs and smart phones have many more buttons.

Figure A-3 A Typical PDA

Power on/off button

Program icons

Hard navigation buttons

Instant Message

The instructions that follow are for Windows Mobile for Pocket PC and Palm OS devices. Since there are various versions for each of these operating systems, your procedures may be considerably different. However, the basic features are roughly similar. Use your help system or consult with team members on how to complete the steps that follow on your particular device.

Learn: Using the Stylus

Many PDAs require input through the use of a stylus or digital pen, as seen in Figure A-4. The stylus works a lot like a digital pen on a tablet PC. Table A-2 summarizes a few of the actions this tool can perform.

Figure A-4 A Typical Stylus

© PHOTODISC GREEN/GETTY IMAGES

Tip

A new PDA should be fully charged before its first use. Allow the PDA to charge overnight. This will charge both the primary and backup batteries to their full capacity.

Table A-2

Stylus Action	Result
Tap	Like clicking a mouse
Touch, drag, and hold	Used to select text
Touch and hold	Used to open pop-up or context menus

Set It Up

When you first turn on a brand-new PDA, you will need to complete some basic setup steps. Turn on the PDA by pressing the power button. You will then be taken step by step through the startup sequence, which usually includes:

- Calibrating or aligning the screen
- Setting the time zone location, time, and date
- Learning a few basics

If you have a digital pen or stylus for your PDA, you will be asked to calibrate the device. **Calibration** normally requires tapping on targets to make sure your stylus and screen know exactly where you are tapping. (See Figure A-5.)

Figure A-5 A New PDA Will Require Calibration

Tap the target firmly and accurately at each location on the screen. The target will continue to move until the screen is aligned.

Tap the center of each target with your stylus. This aligns the touchscreen.

Follow the on-screen instructions to finish the setup process. This usually includes verifying your time zone location, the time of day, and the date. Each PDA
may have additional setup steps for you to perform. The instructions are easy to
follow. If you have any difficulties, consult your owner's manual.

Preview Your Applications

Applications are software programs that allow the user to accomplish certain tasks.
Nearly everyone is familiar with common PC applications such as word processors,
spreadsheets, Web browsers, and games. Many of the same applications can be
found on PDAs. Table A-3 lists common PDA applications:

Table A-3　　　Common PDA Applications

Notes or memos	E-mail	Word processors
Contacts or address lists	Instant messaging	Spreadsheets
Calendars or date books	Alarms or reminders	Calculator
Tasks or to-do lists	Phone dialing (smart phone)	Expense tracking
Camera and video applications	Web surfing	E-book reader
Backup or synchronization applications	Games	Music playback

A PDA is really a miniature personal computer. And like PCs, PDAs have many
programs and applications to choose from. The programs can be opened from the
Today and Programs screen on a Pocket PC. (See Figure A-6.) On a Palm OS device, they can be opened by clicking on the Home icon and the Application
launcher. (See Figure A-7.)

Figure A-6　　　The Today and Programs Screens on a Pocket PC

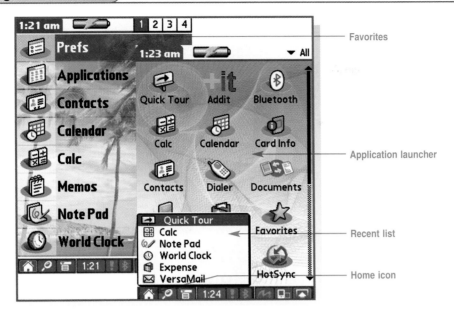

Exercise A2A

What's New at Home Today?

In this exercise, you will use a PDA to plan a vacation to New Zealand. Follow the instructions that most closely match your handheld device.

Pocket PC Instructions	Palm OS Instructions
1. Open the Today screen by choosing **Start**, **Today**.	**1.** Tap the **Home** icon until the **Favorites** list appears as seen in Figure A-7. (On older Palm OS devices, continue tapping the **Home** button until a category **All** appears in the top righthand corner.)
2. Tap the **Programs** icon.	
3. Open, preview, and close several applications, including:	**2.** Open and preview several applications, including:
• *Word Mobile* (or *Pocket Word*)	• *Notepad* or memos
• *Excel Mobile* (or *Pocket Excel*)	• Calendar
• Notes	• Contacts
• Calendar	• Expense
• Contacts	• World clock
• Tasks	**3.** Open the **Calculator** application. Calculate the following expenses:
4. Open the **Calculator** application. Calculate the following expenses:	• $1,780 flight to New Zealand
• $1,780 flight to New Zealand	• $650 hotel accommodations in New Zealand
• $650 hotel accommodations in New Zealand	• $430 car rental in New Zealand
• $430 car rental in New Zealand	• $500 food budget for New Zealand trip
• $500 food budget for New Zealand trip	• $500 souvenir and activities budget for New Zealand trip
• $500 souvenir and activities budget for New Zealand trip	

Hard Button Controls

PDAs are designed to make their users more productive, so they are loaded with helpful shortcuts. For example, most PDAs have hard buttons that open frequently used programs at the touch of a thumb (see Figure A-8). Since the buttons are programmable, every manufacturer can change the application each button will activate. Also, some devices may only have a few buttons while other manufacturers use many of them. To learn what they do, check the documentation on your device and experiment, as explained in Exercise A2B.

Figure A-8

Hard Buttons: Your Buttons May Be Programmed Differently

Home
Calendar
5-way navigator
Contacts
Files

Exercise A2B

Experiment with the Hard Buttons

Instant Message

The **5-way navigator** (see Figure A-8) can move up, down, left, and right by tapping the edges of the outer button. Tapping the center button is the same as tapping the ENTER key on a PC keyboard.

1. Open your notes file *Handheld Tools* from the previous lesson.

2. Start your PDA and tap the first hard button on the left side of your PDA. What application does it open? Record this in your notes.

3. Tap all of the buttons on your PDA from left to right and record in your notes what each button activates.

4. It is very likely that one of the buttons on your PDA will open the **Calendar** application. Tap that button once. Tap it several times in succession to view the Calendar in various modes, such as a daily, weekly, monthly, or yearly view.

5. As you change views in the Calendar application, test the buttons on the 5-way navigator. Observe how in the yearly view the navigator can flip through several years at a time. In the monthly view, the months skip by. In the daily view, you can move between days of the week quickly.

Exercise A2C

Reset Time Zone Settings

1. Locate the settings and preferences that will allow you to change the time zone, time, and date settings.

   - Palm OS users, choose **Prefs** from the Application launcher.

   - Pocket PC users, choose the **Clock** icon just below the Start icon (or choose **Start**, **Settings**, **System**, **Clock & Alarms**).

2. Make sure your time zone has been selected.

   - Choose the city nearest you from your Palm OS device's menu.

   - On a Pocket PC, choose the correct time zone from the drop-down list.

3. Adjust the time and date. Tap on any incorrect date or time, and then use the arrows found on the calendar to adjust the dates and times.

> (>) To use the on-screen standard, shifted, numeric, and international keyboards.

> (>) To practice the Graffiti input with the Wide/Letter Recognizer or the Classic/Block Recognizer input panels.

> (>) To key and edit owner information.

> (>) To key tasks.

> (>) To take a note.

Communicating with a PDA

There are many ways to input information into a handheld computer. Data may be entered using:

- On-screen alphanumeric keyboards
- Graffiti input panels
- Natural handwriting recognition (on some models only)
- Speech recognition (on some models only)
- Docked or external keyboard
- Laser keyboard
- Infrared beaming from another device
- Wireless Internet connection
- Cable to and from a PC
- A phone service provider (smart phone only)

This lesson will cover in detail the first two input methods on the list, which are the most dominant input tools used on Palm OS and Pocket PC devices.

On-Screen Keyboards

On-screen keyboards often provide the most convenient way to input information into a handheld PDA. These tappable keyboards are also called **virtual keyboards**. Virtual keyboards don't really exist; they are just pictures—a series of alphanumeric icons on your PDA screen in the shape of a keyboard. There are several keyboards to choose from. (See Figures A-9a and A-9b on the following page.)

- The standard keyboard lets you tap lowercase letters.
- The shifted keyboard has capital letters.
- The numeric keyboard provides numbers, special characters, and symbols.
- The international keyboard features accented letters and special marks used in languages such as Spanish, French, or German.

Virtual keyboards look a lot like the QWERTY keyboard found on personal computers. Simply tapping the letters, numbers, punctuation marks, or special characters with your stylus will type them on the screen. On-screen keyboard entry is a bit slow, but at times it is the most precise input alternative. Here are a few hints to remember when using the on-screen keyboards:

- To use lowercase letters, tap the keys. (Palm OS users can also tap abc.)
- To use uppercase a letter, tap the SHIFT key. (Palm OS users can also tap ABC.)

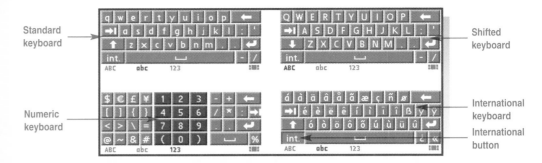

Standard keyboard

Numeric keyboard

Shifted keyboard

International keyboard

International button

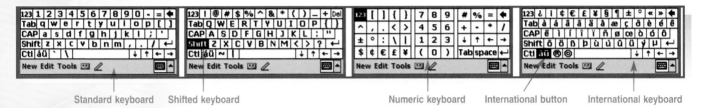

Standard keyboard   Shifted keyboard   Numeric keyboard   International button   International keyboard

- To use numbers and special symbols, tap the 123 icon.
- To use foreign language characters, tap the International button (int. on Palm OS, áü on a Pocket PC). Tap the SHIFT key for international characters in uppercase.
- Tap the ENTER button to move down one line.
- Tap the BACKSPACE button to move backwards and delete mistakes.

Exercise A3A

Tap in Your Owner Information

Figure A-10a   Select Keyboard Icon from the Input Methods List on Newer Palm OS Devices

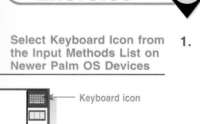

Keyboard icon

Input methods list

1. To open the owner information input window:
   - Palm OS users, tap **Home** and then **Preferences (Prefs)**. Then scroll down to the *Personal* section and choose **Owner**.
   - Pocket PC users, choose **Start**, **Settings**, choose the **Personal** tab, and select **Owner Information**.

2. Choose the **Keyboard** option from the input methods list. See Figures A-10a, A-10b, and A-10c.

Figure A-10b   Select ABC or 123 from the Input Panel on Older Palm OS Devices

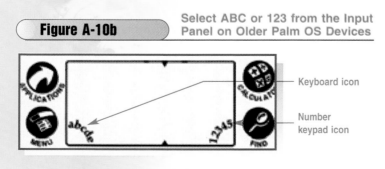

Keyboard icon

Number keypad icon

Figure A-10c   Select Keyboard from the Input Methods List on a Pocket PC

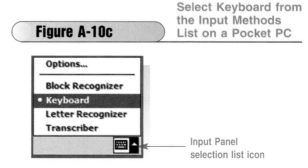

Input Panel selection list icon

3. Key your name. To capitalize, tap the SHIFT key and then the letter.

4. Key the following information:
   - Street address
   - Telephone number
   - E-mail address

5. Close your owner information input screen and return to either your **Today** or **Home** screen.

Marking It Up with Graffiti

Created by Palm, Graffiti is a shorthand way of writing the letters of the alphabet. In fact, it was the original method used to input information into PDAs. Nowadays, there are two Graffiti systems, the original and the expanded Graffiti®2. Older Palms use the original Graffiti system. Newer Palms favor Graffiti2 characters. Pocket PCs permit both systems.

The Original Graffiti

Many people find Graffiti to be more convenient than on-screen keyboards, though forming the letters correctly takes practice and memorization. Figures A-11a and A-11b show how the alphabet and numbers look in the original Graffiti system. The dot in each letter is the starting point.

Figure A-11a	The Original Graffiti Alphabet

ΛBCDEΓGhIJⱭLM
NOPΟRS⌐UVWXYZ

Figure A-11b	Numbers in the Original Graffiti

O123⌐567891

Helpful Gestures

Graffiti uses special keystrokes called gestures. A gesture is a quick motion with a stylus. For example, in the original Graffiti, an upward stroke preceding a letter will create a capital letter. The stylus is set at the bottom of the input area, and a clean upward stroke is made. Nothing will appear on the screen, but the very next letter keyed will be capitalized. The capitalization gesture has the same result as pressing the SHIFT key followed by a letter on the keyboard. For example, the two keystrokes in Figure A-12 will make a capital A.

While there are dozens of gestures that you can learn from your Help files, three additional gestures are very important: Space, Backspace, and Return or Enter. Table A-4 illustrates these three key gestures.

Figure A-12	Use the Capital Gesture to Create a Capital *A* with Original Graffiti

Gesture	How It Is Made	Its Purpose
Space	*Touch the stylus and then slide horizontally to the right.*	The **Space** gesture adds a single space between words.
Backspace	*Touch the stylus and make a quick stroke to the left.*	The **Backspace** gesture erases one character to the left.
Enter or Return	*Touch the stylus and drag diagonally from right to left.*	The **Enter** or **Return** gesture moves down one line, like tapping ENTER or RETURN on a computer keyboard.

The New and Improved Graffiti2

Many people complained about having to memorize special Graffiti characters like *K* or *F*. They wanted to write using more familiar letters. Eventually, Graffiti was improved to include more standard styles of handwriting, including the traditional letters learned by third-graders. And all of the original Graffiti characters still work in Graffiti2 except for the *i*, *t*, and *k*. Figure A-13a shows how to write letters in Graffiti2. Figure A-13b shows how to write Graffiti 2 numerals.

Figure A-13a Letters in Graffiti2

a b c d e f g h i j k l m
n o p q r s t u v w x y z

Figure A-13b Numbers in Graffiti2

0 1 2 3 4 5 6 7 8 9

Figure A-14 Optional Ways to Write the Letter *A*

Graffiti2 also permits several forms of the same letter. For example, Figure A-14 illustrates two more ways Palm and Pocket PC users can write the first letter of the alphabet. (Does this remind you of your elementary penmanship class?)

To accommodate standard handwritten characters, Palm has two input panels—the **Classic** and the **Wide**. On a Pocket PC, these are called the **Block Recognizer** and the **Letter Recognizer**.

The Classic Palm OS and Pocket PC Block Recognizer input panels are divided into two cells. Lowercase letters are written to the left of the center line. Numbers are written to the right of the center line. Upper-case letters are written on the center line on a Palm OS device, but on a Pocket PC you must use the capitalization gesture explained in the previous section. See Figures A-15a and A-15b.

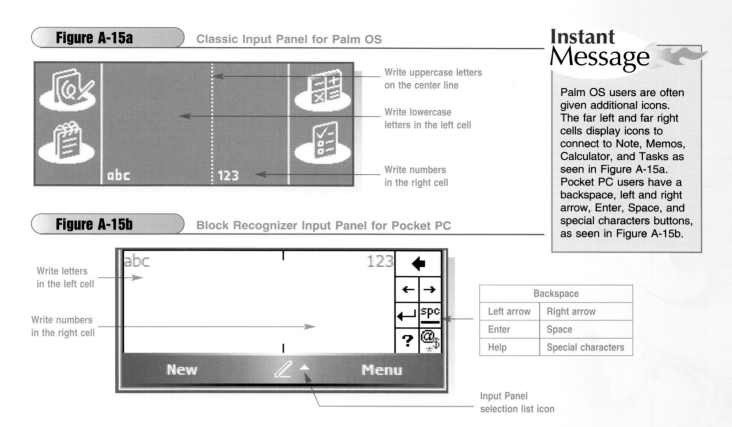

Figure A-15a — Classic Input Panel for Palm OS

Write uppercase letters on the center line

Write lowercase letters in the left cell

Write numbers in the right cell

Figure A-15b — Block Recognizer Input Panel for Pocket PC

Write letters in the left cell

Write numbers in the right cell

Backspace	
Left arrow	Right arrow
Enter	Space
Help	Special characters

Input Panel selection list icon

The Wide or Letter Recognizer Input Panel

The Wide input tool for Palm OS and the corresponding Letter Recognizer for Pocket PC are divided into three cells. Lowercase letters are written in one cell, uppercase letters in another, and numbers in the final cell. Most users prefer this three paneled approach to the Classic or Block Recognizer tools. See Figures A-16a and A-16b to learn how each panel works on your device.

Figure A-16a — The Wide Input Panel for Palm OS

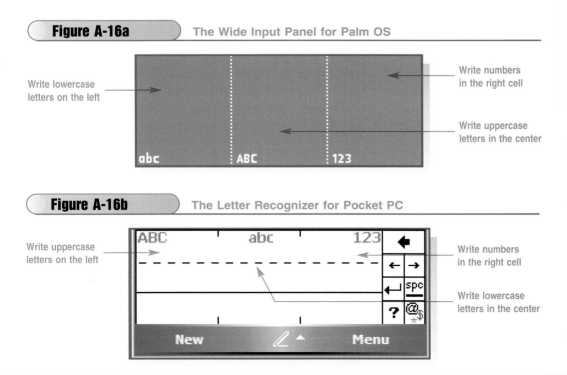

Write lowercase letters on the left

Write numbers in the right cell

Write uppercase letters in the center

Figure A-16b — The Letter Recognizer for Pocket PC

Write uppercase letters on the left

Write numbers in the right cell

Write lowercase letters in the center

Pinpoint Punctuation

PDAs place the most frequently used punctuation marks on a keypad. (See Figures A-17a and A-17b.) These can be viewed by tapping the 123 icon on a Palm OS device and the Special Characters icon on a Pocket PC tool.

Figure A-17a The Special Characters and Numeric Keypad in Palm OS

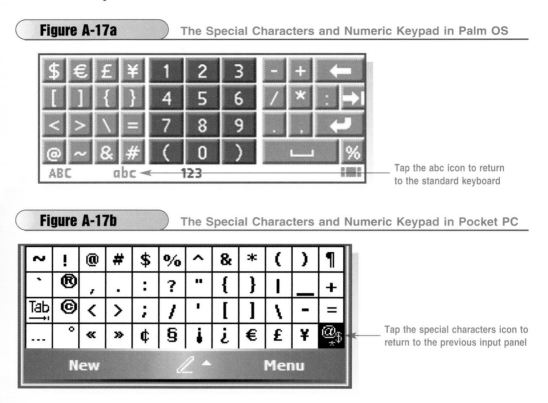

Tap the abc icon to return to the standard keyboard

Figure A-17b The Special Characters and Numeric Keypad in Pocket PC

Tap the special characters icon to return to the previous input panel

Entering Tasks or To Do Items

Everyone has a list of things that they must accomplish or complete every day. PDAs have created applications to help people organize and keep track of these things. On a Pocket PC, the application is called a **Tasks list**. On a Palm OS device, it is called a **Tasks list** or a **To Do list**.

To do or task lists may record things as simple as going to the dry cleaners or the post office. They may also be as involved as planning a vacation. PDAs are wonderful tools to keep track of such items. They can keep such a list perfectly organized, allowing you to check off things that you have completed and prioritize items by their importance or urgency. Using Graffiti or Graffiti2, key the following tasks or to do items into your PDA.

Exercise A3B

Creating a To Do List

Follow the instructions that most closely match your handheld device.

<table>
<tr><td valign="top" width="50%">

Palm OS Instructions

1. Choose the **Home** button to launch the **Application launcher**; then choose **Tasks**.

2. Choose **New**. (See Figure A-18.)

Figure A-18   Create a New Task or To Do Item

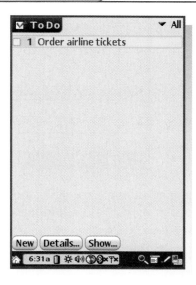

3. Key **Order airline tickets**.

4. Choose **Details** and select the following settings as seen in Figure A-19:

   - Set Priority to **1**.
   - Set Category to **Personal**.
   - Choose **Due Date** and set for **Tomorrow**.

Figure A-19   Set the Following Details

</td><td valign="top" width="50%">

Pocket PC Instructions

1. Choose the **Start** button, **Programs**, and then choose **Tasks**.

2. Choose **Tap here to add a new task**. (See Figure A-22.)

Figure A-22   Create a New Task or To Do Item

> ! ↓ **Tap here to add a new task**

3. Key **Order airline tickets** and tap the ENTER key to accept the new entry.

   Instant Message

   A Pocket PC will try to guess the words you are keying. If the word appears in a little window, tap it!

4. Choose the newly entered **Order airline tickets** task, and then choose **Edit** followed by the **Task** tab:

   - Set Priority to **High**.
   - Choose **Due** and set the due date for **tomorrow**.
   - Choose **Occurs** and then **Once**.
   - Choose **Reminder** and then **Remind me** to set the alarm.
   - Choose **Categories** and then **Personal**.

Figure A-23   Set the Following Details

(continued on next page)

</td></tr>
</table>

5. Click the **Note** button. (*Note:* Your Note button may look like an icon.)

Key the following note as seen in Figure A-20:

American Airlines $1,780 with no layover

Qantas Airlines $1,650 with two-hour layover in LA

Figure A-20 Insert a Note on Airline Prices

6. Choose **Done**.

7. Key these additional task items, but only set a priority setting with no additional details as seen in Figure A-21.

  1 Give dog to Helena

  2 Make hotel reservation

  2 Reserve a rental car

  3 Shop for my vacation

Figure A-21 Create a Task or To Do List

8. Mark the task item **1 Give dog to Helena** as complete as seen in Figure A-21.

9. Close your **Tasks** or **To Do** list.

5. Choose the **Order airline tickets** task again, and then **Edit**. Then choose the **Notes** tab.

Key the following note as seen in Figure A-24:

American Airlines $1,780 with no layover

Qantas Airlines $1,650 with two-hour layover in LA

• Choose **OK**.

Figure A-24 Insert a Note on Airline Prices

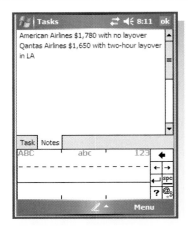

6. Key these additional task items, but only set a **Priority** setting with no additional details as seen in Figure A-25.

High: Give dog to Helena

Normal: Make hotel reservation

Normal: Reserve a rental car

Low: Shop for my vacation

7. Mark the task item **Give dog to Helena** as complete as seen in Figure A-25.

Figure A-25 Create a Task List

8. Close your **Tasks** list.

Get Help!

If you ever forget how to write in Graffiti, you can get a refresher course from your help files and learn much more about your device. On a Palm OS device, choose your Home button, and choose Quick Tour from the Application launcher.

On a Pocket PC device, you can reach the help section by choosing Start, Help. There you can choose from among a list of possible topics.

Exercise Investigate Help Files

Follow the instructions that most closely match your handheld device.

Palm OS Instructions	Pocket PC instructions
1. To take the Graffiti Quick Tour, use the **Home** icon to open the **Application launcher**.	**1.** To review the help files, tap the **Start** icon and choose **Help** from the list.
2. Tap **Quick Tour**.	**2.** From the Help topics list, choose **Transcriber** (or choose **Contents**, **Entering Text**, or **Write with Transcriber**) and research that input technology in more detail. You may wish to use this input method in the future.
3. From the Quick Tour menu, tap **Graffiti®2** to start the tour on that topic.	
4. Choose three additional topics to research from the list.	**3.** Return to the original Help list by choosing **Start, Help**.
	4. Choose three additional topics to research from the contents list.

LESSON 4 USING PDA APPLICATIONS

OBJECTIVES

- To key contact information.
- To create a personal business card.
- To beam information from one device to another.
- To key calendar items.
- To synchronize your data.

Powerful Applications

The first PDAs only offered a limited assortment of programs and applications. The most essential were *contact lists*, *calendar features*, *task* or *to do lists*, and *notetaking* tools. These applications still comprise the core ingredients making PDAs and smart phones necessary business tools. Each, in its own unique way, helps busy businesspeople organize their time and business relationships.

Over the years, thousands of new PDA and smart phone applications have been created. Most are very specialized, such as:

- An application allowing building inspectors and appraisers to accurately calculate the square footage and value of a home or an apartment.

- Games specifically for handheld devices.

- Financial planning and expense applications for business travelers.

Instant Message

You created a task list with a note in the previous lesson. In this lesson, you'll work with the contact management and calendar features, as well as explore data transfer by beaming and synchronizing.

- Internet searching and e-mail capabilities.
- GPS (global positioning systems) and mapping software to assist travelers.

These new, diminutive handheld devices even come with scaled-down versions of popular desktop computer applications, such as *Pocket Word*, *Pocket Excel*, and *Pocket PowerPoint*.

One thing all of these powerful applications have in common is the operating system that allows them to run on a PDA or smart phone. Because each OS provides a common interface for all applications, after you learn to use the basic core applications—contact, calendar, task, and notetaking tools—you should be able to use almost any other PDA or smart phone application.

Learn: Contacts

A contact list, also called an address list, is one of the most helpful programs on any handheld. Such an application provides a powerful way to organize business friends and personal associates. This tool allows you to collect the following types of information:

- Names
- Addresses
- Titles
- Company names
- Phone and fax numbers
- E-mail addresses
- Mailing and shipping addresses
- Web pages (on some models)
- Photos (on some models)
- Birthdates
- Other personal contact information

In this next exercise, key the personal contact information for Helena Petsgo, a friend and a manager at a local business, who has graciously agreed to take care of your dog Mazie until you return from your vacation in New Zealand.

Exercise A4A

Entering A Contact

Follow the instructions that most closely match your handheld device.

Palm OS Instructions	Pocket PC Instructions
1. Open the **Contacts** (sometimes called **Address**) application and tap **New**.	**1.** Open the **Contacts** application and tap **New**.
2. Tap to the right of the **Last name** field and key **Petsgo**. Tap next to the **First name** field and key **Helena**, as shown in Figure A-26.	**2.** Tap the down arrow next to the **Name field** to open a pop-up box. This box will allow you to key **Helena Petsgo**'s name. Key the first name and the last name, as shown in Figure A-27.
• Last name: **Petsgo**	
• First name: **Helena**	
	(continued on next page)

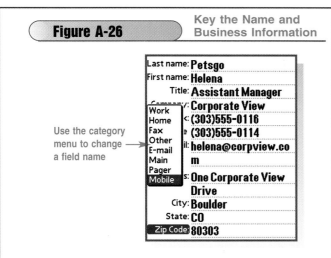

Figure A-26   Key the Name and Business Information

Use the category menu to change a field name

Last name: **Petsgo**
First name: **Helena**
Title: **Assistant Manager**
Company: **Corporate View**
Work (303)555-0116
Home
Fax (303)555-0114
Other
E-mail helena@corpview.com
Main
Pager
Mobile One Corporate View Drive
City: **Boulder**
State: **CO**
Zip Code: **80303**

Figure A-27   Key the Name

3. Key Helena's job title and the name of the company for which she works in the appropriate fields.

- Company: **Corporate View**
- Title: **Assistant Manager**

Tip

Choose the down arrow next to any of the fields to change its title, as seen in Figure A-26.

4. Key her work and mobile phone numbers along with her e-mail address in the appropriate fields.

- Work Telephone: **(303) 555-0116**
- Mobile Telephone: **(303) 555-0114**
- E-mail: **helena@corpview.com**

5. Scroll down to the **Work address** fields and key this information.

- Street Address (W): **One Corporate View Drive**
- City: **Boulder**
- State: **CO**
- ZIP Code: **80303**
- Country: **USA**

6. Tap **Done** to return to your contacts list.

3. Key Helena's job title and the name of the company for which she works in the appropriate fields.

- Job Title: **Assistant Manager**
- Department: **Human Resources**
- Company: **Corporate View**
- Work Telephone: **(303) 555-0116**
- E-Mail: **helena@corpview.com**

4. Tap the down arrow next to the **Work address** field to open a pop-up box.

- Street: **One Corporate View Drive**
- City: **Boulder**
- State: **CO**
- ZIP Code: **80303**
- Country: **USA**

5. Key the remaining information seen here:

- E-Mail: **helena@corpview.com**
- Mobile Telephone: **(303) 555-0114**

6. Tap **OK** to return to your contacts list.

Learn: Personal Business Cards

One of the most common business activities is to hand out personal business cards to potential customers, clients, and partners. With the advent of PDAs and smart phones, business cards have gone digital. All one has to do to create an electronic business card is to create a personal contact and then beam it to other PDA and smart phone users. Try creating your own personal business card in this next exercise, then **beam** it (transfer it wirelessly with infrared technologies) to another PDA or smart phone in the subsequent exercise.

Instant Message

Create a Personal Business Card

Follow the instructions that most closely match your handheld device.

© TERRI MILLER/E-VISUAL COMMUNICATIONS INC.

Palm OS Instructions

1. Open the **Contacts** (or **Address**) application and tap **New**.

2. Key your name in the **Last Name** and **First Name** fields. (If you wish, key a job title in the **Title** field.)

3. Key your mailing address, e-mail address, and phone number in the appropriate fields and then tap **Done**.

4. Return to your **Contact** list and open the contact with your name on it.

5. Tap the **Contact** or **Address** menu tab in the top left corner of the screen. It will open the **Record** menu as seen in Figure A-28. Choose **Select Business Card**.

Figure A-28 — Choose the Select Business Card Option

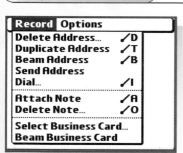

6. When asked if you want to *Make this name your business card*, tap **Yes**.

Pocket PC Instructions

1. Open the **Contacts** application and tap **New**.

2. Tap the down arrow next to the **Name** field to open a pop-up box and key your name. (If you wish, key a job title in the **Title** field.)

3. Key your mailing address, e-mail address, and phone number in the appropriate fields.

4. Tap **OK** to save your information and return to your contacts list.

Beaming with Pride

Your personal business card—along with every other contact, calendar item, and task item—can be beamed to another handheld device using infrared or **IrDA** technologies. The IrDA standard was created by the **Infrared Data Association**, which sets infrared wireless communication standards for the technology industry.

You are already familiar with infrared transmissions. IrDA is the technology used to communicate between a remote control and a television. Beaming from handheld computers is almost as easy as using a remote control. If you have created a personal electronic business card, you can beam that information to a prospective colleague or client with the tap of a few buttons. The contact information can then be accepted by the receiver and stored on their smart phone or PDA. Follow these steps and see how easy beaming is.

Exercise A4C

Beaming Contact Information and Business Cards

Follow the instructions that most closely match your handheld device.

Palm OS Instructions	Pocket PC Instructions

Palm OS Instructions

1. Team up with a partner who has a personal business card on their PDA or smart phone, and align your infrared or IrDA ports.

2. Open your **Contacts** and find the personal business card you designed in the previous exercise.

3. Tap the **Contact** or **Address** tab to drop down the **Record** menu.

4. Tap **Beam Business Card**, as seen in Figure A-29.

Figure A-29 Beam Your Business Card

Tip:

If you hold the Contacts button down continuously on most Palm OS Devices, your business card will be sent automatically.

5. After contact is made between the two devices, follow the instructions on the screen to upload.

6. Have your team members beam their business cards to you.

Pocket PC Instructions

1. Team up with a partner who has a personal business card on their PDA or smart phone, and align your infrared or IrDA ports.

2. Find and open your personal business card on your PDA from the list of **Contacts**.

3. Choose **Menu**, **Beam Contact** (or **Tools**, **Beam Contact**) from the open **Contacts** window to send your business card as seen in Figure A-30.

Figure A-30 Beam Your Business Card

4. After contact is made between the two devices, follow the instructions on the screen, such as **Tap to send**.

Tip:

If your PDA is not beaming properly, choose **Start**, **Settings**, **Connections**, followed by **Beam**. Make sure a check mark appears next to **Receive All Incoming Beams**.

5. Have your team members beam their business cards to you.

Learn: Calendar Applications

The Calendar application organizes timed events. Timed events include meetings, classes, interviews, appointments, flight departures, business lunches with colleagues or clients, or any other event you must attend that begins at a specific time.

In the exercise that follows, calendar your flight to New Zealand, a lunch meeting with friends, and an 8 a.m. meeting with an ocean-kayaking instructor.

Exercise (A4D)

Schedule a New Zealand Flight

Follow the instructions that most closely match those of your specific PDA or smart phone.

Instant Message

To get to New Zealand from North America, you will travel by air nearly a full day and then cross the international date line, making it two days later when you actually arrive. In short, everything across the date line happens tomorrow; so to get there tomorrow, you must have flown out yesterday.

Palm OS Instructions

1. Open the **Calendar** and tap the **Weekly view** button. Move ahead to the next week by tapping the **forward** arrow button, which advances one full week with each tap. (See Figure A-31.)

Figure A-31   The Weekly View

Aug '07	◀ Week 34 ▶
S M T W T F S
19 20 21 22 23 24 25
8:00
10:00
12:00
2:00
4:00
6:00
· ▦ ▦ ▤ (Go To)

2. Tap the **M** (for Monday). Notice how you are taken automatically to the daily view seen in Figure A-32. (Choose the **Daily View** icon if necessary on your PDA.)

Pocket PC Instructions

1. Open the **Calendar** application. Choose the **Monthly** view as seen in Figure A-35. Move ahead to the next week and tap on Monday.

Figure A-35   The Monthly View

Calendar	11:24
February 2006
S M T W T F S
29 30 31 1 2 3 4
5 6 7 8 9 10 11
12 13 14 15 16 17 18
19 20 21 22 23 24 25
26 27 28 1 2 3 4
5 6 7 8 9 10 11
Year	Menu

2. Notice how you are taken automatically to the daily view. (Choose the **Daily View** icon if necessary on your PDA.)

(continued on next page)

Figure A-32   The Daily View

3. Tap **3 p.m.**, which is near the departure time for the flight to New Zealand. (If you tap directly on 3 p.m., the **Set Time** screen will open.)

4. In the Set Time box, key the departure time of **3:30 p.m.** and choose **OK**. (See Figure A-33.)

Figure A-33   Set the Departure Time

5. On the subject line, key **Depart**.

6. Choose the **Details** button and then tap a check mark in the **Alarm** box. Set the alarm for **5 Hours**, which should give you time to drive to the airport and clear airport security. (See Figure A-34.)

Figure A-34   Set the Alarm for 5 Hours in Advance

7. Click **OK** to finish. (Notice the small alarm next to your Depart entry.)

3. Tap **3 p.m.** and choose **New** at the bottom of the screen, as seen in Figure A-36.

Figure A-36   The Daily View

4. On the Subject line, key **Depart**. On the Location line, key **DEN**, short for Denver International Airport.

5. In the Starts box, key the departure time as **3:30 p.m.** on **Monday**.

6. In the Reminder field, choose **Remind me**. Set the timer for **5 hours**. (See Figure A-37.)

Figure A-37   Input the Scheduling Information

7. Choose **OK** to record the entry.

Schedule Additional Events

1. Open your Calendar application, choose the **Weekly** view, and move ahead one week (the same week as your scheduled departure to New Zealand).

2. On Thursday, at 12 p.m., schedule a lunch with friends. Give yourself 30 minutes warning.

3. The next day, on Friday, schedule a class with your ocean-kayaking instructor at 8 a.m. Give yourself a 1 hour warning.

Learn: Backup and Synchronization Applications

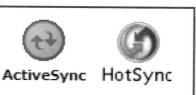

Figure A-38 ActiveSync and HotSync Icons

Synchronization means to exchange data between electronic devices. Synchronization has two purposes: to protect your data in case of a device or battery failure, and to make your data available on your computer as well as on your handheld device. Naturally, not every piece of data needs to be shared. You must be selective about which information is transferred back and forth between the two devices.

Pocket PC users synchronize with the **ActiveSync** application. Palm OS users use an application called **HotSync**. (See Figure A-38.) The software usually comes pre-installed on your PDA or smart phone. A CD that can be used to install ActiveSync or HotSync on your PC is usually included with every handheld. If you lose the CD, you can always download the synchronization software from http://www.microsoft.com for Microsoft Pocket PC tools or from http://www.palm.com for Palm OS devices.

After synchronization, the calendar items, task items, and contacts that you have created can be displayed in *Microsoft Outlook* for Pocket PC users. Palm OS users can also display their data in *Microsoft Outlook* or in another program called *Palm Desktop*. (See Figure A-39.)

Figure A-39 Data Displayed in *Microsoft Outlook*

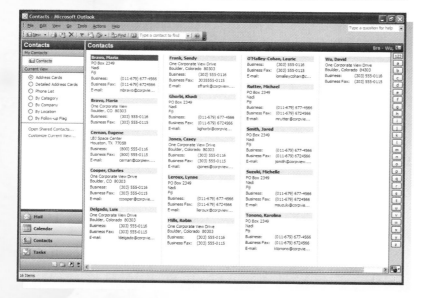

Synchronize Your Devices

1. Confirm that your synchronization software has been installed on your computer.

2. Connect the synchronization cable between your PDA or smart phone and your personal computer.

3. Turn on your PDA or smart phone. Let your computer and your hand-held device locate each other and begin the synchronization process. If synchronization does not start immediately, follow the steps in your owner's guide to troubleshoot problems or start the synchronization process manually. As a synchronization session begins, the ActiveSync or HotSync status screens will appear. The screens will track and report on the synchronization process.

4. View your data on your personal computer in either *Microsoft Outlook* or *Palm Desktop*.

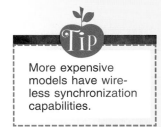
More expensive models have wireless synchronization capabilities.

Appendix A

LESSONS 1–4

PDAs, Smart Phones, and Handheld Computers

LESSON ① **ASSESS KNOWLEDGE OF HANDHELD DEVICES**

OBJECTIVES

⊙ To assess research skills.

⊙ To assess knowledge about PDAs and smart phones at various price points.

⊙ To assess knowledge of memory, expansion, processors, connectivity, battery life, and other applications and features on PDAs or smart phones.

Exercise A1A

Sell a PDA or Smart Phone

In Lesson 1, you and your team selected the PDAs and smart phones you liked best from among all the choices available. Now refine your list by using the Internet to include top picks in specific price ranges. Here are five different price points for PDAs and smart phones.

- Under $150
- Between $150 and $250
- Between $250 and $350
- Between $350 and $450
- Over $500

1. Have each team member pick a different price point before continuing.

2. As individuals, research online a single PDA or smart phone as your top pick at your designated price point.

3. Using *PowerPoint*, prepare an individual sales pitch for the PDA or smart phone that you have selected. Create slides listing all the features and reasons why your individual PDA or smart phone is the best possible choice at your particular price point. Account for the *memory, expansion capability, processor speed, wireless conductivity, battery life, synchronization,* and *other features* on your device. Other important factors, such as *size, ease of use,* and the *applications* available on the handheld device, should be part of the sales pitch.

---

4. Reuniting as a team, have team members try to sell their PDA or smart phone to the rest of the group. Each individual member should make a sales presentation.

LESSON 2 — ASSESS HOW TO CHANGE SETTINGS AND LEARN MORE

⊘ To assess the ability to learn more about PDA features.
⊘ To change device settings.

Exercise A2A

What Time Is It In . . . ?

1. After you arrive in New Zealand, you give some thought to traveling around the world. Investigate in your help system or Quick Tour how to use your Pocket PDA time zone features or the Palm's World Clock to plot the current time in the following possible destinations moving west:

   • Sydney, Australia

   • Tokyo, Japan

   • Bangkok, Thailand

   • Moscow, Russia

   • London, England

   • New York, New York

   • Your hometown

2. Answer the following:

   • How many hours' difference is it between London and New York?

   • How many hours' difference is it between Tokyo and New York?

   • How many hours' difference is it between Sydney and New York?

Exercise A2B

Change Preference Settings

1. Personalize your PDA or smart phone. Change the color background settings or even its graphics. Use your help feature to learn how to make these types of changes.

Exercise A2C

Learn More About Input Techniques

1. Use the help feature provided in your PDA to learn faster and better ways to input information into your PDA. For example, study how gestures can be used to erase, cut, copy, paste, tab, and undo. Pocket PC users, review how to use Transcriber and how to record Notes in your own handwriting. Palm OS users, learn how to use *Notepad* for handwritten notes.

LESSONS 3-4 USE A PDA OR SMART PHONE FOR PERSONAL PRODUCTIVITY

OBJECTIVES

- ⊘ To assess the ability to use a PDA or smart phone for personal productivity planning and personal success.
- ⊘ To assess the ability to manage personal contacts.
- ⊘ To assess the ability to manage personal tasks.
- ⊘ To assess the ability to manage a personal schedule.

Improve Your Personal Productivity with Handheld Tools

In the next four exercises, experiment with your PDA or smart phone. Use it to keep track of tasks, contacts, and calendared events. Evaluate, over a period of one week, whether a handheld device can increase your personal productivity.

Exercise A3-4A

Enter Friends or Family Members into a Contact List

In this exercise, use your PDA or smart phone to keep track of your personal contacts. Enter a minimum of five friends, family members, team members, or colleagues into your PDA's contact list. Enter additional contacts as you see fit during this weeklong project.

Exercise A3-4B

Keep a Personal Schedule on a PDA or Smart Phone

Enter all of your appointments, meetings, and other timed events into your PDA for a least one entire week. Set alarms and use the system to help you remember where you are supposed to be and when.

Exercise

Keep a Task List

Create a to do or task list. Keep track of all the things that you must accomplish for no less than one entire week. Prioritize your tasks to rank the relative importance of each task. Check off items that you have accomplished.

Exercise

Report on Your Personal Productivity Experiment

After using your PDA or smart phone to keep track of personal tasks, contacts, and calendared events for a week or more, report on your experience.

1. Create a short report on your PDA. Use an application such as Notes or Memos or *Pocket Word*. In your report, explain the pluses and minuses of using a PDA, smart phone, or other handheld device to plan and execute your personal schedule and tasks and to manage contacts.

2. Answer these questions in your report:
   - Does a handheld device efficiently help you organize your time, tasks, and contacts?
   - Would you like to continue using a PDA or smart phone to manage your personal productivity in the future?
   - Is there anything about your handheld device that you would change or want to see improved? (For instance: Are there any features missing on your handheld device that you would like to see added?)
   - Which application have you found to be the most useful and why?
   - Which application have you found to be the least useful and why?

3. If possible, beam your report to an instructor or team member.

Appendix *B*

Leadership

LESSON ① LEADERSHIP

OBJECTIVES

- ⊙ To learn about the need for effective leaders.
- ⊙ To learn the attributes of effective leaders.
- ⊙ To explore leadership opportunities in school, in the community, and in a profession.

Exercise B1

Leadership

1. Read the following three sections to learn about leadership.

© PHOTODISC BLUE / GETTY IMAGES

Leadership

Leadership is the foundation for all things in our society. Effective leadership is needed in our schools, homes, government, and places of worship, work, and play, etc. Therefore, much has been written about the attributes that many believe are essential for effective leadership.

Leadership Can Be Learned

It is a popular opinion that leaders are born not made. However, in reality leadership is a set of characteristics that can be learned. You will have many opportunities during your school years to develop leadership qualities. You may have opportunities to be a leader in student government, a student club or other extracurricular activity, and in your community or church. If you work, you will have opportunities to develop leadership qualities for the workplace.

Leadership Defined

Leadership can be defined as getting other people to follow you towards a common goal. For example, imagine that 12 students from your class, including yourself, were asked to move to the front of the room. Once there, the group is directed to line up in the order of their ages from the youngest to the oldest by year, month, and day. Also, the group is told they have five minutes to do this. No further instructions are given.

The question you are to consider is whether or not this group of students could perform this simple task without one of the students assuming a leadership role.

Would you be the one who assumes the leadership role? If so, would you do so immediately or would you wait to see if someone else was willing to step forward to lead the group?

If you assumed the role as leader, would you show any signs of frustration if you could not get others to follow your directions?

If you did not assume leadership responsibilities, would you resent being "bossed" around by someone who assumed the leadership responsibilities? Or would you willingly follow the leader's directions and help the group meet its goal? If so, you would be demonstrating an equally important set of qualities—being a good follower or team player.

2. Open a blank *Word* document and list at least two instances when you successfully fulfilled leadership responsibilities. Indicate why and how you became the leader and give reasons you believe you were an effective leader in each instance.

3. Save as *App B-Exercise B1*.

Exercise B2

A Classmate as a Leader

1. Think of a student in your school whom you consider to be an effective leader. It doesn't matter whether he or she is a leader of a student club, on an athletic field or court, in student government, or in the community. What matters is that you believe this person is an effective leader.

2. Open *CD-App B-Exercise B2* and print the file.

3. As you read each of the following 10 attributes of a successful leader, use the four-point scale to rate the student you consider to be a leader. If desired, use the space at the bottom to explain your ratings.

1. **A successful leader accepts responsibility and accountability for results.** True leadership involves not only the exercise of authority, but also full acceptance of responsibility and accountability. Leaders accept responsibility for those whom they lead. The leader is accountable for everything that occurs, even the errors. Don't fault others; just shoulder the blame when things go wrong. On the other hand, good leaders always share credit for their successes. Leaders always try to exhibit an attitude of sharing, except when things go wrong.

2. **A successful leader has self-discipline, good character, and is committed to personal development.** The best leaders commit themselves to a life of ongoing personal development. An effective leader understands his or her own shortcomings and seeks

improvement from within. The great leaders also give others the opportunity and encouragement to develop. The best leaders love to read. Most subscribe to a lot of different magazines, many of which are outside their area of expertise or current knowledge. They also read books about strategies for leading and biographies or autobiographies about respected leaders.

3. **A successful leader is a great communicator.** What separates many great leaders from others is that they have truly mastered the art of listening. They ask questions and they really listen to the answers. They have learned the power of silence and remember the wise saying, "You can't learn with your mouth open!" Leaders follow up verbal communications with written communications to lessen misunderstandings.

4. **A successful leader has great people skills.** Leaders are open enough so that everyone around them can get to know and trust them. Leaders are also approachable. True leaders are recognized as warm and likable people. Great leaders have a genuine concern for those whom they lead. People expect their leader to safeguard their future.

5. **A successful leader builds momentum and takes action.** To be appointed or elected to a leadership position is not sufficient to make you a leader. You must, after being appointed or elected, take charge and begin leading. Leaders must have strong personal energy to get a project up and running. They must also maintain that energy to see the projects through to completion. Remember, effective leaders perform for results, not recognition.

6. **A successful leader sets high standards and expectations.** Leaders expect excellence of themselves and the people they lead, because they realize that for the most part leaders get what they expect. That is, if they have low expectations, they are likely to get low performance. Conversely, if they have high expectations, they are likely to get high performance.

7. **A successful leader can be trusted and is loyal to his or her followers.** Trust is the single most important factor in building personal and professional relationships. Trust implies accountability, predictability, and reliability. More than anything else, followers want to believe in and trust their leaders. People must believe in and trust their leaders before they will follow them. Trust must be earned day by day. It calls for consistency. Some of the ways a leader can betray trust include breaking promises, gossiping, withholding information, or being duplicitous.

8. **A successful leader delegates tasks.** The question leaders must ask themselves is whether a task can be done by someone else. If so, it should probably be delegated. Good leaders focus on performing tasks that no one can do as well. Oftentimes these tasks relate to long-term planning and strategic thinking.

9. **A successful leader makes decisions.** Successful leaders do not agonize over a decision because they're afraid of making a mistake. They know mistakes are likely to happen, and they are

willing to live with the consequences of their decisions. Also, leaders do not second-guess decisions they have already made. Rather, effective leaders focus their attention on doing the best thing in the present moment and planning for a better future.

10. **A successful leader is friendly, teachable, and can control his or her ego.** Leaders put empathy ahead of authority. Leaders are friendly, not arrogant or egotistical. They are friendly with all kinds of people regardless of their position or status.

Successful leaders don't have fragile egos. They recognize that no single person can have all of the correct answers all of the time and that they can always learn from others. Leaders don't let their ego get in the way.

Attributes of a Successful Leader

- A successful leader accepts responsibility and accountability for results.

- A successful leader has self-discipline, good character, and is committed to personal development.

- A successful leader is a great communicator.

- A successful leader has great people skills.

- A successful leader builds momentum and takes action.

- A successful leader sets high standards and expectations.

- A successful leader can be trusted and is loyal to his or her followers.

- A successful leader delegates tasks.

- A successful leader makes decisions.

- A successful leader is friendly, teachable, and can control his or her ego.

These attributes of leadership apply in all settings. They apply while attending school, playing with friends, participating in sports or other extracurricular activities, working with others, governing others, and being a family and community member.

4. Write any additional comments you have in the space provided on the rating form.

5. Submit your rating to your teacher.

Leadership Opportunities Through High School Student Organizations

1. Read the following information about FBLA.

FBLA-An Opportunity to Lead

One school organization that is popular with students who study business and computers is FBLA. FBLA stands for the future business leaders of America. It exists primarily to provide students with opportunities to learn and apply leadership and competitive skills. Members of FBLA have opportunities to become leaders by holding office at the local, regional, state, and/or national levels. In addition, you will have many opportunities to serve and use leadership skills while serving on committees and participating in activities. FBLA sponsors numerous leadership conferences to help students develop specific leadership skills.

Another aspect of participating in FBLA is the opportunity to take part in competitions at the local, regional, state, and national levels. These competitions are centered around business and computer subjects commonly completed in high school. Students who do well at the local level advance to the regional level. Those who do well at the regional level advance to the state level, and likewise those who do well at the state level can compete at the national level. Students who are successful in these competitions bring favorable recognition to themselves, their teachers, and their schools.

2. Access http://www.fbla-pbl.org (see Figure B-1) to locate information about FBLA and how it is organized to serve middle school, high school, and college/university students and alumni.

3. Print at least one page of the information you find.

4. Access the FBLA-PBL website at http://www.fbla-pbl.org, or if you prefer, link to your state's FBLA-PBL website. Explore either the national or state website to learn how FBLA provides leadership opportunities for high school students. Write a short description of your findings and print one or more pages from the website to support your description.

5. *Save as App B-Exercise B3.*

Figure B-1   FBLA-PBL Home Page

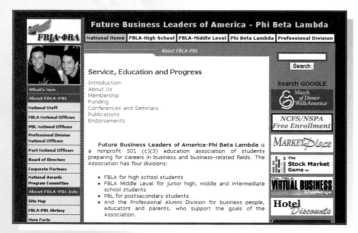

Leadership Opportunities Through Community Service Organizations

1. There are several organizations for service- and community-minded individuals. Among these are Kiwanis International and Rotary International, both of which sponsor organizations for high school students. Choose one of these organizations and access its website.

Kiwanis International—http://www.kiwanis.org (Figure B-2):

Figure B-2 Kiwanis Home Page

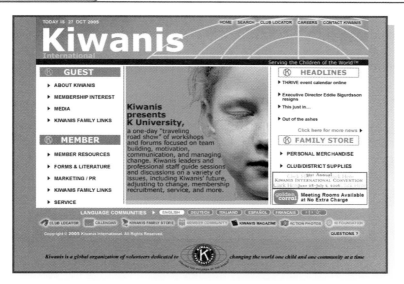

Rotary International—http://www.rotary.org (Figure B-3):

Figure B-3 Rotary International Home Page

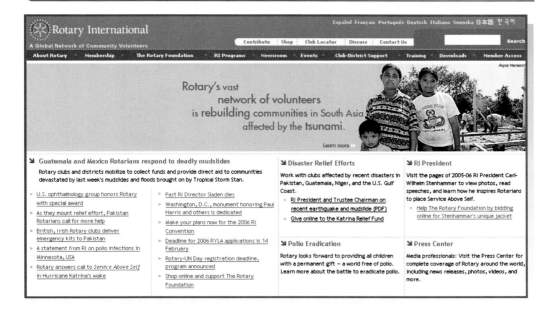

2. Explore the site you selected to learn how the organization provides opportunities for high school students to develop leadership skills. Write a short description of your findings and print one or more pages from the website to support your description.

3. Save as *App B-Exercise B4*.

Exercise B5

Leadership Opportunities in Professional Associations

1. Read the following information about professional associations.

Nearly every profession has an association to serve its members. Many professions have national, regional, state, and local associations. Each provides service to the profession and the members of the association. The associations, regardless of level, also provide opportunities for members to assume leadership positions.

For example, if you are a business education teacher in the Eastern Region of Illinois, there are several professional associations you might want to join. You could join the National Business Education Association (national level), the North-Central Business Education Association (regional level), the Illinois Business Education Association (state level), and/or the Eastern Illinois Business Education Association (local level).

Figure B-4   NBEA Home Page

If you are an architect in the Cleveland, Ohio, area, you may want to join The American Institute of Architects (national level). You could also be a member of the American Institute of Architects Ohio (state level) and/or the American Institute of Architects Cleveland (local level).

2. Identify a profession you want to learn more about. Search the Internet to find associations related to the profession you choose. Look for national, regional, state, and/or local associations. Write a brief description of your findings and a paragraph or two about the benefits of joining and the leadership opportunities they provide for their members.

3. Save as *App B-Exercise B5*.

Appendix C

Careers and Employability

LESSON ① CAREERS AND EMPLOYABILITY

OBJECTIVES

⊙ To explore career options.
⊙ To learn how your personality traits can help you choose a career.
⊙ To identify skills employers want.
⊙ To discover the importance of lifelong learning and career planning.

Introduction

Choosing a career is one of the most important decisions you will make about your future. Your choice will take you down a specific road in your education, training, and personal development. That is why it is so important to plan your career options carefully. You need to explore your talents and passions. You need to develop tools to help in your career search. You need to understand your options so you choose a path that will be rewarding to you both now and in the future.

The information presented in this Appendix will introduce you to some of the many career options available to you. You will learn how your personality traits can help you choose a career you will enjoy. You will be able to identify the skills that employers want so that you can be successful in your professional life. You will discover how ethical behavior relates to employability. And you will read about the importance of lifelong learning and career planning.

Understanding Career Options

Did you know that you currently have many skills that employers look for in an employee? The skills you are learning in this course will be important in your future job. Many companies require employees to have advanced computer skills. They expect you to come to the job knowing how to prepare a spreadsheet, format a letter, and develop a presentation. The word processing and database skills you are learning are necessary for careers in customer service, commercial art, and medical assisting. Excellent verbal and written communication skills are important in careers in sales, teaching, and magazine publishing. Spreadsheet, desktop publishing, and presentation skills are necessary for careers in newspapers, office management, and public relations. As companies become more and more dependent on computers, they will need skilled employees to help them do business.

As you begin to explore careers, you will find countless options to choose from. In fact, the number of career opportunities doubles every few years. New and exciting careers are now available in sports marketing, international banking, health and medicine, hospitality and tourism, and the fast food industry. You have the opportunity to choose a career that is just right for you and to be wildly successful at it! Examine the table in Figure C-1 to see a list of the Top 25 Fastest-Growing Occupations as identified by the U.S. Department of Education.

Figure C-1 Top 25 Fastest-Growing Careers

Top 25 Fastest-Growing Occupations
2000–2010 National Projections

1. Computer software engineers, applications
2. Computer support specialists
3. Computer software engineers, systems software
4. Network systems and data communications analysis
5. Desktop publishers
6. Database administrators
7. Personal and home care aides
8. Computer systems analysis
9. Medical assistants
10. Social and human service assistants
11. Physician assistants
12. Medical records and health information technicians
13. Computer and information systems managers
14. Home health aides
15. Occupational health aides
16. Physical therapist assistants
17. Audiologists
18. Fitness trainers and aerobics instructors
19. Computer and information scientists, research
20. Veterinary assistants and laboratory animal caretakers
21. Occupational therapist assistants
22. Veterinary technologists and technicians
23. Speech-language pathologists
24. Mental health and substance abuse social workers
25. Dental assistants

Source: U.S. Department of Education (http://www.ed.gov), September 2005.

So, how do you make sense of all the options? The U.S. Department of Education has identified 16 career clusters. Beneath each cluster are many different and exciting career opportunities. You can see each cluster, its description, sample careers, sample personality traits, and typical education requirements in the Career Clusters table (see Figure C-2). (*Note:* Additional information about the 16 Career Clusters can be found on the National Association of State Directors of Career Technical Education website at http://www.careerclusters.org/16clusters.htm.)

16 Career Clusters

Career Cluster	Description	Sample Careers	Sample Personality Traits	Typical Education Level
Agriculture, Food, and Natural Resources	The production of consumable goods and services such as food, heat, and light.	• Farmer • Biological Technician • Environmental Scientist • Landscape Architect • Rotary Drill Operator • Veterinarian	• Good at problem-solving • Adept at math and science • Enjoys working alone • Likes working with hands and using technology • Enjoys working outdoors	Most require a bachelor's degree, master's degree, or doctoral degree. All areas require specialized training.
Architecture and Construction	Workers in this career area design, construct, inspect, and maintain homes, offices, recreational facilities, and buildings large and small.	• Architect • Electrician • Carpenter • Surveyor • Construction Laborer	• Good at planning and organizing • Enjoy working outdoors • Analytical/problem solver • Strong in math and science	Highly complex jobs requiring extensive knowledge. Many require a bachelor's degree.
Arts, Audio/Video Technology, and Communications	Careers that deal with the creation, design, and delivery of messages, whether factual, entertaining, serious, or frivolous. These messages can be written, spoken, or performed.	• Art Director • Technical Writer • Photographer • Painter • Animator • Editor • Interpreter	• Enjoy performing or writing • Likes using imagination • Likes to create original ideas or objects • Innovative and creative • Enjoys using music, art, drama, or language	Bachelor's degree and specialized training.
Business, Management, and Administration	Workers in this area manage or provide support for others in the company who create the company's products or services.	• Human Resource Manager • Purchasing Agent • Managing Analyst • Chief Executive Officer • Receptionist	• Enjoys order and procedure • Honest, dependable, responsible • Likes working with people • Enjoys coordinating events	Most careers require a bachelor's degree. Some require an associate's degree.
Education and Training	The creation and presentation of learning materials for preschool, kindergarten, elementary, secondary, college, and adult education students, including corporate training.	• Schoolteacher • Corporate Trainer • Teacher Assistant • Librarian • Coach	• Good interpersonal skills • Knowledge of subjects • Able to work with all types of people • Likes planning/organizing	Bachelor's degree and often teaching certification. Assistants require associate's degree or college training.

16 Career Clusters

Career Cluster	Description	Sample Careers	Sample Personality Traits	*Typical* Education Level
Finance	Careers in this cluster relate to managing money or studying how money is used.	• Economist • Accountant • Tax Preparer • Auditor • Insurance Appraiser • Financial Advisor • Loan Officer	• Enjoy working with money and numbers • Organized and very detail oriented • Enjoys order and consistency • Dependable and honest	Most careers require a college-level degree.
Government and Public Administration	Elected officials, appointed officials, and professional career employees dedicated to running national, state, county, and city level governments for the good of the people.	• President of the United States • Senator • Judge • Court Clerk	• Enjoys interacting with others • Wants order and procedure • Likes solving problems • Good verbal and writing skills	Bachelor's degree or higher degree and specialized training or knowledge.
Health Science	Health science professionals are dedicated to helping people feel their best and live healthy.	• Emergency Medical Technician (EMT) • Pharmacist • Nutritionist • Occupational Therapist • Nurse • Podiatrist	• Desire to help people stay fit and healthy • Sensitive and caring • Good attention to details • Enjoys using math, science, and technology • Investigative	Advanced education and training is necessary. Bachelor's degrees are needed for most careers. Master's and doctoral degrees are necessary for specialty fields.
Hospitality and Tourism	Careers dedicated to helping others enjoy their leisure time, such as eating out, lodging, attractions, recreation events, and other travel-related services.	• Flight Attendant • Chef • Groundskeeper • Tour Guide • Travel Coordinator	• Likes working with people • Good verbal and communication skills • Dependable • Ability to plan and organize	Specialty training. Some positions may require post-secondary education.

16 Career Clusters

Career Cluster	Description	Sample Careers	Sample Personality Traits	*Typical* Education Level
Human Services	Workers in human services careers assist people of all ages from preschoolers to the elderly. Some careers involve helping people with physical or mental handicaps and other special needs.	• Social Worker • Preschool Manager • Physical Therapist • Funeral Director • Occupational Therapist	• Enjoy helping others • Good verbal skills • Cares about others' feelings • Wants to make things better for others	Bachelor's degree and specialized training
Information Technology	Careers dedicated to the design, support, and maintenance of hardware, software, and other technology infrastructures.	• Network Administrator • Computer Scientist • Technology Trainer • Webmaster • Database Manager	• Math, science, and technology skills • Analytical and problem-solving skills • Enjoys investigative work • Very practical	College-level degree and industry-recognized certifications.
Law, Public Safety, and Security	Professionals in this field create or enforce laws, help keep our streets safe, protect our individual rights, and ensure businesses operate honestly.	• Police Officer • Fire Dispatcher • Lawyer • Court Reporter • Judge	• Likes working with people • Caring and sensitive • Wants to make things better • Good verbal skills • Dependable and respected	Some careers require bachelor's degrees and more advanced education. Some careers require associate's degrees or specialized training.
Manufacturing	This career cluster is responsible for the designing, planning, and production of the goods and products we use, drive, and wear.	• Graphic Designer • Production Manager • Machinist • Baker • Electrical Engineer	• Likes working alone • Math, science, and technology ability • Organizational skills • Mechanical ability	Highly trained in machinery, computers, and robotics. Some careers require college-level degrees and advanced certifications.

16 Career Clusters

Career Cluster	Description	Sample Careers	Sample Personality Traits	*Typical* Education Level
Marketing, Sales, and Service	Marketing, retail sales, wholesale sales, and customer support of commodities, goods, or services that are bought, sold, traded, and exchanged in wholesale and retail outlets.	• Market Research Analyst • Sales Manager • Real Estate Broker • Advertising Sales Agent • Telemarketer	• High energy level • Organized, detail oriented • Likes working with others • Enjoys working with words • Likes coordinating events	Bachelor's degree or specialized training.
Science, Technology, Engineering, and Mathematics	Scientists and engineers generally specialize in one specific area of engineering or research, such as marine engineering, hydrology, astronomy, or computer science.	• Zoologist • Astronomer • Electrical Engineer • Microbiologist • Agricultural Engineer • Computer Scientist • Civil Engineer	• In-depth math and science skills • Analytical and problem-solving skills • Likes investigation • Practical • Likes working alone	Requires high levels of education, training, and experience. Bachelor's degrees are required of most fields. Master's degrees and doctoral degrees may be necessary for some fields.
Transportation, Distribution, and Logistics	The planning, management, transportation, and distribution of people, materials, and goods by air, water, railway, and road.	• Truck Driver • Airline Pilot • Transportation Inspector • Air Traffic Controller • Bus Driver	• Highly organized • Attention to detail and scheduling • Mechanical ability • Analytical and problem-solving ability	Many positions require post-secondary education and specialized training.

Thinking About Career Options

1. Review the Career Clusters table in Figure C-2 to identify which clusters or careers interest you.

2. Choose two careers from the table and find out more about them by going to two of these sites:
   - Occupational Outlook Handbook on the U.S. Department of Labor website (http://www.bls.gov/oco/)
   - Careers.Org (http://www.careers.org/)
   - Careers in Business (http://www.careers-in-business.com/)
   - ScienceCareers.Org (http://sciencecareers.sciencemag.org/)

3. Open a blank *Word* document and summarize any information you find about working conditions, special skills or traits, training and education requirements, earnings potential, and related occupations for your chosen careers.

4. Save as *App C-Exercise C1*.

Understanding Your Strengths and Passions

Everyone has their own set of strengths and weaknesses. There are things you excel at and other things that you would rather not do. You have special skills and abilities that make you more likely to succeed in a career than someone who has different skills. The trick is understanding how to identify your skills, passions, and personality traits so you can choose a career that will be right for you.

Identifying Personal Strengths and Passions: There are plenty of ways to help identify your skills and passions. You can begin by making a list of the things you enjoy best, such as working alone or as part of a team, working with numbers and money or working with words, caring for people or working with machines. You can search the many career websites for information on careers and the skills necessary to succeed in those careers. There are also websites with skills profiles to help you identify which type of career will be best suited to you. Some sites you may wish to explore include:
- U.S. Department of Labor (http://www.bls.gov)
- America's Career InfoNet (http://www.acinet.org/acinet/)
- Kidz Online (http://www.kidzonline.org/streamingfutures/)

The screen displayed in Figure C-3 shows the Skills Identifier tool found under Career Tools on the America's Career InfoNet website.

Personality Traits and Aptitude Tests: Another way to identify your strengths and weaknesses is to take a personality test or an aptitude test. Your career counselor may have these tools available at your school. There are also websites that offer personality tests online. Some tests are free and others may require a fee. These tests are designed to help you identify certain career choices that will fit your personality better than others. The tests offer a bank of questions that you answer honestly. At the end of the test, you are provided with scores that describe

Figure C-3   The Skills Profiler on America's Career InfoNet Website

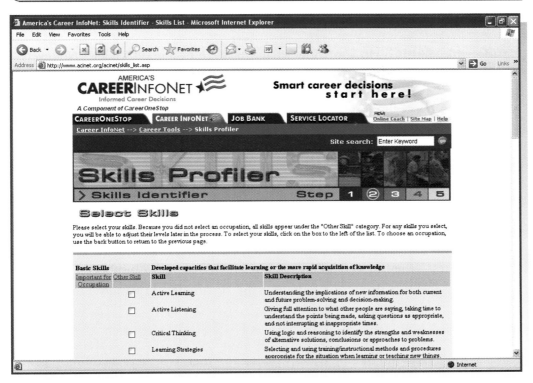

Source: America's Career InfoNet (http://www.acinet.org/acinet/), September 2005.

how you would best fit into the workplace. You can search for online personality tests in your favorite search engine.

Exercise   C2

Exploring Personality Traits

1. With your teacher's permission, visit Kidz Online (http://www.kidzonline.org/streamingfutures/) and take the Career Quiz. If you have additional time, also visit LiveCareer.com and take their free Career Test (http://www.livecareer.com).

2. Print out your test results (if applicable). According to the tests, what type of career would best suit you? Open a new *Word* document and describe whether you were surprised by the results of the tests. How closely do the results align with your current career interests?

3. Save as *App C-Exercise C2*.

Developing the Skills for Success

A company that is hiring a new employee will look for certain skills and traits. Some traits may be basic, such as "Does this person appear to take care of their health and personal appearance?" Other skills may be more difficult to identify, such as "Does this person display leadership capabilities?" You may already have many of the skills necessary to be successful in the workplace. The information below is a sample of the skills and qualities that companies look for in their employees. No matter what path you take, these are skills and traits you will need for your personal development and success.

Leadership Skills. Do you know what it takes to be a good leader? Not everyone has the skills, or desire, to lead a group. However, if you have ever been part of a team that had a good leader, or a bad one, you know how the leader's skills affect the success of the team. The dictionary defines a *leader* as "a person who guides, directs, or commands." Good leaders usually have these skills in common:

- **Good communicator**—they listen to others, provide honest feedback, and keep everyone informed.

- **Trusted**—they are trusted by others to lead a team.

- **Dependable**—they do what they say, say what they mean, make sound decisions, and take responsibility for their actions.

- **Adaptable**—they are able to adjust to new situations.

- **Honest**—they are candid and sincere when dealing with others.

- **Courageous**—they can handle stressful situations and stand up for what they believe is right.

Teamwork Skills. What does it mean to be a team player? In the world of work, a *team* is a group of employees working together to achieve a common goal. People working as teams can usually accomplish more than people working alone. In fact, job success often depends on your ability to work well with others. Here are some things to remember when working with a team:

- **Be part of the team.** Work hard to get along with others, be cooperative, and always do your share of the work.

- **Be considerate.** Be respectful of others by admitting when you are wrong, apologizing if you hurt someone's feelings, and not acting like a know-it-all. In other words, treat others the way you want to be treated.

- **Be helpful.** Help others with their work, give compliments, listen to what others have to say, offer helpful and sincere feedback, and stay focused on the team goal.

Exercise C3

Exploring Teamwork Skills

1. Take the Teamwork Skills quiz in Figure C-4 to determine if you have what it takes to be an effective team member. If you can place a check mark by most of the statements, you could be an effective team member. Take note of items where you might need improvement.

Figure C-4   Teamwork Skills

Teamwork Skills

Read the following statements to determine if you are an effective team member.

_____ I enjoy working with others to solve problems.

_____ I always let others finish talking before I give my views.

_____ I listen carefully to what others have to say and never prejudge their ideas.

_____ When I have a problem to solve, I seek others' opinions before I make a decision.

_____ I consider myself a good leader.

_____ If others disagree with me, I always listen to their opinions before I answer.

_____ I enjoy debating issues and listening to others' opinions.

_____ I am careful not to hurt others' feelings when I offer my views.

_____ I set goals for myself and I usually achieve them.

_____ I like to help my family and friends work out their differences.

Customer Service Skills. Many successful companies place great importance on customer satisfaction. Using good customer service skills means that you put the needs of your customer first. It also means that you are always concerned about how your actions and decisions will affect your customers. Companies with a customer service-based culture will often conduct surveys to make sure they are meeting the goals and standards their customers expect of them. Based on their findings, they may change the way they do business to better serve their customers.

Communication Skills. Most people assume they have good communication skills. However, good communication skills take practice and may be more difficult than you think. For example, as a good communicator, you need to speak clearly when giving instructions to others. When taking orders, you need to listen closely and follow directions without mistakes. When writing letters or e-mail, you need to use clear language with error-free grammar and spelling. When talking with customers, you need to convince others to do or buy something. If you can do all of this well, you can consider yourself a good communicator.

Employability Skills. There are certain skills that _every_ employer is looking for. Do you know what they are? To be the perfect employee, you will need to have certain skills that will benefit any employer. You need to have excellent communication skills and the ability to talk with customers. You must work well with a team and be able to take the lead on group projects. You should be able to adapt to new situations. You should be willing to continue learning to be better at your job. You must be responsible, honest, and dependable. You should be able to prioritize your work to meet important deadlines. And, of course, you need to have the technical skills necessary for your job.

Personal Finance Skills. As you plan for the job of your dreams, you should also understand how that job will financially support your future. Some careers will be attainable after high school. Other careers require additional education, which may mean student loan payments. Usually, the more education you need for a career, the more money you will earn as income. You should be aware of what type of income to expect from your career. Knowing your expected income will allow you to estimate your living expenses and determine if you can pay your bills on your expected salary. Some websites to visit that offer expected salaries are the U.S. Department of Labor (http://bls.gov) and CollegeBoard.com (http://www. collegeboard.com). Figure C-5 shows job information on the CollegeBoard.com website.

Figure C-5 — Job Information on the CollegeBoard.com Website

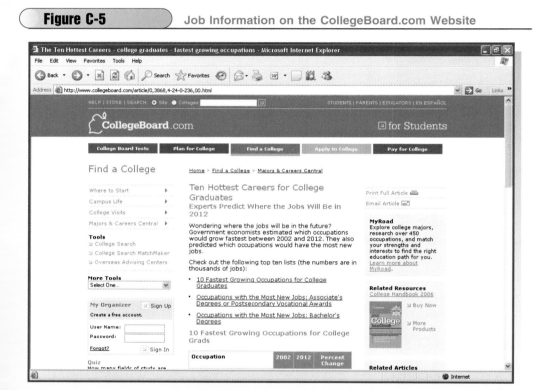

Source: CollegeBoard.com (http://www.collegeboard.com), September 2005.

Exercise C4

Exploring Personal Finance Skills

1. The table in Figure C-6 shows a personal monthly budget. Visit either the Department of Labor (http://bls.gov) or CollegeBoard.com (http://www. collegeboard.com) and look up the salary of a career of your choice.

2. Use the table in Figure C-6 to help you determine your possible monthly income minus expenses. Ask your parents to help you estimate monthly expenses.

3. Create the table in a spreadsheet document. Then fill out the table to establish your monthly budget. *Tip:* Be sure to include formulas to deduct total expenses from total income.

4. Save as *App C-Exercise C4.*

Figure C-6   Sample Monthly Expenses Table

Monthly Expenses Table	
Monthly Income	
Job	
Other	
Monthly Expenses	
Housing/rent	
Utilities	
o Phone	
o Cell phone	
o Gas & electric	
o Sewer & water	
o Cable	
o Other	
Food	
o Groceries	
o Lunch/eating out	
Car expenses	
o Car payment	
o Gas	
o Maintenance & repairs	
Entertainment	
Savings	
Miscellaneous	

Interviewing Skills. You can be the best, most qualified person for a position. You can have the highest grades, know the most in your career area, and have the fanciest suit. However, if you don't interview well, you won't get the job.

Like many other aspects of your career, developing your interviewing skills is critical to your success. Without these skills, you may never get the chance to realize your career dreams. To prepare for an interview, you need to know your skills and you need to practice answering typical interview questions (see Figure C-7).

Exercise C5

Exploring Interview Skills

1. Review the Common Interview Questions presented in Figure C-7. In a word processing document, key the questions and a few sentences to answer each question.

2. Save as *App C-Exercise C5*.

3. With a classmate, trade the roles of interviewer and interviewee and practice answering these questions with self-confidence and conviction.

Figure C-7 Common Interview Questions

© PHOTODISC RED/GETTY IMAGES

Common Interview Questions

- How would you describe yourself?
- What do you consider your greatest strengths?
- What do you consider your greatest weaknesses?
- What are your favorite classes and why?
- What are your least favorite classes and why?
- What are your hobbies and interests outside of school?
- What are your favorite extracurricular activities and why?
- Have you ever been fired from a job? Explain why.
- Why do you want to work for this company?
- Explain your long-term goals and how you plan to achieve them.
- Why do you want this job?
- Why should we hire you?
- What do you look for in a job?
- How would your friends, classmates, or coworkers describe you?
- Explain a situation where you worked with a team to solve a problem.

Developing the Tools for Success

As you begin thinking about your career choices, you need to understand the tools that will help you successfully land your dream job. There are steps to take now, while you are in school, to ensure you are on the right path for your career. Developing a career plan will help you take the right direction in your schoolwork and professional development. Keeping a portfolio of your work will enable you to provide proof of your skills to employers. And, of course, building a top-notch resume is essential for landing an interview.

Career Plan. Landing the perfect career takes careful planning. You need to carefully research the skills, education requirements, and experience necessary for your career choice. Many times, your ultimate career may mean higher-education requirements, industry certifications, or prior on-the-job experience. Developing a career plan will help you outline the steps needed to reach your career goals. For example, if your career goal is to become a computer software engineer, your first step would be to determine if you had the personality traits required for that type of career (e.g., analytical, detail-oriented, math and computer science skills). Your second step would be to study hard in your math, science, and computer science courses in school. Another step would be to attain a bachelor's degree in computer science as well as important certifications in the field. All of these steps would need to be accomplished before actually applying for a job.

Exercise C6
Developing a Career Plan

1. There are websites that offer additional information on developing a career plan. Search for sites you think might be useful. Some sites you might want to visit include the U.S. Department of Labor (http://www.bls.gov), America's Career InfoNet (http://www.acinet.org/acinet/), or Mapping Your Future (http://www.mapping-your-future.org/). Figure C-8 shows the Career Planning tool available on the Mapping Your Future website. Review the career plan information provided.

2. Print a page or two of information from the most useful sites.

3. Using a career of your choice, develop a sample plan of your own.

4. Save as *App C-Exercise C6*.

Figure C-8   Career Planning Information on the Mapping Your Future Website

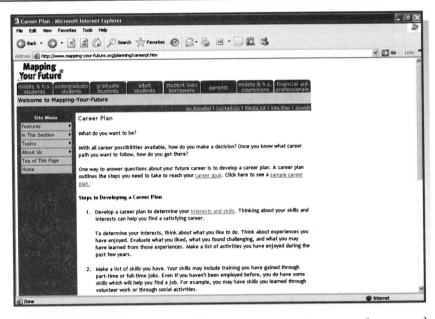

Source: Mapping Your Future (http://www.mapping-your-future.org), September 2005.

Portfolio. A *career portfolio* is a place to store items that show off your best work abilities. For example, if you want to be a photographer, you should store your best photos. If you want to be an architect, you should show samples of blueprints from your best designs. When you create a portfolio, the items you include should be neat, clean, and something to be proud of. Your portfolio should contain evidence of your skills, such as awards, certificates, letters of recommendation, samples of your work, and a flawless resume. Visit America's Career InfoNet (http://www.acinet.org/acinet/) for more information on building your portfolio.

Resume. Ten seconds. That's all you get. Most employers spend about ten seconds glancing over a resume. That means you have ten seconds to show them you have what they need. Developing a resume is serious business. In fact, there are countless businesses whose sole purpose is to help you develop your resume. A *resume* is a one-page document that tells the story of you—the skills and qualifications that make you the best candidate for a job. You do this by showing what job you are seeking, how you are qualified for the job, and how your experience complements the position. Figure C-9 shows some common resume headings and what is included under each heading.

Figure C-9   Common Resume Headings

Resume Headings

Every resume should include the same basic information. Although the headings may vary, below is a description of the most common sections.
- **Name header**—Every resume includes your name, address, phone number, and e-mail address. This information is displayed clearly at the top for easy reference.
- **Objective**—This is a short description of the job you are seeking.
- **Related Experience**—This section includes experience directly related to the job you are seeking. Examples include volunteer work, community service, unpaid internships, or other work experience or activities.
- **Educational Experience**—This section includes information about schools you have attended. List your school, its city and state, and the years you attended. This is also where you would list your favorable grade point average.
- **Work Experience**—This section includes any other work experience you have had. Examples include grass cutting, babysitting, fast food work, grocery bagger or shelf stocker, etc. Listing your past jobs shows that you can be responsible.
- **Achievements**—This section lists awards or deeds you are proud of. Examples include honors, awards, and student-elected positions.
- **References**—For this section, include two or more names of people who know your skills well. References can be teachers, advisors, mentors, former employers, coworkers, neighbors, or others you've worked for.

It is important to note that you should change your resume to reflect the job you are currently seeking. The information you provide under the Objective and Related Experience headings should match the requirements for the job for which you are applying. There are many websites that offer free advice for building a resume. Some sites you may wish to visit are CollegeBoard.com (http://www.collegeboard.com), America's Career InfoNet (http://www.acinet.org/acinet/), and Resume-Resource.com http://www.resume-resource.com/). Additionally, many of the job search engines offer advice on resume building. A few of those sites are Monster Jobs (http://www.monster.com), Yahoo! HotJobs (http://www.hotjobs.yahoo.com), and MSN Careers (http://www.careers.msn.com). Figure C-10 shows the MSN Careers Website.

Figure C-10   MSN Careers Website

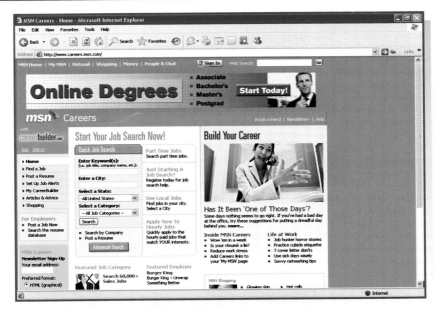

Source: MSN Careers (http://www.careers.msn.com/), October 2005.

Exercise C7

Developing a Resume

1. Do you currently have a resume? If not, visit the websites listed above to assist you in developing a resume. Be sure to use the headings listed in Figure C-9. If you currently have a resume, read through the document and update it to apply for a specific job (of your choice).

2. Trade resumes with a classmate and provide feedback on improving each other's resume.

Ethics and Your Career

Successful companies practice business fairly and honestly. They strive to build trust with their customers, employees, other businesses, and the general public. In turn, companies expect their employees to be fair and honest in the workplace.

Many companies will establish a Code of Ethics or a Code of Conduct by which they expect their employees to act. For example, a company may establish guidelines for using the computer or Internet for non-company work while on the job. There may be standards for how to deal with angry customers on the phone or how to behave when representing the company at a meeting.

If an employee violates a code of ethics, the company may give a warning or suspend an employee without pay. In extreme cases, an employee may even be fired from the job. As an example, if a company discovers an employee lied about an important fact on their resume or application, they may be dismissed.

In order to be a successful, valued, and trusted employee, always act with integrity and honesty. If you are unsure how to act in a certain situation, discuss the situation with your supervisor or human resources director.

Lifelong Career Planning and Learning

Choosing a career is a journey, not a destination. As you learn more about your career, you may decide you have greater interest in one part of your job over another. New technology may change how you complete your work, causing you to focus on a different aspect of your job. You may decide to continue your education to get a better promotion or increase your value to your company. In any case, it is important to always learn on the job, to keep on top of the trends in your business, and to continue your education so you can be the best at what you do.

You should also take the time to update your resume every few years. Make sure it accurately reflects your current skill set. Examine current trends to determine how to keep on top of your career. There will always be new technology and new ways of doing things—make sure you take the time to advance your career and skills along with the times. The competition is tough. Invest the time in your skills and education to make sure you can compete with the best.

Glossary

abacus early mechanical counting device using beads on wires in a wooden frame

absolute cell reference when a cell is copied, the copy of the cell maintains a reference to a specific row and column

action plan guides the implementation of business plan strategies

active cell highlighted cell in a worksheet; stores information that is entered while it is active

Amazon popular e-commerce website

analytical engine early steam-powered programmable computer invented by Charles Babbage

anchor tag tag that defines a hyperlink

animation schemes preset presentation schemes

Arithmetikal Engine early mechanical calculator invented by Gottfried Wilhelm von Leibniz

arithmometer early mechanical calculator invented by Charles Xavier Thomas

ARPANET Advanced Research Projects Agency, created to research how to maintain communications in case of nuclear war or disaster

aspersion statement that casts doubt on a person's integrity

audience customers or viewers of a website

AutoComplete a feature that recognizes a word as you begin to type it (such as the name of a month) and finishes it for you

backbone communications network infrastructure

backspace text at the left of the insertion point is removed

bar graph an illustration that compares one or more sets of data that are plotted on the horizontal X-axis and the vertical Y-axis

blind copy notation part of a letter that indicates a copy of the letter was sent to someone without disclosing this to the addressee

blogger person who creates a weblog

blogosphere the world of blogs

boom arm of the headset that holds the microphone

bound report long report with pages fastened together at the left margin, often prepared with a cover or binder

bullets special characters used to enhance the appearance of text and add emphasis to a list of items

business plan a blueprint for a company

category axis sometimes called the x-axis; used to plot categories of data

cells the intersection of a column and a row

Center alignment a feature that centers a table horizontally on a page

Center page a feature that centers text vertically on a page

change case a feature that changes capitalization

chart sheet appears as a separate worksheet

client/server system of host servers and Internet software on which the Internet is based

closing tag ending tag in a pair of HTML tags

code view view in a Web design program that shows the source code

columns vertical areas in a worksheet; each column has a heading (letters from A to Z, AA to AZ, etc.) running left to right across the worksheet

columns vertical part of a table grid; labeled alphabetically from left to right

compressed method of making graphic files smaller

continuous speech recognition (CSR) software that allowed voice interaction with a computer

copyright form of protection granted to intellectual property

credit report keeps track of a consumer's financial history

customer audience of a website

data labels numbers or words that identify values displayed in the chart

data points the bars, columns, or pie slices that represent the numerical data in a chart

Decrease Indent a feature used to format desired outline levels

defamation harming the reputation of someone by libel or slander

Default Value field property automatically inserts a default value in a record unless other text is specified

delete text at the right of the insertion point is removed

diagram a drawing that explains a process or idea

difference engine early computer invented by Charles Babbage to calculate celestial tables

digital pen computer input tool

digital zoom adjusts the lens of a digital camera to close in on a subject

Domain Name System (DNS) converts domain names into IP addresses

domain name name that identifies computer sites on the Internet

dot leader tab a feature that automatically places dot leaders between columns of designated text; the dots lead the eye from text in the first column to text in the second column

eBay popular e-commerce website

e-commerce doing business on the WWW

electronic presentations computer-generated visual aids (usually slide shows) that can be used to help communicate information

embedded chart appears as an object within a worksheet

emoticons abbreviations used to signal emotions and verbal inflections in e-mail

encryption software security tools that convert information into unbreakable code

end-of-record codes codes that separate records

ENIAC early computer powered by vacuum tubes

ethics moral principles that govern human interaction

fair use doctrine lawful use of a small portion of copyrighted material without permission for educational purposes

field codes codes that separate fields of information

fields the columns in a database table

file sharing sharing of music files over the Internet

financial projections show expected results in a business plan

find a feature used to locate a specific keystroke, word, or phrase

firewall hardware and software that prevents hacker intrusions

flow how visitors use a website

flowchart an illustration that shows steps in a process, connected by arrows

folder tab organizing tab in OneNote

font the typeface or style of the letters in which a document is printed

font effects special font styles, such as shadow, emboss, small caps, and outline

font styles different appearance of the letters in which a document is printed, including bold and italic

Format field property allows numbers, dates, times, and text to be displayed in specific ways in a database

function arguments values to be used for calculating functions in a spreadsheet

graphical user interface (GUI) way of communicating with a computer using a mouse to click on graphics

Graphics Interchange Format (GIF) common graphic type used on the Web

gridlines lines through a chart that identify intervals on the axes

grids on a graph, lines that extend from tick marks to make it easier to see data values

hacker person who accesses computers and networks without permission

handtyping converts handwritten words into typed text

harassment persistent threatening or annoyance

hexadecimal values base-16 system for defining colors used in Web pages

hierarchical design method of organizing a website with main topic pages that have many subpages

horizontal outlining notetaking feature in OneNote; used for definitions and similar two-column material

host/server computer through which other computers connect to each other and the Internet

HTML (HyperText Markup Language) a computer language that uses codes to format documents displayed on the WWW

HTTP (HyperText Transport Protocol) a protocol (or method) that computers use to communicate with each other to move information across the Internet

hyperlink text or graphic that links one document or Web page to another, or to a different place in the same document

identity theft criminal activity in which a criminal pretends to be the victim in order to steal

imaging devices hardware tools that capture images, such as cameras and copy machines

Inbox storage area for incoming e-mail

Increase Indent a feature used to format desired outline levels

index page starting page of a website

infected when a computer has received a virus

infrastructure systems such as roads, electrical lines, and telecommunication links that allow society to function

inking using a digital pen to write, draw or sketch

Input Mask controls the data format allowed in a database field

insert new keyed text appears at the insertion point

Insert Comment a feature that allows the reader of a document to insert comments or annotations

Insert Date a feature that inserts the current date in a document automatically

integrated circuit (IC) chips power source for computers with miniaturized transistors placed on silicon wafers

intellectual property works of individual creativity such as books, music, and artwork

Internet a global network of computers

Internet Explorer popular GUI browser

Internet Service Provider (ISP) provides host computers for customers to connect to the Internet

IP address number that identifies each computer on the Internet

join merge two or more table cells into one

Joint Photographic Experts Group (JPEG) common graphic type used on the Web

justify format left and right margins of text to be aligned evenly

keyword word entered in a search engine

labels names used to identity parts of a graph

landscape an image positioned with the long side at the top

layout the way text and graphics are arranged

legend the key that identifies the shading, coloring, or patterns used for the information shown in a graph

letters column identifiers in a worksheet

libel defamation of a person in print

line graph an illustration that shows quantity changes over time or distance

linear design method of organizing a website with related pages in a specific sequence

liquid crystal display (LCD) display provided by a digital camera

look and feel the artistic appeal of a Web page design

Macintosh early computer from Apple Corporation that used a graphical user interface

macro a time-saving feature that allows the operator to record keystrokes and commands and play them back later

mainframes early supercomputers

market analysis defines the market of a company and specifies strategies to be used to achieve revenues

megapixels millions of pixels; used to measure digital camera resolution

merge used to combine information from two files, such as a letter and an address list, into a third file that is created via the merge process

message purpose of a website

minicomputers smaller versions of mainframes, used by businesses, government agencies, schools, and hospitals

MITS Altair 8800 first personal computer, sold as a hobby kit

mixed cell reference when a cell is copied, the copy of the cell maintains a reference to a specific row or column but not to both

Modern Language Association (MLA) a style often used to document and format research papers

Moore's Law prediction by Gordon Moore that the evolving integrated circuit would increase the power of computers while reducing their cost

Mosaic early GUI browser

Mozilla early GUI browser

multiple sort a sort that arranges records by information in multiple fields

Napster popular file-sharing website

National Science Foundation funded six networked supercomputers for scientific research

navigation bar list of topics to help visitors to a website

NCSA National Center for Supercomputing Applications, research center where the first browsers were developed

nested HTML tags begin and end outside of existing tags

netiquette implied rules of good behavior on the Internet

Netscape Corporation that developed browser software

network the means of connecting one computer to another whether both computers are in the same room or in different countries

noise cancellation headset hardware used with speech recognition

NREN National Research and Education Network; connected colleges and universities in a computer network

NSFNET a system of high-speed phone lines that connected six supercomputers

numbering used to show the proper order of a series of steps

numbers row identifiers in a worksheet

opening tag first in a pair of HTML tags

optical zoom part of a digital camera that adjusts the lenses

orientation the way an image is positioned

orphan first line of a paragraph that appears at the bottom of a page

Outbox storage area for outgoing e-mail

packet bits and bytes of information sent over the Internet

Palo Alto Research Center Xerox Corporation center where computers were developed

Pascaline early mechanical calculator invented by Blaise Pascal

peer-to-peer networking that allows people to download and share music and video files

pen pointer digital pen version of the mouse pointer

personal digital assistant (PDA) handheld computer

phishing e-mails intended to fool customers into giving up important information such as account numbers or passwords

phrase searching method of searching that finds results based on a phrase in quotation marks

pie charts illustrations used to display parts of a whole; they show clearly the proportional relationship of only one set of values

pixel picture elements that make up an image displayed on a computer screen

podcasting audio transmissions over the WWW

portrait an image positioned with the short side at the top

presentation design template a presentation with styles and formats already set up so the user just has to select the slide layout and key in the information

primary key identifies each record in a table with a number

query question posed to a search engine when looking for information on the WWW; or question used to sort a database for specific information to be retrieved from tables that have been created

Recording Industry Association of America protects copyrighted music on behalf of musicians and recording companies

records the rows in a database table

relative cell reference when a cell is copied, the copy of the cell is related to its new address

repetitive stress injuries a category of physical injuries suffered by workers who must repeat the same task over a long period of time

replace a feature that finds a specified keystroke, word, or phrase and replaces it with another keystroke, word, or phrase

Required field property used for fields in a database where some value must be inserted

results answers to a search engine query

rows horizontal part of a table grid; labeled numerically from top to bottom

scale on a graph, numbers on the Y- or X-axis representing quantities

section tab organizing tab in OneNote

Sent storage area for e-mail that has been sent

shading a feature used to enhance or highlight selected text

sheet tabs labels at the bottom of the worksheets that identify the active worksheet in the workbook

slander false oral statements about a person

slide transition describes how the display changes from one slide to the next slide

smart phone cell phone with the capabilities of a PDA

sort a feature that arranges selected text in a specific order

source code the HTML tags that make up a Web page

source document form from which data is keyed

spam unwanted and unsolicited advertising via e-mail

speech recognition software that allows a user to communicate with a computer using speech

speech user file file created by SR software that identifies a particular user

speech user interface (SUI) way of communicating with a computer using voice

split divide two or more table cells

spyware software that tracks data on a computer

stemming search method which finds results based on the stem of a word and finds related words with different endings or tenses

surfing exploring the World Wide Web

tablet PC small portable computer designed to be used with handtyping and speech recognition

telecommute work from home

template pre-designed Web page

text interface early way of communicating with a computer using only a keyboard as an input device

thumbnail small sketch of a webpage design

tick marks on a graph, coordinate marks to help guide the reader

timing a feature in presentation software that controls the speed with which slides replace other slides

title heading that identifies chart contents and axes

traffic visitors to a website

Transfer Control Protocol (TCP) method of keeping track of packets sent over the Internet

transistor computer power source that replaced vacuum tubes

typeface the design of the letters in which a document is printed

typeover new keyed text replaces current text

unbound report short report that is often prepared without cover or binder; if it consists of more than one page, the pages are usually fastened together in the upper-left corner by a staple or paper clip

Uniform Resource Locator (URL) defines the path to a given page or file on an Internet host

UNIVAC first commercially-viable computer, run by transistors

value axis usually the y-axis; used to plot values associated with categories of data

Vertical alignment a feature that centers text vertically on a page

virus malicious computer code

voice-write dictate to a computer; also called *voice-type*

wearable tech future computers that may be built into clothing

weblog online journal; also called *blog*

web-safe colors colors based on the hexadecimal system that appear correctly on all browsers

website collection of linked Web pages

widow last line of a paragraph that appears at the top of a new page

windscreen sponge that covers the microphone on a headset

word art gallery predefined styles of text changed into a graphic object

X-axis the horizontal axis on a graph; usually for categories

Y-axis the vertical axis on a graph; usually for values

Index